W9-BCU-206

DICTIONARY OF NON-CHRISTIAN RELIGIONS

By the same author:

A Book of World Religions (Hulton)
The World's Living Religions (Pan)
What World Religions Teach (Harrap)
Worship in the World's Religions (Faber & Faber)

Dictionary of Non-Christian Religions

by

Geoffrey Parrinder, M.A., D.D., Ph.D.

Professor of the Comparative Study of Religions, University of London

HULTON EDUCATIONAL PUBLICATIONS

ISBN 0 7175 0572 3

First published 1971 by Hulton Educational Publication Ltd.,
Raans Road, Amersham, Bucks,
Set in Great Britain by
Cox & Wyman Ltd., London and
printed in the German Democratic Republic

Introduction

This dictionary covers the whole field of the religions of the world, with the exception of Christianity and the Bible. The reasons for the exclusion of these last two are that they have been treated in many other works of reference, and that to have included them would almost have doubled the size of this book. Special attention is given here to the three next largest religions: Hinduism, Buddhism and Islam, in view of widespread modern interest in their beliefs and terminology. However, considerable space is also devoted to other Far Eastern religions, to the classical worlds of ancient Persia, Mesopotamia, Egypt, Greece and Rome, and to Celtic, Teutonic and Scandinavian religions. Judaism is referred to in detail in the post-Biblical period, and special features are discussions of some of the beliefs and customs of ancient American cultures: Mayas, Aztecs and Incas, and also those of Australasia and Africa.

Many deities, beliefs and practices are considered here, and there are articles on philosophical schools. It is difficult to draw a clear line between divine mythology and human legend and there is some overlapping; but history and traditions which have no connection with faith have generally been avoided. So Zeus and Brahman have places by right, Heracles and Arjuna also through mythology, Odysseus and Harish-chandra less certainly, and Demosthenes and Kubla Khan none at all. Yet Akbar, Ashoka, Abū Hanīfa and Aristotle, and many similar figures, are included for the religious importance of their thoughts or actions.

In addition to names and philosophies a great many subjects are expounded. Here are to be found, alongside different themes: the loves of Zeus, the ten Labours of Heracles, three Graces, nine Muses, the Capitoline Triad and the Vestal Virgins; the ten Avatars of Hinduism, four *Vedas*, Yugas and Yogas, and the principal *Upanishads*; the four Noble Truths of Buddhism, three Jewels, four Brahma Vihāras and the Third Eye; the ten Gurus of the Sikhs, Fire Temples and Towers of Silence of the Parsis, White and Sky-clad Jains; the five *Classics* of Confucianism, eight Trigrams, the Temple of Heaven, the Torii and Sects of Shinto. From Mesopotamia come Ziggurats, Tablets of Destiny, and myths of Marduk and Gilgamesh; from Egypt nine Enneads, the *Book of the Dead*, the Pyramids and the Sphinx; from Islam the five Pillars, four Law Schools, Seven Sleepers, Aqsa Mosque and the Dome of the Rock; from Judaism the eighteen Blessings, thirteen Principles of Maimonides, Kabbalism and Hasidism; from Scandinavia the tree Yggdrasil and the Doom of the Gods; from Celtic lands the *Mabinogion*, Stonehenge and Arthur; from America the Big House, Totem Poles, the Ball Game and the Virgins of the Sun; from Australasia the

Dreaming, Bark Paintings, Taboo and Mana; from Africa the ancestral Stools, Ifa Oracle, and Zimbabwe, and beyond the sea Voodoo, Zombies and Black Muslims. These and thousands of other entries appear in this work. For the information given, reference has been made to countless expert authorities, primary sources and original languages, and no effort has been spared to provide material that is up to date, reliable and impartial. I am grateful to Miss Grace Golden for the interest and great care she has devoted to producing the drawings.

GEOFFREY PARRINDER

A

Ab, Av. The fifth month of the Jewish year, corresponding to part of July and August. The Ninth of Ab, Tishah b'Ab, is the most solemn of minor fasts to Orthodox Jews and is preceded by abstention from meat, wine and marriages. The fast commemorates the destruction of the first Temple of Jerusalem by the Babylonians under Nebuchadrezzar in 586 B.C. and the second Temple by the Romans under Titus in A.D. 70. Ornaments are removed from synagogues during the fast and readings are taken from the Biblical book of *Lamentations*. In recent times this fast day has also been used as a commemoration for those millions of Jews who died under the Nazis.

Abādīya. See IBĀDĪS

'Abbās Efendi. Second leader of the Bahā'is (q.v.), son and spiritual successor of Bahā'ullāh. He died in 1920.

'Abbāsids. A dynasty of caliphs of Islam from the family of the uncle of the Prophet Muhammad, al-'Abbās, of the Meccan clan of Hāshim. They defeated the Umayyad caliphs (q.v.) in A.D. 749, with the support of the Persians and others who wished Islam to be ruled by descendants of the Prophet. The centre of the empire was moved to Iraq and the second 'Abbāsid caliph built a new city at Baghdad, which became a centre of world culture, illustrated in the stories of the Arabian Nights. This was the golden age of Islamic culture and literature; theology and the natural sciences flourished, along with widespread economic and commercial progress. The 'Abbāsid empire slowly declined till Baghdad was sacked by the Mongols in 1258. One of the few who escaped was installed as caliph in Cairo in 1261, and though they had little practical power in the Mamlūk state there, 'Abbāsid influence lingered till the last caliph was carried off to Istanbul in 1517. See also HĀRŪN AL-RASHĪD.

Abbaye. Jewish rabbi (283–338) of Babylon, one of the most active of the Amoraim (q.v.) who interpreted and harmonized the *Mishnah*.

'Abd Allāh, 'Abdullāh. 'Servant of God', father of Muhammad and youngest son of 'Abd al-Muttalib. He died at Medina before the birth of his son who was left in the care of his grandfather till his death eight years later. An 'Abdullāh was cousin of Muhammad, another was one of his secretaries, and yet another was son of the caliph 'Umar and one of the most respected companions of the Prophet.

'Abduh. A leading Islamic modern reformer, Shaykh Muhammad 'Abduh (1849–1905) was born in Egypt and studied at the great mosque of al-Azhar in Cairo. He became a follower of al-Afghānī (q.v.) and was exiled to Paris for implication in a revolt. After their joint review had failed, 'Abduh went to Beirut and then returned to live peaceably in Egypt. He taught a return to the *Qur'ān*, and such reforms as were practicable, in law and university. He wrote several theological books and a commentary on the early chapters of the *Qur'ān*, and his work on Divine Unity is studied as a classic. His commentary on the *Qur'ān* was completed by his disciple Rashīd Ridā (q.v.) who also wrote a long life of his master.

Abhidhamma (Pali; Abhidharma, Sanskrit). 'Higher Dhamma', the third section of the canon of scripture of the Theravāda (q.v.) or Hīnayāna Buddhists contained in *Three Baskets, Tipitaka* or *Tripitaka*. The *Abhidhamma Pitaka* consists of seven works of philosophical and psychological analysis, in systematic expositions of parts of the much larger second section, the *Sutta Pitaka*, which gives the principal Dhamma (q.v.) or doctrine of the Buddha.

Abina. See RABINA.

Abohab, Isaac. Jewish rabbi of the fifteenth century, a leading Talmudic scholar and writer on law. His book 'The Lamp of Life' (*Menorah ha-Maor*) gives moral teachings with interesting stories and became a popular guide of conduct, being translated from Hebrew into Yiddish.

Abraham. See IBRĀHĪM.

Absolute (Latin *absolutum*, past participle of *absolvere*, set free). In philosophy the independent, unconditioned, self-existent, existing without relation to other beings. In Indian philosophy Brahman (q.v.) in the *Upanishads* and later texts is indefinable, 'not this, not this', and is not generally an object of worship but rather of meditation and the goal of knowledge by identification with it. See SHANKARA. See also FĀRĀBĪ.

Abstinence. Refraining from pleasures or necessities of ordinary life, such as marriage or certain foods, animal or liquid, with the aim of disciplining the soul. See ASCETICISM, CELIBACY, and FASTING. TOTAL ABSTINENCE from alcoholic drinks is enjoined of all Muslims in the *Qur'ān* and on all Buddhists in the *Five Precepts*. See SHĪLA.

Abu, Mount. Mountain (c. 1720 metres) in Rajasthan, sometimes called the 'Olympus of India'. It is a centre of beautiful temples of the Jains (q.v.), especially those temples called Dilwara, which contain some of the finest marble fretted ceilings in the world.

CEILING CARVING AT ABU

Abū Bakr. The first Caliph (q.v.) or Successor of Muhammad reigned only from A.D. 632 till his death in 634, but he so faithfully followed his master's policy that the young Islamic community was firmly established. His armies subjugated some of the most important Arabian tribes and defeated Persian and Syrian forces, thus preparing the way for the great successes of the empire. Abū Bakr is the first of the 'rightly guided' Caliphs according to Sunni Muslims, but the Shī'a (q.v.) reject him and consider the fourth, 'Alī, to be the first.

Abū Hanīfa. See HANĪFA.

Abū Jahl. A Meccan, named 'Amr ibn Hishām, who was an implacable opponent of Muhammad, and was nicknamed by Muslims Abū Jahl, 'father of folly'. He is perhaps referred to in the *Qur'ān* (22, 8) as a man who disputes about God without knowledge. He was killed at the battle of Badr in 624, leading the forces of Mecca against the Prophet.

Abū Tālib. Uncle of Muhammad, who took charge of the prophet when his grandfather died. He had a large family, among whom was 'Alī (q.v.) who became a follower of Muhammad and fourth Caliph of Sunni Islam. Abū Tālib not only protected Muhammad as a youth, but later when the prophet was attacked for his preaching. The death of Abū Tālib in 619 was a severe blow to Muhammad and prepared for his migration (see HIJRA) to Medina.

Abū Yazīd. See BISTĀMĪ.

Academy. A school founded in Athens by Plato (q.v.) about 385 B.C. and which continued as a corporate body until it was dissolved by Justinian in A.D. 529. Plato aimed at training men here for state service, but since this entailed a thorough teaching in philosophy and science the Academy became best known for its work in these subjects and was dominated by philosophical interests.

Acca Larentia See ROMULUS.

Āchārya. (Sanskrit) one who knows or teaches the rules, *āchāra*. The title of a Hindu teacher or spiritual director (see GURU), who teaches students the *Vedas* and ceremonies and invests them with the Sacred Thread (q.v.) By extension the title is applied to philosophers, or learned men in general, like our title 'doctor'. See also BRAHMA-CHĀRĪ.

Acheron. A river in southern Epirus in Greece which went underground in several places and so was thought to lead down to Hades, and an oracle of the dead was connected with it.

Achilles. Greek hero in the siege of Troy, described in the *Iliad*, and so a historical or legendary character, though he was worshipped in Asia Minor and round the Black Sea.

Aclla Cuna. See VIRGINS OF THE SUN.

Acrisius. King of Argos, in Greek mythology, father of Danaë and grandfather of Perseus (q.v.). His wife was Aglaia. He was warned by an oracle that Danaë's son would kill him, and so he shut her up in a bronze room. Later he put Danaë and Perseus in a chest and threw it out. Eventually the grown Perseus took part in some funeral games and killed Acrisius accidentally with a discus.

Acropolis, Akropolis. (Greek) 'higher city', citadel, a name for the high place of various towns, but especially of Athens. The Athenian Acropolis was a holy place from early times and was also used as a treasury. It was rebuilt under Pericles in the fifth century B.C., with a monumental gateway (Propylea), small temple of Athena Niké (Victory, q.v.), Erechtheum (q.v.) with Caryatid maidens in the porch,

ACROPOLIS AT ATHENS

colossal statue of Athena, and rebuilt Parthenon (q.v.).

Actaeon. Greek hunter, grandson of Cadmus, who saw Artemis (q.v.) bathing, so that she turned him into a stag and he was torn to pieces by his own hounds. In other versions of the story Actaeon either wanted to marry Artemis or boasted that he was a better hunter, and so brought down the wrath of the goddess.

'Ād. Arabian or nearby tribe, mentioned often in the *Qur'ān* but difficult to locate. It is said that the people of 'Ād were haughty, rejected the prophet Hūd (q.v.) who was sent to them, and were destroyed in a storm (7, 63, etc.). They have been identified with the Arameans, or possibly with the Sabeans of the ruined remains in the Yemen.

Adad. God of the storm in Babylonia and Assyria and popular throughout ancient Mesopotamia, Asia Minor, Syria and Palestine. The Hittites called him Teshub (q.v.), the Syrians Hadad, and in the Bible he is Rimmon, or Ramman, the thunderer. As the storm-god Adad helped to cause the Flood. His symbol was the lightning which he held in his right hand while grasping an axe with his left. His sacred animal was the bull. Adad had famous temples in Babylon and Aleppo, and at Ashur a great double Ziggurat (q.v.) was devoted to him but later shared with Anu (q.v.).

Adae. Ancestral customs of the Ashanti and kindred peoples of Ghana, the name being derived from 'a place of rest' or 'lying down', since work is forbidden on that day. Adae rites are held twice every forty-three days, once on a Sunday (Kwesidae) and once on a Wednesday (Wukudae). Food and drink are placed on or in front of the stools which represent the ancestors, and prayers are addressed to them by name, asking for health and prosperity.

Ādam. The Biblical Adam is mentioned many times in Islamic tradition, and his creation from potter's clay is related in the *Qur'ān* (15, 26), as well as the divine command to the angels to bow to Adam which was obeyed by all except the devil, Iblīs (q.v.). Ādam is called the Chosen (Safi) of God, the father of mankind, the first prophet who received a book from God. In later legend it is said that, after being cast out of Eden, Ādam and Eve met again on the mountain of 'Arafāt near Mecca. Indian and Ceylonese Muslims say that Adam landed in

Sarandib (Ceylon) where a high peak is called Adam's Peak and bears his footprint. This is the Sumanakuta, which in Buddhist tradition bears the footprint of the Buddha.

Adam's Bridge. Chain of islands between southern India and Ceylon, called by this name by Muslim and European geographers but in India Rāma's bridge. The story of the building of the bridge, by Rāma and his monkey allies, is told in the *Rāmāyana* (q.v.). See RĀMA and HANUMĀN.

Adhān, Azān. Arabic 'announcement', the call to prayer made by the Mu'addhin (see MUEZZIN) from the minaret tower or the door of the mosque at the Friday midday service and the five daily prayers. It was instituted by Muhammad shortly after his arrival at Medina, about 623 A.D. The orthodox Muslim Adhān consists of seven formulas: 'God is most great. I testify that there is no god beside God. I testify that Muhammad is the apostle of God. Come to prayer. Come to salvation. God is most great. There is no god beside God.' The first formula is repeated two or four times, and the other formulas twice each except the last. The Shi'a insert an eighth formula: 'Come to the best work.' There is no fixed melody for the Adhān and it may be modulated at will provided that the pronunciation is not distorted. Every Muslim, at home or in the mosque, alone or with his family, must repeat the Adhān and follow it with formal prayers.

Adharma. (Sanskrit) 'unright', vice, the opposite of Dharma (q.v.). In Hindu mythology Adharma is personified as a destructive son of Brahmā (q.v.).

Adhyātman. (Sanskrit) 'that which pertains to the self', or soul, with reference to the individual. This is its general usage in the Hindu *Upanishads* and *Bhagavad-Gītā*, though Adhyātman is sometimes translated as Supreme Self, or Over-soul, and used of the deity.

Ādi Brāhma Samāj. See BRĀHMA SAMĀJ.

Ādi-Buddha. (Sanskrit) 'first Buddha', the primordial and self-existent source of all beings. It is a term particularly connected with Nepal, though found also in Indian and Tibetan texts, and mingled with a good deal of Hindu mythology. The Ādi-Buddha concept has been described as Buddhist only in name but it appears in northern Buddhist terminology. From the Ādi-Buddha are said to have come seven modes of manifestation in the formed and formless worlds, known as Dhyāni-Buddhas (q.v.).

Ādi Granth. 'Original Book', the scriptures of the Sikh religion, also called *Gurū Granth Sahib*, 'Lord Teacher Book.' It is largely the work of the fifth of the ten Sikh Gurūs, Gurū Arjan (1563–1606), who incorporated the poems of his predecessors, his own compositions, and verses of other Indian, Hindu and Muslim, saints such as Kabīr, Nāmdev and Sheikh Farīd. Other hymns were added later, till the tenth Gurū, Gobind Singh, said there would be no more Gurūs and the *Granth* itself would be their living voice to men. The *Ādi Granth* proclaims in simple terms, in the Punjabi language, the Sikh belief in one God who dwells everywhere and is accessible to all men. See GURDWARA and JAPJI.

Ādi-nātha. See Nātha and Rishabha.

Ādi-Purāna. (Sanskrit) 'first Purāna', Hindu traditional tale. This title is generally given to the *Brahma Purāna* (q.v.).

'Adī, Shaikh. The chief saint of the Yazīdis, so-called Devil-worshippers (but see YAZĪDĪS), whose tomb in the valley of Shaikh 'Adī in northern Iraq is the chief centre of their religious and national life.

Aditi, Ādityas. Aditi, 'boundless', (Sanskrit), was one of the oldest Indian deities, representing the limitless heaven. She is sovereign of the sky, sustainer of the earth, and implored for blessings on children and cattle. Aditi was called mother of the gods and had seven sons, the Ādityas, of whom the chief was the sky god Varuna (q.v.) who was thus called the Āditya. Later the number of her sons was increased. The god Vishnu was also called the chief son of Aditi, and it was said that she was his mother in his Dwarf Avatar (q.v.). Aditi is also called wife of Vishnu, or of the sage Kashyapa (q.v.). See also DAKSHA.

Admetus. In Greek mythology husband of Alcestis (q.v.).

Adonis. A Greek god of vegetation and fertility, akin to the Babylonian Tammuz. His name may come from the Semitic Adon, 'lord'. The cult was taken from Cyprus to Athens and was partly identified with that of Eros. It was closely connected with the worship of Aphrodite, who loved Adonis but her passion was not returned. To the Romans Aphrodite was Venus, hence Shakespeare's poem of *Venus and Adonis*. In Greek mythology Adonis was killed by a boar, and in the cult of Aphrodite swine were sacrificed when she was associated with Adonis. Zeus decreed that Adonis should spend part of the year in the underworld and part on earth with Aphrodite, showing that he was a vegetation deity.

ADONIS

Adon 'Olam. (Hebrew) 'Lord of all', one of the few metrical hymns of the Jewish liturgy, which may be sung at the opening and closing of Sabbath morning services and may take the place of the Yigdal (q.v.). Both are chanted on the Eve of Atonement (q.v.).

Advaita. (Sanskrit) 'non-duality', not-twoness, the doctrine of the fundamental identity of the supreme divinity or Brahman with the human soul, Ātman. It is illustrated in nine examples in the *Chāndogya Upanishad* 6, 13 f., each ending with the statement 'that thou art' (*tat tvam asi*), meaning 'you are that universal self'. It is proclaimed most consistently in the very short *Māndukya Upanishad* saying, for example, 'this Ātman is Brahman'. Advaita was worked into a philosophical system by Shankara (788–820, q.v.) who made it into a system of absolute monism, the theory that there is 'only one' reality and all else is illusory or transient. This philosophy of Non-duality claims to derive from the *Vedānta*, the 'end of the Vedas', that is, the *Upanishads*, and it is popularized nowadays as Neo-Vedānta by the Rāmakrishna Mission. But also a very powerful influence in India has been the 'Qualified Non-duality' of the philosopher Rāmānuja (q.v., 11th century) which allowed for the worship of a personal God. See DVAITA, ĀTMAN.

Aediles. Roman religious officials superintending the temple *(aedes)* of Ceres (q.v.). In time their work was extended to general administration of public buildings and archives.

Aegeus. King of Athens in Greek mythology, and father of Theseus (q.v.). Originally he was probably a form of the sea god Poseidon (q.v.) of Aegae in Macedonia, so that Theseus is variously called son of Aegeus or of Poseidon. He married the sorceress Medea, but drove her away when she tried to poison Theseus. When the latter went to Crete to meet the Minotaur (q.v.), he forgot to change the black sails of his ship on his victorious return, and Aegeus, thinking his son was dead, drowned himself in the sea. The Aegean Sea is said to have been called after him.

Aegir. Scandinavian giant god of the 'sea', not one of the Aesir (q.v.) gods, though he was friendly towards them. Aegir invited the gods to a feast but asked them to bring a kettle, which was hard to obtain but eventually found, and at the feast the mischievous Loki (q.v.) killed one of Aegir's servants.

Aeneas. See VIRGIL.

Aeolus. A minor Greek god or mortal, ruler of the winds, who lived in a floating island called Aeolia, with his twelve sons and daughters who had inter-married. The winds when not blowing were thought to be kept in a cave or tied up in a sack. The same name was given to a son of Hellen and ancestor of the Aeolians.

Aeschylus. Greek dramatist (525–456 B.C.), for religious interest particularly notable for his plays on *Prometheus* and the *Eumenides* (qq.v.). His *Choephoroe* tells of the hatred of Electra (q.v.) for her mother.

Aesculapius. Latin form of ASCLEPIUS (q.v.).

Aesir. The collective name for the greater gods in Scandinavian mythology (the feminine is Asynjur, q.v.). The name Aesir may derive from a root meaning 'wind', and so they would be spirits, but they come to be distinguished from another group, the Vanir (q.v.), beings more concerned with fertility. There are tales of war between the Aesir and the Vanir, perhaps reflecting tribal conflicts and mingling of deities. It is said that the Aesir lived in Asgard (q.v.) or Asaland, and they included gods such as Odin, Balder, Thor and even the mischievous Loki.

Afghānī. One of the most famous modern Islamic reformers, Jamāl al-Dīn al-Afghānī (1839–97), was an Afghan about whose early years little is known and who spent the last thirty years of his life in exile. For eight years (1871–9) he lived in Egypt, influencing public opinion through a masonic lodge and by papers and reviews. He was exiled and went to India and then France, where with an Egyptian, Muhammad 'Abduh (q.v.), he directed a review 'The Indissoluble

Bond' (*al-'Urwa al-Wuthqā*), which had widespread influence towards modern reforms. He went to England, Russia and Persia, and died in captivity in Istanbul.

Africa. Islam dominates North Africa, much of West Africa, and parts of East Africa. There is the Coptic church in Egypt with some three million members, and it is the state church of Ethiopia; there are many churches in tropical and southern Africa of modern foundation. In the latter regions the old traditional, 'pagan' or 'animist' (qq.v.) forms of religion survive with over fifty million adherents. Once called 'fetishism' (q.v.); a term now out of favour, African traditional religion comprises belief in a supreme deity, many lesser nature gods, cults of ancestors, and magical practices. It has been compared to a pyramid, with God at the apex and magic at the base, the latter including belief in witchcraft (q.v.). There are no ancient scriptures and so no history of African traditional religion, and reliable information depends upon the writings of observers nearly all in the present century. For ideas of God, see LESA, MULUNGU, NYAMBE. See also VOODOO.

Aga Khan, Āghā Khān. A title bestowed on different noblemen by early Shāhs of Persia, and given in 1834 to Sultān Muhammad, the leader of most Nizārī Ismā'īlī Muslims, commonly known as Khojas (q.v.). The present Aga Khan is the fourth, and is regarded as the forty-ninth Imām by the Nizārīs, in India, Persia, Syria, East Africa and other parts. He is Prince Shāh Karīm al-Husaynī, son of an English mother and grandson of the sporting Aga Khan III whom he succeeded in 1957.

Agamemnon. In Greek legend king of Mycenae or Argos, who commanded the Greek armies in the siege of Troy. He sacrificed his daughter Iphigenia (q.v.) to Artemis. On his return he was killed by Aegisthus, lover of his wife Clytemnestra, who in turn was killed by her daughter Electra (q.v.), according to Euripides.

Agasti, Agastya. A Hindu sage, reputed to be the author of several hymns of the *Rig Veda*. He was said to be the son of the gods Mitra or Varuna. Agasti appears in the epics, especially the *Rāmāyana* (q.v.), where he received Rāma into his hermitage and later accompanied him to his capital. Among the Tamils Agasti is one of the first great teachers, forming their language and literature.

Aggadah. See HAGGADAH.

Aghlabids. Muslim caliphs of North Africa, and Sicily (800–909). Ibrāhīm ibn al-Aghlab was given the province of Africa, chiefly Tunisia, by Hārūn al-Rashīd (q.v.) of Baghdad and, though he paid tribute, the great distance gave him virtual independence. The Aghlabids conquered Malta and Sicily from the Byzantines; and from Sicily Islamic culture spread into Europe, till its conquest by the Normans in the eleventh century. Aghlabid power declined in the ninth century and was finally overthrown by the Fātimids (q.v.).

Aglaia. Greek grace of 'splendour', one of the three Graces (q.v.). Another Aglaia was wife of Acrisius (q.v.).

Agni. God of 'fire' (Sanskrit, see Latin *ignis*, English 'ignite') in the Indian *Vedas*. More hymns are addressed to him than any other god, and he is important both as a deity in his own right and as the mediator and messenger of the gods since prayers were taken to heaven by the sacrificial fire. The sacred fire was also protector of men and their homes and witness of all great occasions in social life. Though no longer worshipped Agni is honoured for his place in home and temple. Agni is described in many terms, particularly with seven tongues for licking up the sacrificial butter. He is identified with other gods and leads the way towards their unification into one deity.

There is an *Agni Purāna*, one of the traditional Hindu books, said to have been communicated by Agni and devoted to the glorification of the god Shiva. Its contents are mixed, with ritual, historical, legal, medical, ethical and grammatical matters.

Agnostic. From Greek 'unknown' (*agnostos*), and Paul's reference to an Athenian altar 'to an unknown god' (Acts 17, 23), the term Agnosticism was coined in 1869 by T. H. Huxley, and was later used to denote the belief that the existence of anything beyond the material world is unknown or cannot be known; it is also applied to scepticism. For Indian possible parallels see ATHEISM, CHĀRVĀKAS, BUDDHISM, JAINISM. See also GNOSTIC and JÑĀNA.

Agones. Greek public festivals of religious origin, comprising games performed in honour of a god or hero. Best known were the Olympic games (see OLYMPIA), and at Athens plays were performed under the patronage of Dionysus.

Ahad Ha-am. See GINZBERG.

Ahamkāra. 'Ego', self-consciousness, individuality (Sanskrit). In Sāmkhya philosophy, Ahamkāra is the production of Buddhi (q.v.) which first evolves from Nature, Prakriti.

Ahi. A snake, serpent of the clouds, in Hindu mythology, which was destroyed by the god Indra (q.v.). It is often a name of Vritra (q.v.), the demon of drought, but Ahi is sometimes distinct and may represent different forms of clouds.

Ahimsā, Ahinsā. (Sanskrit) 'not-killing'. Harmlessness, non-violence, an Indian doctrine of general benevolence, but particularly applied to abstention from harming any living creature, since all life is sacred, and hence to vegetarianism. It was developed especially by the Jains, and also by Buddhists and some sects of Hindus. Buddhists are forbidden to take life, but eat meat if provided by another; all meat is forbidden to Jain monks and laity, and also occupations such as hunting or agriculture which might involve taking life. Jain temples often bear the text 'non-violence is the highest religion.' Mahātma Gāndhi (q.v.) applied Ahimsā to political ends by his technique of non-violent non-co-operation. See HIMSĀ.

Ahl Al-Kitāb. 'The People of the Book' (Arabic), a name given frequently in the *Qur'ān* to distinguish Jews and Christians from heathens who had no scriptures. With Christians (Nasārā q.v.) and Jews (Yāhūd) were linked the Sābi'īn and the Magi (qq.v.), who also believed in one God and the Last Day (2, 59; 22, 17). These received exemption from poll tax (*jizya*; 9, 29), because of their monotheistic worship. Such toleration was later extended to other religions, even Hindu and Chinese, though more fanatical Muslim rulers did not agree.

Ahl-i-haqq. 'People of the Truth' or God (Arabic), also called 'Alī-Allāhī, an extreme Shī'a (q.v.) Islamic sect found in western Persia. The second name was given to them by neignbours, but 'Alī (q.v.) is not their principal religious figure. They believe in seven manifestations of divinity and in the transmigration of souls.

Ahmad. A name of Muhammad (q.v.) in Muslim tradition. In the *Qur'ān* (61, 6) it is said that Jesus foretold the coming of a messenger whose name was *ahmadu*. The standard biography of Muhammad, by Ibn Ishāq, has a similar passage which does not mention *ahmadu*, but refers to the Paraclete, the Comforter announced by Jesus which it identifies with Muhammad. Muslim commentators have taken the passage to mention Muhammad by the name Ahmad, but some modern Western critical scholars consider that *ahmadu* is an adjective, meaning 'celebrated' and referring to the promised Comforter.

Ahmad B. Hanbal. See HANBAL.

Ahmadiyya. The name of the followers of a popular saint in Egypt and North Africa, Ahmad al-Badawī. See BADAWĪYYA.

The name Ahmadiyya is also given to the followers of Mirza Ghulām Ahmad (1839–1908), who founded a religious movement at Qadian in the Punjab. Ahmad was a Muslim who announced himself as the expected Madhī of Islam, the Messiah of Christians and the Avatar of Hindus. He differed from orthodox Islam also in teaching that Jesus had been crucified but taken down alive from the cross, whence he went to Kashmir where his grave was still to be seen, a claim that has often been refuted. There was division after the death of Ahmad, one group based on Qadian, now at Rabwah in Pakistan, and one in Lahore which has drawn closer to Islamic orthodoxy. Ahmadiyya missionaries have been particularly successful in West Africa and to a lesser extent in East Africa; they publish a considerable amount of literature in English.

Ahriman, also **Angra Mainyu.** The evil or destructive spirit in Zoroastrianism, he personifies the Lie (See Druj) and unrighteousness. Ahriman is a devilish spirit who stands over against God,

Ahura Mazdā, being all wickedness and death, seeking to subvert good government and peaceful agriculture (see DUALISM). Ahriman, like Ahura Mazdā, is pure spirit and is accompanied by subsidiary spirits, in his case personifying lust, sloth and heresy. According to one theory both Ahura Mazdā and Ahriman were born of infinite Time, but God is eternal whereas Ahriman will come to an end, or at least will be rendered powerless after great cosmic battles with the good, and neither Ahriman nor his creatures will prevail. As Angra Mainyu, 'the destructive spirit', he is opposed to the bountiful or 'holy spirit', Spenta Mainyu (q.v.). See ZURVĀN.

Ahuna Vairya, Ahunavar. The most sacred prayer of the Zoroastrians, so called from its second and third words, speaking of the Lord, Ahu, whose desire, Vairya, is supreme. It comes in the *Yasna* (q.v.) and consists of twenty-one words and therefore the original *Avesta* (q.v.) is said to have contained twenty-one volumes. The recital of the Ahunavar is said to have conquered the evil Ahriman when he tempted Zoroaster, whereupon the latter taught it as a protective prayer. It is the first prayer learnt by a Parsi child, recited on daily as well as on special occasions, and repeated on strings of beads.

Ah Uoh Puc. 'Lord of the underworlds' in ancient Maya (q.v.) religion, and also called 'lord of seven hells' (Uac Mitun Ahau). He was represented as a skeleton, and was associated with the war god, presiding with him over human sacrifices. He was accompanied by a dog and a moaning bird.

Ahura Mazdā. The Wise Lord, the supreme and only God and creator in Zoroastrianism, later called Ohrmazd. Ahura Mazdā was the creator of truth, holiness and goodness, the giver of health and abundance. Evil could not come from him and was therefore attributed to an opposing principle of darkness and lies, Ahriman. From Ahura Mazdā came six Bounteous Immortals, Amesha Spentas, personifying virtues which God created. These are aspects of God, but man can share in them by practising righteousness and truth. Ahura Mazdā finally defeats Ahriman and so his good will is perfectly fulfilled.

'A'isha. See AYESHA.

Aitareya. Title of one of the principal *Upanishads* (q.v.), called after a sage of that name. It is part of a *Brāhmana* and *Āranyaka* attached to the *Rig Veda*. The *Upanishad* consists of three short parts, and is concerned with creation and the self.

Ajanta. A village in western India where twenty-nine caves are cut into the cliffs of a secluded valley and are some of the finest specimens of ancient Buddhist monasteries and temples. They date from about the second century B.C. to the seventh century A.D., the best work being from the end of this period. Frescoes remain in thirteen of the caves which depict the birth of the Buddha and incidents in his life, along with many Bodhisattvas (q.v.) and Hindu deities, since the Buddha is believed to have passed through many experiences and places of life in previous existences. Many frescoes illustrate parts of the Jātaka stories (q.v.), but although Indian life is depicted in varied phases the general impression is religious, and through the scenes the Buddha moves with grace and compassion. See also VAJRA.

AJANTA CAVE

Ājīvikas. An unorthodox Indian sect contemporary with Buddhism and Jainism. The founder, Gosāla (q.v.), developed earlier doctrines and died about 484 B.C. The Ājīvikas prospered for some centuries and then rapidly declined, lingering in eastern Mysore and Madras till the fourteenth century when they disappeared. No Ājīvika scriptures have survived and knowledge of their doctrines depends on debates recorded in Buddhist and Jain scriptures. The name Ājīvika may mean 'the mode of life' or 'as long as life' and refer to the extreme asceticism which they practised, involving complete nudity. They were atheistic and their principal teaching was determinism, the whole universe being conditioned to the smallest details by an impersonal destiny, Niyati (q.v.).

Akālīs. The 'immortals', a body of militant ascetics among the Sikhs, soldiers of Akāl, 'the Timeless', the true name of God to them. They appeared in 1690 in the days of the tenth Sikh Gurū, Gobind Singh (q.v.), and became the most ardent defenders of the Khālsā, the inner group of initiates. The Akālīs have been prominent in struggles for Sikh independence, against the Mughals, the British and within the Indian state. They rejected Hindu rites of birth, marriage and death, were opposed to the use of alcohol, and were noted as fanatical soldiers. They were strongest in Amritsar and Tarn Taran in the Punjab, and their headquarters has been a building called Akāl Takht, the 'Throne of the Timeless', facing the major Sikh Golden Temple in Amritsar.

Akbar. Greatest of the Mughal emperors of India, he was born in Sind in 1542, was crowned at the age of fourteen, and died in the great fort at Agra in 1605. Although illiterate, Akbar was a man of great intellectual activity, a successful soldier and a fine administrator. He changed the practice of Muslim rulers in India and ruled for the Hindu majority of his subjects, giving justice to the poor, and taking as his motto 'Peace for all'. Although brought up as a Muslim, Akbar was dissatisfied with the orthodox faith, consorted with Sūfī mystics and took a keen interest in other religions, especially those of the Hindus, Parsīs and Christians. He called to his court representatives of different faiths, and gave close attention to the Jesuit missionaries. But eventually Akbar founded his own eclectic religion, Tawhīd-i ilāhī, the 'divine faith'. He accepted belief in God as basic to all religion and added rules of conduct. See also AURANGZEB.

Aker. Ancient earth-god of the Egyptian Delta. He is depicted in art as two lions with their backs to each other, or as one animal but with each end as the head and front paws of a lion guarding the two horizons and the underworld. See JANUS.

Akhenaten. See IKHNATON.

Akiba. A leading Jewish rabbi (50–135) who began systematizing the teaching of traditional law in the form of Mishnah repetition, arranging legal teachings by subject-matter with sub-divisions. He also developed the interpretation of the smallest details of the Biblical text and applied them to religion and morality. Akiba acclaimed Bar Kozeba as military Messiah in the revolt against the Romans in 132—135, and when Hadrian forbade the study of the *Torah* Akiba defied this prohibition publicly and was put to death. He is called the 'father of Rabbinic Judaism' and is remembered in synagogue prayers. See COCHBA and MAASEH BERESHITH.

'Akīka. Arabic name of an Islamic sacrifice performed on the seventh day after the birth of a child. The baby is named, and two rams or goats are killed for a boy, one for a girl, and most of the flesh given to the poor. The child's hair is shaved off, and this also may be called 'Akīka.

Aksa. See AQSA.

Akshobhya. (Sanskrit) 'immovable', imperturbable, name of one of the Dhyāni-Buddhas (q.v.).

Ala, Ale, Ana. The earth goddess of the Ibo of Nigeria. Ala is a mother deity, the most popular in many parts of Ibo country, invoked for fertility of family and land. She is the guardian of morality, laws are made in her name, and oaths taken by knocking a staff against the earth. The dead are said to lie in her pocket or womb. Clay temples to Ala are found in many places and contain sculptures of the goddess with a child in her

arms, usually brilliantly painted. In a region south of Owerri the custom survives of building Mbari houses in honour of Ala, when a priest reports that he has received the command. The houses are square with open verandas, and are full of clay sculptures, in which Ala is the principal figure, flanked by other deities and all manner of human and divine figures, in traditional and modern dress, painted in bright colours.

Alamūt. Fortress of the Assassins (q.v.) and Old Man of the Mountains, overlooking the Caspian Sea in Persia. It was described by Marco Polo in 1273.

Alcestis. In Greek mythology the wife of the pious King Admetus of Thessaly. Admetus forgot to sacrifice to Artemis at his bridal feast and was threatened with death. Apollo intervened and made the Fates promise to spare Admetus if somebody would die in his place, and this Alcestis did. In a further story Admetus, or Heracles in his stead, went down to Hades and gained the release of Alcestis.

Alcheringa. See DREAMING.

Alcoran. See QUR'ĀN.

Alenu. (Hebrew) 'it is our duty', a third century Jewish prayer which is recited at the end of normal synagogue services and festivals. It affirms the unity of God and looks to the coming of his kingdom on earth.

Alexander the Great. The famous Greek soldier appears in the *Qur'ān* under the name of Dhu 'l-Qarnain (q.v.), the 'two-horned'.

Alfar, Alfheimr. The home of the elves in Scandinavian mythology (see ELF). The beautiful light elves lived in this splendid place, to the far east of Norway. It was ruled by Alfr, king of the elves. The gods gave Alfheimr to the rain god Freyr when he cut his first tooth.

Al-Ghazālī, Algazel. See GHAZĀLĪ.

'Alī. Cousin and son-in-law of Muhammad and the fourth caliph according to Sunni Islam. He was one of the first to accept Islam and married Fātima (q.v.), the Prophet's daughter.

'Alī was hailed as caliph after 'Uthmān in the mosque at Medina in 656 and then left to engage in a series of struggles against rivals and was assassinated and buried at Kūfa in 661. His sons Hasan and Husain succeeded him but with short-lived success. 'Alī was notable for piety and transmitted hundred of Traditions of Muhammad. According to the Shī'a, the 'followers' of 'Alī, he was the first legitimate caliph or imām, 'spiritual leader' after the Prophet. He is called the 'friend of God', a title which the Shī'a add to the regular confession of faith in God and in Muhammad. He is in particular the ideal warrior and saint and many legends are told of his miracles and holiness, while judgements and maxims attributed to him are widespread.

'Alī-Allāhī. See AHL-I-HAQQ.

Alkumisi, Daniel. Jewish Karaite (q.v.) teacher of Persia in the ninth century. He was opposed to allegorical interpretations of the Bible but also condemned astronomical calculations as superstitious. Alkumisi disliked speculation, but he considered that angels are natural forces by which God operates in the world rather than personal beings.

Allāh. The Supreme Being of the Muslims, the name God, derived from the Arabic al-ilāh, 'the God'. Faith in him is expressed in the first phrase of the creed and prayer, 'there is no god but God' (*lā ilāha illa 'llāhu*). To Muhammad Allāh was the sole deity and he has no associates and no images; this faith is expressed throughout the *Qur'ān*. The nature of God is indicated in the Ninety-nine 'Most Beautiful Names' of Muslim devotion (see BEAUTIFUL NAMES), recited on prayer beads, many of the names being found in the *Qur'ān* (17, 110 etc). Thus God exists in and by himself, and in relation to others he is creator, ruler and destroyer, the only one who has real power of action. But in a constantly used phrase he is 'the Merciful, the Compassionate' (*al-rahmān al-rahīm*). So God is protector as well as king, and forgiver as well as reckoner. It is said that God has a face, two hands, and so on, but theologians accept these terms 'without asking how'. The Sūfī mystics stressed the love of God to man and some spoke of virtual identification with him.

Allāhu Akbar. (Arabic) 'God is very great' or 'most great', a formula called the *Takbīr* (q.v.) which occurs frequently in Muslim daily prayers, in the funeral office, and has also been used as a war cry.

Allatu, Allatum. Akkadian name of

the Babylonian goddess Ereshkigal (q.v.). She was 'lady of the earth' and of the underworld. She was dragged from her throne by Nergal (q.v.) till she agreed to share her realm with him.

Almamar. See BIMAH.

Almohads. Islamic caliphs of North Africa and Spain (1130–1269). The name means Unitarians, al-Muwahhidūn, and they were protesters against the laxity of Muslim life and faith in Africa. The founder was a Berber, Ibn Tumart, who proclaimed himself Madhī or Guided One and his successor called himself Caliph. The Almohads took over Morocco and its capital Marrakesh from the Almoravids (q.v.), and then occupied all the Islamic parts of Spain with capital at Seville. Algeria, Tunis and Tripoli were also conquered. Then Almohad power declined, they lost all Spain except Granada in 1212, and their African lands were divided among smaller powers.

Almoravids. Islamic caliphs in North Africa and Spain, 1056–1147. They arose in West Africa where a *ribāt* or fortress on the Senegal river trained warrior missionaries. They came to be known as Murābitūn; the Spanish form gave Almoravids and the French word *marabout* meant a holy man. These warriors wore veils, like the modern Tuaregs, and were so-called 'veiled ones'. They conquered Morocco and Algiers, founding the capital of Marrakesh in 1062. They crossed into Spain in 1086 and defeated Alfonso VI, but later retreated. Then the Almoravids were pressed from the rear by the Almohads (q.v.) and succumbed to them.

Alms. See DĀNA and ZAKĀT.

Amahraspands. See AMESHA SPENTAS.

Amarāvatī. In Hindu mythology the 'abode of the immortals' (Sanskrit), the capital of the heaven of the god Indra, situated somewhere near Mount Meru (q.v.).

In southern India Amaravati, near Madras, was once the capital of the Andhra kingdom and a Buddhist centre. It had a splendid Stūpa, perhaps thirty metres high and dating from about the beginning of the Christian era. Little now remains of it, but specimens of the stone sculptures are in the British Museum and at Madras and Calcutta.

Amar Dās. Third Guru of the Sikhs (1479–1574), succeeding to Guru Angad when he himself was an old man. He was a reformer and organizer, gathering Sikh congregations into provinces and making communal eating compulsory. He wrote over nine hundred verses which were incorporated into the Sikh scripture, *Ādi Granth* (q.v.). He was succeeded by Guru Rām Dās.

Amarna. See TELL EL-AMARNA.

Amaru. Mythical dragon in Inca mythology, sometimes identified with the earth mother Pachamama (q.v.).

Amaterasu-ōmi-kami. The 'Heaven-Shining-Goddess', the Sun-Goddess, chief of the Kami (gods) in the Shinto religion of Japan. According to myths in the Kojiki (q.v.) and Nihongi records, Amaterasu was born from the left eye of a primal being, Izanagi, (q.v.), and her brother from his nose. Amaterasu was beautiful and mild, ruling all wisely, but her brother Susano-wo, the storm god, ravaged the rice fields and offended Amaterasu so that she hid in a cave and disorder covered the world. This myth of eclipse, darkness and winter says that eight million gods came together and induced Amaterasu to emerge by performing a ceremonial dance. Later she sent down her grandson, Ninigi, to rule the earth and he married the goddess of Mount Fuji (q.v.), and from their descendants came Jimmu Tenno, first human king of Japan (q.v.). The temple of Amaterasu at Isé (q.v.) on the eastern sea coast is the most sacred place in all Japan.

AMARĀVATĪ

Amazons. Female warriors in Greek mythology who lived on the borders of the world. They were said to have fought Bellerophon and helped the Trojans. One

of the Labours of Heracles was to gain the girdle of their queen Hippolyta, who was captured and married by Theseus.

Ambrosia. Am-brosia was the 'immortal' food of the gods in Greek mythology, like the Indian A-mrita (q.v.). It was sweet-smelling and overcame bad odours. Nectar was the drink of the gods, said in Homer to be red like wine. It was poured out by Hebe (q.v.). It may have been a kind of honey product, like mead, but it is sometimes confused with Ambrosia as the food of the gods.

Amenhotep, Amenophis. A wise man who lived in Egypt in the fourteenth century B.C. and was deified some eight hundred years later. He was a royal vizier and architect, and in art was represented as a bearded man holding a papyrus roll. The Greeks called him Amenophis, son of Paapis, their version of his father's name Hapu. Like Imhotep (q.v.), for the Greeks he represented the deified wisdom of the ancestors. See also IKHNATON.

Amesha Spentas. 'Bounteous Immortals' in Zoroastrianism, who surround the one true God, Ahura Mazdā, and are also his characteristic attributes. In the *Gāthās* of Zoroaster the Amesha Spentas are six abstractions: Good Mind, Truth, Rightmindedness, the Kingdom, Wholeness and Immortality. In later Zoroastrianism they are called Amahraspands and are subsidiary created spirits, like angels, who serve Ohrmazd and help in his fight against Ahriman and his demons. See AHURA MAZDĀ, and SPENTA MAINYU, also ASHA and VOHU MANAH.

Amida. See AMITĀBHA.

Amidah. 'Standing', the Jewish prayer *par excellence*, recited standing at each of the three daily prayers. Called in the *Talmud* Tefillah, *the* prayer, it is now known as Amidah. It consists of nineteen (originally eighteen) blessings, of which the first three praise the greatness and commandments of God, the last three thank him for his continued mercies, and the other thirteen pray for material and spiritual needs, including the rebuilding of Jerusalem and setting up the throne of David. The name Shemoneh Esreh ('eighteen') is also used, although there are now nineteen benedictions and sometimes they are not all recited.

Amina. Mother of the prophet Muhammad, she belonged to a clan of the Quraysh (q.v.). She died when he was six years old, in A.D. 576, and was buried at Abwā, between Mecca and Medina.

Amīr. See EMIR.

Amitābha, Amitāyus. (Sanskrit) a Buddha of 'immeasurable light' or 'immeasurable life' in Mahāyāna Buddhism. In the Lotus scripture he dwells in the west in the world of bliss, Sukhākara or Sukhāvatī, sitting on a throne in a lotus and attended by the great Bodhisattva Avalokiteshvara (q.v.). In countless later writings Amitābha is presented as king of the Western Paradise, the Land of Blessedness, who guides weary travellers in the ship of salvation over the sea of sorrows, to the peace of the western heaven which is described in colourful terms. The Pure Land Buddhists of China and Japan call upon Amitābha constantly as Amida and briefly in the Nanmo or Nembutsu (q.v.) (in Japanese Namu) as Amida Butsu, 'Hail to Amida Buddha'. Repetition of the phrase helps in meditation, is made on prayer beads, and is held to ensure entry to Amida's paradise at death. In a popular Pure Land text, *Sukhāvatī-vyūha*, a monk Dharmākara (Japanese Hozo) took a vow to save all beings and eventually became Amitābha.

Amma. The name of the Supreme Being among the Dogon of Mali and Upper Volta in West Africa. Most African peoples believe in a supreme God, but generally there are no temples for his worship and cults are restricted to lesser deities. The Dogon are one of the few peoples that have altars and rituals for God, and these may be group altars for villages at which the chief officiates, or special altars erected at places where some object is believed to be filled with the divine power, and here sacrifices are made by chosen priests or priestesses. In Dogon mythology Amma was the creator who made the sun and moon of clay, and then the earth. This was like a giant female with whom Amma was united in order to produce other spirits and men.

Amma. See GRĀMADEVATĀ.

Ammon. See AMŪN.

Ammonius Saccas. Reputed founder (175–242) of Neo-Platonism (q.v.). He was born at Alexandria into a Christian family, and taught the Christian father Origen, but reverted to Greek philosophy. Ammonius Saccas wrote nothing, but his teachings were expounded by his disciple Plotinus who quite overshadowed him.

Ammonite. A fossil, from medieval Latin 'Ammon's horn' which it was thought to resemble. In India it is the

Shālagrāma (q.v.), symbol of the great god Vishnu. See AMŪN.

Amogha-siddhi. (Sanskrit) 'unfailing perfection', name of one of the Dhyāni-Buddhas (q.v.).

Amoraim. Hebrew, 'speakers', the title of Jewish teachers who interpreted and harmonized the *Mishnah* (q.v.) and oral teachings, and formulated decisions and judgements for new circumstances. Their work culminated in the *Talmud*, in Palestinian and Babylonian versions. The Babylonian Amoriam were most active under the dialectics of Abbaye (283–338) and Raba (299–352). The mass of interpretative material that accumulated was set in order by Rab Ashi (died 427), who spent over thirty years on Talmudic arrangement. His work was concluded by Rab Abina or Rabina II, last of the Amoraim to teach the Torah on an oral basis. They were followed by the Saboraim (q.v.).

Amphion. In Greek mythology a son of Zeus and Antiope. He and his brother Zethus were abandoned at birth and brought up by a shepherd and Amphion received a lyre from the god Hermes and became a great musician. Later they found their mother and protected her. Amphion married Niobe (q.v.).

Amphitrite. Greek sea-goddess, but with a non-Greek name and rather a vague character, like the Tritons (q.v.). See also POSEIDON.

Amram Gaon, Rav Amram. Jewish writer (died 874) who produced a *Seder* or *Siddur* (order), a prayer book with notes and explanations for Spanish Jews. This was the first Jewish prayer book and had considerable influence on the practices of the synagogue.

Amrita. (Sanskrit) 'Immortal', a name of gods, the immortals, and the Soma juice of Hindu sacrifice. Later it was the nectar or water of life, the story of which is told in the epics. The gods being worsted by demons asked the great god Vishnu for the gift of immortality, and he told them to churn the ocean for the Amrita and other treasures that had been lost. Vishnu himself in an Avatar as a Tortoise (q.v.) served as pivot in the ocean on which the gods twirled the mountain Mandara. The ocean then gave forth its riches and the physician of the gods, Dhanvantari, robed in white, brought out the cup of Amrita. The demons seized it, but Vishnu assumed a female form, recovered the Amrita, and gave it to the gods who after quaffing the nectar put their foes to flight. See also KŪRMA and AMBROSIA.

Amritsar. The sacred city of the Sikhs in the Punjab, India. It was founded in 1577 by the fourth Guru, Rām Dās (q.v.), on a site granted by the Mughal emperor Akbar (q.v.), and is constructed round a sacred tank which gives its name to the city, 'pool of nectar'. See GOLDEN TEMPLE.

Amulet. A charm or protective ornament worn or used against disease, misfortune, harmful magic and witchcraft. It comes from a Latin word of unknown origin. See ANKH, FETISH and TALISMAN.

Amulius. In Roman mythology king of Alba Longa by deposing his brother Numitor. When Numitor's daughter gave birth to the twins Romulus and Remus (q.v.), Amulius had them thrown into the Tiber. Later they killed him and Numitor was made king again.

Amūn. Air and wind god in ancient Egypt who became established at Thebes in the Middle Kingdom and was identified with the old state god Rēʿ as the mighty Amūn-Rēʿ and the father of the reigning king. The name may mean 'what is hidden' and later was connected with the word 'eternal'. Amūn was self-created, lord of time, before all other gods, hearing prayers and fighting sickness. He was represented with a beard, wearing a cap with two tall plumes from the back of which hung a cord, and holding a sceptre and Ankh (q.v.). During the reign of the young monotheistic Pharaoh Ikhnaton (fourteenth century B.C.) the name of Amūn and other gods was chiselled out of monuments in favour of the god Aton, but at his death the priests of Amūn took their revenge. Tut-ankh-Aton's name was changed to Tut-ankh-Amūn, and Amūn dominated. As an oracle Amūn became popular with the Greeks and Syrians and was visited by Alexander the Great. The symbol of Amūn was a ram, and in Egypt, as well as in Greek and Roman art as Zeus or Jupiter Ammon, he had a ram's head or ears. See AMMONITE.

AMŪN

Anāgarikā. See DHARMAPĀLA.

Anāhitā. The 'spotless', goddess of the waters in developing Zoroastrianism. Anāhitā was ignored by Zoroaster but in the *Yashts*, texts composed after his time, it is said that he was told to worship Ardvī Sūrā Anāhitā, the 'humid, strong and spotless' water goddess, and even that the supreme Ahura Mazdā himself had prayed to Anāhitā for her help in inclining Zoroaster to think, speak and act in accordance with true religion. Anāhitā is mentioned in inscriptions of Artaxerxes II, and statues were erected to her as a beautiful young woman crowned with gold and gems. It seems that her cult was most successful outside Persia, in Armenia and Asia Minor.

Analects. The *Lun Yü* or 'Selected Sayings' of Confucius. A short work which contains the basic moral, political and religious thoughts of the great Chinese teacher. Even so, among its twenty chapters or books, critical scholarship considers that chapters 3 to 9 present the oldest material, and other chapters include sayings and ideas of disciples. The usually accepted date of the book is about the fourth century B.C. The *Analects* teach the duties of rulers and subjects, filial conduct towards parents and ancestors, the ideal of the true gentleman who is moderate in opinion and conduct, the Way in which things should be done, and the guidance of Heaven in the sense of Providence.

Anan ben David. Babylonian Jew of the eighth century A.D., founder of the Karaites (q.v.). When he did not become Exilarch, he denounced the *Talmud* and oral tradition, and expounded the *Bible* literally. The letter of the law was strictly followed, especially in regard to the Sabbath. About 770 Anan published *Sefer ha-Mitzvoth*, the 'Book of the Precepts', in Aramaic, and eventually he withdrew to Jerusalem where his Karaite community rejected all rabbinic laws, abolished traditional prayers in favour of Biblical quotations, and forbade marriage with the orthodox.

Ananai-kyō. A Japanese New Religion (see SECT SHINTO), seeking to 'tie God with man'. Founded by Yonosuke Nakano, it is a synthesis of Shinto and Christianity, seeking union with the Great Spirit of the Universe. Ananai-kyō emphasizes 'god-possession' (*kami-gakari*) and tranquillity of the soul. Since it teaches the mystical powers of the sky, the movement has built many observatories throughout Japan. It also expects the coming of a saviour. Ananai-kyō has about a hundred thousand members.

Ānanda. 'Bliss' (Sanskrit), one of the three attributes of the divine principle Brahman in the Vedānta philosophy, combined as Sat-chit-ānanda. Ānanda is also a title of the god Shiva.

Also the name of the beloved disciple of the Buddha. It is said either that Ānanda became a monk in the twentieth year of the Buddha's preaching, or that he had been a monk for twenty years then. Thereafter he was for twenty more years a permanent attendant on the Buddha. From him came some of the stories of the Buddha's birth, which he stated that he heard from his master. His name appears frequently in the *Sutta Pitaka*, the second part of the canon of scripture, as a recipient of the teaching and a companion of the Buddha during his travels and witness of his death. At the Buddha's death it is said that Ānanda recited the teaching of the Buddha, the *Dhamma*, and the monastic rules, the *Vinaya*.

Ananke. (Greek) 'necessity', force. According to Plato, she was the mother of the Moirai, Fates, and later it was said that Ananke presided at the birth of children. See FATE.

Ananta. (Sanskrit) 'endless', a title applied to Vishnu and other Hindu gods, and particularly to Shesha (q.v.), the snake on which Vishnu reposes. As an endless circle An-anta is an apt symbol of eternity.

Anat, Anath. Warrior-goddess of the Phoenicians (q.v.), called goddess of the sky and mother of all the gods. She obtained the help of Baal to conquer the heights of Lebanon and build a temple where many youths were sacrificed.

Anattā. 'No-self', non-ego (in Pali: Anātman in Sanskrit), the Buddhist doctrine denying a permanent self to be identified with the five Skandhas (q.v.) or constituents which make up the personality. In his sermon on the marks of non-self (in the *Samyutta Nikāya*) the Buddha says that the body is not-self, nor are feeling, perception, aggregates or consciousness. These are impermanent and painful and cannot be identified with the soul. But apparently the Buddha did not deny the self of experience, but no permanent entity can be found in the mortal faculties. See NITYA.

Ancestor Worship. Reverence for the spirits of the dead, implying belief in their survival into an afterlife, is one of the oldest forms of religion and can be traced back at least into the Old Stone Age. Found in all cultures, it has been particularly developed in China and some writers called it the real religion of China, though others regarded it as a cult of filial piety rather than religious worship. After funeral rites had been performed, a tablet was set up for the ancestor in his old home, and later old tablets were grouped together in ancestral halls, where regular ceremonies were held. Incense sticks were lit every morning and prayers made for the departed soul. Much of this survives in modern China. Ancestral cults have been practised in all other continents and have been particularly prominent in Africa (see ADAE), where the dead are propitiated for health, family, property, crops and rainfall. See MIAO and HUMAN SACRIFICE.

Andhaka. In Hindu mythology a demon with a thousand heads who was killed by the god Shiva. Another Andhaka was ancestor of the race of Andhaka-Vrishnis into which Krishna was born.

Andromeda. In Greek mythology the daughter of the Ethiopian king Cepheus and his wife Cassiopeia. The sea god Poseidon sent a monster to ravage the land, and Andromeda was chained to a rock as a sacrifice. The hero Perseus rescued her by killing the monster. He then married Andromeda. This may have been a prototype of the legend of St George and the dragon, and it was a favourite subject in art. Andromeda, Cepheus, Cassiopeia and Perseus all became constellations, as did the monster Cetus.

Andronicus. Peripatetic (q.v.) philosopher of the first century B.C. who revived the study of the works of Aristotle and wrote books on them.

Anga. (Sanskrit), a 'limb' or 'member', the name of works auxiliary to the Hindu *Veda* (see VEDĀNGA). The basic canonical scriptures of the Jains are called *Angas* and *Upāngas*. It is said that originally there were twelve *Angas*, but these were transmitted orally and the twelfth was finally lost. There remain eleven *Angas*, which include the principal Jain teachings, lives of the saints, and monastic and moral rules. There are twelve *Upāngas*, which contain further rules, doctrines and narratives. The Digambara sect of Jains declare that all the Angas were lost and have their own scriptures, with doctrines, biographies and customs.

Angad. Second Guru of the Sikhs (1504–52), son of a trader, at first a worshipper of the Hindu goddess Durgā, and then an ardent follower of the first Guru, Nānak. He was chosen by Guru Nānak to succeed him, in preference to his own sons. Guru Angad introduced the Gurmukhi script in which the Sikh scriptures, *Ādi Granth*, are written. Sixty-two of his hymns are in that scripture. He was succeeded by Guru Amar Dās.

Angels. The Greek word for 'messenger' (*angelos*) is used for heavenly envoys in the Bible, but no angels are named till the Book of Daniel mentions Gabriel and Michael, and Jewish rabbis later said that their names came into Israel from Babylon. The *Talmud* speaks of four archangels which surround the throne of God: Michael, Gabriel, Uriel and Raphael. Their names are still found in the Hebrew prayerbook in the prayer before retiring at night: Michael at the right, Gabriel at the left, Uriel in front and Raphael behind. Michael and Gabriel are the most prominent in the *Talmud* and appear on many occasions. Hebrew angelology profoundly affected Islam, where the four archangels are Gabriel (Jibrīl), Mīkhā'īl, Isrāfīl and 'Izrā'īl (Azrael, q.v.). Islamic angels are messengers of God, surrounding his throne, watching over men and recording their deeds. Only Gabriel and Michael are mentioned in the *Qur'ān*, but many others come in later tradition. See MUNKAR.

Angiras. A Rishi, Hindu sage, to whom many hymns of the *Rig Veda* are attributed. He is said to be priest of the gods and lord of sacrifice. The name is used for the father of the fire-god Agni, and the Angirases were luminous deities.

Angkor Wat. 'The temple of the capital', in the ruined city of Angkor, of Hindu and Buddhist inspiration in Cambodia. Built under the Khmer rulers, from the ninth century A.D. onwards, Angkor Wat contains many stone sculptures and images of Hindu gods and attendants. In the centre of the city square of Angkor Thom is the huge Bayon temple, with fifty towers and 172 sculptures of human faces, which are believed to represent the Buddhist Avalokiteshvara (q.v.). Amongst dancing figures the enormous faces look out with the enigmatical 'smile of Angkor', indicating inner peace. The city was in ruins till modern times. Hinduism has disappeared there and the Buddhist sculptures are Mahāyāna, but Cambodia now is firmly Theravāda Buddhist (q.v.).

Angra Mainyu. The 'evil spirit', or spirit of destruction, in early Zoroastrianism, opposed to the good spirit Ahura Mazdā. Later he is called Ahriman (q.v.).

Angrboda. 'Distress-bringer', Scandinavian giantess and mother of the Fenris wolf (q.v.).

Anguttara Nikāya. (Pāli), 'collection of gradual sayings', the fourth section of the second main division of the Theravāda Buddhist canon of scripture. See TRIPITAKA and SŪTRA.

Anicca. See NITYA and ANATTĀ.

Animatism. A modification of Tylor's theory of Animism (q.v.) proposed by R. R. Marett in 1899. Instead of believing in personal souls, Marett said that primitive man thought the world was 'animated' by impersonal forces. Bishop Codrington had said that the Melanesians of the Pacific believed in such a vague spiritual force (see MANA), but later research showed that this was not a power animating the universe but a quality which gave distinctiveness to people and spirits. Marett also opposed Tylor's notion of primitive man as a philosopher and said that he was primarily an actor, his religion being 'not so much thought out as danced out', and so it was similar to magic. Animatism has been generally abandoned as an explanation of the origins of religion or of the practice of primitive religion.

Animism. A term coined in 1871 by E. B. Tylor in his *Primitive Culture* to denote 'the deep-lying doctrine of

ANGKOR WAT

Spiritual Beings' which he regarded as 'a minimum definition of religion.' He related it to the doctrine of the soul, from the Latin *anima*, soul, and included belief in the souls of individuals considered capable of existing after death, and in other spirits up to the powerful deities. Tylor said that Animism characterized tribes low in the scale of humanity and ascended thence in unbroken continuity into high modern culture. Tylor's theory has been criticized as lacking historical evidence, by assuming that the idea of souls led on to belief in celestial gods. Marett proposed a modification (see ANIMATISM). In later use Animism has been applied to pre-literate religions, but these often include elements such as belief in a Supreme Being which can hardly be fitted into a theory of souls or vague forces.

Ankh, 'Nh. The sign of life, one of the most numerous and important amulets used in ancient Egyptian tombs and pictures and symbolizing the triumph of life over death. In the shape of a T or a cross surmounted by a loop the Ankh appears in every kind of material, was placed on mummies or engraved in pictures to the gods. In hymns to Rē' at sunrise in the *Book of the Dead* the Ankh has arms emerging from its neck which support the disk of the sun. It is also called the Crux Ansata, 'handled Cross'.

Ansār. (Arabic) 'helpers', the name given to believers from Medina who received Muhammad after his migration from Mecca. The Ansār are praised along with the Muhājirūn, the 'emigrants' who accompanied the Prophet from Mecca.

Anthropomorphism. From Greek *anthropos,* man, and *morphe,* form, the description of the deity as having a form or attributes similar to those of man. Coleridge spoke of 'the strong anthropomorphism of the Hebrew scriptures', where it is said that God created man in his own image, rode on the wings of the wind or stretched forth his right arm. Islamic theologians were similarly concerned about anthropomorphic expressions in the *Qur'ān,* and al-Ash'arī in the tenth century accepted these scriptural expressions but 'without asking how'. He said, 'we confess that God has two hands, without asking how, as he said: "I have created with my two hands." ' Attempts to dispense with all analogies between divine and human were made in Hinduism (see ABSOLUTE) where some early *Upanishads* said that Brahman had 'no qualities' (*nirguna*), but the later *Shvetāshvatara Upanishad* said that God 'had qualities' (*saguna*) and the *Bhagavad-Gītā* returned to personal theism.

Antichrist. See DAJJĀL.

Antiope. In Greek mythology either daughter of Nycteus, king of Boeotia, or of the river Asopus. She was pursued by Zeus in the shape of a satyr and bore him two sons, Amphion (q.v.) and Zethus. She fled from home and was imprisoned and tortured, but later released, and helped her grown sons to build the walls of Thebes.

Anu. The high God of Sumerian religion whose name means 'heaven'. In the *Enuma Elish* (q.v.), the Babylonian epic of creation, Anu was one of the first gods to be born from the primeval chaos. In early times the position of Anu was obscure, but he emerged to prominence from the beginning of the second millennium B.C., when he was called King of the Gods and Father. In early times he had a colourless consort called Antu, but later he was allied with the great goddess Ishtar. No image of Anu has survived, but his symbol, as a shrine surmounted by a horned cap, is often found on boundary stones. Anu's special city was Der; other centres of his cult existed at Ur, Erech and Nippur and there was a great Ziggurat (q.v.) at Ashur shared by Anu and Adad (see ADAD). Anu was the god of kings rather than ordinary mortals, and in inscriptions royal persons inscribed themselves as 'beloved of Anu'.

Anu. A Celtic mother goddess. See DANU.

Anubis. Egyptian god of the dead, son of Osiris and Nephthys. He was called 'the embalmer', and 'opener of the ways', and was guardian of tombs and cemeteries. Anubis as god of the dead was minister of Osiris and assisted him in judgement by weighing the hearts of the dead. Anubis was usually represented as a man with the head of a jackal, often carrying the

ANUBIS

Ankh (q.v.) amulet in his hand, or else as a jackal sitting down. He was also represented by an ox-skin on a pole.

Anukis. Minor water-goddess of ancient Egypt, whose worship was centred at Aswan. Her name meaning 'to embrace' expressed the floods of the Nile which fertilize the earth. Anukis was depicted as a woman with a feather headdress. She was later identified with Nephthys (q.v.).

Anunnaki. Gods of the underworld in Babylonian mythology; Enlil (q.v.) was said to be King of the Anunnaki. By contrast, the Igigi were said to be gods of heaven and Anu (q.v.) was their king. There is, however, confusion in the use of these two terms; in one text the Annunaki are said to be on earth and the Igigi in heaven, while in another text there are said to be three hundred Anunnaki in heaven. Their numbers vary considerably in different lists.

Anurādhapura. Famous Buddhist remains, called 'the buried city of Ceylon'. Founded in 437 B.C. it was called after the constellation Anurādha. It became a centre of Buddhism and has some of the most extensive monastic remains in the world, including stone baths, Brazen Palace, huge Dāgobas (q.v.) and the sacred Bo-Tree (q.v.) from a shoot brought from India. See MAHINDA and SANGHAMITTA.

Aphikomen. Greek word of uncertain meaning, used in the Jewish Seder (q.v.) ceremony for half of a Matzah which is put aside and hunted out by children.

Aphrodite. Greek goddess of beauty, love and fertility, said to have been born from the 'foam' (*aphros*), though Homer said she was daughter of Zeus and Dione (q.v.). Aphrodite was worshipped all over the Greek world and had great centres in Cyprus and Corinth. Greek and Semitic culture met in Cyprus and it was probably from there that the cult of Aphrodite entered Greece, since she was related to the Semitic Astarte and Ishtar, and it was from Cyprus also that came the cult of Adonis who became the consort of Aphrodite. She was chiefly the goddess of fertility and the family, often personifying the sexual instinct, though her public cult at Corinth was respectable. Aphrodite was also worshipped by agriculturalists and fishermen, since she multiplied their produce. To the Romans she was Venus (see ADONIS).

Apis. A bull-headed god, perhaps son of Osiris, in ancient Egypt. Apis was primarily a manifestation of the god Ptah (q.v.), and like other sacred bulls (see MNEVIS and BUCHIS) represented the god of the city where he was worshipped, Ptah at Memphis. He was a god of the underworld and came to be united with Osiris as Serapis (q.v.). The priests of Apis at Memphis said that after the death of Apis

his soul went to heaven where it became united with Osiris. During the late Graeco-Roman period Osiris-Apis (Serapis) was one of the greatest of gods.

Apollo. The most Greek of the gods and in sculpture the personification of manly beauty. He was the god of flocks and herds, of archery and music, of prophecy and medicine. He often taught high legal and moral principles and his oracles were regarded as supreme. The chief shrine of Apollo was at Delphi (q.v.), where he killed the dragon or Python which guarded the shrine. Then the medium at Delphi, usually a woman, was filled with the god and gave his oracle. Apollo had many loves, among them being Cassandra, the daughter of Priam of Troy, and he gave Cassandra the gift of prophecy. Since she withheld her love from him, however, he decreed her prophecies should not be believed. Apollo favoured the Trojans, Persians and Spartans, yet he was generally respected throughout

APOLLO

Greece. His cult was introduced to Italy at an early date, where he was chiefly revered as a god of healing and prophecy. As Phoebus, the 'bright one', he was the sun-god.

Apophis. Snake god of ancient Egypt and the most important of demons. He symbolized evil, hiding in the clouds and preventing the sun god from taking his daily journey across the sky. He is often identified with Set (q.v.), and a legend of creation tells how the sun, Rēʿ, bound and burnt Apophis. Apophis was often represented as a snake with four heads, like the four sources of the Nile which were supposed to come from the underworld, and as the subterranean ocean it swallowed up the sun at night.

Appar. Tamil poet of Shaiva Siddhānta (q.v.) who lived about A.D. 650. He was a Jain who was converted to Shaivism after being cured from illness. His poems are contained in the Tamil collection *Tevāram*.

Apsaras. 'Moving in the waters' (Sanskrit, see APHRODITE), a class of female divinities or nymphs in Hindu mythology. They are prominent in the epic and later poems and are said to have been produced at the churning of the ocean (see AMRITA). They are heavenly and earthly, fond of the waters, and very numerous, and sometimes these charmers were sent to lure ascetics from their austerities. The Apsaras were wives of the celestial musicians, Gandharvas (see GANDHARVAS), but had many other amours and in Indra's heaven they gave rewards to heroes who fell in battle. They changed their forms at will and gave good luck to those whom they favoured. These gracious beings are common figures in sculpture and painting.

APSARAS

Apsu. The underworld 'ocean' in Mesopotamian mythology which, like the Greek Oceanus (q.v.), was thought to be a great subterranean sea on which the world floated, surpassing the horizon and from which rivers flowed. In the creation epic, *Enuma Elish* (q.v.), Apsu is husband of Tiamat, 'chaos' (q.v.). They produced the gods but their noisy behaviour angered Apsu and, on the advice of his vizier Mummu, he resolved to destroy them. But the all-wise Ea heard this, sent Apsu to sleep with a magical spell, and killed him. Then Ea established his dwelling on Apsu and himself became god of the waters.

Apuleius. African writer of the second century A.D., educated at Carthage, who became a philosopher and chief priest of the province. His amusing Latin novel, *Metamorphoses* (q.v.), probably gives some of his own experiences in the cult of Isis and Osiris, as well as the tale of Cupid and Psyche.

Aqsa. A famous mosque in Jerusalem, said to be the one mentioned in the *Qur'ān* (17, 1), visited by Muhammad at night during a journey from the Sacred Mosque to the Farther (Aqsa) Mosque.

It stands near the Dome of the Rock (q.v.). The present building is on the site of the Church of the Virgin, built by Justinian, but after damage in earthquakes the caliph al-Mahdī changed the ground plan in A.D. 780, and the façade was built in the thirteenth century. It was restored in 1938. There is a fine silvered dome, but some of the Roman and Byzantine capitals have been replaced. There is a fine prayer niche, built by Saladin, and two sets of footprints either side are said to be those of Moses and Jesus. In 1969 an incendiarist, Rohan, damaged the roof of the prayer hall wing and destroyed a pulpit given by Saladin.

Aquila. Jewish proselyte of the second century A.D. whose rendering of the Hebrew Bible resulted in the Aquila Greek version, once a standard text and now only found in fragments. It is disputed whether he was the same as the Aquila (Onkelos, q.v.) who produced an Aramaic *Targum*.

'Arabī. See IBN 'ARABĪ.

Arabian Nights. 'A thousand and one nights', *Alf Laylah wa-Laylah*, was first compiled in Iraq by al-Jahshiyāri (died 942). It was based on a Persian work which contained some Indian stories, and in time additions were made from many other sources: Greek, Hebrew, Egyptian, Indian. It gives ideas of life under the 'Abbāsid caliphs in the time of Hārūn al-Rashīd (q.v.).

'Arafāt, 'Arafa. A hill to the east of Mecca which is famous in the ritual of Islamic pilgrimage. Stone steps lead to the top, and from here on the ninth day of the pilgrimage month a sermon is delivered. All the pilgrims camp there, shouting praise, and chanting texts and prayers. Standing before God they declare their repentance, then all leave the mountain after sunset for Mina (see HAJJ). Legend gives a Biblical touch to what may have been an ancient pagan ritual, by saying that Adam and Eve met again at 'Arafāt after being cast out from Paradise.

Arahat (Pali), **Arhat** (Sanskrit), 'Worthy one', entitled to respect, a Buddhist monk who is on the way to Nirvāna, or who has traversed the Eightfold Path and eliminated the Fetters of error and on death attains Nirvāna. The Arahat is the ideal of the Theravāda (Hīnayāna) Buddhists. In China they are called Lohans (q.v.) and sixteen of them figure frequently in sculpture and painting.

Āranyaka. 'Belonging to the forest' (Sanskrit), religious treatises composed in or studied in the forest in ancient India, attached to the *Brāhmanas* and followed by the *Upanishads*. Four *Āranyakas* are extant: *Brihad*, *Taittirīya*, *Aitareya* and *Kaushītaki*. The names of the *Āranyakas* are sometimes used interchangeably with the *Upanishads*, and the *Brihad* is called either *Āranyaka* or *Āranyaka Upanishad*. They form part of the development of philosophical thought in Hinduism, and amid antique and obscure passages there are others of grandeur and simplicity that anticipate the monism and theism of the *Upanishads*.

Arba Kanfoth. (Hebrew), 'four corners', Jewish undergarment which since the thirteenth century has been worn to recall the need to consecrate all one's being to God. It is a rectangular piece of cloth, about a metre long, with a hole to pass over the head and its four corners are

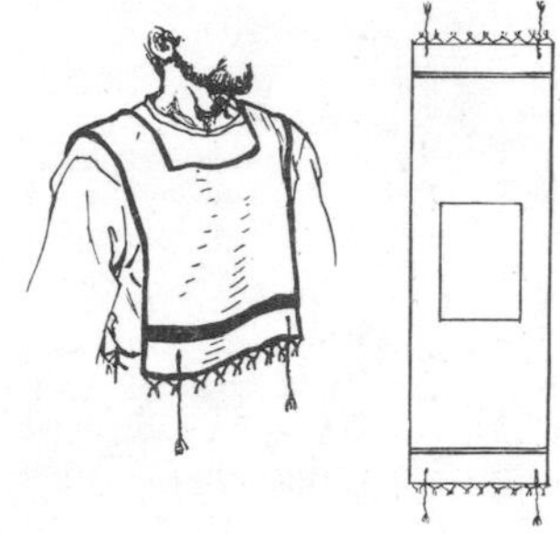

fastened to the Tzitzith fringes (q.v.). It is also called the Small Tallith, prayer shawl (see TALLITH).

Ares. The Greek god of war, said in mythology to be son of Zeus and Hera, and probably originating in the north. The Roman Mars cult adopted the myths of Ares. Ares was violent and quarrelsome, had little moral character, and was associated with Aphrodite and Athena. The Areopagus ('Mars' Hill') in Athens had a temple of Ares, and on this rocky mass also the Senate was held and Paul preached. Ares was not only worshipped by soldiers but also by women, since goddesses like Aphrodite had warlike qualities.

Arges. The 'Bright', one of the Cyclopes (q.v.).

Argonauts. Greek heroes of an ancient saga who set out in the Argo, built by Argos, to fetch the Golden Fleece, perhaps a reference to ancient gold trade in the Black Sea. They were led by Jason (q.v.), who gained the Fleece with the help of the enchantress Medea. The

Argonauts included famous Greek heroes, and all lists include Argos, the keen-eyed, and the helmsman Tiphys. Some (clearly later) lists included Heracles and Orpheus.

Argos. In Greek mythology a three-eyed monster, or four-eyed with two in front and two behind, who was of great strength. Hera set him to watch Io (q.v.), but Zeus sent Hermes to kill him. Argos then was turned into a peacock, or his eyes were put into its tail.

Ariadne. In Greek mythology daughter of Minos of Crete and Pasiphae. She fell in love with Theseus and gave him a thread to guide him out of the Labyrinth (see DAEDALUS) when he had killed the Minotaur (q.v.). Theseus took her away but abandoned her at Naxos where, according to a later legend, she died in childbirth. Later celebrations of this event probably show that she was a woman's deity.

Aricia. City 25 kilometres south of Rome, which had the most famous temple of Diana (q.v.), called Nemorensis, whose ruins survive in the woods by Lake Nemi. See also VIRBIUS.

Arinna. Chief goddess of the Hittites (q.v.), deity of the sun, but also combining

other functions. Her symbol was a lioness and also a dove.

Aristotle. One of the greatest Greek philosophers, 384–322 B.C. When he was seventeen he went as pupil to Plato's Academy (q.v.) in Athens, and stayed

ARISTOTLE

there for twenty years as research student till the death of Plato. For a year Aristotle was tutor to Alexander, later styled 'the Great', and in 335 he founded his own Peripatetic (q.v.) school in Athens, where the students had common meals and a monthly symposium. Here Aristotle founded a library and a museum to illustrate his lectures, especially those on zoology. Aristotle wrote a great many scientific and philosophical works, many of which were lost. He wrote on Analytics, Physics, Metaphysics, Ethics, Politics, Rhetoric and Poetics. His philosophy was profoundly influenced by Plato, but his scientific work and orderly habits of mind led him to introduce terms that have been of great value ever since, such as: *universal* and *particular*, *form* and *matter*, *subject* and *attribute*, *premise* and *conclussion*. His philosophy came to be adopted as the basis for much medieval Islamic and Christian philosophy. See AVERROES.

Arjan, Guru. Fifth Guru of the Sikhs (q.v.), who lived from 1563 to 1606. He compiled the sacred scripture, *Ādi Granth* (q.v.), in 1603–4, and built the Golden Temple at Amritsar. He was killed by the Mughal emperor Jahangir and became the first Sikh martyr. Arjan followed Guru Ram Dās and was succeeded by Har Govind.

Arjuna. The third of five brothers famous in Hindu mythology, son of Pāndu and Kuntī (q.v.) or Prithā, whence Arjuna is called Pārtha. He was also said to be son of the great god Indra and his name means 'white' (argent). Arjuna was a brave and handsome warrior, prominent in many exploits with

ARJUNA

men, nymphs, demons and gods, and in the great epic *Mahābhārata* he helps his eldest brother Yudhishthira to recover his kingdom from the Kurus. After all the enemies were killed, and the Pāndu brothers had enjoyed their kingdom, Arjuna retired to the Himalayas and finally went to heaven. Arjuna is particularly known for his dialogue with the god Krishna, who acts as his charioteer, in the religious poem *Bhagavad-Gītā* (q.v.). Here Arjuna is smitten with compassion and despondency at the thought of the fratricidal battle about to begin, and Krishna gives long teachings to assure him of the necessity of fulfilling his caste and warrior's duty. Penance of Arjuna, see MAHABALIPURAM.

Ark. Aron ha-kodesh, a cupboard in a synagogue, in the wall that faces Jerusalem, where are kept the scrolls of the Law.

Each scroll contains the *Torah* in Hebrew, written by hand on parchment. The scrolls are mounted on wooden rollers, which often have silver or gilded heads, and covered with velvet and fine wrappings. They are taken out of the Ark during service and carried round the synagogues before reading, while everyone faces them and bows as they pass. In front of the Ark is a perpetual light to symbolize the constant presence of God and also perpetuate the altar-fire of the old Temple.

Arkān. See PILLARS.

Armilustrium. Temple on the Aventine hill in Rome where soldiers' arms were ritually purified in a ceremony of this name on 19 October, the end of the campaigning season, in which the Salii (q.v.) played an important part.

Aron. See ARK.

Artemis. A popular goddess of Greece, connected with the earth, forests, hills and wild beasts, though with temples in cities. She has not much mythology, although she is a daughter of Zeus in the *Iliad*, but her chaste nature is shown in the story of Actaeon who while hunting saw her bathing; she turned him into a stag and he was torn to pieces by his own hounds. Artemis was a giver of fertility and appears in tales of women who bear children. She was often identified with similar goddesses, notably with the great goddess of Ephesus (the Biblical translation 'Diana of the Ephesians' should read 'Artemis', *Acts* 19, 28). Artemis was also identified with other goddesses, such as Hecate and Selene.

Arthur. The famous Celtic hero may have been a legendary king, of the Lowlands of Scotland or of Wales and the west of England. His name has been said to come from Artor, a 'ploughman', which would connect him with agriculture. There may have been an Arthur deity, a culture-hero or god of farmers, or perhaps a war-god who thus became linked with the warrior Arthur. See AVALON and MERLIN.

Arval Brethren. Fratres Arvales, a priestly brotherhood in Rome made up of twelve members chosen from distinguished senates, the emperor being always one. Their chief ceremony was in May, honouring the goddess Dea Dia, an agricultural deity. A famous song was the *Carmen Arvale* (q.v.); See also SODALES.

Āryan. 'Noble' (Sanskrit), honourable, belonging to the Āryan people of India (related to Iran and Eire). This was the name given to themselves by the peoples who invaded India and Iran from central Asia between 2000 and 1500 B.C. (nothing to do with Hitler, see also SWASTIKA). They entered the plains of the Indus river with horses and chariots, and destroyed the cities of the more cultured Indus Valley peoples. The Āryans were illiterate and despised the religion and civilization of the literate peoples they conquered and enslaved, thus strengthening their class system (see CASTE) in which their own priests and warriors were leaders. They were lighter-skinned than the Indus Valley peoples, and class distinctions were reinforced by colour and conquest. The religion of the Āryans was expressed in the hymns of the *Vedas* and developed in the *Upanishads*. See also DĀSAS and HARAPPĀ.

Ārya Samāj. 'Society of the noble' (see ĀRYAN), a modern reform movement of Hinduism founded in 1875 in Bombay by Dayānanda Sarasvatī (1824–83, q.v.). He sought to go 'Back to the *Vedas*' and rid Hinduism of Muslim and Christian influence. He believed that there is only one God and that there was no polytheism or idolatry in the *Vedas*, but that the divine names which occur there are epithets of the one true God. The Avatars of later Hinduism were rejected, and animal sacrifice. The official creed of the Samāj teaches that there is one God who alone must be worshipped, the *Vedas* are the books of true knowledge and every Āryan should read or hear them. The aim is still to make Hinduism the religion of all India and convert those Indians who follow other religions.

Asaland, Asaheimr, Home of the Aesir gods in Scandinavian mythology, whose chief city was Asgardr (q.v.).

Āsana. (Sanskrit) 'sitting', posture, especially for meditation and religious exercises. There are many kinds of Āsanas, one of the commonest being Padmāsana, 'lotus seat', in which the legs are crossed and feet tucked on to the opposite thigh, with soles turned up. A variant of this is the Yogāsana, 'yoga posture', in which the hands are placed on the ground with palms turned upwards.

Asanga. Buddhist philosopher, of about the fourth century A.D., who with his brother Vasubandhu (q.v.) is said to have founded the Yogāchāra (q.v.) school. He lived in Peshawar and studied the doctrine of the Void (see SHŪNYA), but despaired of grasping it until a teacher called Maitreya, either the Buddha-to-come or a teacher of this name, explained it. Asanga wrote commentaries on the Buddhist scriptures and notably expounded the Trikāya (q.v.), doctrine of the three bodies of a Buddha.

Asase Ya. 'Earth Thursday', the name of the earth goddess among the Ashanti of Ghana. Ya is the name given to women born on a Thursday, and that is the day sacred to this deity who is called Old Mother Earth, and Creator of the Underworld. Although there are no temples for this deity, sacrifices are made on the land for her at time of ploughing and harvesting. Thursday is set aside for her honour and all work on the land is forbidden on that day, a taboo which has caused difficulties in modern times for members of other religions. Since the dead are buried in the earth, libations are poured and traditional songs are chanted to Asase Ya when graves are dug.

Asat. (Sanskrit) 'not being', non-existence, unreality. It is used for untruth, nonentity, and of evil men. In philosophy Asat is non-existence or unreality, the opposite of Sat (q.v.).

Āsava. Pali Buddhist term for 'defilement' or mental intoxication. There are four Āsavas: sensuality (*kāma*), lust for life (*bhava*), false views (*ditthi*), and ignorance (*avijjā*). The Āsavas cloud the mind and hinder attainment of enlightenment, but the true Arahat (q.v.) breaks free from them.

Ascetism. Religious self-denial, austerity and bodily mortification. The Hindu *tapas* (q.v.) for asceticism indicated also 'heat', the five fires to which ascetics submitted themselves, and the power acquired by extreme mortification. Many Hindu holy men have engaged in ascetic practices, ranging from abstinence from foods (see ABSTINENCE) to torture or maiming of the body. Jain monks wear cloths over their mouths and sweep the path in front of them to avoid treading on insects, and some of them wear no clothes. The Ājīvikas (q.v.) were even more extreme, went naked and ate refuse. In reaction against such practices the Buddha renounced asceticism and taught the Middle Way between the extremes of sensuality and austerity.

Asclepius. A Greek hero and god of healing, called the 'blameless physician' in the *Iliad*. He is said to have been son of Apollo and born at Epidaurus, and he may have been a hero who was exalted into divinity. The cult may have originated in Thessaly, but became popular and fervent in the Greek world and outside, with temples at Athens, Pergamum, Rome (see AESCULAPIUS) and elsewhere. The temples used both ritual and physical methods of treating the sick, with baths, gymnasia and theatres. At Pergamum in Asia Minor there were baths in radio-active springs and underground passages where mental diseases were treated. Asclepius was associated with his daughter Hygieia, 'health', with dogs and sacred snakes. In art he appears as a bearded kindly man, with a staff round which a snake or snakes are coiled, and these became the symbols of medicine.

Asgard. The district or citadel of the gods in Scandinavian mythology, either in heaven or raised above the surface of Midgard or Middle-earth where men dwelt. In the *Prose Edda* Asgard is identified with Troy near the Black Sea, and its chief was the god Odin, then a warrior, who travelled thence to Scandinavia. The heavenly Asgard had a great golden house or hall called Gladsheim, where there were seats for all the gods. Besides their general home there were separate dwellings for special people; Valhalla in Gladsheim was Odin's heaven for warriors and the most beautiful of all places. See UTGARD.

Asha. Avestan, 'truth', righteousness, the principle of goodness in Zoroastrian theology, which was in constant conflict with Druj (q.v.), the Lie. Zoroaster and his disciples were called upon to side with Asha and ensure the victory of righteousness; all such followers of truth were Ashavans. Asha was one of the highest of the Bounteous Immortals (Amesha Spentas) and closely joined to Good Mind, Vohu Manah (q.v.).

Ash'arī, Al-ash'arī. One of the most famous orthodox theologians of Islam, born in Basra in 873 and died in Baghdad in 935. He successfully justified the use of reasoning in theology, and opposed Mu'tazilite (q.v.) and other heretics. Ash'arī is regarded as the founder of orthodox Islamic scholasticism. He wrote about three hundred books, discussing the existence and attributes of God, the eternity of the *Qur'ān,* faith and predestination, and the orthodox Sunni caliphs. Two creeds are attributed to him, in which he justified the use of anthropomorphic expressions about God because they occur in the *Qur'ān* (see (ANTHROPOMORPHISM). See QADAR and QADARYĪA.

Asherah, Asherat. Goddess of the Phoenicians (q.v.), associated with El and Baal. She was also known as Qadesh, 'the holy'. Her symbol was a lion.

Ashi. See RAB ASHI.

Ashkenazim. Ashkenaz, a grandson of Japheth (*Genesis* 10, 3), was identified with Germany in medieval Hebrew, and the name Ashkenazim was extended to include the Jews of Poland, Russia and eastern Europe, and their descendants in Britain and America. They followed local customs and usages, Minhag (q.v.), which differentiated them from those of the Sephardim (q.v.), the other great branch of Jewry. Today the Ashkenazim constitute the majority of all Jews.

Ashoka. Emperor of India, 273–232 B.C., and grandson of Chandragupta founder of the Maurya dynasty. Ashoka was one of the greatest rulers of India and the world. There was delay at his accession and he was not crowned till 269. He then went to war against the Kalingas in the east. But the ensuing bloodshed horrified the king, who thereupon renounced war and the taking of all life. Ashoka became a Buddhist and some say he was a monk; he convened a council and regulated the monastic order and lay worship. He issued decrees ordering morality, forbidding taking life even for food, and instituting hospitals for men and animals. It is said that he sent missions to Ceylon and elsewhere. Many of the edicts of Ashoka were inscribed on rocks and pillars and survive to this day, giving the earliest written evidence for Buddhist and Indian teaching. They were deciphered by James Prinsep in 1837. Ashoka visited the sites connected with the life of the Buddha and erected monuments there, some of which still remain.

Āshram, Āshrama. A 'hermitage' (Sanskrit), or dwelling of ascetics or sages in India. In modern times an open monastery or retreat-house for meditation, self-discipline and service, such as those founded by Mahātma Gāndhi, Rabindranath Tagore or Shri Aurobindo Ghose. There are also Christian Āshrams.

In Indian tradition an Āshram is also a stage in the life of a Brahmin, in four periods or conditions, those of: student of the *Vedas*, householder, forest dweller, and complete renouncer or religious beggar (Brahmachārin, Grihastha, Vānaprastha, Sannyāsin). Many only complete the first two Āshrams, but, if a man has seen his children's children, then he may retire to the forest and perhaps eventually become a beggar at a holy place till death.

Ashtoreth. See ASTARTE.

Ashur. The chief god of Assyria and deity of the city of Ashur. The derivation is uncertain, though a connection with the Egyptian Osiris has been suggested. He was particularly a god of war and was commonly symbolized by a winged disk which enclosed the god shooting an arrow from his bow. This symbol was engraved on royal rings and monuments

as a mark of devotion. Ishtar, the greatest goddess, was the consort of Ashur. In the Assyrian version of the creation epic Ashur takes the place of Marduk (q.v.) as the hero of the great battle.

'Ashūrā. An Islamic fast day on the tenth of the first month, Muharram, from Hebrew *'asor* (tenth; *Leviticus* 16, 29). Legend says that on this day Noah left the ark, and Sunnis observe it as a fast. In Shī'a Islam the day is the climax of the memorial of Husain (q.v.).

Ashvaghosha. A Buddhist writer and poet of the first or second century A.D. According to tradition he was a brilliant Sanskrit writer, living at the court of King Kanishka (q.v.), a Buddhist monarch of north-west India. Ashvaghosha wrote the *Buddha-charita*, a life of the Buddha in verse up to the time of his enlightenment, describing him as the hero of an epic but with many miracles. Another work, *The Awakening of Faith*, has also been ascribed to Ashvaghosha, but this is disputed.

Ashva-Medha. (Sanskrit) 'horse sacrifice', the great sacrifice performed by ancient Hindu kings when they wanted offspring or celebrated a great victory. It was performed by Yudhishthira (q.v.) after the final victory recounted in the *Mahābhārata* epic. A horse was consecrated and set free to wander at will for a while, followed by the king with an army, and if the horse entered another country the ruler had to submit or fight. After the successful return, both king and queen figured in a real or symbolical horse-sacrifice. See also RĀJASŪYA.

Ashvins. Twin 'horsemen' in the Indian *Rig Veda*, like the Greek Dioscuroi (q.v.). They were said to appear before dawn riding in a golden chariot drawn by horses or birds. They were children of the sun by a nymph who had taken the form of a mare. Many hymns were addressed to them as harbingers of daylight, and the Aśhvins were believed to bring treasures to men, and particularly to send away misfortune and sickness by their warmth. So they were the physicians of heaven, with the attributes of youth, light, speed, curative powers and benevolence.

Asita. A sage who foretold the future of the Buddha. In an introduction to a section of the *Sutta Nipāta* (q.v.), Asita in the Himalayas saw the gods rejoicing and heard from them of the birth of the future Buddha. He went to his father's house, saw the child, recognized in him the thirty-two marks of a Great Man, but was sad that he himself would die before hearing the preaching of the Buddha's doctrine. Asita returned home and told his nephew, Nālaka, to watch for the appearance of the Buddha. Later versions of the story greatly magnified the powers of Asita, crediting him with supernatural vision to see the child from the Himalayas and flying through the air to visit him. Asita has been called the 'Buddhist Simeon', because of superficial resemblances to the story of Simeon in the Gospel. But there are basic differences of approach and there is no evidence that the Asita story is pre-Christian.

Asoka. See ASHOKA.

Asram. See ASHRAM.

Assassins. A term adopted by the Crusaders from the Arabic word *hashishi*, meaning a consumer of hashish or hemp. In Syria this was applied to followers of the Nizārī sect of Ismā'īlis (see ISMĀ'ĪLĪ) who got rid of their enemies by assassination. In Muslim sources they are generally called Ismā'īlis or Nizāris. The sect was founded by Hasan ibn Sabbāh (q.v.) when he conquered the fortress of Alamūt in 1090. From this and other fortresses in Persia a powerful movement was built up which lasted till the destruction of Alamūt by the Mongols in 1256. Assassins were supposed to intoxicate themselves with hashish and then commit desperate assassinations. The Crusaders feared the 'Old Man of the Mountains' (q.v.) and Conrad of Montferrat was killed by an Assassin, but the attacks of the movement were much more violent against fellow Muslims. A few of their descendants remain peacefully in Syria, Persia and India.

Astarte, Ashtoreth. Principal goddess of the Phoenicians and Canaanites, and counterpart of Baal. Goddess of fertility, with a strong sexual character, Astarte was regarded as responsible for the increase of herds of sheep and goats. Trees, especially the cypress, were prominent in her worship, and images of the goddess often show her as a woman with two horns. Her cult was introduced

into Egypt, as the daughter of Ptah, and she became goddess of healing. She was akin to Ishtar of Mesopotamia and Aphrodite of Greece. See also KEDESH.

Astrology. See MAGIC and ZODIAC.

Asuras. (Sanskrit) 'spiritual, divine', used of the supreme deity or the gods in general in early Hinduism, and akin to the Persian *ahura* (see AHURA MAZDĀ). Later they came to be regarded as inferior beings, made from the lower breath of the creator, and finally as enemies of the gods and demons in general. See POLYDAEMONISM.

Asvaghosa. See ASHVAGHOSHA.

Asva-Medha. See ASHVA-MEDHA.

Asvins. See ASHVINS.

Asynjur. The name given collectively to the goddesses (see AESIR) in Scandinavian mythology. They include Frigg, Freyja and Gerd (qq.v.), but of others named little is known except that they are called attendants upon or consorts of the gods.

Ātar. In Zoroastrian religion the fire, Ātar, was the centre of the worship and symbol of truth. Zoroaster spoke of it as mighty through righteousness, and identical with the holy Spirit, a joy to God (see AHURA MAZDĀ), and later it was called a son of Ahura Mazdā. As with the Indian fire god Agni (q.v.), in Persia the fire was honoured in home and in temple, but the Zoroastrian fire has remained in the central place, whereas Agni has declined, and fire is focal to the Parsi Fire Temples today (q.v.). See FIRE.

Atargatis. A Syrian goddess, Atar-Ata, perhaps meaning 'divine Ata'. She was also called Derceto and was the consort of the great god Adad. At Ascalon she was depicted as half woman half fish (see DAGON) and fish and doves were sacred to her, as doves were also to her daughter Semiramis (q.v.). Atargatis was chiefly a fertility goddess, and Greeks often identified her with Aphrodite.

Ātash Behrām. See FIRE TEMPLES.

Atatürk. See MUSTAFĀ.

Ate. The personification of folly or moral blindness in Greek mythology. In the *Iliad* she was the daughter of Zeus, and showed the problem of the moral responsibility of God. She was also daughter of strife and sister to lawlessness. By the incitement of Ate it was supposed that right and wrong, helpful or ruinous conduct, could not be distinguished.

Aten. See ATON.

Atharva Veda. The fourth of the *Vedas*, the most ancient religious texts of the Hindus. Said to have been compiled by a priest, Atharvan, it is clearly later than the other three *Vedas* and is not mentioned in some early lists. It contains about 760 hymns and some prose passages, and about one sixth of the hymns are found in the *Rig Veda*. The *Atharva Veda* contains many incantations and magical texts, particularly directed towards healing sickness. Some hymns are concerned with a single rite or ceremony. It portrays popular Indian religion and the magic power of knowledge, but also includes some philosophical speculations that lead on to the *Upanishads*. The neuter divinity Brahman appears here, the soul (*ātman*), and the cosmic power of Time.

Atheism. 'Denial of the gods' (Greek *a*, not, *theos*, god) to the Greeks might mean complete scepticism or dislike of the myths of the traditional deities. Socrates criticized the immoral myths, but had a deep personal faith in divine inspiration. Pindar and Euripides did the same, and there was no room for such personal deities in Aristotle's intellectual concept of divinity. 'Atheist' also meant godless in the sense of wicked. In Hinduism *na asti*, 'it is not', meant primarily a denial of the revelation in the *Veda* scriptures, and also atheistic or impious. The Chārvākas were materialists who rejected the *Vedas*, and so did the Buddhists and Jains. Yet Hindu gods appear in these systems, though subservient to the Buddhas and Jinas. Rather than atheistic they have been called 'transtheistic', by-passing the great gods, or 'transpolytheistic' in that they relegate the many gods to a low place and have no knowledge of a Supreme Being.

Athena, Athene. The patron goddess of Athens, but also worshipped in many other parts of Greece and the islands. Her most famous cult was on the Acropolis hill at Athens where the Parthenon temple of the virgin (*parthenos*) goddess contained a great gold and ivory statue made by Phidias in 438 B.C. Here and elsewhere Athena was depicted as a female yet fully armed, and she was a goddess of war and patron of the warrior rulers. She was always regarded as a virgin, but was interested in animal and vegetable fertility. She was a state goddess, but also concerned with arts and crafts, pottery, goldsmithery, and particularly women's work such as spinning and weaving. Sometimes she took the form of a bird, especially the owl. Athena was said to have been born from the head of Zeus whence she sprang out fully armed. See ACROPOLIS, PARTHENON and METIS. See also PALLAS.

Atiedii, Brethren. Fratres Atiedii, a priestly fraternity of ancient Italy, not unlike the Arval Brethren (q.v.), whose proceedings and liturgy were inscribed on the Iguvine Tablets (q.v.).

Atisa. Indian Buddhist (died 1052) who reformed the Lamaistic (q.v.) Buddhism of Tibet. He founded an order named Kah-dam-pa which was itself reformed nearly four hundred years later by Tsong-kha-pa (q.v.) who called it Gelugspa, 'virtuous.'

Ātman. The 'soul', principle of life, self, individual or universal, in Hindu thought. The word is said to be derived from a Sanskrit root meaning 'breath', and is perhaps related to Greek *atmos*, vapour, and atmosphere. Ātman is sometimes the individual soul or self, but in the *Upanishads* it is often the soul of all and means practically the same as Brahman. The *Chāndogya Upanishad* says that one should venerate the Ātman which consists of mind, with body as its breath, light as its form and space as its self. This soul within the heart is Brahman. This non-dualism (see ADVAITA) of Ātman and Brahman, called monism or pantheism, indicates that at the deepest level the self is one with the essence of the universe. The Ātman as individual soul rides in the body as chariot, but is unaffected by bodily conditions. See also ANATTĀ and JĪVA.

Atomism. See DEMOCRITUS, EPICURUS, and VAISHESHIKA.

Aton, Aten. The sun or disk of the sun in ancient Egypt, whose worship was patronized by Amenophis IV under the name of Ikhnaton. Aton was called the good god, lord of every land and lord of eternity. He was represented at first by a man with a falcon's head above which was a red disk, but later by a red disk alone having long rays spreading out like a fan,

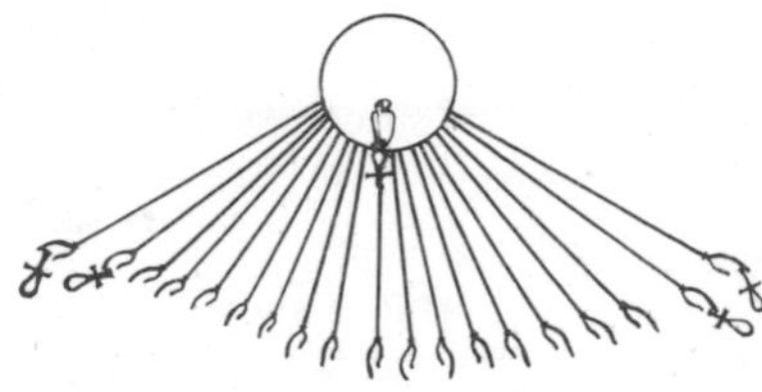

and a cobra on the lower edge. Aton worship was closely connected with that of Rēʿ, the great sun god, but Pharaoh Ikhnaton (q.v.) opposed that of the popular Amūn (see AMŪN), effacing his name from inscriptions. In revenge Aton's name was effaced after the death of Ikhnaton, but many hymns and prayers to Aton as king have survived in the rock-tombs of Tell el-Amarna.

Atonement, Day of. In Hebrew Yom Kippur, the holiest day in the Jewish year, on the tenth day of Tishri, the first month. It is a time of total abstinence from food and drink from the evening of the ninth Tishri to that of the tenth. Originally the ceremonial was performed by the High Priest in the Temple at Jerusalem, and now Jews spend the whole Day of Atonement in synagogues where the central part of the liturgy recalls the Temple service. Collective confession is made of social and moral sins, and repeated several times, but in the liturgy when the Temple rites are remembered the worshippers kneel at the divine name and feel the presence of God most nearly. The service closes at sunset with a sevenfold proclamation of the unity of God and the sounding of the Shofar, the ram's horn which announces the end of the fast.

Atropos. (Greek) 'inflexible', cannot be stayed, the one of the Moirai or Fates (q.v.) who could not be stopped from severing the thread of life.

'Attār. The surname of the Persian Sūfī mystic Farīd al-Dīn. Born near Nishapur, about A.D. 1150, he was killed by Mongol invaders in 1230. As a young man he followed his father's profession of seller of drugs and perfumes, and hence was later called 'Attār, but he gave it up to follow the example of an ascetic dervish who pointed out the vanity of his treasures. 'Attār travelled widely, to Mecca, Egypt and India, extending his knowledge of Sūfism. He compiled *The Memoirs of the Saints*, biographies of Sūfī mystics, giving not only their lives and teachings, but many legends connected with them. His life of Rābi'a (q.v.) is the most extensive among the old narratives. 'Attār's own mystical teachings speak of the love of God and the union, even identity, of the divine lover and beloved.

Attis. A god of the Phrygians of Asia Minor, in one story said to have been killed by a boar, like Adonis. Attis was god of vegetation and youthful lover of Cybele, the great mother-goddess of Asia Minor and giver of fertility. At the spring equinox there was a festival which centred on the death and return to life of the vegetation deity. Attis did not appeal much to the Greeks, but was officially adopted by the Romans in the time of Claudius. Then he became a sun god, all-powerful and promising immortal life to his followers. In art Attis was represented as a youth wearing the distinctively Phrygian cap.

Atua. The 'gods' in Maori religion, children of the primeval heaven and earth, Rangi and Papa (q.v.). The most important god was Tane (q.v.), and others were: Rongo, god of agriculture and peace, Tangaroa, the god of the sea, and Tu, the god of war. The Atua were served by priests (Tohunga, q.v.), and were in constant contact with them, in rituals, in the sending of messages, and in possession.

Atum. The first god of Heliopolis in ancient Egypt, whose name perhaps meant 'the Accomplished One'. He arose out of primeval chaos and came into existence by himself, so being called the oldest and only one of the gods. He produced eight other gods and goddesses, and with them formed the Great Ennead (q.v.), being regarded as the chief and called 'bull of the Ennead'. Later he was regarded simply as a form of the sun god Rē'. Atum is depicted as a man with a beard, wearing a double crown, though sometimes he was symbolized by a bull.

Augean Stables. The fifth Labour of Heracles (q.v.) was to clean the cattle yard of King Augeias in one day. He did it by diverting two rivers through the filthy yard and also tamed a bull with his bare hands.

Augurs, Augures. Official diviners in Roman religion, at first three and later sixteen, who sought to discover the will of the gods by observation of signs. The cries of wild birds were interpreted according to the direction in which they were heard, and armies caught chickens to provide signs for them. If they ate food given them, but dropped some, that was a good sign. In later times Haruspices (q.v.), interpreting from animal organs, encroached upon the work of Augurs.

Aum. See OM.

Aurangzeb. Indian Mughal emperor (1659–1707), great-grandson of Akbar (q.v.). Akbar's policy of religious toleration was reversed, and Aurangzeb became a fanatical Muslim, persecutor of the Hindu majority of his subjects. Thousands of Hindu temples were destroyed and statues mutilated, while Hindu rites were restricted and court preferment was confined to orthodox Muslims. This brought violent reaction from Hindus, led by the Marāthā chief Shivājī (1627–80), and from the Sikhs (q.v.) who became a militant brotherhood. When at last Aurangzeb died, the Mughal empire was almost at an end.

Aurelius. See MARCUS AURELIUS.

Aureole. See NIMBUS.

Aurobindo Ghose or **Ghosh.** Modern Indian philosopher (1872–1950). Brought up in a Bengali high-caste family, his education was thoroughly English, with Roman Catholic, Congregationalist and Anglican influences. From St Paul's School he gained a classical scholarship to Cambridge, but there got involved in politics. On return to India he began the study of Sanskrit and joined the Indian nationalist movement, editing the journal *Bande Mātaram*. Imprisoned in 1908 he began to study Yoga, had a vision, and on release withdrew to the French enclave at Pondicherry where he passed the rest of his life. Aurobindo began a great output of poetry and philosophical writing in English, chief among his books being *The Life Divine*, *Synthesis of Yoga*, and *Essays on the Gita*. His themes of Integral Yoga, covering all aspects of life, and entry into the Life Divine by union with Supermind, are continued in his Ashram at Pondicherry, governed by the now retired Mother of the movement. His followers call him Shrī, and do much literary, educational and meditational activity.

Aurora. The goddess of the dawn in Roman mythology. See the Greek Eos.

Australian Religion. The old religious beliefs of Australian aboriginal tribes have been best studied in central and northern areas, and are closely linked to pictorial art (see BARK PAINTINGS). The Aranda (Arunta) and other inland tribes thought the earth was eternal, but many supernatural beings, called 'totemic ancestors', emerged from their endless sleep under the plain (see DREAMING). The sites where they emerged were sacred, and most of these beings were linked with a particular animal or plant. Human beings also were believed to be descended from the same ancestor as some animals or plants, and Australian totemism was belief in the link between a man and an animal with which he shared the same life. After making the landscape the supernatural beings returned to the earth, or changed into trees, rocks or Tjurunga (q.v.). They were celebrated in songs, myths, rituals and artistic works. See also WANINGGA, TOTEM POLES, and the names listed under BARK PAINTINGS.

Avagddu. In Celtic mythology the ugly child of Tegid Voel and Cerridwen (q.v.) who lived in Lake Tegid. Cerridwen made a 'cauldron of inspiration' to help Avagddu, but three precious drops were taken by Gwion who gained the inspiration instead.

Avalokita, Avalokiteshvara. The Lord (*īshvara* in Sanskrit) who is seen or who looks and surveys, one of the greatest Bodhisattvas (q.v.), beings of enlightenment, of Mahāyāna Buddhism. Avalokita constantly surveys the world in compassion for all beings and hears every cry. The name occurs in the great Mahāyāna scripture, the *Lotus Sūtra*, where in chapter twenty-four this being is praised by the Buddha for conferring all kinds of benefits on his worshippers. This great saviour, though strictly not a god, became ever more popular. In China he became female and was called Kuan Yin, the Lady-Giver of Children, and in Japan the male Kwannon. As Chenresi he was lord of Tibet and the Dalai Lama is regarded as the incarnation of this Bodhisattva and not of Gautama the Buddha.

Avalon. A Celtic wonderland, perhaps connected with a word *aballos*, 'apple', filled with marvellous apple-trees. The divine hero Arthur (q.v.) is said to have been taken there to recover from his wounds. It was supposed to be a beautiful place, like Elysium (q.v.), beyond or under the sea, where people were immortal.

Avatamsaka. (Sanskrit) 'Garland', a sūtra of Mahāyāna Buddhism, which adorns or glorifies the Buddha and Bodhisattvas. As Hua Yen (q.v.) in Chinese it is the chief inspiration of the Garland School.

Avatar, Avatāra. Sanskrit term for a 'down-coming', descent, manifestation or incarnation of a Hindu divinity. Many gods have Avatars in the *Mahābhārata* epic, but they are particularly associated with Vishnu whose Avatar as Krishna appears in the *Bhagavad-Gītā*, where though the term Avatar is not used it is said that Krishna appears on earth age after age to restore the right. Ten or more Avatars are named in the *Mahābhārata* in which Vishnu appears as swan, fish, tortoise, boar, man-lion, dwarf, Rāma with the axe, Rāma, Krishna, and Kalkī the Avatar to come (see separate articles). Later books increase the number and twenty-two Avatars appear in the *Bhāgavata Purāna*, including the Buddha, perhaps with the aim of attracting

KRISHNA AVATAR

Buddhists back to Hinduism. Rāma is the principal Avatar of the *Rāmāyana* epic, but Krishna is the most popular elsewhere and devotions to him extended widely in the Middle Ages with many tales of his childhood and youthful loves, showing the importance of the Avatar as a personal deity.

Averroes or **Ibn Rushd.** Islamic philosopher (1126–98). Born in Cordova he spent much of his life as judge there and in Seville. Averroes was convinced that religion and philosophy are both true and he sought to harmonize them in his writings, against contemporary trends in Islamic theology. His chief importance was as a commentator on Aristotle and his works were so esteemed by Christian and Jewish scholars in Spain that they were translated from Arabic into Latin and Hebrew. Averroes was thus responsible for the first general introduction of Aristotle into medieval Europe and he was regarded as a master by the Thomist philosophers. His influence in Islam was much less than that in Europe and he failed to convince his fellows of the need for philosophy. See AVICENNA.

Avesta. The scriptures of the Zoroastrians, sometimes wrongly called *Zend-Avesta* which means 'commentary on the Avesta'. *Avesta* may be from a root similar to the Sanskrit *Veda*, meaning 'knowledge', or it may derive from another word meaning 'original text' or 'scriptures'. Only a fragment of the original *Avesta* survives, though it is about one and a half times as long as the *New Testament*. The oldest part, in an earlier form of Persian, is the *Gāthās*, 'songs' or 'hymns' (like Sanskrit *Gītā*) of Zoroaster himself, and they form the heart of the liturgy or Yasna. The *Gāthās* describe Zoroaster's own religious experience and beliefs. Next and later are the *Yashts* (q.v.) and other texts known as *Little Avesta*, which include hymns to various divinities. Lastly comes the *Vendidad* or rather *Vidēvdāt*, the 'law against demons', which is mainly concerned with ritual purity.

Avicenna or **Ibn Sīnā.** Islamic philosopher (980–1037). A Persian born near Bukhara, he first learnt the *Qur'ān* and Arabic poetry and was introduced to Aristotle's writings at the age of fourteen. He read his *Metaphysics* forty times. He had to earn his living as vizier or chief minister in Hamadhan and finally settled under princely patronage in Ispahan. Avicenna taught that God is the One, the necessarily existent, from whom everything emanates. His ideas are generally those of Aristotle, but modified to include the Prophet Muhammad. Avicenna seems to have felt that there was no real opposition between Greek scientific and philosophical learning and Islamic theology and religion. He wrote a number of mystical books and because of this some think that he was closer to the spirit of Plato than that of Aristotle, and like Plato he appealed to religious people. See AVERROES.

Avidyā. (Sanskrit) 'not-knowing', ignorance, spiritual blindness. In Hindu Vedānta philosophy salvation comes by the displacement of Avidyā by the right outlook or true knowledge, Vidyā (q.v.). Avidyā is sometimes personified as Illusion (*māyā*, q.v.). In Buddhist thought (*Avijjā* in Pali) it is the root of evil and the cause of the desire which creates the suffering of existence. It is first of the twelve links in the chain of causation and last of the ten fetters. The goal of the Buddhist path is the total elimination of ignorance in perfect enlightenment.

Ayesha, 'A'isha. Youngest wife of Muhammad and daughter of the first caliph Abū Bakr, she was born in Mecca about A.D. 613 and buried in Medina in 678. She was married to the Prophet at about seven years of age and brought her toys to his house, but the marriage was not consummated till later. She was eighteen when he died and became a powerful influence in struggles for the caliphate. She opposed 'Alī at the Battle of the Camel in 656 and was taken prisoner but treated kindly. Many *Traditions of Muhammad* are recorded as coming direct from 'A'isha; she could read and recite poetry. She holds a high place in Muslim regard and is called the Mother of Believers.

Ayodhyā. One of the seven sacred cities of ancient Hinduism, capital of Rāma (q.v.), whose exact site is not known but was somewhere near modern Oudh.

Ayur-Veda. Class of writings belonging to the *Upavedas* (q.v.), subordinate to the *Vedas*, and concerned with the science of medicine. It is said to have been produced by the divine physician, Dhanvantari (q.v.).

Ayyūbids. Islamic caliphs in Egypt, Syria and the Yemen from the twelfth to the fifteenth century. The founder of the dynasty, Ayyūb, was a Kurd in Turkish service. His son Saladin (Salāh ad-Dīn, q.v.) became ruler of Egypt in 1169, ending Fātimid (q.v.) rule, and restoring orthodox Sunni Muslim teaching. Saladin's holy wars against the Crusaders brought together armies of Kurds, Turks and Arabs, and Jerusalem was restored to Muslim care after being under the Franks for eighty years. After Saladin's death peaceful relations were maintained with the Franks who remained in fortresses, and trade spread over the Mediterranean. The Ayyūbid dynasty was divided by quarrels, and fell before the Mongol armies.

Āz. (Old Persian) 'lust', a weapon which was delivered to the evil Ahriman, in Zoroastrian belief, in the fight against the good Ohrmazd. Āz was black and ashen, and was offered to Ahriman by Zurvān, infinite time (q.v.). Ahriman chose it freely, but in the end it would bring destruction to him and all his followers. Āz was not only sensual lust, but also doubt and essential imperfection.

Azalīs. A sect of followers of the Bāb (q.v.).

Azan. See ADHĀN.

Azhar. Mosque and college in Cairo, sometimes claimed as one of the oldest universities in the world. Built by the Fātimid caliphs (q.v.) on the foundation of their new capital al-Azhar rapidly grew from a simple mosque to be an academy with almshouses and endowments. In the courtyards and loggias instruction was given, libraries kept, and students lived partly inside and partly out, as they still do. Students came to al-Azhar from all over the Islamic world and its international authority has remained. Until last century it was the only place of advanced education in Egypt, concentrating on theology, law and language. Reforms were inspired by 'Abduh (q.v.) in 1895, and further changes have been made since. Teaching is in modern college buildings, women are admitted, and since 1962 there have been added faculties of medicine, agriculture, engineering, industry, management and administration.

AZHAR

Azrael or **'Izrā'īl.** The angel of death in Islamic mythology, one of the four archangels next to Gabriel, Michael and Isrāfīl. Not named in the *Qur'ān*, but a verse which mentions the angel of death is applied to Azrael. The name may be derived from a Hebrew word for the prince of hell and, as in Jewish literature, Islamic tradition mentions several angels of death. 'Izrā'īl is the chief, with four faces and four thousand wings, and he was appointed angel of death above all others because of his hardness of heart. 'Izrā'īl keeps a roll of mankind but he does not know the date of a man's death till God decides it, whereupon the angel has to take his soul away within forty days. Jesus and several others, such as Idrīs or Enoch, were not subject to death in Islamic belief. See ANGELS.

Azriel ben Menachem. Jewish Kabbalistic teacher (1160–1238), disciple of Isaac the Blind and leading exponent of the doctrine of God as the En Sof (q.v.), the Endless.

Aztecs. A conquering people who entered the Valley of Mexico in the twelfth century A.D. Their religion was a mixture of worship of their own national gods, those of people they conquered, and nature deities. Their chief god, Huitzilopochtli (q.v.), from one of whose names Mexico was called, was not one of the ritual calendar gods. In Aztec myth the earth was once a great toad which was brought from heaven by the gods Tezcatlipoca and Quetzalcoatl, and from its body the mountains, waters and plants were made. At the end of the last age the sky fell down and these two gods made themselves into trees to support it. The Aztecs built great pyramids (q.v.) orientated to the sun, and were notorious for countless human sacrifices which they made in the belief that this was a glorious fate and also to keep the sun in the sky.

AZTEC SACRIFICIAL KNIFE

Almost every temple had a court in which a ball game Tlachtli (q.v.), was played by two teams with a rubber ball representing the planets. The Aztecs did not practise many elaborate burials, and although magic was important to doctors and diviners, the life of the people was dominated by the priests. See also TONATIUH, and gods listed under letter X., also CALENDAR.

B

Ba. An Egyptian word meaning 'animation' or 'manifestation', generally translated as 'soul', but referring to the whole person after death. The dead were thought to appear in bird form and in tombs they are shown as birds with human heads, often holding an Ankh amulet (q.v.). The Ba was believed to stay by the corpse in the journey to the world beyond, and to become divine with the blessed ones. It was said that the perfect Ba's would speak to the new arrival, it would receive eyes and ears, mouth and feet, would have power over water and mount up to the sky or descend below at will. In pictures the Ba-bird often appears hovering over the body or flying down a shaft to visit the mummy.

Baal. 'Lord', 'possessor', the chief male deity of the Phoenicians (q.v.) and Canaanites. This rain and fertility god plays the leading role in tablets found at Ugarit (Ras Shamra) on the north Phoenician coast, with his consort the warrior-goddess Anath. As the name of the Phoenician god, and many local deities (in the plural Baalim), it occurs often in the Bible. From the Eighteenth Dynasty (fourteenth century B.C.) Baal is the most frequently mentioned Asiatic god worshipped in Egypt, and as god of

heavens and thunder he is the counterpart to Set. See BEL.

Bāb. 'Gate' in Arabic, a term used among Ismā'īlī Muslims for a spiritual leader who guides them into religious mysteries. The name became known in wider circles from 1844 when 'Alī Muhammad of Shiraz declared himself as the Bāb to divine truth. He was executed in 1850, charged with sedition against the Shah of Persia, but his followers took his body first to Teheran and then, it is said, to Haifa. The disciples preached a new revelation in the Bāb, to which persecution added political overtones. They became divided into two groups, the Bābīs or Azalīs, and the Bahā'īs. The former are named after Subh–i–Azal who proclaimed himself the successor of the Bāb, but they are few in number. The Bahā'īs follow his half-brother, Bahā'ullāh, regard the Bāb simply as his forerunner, and have spread to many countries. See BAHĀ'ĪS and NUSAIRĪS.

Babel, Bābil. Named in the *Qur'ān* (2, 96) as a place where two angels received false doctrine. See HĀRŪT.

Bacchus. A Phrygian god of vegetation, identified with Dionysus (q.v.). Especially connected with the fruit of trees and the vine, Bacchus was the god of wine and corn. The Bacchanalia were similar to the Dionysia (q.v.), but Dionysus proper was much more the god of emotional cults than of wine. For BACCHAE, see DIONYSUS.

Bacis, Bakis. Greek name for inspired prophets who became prominent in ecstatic religious movements from the seventh century B.C.

Bādarāyana. Hindu philosopher, perhaps living in the early Christian centuries, to whom is attributed the *Brahma Sūtra* or *Vedānta Sūtra* (q.v.).

Badawiyya or **Ahmadiyya.** The followers of the most popular Muslim saint of Egypt, Ahmad al-Badawī (1200–76). He was born in Fez (Fās) in Morocco and claimed descent from 'Alī, the cousin and son-in-law of Muhammad. Badawī lived an ascetic life and wore a veil like African Tuareg Bedouins and so was called al-Badawī, the Bedouin. After travelling widely visiting tombs of saints, he settled at Tanta in Egypt and remained there till his death. His shrine at Tanta is very popular; three festivals are celebrated there and in many other places every year. The Badawiyya wear red turbans and have played considerable roles in public life, in Egypt and beyond.

Badr. Site of a battle between Muhammad and his followers from Medina and the Quraysh from Mecca. With three hundred men, the Prophet defeated a force of about a thousand, led by Abū Jahl (q.v.) who was killed. This was a turning point in the fortunes of the young Islamic movement and is regarded as signal proof of divine assistance. The Battle of Badr took place in March, A.D. 624.

Baghdad. See 'ABBĀSIDS and HĀRŪN AL-RASHĪD.

Bahā'īs. Followers of the doctrine of Bahā'ullāh, 'splendour of God', the title taken by Mīrzā Husain 'Alī (1817–92). Born at Nur in Persia he accepted the teaching of the Bāb (q.v.), although he never saw him. After civil disturbances he was exiled to Baghdad and in 1852 declared that he was the man whom the Bāb had prophesied that God would manifest. Here he planned a universal religion, and continued this at Acre in Palestine till his death. His son 'Abbās Efendi was named as spiritual successor; he died in 1920. Bahā'ī teachings have spread to many countries, with publishing activities and many properties. The administrative centre is at Haifa, in a great golden-domed edifice containing symbols from different religions. The

Bahā'ī faith teaches the unity of God, the truth of his prophets, and continuous revelation in every age. It has no priesthood, gives equal rights to men and women, and declares its unity with science. All religions are said to be in basic harmony. Men should love one another and seek universal peace.

Bahīra. Christian monk in Muslim tradition who is said to have recognized the young Muhammad, aged twelve, as a prophet from a Seal (q.v.) of prophethood between his shoulders. The story is told in the standard life of Muhammad by Ibn Ishāq (q.v.).

Baiami. The 'all-father' in the belief of many south-eastern Australian aboriginals. He is the creator of the world, of men and animals, and of their laws and customs. He was a model for ordinary life, and in addition gave magical power to doctors. Baiami lived in the sky, with several wives, and sent a one-legged hero, Daramulun (q.v.), to visit the earth and initiate men. He is depicted on rock engravings and bark paintings as a gigantic superhuman figure.

Baidāwī. One of the most famous Muslim commentators on the *Qur'ān*; who died in Tabriz about 1282 or 1291.

His work is voluminous, using Christian as well as many Islamic sources, and is regarded almost as a holy book, though it has numerous inaccuracies. Baidāwī opposed the Mu'tazila point of view of Zamakhsharī (q.v.) and tried to surpass him in grammatical exposition. See TAFSĪR.

Bairam. A Turkish word for the two great festivals of Islam. The Great Festival, Corban or Kurbān-Bairam, is the feast of sacrifice during the Pilgrimage to Mecca, in the twelfth month of the Islamic year. The Little Festival, or 'feast of sweets', Sheker-Bairam, comes at the end of the month of fasting, Ramadān, the ninth month (see 'ĪD).

Bakkah. See MECCA.

Baktāshi. See BEKTĀSHI.

Bala-rāma. Elder brother of Krishna (q.v.) and sometimes called a 'partial Avatar' of Vishnu. In the epic *Mahābhārata* it is said that when Vishnu was to descend to earth he took two hairs from his body, one white and the other black, and these became Bala-rāma and Krishna, the latter being black. Bala-rāma grew up with Krishna, fought demons as a child, and shared in many heroic exploits, dying just before his brother. Stories of Bala-rāma are popular among the followers of Krishna.

Balder, Baldr. The most beautiful and wisest of the Scandinavian gods, son of Odin and Frigg. His name means 'bright' or 'shining' and his home was Broad Splendour in the sky. Although Balder was the fairest of speech, his judgements were not upheld, and he would be of little interest were it not for the moving myths of his death. Balder dreamt that his life was threatened and his mother, Frigg, made all trees, animals and elements swear not to touch him. But she told the evil Loki that she had not taken an oath from the mistletoe because it was too young. Loki took a mistletoe shoot and gave it to the blind god Hödr, directing his hand till Balder fell down dead. This was the greatest tragedy that ever befell the gods and Balder was cremated with his wife. Hermodr, a son of Odin, galloped to Hel to ransom Balder, and the goddess of death promised to release him if all creatures would weep for Balder. All beings wept except Loki, as a giantess in disguise, and so Balder remains in Hel on a seat of honour.

Bali. In Hindu mythology a king whose austerities were so great that he humbled the gods and they appealed to the great god Vishnu for help. Vishnu came down in an Avatar (q.v.) as a dwarf (Vāmana, q.v.) and craved three steps of land from Bali, who granted it whereupon Vishnu strode over earth, air and sky (see TRILOKA). It is said that Bali's capital was Maha-bali-puram, whose famous temples (or Seven Pagodas) on the east coast of India below Madras date from about the seventh century A.D.

Balkis. See BILQĪS.

Ball Game. Mexican sport and symbolical contest; for details, see ṬLACHTLI.

Balor. God of the Fomorians (q.v.) of ancient Ireland, or perhaps a personification of an evil eye which had been poisoned by magic. It took four men to lift his eyelid, and then his eye destroyed whatever it gazed upon. The god Lug, of the Tuatha Dé Danann (q.v.), eventually destroyed Balor's eye with a stone.

Bānī. (Hindi) inspired 'utterances' or oracles name given to the hymns of the sixteenth century mystic Dādū (q.v.).

Baptist, John. See MANDEANS and YAHYĀ.

Barai. See HARAI.

Baraitha. See TOSAFOTH.

Baraka. An Arabic word which means 'blessing', and which is widely used throughout the Islamic world to denote a mysterious and wonderful power, a blessing from God, indicating holiness or 'blessed virtue'. Baraka (sometimes pronounced Barka) is possessed by saints, and the Prophet Muhammad possessed it in the highest degree. He transmitted his Baraka to the Sharīfs (his descendants in the male line through his daughter Fātima) who are much revered and in some places, such as Egypt, distinguished by a green turban. The Sharīfs thus inherited Baraka, but not all of them are saints and the power is diluted on the female side. Baraka is seen in miracles, holy places and people, strange objects prayers, blessings and curses.

Bar Cochba, Kozeba. See COCHBA.

Bardo. In the teachings of Tibetan Buddhism, Bardo is an intermediate state between death in this world and rebirth on earth. The word means literally 'between two', and so an intermediate or transitional state. It is a purely mental state and the conditions there depend upon the personality, while the length of time depends on Karma previously acquired. Visions and other experiences on the Bardo plane are described in the Tibetan Book of the Dead, *Bardo Thödol*, 'Liberation by Hearing in Bardo'.

Bark Paintings. Painting or scratching pictures on the bark of trees has been widespread among Australian aboriginals, and is recorded from 1807. It occurred throughout the continent, though there are none surviving from Tasmania. Sheets of bark are stripped from stringy-bark trees, the outer fibre is removed and the inner bark flattened and dried. Brushes are made of bark or palm-leaf, and colours are in red, yellow, black and white pigments. The Bark Paintings depict many mythical scenes, or supernatural figures. See BAIAMI, DARAMULUN, DJANGGAWUL, GURUNGA, JULUNGGUL, MIMI.

Barlaam and Josaphat. Popularly acclaimed as Christian saints, though never officially canonized, and commemorated on 27 November in the West and 26 August or other dates in the East. The stories of these holy men are now known to have been derived from Indian Buddhism. Their romance was included by Caxton in *The Golden Legend*, and a story of Caskets inspired an episode in Shakespeare's *Merchant of Venice*. The various versions of the tale speak of an Indian prince Josaphat or Iodasaph (from Bodhisattva), and his conversion to a holy life by a hermit Barlaam or Balahvar. Buddhist narratives and teachings are only thinly presented, but they include wise men hailing the child at his birth, his sight of old, sick and dead men, renunciation of the world, teachings in parables, the death of Josaphat and burial of his relics in a golden urn.

Barmecids, Barmakids. Persian viziers or ministers under the 'Abbāsid caliphs (q.v.) of Islam. The name was derived from Barmak, a priest, and the first holder Khālid ibn-Barmak (765) was son of a Buddhist priest in Balkh. The Barmakids had great palaces in Baghdad, with splendid gardens and precincts; their generosity was proverbial and is still quoted, Barmecid indicating generosity. See also HĀRŪN AL-RASHĪD.

Bar Mitzvah. (Hebrew) 'son of the commandment', the term applied to a Jewish boy on the completion of his thirteenth year when he attains his legal majority. On the following Sabbath he puts on the *tefillin* (phylacteries) and is called up among the men who read the weekly portion of the Law or the lesson from the Prophets. The Bar Mitzvah recites a special prayer when called to the Law or after being addressed by the minister.

BARK PAINTING

Barsam. Twigs from certain trees, sometimes pomegranates, used in ancient Zoroastrian worship. In the Avesta scriptures called Baresman, the word may be derived from a root meaning 'to grow', and it was the symbol of the vegetable creation. In modern Parsi ritual the old vegetable Barsam has been replaced by metal or wire placed on two crescent-shaped metallic stands, and used in various rituals, such as grace before meals.

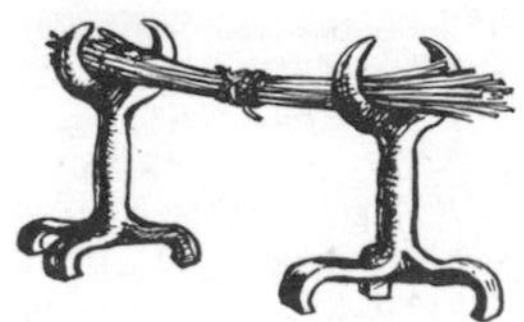

Basil. See TULASĪ.

Basin of Paradise. See HAWD.

Basket. See PITAKA.

Basmala. See BISMILLĀH.

Bast. A sun-goddess of ancient Egypt, 'she of the city of Bubastis' or 'lady of the east'. Bast was represented as a cat or a woman with a cat's head, and often identified with Sekhmet, the lioness-headed goddess. She was daughter of the

sun god Rē' and sometimes thought of as personifying the moon. By the Greeks she was identified with Artemis. The chief centre of the cult of Bast was at Bubastis, but there were other sanctuaries as well.

Bātinīya. Title of a number of Shī'a Islamic sects. The name means 'inner', for those who seek the inner meaning of the *Qur'ān* instead of formal and legal interpretation. It is applied particularly to the Qarmatians and Ismā'īlīs (q.v.).

Bāuls. Bengali nickname, meaning 'mad', for a sect which claims to have been founded by Chaitanya (q.v.) but may well be older. Their principal doctrine is the presence of God in the human body and the importance of worship of everything connected with it, including sexual union. The love of Krishna for Rādhā (q.v.) is taken as the model of activity and worship, but the Bāuls are notable for their rejection of images in worship.

Bāyazīd. See BISTĀMĪ.

Bayon. Great temple of Angkor Thom in Cambodia. See ANGKOR WAT.

Beautiful Names. The *Qur'ān* speaks several times of the Most Beautiful Names of God (*al-asmā' al-husnā*, 7, 179, etc.). Muhammad relished such descriptions and their importance for devotion was soon realized. Tradition said that there were ninety-nine Beautiful Names, and various lists were compiled amounting to more than that number. Many of these names are found in the *Qur'ān*, and some afterwards, and they are attributes of God: wise, knowing, strong, generous, merciful, etc. It was said that the hundredth name of God was unknowable, or revealed only to his saints or in heaven, perhaps from the unutterable or unknowable name in Jewish and Christian belief. Muslim prayer beads (q.v.) number ninety-nine for telling over the Beautiful Names (see SUBHA).

PRAYER BEADS

Begging bowls. See BHIKKHU.

Bektāshi, Baktāshīya. A Turkish order of dervishes, said to have been founded in the twelfth century by Hajjī Bektāsh, though his existence is disputed. The Bektāshis sometimes claimed to be orthodox Sunni Muslims, but they disregarded ritual, even prayer, and revered the twelve Imāms of Shī'a Islam. They reverenced 'Alī and had traces of Christian influence, with a communion of bread, wine and cheese. Women took part in their rites unveiled, but some Bektāshis were vowed to celibacy. They became closely associated with the Janissaries, 'new troops', Turkish soldiers largely recruited from Christian captives. The Bektāshis were banned in Turkey in 1925, along with other dervish orders, but some survive in neighbouring lands and there is a famous centre on the Muqattam slope near Cairo.

Bel. God of the earth in Babylonian religion whose worship was centred at Nippur. With the growth of the cult of Marduk (q.v.), tutelary god of Babylon, he came to be identified with Bel, as 'the lord' over all. The name means the same as Baal (q.v.). The apocryphal book of *Bel and the Dragon* or *Snake* says that Cyrus the Persian worshipped the Babylonian idol called Bel, but Daniel overthrew it and a serpent which was also worshipped.

Belenos. A sun god of Celtic mythology, from *belos*, 'bright'. His worship was widespread in Gaul, and perhaps in Britain too, and the Romans identified him with Apollo. Images have been found of a nameless god who has a wheel, often a symbol of the sun, and this may be Belenos. Geoffrey of Monmouth in his *History* said that the ashes of Belenos were preserved at Billingsgate in London, so named after him. See BELTANE.

Bellerophon. Hero of ancient Greek

BELLEROPHON

mythology who was set to fight the Amazons and the Chimaera (q.v.), which he did on his winged horse Pegasus (q.v.). He is a prototype of St George fighting the dragon, may be seen in a mosaic at Lullingstone in Kent, and may be compared also with Perseus in the deliverance of Andromeda (q.v.) from the monster.

Bellona. Roman war-goddess, related to Mars; her name occurs in early formulas of devotion, mentioned by Livy. However, her temple was not built till the third century B.C., near the altar of Mars, and in front of it stood a column used in declarations of war.

Beltane, Beltain. One of the two major festivals of the Celtic year, the summer half celebrated on 30 April or May Day, corresponding to Samhain (q.v.) on 31 October or 1 November. Beltane is perhaps connected in name with Belenos, an ancient Celtic god associated with pastoralism. Druids presided at Beltane festivals and apparently drove cattle between fires, and no doubt made sacrifices. Sacred fires were lit at both these festivals, round which people danced sunwise, to encourage the growth of the sun and health to cattle and crops. Beltane cakes were rolled down slopes, in imitation of the sun in the sky, and Maypole festivals, May-queens, and May Day parades, continue the old customs.

Benares, Vārānasī, Kāshī. The most sacred Hindu city, situated on the holy river Ganges. It is one of the seven sacred cities of the Hindus, the most important place of pilgrimage, and the northern centre of the worship of Shiva. Shiva made the city his abode and has many temples dedicated to him, especially a Golden Temple, the roof of which is covered with gold leaf. There are also temples to Vishnu and many other gods. A million pilgrims a year visit Benares, and many go there to die, regarding every stone in the city as sacred and death there leading direct to heaven. Many of the temples, however, have been destroyed or mutilated during Muslim wars and rule. Others crowd along the banks of the Ganges; down the steps (ghats) in front of them people go to bathe, or sit and recite texts. 'Burning ghats' are steps on which cremations are made, before the ashes and sacred marigold flowers are placed in the river.

Ben Asher. Jewish rabbi of the ninth century who lived in Palestine and transmitted the traditions of the Palestine Masora (q.v.).

Beowulf. Old English poem of a Swedish hero who delivered the Danes from a sea-monster, Grendel, and its mother a water-hag. He dived into a lake and fought them in a cave, cutting off their heads with a giant's sword. After his return home and succession to the kingdom, Beowulf fought a dragon and killed it but was mortally wounded himself, and was buried under a barrow on Whale's Headland.

Bes. An Egyptian god, patron of fun and music, and also of childbirth. He was represented as a dwarf with a beard, often with long hair and a tail, or wearing a lion's skin. Later he became more of a magician, and amulets with his image were popular.

Besant, Annie. A leading Theosophist (1847–1933). Born in London, née Wood, she married Rev. Frank Besant but became a freethinker, worked with the atheist Bradlaugh and the Fabian Socialists. In 1888 she read Madame Blavatsky's (q.v.) *The Secret Doctrine* and turned at once from atheism to Theosophy, becoming the most powerful person in the society after the death of the foundress. She settled in Benares and founded the Central Hindu College which became a university, exerting great influence by championing Hindu religion and culture, though having a colouring of occultism. She translated and lectured on the *Bhagavad-Gītā* (q.v.), and travelled widely in Europe and America. She died at Adyar, near Madras.

Besht. See HASIDISM.

Bhagavad-Gītā. The 'Song (*Gītā*) of the Lord (*Bhagavat*)'. The best known and most important Hindu scripture, written in Sanskrit verse, in eighteen chapters and seven hundred verses. It is part of the Great Epic, the *Mahābhārata*, and occurs in the sixth book. Arjuna, third of the five Pāndu brothers, is leading his forces against the Kurus when he is assailed by conscientious scruples and lays down his arms. His charioteer is the Lord Krishna who in long discourses shows him the path of duty, the necessity of action for all men and even for God, the constant manifestation of Avatars (q.v.) of the deity, and the path of loving devotion or Bhakti (q.v.). The *Bhagavad-Gītā*, attributed to the poet Vyāsa, and probably composed in the fourth or third centuries B.C., is full of lofty sentiments of devotion and action. It is very eclectic, acknowledging good in all ways of knowledge, works, and sacrifice, but holding out its own path of devotion as best for both sexes and all classes of people. There are many English translations, the first being by Charles Wilkins in 1785.

Bhagavat. (Sanskrit) 'fortunate', holy, lord. A title applied to saints and gods, especially Shiva and Vishnu-Krishna. It is used by Jains and Buddhists of their holy ones, and by the latter also used as a prefix to the titles of their scriptures. As a term of address it may be Bhagavan, and in compounds Bhagavad (see BHAGAVAD-GĪTĀ).

Bhāgavata Purāna. The most popular of the *Purānas*, 'ancient tales', of Hindu myth and legend, telling the story of twenty-two Avatars (q.v.) of Vishnu, with special reference to Krishna. Vishnu is the Bhagavat, 'lord'. This *Purāna* is in Sanskrit, in eighteen thousand verses divided into twelve books. The tenth book gives the story of Krishna, his childhood adventures, adolescent sports with the Gopīs (q.v.), milkmaids, and his later life. Little, if any, of this can be claimed as history, but it provides the subject of endless story-telling and dramatic enactment, and has been translated into many Indian languages, though not yet fully into English.

Bhāgavatas. The name of Hindu sects given to the worship of Vishnu or Krishna as Bhagavat, 'Lord'. Their early history is obscure, but they arose before the Christian era and emphasized the importance of loving devotion rather than formal sacrifice, hence they may also be called Bhaktas, practitioners of Bhakti devotion (q.v.). The Bhāgavatas gave special importance to the use of images in their worship, finding them valuable for practising devotion, and some of their leading thinkers were also devout saints who used images to express the 'auspicious bodies' of the deity. In the Middle Ages philosophers like Rāmānuja gave intellectual distinction to the Bhāgavata communities.

Bhairava, Bhairavī. (Sanskrit) 'terrible', male and female names of the Hindu god Shiva and his spouse in their terrible forms.

Bhajana. An Indian song of devotional love, from a root related to the word Bhakti, devotion (q.v.). It is sung to the accompaniment of musical instruments, on traditional themes, and may be chanted in temples or in public gatherings. See also KĪRTANA.

Bhakti. (Sanskrit) 'love' or 'devotion', from a root meaning to 'share', but developing into ardent worship and love. It appears strongly in the *Bhagavad-Gītā* (q.v.) where Krishna is said to 'participate' in his devotees, but it is chiefly used there of the loving devotion of men to the personal God. In later texts the imagery of sexual love is also attached to Bhakti, but never in the *Bhagavad-Gītā*. There the Way of Bhakti, Bhakti-yoga, is the highest of the three Ways of Knowledge, Works and Devotion. Followers of this way, Bhaktas, are very numerous among followers of the gods (both Vishnu and Shiva).

Bharata. Indian hero and king from whom the Bhāratas, Indian warrior people, were said to have come. There are several legendary Bharatas, one of these, of the lunar race, was ancestor of the Kurus or Kauravas and the Pāndus or Pāndavas, and their battle is the theme of the great epic poem, *Mahābhārata* (q.v.), 'the great (war of the) Bhāratas'. See also JAMBUDVIPA.

The land of India is often now called Bharata. The nineteenth-century reformer Keshab Chandra Sen (q.v.) called the Brāhma Samāj of India, Bharatvishya.

Bhave. See VINOBA.

Bhikkhu. A Buddhist monk, member of the Sangha (q.v.). This Pali term comes from the Sanskrit Bhikshu, for a 'beggar' and particularly a religious mendicant. In some Buddhist lands, notably Burma and Thailand, Bhikkhus set out each morning with begging bowls to receive gifts of food which are shared at a communal meal in the monastery. A Bhikkhu is thus one who relies for his upkeep on lay gifts, since he has devoted himself to following the way of the Buddha without worldly distractions. His life is governed by the rules of the Order (see PĀTIMOKKHA). A Bhikkhu only possesses his robes, alms bowl, water-strainer, needle and razor. He generally

BHIKKHUS

eats one meal a day. His head and face are shaved, and he wears robes of yellow, orange or brownish-purple colours. A nun is a Bhikkhunī. See also THERAGĀTHĀ.

Bhilsa Topes. See SANCHI.

Bhīma. The 'terrible' (Sanskrit), second of the five Pāndu princes in Hindu mythology, and also said to be son of Vāyu, god of the wind. See MAHĀBHĀRATA.

Bhīshma. The 'terrible' (Sanskrit), warrior and wise counsellor in the Hindu epic battle of Pāndus and Kurus (see MAHĀBHĀRATA). He was said to be son of King Shāntanu and the river goddess Ganges.

Bhoodan. See VINOBA.

Bhrigu. A sage of the Indian *Vedas*, one of the creators and founder of the race of Bhrigus.

Bhūmi. See PRITHIVĪ.

Bhūta. (Sanskrit) 'ghost' or goblin. In Hindu mythology the Bhūtas haunted cemeteries and ate flesh. They were also said to be attendants upon the god Shiva in his fearful aspect. He is then called Bhūtesha or Bhūteshvara.

Bidpai, Pilpay. European name, from Persian, of the Indian Vidyāpati or Vishnu-sharma, who recounted the popular fables in the *Pañcha-tantra* (q.v.). The *Fables of Bidpai* (or *Pilpay*) were current in the Middle Ages.

Bifrost, Bilrost. Rainbow bridge in Scandinavian mythology beside the rocks of heaven, Himinbjörg, where dwelt Heimdall (q.v.), the watchman of the gods.

Big House. Building and cult among North American Indians, known particularly from the Delaware. It was a rectangular hut in the forest, orientated to the cardinal points and with gabled roof. In the middle was a massive wooden pillar, with two large sculptured faces representing Gicelemukaong, the creator who lives in heaven. The Big House represents the universe, with the floor as earth, the roof as sky, and the four walls as the four sides of the horizon. The Big House ceremony took place after harvest in October and was based on the idea of 'beginning', a new year and new world. There were prayers to the creator, passed upwards by Manito spirits (q.v.), dances, recitals, hunting, extinguishing and re-lighting of fires. The Big House ceremonies lasted for twelve days, the final one being reserved for women. See LONG HOUSE.

Big Rabbit. See MANABUSCH.

Bījak. (Hindi) 'seed', document which contains a hidden treasure, a name of the collection of verses which contains the principal teaching of the Indian mystic Kabīr (q.v.).

Bilāl. Abyssinian slave in Arabia who

became a disciple of Muhammad, went with him to Medina in 622 and, when the call to prayer (see ADHĀN) was introduced, became the first Muezzin (q.v.). When Mecca was occupied by the Muslims, it was Bilāl who called them to prayer from the roof of the Ka'ba. He died in 641, in Damascus, at the age of sixty.

Bilqīs. The name given in Muslim legend to the Queen of Sheba. In the *Qur'ān* (27, 23–45) she received a letter from Solomon and on visiting him thought his sea of glass was water, but the name Bilqīs does not occur. Many

variants and legends were added later, like the ones in Kipling's *The Butterfly That Stamped*.

Bimah, Almamar. Desk, or pulpit, in a Jewish synagogue (q.v.). It is a raised platform, which formerly stood at one end of the synagogue, but now is usually in the centre. Candles stand at the desk for the readers of the Law and prayers are made in front of the Ark (q.v.) or facing it.

Bimbisāra. A king of Magadha, where the Buddha preached, said to have built the city of Rājagriha, modern Rājgir. He was converted to Buddhism and presented a Bamboo Grove, Veluvana, for the use of the Sangha monastic order.

Bīrūni. One of the most original thinkers of mediaeval Islam, al-Bīrūni was a Persian, who wrote in Arabic, and knew Turkish, Hebrew, Syriac and Sanskrit. He was a physician, astronomer, mathematician, physicist, geographer and historian. Bīrūni wrote on the calendars of ancient peoples and studied Hindu philosophy. He discussed the theory of the rotation of the earth upon its axis, and sought to determine latitudes and longitudes. He wrote on geometry and astronomy, and on medical abnormalities. He lived from A.D. 973 to 1048.

Birthday. See MAWLID.

Bismillāh. (Arabic) 'in the name of God', *Bi'smi 'llāhi*, an invocation used by Muslims on many occasions. In the form 'In the name of God, the merciful, the compassionate', it occurs at the head of every chapter (sūra) of the *Qur'ān* except the ninth. In the form 'In the name of God, God the most great', it is used when slaughtering animals or before a battle. The Bismillāh is used as a grace before meals, on putting on new clothes, beginning a new work, and at the beginning of new books. It is written in Arabic on walls or as a protective text on motor lorries.

Bistāmī, Abū Yazīd. Islamic mystic from Bistam in Persia, who is also called Bāyazīd. Little is known about his life, but he died in A.D. 874. No works of Bistāmī survive, but with him the pantheistic or monistic tendencies which appeared in Sūfī mysticism come to light. He regarded himself as so close to, or identical with, God that he cried, 'Glory to me, how great is my majesty.' This sentence was condemned as madness by more sober mystics, such as Junaid (q.v.). Since he was taught by al-Sindi (q.v.), probably from Sind in India, it is possible that Hindu monism affected Bistāmī.

Black Magic. See MAGIC.

Black Muslims. American Negro movement introduced by W. D. Fard in 1930. He disappeared in 1934 and his successor Elijah Muhammad (born 1897) declared that Allāh had appeared in Fard and appointed him prophet. The next in command, Malcolm X, founded a movement of his own but was assassinated in 1965. The Black Muslims have Negro racial teachings, exclude white people from their temples, and have strict morals. A militant group, the Fruits of Islam, acts generally peaceably. Prayers in temples are in English and Arabic, and both *Qur'ān* and *Bible* are used. But the claim of Black Muslims to have a prophet after Muhammad is rejected by orthodox Muslims. See MUHAMMAD and ISLAM.

BLACK PAGODA WHEEL

SCULPTURES FROM BLACK PAGODA

Black Pagoda. Popular name of the temple of Sūrya (q.v.), the sun-god, at Konarak in eastern India. Built in the thirteenth century it was one of the largest Indian temples, but although the central tower is ruined the assembly hall remains. Round these two was built a platform with twelve carved stone wheels of the sun-god, often illustrated in books, see photographs (left).

The temple sculptures are highly erotic, as expressions of the mysticism of Tantra (q.v.) which flourished there – see bottom photograph.

Black Stone. Arabic, al-Hajaru 'l-Aswad, 'the Black Stone', is a sacred object set in the south-east corner wall of the Ka'ba shrine in Mecca. Tradition says that it was received by Ishmael from the angel Gabriel when the ancient edifice was rebuilt. It was certainly pre-Islamic and is mentioned by the Greek writer Maximus of Tyre in the second century A.D. Muhammad included this in his adoption and reform of ancient religious customs of Mecca. In the rite of pilgrimage the faithful try to kiss or touch the Black Stone during ritual circling of the Ka'ba, though among the hundreds of thousands this is difficult. Burkhardt and Burton who visited Mecca in disguise described the Black Stone as an oval about 18 centimetres in diameter, grey or black and mounted in a circular silver band. They considered it to be an ancient meteorite round which perhaps Mecca itself grew up as centre of pilgrimage.

MUHAMMAD PLACING BLACK STONE

Blavatsky, Madame. Born in Russia in 1831 of a German family, Helena Petrovna Hahn married in 1848 a Russian official, N. V. Blavatsky, but left him and travelled to many lands, later claiming to have spent seven years in Tibet receiving instruction in the 'ancient wisdom' from

Mahātmas ('great souls') or the Great White Brotherhood. In 1875 she was in New York and met Col. Henry Olcott and together they founded the Theosophical Society. In 1877 Madame Blavatsky published *Isis Unveiled*, a defence of spiritualism, and the following year with her partner she went to India where many converts were won to Theosophy and the Tibetan experiences were announced as giving a new occult wisdom. In 1888 she published *The Secret Doctrine*, claiming to be based on ancient works only found in Tibet. See MAHĀTMĀ. She died in London in 1891.

Blessings, Eighteen. See AMIDAH.

Boand. Celtic goddess, wife of the great god Dagda (q.v.).

Boar Avatar. See VARĀHA.

Bodhi. (Sanskrit) 'wisdom', and with Jains and Buddhists the perfect wisdom by which one attains enlightenment, and becomes a Buddha, or Bodhisattva (q.v.). The word is used also of the tree under which enlightenment comes, see BO-TREE. See also MAHA BODHI.

Bodhidharma. An Indian Buddhist monk of the sixth century A.D. who took to China the Meditation doctrine which became the Chinese Ch'an and Japanese Zen (q.v.). Some Chinese scholars doubt the existence and claims made for Bodhidharma, but the Zen school holds that he arrived in Canton about 520 and count him as the first of six great Chinese patriarchs. Bodhidharma is said to have tried to simplify Buddhist doctrine and practice, placing no reliance on scriptures, but teaching the awakening of the Buddha-nature in everyone by direct perception. In China he is known as Putitamo or Tamo, and in Japan as Daruma (q.v.).

Bodhisattva (Sanskrit), **Bodhisatta** (Pali). A 'being' (*sattva*) destined for 'enlightenment' (*bodhi*) in Buddhist terminology. In Theravāda or Hīnayāna Buddhism a Bodhisatta is one who is on the way to becoming a Buddha, and the term is used of Gotama himself before his enlightenment. In Mahāyāna Buddhism there are countless Bodhisattvas, who are ideals of life and embodiments of compassion, sometimes loosely called 'Buddhas of Compassion'. In the *Lotus Sūtra* (q.v.) the great Bodhisattva is Avalokita (q.v.), called Kuan Yin in Chinese, also later regarded as incarnate in the Dalai Lama. The Bodhisattvas were said to take Ten Inexhaustible Vows which bound them to defer their own Nirvāna until all beings were saved, so they were

destined for enlightenment, ready for Nirvāna, but sacrificed their own good till all others were saved by their merits; hence they are popularly called upon for help.

Bodhi-Tree. See BO-TREE.

Boehme, Behmen, Jakob. German mystic (1575–1624) who taught the doctrine of the inner light, and has often been called a Theosophist (q.v.).

Bogdo. Name of the principal Lama of the Tibetan Buddhists in Mongolia. See LAMA.

Bon, P'ön-Po. The ancient religion of Tibet, pronounced 'pern'. Though much mingled with Buddhism since its introduction into Tibet in the sixth century A.D., the ancient religion was a form of animism and polytheism such as was found right across Asia, with Shamanistic (q.v.) priests like those of Siberia. The ancient gods (Srong ma, q.v.) were guardians of mountains and other natural objects, often represented as fierce and fighting demons. With the triumph of Buddhism they became 'guardians of Buddhist doctrine', and are still to be seen in many religious pictures and statues. Bon literature is scarce, but magical books have survived concerned with control of the elements and curing of disease. Some of the Bon gods resemble those of India, and a great guardian goddess, Palden Lhamo (q.v.), is depicted in horrific form like Kāli (q.v.). See also LAMA and PRAYER WALLS.

Bona Dea. (Latin) 'good goddess', of Rome worshipped by women, and sometimes identified with Fauna (see FAUNS). She had an annual ceremony at night, led by the wife of the chief magistrate with Vestals (q.v.). Wine was used in the ceremony and the room decorated with vine branches. Sows were sacrificed to Bona Dea.

Bonze. From the Japanese *Bozu*, 'head of a monastery', which was originally an honorary title but has now declined in value and Buddhist priests or monks should not be addressed as Bozu.

Book of the Dead. One of the oldest collections of religious texts and hymns, from ancient Egypt, and known there as the *Chapters of Coming Forth by Day* referring to the lot of the dead in the world beyond the grave. Portions of it were known before the First Dynasty, from about 4,000 B.C., in prayers and petitions recited from memory and when oral tradition became doubtful the priests wrote down the texts and added to them. One of the best versions is the Theban Recension which was copied by scribes for the use of kings and queens, rich and poor, from about 1600 to 900 B.C., and the British Museum has a splendid collection of it. The prayers and exorcisms for the use of the soul were placed in the tomb or inscribed on the wall so as to be ready when needed. Similar texts are in the *Book of the Two Ways* and the *Book of Gates*. For the Tibetan *Book of the Dead*, see BARDO.

Boomerang. New South Wales name for a curved wooden missile, used as a weapon, which returns when thrown. It can also be used as a musical instrument, clapping one in each hand or beating

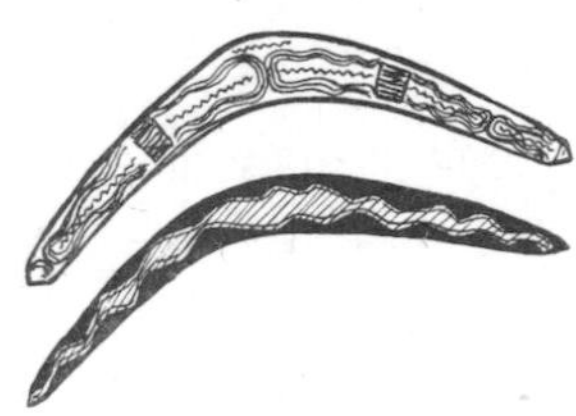

them on the ground in rhythm. Many Boomerangs are decorated with designs, such as creeks and channels, which have mythical significance. Bark paintings of supernatural beings often show them holding Boomerangs.

Booths. See TABERNACLES.

Boreas. Greek name for the north wind which was personified and worshipped in Attica. In mythology he was son of Eos, the dawn (q.v.). Boreas was said to beget horses, perhaps from the idea that the speed of the wind seizes galloping mares.

Borobudur. Great Buddhist monument in Java, built from the eighth century A.D. It is a gigantic pyramid with rising stone terraces decorated with reliefs of the life of the Buddha and a large central stūpa (q.v.) surrounded with lesser stūpas, making a mystical diagram in stone. From the fifteenth century Islam spread over the whole of Java, and Borobudur remained hidden in ruins till modern times.

SHRINE AT BOROBUDUR

Bosatsu. Japanese term for Bodhisattva (q.v.).

Bo-Tree, Bodhi-Tree. The 'tree of enlightenment' (*bodhi*) under which Gautama sat in meditation until enlightenment came to him and he became a Buddha. This was on the banks of a tributary of the Ganges, near a shrine of Vishnu at Gayā (q.v.). The site is now called Buddha-Gayā or Budh-Gayā. The Bo-tree is a pipal (or peepul, sacred fig tree, *ficus religiosa*), which often occurs as a sacred tree in religious literature and practice. Legend said that all Buddhas were enlightened on the Diamond Seat under this tree. A shoot of the tree from Gayā was taken to Ceylon

BO-TREE

in the third century B.C. by the nun Sanghamitta, a daughter of the emperor Ashoka, and planted at the famous Buddhist centre at Anurādhapura where it is said to be the oldest historical tree in the world. Shoots were planted in many Ceylonese temples and also returned to India after the destruction of the original Bo-tree there. Bronze pīpal leaves hang from the spires of many pagodas in Burma and tinkle in the wind.

Boxers. Chinese society, of partly Taoist inspiration, known as I-he-ch'üan, the 'Harmonious Fist' society, and known to the West as Boxers. Taoism was long associated with secret societies which served as opposition to the state, particularly under the Manchu dynasty. The society existed all over China, but the Dowager Empress cleverly blamed the misfortunes of China on the Western powers, and in 1900 the 'Boxer Rebellion' took place. In this more than two hundred foreign missionaries and several thousand Chinese Christians were killed, but the uprising was not so much anti-Christian as anti-foreign. In 1901 the allied forces, chiefly British and French, took Peking and forced a treaty on the Empress, entailing the suppressing of the Harmonious Fist society, but other Taoist secret societies flourished till the nineteen fifties (see TAOISM). See T'AI P'ING, and FÊNG SHUI.

Bragi. Scandinavian first of poets, perhaps originally a maker of verse (*bragr* sometimes means poetry) and eloquence, and revered by poets. It is said that verse and spells were carved on his tongue. Then he was made a god of poetry, rival of Odin, and husband of Idunn who guarded the apples of immortality.

Brahm. See BRAHMAN.

Brahmā (masculine). A Hindu creating deity, sometimes said to be the first member of a triad with Vishnu and Shiva. Brahmā does not appear in the *Veda* scriptures, but emerges in the Great Epic, the *Mahābhārata*, and later texts. Then he declined in importance and it is said that there is only one temple to him in all India today, at Pushkar (q.v.), near Ajmer in Rajasthan. Here he is represented with four faces, looking at the four points of the compass. Brahmā fulfilled for a time the role of a creator, and was the Prajā-pati or Lord of creatures. But his consort Sarasvati, the goddess of learning, was more popular

and eventually Brahmā faded away and was completely overshadowed by the great gods Shiva and Vishnu. For Brahmā's Heaven, Brahmā-Loka, see SATYA-LOKA. See also TRIMŪRTI.

Brahma-Chārī. A Brahmin student, one who is in the first stage or Ashram (q.v.), serving and learning from a spiritual teacher of the *Vedas*. He is the Chela, disciple, of a Guru. See also BRĀHMANA and ĀCHĀRYA.

Brahman (neuter). The all-pervading divinity, the supreme soul of the universe, the Absolute (q.v.), in Hindu philosophy. Perhaps from a root *brih*, meaning generally 'to grow' and in connection with sounds 'to roar', Brahman came to mean 'sacred utterance' or 'holy power'. The power of Brahman in man was regarded as the power or Brahman in the universe. This is developed especially in the *Upanishads*. Brahman sustains the earth, pervades the entire universe, is present everywhere, and man is the city of Brahman. The identification of the individual soul (ātman, q.v.) with the ground of the universe or Brahman is affirmed, and in the *Upanishads* Ātman is often another name for Brahman. Brahman is indescribable, has no attributes, and can only be spoken of as 'not this, not that'. Hence it must be neuter, and it is an error to speak of it as God. In fact, this impersonal and ethereal conception proved unsatisfactory, and in the *Bhagavad-Gītā* there was a return to a personal God. See ANTHROPOMORPHISM.

Brāhmana. The English rendering 'Brahmin' is a convenient misspelling to distinguish the name of the priestly caste of Hinduism. The Brāhmanas or Brahmins are the first of the four classical classes traditionally priests though many of them, like Prime Minister Nehru, are not priests. The Brahmins were held to be first after the gods, or were human gods, entitled to all reverence. Their duty was to study and teach the *Veda* scriptures, and perform sacrifices and other ceremonies. Their life was divided into four stages (see ĀSHRAMS). Brahmins were first of the 'twice-born' and at the initiation ceremony for this state were invested with sacred white threads, worn from the left shoulder across the body under the right arm and never left off. See SACRED THREAD, CASTE and GOTRA.

Brāhmanas. 'Belonging to Brahmins', ancient Sanskrit scriptures, following on the *Vedas*, and giving guidance to Brahmin priests for the use of their hymns. There are various Brāhmanas, mostly in prose, giving details of ceremonies and instructions in their meaning and use, expositions of verses and metres, and many curious legends to illustrate rituals. They may date from about 800–500 B.C. As literary productions they are not exalted and much is tedious, but scattered about there are striking thoughts about the individual and universal souls (Brahman and Ātman, qq.v.). See SHATAPATHA.

Brahmanaspati. See BRIHASPATI.

Brahmānda. (Sanskrit) 'egg of Brahmā', a name for the universe in Hindu cosmology. It was divided into twenty-one zones, at the top six heavens and then the earth, followed by seven regions of the nether world, Pātāla, where dwelt snakes and other mythical beings. The bottom seven zones were Naraka (q.v.), Hell or Purgatory, places of increasing misery. A text called *Brahmānda Purāna* in twelve thousand verses is said to have existed and to survive in fragments.

Brahma Purāna. Placed first in lists of the Hindu *Purānas* or traditional tales. It was said to come from the creator god Brahmā and contains over seven thousand verses. Its particular concern is to promote the worship of Krishna as 'world-lord', Jagannātha (q.v.). See ĀDI PURĀNA.

Brāhma or **Brāhmo Samāj.** The 'society' (*samāja*) of one God, a reform movement of Hinduism founded in Calcutta in 1828 by Ram Mohan Ray (q.v.). The Samāj proclaimed a true Hinduism, against traditional teachers and missionaries of other religions. Idol worship and the caste system were denounced, the burning of widows (*sati*) opposed, and education and a rational theism encouraged. The founder went to England where he died, and in 1842 the Samāj was revived by Debendranath Tagore (q.v.), father of the poet Tagore, but in 1865 there was a split between his followers and those of a leader more influenced by Christianity, Keshab Chandra Sen (q.v.). Further schisms weakened the movement and today the membership of the Brāhmo Samāj is very small, but its influence has always been far greater than its numbers. It has been responsible for intellectual progress and has been active in social reforms. Those who held to the first Samāj called it the Ādi ('original') Brāhma Samāj. The secession was called the Brāhma Samāj of India, and a later branch was the Sādhāran ('general') Brāhma Samāj (q.v.). See MOZOOMDAR.

Brahma Sūtra. See VEDĀNTA SŪTRA.

Brahma Vihāra. See VIHĀRA.

Brahmin. See BRĀHMANA.

Bran. An early Welsh deity, later included among the saints as Bran the Blessed. He was son of Llyr (q.v.). In the Mabinogion Bran was a giant whose sister Branwen was sought in marriage by the king of Ireland. Branwen was reduced to a menial state, and Bran waded across to Ireland, was wounded by a poisoned spear and, as he lay dying, told his followers to cut off his head and take it to London for burial. This was eventually done and it was buried at the White Hill looking towards France.

Branwen. See BRAN and MABINOGION.

Bres. King and god of the Fomorians of ancient Ireland. He was captured in battle with the Tuatha Dé Danann (q.v.) and offered to give them cows always yielding milk and a harvest every quarter. For teaching them how to sow and reap he was freed, and these stories suggest that he was a god of fertility.

Brethren, Muslim. Al-Ikhwān al-Muslimūn, a movement founded in Egypt in 1928 by Shaykh Hasan al-Bannā', as a reforming but conservative organization opposed to secular and Western influences in the Muslim world. The Brethren founded clinics and industrial schools, and also military groups in Palestine. Extremists within the movement caused it to be banned in 1948, Shaykh al-Bannā' to be assassinated in 1949, and an attempt to be made on the life of President Nasser (Jamāl Abd al-Nāsir) in 1954. Some Brethren were executed, and the movement suppressed, but it still has a following and a centre in Switzerland.

Bridge of Judgement. See CHINVAT and RASHNU.

Brigid, Bridget, Brig, Brigantia, Bride. Celtic goddess of rivers and waters and popular among pastoral people. She was particularly associated with knowledge, culture and poetry. But in later accounts there were other Brigids connected with smithery and leech-craft. In Gaul she was known as Brigindu and in Britain as Brigantia, the High One, goddess of the Brigantes and personification of tribal leadership. When the early Irish church allocated the functions and even the names of pagan deities to saints, she became known as St Brigid of Kildare, where her sacred fire was always tended by nine virgins, and there were other dedications throughout Ireland. As flocks and herds were important to Brigantia, so St Brigid was concerned with flocks and the produce of the earth.

Brihad-Āranyaka Upanishad. 'Great forest', the oldest of the classical *Upanishads* (q.v.), and forming the concluding part of the *Shatapatha Brāhmana*. This *Upanishad* forms a link between the ritualistic concerns of the *Brāhmanas* and the speculations of the *Upanishads*. It discusses questions of the origins of things, Brahman and Ātman, and life after death, amongst a great variety of matters not always or easily comprehensible to later minds, so that there have been many commentaries on this *Upanishad*.

Brihaspati, Brahmanaspati. 'Lord of speech', names of a Hindu deity which alternate in the *Veda* scriptures. He is a sacrificer and priest who intercedes with the gods for men, and so is a prototype of priests and called priest of the gods or even father of the gods. The name is also used for the planet Jupiter whose wife was carried off by the moon, causing a heavenly conflict. Teacher of the gods, Brihaspati later becomes an earthly sage.

Brindāban, Vrindāvana. A centre of the worship of Krishna on the river Jumna south of Delhi. According to tradition this was the site of the play (*līlā*) of Krishna with the Gopīs (q.v.) or cowgirls, but most of it remained woodland till the end of the sixteenth century, when the modern temples were built under the influence of mystics such as Chaitanya (q.v.). There are more than a thousand temples, and some thirty Ghats, to which endless streams of pilgrims go. Here there have been many religious teachers, Goswāmīs, (literally, 'cow-lords') as the original descendants of Chaitanya were called, and the life of the saint was written there and then sent to Bengal.

Britomartis. Cretan goddess whose name meant 'sweet maid'. She was identified with Artemis (q.v.) or associated with her. She was pursued by Minos, king of Crete, and to escape him jumped into the sea and thence took refuge in a grove of Artemis.

Brontes. The 'Thunderer', one of the gigantic Cyclopes (q.v.) in Greek mythology. Like his brothers he had only one eye, was son of earth and heaven, and was a fine craftsman.

Brynhild, Brunhild. A Valkyrie (q.v.) in Scandinavian and German mythology. In the *Edda* (q.v.) she slept in armour in the mountain Hindarfjall which was surrounded by glowing shields. She was called Sigrdrifa, 'victory-giver', but the god Odin had put her to sleep with a thorn because she had given victory to the wrong man. She was awakened by Sigurd (q.v.) and was betrothed to him (like the fairy tale of the Sleeping Beauty). Sigrdrifa spoke of herself as a swan-maid, and the name Swanhild given to her combines the notion of swan-maid and warrior or Valkyrie. Sigrdrifa was Brynhild and her betrothal and also rejection by Sigurd was sung in poetry. When Sigurd died, Brynhild killed herself and was burnt on a neighbouring pyre, in a hearse covered with a rich cloth, and she rode the hearse down the Hel-way after her lover.

Bubastis. See BAST.

Buber, Martin. Jewish philosopher and mystic (1878–1965). Born in Vienna he was early attracted to Hasidic mysticism (q.v.) of which he became a foremost exponent. He joined Theodore Herzl (q.v.) and became a Zionist, settling in Jerusalem in 1938 but seeking peace with the Arab population. His most famous work on the relationships of man and God was *Ich und Du*, published in 1923 and translated into English in 1937 as *I and Thou*.

Buchis. A black bull worshipped in later periods of ancient Egypt. Like other bulls (see APIS and MNEVIS) he was regarded as the representative of the chief gods of his city, in his case Rē' and Osiris at Hermonthis. Buchis was depicted with the symbols of these gods, solar disk and two feathers, between his horns.

Buddha. A title meaning 'enlightened' (Sanskrit) which can be used of other people but is particularly applied to Gautama (q.v.) the founder of Buddhism. Theravāda Buddhists believe in relatively few past Buddhas, and some to come, but hold that there is only one Buddha for the present long world eon, namely Gautama. Mahāyāna Buddhists believe in countless Buddhas and Bodhisattvas (q.v.). The

Lotus Sūtra speaks of nearly two million Buddha-fields (perhaps poetical descriptions of the starry heavens), each with its Lord Buddha living there and teaching the doctrine to all beings.

Buddha-Charita. A life of the Buddha in verse by the second century writer Ashvaghosha (q.v.).

Buddha-Fields. See BUDDHA.

Buddha-Gayā. See BO-TREE and GAYĀ.

Buddhaghosa. A great Buddhist writer of the fifth century A.D. According to an appendix in the *Chronicle of Ceylon* he was born in a Brahmin family near Gayā in India and converted by a Buddhist monk. He went to Ceylon to get access to the most ancient commentaries on the Buddhist canonical scriptures. There he wrote *Visuddhi Magga*, 'the Path of Purity', and composed a great body of commentaries. He was an industrious rather than an independent thinker, but his extensive works are held in high honour. It is said that when Buddhaghosa's work was finished he returned to India. Burmese traditions claim him as a native of their land and it may be that he strengthened Theravāda Buddhism in that country, since it became much stronger in Burma than in India.

Buddha Rūpa. See RŪPA and MUDRĀ.

Buddha-Vamsa. *The History of the Buddhas*, one of the latest books of the canonical Pali scriptures of Theravāda Buddhism. In response to a question of his disciple Sāriputta, the Buddha relates in verse how he first took the resolve to become a Buddha long ago in the presence of the first Buddha Dīpankara. He gives an account of the life of Dīpankara and twenty-four Buddhas who followed, down to and including Gotama Buddha himself.

Buddhi. 'Mind', soul, the intellectual principle (Sanskrit), in Hindu Sāmkhya philosophy and followed in the *Bhagavad-Gītā* and elsewhere. Buddhi, also called Mahat, the 'great', is the first production from Nature, Prakriti (q.v.), and is the 'great' source in turn of Ego or self-consciousness (Ahamkāra) and Manas, reason. For Buddhi-Yoga, see YOGA.

Buddhism. One of the world's great missionary religions, it arose in India in the fifth or fourth century B.C. at the teaching of Gautama (q.v.) the Buddha. Buddhism flourished in India for over a thousand years, but eventually almost disappeared there due to renascent Hinduism and destruction of monasteries by Muslim invaders. Buddhism took Indian culture and religion to farthest Asia, and is found in two major forms. The Theravāda (q.v.), 'tradition of the elders', or Hīnayāna, 'little vehicle', is in south-east Asia: Ceylon, Burma, Thailand (Siam), Cambodia and Laos. The Mahāyāna (q.v.), 'great vehicle', is in Tibet, China, Korea, Japan and Vietnam. The Theravāda scriptures are in the Pali language, and comprise the *Tripitaka* (q.v.), Three Baskets, of Discipline, Doctrine, and Exposition. Mahāyāna scriptures include these and many more writings, in Sanskrit, Chinese and other languages. The numbers of Buddhists are difficult to calculate, and estimates range between two and four hundred millions.

Bugamani, Pukamuni. Mortuary rituals of northern Australia, during which carved and painted posts are erected as gifts to the deceased. The rites extend over several months, and the participants grow their beards and decorate themselves with feathers. The poles are erected on or round the grave, and represent the dead person or his close relatives in stylized form. See also Totem Poles.

Bukhārī. Arab traditionist born at Bokhara in Turkestan in 810. He began to study the Traditions, *Hadīth*, attributed to Muhammad at the age of eleven, and at sixteen made the pilgrimage to Mecca and studied under notable teachers of tradition. He travelled to Egypt and widely in Asia, returning home to Bokhara where he died in 870. Bukhārī sifted the enormous mass of material that he had gathered and only regarded a small part as authentic sayings of Muhammad. He was critical and scrupulous, but where necessary added notes distinct from the text. The present edition of the *Tradition* is largely the work of Bukhārī. There is a French translation. See Muslim ibn al-Hajjāj and Tirmidhī.

Bull-roarer. A thin long wooden blade to one end of which a cord is fastened. When whirled around in the air, the blade spins rapidly, producing a sound which varies in tone with the speed of the spin. A deep sound may resemble the roar of a bull, hence the name, or the snapping of a dog, and it may be interpreted as the voice of a supernatural being. Bull-roarers have been used in all continents, and have been particularly noted among the Aboriginals of Australia. But they were used in ancient Greece and America and are popular in modern Africa. Secret societies employ them for the voices of spiritual beings, and at initiation ceremonies they serve to warn women to keep at a safe distance. The use of bull-roarers is chiefly ceremonial and their sight and use may be forbidden to the uninitiated.

Bull-worship. See Apis, Cybele, Mithraism, Minos, Cretan Bull.

Bundahishn. A Zoroastrian book of the ninth century A.D., in Pahlavi where the title means 'original creation'. It begins with the two primeval spirits, Ohrmazd and Ahriman, and the creation of the world, but proceeds to deal with many other topics, from the resurrection of the dead to the nature of plants and animals.

Bunjiro Kawaté, Konkō Daijin. Japanese Shintoist (1814–83), founder of the Konkō-Kyō sect (q.v.).

Burāq. In Islamic tradition the fabulous winged mare, with a woman's head and a peacock's tail, on which Muhammad flew to Jerusalem and thence to heaven on his night journey (see Mirāj). The name Burāq is derived from 'lightning'.

Burning Ghāts. See Benares and Ghāts.

Burqa'. Arabic term for a veil or covering worn by women walking outside

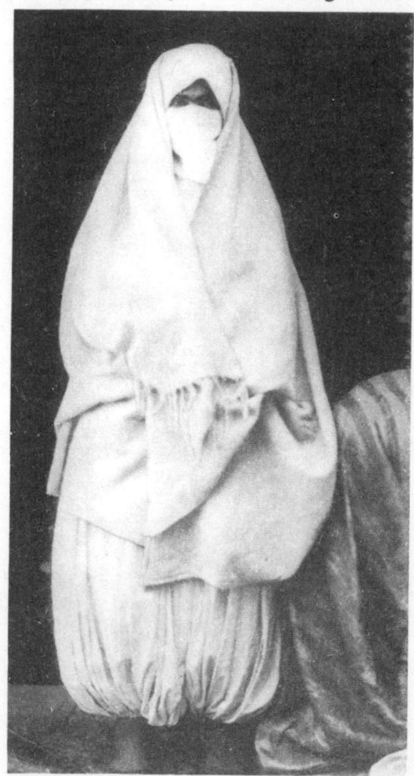

their homes. It covers the body completely, from the crown of the head to the feet, with a slit or net for the eyes. In its complete form it is found in Arabia and neighbouring lands, but much less away from there than at former times. The veiling of Muslim women seems not to have been practised much in the early days, but was in full force by the time of the caliph Hārūn al-Rashīd in 786. But some Muslim women, including some Africans, have never veiled, and modern times have brought a decline in the practice. In 1836 E. W. Lane, in his *Modern Egyptians*, remarked that many women of the lower orders never concealed their faces, and today perhaps ninety per cent of Egyptian townswomen are unveiled. The veil has been officially abolished in some lands, such as Turkey and Persia, though it survives in villages. See HAREM and PURDAH.

Bushidō. Japanese Bu-shi-dō means literally 'military-knight-ways', or the way of the warriors, used to describe training and ethics of the Samurai warriors of Japan. Bushidō was the scheme of training for the ruling Samurai class, the code of principles or chivalry. It was largely an unwritten code, consisting of maxims passed down from mouth to mouth, but applying to every act, in speech, salutation, fencing, swordsmanship and even suicide (called Seppuku rather than the western name Harakiri). Bushidō training was quiet but stern, deriving inspiration from Zen (q.v.) Buddhism with its emphasis on nature and quiet activity. Confucian influences from China taught respect for the emperor and authority, and native Japanese Shinto provided veneration of the ancestors and traditional sanctuaries.

Busshin. (Japanese) 'Buddha nature', the ultimate Buddha reality. Saicho, who took T'ien-T'ai (q.v.) Buddhism from China to Japan, held the unity of all existence, all Dharmas are the same, and everything partakes of the Buddha nature. Realization of and conformity to this nature brings liberation.

Buto. Originally called Wazit, this was an ancient snake goddess of the Egyptian Delta and regarded as guardian of lower Egypt. She was represented by the Uraeus or cobra, which appears in early inscriptions. Greek writers transformed Wazit into Uto and then Buto, for the city and the goddess. Wazit was closely linked with the gods Horus and Osiris.

Butsu. Japanese term for Buddha (q.v.), and see also NEMBUTSU, AMITĀBHA.

Butsu-Dan. 'Buddha-shelf' or altar, a Japanese household Buddhist altar, corresponding to the Shinto Kami-dana, 'god-shelf'. The Butsudan contains images, vessels of worship, and memorial tablets to the ancestors. The central figure may be an image or painting on silk of Amida Buddha, and the Japanese saint Prince Shotoku in front. There are flowers, lanterns and incense, and often food and drink are offered as well. In daily prayers hands are clapped to attract the spirits and Buddhist texts and hymns are chanted.

C

Caaba. See KA'BA.

Cabala. See KABBALAH.

Cadi. See QĀDĪ.

Cadmus. Son of Agenor, king of Tyre, in Greek mythology, and brother of Europa (q.v.). When the latter had been taken away by Zeus, Cadmus and his brothers Cilix and Phoenix went off to find her. He went to Delphi and was told to follow a cow which led him to Thebes, where he built the citadel called the Cadmea. Cadmus was advised by Athena to sow dragon's teeth and warriors came up out of the ground whom he tricked into killing each other till only five were left, and these became the ancestors of noble Thebans. Cadmus was said to have introduced writing to Greece. He married Harmonia (q.v.).

Cairo. Al-Qāhirah, 'the triumphant' (Arabic), so called after the planet Mars, and corrupted by Venetians into Cairo. The new capital of Egypt, replacing al-Fustāt, was built by a Fātimid (q.v.) caliph in A.D. 973, and beautified with many fine mosques over the centuries (see AZHAR). It is today the most populous city of Africa, and the Pyramids (q.v.) are nearby. See also BEKTĀSHIS.

Caitanya. See CHAITANYA.

Cakra. See CHAKRAVARTIN.

Calcutta. English version of Kālīghāt, 'steps of Kālī', the goddess whose original temple was built here in the sixteenth century, the present chief temple dating from 1809. A collection of villages became trading centres and eventually the vast agglomeration which for some time was the Indian capital and now is the second largest city of the British Commonwealth, and not the most beautiful. There are many other temples, of different religions, but the chief festival is still that of Kālī, the Durgā-pūjā, in October. See Kālī and Durgā.

Calendar. Most ancient cultures had a calendar, lunar or solar, with months numbered or named after festivals. One of the oldest recorded was Egyptian, once thought to be dated to the fifth millennium B.C., but now generally dated from 2781 B.C. The Athenian calendar began at the summer solstice, the longest day, and the Roman was of ten months, from March to December. Janus (q.v.), the god of gates, eventually gained the first month.

AZTEC CALENDAR

The Indian Yugas (q.v.) were mythical time spans, and one or more of the Avatars (q.v.) were connected with them. The Mayas and Aztecs of America had divinatory calendars derived from the count of days by priests, consisting of thirteen months of twenty days each, the days corresponding to gods and their relationships with men. The day signs showed good, bad or indeterminate associations with men. Major religious festivals were held on the last day of these Aztec and Maya months. See Marduk

Caliph, Khalīfa. (Arabic) 'successor' or 'vicegerent', the ancient title of the heads of the Muslim community as successors of the Prophet Muhammad. The word is used in the *Qur'ān* for successors of blessings enjoyed by their forefathers. It is said, though disputed, that the title was used by the first Khalīfa, Abū Bakr (q.v.), but it was more certainly from the time of his successor 'Umar (Omar). The Sunni Muslims, the great majority, accept the first four 'rightly guided' Khalīfas: Abū Bakr, 'Umar, 'Uthmān, 'Alī. But Shī'a Muslims hold 'Alī (q.v.) as the first. After these the Sunni count dynasties of Umayyad, 'Abbāsid (q.v.) and many other Khalīfas. Under the Ottoman Turks the caliphate moved to Istanbul, and with the republican regime of Mustafā Kemāl the last Khalīfa, 'Abd al-Majīd II, was deposed in 1924 and the caliphate ended.

Calliope. One of the nine Muses (q.v.), that of epic poetry, in Greek mythology.

Cao-Dai Religious and political movement of southern Vietnam, mingling Taoism and Buddhism, developed by Le Van Trung about 1920. It believes in a Supreme Being. (Cao-Dai), symbolized by an eye surrounded with clouds, and in other divine beings such as Lao Tzŭ, the Buddha, Confucius and Christ. There are many temples, the largest at Tay-Ninh having been consecrated in 1937. A new sect, the Hoa-Hao, emerged in 1939 which had more Buddhist beliefs but played a similar role to Cao-daism in opposing the government. The two movements claim over a million adherents.

Capac Cocha or **Hucha.** The most sacred religious ceremony of the Incas, but the meaning of the name is not known. During the rite a sister of the Inca king would be sent to one of the cities that he had conquered. Alternatively, a provincial ruler would send his own daughter as a Virgin of the Sun (q.v.), to the capital and in due course she was returned to be sacrificed in the Capac Cocha.

Capitoline Triad. The gods Jupiter, Juno and Minerva (qq.v.) who were worshipped on the Capitol hill in Rome. A temple to them was dedicated by the Tarquins in 509 B.C., the platform of which still exists, but the building itself was destroyed and rebuilt a number of times. Other temples stood nearby, and

the Tarpeian Rock from which murderers and traitors were thrown.

Carmathians. See QARMATĪ.

Carmen. Latin term for lyric poetry and song, and extended to cover oracles, incantations, prophecies and epitaphs. The *Carmen Arvale* is a fragment of a litany used by Fratres Arvales (see ARVAL) who performed spring ceremonies of dance, prayer and sacrifice. The *Carmen Saliare* were hymns of the Salii (q.v.) priests.

Carpet. See KISWA.

Carthage. Phoenician (q.v.) settlement in North Africa. They took their gods, which became known under different names, and later under Roman titles. The Phoenician El (q.v.) became Baal Hammon in Carthage, and his consort Elat or Asherah was Tanit. The latter was called Mother and had colleges of priests. In Roman times she was called Juno and Caelestis, while El became Kronos-Saturn. Punic (Carthaginian) texts also mention Melkart and Baal Saphon or Hadad.

Carvakas. See CHĀRVĀKAS.

Caryatid. See ACROPOLIS.

Cassandra. Daughter of Priam of Troy in Greek mythology and later, by the fifth century B.C., regarded as a prophetess. She figures in Greek tragedy as foretelling evil events and warning of their consequences but she was not heeded. See also APOLLO.

Cassiopeia. In Greek mythology wife of Cepheus, king of the Ethiopians and mother of Andromeda (q.v.). Cassiopeia boasted that her daughter was more beautiful than the sea nymphs, Nereids, and the sea god Poseidon sent a monster to ravage the land, who was eventually killed by Perseus. Like other actors in this story Cassiopeia became a constellation.

Caste. In Indian society two terms have caused confusion: 'class' or 'colour' (*varna*), and 'caste' or 'birth' (*jāti*). The four classes are the Brahmin priests (q.v.), the Kshatriya ruler-warriors, Vaishya merchants and farmers, and Shūdra servants. The three top classes were 'twice-born' by initiation ceremonies in adolescence. The classes corresponded to divisions of society which were accentuated when the Aryan invasion (q.v.) gave victory to the light-coloured northerners over the darker indigenous inhabitants of India. When the Portuguese arrived in India in the sixteenth century, they applied their word *casta* to any tribal or family group. The castes proper, amounting to some three thousand, go far beyond the four classes; they rise and fall, or disappear, while the four classes remain. Castes are groups of crafts and occupations, entailing marriage and eating restrictions on their members. Outcastes were beyond the whole system, and subject to many prohibitions. Mahātma Gāndhi tried to elevate them, by leading them into forbidden temples and calling them God's 'People', Hari-jans. See OUTCASTES.

Caste Marks. Name loosely given to decorative marks of various kinds on the face or body of Indian men and women. The 'mole' (*tilaka*) or 'spot' (*tīkā*) is of red, white or yellow paste. Placed on the middle of the forehead it is a simple sign of marriage, and even Christian women use it. A married woman may also have a red mark in the parting of her hair, and ornaments in the parting and the nose. In north India some women have green tattoos in the middle of the forehead and on the wrists, or a star on the chin. Sectarian religious marks called 'lotus' or 'line of ashes' (*pundra*) are worn by male ascetics, three vertical lines like an enlarged V for the devotees of Vishnu, and three horizontal lines for Shiva. These are worn on the forehead, but similar marks may be streaked on the arms and body.

Castor. See DIOSCUROI.

Cat Goddess. See BAST.

Cat-rule. See PRAPATTI.

Celibacy. The unmarried state is not common in many societies and in some is almost unknown. Even priests are normally married since this completes manhood and perpetuates the family. Only in monasteries and nunneries is celibacy necessary for the members of all-male or all-female communities. In Islam there are no priests, but members of Sūfī mystical communities may live in temporary or permanent celibacy. For a Brahmin priest in India the life of a householder is the normal second stage of life, only renounced when the priest has seen his children's children. Where there are Buddhist priests, as in Japan, they are normally married, and celibacy is reserved for the Buddhist monastic order, the Sangha.

Celtic Religion. The ancient Celts occupied much of central Europe, and from the fifth century B.C. advanced into Greece, Italy and western Europe including Britain. Their earliest worship was that of the forces of sky, sea, rivers, mountains and trees, and some of these in time became more personal deities. The priests of Celtic religion were the Druids (q.v.).

Centaurs. Beast-like monsters of Greek mythology, usually with human head and shoulders and horse-like in lower body and legs. They fought against the Lapiths (q.v.), and Heracles clashed with them. There are myths of individual

Centaurs, of Nessus (q.v.) who had a garment that killed Heracles, and of Chiron (q.v.) the medicine-man who taught Achilles, Asclepius and Jason.

Centzon Totochtin. 'Four hundred rabbits', in Aztec mythology, they were gods connected with the moon where the shape of a rabbit was thought to be seen. They were depicted with black and white faces and with crescent-shaped nose ornaments. They were particularly associated with Pulque beer (q.v.).

Cerberus. The dog of Hades, who guarded the entrance to the underworld in Greek mythology. Hesiod says that he

has fifty heads, and in later art Cerberus appears with three heads and a snake's tail. Somewhat similarly in the Indian Vedas a four-eyed dog (with spots above its eyes) guards the road of death (see YAMA). See also HERACLES and TARTARUS.

Ceres. An ancient Italian corn-goddess, the name being related to the English word 'cereal'. She was commonly identified with the Greek Demeter (q.v.). She was naturally associated with the goddess of the earth, Tellus, and the festivals of both deities occurred in the spring sowing in April. But Greek influence became powerful in popular worship, in a women's festival in August, and in tales of her occasional visits to the underworld which would more properly have belonged to Tellus. See AEDILES.

Cernunnos. Celtic horned deity, so called by Roman writers, from Latin *cornu* and *cernu*, for a 'horn'. Cernunnos represented a developed animal deity, sometimes with three horns to show its strength, or with three heads. He was a popular national god, with a horned serpent as his companion. His worship

seems to have been taken from Gaul to Britain, he appears on stone in Gaul and a head of his type was found at Cirencester. Cernunnos is sometimes identified with Dispater (q.v.), the god of the underworld, and this would fit his character as a fertility deity and the association with a snake. See MOHENJODARO horned figures.

Cerridwen. An ancient Welsh deity and enchantress, who with her husband Tegid Voel lived in Lake Tegid. They had three children; Avagddu the ugly, and Creirwy and Morvan the beautiful. Cerridwen was an enchantress and had a cauldron of poetic inspiration with which she planned to help the ugly Avagddu. But three drops from the cauldron were taken by Gwion (q.v.) who was guarding it and he became inspired. Cerridwen pursued him, both changing their shapes till as a hen she swallowed Gwion as a grain of wheat. Gwion was then born of her as the poet Taliesin, and the story is told in the *Hanes Taliesin.* Cerridwen's cauldron may be a symbol of fertility, and so she would be a goddess of fertility and of poetic inspiration.

Ceryneian Hind. The third Labour of Heracles was to capture this beast which grazed on the Ceryneian Hill. It had golden horns and hooves of brass and was sacred to the goddess Artemis. Heracles pinned its legs with an arrow, without harming the hind, and took it on his shoulders to Mycenae. In another version he sacrificed the hind to Artemis.

Cetiya, Chaitya. See STŪPA.

Chac. The rain and vegetation god of the Maya (q.v.) of Central America. Sometimes called the 'long-nosed god' he has some non-human features: nose like a trunk, and lower jaw with tusks or fangs like the serpents of other Maya art. He had an alternative form or aspect in a deity with a shredded or turned-up nose, who was a wind or water god. Chac was very popular, the most-worshipped god in the late Maya period, surviving even the

Spanish conquest. He rode on a serpent, which was a symbol of rain, and also carried a water bottle in the form of a snake, and torches which symbolized lightning. He had a pyramid temple at Izamal (q.v.) in northern Yucatan.

Chaitanya. An Indian mystic (1486–1534). Born of devout Brahmin parents in Bengal, Chaitanya at twenty-two turned from study to religious devotion after visiting the famous shrine of Vishnu's foot at Gayā. He fell into trances and danced and sang about the love of Krishna and Rādhā (q.v.). He engaged in kīrtans, song-dances, telling men to call upon Krishna and lead holy lives. His followers regarded him as an Avatar (q.v.) of Vishnu, though critics have said that his devotions were pathological in their intensity. Chaitanya visited the sacred sites associated with the life of Krishna, and gave stimulus to building of great temples there, especially at Brindāban (q.v.). He spent his last years at the great Krishna centre at Puri on the east coast of India, and may have died by drowning during ecstasy. His followers, celibate and married, have communal centres and sing and dance in honour of Krishna and Chaitanya. Their poetry contributed to the development of Bengali literature.

Chakravartin. (Sanskrit) 'wheel-rolling', a ruler whose chariot wheels roll everywhere without obstruction, a universal emperor. The Mauryan kings of India, in the fourth and third centuries B.C., gave the ideal of universal emperors which entered into Buddhist tradition. When Gautama the Buddha was born, sages said that he would be either a universal emperor or a universal teacher; both these high figures bore on their bodies the thirty-two marks of a superman. Later it was said that whenever a Buddha appears to lead all beings to enlightenment, there also appears a universal emperor to rule all things righteously. The Jains said that every world eon has twenty-four Jinas (q.v.) and twelve universal emperors. The idea was taken over by Hinduism and some medieval monarchs claimed that they themselves were Chakravartins.

Chalchihuitlicue. 'Precious Jade Skirt', in Mexican mythology, wife of the

rain god Tlaloc (q.v.); she was goddess of spirits and streams.

Ch'an. See ZEN.

Chandi Dās. A Bengali religious poet of the fifteenth century A.D. His exact dates and the facts of his life are obscure, but he was perhaps born in Nannur or Chhatna in west Bengal, was a priest of a village temple, and lived with a washer-maid called Rāmī. The fame of the poet priest became so great that a number of other poets composed songs under his name, and of the thousands ascribed to him perhaps about two hundred are authentic. Chandi Dās, like other mystical poets of the time, sang of the loves of the god Krishna and his human lover Rādhā, and the divine love-making symbolizes the relationships of God and the soul. These poems are still chanted all over Bengal and people gather at night in the open air or temple courtyards to hear professional singers chant of the loves of Krishna and Rādhā (q.v.).

Chāndogya. One of the earliest of the Indian classical *Upanishads* (q.v.), named after a class of priests who chanted the sacred texts. It forms part of the *Sāma Veda*. Many important doctrines appear in it: the transmigration of souls, the union of Brahman and Ātman, and the famous phrase 'thou art that' (*tat tvam asi*, q.v.).

Chang Chüeh. Chinese Taoist leader, of the second century A.D., who founded a movement called 'the Way of Grand Peace', T'ai P'ing Tao, inspired by a book of similar name which is now lost. Chang Chüeh organized his followers well, sent out missionaries, and held great public ceremonies of magic and healing by faith. When the government decided to suppress the movement, these Taoists put on Yellow Turbans, after which they were named. Chang Chüeh was executed, but the rebellion lasted many years.

Chango. See SHANGO.

Cha-no-Yu. See TEA CEREMONY.

Chanukah. See HANUKKAH.

Chanul, Nahualli. Maya and Aztec respectively for the notion of 'counterparts in disguise', whereby every person was supposed to have a counterpart, or several, disguised as an animal whose fate was linked with that of the human being. The idea was particularly developed by the Maya, and each animal counterpart shared a soul with the person with whom it was connected.

Chaos. The 'gaping void' in ancient Greek thought. Hesiod says that Chaos was the first to come into being, but his words suggest that it was not everlasting, and he does not describe it. Chaos is said to have given birth to Gaea, the Earth, who in turn begat Heaven, Ouranos (q.v.). Later Chaos is regarded as a mixture of the seeds or potencies of matter of all kinds.

ASSYRIAN CHAOS

Charm. See AMULET.

Charon. The ferryman in Greek mythology who for a coin rowed dead shades over the Styx, river of death. He is a Psychopomp, guide of souls. So a coin was put in the mouth of a corpse as fee for his journey.

Charoset. A mixture of fruits, chopped fine, with a little wine, placed on a dish and used in the Jewish Seder (q.v.) ceremony. It is said to have been a condiment formerly, but is taken as a representation of the mortar with which the Israelites had to work during their captivity in Egypt.

Chārvākas. One of the three heterodox systems of Indian thought, the others being Jainism and Buddhism. Named after a legendary founder Chārvāka, the system was materialistic or atheistic and was also called Lokāyata, meaning that only this world (*loka*) exists and there is nothing beyond it. It is mentioned in the Hindu epics and Buddhist dialogues, but the original Chārvāka texts are lost and the doctrines have to be reconstructed from criticisms of opponents. Apparently it was held that the soul has no existence apart from the body, consciousness is only a transitory modification of material elements, and there is no future life. What is not perceived does not exist, and matter is the only reality. See ATHEISM.

Charybdis. A whirlpool in a narrow channel, in Greek myth, opposite the cave-monster Scylla (q.v.). These have been identified with the Straits of Messina, where there is no whirlpool. The hero Odysseus escaped from Charybdis by grasping a tree which grew above it.

Chassidism. See HASIDISM.

Chela. See BRAHMA-CHĀRI.

Chelebi, Raphael. Jewish banker of Egypt who supported the pseudo-Messiah Shabbethai Zvi (q.v.), and encouraged him to declare himself openly at Salonica in 1665.

Chenresi, Chenresik. Form of the Tibetan *sPyan-ras gzigs*, the name of Avalokiteshvara (q.v.), the great Bodhisattva (q.v.) who is patron of Tibet and incarnated in the Dalai Lama. Chenresi is the great being of mercy and has a female counterpart in the great saviour Tāra. Although the Dalai Lama, head of the orthodox Yellow Hat monks, is regarded as the reincarnation of Chenresi, both this being and Tāra are important also for the monks of the old Red Hat communities. The Red Hats, or Old Sect, regard their founder of the eighth century, Padma Sambhava (q.v.), as an incarnation of Chenresi and both as the essence of the supreme Buddha. Images are everywhere in which Chenresi sits crowned and cross-legged, with one hand upraised in teaching and the other outstretched in compassion. See DALAI LAMA.

Chên Yen, Mi Tsung. Chên Yen, 'True word', is a Chinese form of Tantric (q.v.) Buddhism, introduced from India in the eighth century A.D. It paid special devotion to Vairochana (q.v.) Buddha, and taught that man has the Buddha-nature within him. Much use was made of magical symbols: mantras, mudrās and mandalas (qq.v.). Chên Yen merged with other schools in China, but flourished in Japan as Shingon (q.v.). In China Chên Yen was sometimes called Mi-chiao, 'secret teaching', because of its esoteric nature.

Cheops. Greek form of the name of Egyptian Pharaoh Khufu, who in the third millennium B.C. had built the Great Pyramid on a plateau on the edge of the desert, 8 kilometres west of Giza. One of the wonders of the world, it was built at vast expense and great human suffering. See PYRAMIDS.

Chephren. Egyptian Pharaoh of the Fourth Dynasty, next but one after Cheops (q.v.), who had a smaller pyramid built on the same plateau as the Great Pyramid, and whose face is probably represented in the Sphinx. See PYRAMIDS.

Chiang Ch'ao-Tsung. Founder in 1922 of Chinese syncretistic religious 'society for Common Good'. See TUNG SHAN SHÊ.

Chicomecoatl. A maize goddess of the Aztecs of Mexico. She was very popular and there are numerous images in which the goddess wears a huge four-sided headdress. She carries a twin maize cob and its name, 'for giving strength',

reveals that it was employed when magical ceremonies were performed to make the fields fertile.

Chie. Japanese form of Prajñā (q.v.).

Chih-i, Chih-K'ai. Chinese Buddhist monk (538–597) who at a monastery in the T'ien T'ai mountains of Chekiang province founded the harmonizing school of T'ien T'ai (q.v.).

Chih-Yen. Chinese Buddhist monk

(602–668), and second master of the Garland school. See HUA YEN.

Chilam Balam. A book in the Maya language of Yucatan, written after the Spanish conquest though based on older traditions. It contains much mythology, prophecy and details of ritual and a small amount of history. See POPOL VUH.

Chillul Hashem. Jewish term for any action which discredits the religion or dishonours the name of Jews, opposed to the Kiddush Hashem (q.v.) which is the sanctification of the name of God.

Chiluf. See TZIRUF.

Chimaera. (Greek) a she-goat (Latin *capra*), but in mythology a monster composed of three beasts: lion, serpent and goat. The Chimaera breathed fire and was killed by the hero Bellerophon riding the winged horse Pegasus (q.v.). The

scene is depicted on the Roman mosaic at Lullingstone in Kent, of the fourth century, but in the fourth-century mosaic of Hinton St Mary, now in the British Museum, the Chimaera is alongside a head of Christ.

Chinese Religions. See separate articles on CONFUCIANISM, TAOISM and MAHĀYĀNA BUDDHISM. These have sometimes been called the 'three religions of China', but they have not been so much separate organizations as originally independent schools of thought which have overlapped, and many Chinese have followed elements of all three. For distinction of temples, see MIAO.

Ch'ing T'an. (Chinese) 'school of Pure Conversations', a form of philosophical Taoism (q.v.) which developed from the third to fifth centuries A.D. Sages repudiated all worldly pleasure and met together to talk, drink and write poetry, until they reached 'the Unnameable' and were silent. These philosophers rejected ordinary morality and sought to follow nature, and they inspired some of the greatest Chinese poetry and painting.

Ching T'u. Chinese name for the Pure Land (q.v.) sect of Buddhism, the most popular and least philosophical.

Chinvat, Chinvant. Avestan, 'Bridge' of the Requiter or Separator (Peretu), to which all the departed must come in Zoroastrian belief. Here the deeds of the soul are weighed in a balance by Rashnu, the Requiter, helped by the gods Mithra (q.v.) and Sraosha. Good men are guided across the bridge by Zoroaster himself, but the wicked go to the House of the Lie (Druj, q.v.).

Chiron. One of the Centaurs (q.v.) in Greek mythology, half man and half horse. He was said to be of divine origin and was a wise and kindly medicine-man. He taught Jason, Achilles and Asclepius, and was worshipped in Thessaly.

Chishti. Name of several Indian Islamic mystics and of an order that follows them. They originated in Chisht in Persia. The founder of the brotherhood was Mu'in al-Din Chishti (1142–1236) who died at Ajmer in India. His tomb was visited annually by the great Mughal emperor Akbar (q.v.). It is covered with silver and hung with horseshoes as votive gifts from local horse-dealers. Tombs of other Chishtis are in the Punjab, near Delhi and Agra, and in the Deccan.

Chitra-Ratha. (Sanskrit) 'having a bright chariot', name of various gods and heroes in Hindu mythology, and particularly applied to the king of the heavenly Gandharvas (q.v.).

Chiu Ko. (Chinese) 'Nine Songs', a collection of ancient poems which throw light on the activities of Shamans (q.v.). See CH'U TZ'Ŭ.

Chloë. Greek word for 'the green', a title of the earth goddess Demeter (q.v.), as patroness of the new green crops. See DAPHNIS.

Choice-God. See DEVATĀ.

Chorten, Chöten. The Tibetan 'support for worship' (*mchod-rten*) is a monument such as is found in every Buddhist country, derived from the Indian stūpa, a relic-shrine, which came to be a symbol of universal Buddhahood. If there are no relics, images or texts may be enclosed in the monument. The Tibetan Chorten has five parts, identified with the five elements. The square base is the earth, then comes a dome identified with water, a spire as fire, a crescent as air, and a solar disk as space. Chortens are found all over Tibet and neighbouring Buddhist countries, by the roadside or in the midst of fields and it is a meritorious act to go round them clockwise, chanting texts. Entrance-chortens guard gateways,

CHORTENS

often painted with two eyes, and the dome may be replaced with a double tier.

Chou Li. See LI.

Christmas. See SOL and YULE.

Chrysippus. Greek philosopher (280–207 B.C.) who succeeded Cleanthes (q.v.) as head of the Stoics. He wrote many books which were regarded as central to orthodox Stoicism, and defended its beliefs against the Academy (q.v.).

Chuang Tzŭ, Chuang Chou. Greatest of the Taoist philosophers of China, who lived in the fourth and early third centuries B.C., though his dates are uncertain. He is said to have written a great deal, but the classic principally connected with him, the *Book of Chuang Tzŭ*, has only thirty-three chapters and it is thought that more than half of them were written by his followers. The book has always been a great favourite, along with the *Tao Tê Ching* (q.v.). Chuang Tzŭ was a naturalist, believing in living according to the way of nature in disregard of the conventions taught by the Confucians. Yet final reality was different from the material world, and was indicated by the indescribable Tao, the eternal and absolute, the origin and end of all existence. In lyrical and mystical passages the *Chuang Tzŭ* taught an intense spiritual discipline, with meditation on the formless Tao. See also YANG and YIN.

Chu Hsi. Chinese philosopher (1130–1200) who was for long regarded as the orthodox interpreter of Neo-Confucianism. As late as 1894 the emperor, Kuang Hsü, forbade the sale of any books which attacked his teachings, though there were numerous scholars who held more idealistic beliefs than the rather pedantic expositions of Chu Hsi.

Ch'un Ch'iu. *The Spring and Autumn Annals*, one of the five Confucian Classics (q.v.), giving the history of the state of Lu, where Confucius lived. It is said to have been written by Confucius, but it is a dry chronicle of the events in Lu during the *Ch'un Ch'iu* period, from 722 to 479 B.C., with no indication that Confucius wrote it. Mencius (q.v.) said he did, and it has been supposed either that he was wrong, or that what Confucius wrote, if anything, was different from the *Ch'un Ch'iu* as it has survived.

Ch'un Ch'iu Fan Lu. See TUNG CHUNG-SHU.

Chung Yung. (Chinese) 'doctrine of the mean' or middle way, early Confucian writings attributed to Tzŭ Ssŭ, grandson of Confucius (q.v.). The *Chung Yung*, emphasized the Way of Heaven, which is eternal and brings harmony throughout the universe. At the same time it recognized the importance of sacrifice to gods and of divination. For human behaviour the sage must understand the Way of Heaven and co-operate in promoting the harmony of all things.

Chuppah. See HUPPAH.

Churinga. See TJURUNGA.

Ch'u Tz'ŭ. (Chinese) 'poems of Ch'u',

a collection of elegies of the fourth and third centuries B.C., of the kingdom of Ch'u in south and eastern China. They are valuable in revealing the religious beliefs of the time, particularly animism and ancestral cults. Some of the poems, the *Nine Songs* (*Chiu Ko*), shed light on Chinese forms of Shamanism (q.v.), in which male and female Shamans were possessed by the gods.

Cinteotl. Maize god of the Aztecs, as the deified maize plant, protected by gods of water. Generally male, he also had feminine forms. The festival of Cinteotl was in April, when reeds were put at doors of houses and blood was put on them as an offering to the maize.

Cinvat. See CHINVAT.

Cipactli. See COATLICUE.

Circe. Goddess and magician of Greek mythology. By her spells she changed men into animals, and the sailors of Odysseus into swine. Odysseus was helped by the god Hermes (q.v.) to overcome Circe's magic, and he lived with her for a year before continuing his journey home.

Circumcision. Removal of the male foreskin, an ancient infant or adolescent operation, often with religious significance, especially to Jews and Muslims, but practised in many parts of the world. It is virtually unknown among European and non-Semitic Asian peoples, but found in many parts of Africa, the Middle East, the Pacific islands, and some Australian and American tribes. Some Reformed Jews attempted unsuccessfully to abolish circumcision in the last century. Circumcision is not mentioned in the *Qur'ān*, but Muslims regard it as obligatory following the *Traditions* of the Prophet. It is practised by Christians in Ethiopia. Female circumcision, or excision, is performed in Egypt and Arabia, among many African tribes, in Malaysia, and among some Australian and American tribes. The purpose of the rite may have been to ensure purity and virility, and as an adolescent ceremony it marks the passage from childhood to manhood or womanhood.

Cit Chac Coh. 'Image of the red puma', a war god of the Mayas of central America. At his festival the chief general was honoured like the god himself and carried to his temple, where soldiers danced and sacrificed a dog to the image of the deity.

Clairvoyance. The ability to see objects mentally while at a distance from them, or to discover hidden objects, is attributed to some people, often in a trance state. The practice is worldwide, but has been particularly associated in Europe and America with Spiritualist societies from their beginnings in 1848. *Clairaudience* is distinguished as the faculty of hearing things mentally which are beyond the range of normal hearing.

Classics. See CONFUCIANISM.

Cleanthes. Greek philosopher (331–232) who succeeded Zeno (q.v.) as head of the Stoics. He was deeply religious, considered God was the soul of the universe, and wrote a famous hymn to Zeus.

Clio. In Greek mythology one of the nine Muses (q.v.), that of history, and identified in Egypt with Seshat, the goddess of writing.

Clotho. In Greek mythology the one of the Moirai or three Fates (q.v.) spinning the thread of life. See KLOTHES.

Clytemnestra. See AGAMEMNON and ELECTRA.

Coatlicue. 'Serpent skirt', Aztec earth goddess, both womb and grave, being the

earth in its destructive aspect who swallowed up all living beings as a monster called Cipactli. Stone statues of Coatlicue in her temple, the House of Darkness, show her with claws and a skirt of snakes. She was mother of the sun god, Huitzilopochtli (q.v.). See also COYOLXAUHQUI.

Cochba, Kozeba, Bar. 'Son of the star', Jewish revolutionary who led the final revolt against the Romans from 132–135 and was hailed as Messiah by Rabbi Akiba (q.v.). It was put down with great harshness, the final struggle taking place at Masada. Jews were banned from Jerusalem, which was renamed Aelia Capitolina, and a shrine to Zeus was erected on the site of the Temple, which remained till Christian times.

Cohen. See KOHEN.

Collegium, Conlegium. Latin for any official body, 'company' or 'college'. In religious usage *Collegium* indicated the great priesthoods of Pontifices and Augurs (q.v.), and the Decemviri who kept the Sibylline books. There were minor colleges, such as the Compitalicia who directed the worship of the Lares at the cross-roads (Compita), the Capitolinorum who were concerned with the Capitoline games, and the Mercatorum who were associated with the worship of Mercury. For lesser Roman priesthoods, see SODALES.

Compitalia, Compitalicia. See COLLEGIUM and LARES.

Confucianism. Sometimes considered as the traditional religion of China's (see K'ANG YU-WEI) three religions, or not a religion at all, it has of course been closely associated with Confucius (q.v.). However, to the moral and social teachings of Confucius were added ceremonies for the ancestors, and with state rituals this complex formed Confucianism. The Chinese called it Ju Chiao, the Teaching of the Learned. Five Classics were established as Confucian: the *Book of Poetry*, the *Book of History*, the *Book of Changes*, the *Spring and Autumn Annals*, and the *Book of Rites*. These were the basis of civil service examinations till the end of the empire in 1911. Confucianism was humanistic, though Confucius was adored and the supremacy of Heaven was recognized. Today the Confucian scholars are discredited and the Classics neglected, but the great Communist state ceremonies continue some of the ancient show, and ancestral rites are still performed (see ANCESTORS). For the Five Classics, see separate articles on: CH'UN CH'IU, I CHING, LI CHI, SHIH CHING, SHU CHING. For a sixth Classic, see YO CHING.

Confucius. Latinized form of K'ung Fu'tzŭ, Grand Master K'ung, the greatest sage of China, 551–479 B.C. Born in a poor family in the state of Lu (in Shangtung), Confucius was largely self-educated and gathered round him a group of pupils to whom he taught moral and social precepts; there are said to have been 3,000 pupils. He held minor public office, and travelled widely to find more, without success. Then he is said to have written the Five Classics (see CONFUCIANISM), though perhaps he edited the *Spring and Autumn Annals*. The teachings of Confucius are in a little book called *Lun Yü*, The *Analects* (q.v.) or aphorisms, in twenty chapters of which critical opinion holds chapters 3 to 9 to be most authentic. Here are taught filial piety, the conduct of a gentleman, the duties of rulers and ruled, and not doing to others what one does not wish for oneself. There are brief indications of the life of Confucius and his simple religious faith in Heaven (T'ien) and the ancestors. Later Confucius was adored, though not deified, and called Grand Perfection and Teacher of Ten Thousand Generations. In modern times he has been attacked as feudalistic, but even under the Communists his tomb has been restored. See JU, LI, JÊN. For biography, see SSŬ-MA CH'IEN. See Neo-Confucians.

CONFUCIUS

Consentes Di. (Latin) 'consenting gods', six pairs of gods, male and female, whose images stood in the Forum in Rome and may have been worshipped at the Lectisternium or meal for the gods. The twelve were: Jupiter and Juno, Neptune and Minerva, Mars and Venus, Apollo and Diana, Volcanus and Vesta, Mercury and Ceres. See OGDOAD and ENNEAD.

JUPITER

JUNO

NEPTUNE

MINERVA

MARS

VENUS

APOLLO

DIANA

VULCAN

VESTA

MERCURY

CERES

Consus. Roman god of grain and harvests, who had a temple on the Aventine hill. His festivals, Consualia, were 19 August and 15 December, perhaps at the end of harvesting and sowing. His dates connected him with the agricultural goddess Ops (q.v.).

Corban. (Arabic). Kurbān is a 'sacrifice', used generally in the *Qur'ān*, where prayer or the Friday service is said to be Kurbān. The term is used for the sacrifice of an animal which forms part of the ritual of pilgrimage (see HAJJ) and is celebrated throughout the Muslim world at the same time. Christian Arabs used the word Kurbān for the Eucharist. See BAIRAM.

Cordelia. In Celtic mythology Creiddylad, daughter of the god of the sea, Lear or Llyr (q.v.).

Cordovero, Moses. Jewish mystic (1522–76) and one of the leaders of the school of Safed (q.v.). His Hebrew work Pardes, 'Orchard', is based on the Zohar and is one of the clearest expositions of Kabbalistic doctrine (q.v.).

Core. See KORE.

Coreish. See QURAYSH.

Coricancha. See TEMPLE OF THE SUN.

Corroboree. Australian aboriginal folk dances, festive or warlike, but not sacred in character. Performers wore decorative patterns and used particular songs and dances, but these were copied from one area to another, and in modern times have included European and American dance and jazz forms.

Corybantes. Priests of Cybele (q.v.).

Counterpart, Animal. See CHANUL.

Cow. See KĀMADHENU.

Coyolxauhqui. 'Golden Bells', the Moon in Aztec mythology with the golden bells on her cheek. In a popular myth the stars tried to kill the earth, Coatlicue (q.v.), but Coyolxauhqui tried to warn her, and was decapitated by the newborn child

of Earth, the sun god, Huitzilopochtli (q.v.). The stars were also destroyed. This myth came from the disappearance of moon and stars before the sunrise.

Creirwy. In Celtic mythology the beautiful daughter of the gods Tegid Voel and Cerridwen (qq.v.), who dwelt in Lake Tegid with the ugly Avagddu (q.v.).

Cremation. Burning corpses is the regular practice in Hindu, Buddhist and some other communities, except for very holy saints whose bodies may be supposed to have become incorruptible in a state of Samādhi (q.v.), contemplation. The origins of cremation are obscure; it may have been practised by nomadic peoples who feared that enemies might violate the bodies of their ancestors. Bodies are burnt on mounds or ghāts (q.v.), and the

CORROBOREE GROUND

funeral ceremony is followed by a memorial or Shrāddha (q.v.). Cremation has been opposed by Islam, and until recently by most Christians, in the belief that at the resurrection the physical body will be re-assembled. For the Parsi exposure of the dead, see DAKHMĀ. See also MUMMY and SARCOPHAGUS.

Cretan Bull. See MINOS, THESEUS, HERACLES.

Cronus. See KRONOS.

Cúchulainn. 'Hound of Culann', Irish hero and demigod, who according to story gained his name by killing a savage dog owned by Culann, a smith. Cúchulainn was the hero of Ulster, said to have been son of the god Lug (q.v.), but also of a human father Sualtam. He was a miraculously strong boy and fought many champions in his battle frenzy. He visited Scotland and also a divine land of plenty. In an invasion of Ulster, Cúchulainn fought many heroes, was wounded, but healed by Lug. He died of breaking a taboo of eating dog's flesh and perished in an ensuing battle. For his name as Cuthullin, see FIONN. See also MORRIGAN and EMER.

Cumaean Sibyl. Famous oracle in a cave at Cumae, near Naples, which still exists. See SIBYL.

Cumal. Mythical Irish hero, identified with Camulos of Gaul and with Mars, the god of war. He was father of the hero Fionn (q.v.).

Cupid. The god of love in Roman mythology, son of Mercury and Venus, and identified with the Greek Eros (q.v.). He is represented as a wanton boy, sending his love-arousing arrows indiscriminately. The fable of Cupid and Psyche is the most famous in the *Metamorphoses* or *Golden Ass* of the Roman African writer Apuleius, and it may be derived from an earlier Greek work. Psyche (q.v.) as the soul was the seat of the passions and was liable to be tormented by Cupid.

Cybele. The great mother-goddess of ancient Asia Minor and worshipped with the god of vegetation, her young lover Attis (q.v.). Her chief sanctuary was at Pessinus in Phyrgia. Cybele was goddess of fertility, of wild nature and mountains, but she also gave oracles, healed disease and protected her followers in warfare. The priest, Korubus (Corybantes), would dance ecstatically, go into prophetic rapture, and become insensible to pain. Cybele was known in Greece from the fifth century and taken to Rome in the third century B.C., though her cult was

CYBELE

restricted under the Republic; later it gained official status and spread to Gaul and Africa where its agricultural associations made it popular. The Taurobolium, bull-sacrifice (q.v.), originated in Asia Minor and was performed in the cult of Cybele and other deities. Belief in immortality was also associated with this goddess who, with Attis, was guardian of graves, perhaps because of the reunion of the soul with the earth. In art Cybele sits on a throne, wearing a crown, and flanked by lions.

Cyclopes. Giant beings with one eye in Greek mythology. According to Homer they were wild beings who had no law. Odysseus (q.v.) and his companions visited the Cyclop Polyphemus. Polyphemus ate one man after another until Odysseus escaped by blinding him.

Polyphemus threw rocks at Odysseus and persuaded his father, Poseidon, the god of sea, to hinder the efforts of Odysseus to sail home. Hesoid says, however, that there were three Cyclopes: Brontes, Steropes and Arges, sons of Earth (see GAEA) and Heaven, fine craftsmen, but with one eye each. They worked for the god of fire, Hephaestus, and were said to have made the fortifications of Tiryns and other towns.

Cynics. Greek 'dogs', nickname given to followers of Diogenes of Sinope (400–325 B.C.) who rejected morality and tried to live on nothing. The Cynics were not organized into a philosophical school and included depraved beggars as well as more noble characters.

D

Dādū. An Indian saint who lived at Sambhar in Rajasthan (1544–1603). His family bore Muslim names, though comparatively recently it has been said that he was a Brahmin. Probably the family had been recently converted to Islam, like that of Kabīr (q.v.). Dādū was a cotton-carder, and spoke a dialect of Hindi; he was affected by the Sūfī mysticism of Islam, but a much greater influence was the monotheistic influence of Hindu teachers, and especially Kabīr. Like him Dādū taught that the one God has many names, though the name that he preferred was Rām. Devotion to the gracious God was his chief theme. His followers are Dādū-panthis, followers of the 'way' of Dādū. They worship in temples of Dādū, Dādū-dwāra, where there are portraits of Dādū as a child but no images. His teachings are preserved in hymns called Bānī, inspired utterances or oracles.

Daedalus. Legendary Greek craftsman, in metalwork and carpentry. It is said that he was born in Athens, but went to Crete where he made the Labyrinth for Minotaur (see MINOS) and the thread for Ariadne by which she enabled Theseus to get out of the Labyrinth. He and his son Icarus were imprisoned by King Minos, but Daedalus made some artificial wings and they flew away. Icarus flew too near the sun, the wax of his wings melted and he drowned in the sea. Daedalus is said to have made many statues, some of which could walk like robots.

Daeva. An ancient Persian word which originally indicated a class of gods, like the Sanskrit *deva* (q.v.). After Zoroaster's reform, however, these Daevas were regarded as demons and followers of Druj, the Lie (q.v.).

Dagda, Daghdha. 'Good God' of ancient Celts, called the Great Father, the God, and the Red One of Great Knowledge. He may originally have been an earth fertility god, and a popular story was told of his mating with the Irish raven goddess, the Morrigan, while straddling a river. Dagda is said to have lived with his sons at the great tumulus at New Grange on the Boyne. Dagda carried a club; he had a cauldron which was always full, a pig always ready for cooking, and trees full of fruit. He was a warrior dealing death blows, but also a healer, and though some of his aspects were crude he was generally inoffensive. His wife was Boand, goddess of the river Boyne, and among his children were Brigit, Danu and Oengus. Dagda divided the tumuli among the gods, and in one story Oengus (q.v.) expelled him from New Grange, which may reflect the greater popularity of the son's worship.

Dāgoba, Dāgaba. The Singhalese name for the Indian Stūpa and Burmese Pagoda (q.v.), from Sanskrit *dhātu-garbha*, 'relic-chamber'. Many kinds of Dāgoba range from tiny stone shrines to towering mounds as high as St Paul's Cathedral.

The Dāgoba is bell-shaped, and encloses a relic of the Buddha or one of his disciples in its centre, but the mass of it is solid, and crowned by a short spire. At the ancient Buddhist centre of Anurādhapura in Ceylon four great Dāgobas tower over the forest. The Ruanweli has been restored and painted white over its brick and plaster, on the four sides are chapels at the cardinal points, containing Buddha images and tables for gifts from worshippers. The Abhayagiriya Dāgoba is the largest and stands about seventy metres high; until recently it was in ruins, covered with grass and scrub; it has now been restored. It is said to contain enough bricks to build a wall three metres high from London to Edinburgh. Under the solid bell a small passage leads to the relic-chamber.

Dagon, Dāgan. An ancient Mesopotamian god. Although not in the oldest pantheon he became a national deity, was called 'king of the land' at Mari, and it

DAGAN

was thanks to him that Sargon of Akkad was said to have conquered territory as far as northern Syria. The name of Dāgan is found in ancient Assyrian inscriptions and in royal titles. He was associated with Anu, and his spouse was called Shalash or Ninlil. Dāgan was probably the same as the biblical Dagon, god of the Philistines. It has often been thought that this was a fish-god, whence the Hebrew word *dāg* for a fish; but it is more likely that Dāgan was a corn deity, and a Hebrew word *dāgān* for corn supports this view.

Daibutsu. Great Buddha, a colossal metal image of the Buddha Roshana or Vairochana in the Todaiji temple at Nara in Japan. It was ordered by the Emperor Shomu and took three years to make, from A.D. 747–749. It still stands as the greatest metal figure in the world, composed of over half a million Japanese kilos of copper, gold and lead. The head and neck were cast in one piece, and the body formed of metal plates. The Buddha is over fifteen metres high, and sits cross-legged on a lotus of fifty-six petals, about twenty metres in diameter. The emperor himself took part in the work, carrying earth in his sleeves to build up the platform needed for the work. See photograph below of head. See also LOCHANĀ.

Another great bronze Buddha, sometimes also called Daibutsu, is that of Amida at Kamakura. It replaced a statue destroyed in warfare, was cast in 1252, and stands about fifteen metres high. The Kamakura Buddha was once enclosed in a temple, as that of Nara still is, but tidal waves washed the structure away and Amida sits calmly under the sky. See photograph immediately below.

Daimon. In Homeric Greek this word was used only in the masculine singular, applied to any of the great gods, but indicating a supernatural power. Later in relation to men it was almost like the notion of 'fate'. Then it came to denote intermediate beings between gods and men, such as the Daimon which inspired Socrates (q.v.). In the Christian era the gods were regarded as evil and 'demon' took on this meaning.

Daimyō. (Japanese) 'great name' a title given to feudal lords, to whom the Samurai (q.v.) were attached.

Dainichi. Japanese name of the Buddhist 'Illuminator' Vairochana (q.v.).

Daityas. Hindu titanic beings, descendants of Diti, a complementary deity to Aditi (q.v.). They were giants and demons who fought the Vedic gods and interfered with their sacrifices.

Dajjāl. Name of the Antichrist in Islamic legend. It is not found in the *Qur'ān*, and perhaps comes from a Syrian word meaning 'false prophet'. Dajjāl is sometimes identified with Satan, fighting against God. He is red-coloured and has an eye in the middle of his forehead. Dajjāl is especially an eschatological figure, who it is believed will set up his kingdom in Jerusalem at the end of time and will be destroyed by Christ returning to earth.

Dakhmā. A receptacle for the dead in the Parsi religion, generally described in English as a 'Tower of Silence'. The ancient Persians buried their dead, covered in wax, but the later Magi priests considered that this would defile the earth and as fire also was sacred bodies could not be cremated. Therefore they were exposed to vultures who destroyed them. In Bombay the Parsi community has five tall Dakhmās in a park on a hill secluded from the public. At the end of funeral ceremonies a corpse wrapped in cloth is carried to the Dakhmā and placed on a stone slab at the top of the tower, open to the sky. The clothes are removed and placed in a lime-pit, into which also the bones fall after the vultures have operated.

Dākinī. In Hindu mythology female imps who attended on the fierce goddess Kālī (q.v.).

Daksha. Ancient Indian divine sage whose Sanskrit name, meaning 'able' or 'intelligent', was associated with creative powers. In the *Rig Veda* he is born from the infinite Aditi (q.v.), who was also born from him. Later he is identified with the creating god Prajāpati, or he is said to have sprung from the right thumb of the creator Brahmā. Aditi is important in mythology as father of seven sons, and of many daughters, especially Umā and Vāch. There are several versions of his conflict with the great god Shiva, who interrupted Daksha's sacrifice, and took his daughter Umā.

Dakshināchārīs. (Sanskrit) 'right-hand worshippers', those who observe open and regular rituals of Shakti. See SHĀKTAS.

Dalai Lama. The traditional head of of the Tibetan state and religion. The title was bestowed in the sixteenth century by the Mongol Altai Khan, calling the Grand Lama or abbot of Tibetan Buddhism as Dalai Lama Vajradhara, or 'Ocean Lama, Thunderbolt bearer'. The Dalai Lama is head of

the Yellow Hat monks, the dominant sect of Tibet. He is regarded as the reincarnation of the Bodhisattva Chenresi or Avalokiteshvara (qq.v.). After the death of a Dalai Lama he is thought to be reincarnated in a newborn baby, usually forty-nine days afterwards. However, this baby has to be found and that may take months or years. Leading monks tour the country to find a child bearing marks that prove its supernatural birth. When it is chosen, it is taken to Lhasa with its parents, and trained for future office. The present Dalai Lama has lived in exile in India since fleeing from Tibet in 1959.

Damayantī. In Indian epic story the beautiful daughter of the king of Vidarbha, whose love for Nala (q.v.) is told in the *Mahābhārata* and remains a favourite romance, including their sufferings and final reunion.

Damkina. Mesopotamian goddess, consort of the great god Ea (q.v.). In one text Damkina and Ea are said to be the ears of the god Nergal (q.v.).

Dāna. (Sanskrit) 'gift', donation. In Hindu and Buddhist usage Dāna is giving to holy men and monks, and also almsgiving to the poor. In Buddhism it is one of three 'acts of merit', the others being moral conduct and meditation.

Dance of Shiva. A common representation of this great Hindu deity, in stone or metal, depicts him as the Natarāja, Lord of Dance, doing his Tāndava or world-shattering dance. He dances in a ring of fire which symbolizes the life–process of the universe. Shiva has four hands; the two upper ones balance creation and destruction, one a small drum the sound of which is the first to evolve at creation, and the other the fire of destruction at the end of the present world cycle. The two lower hands hold out the prospect of salvation and protection. Shiva dances on a dwarfish demon which represents the ignorance which must be destroyed in order that the souls of his followers may find enlightenment. Shiva is thus both creator and destroyer, and he also reveals himself to the faithful who call upon him as sole deity.

Dandīs, Dandins. An order of Hindu ascetics who carry a staff, Danda. They worship the god Shiva and their order is said to have been founded by the philosopher Shankara. In theory they should wander from place to place, but many are found in holy places like Benares, with the staffs stuck in the ground beside them. They wear salmon-coloured clothes in five pieces, though in the jungle some go naked. The Dandins are Brahmins, and beg from Brahmins, but they discard the sacred thread of the Brahmin caste (see BRĀHMANA) and bury their dead instead of cremating them.

Danaë. In Greek mythology daughter of Acrisius who was warned by an oracle that her son would kill him. Danaë was shut up in a bronze chamber, but there the god Zeus visited her in a shower of gold and she gave birth to the hero Perseus. Eventually the latter accidentally killed Acrisius when throwing a discus.

Danu, Anu. A mother goddess of Celtic religion, not only presiding over mortals but also the divine mother controlling the gods themselves. It is not sure whether Danu and Anu were distinct or the same, but they have a parallel in Don, mother of some Welsh gods. The deities of Ireland were called Tuatha Dé Danann (q.v.), 'the people of the goddess Danu', but this title is applied particularly to her three sons who were earth gods. Danu was associated with hills and the earth, and the fruits of the earth were her gifts. Two hills in Kerry were called the breasts of Danu or of Anu. Danu is said to have been daughter of the Celtic father god Dagda, and later much of her cult passed over to Brigit (q.v.).

Daphne. The 'laurel' bush in Greek mythology, personified as daughter of a river god. She was pursued by the god

Apollo and called on the gods for help, so that she was turned into the bush which bears her name.

Daphnis. A Sicilian shepherd in Greek mythology, son of the god Hermes. In one story he was loved by the nymph Echenais, but being unfaithful was blinded by her and so he invented pastoral music to console himself. In another story he was loved by the goddess Aphrodite but did not return her love (like Adonis, q.v.), so that she punished him with unsatisfied passion of which he died. He is associated with Chloë, 'green', from the goddess of green crops (q.v.), in a Greek romance, written perhaps by Longus in the second century A.D. In this story, however, two children were discovered by shepherds, grew up, loved and were separated, and finally united after finding their wealthy parents.

Dār al-Islām. (Arabic) 'abode of Islam', a term used of a country ruled by a Muslim and where Muslim laws are dominant. It may have non-Muslims who have submitted to Muslim rule, provided that they are not idolaters but are People of the Book. See AHL AL-KITĀB and DHIMMA.

Daramulun. A heroic or divine figure in the mythology of the aboriginals of south-eastern Australia. Sometimes he is supreme and sometimes the envoy of the 'all-father', Baiami (q.v.). Daramulun came down from the sky to visit the initiation grounds, take the novices away and bring them back as initiated men. He had one leg, or had an emu's leg and a human foot, and his head appears in paintings as human, bird or animal. He holds an axe or boomerang, often in the left hand, and may be accompanied by his wife.

Darazī. See DRUZES.

Dar-I-Meher. See FIRE TEMPLES.

Darshana. (Sanskrit) 'showing', seeing, manifestation, vision. The word is used of an audience with a sage or holy man, or any contemplation or demonstration. Particularly it indicates the Six Demonstrations, Shad-darshanas, or six systems of orthodox Hindu philosophy. Although very diverse these all accept the authority of the *Veda* scriptures and seek the emancipation of the soul. These six schools are: Nyāya, Vaisheshika, Sāmkhya, Yoga, Pūrva-mīmāmsā, and Uttara-mīmāmsā or Vedānta (qq.v.).

Daruma. Japanese name for Bodhidharma (q.v.), reputed founder of the Zen school of Buddhism. It is said that he spent nine years sitting looking at a wall

DARUMA

till his legs dropped off. Japanese children have a toy called Daruma, which has no legs and always rights itself.

Darwesh. See DERVISH.

Dāsas, Dasyus. (Sanskrit), 'slaves', title given in the *Vedas* (q.v.) to Indian tribes. They are described as dark-skinned, snub-nosed, irreligious and speaking unintelligibly. This was the point of view of the Āryan (q.v.) invaders of India, but if the Dāsas were the defeated inhabitants of Harappā (q.v.) and other Indus Valley cities, they were more civilized and literate than their conquerors, and their religion has probably survived in the worship of Shiva, Shakti and Krishna, in Yoga practice and in belief in transmigration. In the *Rig Veda* scripture the word Dāsa comes to mean a slave, and Dāsī is regularly used of a slave-girl.

Dashanāmi. (Sanskrit) 'ten names', title of a sect of Shaivites, who carry triple batons. See TRIDENT.

Dasharā, Daserā, Dussehra. Popular Hindu festival of the 'tenth day' in honour of the goddess Durgā (q.v.). It comes in September-October in the month Ashvina, after 'nine nights', Navarātra, in which hymns are recited to Durgā. The Avatar Rāma (q.v.) also marched against Rāvana on this day and so it has added importance. Both these connections make Dasharā important for the warrior class and it is sometimes called the Festival of Warriors. There are processions and military parades, and even in Muslim states Hindu officers have deputized for the rulers. Sacrifices were offered of animals, buffaloes if possible for Durgā representing the demon she killed, especially in Bengal and Mysore. Dasharā is also a special holiday for brides and engaged people who receive presents of jewellery, clothing and sweets.

Dasharatha. A prince of the solar race, in Indian mythology, and king of Ayodhyā. Being childless he performed a horse-sacrifice (see ASHVA-MEDHA), and of the four sons then born to him one was the divine hero Rāma (q.v.).

Dastur. A priest of the Parsi (Zoroastrian) religion. The chief priest is called Dastur-i-Dasturan. The priesthood is restricted to heredity and only the son of a priest can become a priest, or a member of a priestly family. Not all members of these families take up priesthood, but the right can be revived by any male member of a priestly family even if his immediate ancestors were not practising priests. The Parsi religion has little asceticism and priests are allowed to marry, though marriages outside their ranks are not favoured. Dasturs are distinguished by the white turbans that they wear, and a piece of cloth is put over the face during the performance of certain religious ceremonies. They are responsible for rituals in Parsi homes and at the temples, or Fire Temples (q.v.).

Dasyu. See DĀSA.

Dattātreya. A Brahmin sage who was said to incorporate portions of various gods, notably Vishnu. In the *Bhāgavata Purāna* (q.v.) he is said to be one of twenty-two Avatars of Vishnu. Dattātreya had three sons to whom also some of the divine essence came.

Dāwūd. Arabic form of the name of the Biblical David, who is mentioned several times in the *Qur'ān* and to whom are credited the *Psalms*, Zabūr (q.v.).

Dayānanda Sarasvatī, Swāmī. Hindu reformer (1824–83). Born to a Brahmin family in Kathiawar, and named Mūla Shankara, he revolted against the idolatry of Shiva worship at the age of fourteen and in his twenties left home to become a wandering ascetic, being finally received into the Sarasvatī order of Dandins (q.v.) under the name Dayānanda. He practised Yoga, but came to believe in the reality of the world and the personality of God. Then he began public discussion and lecturing and in 1875 founded the Ārya Samāj (q.v.). Dayānanda rejected the teachings of modern Brahmins and the Bhakti cults of Vishnu, and sought to return to the four *Vedas*, which he held to contain all religious truth, and even all science, at least by implication. He was opposed to idolatry and polytheism, and regarded the many divine figures of the *Vedas* as epithets of the one true God. He wrote commentaries in Sanskrit and other works in Hindi. He is commonly called by the honorific title of *Swāmī*, 'master'.

Debendranath. See TAGORE.

Decemviri. (Latin) 'ten men', a name given to various groups of Roman magistrates. In religious usage they were the ones who were in charge of the Sibylline oracles (see SIBYL). Originally only two (duoviri), they were increased to ten and then by Sulla to fifteen (quindecimviri).

Dedication. See HANUKKAH.

Deepavali. See DĪVĀLĪ.

Dei Consentes. See CONSENTES.

Delos. A small island in the Greek Cyclades, regarded in mythology as the birthplace of Apollo and Artemis. It was

an ancient holy place of Apollo and people came from all round the Aegean Sea to his festival. The island today has the remains of many temples and public buildings, including a famous row of lions, carved out of marble, from the sixth century B.C., facing a garden marking the site of an ancient sacred lake.

Delphi. The most ancient and sacred sanctuary in Greece, on the lower slopes of Mount Parnassus above the Gulf of Corinth. The sanctuary was enclosed by a wall, and inside were monuments dedicated by Greek states, of which the Athenian Treasury remains. The main temple of Apollo remains only in broken pillars and foundations. This was supposed to be the centre of the earth, marked by a navel stone, or Omphalos (q.v.). The priestess gave oracles in the Holy of Holies, below its south-west corner. She was the Pythia, a young woman in a state of trance, believed to be possessed by the god. Delphi provided a meeting-place for the divided Greek states, Pan-Hellenic games were held,

and it was connected with a powerful state league, the Delphic Amphictiony. Delphi was sacked several times, and declined under the Romans and Christianity, but at the sacred stream there still stands a small shrine dedicated to St John the Baptist.

Deluge. See FLOOD.

Demeter. The ancient Greek goddess of corn, identified by the Romans with Ceres (q.v.). The second part of her name means 'mother', and the first part has been explained either as 'earth' or 'corn'. As goddess of corn she was naturally concerned with the earth and descended into it at times. In the Homeric Hymn to Demeter it is said that Hades, god of the underworld, carried off Demeter's daughter Koré (Persephone, Prosperina). Demeter in her search came to Eleusis and nursed the king's son, where a temple was built to her. Meanwhile Koré returned but having eaten some pomegranate-seeds had to return to Hades part of each year. The Eleusinian Mysteries were connected with the return of Koré, and the death and rebirth of the corn symbolized human immortality. At another popular festival of Demeter she was celebrated as Thesmophoria, 'bringer of treasures'. *Hymn to Demeter*, see HOMER.

Democritus. Greek philosopher, 460–370 B.C. Born in Thrace, he is said to have travelled in Egypt and the east. A story that he saw Socrates has been denied, Plato never mentions him, but Aristotle studied his teachings, which have only survived in fragments. Democritus taught that the basic principles of the universe are atoms and the void. Atoms are innumerable tiny particles of infinitely various shape, which are solid and cannot be modified, the void is infinite and empty space in which the atoms move in all directions. The motion of atoms is by necessity or natural law, and the worlds are the result of spontaneous origination or chance. Aristotle criticized Democritus for identifying thought with sense, and Epicurus, who followed Democritus in the main, gave more independence to the atoms and avoided the blind necessity or mechanism of the atomic system.

Demon. See DAIMON.

Dengyō Daishi. Japanese Buddhist monk (767–822), also called Saichō, who founded the Tendai sect from the Chinese T'ien T'ai (q.v.).

Dēnkart, Dinkart. A late Zoroastrian philosophical text, of about the ninth century A.D., containing a summary of the *Avesta* (q.v.) and much mythological and legendary material. The text that has survived is corrupt and difficult to read.

Derceto. Another name for the ancient Syrian goddess Atargatis (q.v.).

Dervish, Darwesh. Member of a religious fraternity in Islam, the name being sometimes explained as derived from a Persian root meaning 'seeking doors', namely, a beggar, but this is disputed. In Turkish and Persian it is used for the religious mendicant that in

DERVISHES

Arabic is called a Faqīr, a poor man. In North Africa the dervishes are commonly called Ikhwān, Brethren (q.v.). These fraternities have been powerful influences in Islam since the early centuries, giving special teachings, ordered devotions and communal living. But only a small number of the full members of the orders live in monasteries, while many lay members live in the world but have special devotions. The earliest fraternity seems to have been the Qādirīs (q.v.). The Dancing or Whirling Dervishes are said to have been founded by Jalāl al-Dīn Rūmī (q.v.) in the thirteenth century and they go into ecstasies during dances. There are female dervishes who are trained by women and hold their devotions apart from men. See also SŪFĪ.

Desire. See TANHĀ.

Destiny. See FATE.

Deucalion. The son of Prometheus (q.v.) in Greek mythology who figures in the Greek story of the Flood (q.v.). Angry at the sins of men, the supreme god Zeus flooded the earth, but Deucalion and his wife Pyrrha built an ark on the advice of Prometheus and floated on the waters till the flood subsided.

Deva. Sanskrit name for a god, a heavenly or shining one, from a root 'div' meaning to shine. It is said in the *Rig Veda* that there are thirty-three gods, eleven each for the three worlds of earth, air and sky. The word *Deva* is related to the Latin *Deus* and English *Divine*. It is the same as the Persian word *Daeva* which originally also meant a god, but after the reformation of Zoroaster a *Daeva* (q.v.) came to mean a demon.

Devadāsī. A 'handmaiden of the god' in India, a temple woman and dancer. Hindu literature often speaks of heavenly dancers and musicians, Apsaras and Gandharvas (qq.v.), and temples reproduced the celestial court. The Devadāsīs or Nautch girls were taken by priests in childhood and trained to sing and dance before images of Shiva, Vishnu and other deities, and also when the images were carried outside in processions. Formerly they lived in the temples, but nowadays live and dance outside. From medieval times at least the dancing girls sang suggestive songs and engaged in prostitution, but in modern times some of the abuses have been suppressed. The low status of dancers has been raised with the revival of classical forms of dance and music.

Devadatta. 'God-given', a cousin of the Buddha and one of his early disciples. At first mentioned without any hostility, the chronicles come to regard him as a schismatic or worse. As the Buddha was getting older, Devadatta asked if he might lead the Order of monks, but this was refused. Then it is said that Devadatta tried to kill the Buddha, rolling a rock at him, turning a fierce elephant towards him, and trying to get archers to shoot him, but these seem to be later legends. Devadatta with three others planned a schism, getting permission from the Buddha to institute five rigid rules, but making them compulsory. Two other disciples were sent to win back those who had gone astray, and Devadatta was condemned to hell but not forever. The stories may reflect divisions in early Buddhism.

Devakī. In Hindu mythology, the wife of Vasudeva and mother of Krishna (q.v.). Her name, but not that of her husband, appears in the *Upanishads* as mother of Krishna, but from the *Mahābhārata* onwards she and her husband are linked. Her cousin was the tyrant Kamsa (q.v.), who had heard that Devakī's son would kill him and tried to destroy all her children, but unsuccessfully. Devakī was sometimes called a manifestation of the goddess Aditi (q.v.).

Devaloka. (Sanskrit) the 'world of a god', any of the superior worlds or paradises of Hinduism. In particular it is the Swarga or heaven of the Vedic god Indra, but it is only a temporary abode where the souls of the virtuous receive the rewards of their earthly actions till the time comes for their return to earth in the round of transmigration. The goal of the wise and devout is to get beyond all these heavens to final bliss, or Nirvāna, from which there is no return to earth. For Devaloka in Jainism, see SWARGA.

Devatā. A 'divinity', godhead, or image of a god (Sanskrit). Devatā includes the gods in general, or all the inferior gods. It is common nowadays to say that one should worship the god of one's choice (*ishta devatā*).

Devī. (Sanskrit) 'goddess', and particularly Mahā-devī, the 'great goddess'. She was wife of Shiva and daughter of Himavat, the Himalaya mountains. In the *Rig Veda* there are few goddesses, but many female figures have been found in the ruins of the Indus Valley civilization, and mother goddesses survived and entered powerfully into later Hinduism. Devī appears under various names in the great epic *Mahābhārata*, but is particularly developed in the *Purānas* and later works. She is the Shakti or female energy of Shiva; in a mild form she is Umā the 'light' and Pārvatī the 'mountaineer'. In her terrible form she is Durgā the 'inaccessible' and Kālī the 'black' (qq.v.). She is also the great Mother, and modern saints like Rāmakrishna have had special devotion to her.

Devil. See IBLĪS.

Devil Worshippers. See YAZĪDĪ.

Dhamma. The Pali Buddhist form of the Sanskrit Dharma (q.v.). In Buddhism Dhamma has various meanings as it does in Hinduism. From meaning right, virtue and law, it becomes also doctrine and teaching, as the Dhamma of the Buddha, the second of the three refuges which Theravāda Buddhists constantly repeat, 'I go to the Dhamma for refuge.' Dhamma also means condition, on its causal side, and phenomenon as effect, so it is said that 'all Dhammas are mind-created', meaning all phenomena. In Mahāyāna Buddhism Dharma (the Sanskrit form) is sometimes synonymous with ultimate reality or Tathatā (q.v.).

Dhammapada. The *Path of Teaching* (Pali), the most famous scripture of the Buddhist canon. It is a short work of 423 verses in twenty-six chapters. It teaches moral and mental discipline, includes the Four Noble Truths and the Noble Eightfold Path, and teaches taking refuge in the Buddha, the Law and the Order. It says that a man should 'overcome anger by non-anger, let him overcome evil by good'. A version in the Gandhari language was discovered near Khotan in central Asia in 1892, written on birch bark, and dated to the first or second century A.D., thus being the oldest surviving Indian religious text. The *Dhammapada* comes towards the end of the *Sutta Pitaka*, the second major division of the Buddhist canonical scriptures. It is so short that many Buddhists know much of it by heart.

Dhanvantari. Ancient Indian god who received offering at twilight in the north-east quarter; his name meant 'moving in a curve'. He was also the physician of the gods, who emerged at the churning of the ocean for nectar (see AMRITA). He was the founder of medicine, to whom the *Ayur-Veda* was attributed (q.v.) and was called an Avatar.

Dharma. (Sanskrit) a basic concept with a variety of meanings; right, virtue, morality, righteousness, duty, law, truth, doctrine, religion. It takes the place of Rita (order) of the *Rig Veda*, and in the epics and later writings Dharma is both absolute moral order and the duty and right of this world. The noble king Yudhishthira is Dharma-rāja, 'king of righteousness', son of the god Dharma. The word *Dharma* comes from a root *Dhri*, meaning to have or maintain and is related to our words 'firm' and 'form'. So it is the form of things and the power that maintains them. There is the 'eternal law', Sanātana Dharma, of the universe and of human society. Dharma is the first word of the *Bhagavad-Gītā*, though at the very end one is told to abandon things of Dharma in devotion to God. The *Dharma-Shāstras* are Hindu law books, and this term is particularly applied to the Laws of Manu (q.v. and see also SHĀSTRA).

Dharmakāra. Legendary Buddhist monk who is said ages ago to have taken a vow to become a Buddha, provided that his merits could be used for the benefit of others, and eventually he became Amitābha (q.v.). His story is told in the *Sukhāvatī-vyūha*, a text of the Pure Land school (q.v.).

Dharma-Kāya. (Sanskrit) 'law-body' or body of doctrine, a Mahāyāna Buddhist term for the transcendental Buddha essence. See TRIKĀYA.

Dharmapāla. (Sanskrit) 'guardian of doctrine', title of several Indian princes and poets. It was adopted by a modern Ceylonese reformer, D. H. Hewavitarne (1865–1933), who founded the Maha Bodhi Society (q.v.). He also called himself Anāgārika, a 'houseless' wanderer.

Dhātri. 'Founder', creator (Sanskrit), an abstract deity of the later hymns of the *Rig Veda*, producing life and preserving health. He is also one of the Ādityas (q.v.). In later myth Dhātri is identified with the creator gods Brahmā and

Prajāpati, and his name is given as a title to Vishnu and Krishna.

Dhikr. (Arabic) 'remembrance', the Islamic practice of glorifying God by repeating certain words or phrases, sometimes with special breathings or physical movements. The *Qur'ān* (33, 41) says, 'remember God with much remembering'. In the Sūfī (q.v.) mystical brotherhoods, each one differed by its own special Dhikr. These were repetitions of praises to God, and especially the Beautiful Names (q.v.), often on prayer beads. Love songs were also sung with a divine reference, accompanied by dancing and musical instruments. At various times attempts have been made to reform the Dhikr, clear it of superstitious elements, and revert to the simple praise of God.

Dhimma. 'Covenant', obligation (Arabic), a term applied by Muslims to conquered people who accept Islamic rule and taxation. They became 'people of the covenant', Ahl al-Dhimma or simply Dhimmis. Strictly these should be only the People of the Book, Ahl al-Kitāb (q.v.), but in practice many other peoples have been admitted as Dhimmis. See DĀR AL-ISLĀM.

Dhrita-rāshtra. King of the Kurus in the great Indian epic, *Mahābhārata*. He was brother of Pāndu and the struggle of their sons for the succession forms the subject of the epic. Dhrita-rāshtra was blind, and at the beginning of the *Bhagavad-Gītā* (q.v.) he sits beside the field of the battle between Kurus and Pāndus, while his charioteer Sanjaya tells him what is going on and repeats the dialogue of Krishna and Arjuna. Dhrita-rāshtra was one of the few survivors of the battle, but eventually he and his wife Gāndhārī were burnt in a forest fire. Their eldest son was the evil-minded Duryodhana who opposed the king of righteousness, Yudhishthira.

Dhu 'l-Qarnain. The 'two-horned' (Arabic), name given to Alexander the Great in the *Qur'ān* (18, 82f.), and in Islamic legend. The name is probably connected with stories derived from the imagery of rams and goats with horns in *Daniel* 8, which have been interpreted as referring to Alexander and other rulers. The *Qur'ān* links Dhu 'l-Qarnain with Yājūj and Mājūj, Gog and Magog, (q.v.).

Dhundia. See STHĀNAKAVĀSĪ.

Dhyāna. (Sanskrit) 'meditation', reflection, and especially profound religious meditation. The sixth chapter of the *Bhagavad-Gītā* is called Dhyāna-Yoga, the discipline of meditation which it briefly describes. In Buddhism the Pali form Jhāna indicates a series of stages of mental development. It is one of six Perfections or Pāramitās, with eight states, in the highest of which the idea of self is eliminated and perfect contemplation, or Samādhi, is experienced. Dhyāna is said to be the word from which Ch'an and Zen (qq.v.) are derived.

Dhyāni-Buddha. 'Buddha of meditation'. A term used in Tibet, Nepal and some other northern Buddhist regions but much disputed. The compound is unusual Sanskrit, but it designates perhaps the meditations of Buddhas coming from the primal Ādi-Buddha (q.v.), 'Father of the world.' The term might suggest the transcendent nature of the Buddha-forms which are found on stūpas, and which goes beyond the material images. There are said to be seven Dhyāni Buddhas, of which the first five are concerned with the phenomenal world, and are named as: Vairochana, Akshobhya, Ratna-Sambhava, Amitābha and Amoghasiddhi. See ĀDI-BUDDHA.

Di. See MANES, PARENTALIA, FASTI and DI NOVENSILES.

Dialis. See FLAMENS.

Diamond Sūtra. A popular Mahāyāna Buddhist wisdom book, known in Sanskrit as 'the Perfection of Wisdom

DIAMOND SŪTRA

which cuts like a thunderbolt' (Vajracchedikā Prajñāpāramitā). Compiled about the fourth century A.D. and translated from Sanskrit into other languages, a Chinese copy in the British Museum is the oldest printed book in the world, dating from the ninth century. The *Diamond Sūtra* expounds the vow of a Bodhisattva (q.v.) to save all beings, his Pure Land, and final Nirvāna. The nature of the Buddha is discussed, his knowledge, teaching and true nature. Further words consider the nature of reality, the material world, supreme knowledge, truth and falsehood, peace and freedom. See PRAJÑĀ.

Diana. An ancient Italian goddess comparable to the Greek Artemis (q.v.); a Bible verse formerly translated 'Diana of the Ephesians' is 'Artemis' in the original (*Acts* 19, 28). The name of Diana may mean 'bright one', comparable to Dyaus and Zeus, but this does not prove theories which have sought to identify Diana with the moon; it is more likely that she was a wood-goddess. Her most famous shrine was by a lake near Aricia, where her temple stood in a grove and the priest was an escaped slave who killed his predecessor by plucking a bough of the sacred tree, a story made popular again by Sir James Frazer in *The Golden Bough* (see VIRBIUS). Diana was chiefly a goddess of women, however, who held processions in her honour at Aricia and elsewhere and brought votive gifts in thanks for children and successful births.

Diarmaid. Irish mythical hero, nephew of Fionn (q.v.). He had a 'beauty spot', so that women fell in love with him, including Grainne who was betrothed to Fionn. Diarmaid was protected by several gods, being taught by Manannan and helped to defeat his enemies by Oengus (qq.v.). He eloped with Grainne, but was caught by Fionn who made him break his taboo (*geasa*) of touching a boar so that he was fatally wounded.

Diaspora, Dispersion. The dispersion of the Jews from their ancient homeland, partly and primarily by captivity but also by travel and trade. The Dispersion began with the deportation from the kingdom of Samaria to Mesopotamia in 722 B.C., followed by that from Judaea in 597 and 586 B.C., and by later flights from the Romans in A.D. 70 and 135. Many Jews went also to Egypt, Rome and other parts of the known world. There were Jewish colonies as far away as China surviving into modern times. See JUDAISM and ZIONISM.

Dievaitis, Dievs. Sky god of ancient Lithuania and Latvia, sometimes identified with the god of thunder, Perkunas (q.v.).

Digambaras. One of the two major schools of the Jain (q.v.) religion. Mahāvīra, the great 'conqueror' (Jina), who died about 468 B.C., had spent the closing years of his life in complete nudity. Some two centuries later a great famine led to the exodus of some of his followers from the Ganges Valley to southern India. The monks who remained in the north, owing to cold and hunger, took to wearing white robes and were called Shvetāmbara, 'white-clothed', but those in the warmer south remained naked and were called Digambara, 'space-clothed'. A schism arose over this point of monastic discipline, though most Digambara monks modestly wore robes in public. There was little doctrinal difference, but the Digambaras claimed that the oral sacred literature had been lost, whereas the Shvetāmbaras accepted a reconstructed canon of twelve *Angas* (q.v.) or sections. The Digambara eventually compiled new scriptures for themselves, but many of these have not yet been published.

Dīgha Nikāya. (Pali) 'collection of long discourses', the first section of the second main division of the Theravāda Buddhist canon of scripture. See TRIPITAKA and SŪTRA.

Diké. (Greek) 'right', justice. Personified as one of the Horae (q.v.), goddesses of the seasons, Diké reported the wrongdoings of men to Zeus. Sometimes she is identified with the constellation Virgo.

Dīn. A comprehensive Arabic word to cover judgement, custom, and especially 'religion', the latter under Persian influence. Dīn is religion in the broad sense, any religion, but especially Islam, which is 'the religion with God' (*Qur'ān* 3, 17). Dīn is the whole of religion, and includes the faith and obligations included under the Five Pillars (see PILLARS OF ISLAM).

Dinkart. See DĒNKART.

Di Novensiles. (Latin) 'newly introduced gods', a name given to foreign or immigrant deities in the Roman pantheon. Among the most important were the Etruscan Minerva (see CAPITOLINE TRIAD), Hercules, Mercury, Apollo, Fortuna and Diana (qq.v.).

Diogenes. See CYNICS.

Diomedes. A Thracian king, in Greek mythology, son of the god Ares and Cyrene. He owned a herd of man-eating horses, and to capture them was the eighth labour of Heracles (q.v.).

Dione. The female form of Zeus and associated with him at the oracle at Dodona (q.v.). This suggests that Dione was a sky-goddess, though it has been conjectured that she was the local earth-mother at Dodona. Little is known about her worship elsewhere, and in Homer and later she appears simply as a secondary wife of Zeus, identified with Aphrodite or her mother.

Dionysus. A popular god of Thrace, rarely mentioned in Homeric times, but in the last millennium B.C. the cult entered Attica and Boeotia. The ecstatic nature of the Dionysia, festivals and dances affected women particularly. They left home, roamed the mountains swinging torches, and in frenzy seized animals and devoured them live. These Maenads, or Bacchae, dressed in fawn-skins and sometimes wore masks. Dionysus himself was said to appear sometimes as an animal, and he was called 'bull-horned', his image being composed of a human mask and a robe on a pole. By devouring

animals the Maenads believed that they took the power of the divinity into themselves. When the cult of Dionysus was taken into the state Greek religion, the orgies were tamed, and the god was admitted by Apollo to the great sanctuary at Delphi (q.v.). Another form of Dionysus came from Asia Minor, identified with Bacchus and wine. In the Mysteries Dionysus was associated with the underworld and was popular in Hellenistic and Roman times. See SEMELE and ZAGREUS.

Dioscuroi. Sons of Zeus and Leda in Greek myth, the twins Castor and Polydeuces (Latin: Pollux). They were the brothers of Helen, rescued her from Theseus and took part in the expedition of the Argonauts. It is debated whether the Dioscuroi were heroes who became gods, or gods who faded into heroes. They resemble the Sanskrit twin Ashvins (q.v.) and like them are horsemen; they are connected with the stars and often identified with the constellation Gemini. On the other hand Castor was said to be killed, or shared in the immortality of his twin, so that they spent half their time on earth and half on mount Olympus. They became popular in Rome, where they were connected with horse guards and had a temple on the Forum.

Dīpankara. The first Buddha in the present world cycle, and twenty-fourth before Gotama Buddha, according to late Theravāda and Mahāyāna scriptures. Dīpankara is mentioned in the Therāvada *Buddhavamsa* (q.v.), one of the latest works in the canon and not accepted as such by all schools, and his story is developed in the Mahāyāna *Lalitavistara* and *Mahāvastu*. His principal interest is that he met the young Gotama, who in that life was a Brahmin called Sumedha, and prophesied his career, whereupon Gotama then took a vow to become a Buddha.

Dīpavalī. See DĪVĀLĪ.

Dīpavamsa. The 'Island Chronicle', one of the two major Chronicles of Ceylon. It dates from about the fourth century A.D. and was written in Pali from older commentaries in Singhalese. Much of this material is reproduced and enlarged in the *Mahāvamsa*, the 'Great Chronicle' of the next century (q.v.). The *Dīpavamsa* gives stories of the Buddha, his legendary visits to Ceylon, and accounts of kings and councils.

Di Penates. See PENATES.

Dis, Dispater. *Dis* was the Latin for 'deity', but was applied to Jupiter as ruling the underworld, and to Prosperine there also (see PERSEPHONE). Julius Caesar said that the Gauls believed themselves to be descended from Dispater, perhaps reflecting a belief that men had come to the earth from underground. Dis or Dispater was referred to by other Latin writers as the Celtic god of night and the underworld, and probably the native Dis was a Celtic god of the earth. He was sometimes identified with the horned god Cernunnos (q.v.).

Disciplinary School. See Lü.

Dis Manibus. See Manes.

Dispersion. See Diaspora.

Ditheism. Belief in 'two gods', and applied erroneously to the Dualism (q.v.) of Ahura Mazdā and Ahriman in Zoroastrian religion.

Dithyramb. The origin of this word is unknown, but it appeared as a choral song to Dionysus and was said to be sung under the influence of wine (see Dionysus). It was sung in an orderly way by choirs at Corinth from about 600 B.C. and in Athens was open to competitions where great poets won prizes. The Dionysian element disappeared, solos were introduced and pompous language led to protest against degeneration of the text. The competitions lasted in Athens till Roman times.

Diti. See Daitya.

Dīvālī, Dīwālī, Dīpāvalī. The 'Cluster of Lights', or 'Feast of Lamps' at the end of the Hindu old year and beginning of the new. It comes in October-November, at the end of the month Ashvina, and is particularly associated with the goddess Shrī Lakshmī, the consort of the great god Vishnu, and goddess of wealth. Houses are cleaned and decorated, vessels polished, new clothes put on and homes illuminated with oil lamps. On the second day ghosts and witches are said to be abroad and people stay at home or recite spells to lay the spirits. But on the third day people rise early, children let off crackers, bigger lights are lit, and friends are entertained. Businessmen open new account books for the new year and write the word *Shrī* for Lakshmī over and over again to bring good fortune. For them, especially in western India, it is the most important of all festivals.

Divination. Methods of seeking to discover the unknown or foretell the future. The Latin root word referred to miraculous or 'divine' knowledge and inspiration, coming from the gods. Such practices of Magic (q.v.) have been found all over the world (see Augures and Haruspices). Fortune-telling, by cards, tea leaves, bird flights, markings on the liver, etc., are ancient and modern methods. See Ifa.

Dīwān. Arabic and Persian for an account book, a court of justice, and from this a part of the floor raised and cushioned (whence 'Divan'). A Dīwān was also a collection of poems, or mystical odes, such as those of Hāfiz or Hallāj (qq.v.).

Djanggawul, Djanggau. Hero of a north Australian aboriginal myth. With his two sisters, Bildjiwuraroju and Miralaidj, he left a land beyond the sunrise and travelled west by canoe to land on the shores of the Gulf of Carpentaria. Jelangbara (Port Bradshaw), the site of their arrival, is sacred. They were creating beings, and the main theme of the myth is fertility. They walked across Arnhem Land, making the hills, springs, trees, and especially human beings. The sisters gave birth to many children who were the ancestors of modern tribes. The myth is illustrated on bark paintings, showing different incidents in the story. Sometimes the sisters are said to be daughters of the sun and they are great fertility mothers.

Dodona. The most ancient oracle of Zeus, in the Epirus mountains of north-west Greece. A myth said that a pigeon flew from Thebes in Egypt and lighting on an oak tree at Dodona gave instructions in a human voice for founding an oracle there. The oracle of Zeus was heard in the rustle of the oak leaves, and perhaps also in the cooing and flight of pigeons and the sound of a running spring. Visitors wrote questions for the oracle on lead tablets, some of which remain. The priests were called Selloi or Selli ('of unwashed feet'), and the priestesses of Dione (q.v.) were called 'pigeons'. The oracle had a great reputation, though overshadowed by Delphi (q.v.). The temple became a Christian church and was destroyed by the Goths in the seventh century.

Dome of the Rock. In Arabic 'Qubbat al-Sakhra'. Erroneously called the Mosque of Omar, it was not built by him, but by the Umayyad caliph 'Abd al-Malik (688–691), though when Omar conquered Jerusalem he ordered the derelict Temple site to be cleared. The Dome is on the site of the old Temples of Solomon and Herod, a shrine rather than a mosque, though prayers are said there. It covers a large slab of bare rock, perhaps the threshing-floor of Araunah the Jebusite (2 Samuel 24, 16), and Muslim legend says that marks in the rock came from Muhammad's night visit (*Qur'ān* 17, 1). The Dome is one of the most beautiful and ancient buildings, the style copied from the Holy Sepulchre church. It is covered with gold, and the walls are of marble and mosaics, outside and inside. There are many Arabic inscriptions, including Quranic verses mentioning Jesus. The whole temple site is sacred to Muslims, Jews and Christians. At the

DOME OF THE ROCK

end of the courtyard is the Aqsa mosque (q.v.).

Doms. Outcaste or Scheduled Class Indians, some of whom are scavengers and provide lighted straws for funeral pyres, while others are craftsmen and hill inhabitants. They are probably related to our Gipsies (q.v.). See OUTCASTES.

Don. Ancient Welsh goddess, mother of Gwydion, Gilvaethwy, Govannon and Arianrhod, whose stories come in the *Mabinogion* (q.v.). This divine group is comparable with that of the Irish goddess Danu (q.v.).

Donar. The ancient Thunder god of Germany, called Thunor by the Saxons and Thor in Scandinavia. See THOR.

Dönmeh. 'Apostates', name by which the Turks knew the surviving followers of the pseudo-Messiah Shabbethai Zvi (q.v.). They called themselves 'believers', and despite some persecution and ostracism from Turks and orthodox Jews, they survived down to this century.

Doom of the Gods. See RAGNARÖK.

Dorje. See VAJRA.

Dosa, Dosha. (Pali) 'depravity', evil of mind due to anger, malevolence or hatred. It is one of the three major blemishes of character, or fires for Theravāda Buddhism. See MOHA.

Dragon King. See LUNG WANG.

Draupadī. Also called Krishnā, she was the common wife of the five Pāndu princes, in the Indian epic *Mahābhārata*, and bore a son to each. Arjuna was her favourite, but the eldest prince, Yudhishthira, gambled away all his kingdom and belongings, including Draupadī. She was insulted by this and went with the Pāndus into exile in the forest for twelve years, but returned to reign with them after their final victory. When her husbands eventually retired and went to the Himalayas and Indra's heaven, Draupadī was the first to die on the way.

Dravidians. Peoples and languages of southern India and northern Ceylon, different from the Āryans (q.v.) who entered northern India. The four great Dravidian languages are Tamil, Telegu, Kannada and Malayalam, which are sometimes claimed to be related to Finnish. The ancestors of the Dravidians may have been the Indus Valley peoples (q.v.) whose religion mingled with that of the Aryans to form developed Hinduism, though it has also been held that they came by sea to India at a later date. In southern India today there are countless great Hindu temples and holy places, and sacred texts include Sanskrit *Vedas* and other classics as well as Tamil and other scriptures. See SHAIVA SIDDHĀNTA and GOPURAM.

Dreaming. Australian aboriginal concept, called Alcheringa or Wongar, the heroic period of the past but timeless, as the real world. It is reborn through ritual art, painting, chanting and dancing, to the initiated in Totem (q.v.) and cult ceremonies. Some of the great heroic or Totem beings are said to have made themselves into Dreaming, and so immortal, and left their images in paintings on cliffs and shelters. A Totem centre is a Dreaming, and may be a medium of giving children to women who pass by. The Dreaming centres are preserved by the performance of rituals, and repetition of myths, emblems and designs. An artist communicates with the Dreaming by depicting, not just natural objects, but the symbols of the pre-existent spirits. See BAIAMI, DJANGGAWUL and WANDJINA. See also AUSTRALIA.

Drona. A Brahmin and teacher (*āchārya*) of both Kuru and Pāndu princes in the Indian epic *Mahābhārata*. In the battle between them Drona sided with the Kurus and was killed in combat, but as a Brahmin and Āchārya it is said that he carried himself to heaven in a glittering state like the sun, so that only his body was killed.

Druids. The priests of Celtic religion, particularly in Britain and Gaul. They seem to have been associated with oak trees, but the suggestion that their name means 'knowledge of the oak' is denied. Little is known of the Druids, apart from references in classical Roman writers and some archaeological remains. They may have been connected with La Tène sanctuary in Switzerland, but there is no evidence at all for linking them with Stonehenge (q.v.). The Druids came from Celtic warrior aristocracy and practised rituals and magic, interceding with the gods of the Celtic tribes. They were priests or Shamans (q.v.) and probably not the philosophers that some classical writers supposed. Pliny said that Druids dressed in white, climbed oak trees and cut mistletoe (q.v.) with golden sickles, after which white bulls were sacrificed and a feast followed. Tacitus speaks of howling priests in Anglesey, and black-clad women, whirling torches when their stronghold was destroyed by Roman soldiers. No doubt Druids directed pastoral festivals, such as Beltain and Samhain (q.v.).

Druj. (Avestan) the 'Lie', the principle of evil and disorder in Zoroastrian religion. Druj was in endless conflict with Asha, truth and right. His followers (Drvants) were the worshippers of the demons (Daevas, q.v.), and Zoroaster and his disciples were all called upon to join in the fight against the Lie. The wicked who are condemned at the Chinvat Bridge (q.v.) are bound by demons and dragged off to the House of Druj.

Druzes. Communities in Lebanon, Syria and Israel whose religion originated from Islam and perhaps also from older roots. The name is taken from one of the founders, Darazī, who died in 1019 fighting the Turks. Another leader, Hamza, supported by Darazī, claimed that the Fātimid caliph Hākim was the manifestation of God. This was an Ismā'īlī (q.v.) doctrine that God was manifest in man in all ages and, despite the notorious cruelties and eccentricities of Caliph Hākim, these were explained symbolically by the Druzes, and he was regarded as the last divine manifestation. He was said not to die, but to be hidden and due to reappear one day like a Mahdī. Druzes have an Emir at their head whose power is passed down in the same family. They seek truth, recognize the divine in humanity, renounce evil, and care for each other's safety. It is estimated that there are about 300,000 Druzes in the Middle East: 150,000 in Syria, 110,000 in Lebanon, and 30,000 in Israel.

Du'ā'. (Arabic) 'blessing', and 'prayer'. It is used of different forms of prayer, and in particular of the first chapter (sūra) of the *Qur'ān* which is the basis of all formal prayer, and is called the *Sūrat al-du'ā'*. See FĀTIHA and SALĀT.

Dualism. Belief in the existence of two principles, of good and evil, in the universe. Traces are found in many religions, the two chief being Manichaeism and Zoroastrianism, very different from one another. In Manichaean (q.v.) belief the world is evil, made from the substance of an evil being, while good is spiritual. Hence arose world-denial and asceticism, which affected Islamic mystics and Christianity through St Augustine who had been a Manichaean. Zoroastrianism, on the contrary, believed that the world was good, the creation of the wise god Ahura Mazdā or Ohrmuzd. Any corruption in the world was introduced later by the evil spirit Ahriman. Ahura Mazdā and Ahriman were eternal twins, though there was some effort made to give them a single parent, Zurvān (q.v.) or Time. It has been said that Zoroastrian dualism is not complete, because in the end the good Ahura Mazdā will triumph, the world will be restored to goodness,

MOSQUE IN CAIRO BUILT BY
MUHAMMAD ʿALĪ (1824)

MUSLIM PULPIT (MINBAR),
MUSEUM OF ISLAMIC ART,
CAIRO.

PAGE FROM QUR'ĀN,
ARABIC, 10TH CENTURY A.D.

and Ahriman will be rendered powerless or perish. See DVAITA, YANG and YIN.

Dukkha. 'Suffering', or ill, in Pali (*Duhkha* in Sanskrit), diagnosed by the Buddha as universal in the first of his Four Noble Truths (q.v.). Its opposite is Sukha, happiness (q.v.).

Dumuzi. See TAMMUZ.

Duoviri. See DECEMVIRI.

Durgā. 'Inaccessible' (Sanskrit), one of the names of the Hindu mother goddess, Devī (q.v.). According to one of the *Purānas* (q.v.), there had been a long war between the gods and demons in which the powerful demon Mahisha seized heaven and the gods wandered homeless on earth. The goddess Durgā, riding a lion or tiger, fought Mahisha who changed into many shapes and finally into a buffalo, symbol of death. Durgā

pierced the buffalo's throat and when the demon came out she cut off his head with a sword. The gods returned to heaven, and Durgā fighting the buffalo appears in picture and sculpture. Durgā-pūjā, 'worship of Durgā', is another name for Dasharā (q.v.), the festival held in honour of the warrior-goddess. Durgā is wife of Shiva and is attended by Bhairavīs, 'fearful ones', Shākinīs, 'able ones', and Yakshinīs (q.v.).

Duryodhana. Eldest son of King Dhrita-rāshtra (q.v.) in the *Mahābhārata* epic of Hinduism, and leader of the Kuru or Kaurava army in the great battle of Kurukshetra. His name means, 'hard to conquer' (Sanskrit), and when he was winning in the battle his adversary, Bhīma, unfairly hit him below the waist so that he fell and died thinking, mistakenly, that he was crushing Bhīma's head. He is called 'evil-minded' in the *Bhagavad-Gītā*.

Dvaita. (Sanskrit) 'duality', dualism, the opposite of Advaita (q.v.). A Dvaita-vādin is a 'dualist', who asserts that there are two principles, a human soul separate from the Supreme Being. See MADHVA.

Dvi-Jā. See TWICE-BORN.

Dwāpara Yuga. The third age of the world in Indian mythical chronology (see YUGA). Righteousness was diminished by one half, the *Vedas* were divided from unity into four and some neglected their study altogether. The Avatar Krishna appeared then. The Dwāpara Yuga lasted 864,000 years and was followed by the present Kali Yuga.

Dwarf. In Scandinavian mythology a long list of names of dwarfs (*dvergar*) is given in Snorri's Edda (q.v.). They were supposed to live underground and be skilled in metal-working, making Thor's hammer, Odin's spear and gold ring, and also gold hair for Thor's wife Sif (q.v.). Four dwarfs were said to hold up the sky which was called the 'burden of the dwarfs', and others dwelt in huge stones, but apparently they were not worshipped. See also TROLLS. Dwarfs are thought to have uncanny powers in many parts of the world. African chiefs had dwarfs as court officials, and sacrifices of them were sometimes made. In Hindu mythology Vāmana (q.v.) 'dwarf', was an Avatar (q.v.) of the god Vishnu. King Bali (q.v.) dominated the universe and Vāmana asked him for as much land as he could step over in three paces. Bali agreed and Vāmana took two strides over earth and heaven, but left hell to Bali. In the *Rig Veda* Vishnu himself took three strides over earth, air and sky.

Dwat. Name of the underworld of the god Osiris in ancient Egyptian religion. In the pyramid texts it sometimes refers to heaven, but later Dwat regularly indicates the subterranean kingdom of Osiris. It was a duplicate of the present world, with an Upper and Lower Dwat, like Upper and Lower Egypt, and a river running down the midst like the Nile. It had many halls, divisions and gates, and the judgement hall of Osiris was between the fifth and sixth divisions, according to the *Book of the Dead* (q.v.).

Dyaus. An ancient Indian god of 'heaven', from the same root as Zeus, Deus and Jove. In the *Rig Veda* he is sometimes called 'heavenly father', Dyaus-pitri, like Ju-piter. He is father of the dawn, Ushas, and male partner to mother-earth. Heaven and earth, Dyāvā-Prithivī, are parents of men and gods but are also at times said themselves to have been created. Despite his fatherly function Dyaus is not very prominent even in the *Vedas*, and later he disappears before more powerful creating gods such as Vishnu and Shiva.

Dylan. A Celtic god of the sea, called Dylan Eil Ton, 'son of the wave'. He was identified with the waves, or it was said that they mourned for him.

E

Ea. The third of the great Babylonian gods, also called Enki. Anu was god of heaven and Enlil of the lands, so Ea dwelt in the *apsu* (q.v.) or abyss of waters on which the world rested. He was favourable to men and, since the 'water of life' delivered men from disease and demons, Ea was invoked in incantations. Ea comes in Akkadian creation and flood myths, and it was at his warning that some men were saved from the Flood. The chief temple of Ea was at the old Sumerian city of Eridu, at the top of the Persian Gulf. His consort was Damkina and Marduk (q.v.) was his son. In magical texts Marduk consults Ea for efficacious spells. Ea was associated with stars and particularly the constellations Pisces and Aquarius. His symbol was a ram's head or a goat's head with the body of a fish. See also KUMARBI.

The Babylonian cuneiform (topright) gives an account of the Creation.

Earth God, Chinese. See T'U TI.

Eblis. See IBLIS.

Echenais. A nymph in Greek mythology who loved a Sicilian shepherd Daphnis (q.v.). She demanded that he should be faithful, which he was until he was made drunk and unfaithful by a princess; Echenais in anger blinded him.

Echo. In Greek mythology Echo was a nymph who was loved in vain by the god Pan (q.v.), and was torn in pieces by mad shepherds, but fragments of her were hidden in the earth and can still imitate sounds. Another story says she was repulsed by Narcissus (q.v.).

Ecstasy. (Greek) 'put out of' one's senses. In classical Greek this described anger, madness or a diseased condition of mind. Later it was used of a state of trance in which the soul was thought to leave the body, and in Neoplatonic writings it was applied to union with the deity. The trance state of ecstasy is worldwide and the normal practice of Shamans (q.v.). The Prophet Muhammad received some of his revelations in a comparable state.

Eddas. Scandinavian works which are the chief source for information about the ancient religions of those countries. The *Poetic Edda* contains poems about gods and heroes, myths about heaven and earth, future life and the Doom of the gods. The latter is particularly found in the poem *Voluspa* (q.v.) in which the god Odin consults a wise woman about the future. The *Poetic Edda* was composed in the pagan period, from about the tenth century A.D. The *Prose Edda* was composed by an Icelandic Christian chief, Snorri Sturluson (q.v.), who lived in the twelfth and thirteenth centuries. The prologue to his Edda tells of the Creation and Flood and how the gods came from Troy. But then he proceeds to set down the more native Scandinavian myths of Asgard, the home of the gods, the stealing of apples of immortality, and how Odin gained the mead of poetry. There are descriptions of gods and men taken from more ancient poets.

Eden, Islamic. See JANNA.

Egeria. Roman water goddess, the meaning of whose name is uncertain. She was favoured by pregnant women and worshipped along with Diana (q.v.).

Egyptians, Ancient. With its buildings, pictures and texts ancient Egypt presents some of the earliest and most lasting forms of religion, from before 3000 B.C. till well into the Christian era. There were many gods, of whom the jackal-headed Anubis of the dead, Rē' the sun-god, the pair Isis and Osiris, and others are referred to under separate articles. The attempted imposition of a kind of monotheism was made by Ikhnaton (see ATON). The famous Pyramids (q.v.) were royal tombs, in which the embalmed body was placed with protective texts for the journey to the world after death. Commoners also adopted modified forms of pyramid at an early date. In the sixteenth century Thuthmosis I began a new type of royal tomb cut in the rock in the Valley of Kings at Thebes. Egyptian worship in temples was conducted by priests, serving the images of the gods, but beside the official religion there were many popular cults varying in different places. In A.D. 391, on the orders of emperor Theodosius I, the Egyptian temples were closed.

RĒ'

ISIS

SET

PTAH

OSIRIS

THOT

Eid. See 'ĪD.

Eightfold Path. See NOBLE EIGHTFOLD PATH.

Eight Trigrams. See TRIGRAMS.

Eir. A Scandinavian goddess named by Snorri in the *Edda* (q.v.) among a group of goddesses known as Asynjur. Eir was a youthful goddess of healing, and she is also called one of the maidens of Mengloth, also a healing goddess, who was perhaps better known as Frigg (q.v.).

Eirene. See IRENE.

Eisai. Japanese Buddhist monk (1141–1215), who went to China and brought home the doctrine of Zen (q.v.).

Ekayāna. (Sanskrit) 'one way', vehicle or career. A term of Mahāyāna Buddhism, declared in the *Lotus Sūtra* (q.v.) to be the way of salvation for all, but implying that the Mahāyāna, 'great vehicle', is superior to the Hīnayāna, 'small vehicle'. See YĀNA.

Ek Chuah. Black scorpion-tailed god of the Maya of central America. He was a patron of merchants and cocoa-planters in one aspect and in another aspect he was god of war. At his festival a dog with cocoa-coloured markings was sacrificed and participants were not allowed to get drunk, as they often did at other Maya festivals.

El. Name of the great God, head of the pantheon, among the Canaanites and Phoenicians. El was the master of the gods, the king, 'creator of creation', and also wise and a judge. In the *Ras Shamra* texts of Ugarit everything comes from the orders of El, given to the gods but communicated to men in dreams. He was called 'bull', but also 'kindly bull'. When Ikhnaton of Egypt exalted his god Aton (q.v.) as supreme throughout his empire, the Phoenician priests said that Aton was the same as El and that El ruled over Egypt and Crete. The names 'El' and 'Elohim' were used in the Bible, and in Islam Ilāh and Allāh are related to the same root. The consort of El was Elat, or Asherah, and among the Phoenicians in Carthage he became Baal Hammon and Elat was Tanit. (See also CARTHAGE and PHOENICIANS.)

Eleatics. A Greek philosophical school, said to have been founded at Elea about 540 B.C., by Xenophanes (q.v.). Its special tenet was Monism (q.v.), and this was expounded by Parmenides who denied plurality and change, and by Zeno of Elea.

Electra. One of the Pleiades in Greek mythology. A more historical, but legendary, Electra was daughter of Agamemnon and Clytemnestra. According to the dramatists Aeschylus and Sophocles she hated her mother, and Euripides makes her kill her and then go demented with remorse. Some modern psychologists see in this 'Electra complex' a parallel to the theory about Oedipus (q.v.) and the origins of religion. See FREUD.

Eleusis. One of the most ancient and largest towns of Attica where the Mysteries (q.v.) were celebrated for over a thousand years. The sanctuary was principally of the goddesses Demeter (q.v.) and Koré or Persephone, who were basically connected with agriculture. Although Eleusis attracted pilgrims from all over Greece and there were great processions, the details of the rituals are unknown, yet the visit of Persephone to the underworld and her return were clearly central. There were Little Eleusinia celebrations in the early spring and Great Eleusinia in the autumn and at the latter times Greeks from many parts were initiated. The cult remained popular during Roman times and was finally prohibited by Theodosius II in the fifth century A.D. See HIEROPHANTES.

Elf. A word that perhaps meant a 'spirit' (Norse *alfar*) in Scandinavian religion. In the *Edda* (q.v.) elves are mentioned along with gods and dwarfs. Snorri's *Edda* speaks of the Light-elves, fairer than the sun, whose home was Alfheim, and Dark-Elves who were black and lived in the earth. It is not sure whether any of the elves were worshipped, and in some instances they seem to be the same as or akin to the souls of the dead. In Iceland the Alfar or Huldu, the hidden people' were also called 'darlings', and were said to dwell in rocks and hills. Sometimes they were friendly to men, and sometimes hostile, like fairies.

Elias. See ILYĀS.

Elkesaites. A Jewish-Christian sect, which has sometimes been taken as the Sabaeans (q.v.) referred to in the *Qur'ān*. The original Elkesaites are said, from references in the writings of the church fathers Hippolytus and Epiphanius, to have believed in a revelation given to Elkesai, 'holy power', by a gigantic angel. This was contained in the *Book of Elkesai*, which taught strict observance of the law, rejection of the writings of Paul, and taught a Docetic or 'appearance' doctrine of Christ.

Ellora, Elura. A group of Cave Temples in western India. There are twelve Buddhist, seventeen Hindu, and five Jain Cave Temples here, and they are different from those of Ajanta (q.v.) in being cut into a sloping hill rather than a cliff. One of the finest is the Kailāsa temple, dated in the eighth century A.D., and carved out of solid rock as a monolithic shrine. It is dedicated to the god Shiva and the temple tower, thirty metres high, stands for Mount Kailāsa in the Himalayas where Shiva dwelt. Sculptures also show his wife Pārvatī and the demon Rāvana. The Buddhist shrines have standing and seated Buddha figures and other carved characters, while the Jain caves figure their principal Jinas (q.v.). One Jain temple, the Indra Sabha, is also a monolith cut out of solid rock.

Elysium, Elysian Fields. In Homer and Hesiod Elysium was the name of the Isles of the Blessed, to which special heroes were taken by the gods without dying. There was no rain, storm or snow there, but sweet western breezes blew always from the ocean. The idea of Elysium may have come from Minoan religion, but the later Greeks who thought the dead survived underground transferred Elysium to those nether regions. In ancient Egypt the Fields of Peace of the afterworld were later called Elysian Fields, and they included a Field of Reeds and a Field of Offerings. A vignette in the *Book of the Dead* (q.v.) shows these fields, surrounded and cut by streams, with the dead ploughing, reaping and threshing. See AVALON.

Emanation. A flowing forth, or issue from, usually, the Divine Being. In general it is similar to pantheism, in the doctrine that all things have come from, and are identical with, absolute Being or Reality. In Hinduism the doctrine of the Pancharātras teaches four emanations or manifestations (*vyūha*) of the Supreme Being Vāsudeva or Vishnu. These are similar to Avatars (q.v.), creating and maintaining the world, protecting all beings, and helping those who seek salvation.

Emer. In Celtic mythology, daughter of Forgall and wife of Cúchulainn (q.v.). When the latter fell in love with Emer, Forgall sent him on a journey, thinking that he would not survive the perils of the way. On his return, however, Cúchulainn slew Forgall and married Emer.

Emir. The Arabic *amīr* is a leader or nobleman, and in religious usage it indicates 'the commander of the faithful', Amīr al-Mu'minīn. The title was first used by 'Umar, the second Caliph of Islam, and for centuries was only adopted by leaders of the principal caliphates, but after the fall of Baghdad to the Mongols in 1258 many smaller rulers took the title. It was used in North and West Africa and Spain and is still borne by the king of Morocco.

Endogamy. 'Marriage within' a restricted group, a common practice in many parts of the world in order to maintain family or racial purity, as opposed to Exogamy (q.v.). It is one of the principles upon which the Indian Caste system (q.v.) is founded, and all the principal castes are endogamous. However, some subcastes are not so and people may intermarry with others of a subcaste within the same major caste. There are some subcastes, however, which have such strict taboos against exogamy that marriage is restricted to a very few families.

Engi-Shiki. The 'Institutes of the Engi Period' of Japanese history (901–923 A.D.). This is a collection of fifty volumes of Japanese government regulations which were promulgated in 967. The first ten books are valuable for the detail that they give of Shinto ritual, and they list over three thousand gods worshipped in some two thousand temples. Any Shinto temple mentioned in the list is proud of its tradition. Very little of the *Engi-Shiki* has been translated into any European language.

Enki. Third of the first triad of Babylonian gods, and in the later texts called Ea (q.v.).

Enkidu. In Babylonian mythology Enkidu was a wild man who was created by the gods to reduce the pride of King Gilgamesh (q.v.). Enkidu first lived with animals and ate grass, but Gilgamesh sent

ENKIDU

a prostitute to ensnare him, so that when Enkidu returned to the animals they fled from him. After a great fight with Gilgamesh the two heroes became friends and together fought the Bull of Heaven which had been created to destroy Gilgamesh. For this the gods killed Enkidu and the seventh tablet in the *Epic of Gilgamesh* described how Enkidu went to the House of Darkness, on the road from which there is no return, where the dead dwell in darkness and are clothed like birds. Later the spirit of Enkidu gave information to Gilgamesh about the state of the afterworld.

Enlightenment. See HASKALAH.

Enlil. The second great god of Babylonia, with Anu and Ea. Enlil or Ellil means 'storm god' in Sumerian, and in mythology he was chiefly responsible for bringing about the Flood and was angry when one man escaped. Yet he was creator and helper of men and his favour is suggested by the personal names that were compounded with Enlil. He guarded the 'tablets of destiny' (q.v.) giving him power over everything. An early myth tells how a storm-bird, Zu, stole these tablets from Enlil and how he got them back again. His chief temple, the 'house of the mountain' was at Nippur, though he was worshipped in other cities and had gods attendant upon him, notably the fire-god Nusku (q.v.). Among the constellations Enlil was symbolized by the Pleiades.

Ennead. (Greek) 'nine', applied to a set of nine. It is used of collections of nine books in the philosophical works of Plotinus (q.v.). In Egyptian religion the term is applied to groups in which the theologians of Heliopolis arranged the principal gods. The Great Ennead comprised Atum the creator, Shu the god of air, Tefnut the goddess of moisture, Geb the god of earth, Nut the goddess of the sky, the male Osiris and female Isis, the male Seth and female Nephthys. There was a Little Ennead whose members are not fully known, but included Horus, Anubis, Thoth and Maat. Atum (q.v.) was probably the chief of the Great Ennead but he was replaced by Rē', or combined with him as Atum-Rē'. See OGDOAD and CONSENTES DI.

En Sof. The 'endless', without limit or definition, a Kabbalistic (q.v.) term for God or the Absolute. Expounded from the twelfth century by Isaac the Blind, and Azriel ben Menachem, the doctrine of En Sof was particularly developed in the Zohar (q.v.). God is both hidden and the All, projecting light from his infinite self. There are ten channels of light, Sefiroth ('countings'), the first coming directly from En Sof and the others from each other down to the creation of the world. The last is called Shekhinah ('indwelling') which manifests God in individuals and communities. Owing to sin the Shekhinah is in exile, and to achieve its reunion with En Sof is the aim of communion with God in religion and life.

Enuma Elish. 'When on high', the Akkadian name of the *Epic of Creation*, taken from its opening words, 'when on high heaven had not been named, and firm ground below had not been called by name'. It consists of seven tablets, and was recited on the fourth day of the New Year festival. The struggle between order and chaos was a great drama to the ancient Mesopotamians and it was renewed at the turn of every new year, hence the importance of chanting the epic which told of the coming of order out of the watery chaos.

Eos. The Greek goddess of dawn, the Ushas of India, and Aurora of Rome. Eos was daughter of Hyperion, who was also father of the sun, and she drove across the sky in a chariot drawn by two horses called Shining and Bright. Homer called her 'rosy-fingered' and 'saffron-robed', referring to the colour of the sky at dawn, but she was less important than the sun in his car with four horses. She was said to be very amorous, kidnapping handsome men to live with them, and Aphrodite was jealous of her love for Ares. She is a popular figure in ancient and modern art. See ORION.

Epictetus. A Stoic philosopher, A.D. 55–135. Born in Asia Minor he was a slave in Rome but held high office and was later freed. He studied philosophy and was banished to Greece in 89 where he taught many distinguished people till his death. His lectures were published and later influenced Marcus Aurelius. Epictetus taught the crowd as well as scholars, and said that men should be self-reliant, indifferent to pain, bereavement and even death. Yet he believed in the Divine Providence that is manifested in the unity and order of the world and is always good.

Epicurus. An Athenian philosopher, 342–270 B.C. He studied Platonic and Democritean philosophy, and founded his own school, to which women were admitted, for the first time in such an academy. He lived most of his life in retirement in Athens, and was highly honoured by his followers. Most of the works of Epicurus are lost. Like Democritus (q.v.) he taught that atoms are the basic element of all objects, and the world, including men and gods, is due to the atoms and their movement. Epicurus recognized that 'pleasure' (Hédoné, whence Hedonism) is the highest aim, but he understood this in a negative way as meaning freedom from pain, and he advised men to avoid public life, marriage and children. The later notion of an Epicurean as seeking physical pleasure was far from the simple and pure existence of the philosopher.

Epimetheus. (Greek) 'after thinker', the simple brother of Prometheus the 'fore thinker'. He married Pandora, in spite of warnings from Prometheus, and she released the evils from her store jar which brought woe to mankind. See PROMETHEUS and PANDORA.

Erato. One of the nine Muses (q.v.) in Greek mythology, that of lyric poetry.

Erechtheus. Legendary king of Athens, son of Earth and brought up by Athena. Both Athena and Erechtheus may have been worshipped in an earlier form of the Erechtheum on the Acropolis (q.v.), which was perhaps a royal palace.

Ereshkigal. 'Lady of the Kigallu', the great earth, in ancient Mesopotamia, also known as Ninkigal and Allatum, and ruler of the underworld. She was vanquished by the god Nergal (q.v.), who dragged Ereshkigal from her throne by the hair until he could share her rule over the earth and underworld.

Erinyes. Greek spirits of punishment, who avenged particularly wrongs done within the family. They may originally have been thought of as the ghosts of persons who had been wronged or killed, or they may have been the personification of curses in mysterious powers which these words set in action. They were connected with the Earth, and Demeter (q.v.) was regarded as associated with the powers of vengeance of the Erinyes. Sometimes they are milder and, like the Earth, give fertility to crops and human beings, being confused or identified with the Eumenides (q.v.).

Eros. The Greek god of love, though in Homer the word Eros is used of passionate desire rather than a personified deity. Hesiod connects him with Aphrodite and makes Eros one of the oldest gods. The poets sang of the tricks which he played on mortals, and Euripides was the first to mention his bow and arrows. Eros was the god of male as well as female beauty and his images were in the gymnasia. Along with Aphrodite he had a cult on the north slopes of the Acropolis in Athens where phallic symbols have been found. Eros is a god of fertility, but images represent him as young, a boy or even a child. In Rome he was identified with Cupid (q.v.).

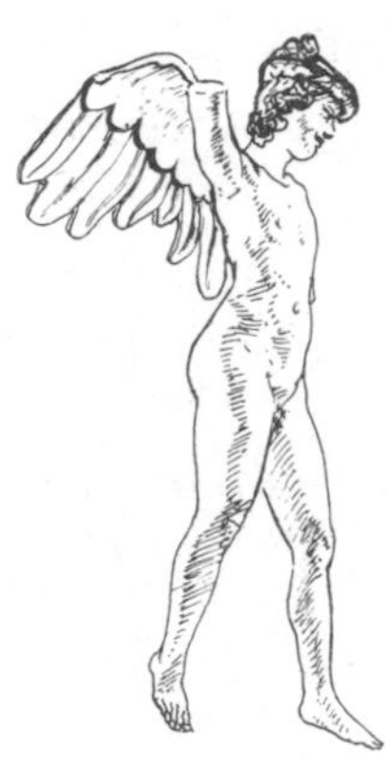

Erymanthian Boar. The fourth labour of Heracles was to kill an enormous boar which lived on Mount Erymanthus. He bound it with chains and carried it on his shoulders to Mycenae. It is not known who killed the boar, but its tusks were said to be in the temple of Apollo at Cumae (q.v.).

Eschatology. Doctrines of the 'last things' are found in most religions. Jewish and Christian ideas may have been influenced by Zoroastrianism, which held that the eschatological drama would be inaugurated by Saoshyans, a posthumous son of Zoroaster. The evil spirit Ahriman (q.v.) would be destroyed or made powerless, the dead would rise again and all creation would be renewed and made immortal. Hindu belief looks to the coming of Kalki, the tenth Avatar of Vishnu. Kalki will appear at the end of the present Iron Age, riding a white horse, bearing a flaming sword, destroying the wicked, renewing the good, and restoring purity to the world. Buddhism looks to the Buddha-to-come, Maitreya. Goodness will decline, poverty, enmity and warfare will abound, the law will be neglected and holy places abandoned. Then will arise a righteous king and the fully awakened Buddha Maitreya, who will know all things, and proclaim the Truth in its purity, for the renewal of all things. For Islam, see MAHDĪ.

Etruscans. The inhabitants of Etruria, modern Tuscany, mingled with the Romans from the fifth century B.C. and undoubtedly influenced Roman religion, but it is not easy to gain a clear picture of Etruscan religion. Etruscan documents are largely unintelligible, and references in Roman and Greek authors are derivatory and fragmentary. Etruscan myths include their own along with Roman and Greek gods, among the most important being Juno, Minerva, Mars, Neptune, Silvanus and Janus. Other gods were related to cities, families, and spheres of life. Their temples, statues and priestly dress all influenced the Romans. The Etruscans paid great attention to the dead, built house-like tombs for them, and held funeral games in their honour. The Romans paid great attention to Etruscan prophecy and divination, though this formed only a part of their religion. Some of their mythology and rituals of agriculture may go back beyond Greek to oriental influences. See HARUSPICES and DI NOVENSILES.

Euhemerus. A Greek writer of Messene, fourth century B.C., who in a travel novel, *Sacred Scripture*, claimed to have visited an island in the Indian Ocean. Here he saw a golden column on which were written the deeds of the gods Ouranos, Kronos and Zeus, and he claimed that this proved the gods to have been once men. This theory that the gods were really deified heroes was later popularized in Latin, and Christian writers used it to show the real nature of the Greek gods. In modern times 'euhemeristic' theory has again been revived to support the view that the gods were originally heroes, or even that all religion derived from ancestor worship, a theory now generally discredited.

Eumenides. The 'well-disposed', or gracious goddesses in Greek religion. They were earth deities and kindly to men in sending fertility. The Erinyes (q.v.) were identified with them when viewed, or wished for, under a kindlier aspect than that of punishment. See AESCHYLUS.

Euphrosyne. (Greek) 'merriment', one of the three Graces (q.v.).

Euripides. Greek dramatist (485–406 B.C.), who was strongly critical of the gods and myths of traditional Greek religion and, in using old stories, altered and added to them. His play *Oedipus* is lost, but in *Orestes* he attributes the murder of her mother to Electra (q.v.), which has been thought significant to theories of religious origins by some modern writers. See FREUD.

Europa. In Greek mythology daughter of the king of Tyre, Agenor. She was loved by Zeus who turned himself into a bull (or sent a bull) and, when Europa had climbed on its back, she was borne over the sea to Crete. There she bore Zeus children, including Minos (q.v.). Europa

was worshipped as a goddess or identified with a Cretan goddess. She is depicted riding the bull in the mosaic at Lullingstone in Kent.

The name Europé was given originally to central Greece, and later to the whole mainland and the land behind it, the frontier with Asia being fixed at the river Don.

Euryale. (Greek) 'wide-leaping', one of the three Gorgons (q.v.) in Greek mythology.

Eurydice. (Greek) 'wide-judging', princess, the name of many characters in mythology. The best known was the wife of Orpheus, who died of a snakebite, and was pursued by her husband to the underworld. See ORPHEUS.

Euterpe. In Greek mythology one of the nine Muses (q.v.), that of flutes.

Exogamy. A social rule which prohibits marriage within a specified group (see ENDOGAMY). It is worldwide and may be illustrated by the Table of Affinity in the *Book of Common Prayer*. Exogamy is one of the principles underlying the Indian Caste system. The social group within which marriage is prohibited is generally a clan, with blood-relationship and links with a common ancestor. The closest relationships of prohibited unions are those of parents and children, and brothers and sisters, but marriage of cousins is often forbidden. Marriage may be taboo between people of common descent, but the rules are complicated according to whether descent is counted through the father's (patrilineal) or the mother's side (matrilineal). See TOTEM.

F

Fa. See Ifa.

Fafnir. Son of Hreidmar in Scandinavian mythology and brother of Regin. The sons killed Hreidmar to gain his treasure and then Fafnir turned himself into a dragon and refused to share the gold. Regin went to get help from Sigurd the Volsung (q.v.) and helped him kill Fafnir by stabbing it from a pit. The dragon's blood splashed all over Sigurd and made him invincible except for one spot which the blood missed. When the dragon's blood touched Sigurd's tongue, it enabled him to understand the language of birds. Regin plotted Sigurd's death; but Sigurd was warned by two birds so he cut off Regin's head and rode away with the treasure.

Fa Hsiang. The 'Mere Ideation' school of Chinese Buddhism, also known as Wei Shih. It was based upon the teachings of Asanga (q.v.) and Vasubandhu, of the fourth century A.D., who taught that mind is the only reality, the external world being the product of our ideas. See also Hsüan-tsang.

Fa-hsien. A Chinese Buddhist monk who visited India in the fourth century A.D., during the reign of Chandra Gupta II, and gave valuable descriptions of religious conditions there. He provided information about temples and monasteries, and noted the peacefulness of society and the fact that many people were vegetarians. He found that Buddhism was flourishing in India, but that Hindu theism was strong and widespread. Fa-hsien collected Buddhist manuscripts and relics which he took back to China. He repeats many Buddhist legends, but says little of social conditions and never mentions the emperor Chandra Gupta himself.

Fairy. See Elf.

Fakir, Faqīr. A needy man, either physically or spiritually, in Arabic. Hence the term is used of those who need God and in Arabic-speaking lands it is used for a mendicant dervish (q.v.). In India the term has been loosely applied to ascetics (sannyāsis) and Yogis.

Falāshas. Groups of people, descended from Jews, who are called Falāshas or Esrā'ēl in Ethiopia where they live. They came from Jews from Egypt and Arabia, some of whom had migrated to Ethiopia before the Christian era. They number now about sixty or seventy thousand. Falāsha places of worship are called 'mosques' (masjid) and there sacrifices are performed, unique in Judaism. They also have monasteries. They practise circumcision and observe Passover, Harvest, Tabernacles, the Day of the Covenant and Abraham's Day. The Falāshas have no knowledge of Hebrew, but their priests use the *Old Testament* and *Apocrypha* in the Ethiopian liturgical language, Ge'ez. Most of them are agriculturalists and others practise metalwork and pottery.

Fanā'. A technical term in Islamic mysticism, from the Arabic for 'passing away' or 'annihilation'. The origin of the term may be in Christian mystical notions of the annihilation of the will before God. Early Islamic writers speak of Fanā' as seeing only God, annihilating human attributes, and obliterating consciousness when the vision of God is attained. However, orthodox writers maintained that Fanā' was not cessation of the self, as in Buddhist Nirvāna, but continuation of the self in God. The word *Fanā'* is often used interchangeably with *Safā'*, meaning 'purity', and indicates that the mystic should be free and pure from attachment to creaturely things. See Tawhīd, Ittihād and Junaid.

al-Fārābī. An Islamic philosopher (875–950) who was called 'the second teacher', after Aristotle. He was born in Turkestan, but studied Greek philosophy and science in Baghdad, where he lived an ascetic life. Al-Fārābī based his philosophy on the Aristotelian belief in a First Being or Absolute, whom he identified with the God of the *Qur'ān*. From God all existing things emanated in the order of a hierarchy, just as in a state all authority emanates from the head. The ideal state, according to al-Fārābī, would have a prophet at its head, and he would be followed by a second head rather like an 'imām' in the belief of Shī'a Muslims, which made his teaching attractive to them.

Fard. An Arabic word meaning 'duty' or obligation, which will be rewarded and the omission of which merits punishment. Islamic law has distinguished between Fard which is binding on everyone, and that which applies only to a sufficient number, such as the attendance of ten for prayer in a mosque, or adequate supplies of soldiers for a holy war.

Farīd, Shaikh. Muslim mystic of ancient India (1173–1265), whose teachings were appreciated in other religions.

He left 134 hymns in the Punjabi language, which were incorporated into the sacred book of the Sikhs, the ĀDI GRANTH (q.v.).

Farīd al-Dīn. See 'ATTĀR.

Fasti, Nefasti. Dies Fasti in the Roman calendar were marked F, 'days of speaking' (*Fas* or *Fastus*), meaning that courts were open and the days were not festivals. The Nefasti were days, such as Dies Religiosi, when legal business might not be performed except by an expiatory sacrifice.

Fasting. Abstention from food and drink on special occasions is practised in many religions. In Judaism total fasting is observed on the Day of Atonement (q.v.), from sunset to sunset. There are minor fasts, such as Ab (q.v.). In Islam the whole of the ninth month, Ramadān (q.v.), is a time when no food or drink may be taken during the hours of daylight, though eating is done at night. The Zoroastrians, however, deprecated fasting. Devout Hindus may fast on the eleventh day of the month, and in fulfilment of vows or performance of special ceremonies. Jain monks practise many fasts, some starving themselves to death following the example of their great teacher Pārshva (q.v.). The Buddha fasted rigorously during his search for enlightenment, but abandoned it as unprofitable. Buddhist monks hold a fast day (Uposatha) every fortnight, when monastic rules are recited, and laymen are encouraged to observe it. See ABSTINENCE.

Fate. From the Latin *fatum*, 'decreed', comes the notion of necessity or predestination. In ancient Greece the word *Moira* was used of the human lot and personified as Fate. In Hesiod the Moirai (or Klothes, Spinners) were three goddesses: Lachesis assigned the lot, Clotho spun the thread of life, and Atropos cut it off. Plato spoke of Ananke, Necessity, as their mother. In the myth at the end of the *Republic* Plato described the three Fates allotting the destiny of those about to be born. In Latin poetry three goddesses, Parcae, were identified with the Moirai. For Norse Fate, see NORN. In Islam the Turkish word *Kismet*, from Arabic *Qisma*, is used for lot or fate, but it is better to speak of Predestination. In Hinduism the word *Karma* (*Kamma* in Pāli) means 'deeds' and their result in a destiny in a future life (see KARMA). See also GOSĀLA and NIYATI.

Fātiha. The first chapter or sūra of the *Qur'ān*, meaning 'the opener'. It is a short ascription of praise and prayer, and forms part of each of the five daily acts of prayer of all Muslims, whence it has been compared with the Lord's Prayer in Christian usage. It is always recited in Arabic, and is used on many other occasions. Muslims regard the Fātiha as containing the essence of their doctrine. It is difficult to date, and it contains epithets of Allāh ('the merciful, the compassionate',) for the first time, but it probably belongs to an early period in the ministry of Muhammad, perhaps about A.D. 613. See DU'Ā'.

Fātima. The daughter of Muhammad and his first wife Khadīja, she was born at Mecca about A.D. 605 and died at Medina in 633. Fātima married 'Alī, cousin of the Prophet, and bore his sons Hasan and Husain, all these three men are prominent in Shī'a faith. There are few sure historical details of the life of Fātima, but tradition reports hostility between her and Ayesha (q.v.), the youngest wife of Muhammad. The early Shī'a were divided between supporters of the Fātimid line and those who supported the non-Fātimid descendants of 'Alī. Later legend enhanced Fātima's position; she was said to have been born miraculously and to be the embodiment of perfect womanhood. Fātima's hand was a common symbol in Islamic painting.

Fātimids. Islamic dynasty in North Africa, Egypt and Syria (909–1171). They claimed descent from Fātima, daughter of Muhammad and wife of the fourth caliph 'Alī (qq.v.), but their enemies denied this. The Fātimids were followers of Shī'a (q.v.) doctrine, which taught the primacy of 'Alī as Caliph and Imām. They built a new capital in Egypt, Cairo (al-Qāhira, 'the Victorious') and the mosque-college of al-Azhar (qq.v.). The Fātimids had peaceful relationships with Christian Byzantium, and even with the Crusaders at first, till they lost Ascalon to them. The Fātimid kingdom was crumbling internally when Saladin (q.v.) overthrew it, to restore Sunni Islam and fight successfully against the Crusaders.

Fa-Tsang. Chinese Buddhist monk (643–712), one of the early teachers of the Garland School. See Hua Yen.

Fatua, Fatuus. Titles of identifications of the Roman gods Fauna and Faunus (see Fauns).

Fatwā. A formal legal opinion among Muslims, given by a canon lawyer or Muftī, in answer to a question from a judge or a private person, and based on canonical texts and precedents. A case of law or behaviour may be decided on the authority of this Fatwā. Under modern conditions in the Islamic world, where times have brought many changes, the Fatwā advice applies chiefly to marriage, divorce and inheritance. Some Muslim states have favoured one of the four legal schools (see Fiqh) and only the Fatwās of that school have been admitted.

Fauns. Latin rural divinities, like Greek Satyrs (q.v.), often provided with horns and tails. The god Faunus was identified with the Greek Pan. His name came from *favere*, 'kindly one', a pleasant designation which hid his mysterious and sometimes fearful side. He was chiefly a spirit of the forests, and was identified with mysterious sounds that are heard there and also with Incubo, a spirit of nightmares. Faunus had female associates in Fauna and Fatua, and occasionally gave oracles. See Lupercalia.

Feast of Weeks. See Pentecost.

Feathered Serpent. In Mexican religion, perhaps a hieroglyph for the god Quetzalcoatl (q.v.), though it may be

a symbol of the earth swallowing the planet Venus.

Februum. A Roman term for objects used in rituals of purification. In the Lupercalia (q.v.) festival on 15 February, two youths wore strips of goat's hide which were called Februa, and February was the month of purification, an idea perpetuated in the Christian feast of the Purification on 2 February.

Felicitas. (Latin) 'fortune', luck, personified as a goddess from the second century B.C. She became important in the Roman empire with the figure of the goddess often appearing on coins.

Fêng Shui. 'Wind-water' in Chinese, a term used for geomancy, the art of selecting fortunate sites for buildings and graves. It is said to have been founded by Kuo P'o, a Taoist sage of the fourth century B.C., but it includes ancient ideas: of the Yin and Yang (q.v.), of the elements, and Taoist views on hygiene. Fêng Shui was based on the notion that man must be in harmony with the universe, with natural forces, and so with wind and water. The geomantist would look for a site that sloped to the south, with a hill on the east, so that Spring might prevail against Autumn and Yang dominate Yin. There should be no higher erections nearby, and telegraph poles that went against Fêng Shui were a cause of the Boxer Rebellion. Much of this has declined nowadays, but the idea was dominant till the nineteenth century.

Fenrir, Fenris. The fiercest of all wolves in Scandinavian mythology, child of the mischievous Loki and the giantess Angrboda, and brother of the World Snake and Hel the goddess of death. The

gods brought Fenrir home when he was small but, as he grew, it was decided to chain him. He broke all the fetters till he offered to hold one of the gods' hands in his mouth while he was being bound. The war god Tyr (Tyw) volunteered and Fenrir was bound but Tyr's hand was bitten off. At the Doom of the gods Fenrir devoured the great god Odin who was avenged by his son Vidar stabbing Fenrir to the heart.

Fensalir. 'Sea halls', in Scandinavian mythology, the abode of the great goddess Frigg (q.v.).

Feralia. In ancient Roman religion the last of the Parentalia (q.v.), days when offerings and prayers were made for the dead. It was on 21 February.

Fetiales. Roman priests who conducted treaties between states. There were twenty of them in a Collegium (q.v.). On making a treaty one of the Fetiales carried herbs, and another killed a pig and uttered a curse on Rome if she broke the treaty. If another state had offended Rome, a Fetialis crossed the border with his head veiled, and called on Jupiter and the boundaries to witness. This was repeated several times and, if satisfaction was not given, the Fetialis cast a spear across the border in the presence of witnesses and formally declared war. The Fetialies were chief of the Sodales (q.v.).

Fetish. Portuguese traders to West Africa in the sixteenth century applied their word *feitiço* to the images and magical charms which they saw there. It was derived from the Latin *factitius*, meaning a thing made by art, and was used of the talismans worn by the Portuguese themselves. Later writers came to apply it to all African religion or to the worship of 'stocks and stones'. The term was unsatisfactory for description of African worship, which included a Supreme God and reverence of ancestors, and attempts were made to restrict the use of Fetish to magical charms, and call the rest of the religion Animism (q.v.) or Polytheism. But such magical charms are not peculiar to Africa, being worldwide, and Fetish is now no longer used by serious writers, though it lingers in popular speech. See IMAGE and MASK.

Fides. (Latin) 'faith', trust, personified as the goddess of good faith, and having an ancient cult. In sacrifices to Fides the priest had his hands covered with white cloth. The symbol of the goddess was a pair of covered hands, perhaps connected with shaking hands in sign of agreement.

Fields of the Blessed. See ELYSIUM and AMITĀBHA.

Filial Piety. See HSIAO, MAKOTO and ANCESTOR WORSHIP.

Fingal. See FIONN. Fingal's Cave is a vast cavern in the island of Staffa, described by Sir Walter Scott and others. The title *Fingal's Cave*, or *The Hebrides*, was given to an overture by Mendelssohn.

Fionn, Finn. Mythical hero of Ireland and western Scotland, with his followers the Feinne or Fians. He was son of Cumal or Camulos (q.v.) and father of Ossian (q.v., Oisin). He gained supernatural knowledge from salmon, and fought many giants and even gods. He was betrothed to Grainne, who eloped with Diarmaid (qq.v.) whom he caught and caused to die. Fionn and his followers were killed in fight, and later it was said that St Patrick interceded for him in hell. In Macpherson's *Fingal* (see OSSIAN), Fionn, called Fingal, is son of the giant Comhal, and King of Morven, which makes him a Scot who crossed to Ireland to help Cuthullin (Cúchulainn, q.v.). This was romancing and mingling of stories.

Fiqh. 'Intelligence' or 'knowledge' in Arabic, the name given to Islamic law covering all aspects of public and private life, political and religious. It is jurisprudence or the science of law in general. Fiqh has developed in four directions in orthodox Sunni Islam, differing in small details, from founders who have given their names to the four schools of law. The Hanafī is followed in central Asia and India; the Shāfi'ī in lower Egypt, Syria, South Arabia, East Africa and Indonesia; the Mālikī in upper Egypt, North and West Africa; and the Hanbalī in Arabia. See also SHARĪ'A.

Firdaws. Arabic word from Greek *Paradeisos*, 'Paradise', and used in the sense of a walled garden. In the *Qur'ān* it is used twice in the sense of Garden of Eden. See JANNA.

Fire. Fire is sacred in many cultures, because the discovery of fire was a great step forward in the progress of mankind. Those who tend the fire, such as blacksmiths, are often priests. In Greek mythology Prometheus stole fire from Zeus to give it to men. In Zoroastrianism fire, Ātar (q.v.), was the centre of the cult and has remained the focal point of worship in Parsi Fire Temples (q.v.).

In ancient India the fire god Agni (q.v.) was one of the most popular deities in the hymns of the *Rig Veda*, both as messenger of sacrifice to all the gods and as a deity in his own right. In China the Kitchen God (q.v.) was one of the most popular, and his picture was found at every hearth. Fire was located both in the home and in temples or places of public worship, and in communal rituals could be tended by priests who kept it ever burning. It came to be regarded as an apt symbol of the power and intangibility of the divine. See the Mexican fire god XIUHTECUHTLI. See also HERACLITUS.

Fire Temples. Ātash Behrām, the 'Fire Temples' of the Parsis, also called Dar-i-Meher, 'Door of Mithra'. Fire is sacred to the Parsis, as to the ancient Hindus and many other peoples. There

are no images in Parsi temples, but a stone slab stands under a central dome from which hangs a metal tray called the crown of the sacred Fire. The fire burns in a censer on the stone slab, is fed with sweet-smelling sandalwood and is never allowed to go out once the temple has been consecrated with fire from another temple. The sacred fire is the best symbol of the invisible God, Ahura Mazdā (q.v.), and is called his son Ātar (q.v.).

First Fruits. The first produce of the harvest, often cut symbolically by a priest or tribal leader, is generally regarded as sacred to the deity or the ancestors: no human may eat until the First Fruits have been offered. Similarly, the firstborn of flocks and first fish caught in the sea would be offered to the deity, and sometimes the firstborn children of men (see HUMAN SACRIFICE). After the First Fruits had been presented, or a ceremonial eating by a priest had taken place, there would be communal eating and a general harvest festival. Many temples drew much of their revenue from the offering of first fruits at different times in the agricultural and pastoral year. See PASSOVER and THARGELIA.

Fish Avatar. See MATSYA.

Five Agents, Forces. See WU HSING.

Five Pillars. See PILLARS OF ISLAM.

Five Precepts. See SHĪLA.

Flamens, Flamines. The Latin word *flamen* probably meant a priest or sacrificer. In Rome the Flamens were fifteen priests, three major and twelve minor, who formed part of the college of pontiffs. Each Flamen was assigned to a special god, though he might worship others on occasion. The three major ones

were the Flamen Dialis, priest of Jupiter, the Flamen Martialis of Mars, and the Flamen Quirinalis of Quirinus. These priests were surrounded with many taboos to preserve their sanctity from pollution, were not allowed to touch corpses or unclean things, and had a place in the Senate. The major Flamens wore white caps and woollen togas, and carried knives and rods when going to the altars. The minor Flamens were also attached to gods and temples in Rome and the provinces.

Flood, Deluge. The ancient Sumerian form of the Flood myth is preserved only in fragments of tablets but tells of the decision of the gods to destroy mankind. A pious king, Ziusudra, was warned and built a huge boat which was tossed on the waters for seven days. When light came forth, he opened a window of the boat, later offering an ox and a sheep, while the gods Anu and Enlil sent breath, and vegetation grew from the earth. In a Babylonian epic the god Ea revealed to Ut-napishtim (q.v.) the intention of Enlil to destroy mankind, whereupon he built a boat and escaped the flood. An

Indian story, in the epic *Mahābhārata*, told how an early man, Manu, cared for a fish and at the dissolution of the world the fish told Manu to make a ship and take seven sages, and different seeds from the earth, then it towed the ark to the peaks of the Himalayas. The fish told Manu that it was the Lord of Creatures, Prajāpati, and later it was identified with one of the Avatars (q.v.) of the great god Vishnu. See DEUCALION.

Flora. Italian goddess of flowers and blossoming plants. There was a Flamen Floralis (see FLAMEN) in Rome which shows that her cult was ancient, but her festival was probably moveable until in the third century B.C. it was fixed on 28 April and games were celebrated annually on that date. The games included farces, some of which were immoral, and may have been affected by Greek influence from the cult of Aphrodite (q.v.).

Folkvangr. In Scandinavian mythology the 'field of the folk', the celestial mansion of the beautiful goddess Freyja (q.v.).

Fomorians, Fomhoire. Deities of the pre-Celtic people, regarded as evil spirits by the Irish annalists. They were perhaps gods of fertility. One of them was Bres, a king who was captured in battle but set free when he promised to tell the men of Erin how to plough, sow and reap. This suggests his fertility character. Another was Balor, who seems to have personified the evil eye, for nobody could resist his evil gaze. The Celts derived the name Fomorian from *muir*, the 'sea', and regarded them as demons of the sea or pirates, who were defeated by the more beneficent prehistoric deities, the Tuatha Dé Danann (q.v.).

Fordicia. Roman festival of the earth goddess, Tellus (q.v.), celebrated on 15 April when a *forda*, a cow in calf, was sacrificed to Tellus.

Forseti, Fosite. Minor Scandinavian deity, son of Balder and Nanna (qq.v.). He may have had a grove in eastern Norway whose memory is preserved in the name Forsetalundr.

Fortuna, Fors. An Italian goddess of fertility, whose name meant 'the bringer'. She was worshipped by gardeners and by women seeking children; a shrine of hers near Rome could only be used by women in a first marriage. She had no ancient Flamen in Rome and it is said that her cult was introduced there in the sixth

century B.C., but it was older in other parts of Italy. Later Fors Fortuna was identified with the Greek goddess Tyche (q.v.) and adopted her character of good 'fortune'.

Four Noble Truths. The basic teachings or analysis of suffering, as taught by Gautama the Buddha in his first sermon. The first is the Noble Truth of Suffering or Pain (*dukkha* in Pali), that all life is painful. The second is the Noble Truth of the Cause (*samudaya*) of suffering, which is desire or craving (*tanhā*, q.v.). The third is the Noble Truth of the Cessation (*nirodha*) of suffering. And the fourth is the Noble Truth of the Way (*magga*) which leads to cessation of suffering, and that is the Noble Eightfold Path (q.v.).

Four Schools of Islamic Law. See FIQH, and separate articles on HANAFĪ, HANBALĪ, MĀLIKĪ and SHĀFI'Ī. See also ZAIDĪ.

Fratres Arvales. See ARVAL, SODALES and CARMEN.

Fratres Atiedii. See ATIEDII, IGUVINE TABLETS.

Fravashi, Farohar. In developing Zoroastrianism, in the Yasna composed after Zoroaster, appear the Fravashis or immortal human souls. The Fravashi exists before the body, but it is a creature of the supreme God, Ahura Mazdā, and does not exist eternally independently of him as in Indian religions. But all the human race was present in the Fravashis before the Creator, who sustained heaven and earth through them, causing plants to grow and sun and moon to shine by their spiritual power. The final victory over evil would also be accomplished through the help of the Fravashis, so that the souls worked together with God to overcome evil, rather than everything remaining solely in his power.

Frazer, James George. British anthropologist (1854–1941). Prolific writer, in a charming style; his opinions, based on the field work of others, had great influence but are mostly now abandoned. For his *Golden Bough*, see DIANA and VIRBIUS. For other theories, see MAGIC and TOTEM.

Freud, Sigmund. Austrian psychologist (1856–1939) whose theories on the origins of religion (see OEDIPUS and TOTEM) were notorious but are not generally accepted now. See also ELECTRA.

Frey, Freyr. One of the chief Vanir, a major group of Scandinavian gods described in the *Edda* (q.v.). He was son of Njörd and brother of Freyja. Frey ruled the rain and sunshine and was a god of fertility upon whom men called for fruitful seasons. He had a magic ship, Skidbladnir, and a boar called Goldbristles. He was popular in Iceland, Norway and Sweden, and his chief temple was at Uppsala where he was called lord of the Swedes who gave peace and plenty. At the end of the winter his image was drawn on a waggon through the land and his priestess received sacrifices. Fields were sacred to Frey and his name remains in many place-names in Scandinavia. The name *Frey* meant 'lord', as chief of gods, but he had other titles. The wife of Frey was Gerd (q.v.).

Freyja, Freya. Scandinavian deity, goddess of the Vanir, daughter of Njörd and sister of Freyr. Her name meant 'lady' and was simply a title, but she had other names in different localities. She was a goddess of love, a beautiful lady, who lived in a heavenly mansion called Folkvangr, 'Field of the folk.' Like her brother she was concerned with fertility, pigs were sacred to her, and she rode in a chariot drawn by cats. She also wore a feather-dress and was goddess of riches. Freyja was married to Odr or Odin, and devoted to him, but she had other lovers and the giants sought her favours. Little is known of her worship, but many place-names still include her name.

Frigg. Scandinavian goddess, consort of Odin and mother of Balder. Because of her age and importance Friday was named after her. Frigg was a goddess of love and giver of children, though her loose morals are mentioned. On the other hand, she was the weeping mother of Balder, for when she asked all things not to hurt him she omitted the mistletoe because it was too young; when she told the evil Loki (q.v.) he took a mistletoe shoot and had Balder killed. Frigg had a glorious mansion at Fensalir, 'sea halls', and was said to know the fates of men. There is little evidence of her worship, though some place-names in Sweden are claimed to come from her name.

Fuji-san, Fuji-yama. Mount Fuji in Japan, the most sacred mountain of the country, with eight summits round its crater which have been praised and painted innumerable times. It is a place

of popular pilgrimage, with over a hundred thousand persons, in special straw sandals, climbing to the top every year. Fuji-san is believed to be the abode of a goddess, Kono-hana-sakuya-hime, who married Prince Ninigi, son of the supreme sun-goddess Amaterasu (q.v.), and from their descendants the kings of Japan are believed to come. See FUSŌ-KYŌ and JIMMU TENNO.

Fulla. One of the goddesses known as Asynjur (q.v.) in Scandinavian mythology. She was servant of Frigg (q.v.), bearing her sandals and knowing her secrets. Gold was associated with her, called Fulla's fillet since she wore a golden band round her hair.

Fung Shui. See FÊNG SHUI.

Furies, Furiae. Latin version of the Greek Erinyes (q.v.), both in name and character; there is no evidence of an independent cultus.

Furqān. 'Revelation', salvation (Arabic), a word used in the *Qur'ān* of various scriptures. Moses and Aaron received the Furqān (21, 49), but this term is applied to the *Qur'ān* itself, since it is said that God 'sent down the Furqān upon his servant' (25, 1). In the sense of salvation Furqān is referred to the deliverance at the battle of Badr (8, 42).

Fusō-kyō. A Japanese Shinto sect, founded by Shishino Nakaba (d. 1884) as an amalgamation of several groups (*kō*) which worship Mount Fuji. It is a mountain sect whose chief discipline is to climb Mount Fuji, and it worships three great gods listed in the Kojiki traditional history who are believed to dwell on top of the mountain. See FUJI-SAN.

G

Gabars, Ghebers. The remaining Zoroastrians of Persia as distinct from the Parsis of India. The origin of the name Gabar is uncertain, but may come from the Arabic *kāfir*, 'infidel', a title given to them by the Arab conquerors of Persia from the seventh century A.D. After the conquest of Persia by Islam, the Zoroastrian religion was, in theory, to be respected as being monotheistic and non-idolatrous, like Christianity and Judaism. But social and military pressures increased and eventually many Zoroastrians migrated to India where they became Parsis. The Gabars continued the old worship in Fire Temples (q.v.) or private houses, and have much the same customs as the Parsis. Today some of them adopt the name *Parsi*, 'Persian'. Their numbers are very small, about seventeen thousand, and seem to be declining though there has been some help from Indian Parsis (q.v.).

Gabriel. (Hebrew) 'God is mighty', an angel of Jewish tradition. The name occurs in the *Bible* only in *Daniel* (8, 16; 9, 21) and *Luke* (1, 19; 1, 26), but in the *Talmud* Gabriel is one of the four archangels round the throne of God. The others are Michael, Raphael and Uriel, and their names are still in the Hebrew prayer book named before retiring at night, like the apostles in Christian tradition. In the *Talmud* Gabriel acted with Michael as groomsman at Adam's marriage, and was often a messenger from God to the Patriarchs. He is said to have made the mud-bank on which Rome was built. As the angels ruled over the elements, Gabriel was the prince of fire. For Gabriel in Islamic legend, see JIBRĪL.

Gaea, Ge. The 'Earth' in Greek mythology, perhaps originally the vague power of the earth, and later made more personal as a goddess, daughter and wife of Chaos, and both mother and husband of Heaven (Ouranos, Uranus). This represents ancient notions of the marriage of Earth and Heaven, and their separation by their children. Gaea was also said to be mother of the Titans and Cyclopes, and of mountains and seas. Vague cults of the Earth can be traced, though later supplanted by more personal gods. It is said that Gaea was the original deity at Delphi, and here Apollo killed Python, a creature of the earth. Gaea was identified with Themis (q.v.), whose name 'steadfast' was suitable to the Earth.

Galeru, Kaleru. The rainbow serpent of much Australian aboriginal mythology, called Ungud in the northern Kimberley region. It is a huge snake, often depicted in cave paintings, which is held to live in sacred pools which it fills with the spirits of babies, so that it is a fertility spirit. Galeru is closely associated with the Wandjina ancestors (q.v.), who also are concerned with fertility. See also JULUNGGUL.

Ganas, Gana-devatas. (Sanskrit) 'troops' of deities, various classes of secondary Hindu divinities, often said to be in nine groups. Ganesha (q.v.) is Lord of the Ganas, Gana-pati.

Gandhāra. Ancient name for a district of north-west India and eastern Afghanistan, which was once a Buddhist stronghold and has become famous for its art. Gandhāra art blended Persian and Greek styles and, whereas the Buddha figure was not represented in early Buddhism, at Gandhāra the figure was shown in series of illustrations from stories of his life.

Gandharva. In the *Rig Veda* a heavenly being, guardian of the sacred drink Soma, knowing celestial secrets, having power over women, and invoked in marriage ceremonies. Later the Gandharvas are a class, some six thousand or more, with much the same functions. They dwell in Indra's heaven and are singers and musicians for the gods. They are said to have been born from the creator Brahmā and are married to the nymphs Apsaras (q.v.). Their chief is Chitra-ratha and they fight with the Nāga snakes. They appear as graceful figures in sculpture.

Gāndhi, Mohandas Karamchand (1869–1948). Hindu leader, called Mahātmā, 'great soul', or Gāndhiji. Born into the third caste, Vaishya, he studied law in London and went to South Africa to defend Indian rights in Natal and then returned to India to lead the struggle for independence. He died at the hand of an assassin of the extreme Hindu Mahāsabha (q.v.) the year after independence was achieved. Gāndhi's religious ideas reinforced his politics. He was influenced by the non-violence of the Jains, the *Bhagavad-Gītā*, the *Sermon on the Mount*, and Tolstoy. He practised Satyagraha, 'soul-force' in South Africa and India. He sought to raise the lot of the outcastes and untouchables by calling them Harijans, 'God's people', leading them into forbidden temples, and getting them the vote. He practised fasting, against governments and people. He opposed child-marriage and the enforced celibacy of virgin widows. He tried to revive village industries. His bust is found in all Indian towns, garlanded with marigolds, and his grave in Delhi is a place of pilgrimage. Some have called him a modern Avatar.

Ganesha, Ganapati. Lord of the Ganas (q.v.) or inferior deities in Indian religion, son of Shiva and Pārvatī. He is the elephant-headed god, shown as yellow or pink, and very popular as god of wisdom and fortune. In myth Shiva burnt or cut off his son's head in anger and then to please Pārvatī replaced it with an elephant's head. More probably, Ganesha is an ancient forest god, and he rides on or is accompanied by a rat. There are countless temples of Ganesha and wayside shrines where his image is daubed with red. As god of wisdom he is invoked at the beginning of books and any important undertaking.

Gangā, Ganges. The most sacred river of India is said to have come from the toe of Vishnu and was brought from heaven at the prayers of sages. To break the fall of the river from heaven the god Shiva caught it on his head with his matted locks, and so he is called 'upholder of Gangā'. As a goddess the river is daughter of the Himalayas. The Ganges is held to be sacred for the 1,500 kilometres of its length and many temples line its banks, particularly in holy cities such as Benares. Pilgrims trace the course of the river and bathe in its waters to wash away evil. The dead are cremated on its banks and the ashes thrown into the river. Mother Gangā is said to have absolutely pure water and to sanctify all that enter it. See also YAMUNĀ and KUMBHA MELA.

Ganymede. Cup-bearer of Zeus in Greek mythology, he was said to be a son of a Trojan prince who was renowned for his beauty. He was taken away by the wind, and Zeus gave his father a breed of horses or a golden vine in exchange. The pretty figure of Ganymede was a popular theme in art.

Gaon. See GEONIM.

Garland School. See HUA YEN.

Garm. Watch-dog of Hel, in Scandinavian mythology. At the Doom of the gods (see RAGNARŌK), Garm fights the god Tyr and each kills the other.

Garuda. A bird of Hindu mythology, half-man and half-vulture, on which the god Vishnu rides. He is the king of birds and enemy of snakes, and was so bright at birth that the gods worshipped Garuda for the fire deity Agni. It is said that Garuda stole the nectar, Amrita, from the gods in order to free his mother Vinatā from captivity. Indra fought him and recovered the nectar but had his own

GARUDA

thunderbolt smashed in the process. Garuda has many names and is popular in sculpture and painting with Vishnu riding on his back. He is also called Vainateya, son of Vinatā.

Gāthās. The most ancient Zoroastrian scriptures, being that part of the *Avesta* which can most confidently be ascribed to Zoroaster himself. The *Gāthās* are 'songs' or 'odes' (like the Hindu *Gītā*) and contain the principal teachings of Zoroaster, which form the oldest part of the liturgy or Yasna. They are in an earlier form of Avestan, an ancient Persian language. It is not known in what order the *Gāthās* were composed, and the traditional order which arranges them according to the length of the verses is highly artificial. Some modern translations try to arrange them according to subject matter, and in these the characteristic beliefs of Zoroaster appear, in the supreme God Ahura Mazdā, his call of Zoroaster, and fight against evil.

There are also Hindu *Gāthās*, poems which do not belong to the *Vedas*, and Buddhist verses such as the *Thera-gāthā*, 'songs of the Brethren' (q.v.).

Gautama. A common Sanskrit name, applied particularly to the founder of Buddhism. He belonged to the Shākya tribe and Gotama clan, known by the derived name of Gautama. In the Pāli texts of southern Buddhism he is always Gotama. His personal name was Siddhārtha (Siddhattha in Pali), and he is also called Shākyamuni, the 'sage of the Shākyas'. The date of Gautama's birth is uncertain: a common date reckoned from Ceylonese Chronicles is 563 B.C., but some Western scholars put it later, and other Buddhists earlier. He was born in the Lumbini Grove near Kapilavastu (q.v.) in the foothills of Nepal. His father was a ruler of the Kshatriya caste, called Suddhodāna, and his mother was Māyā. He married Yasodharā and they had a son Rāhula. At 29 Gautama left his home and wandered about seeking the cause of suffering. He found Enlightenment, became a 'Buddha' under the Bo-tree (q.v.), and preached his doctrine till his death at Kusinārā at the age of eighty. He was cremated and his relics divided between eight towns. For the Gautama, founder of Nyāya philosophy, see GOTAMA. See BUDDHA and BUDDHISM.

Gayā. A city in Bihar, India, which is one of the seven most sacred cities visited by Hindu pilgrims. Here is a footprint of the god Vishnu, Vishnu-pad. Nine kilometres further on is Buddha-Gayā, or Bodh-Gayā one of the four most holy places for Buddhists since the Buddha was enlightened here. A great stone temple marks the place and is surrounded by pīpal trees descended from the ancient Bo-tree (q.v.).

Gāyatrī. The most sacred verse of the *Rig Veda*, so named from its metre. It is called the 'Mother of the Vedas', and every Brahmin repeats it on rising, at noon, and going to bed, as grace before meals and on many other occasions. It is also called Sāvitrī, as it is addressed to the sun, under the name of Savitri. Its reference in the *Rig Veda* is 3, 62, 10 and the Gāyatrī may be translated: 'Let us meditate on the splendour of Savitri, may he inspire our minds.' See also SANDHYĀ.

Gayōmart. 'Dying life' and 'Blessed Man', in Zoroastrian mythology. Gayōmart was the Primal Man, created by Ahura Mazdā in the sixth stage of creation. He shone like the sun and was four cubits high. Ahura Mazdā fashioned him from the earth and gave him sleep for repose. Gayōmart was attacked by the demon Ahriman and by a demon Whore (perhaps an aboriginal woman). Gayōmart suffered for thirty years and then died, but his seed was preserved and after forty years the first human couple, Mashyē and Mashyānē, were born, joined together like a rhubarb plant but eventually separated out. At the end of time the Saviour, Saoshyans (q.v.), is given the power of raising the dead and Gayōmart is the first of them and lives for ever.

Ge. See GAEA.

Geasa. Ancient Irish word for a taboo (q.v.) or obligation. See DIARMAID.

Geb, Keb. The personification of the earth and in some accounts the greatest and oldest of the gods of Egypt. Geb was called 'Leader of the gods' and 'Father of the gods'. He was son of Shu and Tefnut, married to Nut, and their children were Osiris and Isis, Set and Nephthys. Geb was sometimes also called father of the sun and moon. His symbol was the goose (Gb), and he was represented as a goose or a bearded man with a goose on his head. He also appears as a man lying on his back with plants coming up from his body, or with a snake's head. Later he was shown with a crown and the diadem of Osiris. Geb had no temple but the centre of his influence was Heliopolis.

Gefjun. One of the goddesses known as Asynjur (q.v.) in Scandinavian mythology. In one story she was a virgin, but in another she had four sons by a giant and turned them into oxen which ploughed the land and turned much of Seelund into sea. She was said to know fate and may have been a form of Frigg or Freyja.

Gehenna. See JAHANNAM.

Gelusgpa, Gelugpa. 'Virtuous ones', the dominant order of Tibetan Buddhism, often known from their headdress as the 'Yellow Hat'. Founded in the fourteenth century by Tsong-kha-pa (q.v.), the reformed order became the state religion of Tibet, whose principal doctrines differ little from other forms of Mahāyāna Buddhism. See LAMA.

Gemara. 'Completion' or 'learning' in Aramaic, a term applied to the comments of rabbis on the Mishnah (q.v.), the code of Jewish law. These were much discussed in the academies in Palestine and Babylon, and both Mishnah and Gemara were incorporated into the Palestinian and Babylonian *Talmuds*, from the third century A.D. onwards.

Gematria. In Jewish Kabbalah (q.v.) Gematria (from the Greek *geometra*) was a method of interpreting words of scripture by taking the numerical value of their letters and interchanging them with words which had the same numerical value when added together. See also NOTARIKON, TEMURAH and TZIRUF.

Gemini. See DIOSCUROI and ZODIAC.

Genie. From a French word from the Latin *Genius*, but generally applied to the Arabian Jinn (q.v.).

Genku. A name of Honen (q.v.), founder of Japanese Jodo or Pure Land Buddhism. Genku was made up from the names of his two teachers, Genko and Eiku.

Geomancy. From Greek words meaning 'earth-divination', geomancy indicates methods of discovering the past, unknown present, or future by means of handfuls of earth or sand, or by using signs marked on the ground or on wood. A modern method of geomancy is the African Ifa (q.v.). See FÊNG SHUI.

Geonim (singular: *Gaon*, 'eminence'). The name applied to the heads of the two great Jewish academies in the Babylonian cities of Sura and Pumbeditha. Their importance increased as the Islamic capital developed at Baghdad, and the Geonim gained authority as pre-eminent expounders of the many difficult passages in the *Talmud*. They attracted students from the Christian as well as the Islamic world, sent Talmudic explanations to distant communities, and their influence was felt as far away as Spain. They compiled legal codes to illustrate the application of the *Talmud* in civil and religious matters. The influence of the Babylonian Geonim lasted nearly five hundred years, till the fall of Baghdad in 1258 to the Turks. See RESPONSA.

Gerd, Gerda, Gerdr. One of the Scandinavian goddesses called Asynjur. She was an earth deity, daughter of a hill giant named Gymir and wife of the god Frey. The brightness of Gerd shone everywhere and made Frey sad, so that he could neither eat nor sleep. Frey sent his servant Skirnir to woo Gerd and, as her father's house was surrounded by flames, he rode on a horse which would go through fire and carried a sword which fought by itself. At first Gerd refused to meet Frey, but at last agreed to meet him nine nights later in the forest. The story is told by Snorri in the poem *Skirnismal* in the *Edda* (q.v.).

Gershom ben Judah. A Jewish rabbi of Mainz (960–1040) whose systematization of the Talmudic laws was used for centuries in Germany and France. He was called the 'Beacon of Light' for his reforms and encouragements in persecutions. Most notably he defended the rights of women, forbade polygamy, and ruled that a divorce could not be obtained without the consent of the wife. This was a departure from the laws of the *Bible* and the *Talmud*, but it was accepted by most Jews.

Geryon. A monster of Greek mythology, with three heads or bodies, perhaps once a sun hero who became a god of the dead. His cattle were stolen by Heracles (q.v.) as one of his Labours.

Ghāts. In India, ranges of hills, temple steps, bathing places, or cremation grounds. In Benares several kilometres of ghāts or flights of steps line the river Ganges from the temples on its banks down into the waters and are used by countless pilgrims. In Calcutta the temple of Kālī, Kālīghāt, with its steps into the Hoogly, gave its name to the city. 'Burning Ghāts' are places for cremation, usually on river banks as in Benares, where the dead are placed on piles of sandal-wood and burnt.

Ghazālī, al-Ghazzālī. Generally regarded as the greatest theologian and philosopher of Islam, he was born at Tus in Persia in 1058 and died there in 1111. In 1091 Ghazālī was appointed a professor in Baghdad, where he was a popular lecturer, expounding and criticizing the views of al-Fārābī and Avicenna (qq.v.). In 1095 he left Baghdad to seek a more profound knowledge of God as a Sūfī mystic. He went on pilgrimage to Mecca and Jerusalem, also visited Damascus and then returned to live an ascetic life at Tus. He was persuaded to lecture at Nishapur for three years, but because of ill health returned to Tus to die. Ghazālī sought to justify orthodox Islamic teaching yet used the methods of the Greek philosophers. Among his many books *The Revival of the Religious Sciences* included a creed and an exposition of orthodox Sunni doctrine.

Ghazzati, Nathan. Nathan Levi of Gaza, often called Nathan Ghazzati, became an enthusiastic follower of the pseudo-Messiah, Shabbethai Zvi (q.v.), in the seventeenth century and won him many followers.

Ghee, Ghī. Clarified butter used in Hindu religious ceremonies, for sacrificial fire, and for cremation. Butter is melted, the solid fat is skimmed off, and the liquid clarified portion which remains is the Ghee which keeps well in a hot climate.

Ghetto. Italian term, perhaps from *Borghetto*, 'little borough', for the quarter of a city where Jews were restricted. It appears first in Venice in 1516, but the restriction had been practised long before, at least since the persecutions of Jews began in the Crusades of the eleventh century. The mental isolation caused by the Ghettos began to break down with the Enlightenment movement (from the eighteenth century onwards) and the study of non-Jewish subjects. See HASKALAH.

Ghose, Ghosh. See AUROBINDO.

Ghulām Ahmad. See AHMADIYYA.

Gicelemukaong. See BIG HOUSE.

Gilgamesh. The *Epic of Gilgamesh* is on twelve tablets of which the eleventh contains the Babylonian version of the story of the Flood (q.v.). Gilgamesh was a legendary king of Erech and said to be

GILGAMESH

two-thirds god and one-third man. In the first tablets he struggles with a wild man, Enkidu (q.v.), who had been sent by the god Anu to reduce his arrogance, but they become friends and together destroy the Bull of heaven. Enkidu is then killed and Gilgamesh sets out to seek immortality for himself. He finds his ancestor Ut-Napishtim, who tells him how he had escaped the Flood, but he was the only one to become immortal and Gilgamesh cannot attain that state. However, he dives into the sea to get a magic herb which makes the old young again, but loses it to a serpent on his way back to Erech. The twelfth tablet is an addition in which the spirit of Enkidu tells Gilgamesh about the state of the dead, and other fragments relate the death of Gilgamesh.

Ginzberg, Asher. Russian Jew (1856–1927), commonly known as Achad Ha-am, 'one of the people'. Founder of 'cultural Zionism', he supported the foundation of a Jewish state in Palestine, but looked for a new form of Judaism which would be a spiritual centre (later called a 'spiritual Zionism'), in which the prophetic ideals would be applied to modern conditions. While most Jews would remain in the Diaspora, a community of élite would radiate the highest way of life to all other communities.

Gipsies, Gypsies. Name derived from Egyptian, but the Gipsies probably came from India and have been identified with the low-caste Doms (q.v.), since in Syria they are called Doum and further west call themselves Rom and Romany.

Gītā. See BHAGAVAD-GĪTĀ.

Gīta Govinda. 'Songs of the Cowherd', a series of religious love poems composed in Sanskrit in the twelfth century A.D. by the Bengali poet Jayadeva (q.v.). The work opens with an invocation to the ten Avatars (q.v.) or incarnations of the god Vishnu, and it is still sung by Bengalis of the Vaishnavite sects at their festivals. The final verse of each poem includes the author's name. The main theme of the poems is the love of Krishna, Avatar of Vishnu, for Rādhā (q.v.) and the cowgirls, and the verses tell of the absence and estrangement of Krishna and Rādhā, the anguish of Rādhā, and their final rapturous reunion. Although the songs are apparently erotic, their purpose is to depict under this symbolism the love of God for the soul, struggles and separation, and blissful union.

Gjallarhorn. The 'ringing horn' of the god Heimdall (q.v.) in Scandinavian mythology. It was stored beneath the Yggdrasil tree, or in a holy well, but at the Doom (see RAGNARÖK) it will ring through all the worlds and wake the gods.

Gladsheim. The 'world of joy' in Scandinavian mythology, in which stood Valhalla (q.v.). See also ASGARD.

Gna. One of the Scandinavian goddesses called Asynjur (q.v.). She was the messenger of Frigg and rode over sea and sky on her horse named Hoof-tosser.

Gnostic. From Greek, 'pertaining to knowledge', this word has been applied to early Greek interpretations of Christian doctrine. In a broader sense Gnostic is applied to those who claim occult or esoteric or mystical knowledge, such as certain Theosophists (q.v.). The Indian word *Jñāna* is related to Greek *Gnosis*, but is used in different ways (see JÑĀNA).

Gobind Singh. Tenth Guru of the Sikhs (1666–1708). He became Guru at an early age, on the death of his father the ninth Guru, Tegh Bahadur, in 1675. Guru Gobind Singh realized that the persecution which Sikhs were suffering demanded a strong organization and at the Hindu New Year in 1699 he initiated five of his followers, the Five Beloved (Panj Payara), into a new community, the Khālsā, 'the pure'. The five drank from the same bowl and took the name Singh, 'lion'. They vowed to observe the Five K's (see K's). Gobind Singh built fortresses in the Punjab, but Mughal armies advanced on him, his sons were killed, and he took refuge in the Deccan where he died at the hand of a Muslim retainer. Gobind Singh declared that the scripture itself, *Ādi Granth* (q.v.), would be the continuing Guru, and power in the Sikh community was vested in the Khālsā (q.v.).

God. The concept of a Supreme Being or High God is found in many religions, as creator of gods and men, father or father-mother, Great Spirit, giver and upholder of the moral law. Often connected with the sky, sun or thunder, God is usually spoken about as male, though formally he may be beyond description and with no attributes. The Muslim Allāh is similar to the Jewish and Christian God. The Greek Zeus is related to Roman Ju-piter and Indian Dyaus Pitar. In Persia Ahura Mazdā was supreme in Zoroaster's reform of religion. In Buddhist and Jain belief there was no supreme deity, but the Buddha, for example, was 'teacher of gods and men'. In China the supreme God was called T'ien or Shang Ti, and in Japanese Shinto it was the sun goddess Amaterasu who was supreme. In the popular Hindu religions the old sky gods faded away and Vishnu or Shiva were supreme for their followers.

Gods. The word 'gods' with a small 'g' indicates a multiplicity of divine spirits in the belief of many peoples, commonly called Polytheism (q.v.). Some religions which have been called 'atheistic' are not strictly so, because their scriptures and popular beliefs tell of many gods, who act as attendants upon other figures; however, these gods have little vital function, and they serve as background for the mighty acts of the Buddhas or Jinas who are the saviours of the religions.

Gog and Magog. These mysterious heathen powers appear in Biblical apocalyptic (*Ezekiel* 38 and 39; *Revelation* 20, 8), and were regarded in the *Talmud* as fomenters of strife before the coming of the Messiah. The world would be partly destroyed by the wars of Gog and Magog, and Rabbi Akiba declared that they would be punished for twelve months in the hereafter. In the *Qur'ān*, as Yājūj and Mājūj, they appear with Alexander the Great, Dhu 'l-Qarnain (q.v.) and work corruption in the earth (18, 93). The commentator Baidāwī said they were two tribes descended from Japheth, no doubt by reference to *Genesis* 10, 2.

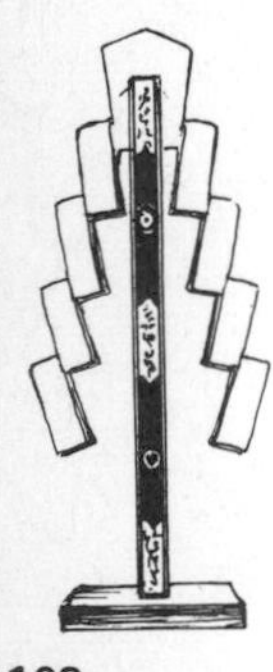

Goheï. An instrument of purification in the Shinto religion of Japan. The word *Goheï*, used by nearly everybody, is Chinese and its Japanese equivalent, *Mitegura*, is variously explained as an offering or seat. The *Goheï*, is a stick with strips of paper folded in elaborate patterns hanging from either side; there are said to be more than twenty patterns which have esoteric significance. The Goheï are used in Shinto halls of worship both as symbolic offerings and as signs that the god is present. They can be made of paper of various colours, and also from strips of metal which on great occasions may be gilded.

Golden Bough. See FRAZER, DIANA and VIRBIUS.

Golden Fleece. See ARGONAUTS.

Golden Stool. See STOOL.

Golden Temples. Many temples in India and neighbouring countries are covered partly with gold leaf. At Amritsar (q.v.) the Golden Temple of the Sikhs (Hari Mandir or Darbar Sahib) was founded by Guru Arjan about 1600 and roofed with gilt by Ranjit Singh in 1802.

The entire upper part of the temple is now covered with gold, and reflects beautifully in the lake that surrounds it (see GURDWĀRĀ). In Benares a Golden Temple of Shiva (Biseswar or Vishveshvara) stands hemmed in the bazaar, overshadowed by the mosque which occupies some of its former land. This temple also had its roof covered by Ranjit Singh with gold plates over copper. In Rangoon the Golden Pagoda, Shwe Dagon, is a pyramid, higher than St Paul's Cathedral, London, covered with gold leaf, and containing solid golden statues of the Buddha as well as reputed hairs from his head as relics. It is on the site of a very ancient shrine and has remained in its present shape since 1564.

Gommata, Gommateshvara. A saint of the Digambara Jains (q.v.) who is said to have stood so long in meditation that creepers twined round his legs and anthills rose beside him. A famous and colossal statue of the saint stands on a hill at Shravana Belgola in Mysore. The

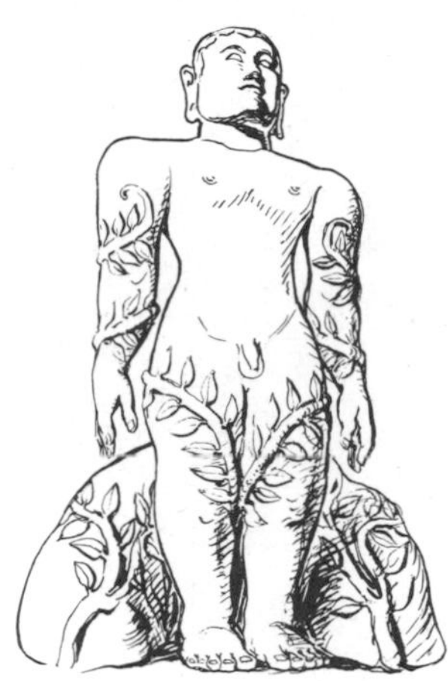

image is cut from a single piece of rock and stands about seventeen metres high, towering above the surrounding buildings. It is completely nude, facing north, with a serene smile on its face while the legs are entwined with stone representations of plants. It was carved in the tenth century A.D.

Gopā. Name occasionally given to the wife of Gautama the Buddha, though she is generally known as Yasodharā (q.v.).

Gopī. The wife or daughter of a cowherd in Sanskrit, and so a 'cowgirl' or milkmaid. In the mystical and erotic poems of medieval India the Gopīs were especially the cowgirls of Brindāban (q.v.) or Vrindāvana, who were companions of Krishna in his youthful sports; they came to symbolize human souls or were considered sometimes as celestial beings. Krishna played on his flute and called the women to leave their husbands and dance with him in the moonlight. This illegitimate love, on the human plane, was regarded as a representation of the divine love which takes precedence of all human ties. Krishna danced a circular dance in which he multiplied himself so that each Gopī

GOPĪS

thought that she alone was dancing with him, but he pursued particularly Rādhā (q.v.).

Gopuram. A tower over the 'gate' of a temple in south India. Developing from watch-towers or gate-houses, these Gopurams came to take the form of flat-topped pyramids in carved stone, and some of the greatest stand over sixty metres high. This architectural style is sometimes called Dravidian (a general term for southern Indian populations), or more specifically Pāndyan, after the dynasty which dominated the country from about the twelfth century A.D. and whose kings built walls and Gopurams round many temples. Gopurams stand at the entrance and cardinal points of the temple walls, and are to be seen in many villages as well as in countless temples of south Indian cities. They are lavishly carved in stone, with animal, human and divine figures in great profusion, sometimes painted, sometimes in brown or blackened stone. See SHIKHARA.

Gorakhnāth. One of the leaders of the Nāthas, orders of Indian Yogīs, who lived in the twelfth century A.D. Many legends are told about him and he is said to have been born from the god Shiva. Gorakhnāth composed verses which embodied his teachings and founded the Kānphata Yogīs (q.v.), the 'ear-split', so called from the earrings which are inserted at initiation into the order. Such Yogīs are not cremated but are entombed in the sitting posture of *samādhi* or contemplation in which they passed away.

Gorgon, Gorgo. Three sisters who were monsters in Greek mythology, called Medusa the Cunning, Sthenno the Strong and Euryale the Wide-leaping. Medusa was the worst, with a horrible face, snakes for hair, huge wings, and eyes that turned men to stone. They lived in the far west, where Medusa was

GORGON

loved by the sea god Poseidon and bore him the winged horse Pegasus. The hero Perseus (q.v.) killed Medusa and carried off her head to turn his enemies into stone. The Gorgon may also have been an earth goddess and she was said to have been buried at Argos.

Gosāla, Goshāla. The founder or principal teacher of the Ājīvikas (q.v.). He is called by various names, among them Makkhali Gosāla and Goshāla Maskarīputra. According to some texts he was the twenty-fourth Ajīvika teacher, born in a poor family, and died a year or two before the Buddha, so perhaps in the fifth or fourth century B.C. It seems that Gosāla met Mahāvīra, the Jain leader, but after some association the two saints parted company. The Ājīvikas were even more ascetic than the Jains, and their particular doctrine was a rigid determinism which taught that the whole universe, down to the smallest detail, was fixed by an impersonal destiny. Both the sect and its scriptures disappeared, and the life of Gosāla has to be reconstructed from Jain and Buddhist sources.

Go-Shintai. See HONDEN.

Goswāmī. (Sanskrit) 'lord of cows', a title of Krishna, or of an honoured person or a religious mendicant. It is used to describe teachers (Gurus) of most Vaishnava sects and is often written Gosain; it is applied especially to the descendants of the disciples of Chaitanya. See BRINDĀBAN.

Gotama, Gautama. A name of the Buddha (see GAUTAMA). The founder of the Nyāya school of orthodox Hindu philosophy was another Gotama (also called Gautama) according to tradition. He is a shadowy figure, sometimes called Akshapāda, 'with eyes fixed on his feet', and may have lived in the third or second centuries B.C. The *Nyāya Sūtra*, attributed to him, may contain some verses derived from the master, but it is believed that much of it was composed centuries later. See NYĀYA. Another Gotama was one of the seven ancient seers (see RISHI).

Gotra. (Sanskrit) 'cowshed', and so enclosure, lineage, family name and clan. Orthodox Hindu Brahmins (q.v.) attach great importance to descent from legendary sages from whom their Gotras are named, forty-nine of them reckoned to have sprung from celebrated teachers. Other high castes have imitated this with less zeal. See PRAVARA and SHĀKHĀ.

Go-Vinda, Go-Pāla. The 'cowkeeper', a title of Krishna indicating his role as god of herdsmen and his life among the cowherds of Brindāban (q.v.).

Govind Singh. See GOBIND SINGH.

Graces. Three minor classical goddesses of loveliness, attendant upon Venus. The Three Graces were generally

known by their Greek names: Aglaia, splendour; Euphrosyne, merriment; and Thalia, abundance (also known as one of the Nine Muses (q.v.), that of comedy).

Gradual Sayings. See ANGUTTARA NIKĀYA.

Grainne. In Irish legend a beautiful woman who was betrothed to the hero Fionn, but eloped with Diarmaid (q.v.).

Gramdan. See VINOBA.

Grāmadevatā. A 'village god' (Sanskrit) of India. These may be seen in image or shrine in most towns and villages, especially in southern India. The shrines are smaller and less elaborate than the temples of the orthodox Hindu gods, Vishnu and Shiva, but they receive great attention and have regular ceremonies. The village gods probably continue very ancient traditions, mostly concerning fertility and protective deities. Most of them are female, and often have the termination *-amma* or *-amman*, 'mother', to their names (see SHĪTALĀ). Many of them are deities of disease, cholera, smallpox, or cattle disease, and others are snakes (see NĀGAS).

Granth. See ĀDI GRANTH.

Gree-gree. A term derived from the French word Gris-gris, and formerly applied to religious and magical objects in Africa. The origins of the word are obscure, and it may come from an African term or be a fanciful reduplication. It is declining from modern serious usage and suffers from the same disadvantages as Juju (q.v.).

Grendel. Sea-monster who ravaged the land of the Danes and was killed by Beowulf (q.v.).

Grettir. A hero of Scandinavian mythology, whose struggles with a huge Troll-woman (q.v.) are told in the *Grettis Saga*. After a long fight she dragged him towards a river, but he worked his hand free and cut off her arm so that she fell into the river instead.

Grihastha. (Sanskrit) 'householder', the second stage of religious life for a high caste Hindu. See ĀSHRAM and CASTE.

Grihya Sūtras. Hindu religious texts which regulate life from birth, with special reference to personal sacraments and 'domestic' rites.

Gris-gris. See GREE-GREE.

Guide for the Perplexed. See MAIMONIDES.

Gunabibi, Kunapipi. A 'great mother' in northern Australian mythology, whose rituals are chiefly concerned with fertility. Her husband is the Lightning, represented as a snake, and in paintings and engravings he is the rainbow serpent on the symbolic earth-womb of the mother goddess.

Gunas. (Sanskrit) 'strands', qualities or subtle elements which compose and permeate primal matter (Prakriti) in Hindu thought, and particularly in the Sāmkhya philosophy (q.v.)). The Gunas, like Strands of a rope, are three: Goodness or brightness (*sattva*), Passion or energy (*rajas*), and Darkness or dullness (*tamas*). Matter contains all three Gunas, in equal balance, but as beings and objects develop the Gunas come to dominate differently and they are better or worse accordingly. Where Goodness dominates, there is truth and virtue; where there is Passion, violence and force dominate; and Darkness prevails in gloomy and stupid beings. Sattva Guna is nearest to the supreme Spirit and leads to liberation, while Rajas binds the soul to transmigration, and Tamas keeps it in even greater darkness.

Gungnir. Magic spear of Odin (q.v.) the great Nordic deity. It was forged by dwarfs and Odin was known as the 'shaker of Gungnir'.

Gurdwārā. Punjabi name for a Sikh temple or similar building, from the Golden Temple at Amritsar (q.v.), to a small village shrine. Many Gurdwārās have golden domes, but there are no images inside. The central object is the sacred book, *Ādi Granth* (q.v.), which is read all day in a low chant, sometimes accompanied by musical instruments. Worshippers touch the ground with their foreheads on entering and make an offering, frequently receiving small portions of sweet food in return. At intervals all present recite Sikh prayers, Anand and Japji, invoking God and recalling the history of the community. A Langar, public kitchen and refectory, often adjoins the Gurdwārā where visitors are fed freely.

Gurunga. A spirit woman in a myth of north Australia. Three brothers and two sisters were performing a ritual and when they called the secret sacred name for the fire, Nereirei, it flared up and spread. One of the sisters, Gurunga, tried to put it out, but it spread even further, burning many people. She is depicted in bark paintings with her head in a sacred hut, while the fire blazes around her.

Gwion. A spirit in Welsh tales of divine combat and rebirths. Gwion was charged by Cerridwen (q.v.) to watch her magic cauldron, but three drops from it fell on his finger and when he tasted them he became inspired. Cerridwen pursued him and both changed their shapes until as a hen she swallowed him in the form of a grain of wheat. Cerridwen then gave birth to Gwion and threw him into the sea, but he was rescued and became the greatest of poets. The story is in the *Hanes Taliesin*.

Guru. A 'teacher' in Hinduism, a spiritual instructor who has himself attained insight, and who initiates his pupil, instructs him in sacred and moral texts, and conducts the ceremonies of his investiture with the Sacred Thread (q.v.). The Laws of Manu contain many ancient instructions for the behaviour of pupils to their Gurus. Among the Sikhs there are ten Gurus, from Guru Nānak, the founder, to Guru Gobind Singh. After him the scriptures, *Ādi Granth* (q.v.), were to be the Guru of the Sikhs and were called the Guru Granth Sahib. The ten Sikh Gurus were: Nānak, Angad, Amar Dās, Rām Dās, Arjan, Har Govind, Har Rai, Harkishan, Tegh Bahadur, Gobind Singh (see separate articles on them).

Gylfaginning. The 'deceiving of Gylfi', the first part of the *Edda* of Snorri (q.v.), which is of great literary and mythological interest. It tells of Gylfi, a

Swedish king, who goes to Asgard the city of the gods and asks questions about the past and future.

Gymir. Giant of the hills in Scandinavian mythology, who dwelt in a castle in the world of giants. His daughter was the beautiful Gerd (q.v.), who was sought in marriage by the sun god Freyr.

Gymnosophists. 'Naked sages', a Greek term used by early Christian writers for Indian, probably Jain and Buddhist, monks. Clement of Alexandria in the second century said that the Indian Gymnosophists knew neither marriage nor begetting of children. Jerome in the fourth century said that among the Gymnosophists of India there was the belief that the Buddha was born of a virgin, but he was mistaken because all the early Buddhist accounts make the Buddha's mother a married queen. The Buddhist monks did not go naked, but some of the Jains did so.

H

Hachiman. A Shinto deity, sometimes called the War God, and linked with the Emperor Ojin (third century A.D.). The Emperor was a peaceful man who did much to raise the cultural level of Japan. After his death it is said that a god (*kami*) appeared and declared that its name was Yawata, which was identified with the Chinese name Hachiman. The Hachiman-Ojin identification was thus a union of a human emperor with a divine being. Although not mentioned in the ancient scriptures, Kojiki or Nihongi, the cult of Hachiman became popular and today has thousands of temples. Soldiers often took relics from his shrines, but he was also a god of peace and protector of human life. Hachiman is also regarded as a protector of Buddhism, in oracles he is called a Bosatsu (Bodhisattva, q.v.), and as God of Eight Banners he protects the Eightfold Path of Buddhist morality.

Hadad. See ADAD.

Hades. The lord of the underworld, a son of Kronos. In classical Greek he is always a person and not a place, and the dead go to Hades or the House of Hades. There he is portrayed as a grim punisher of the wicked, but he is not evil and does not torment the dead, leaving that to the Erinyes (q.v.). There is very little mythology of Hades, apart from the myth of Persephone (q.v.) whom he married and retained underground for three months of the year, in the same way that seed remains in the earth during winter. Hades is also associated with wealth, Plutus. He had a temple at Elis, but little cult elsewhere. Various people tried to get out of Hades. See ALCESTIS and EURYDICE.

Hadhayans. A bull in Zoroastrian mythology which will be sacrificed in the last days by the saviour Saoshyans (q.v.).

Hadīth. 'Tradition', in Arabic, a term used for collections of traditions of Muhammad and his followers. Six collections of *Hadīth*, all made in the third Islamic century, came to be regarded as authoritative by orthodox Sunni Muslims, and the most important were those compiled by Bukhārī and Muslim (qq.v.). The Shī'a Muslims esteemed their own collections of five works of *Hadīth*, based on the authority of 'Alī and his followers. The *Hadīth* have been regarded with great reverence, next to the *Qur'ān* itself, but tradition has been criticized according to the status of its origin and the lists of authorities who supported it; in modern times there have been considerable criticisms of *Hadīth* but virtually none at all of the *Qur'ān* in the Islamic world. See ISNĀD, BUKHĀRĪ, MUSLIM IBN AL-HAJJĀJ and TIRMIDHĪ.

Hadj. See HAJJ.

Hāfiz, Shams al-Dīn. Persian mystical poet of Shiraz (1320–89). He was a devout student of the *Qur'ān* and competent in the sciences of his day. Hāfiz is agreed to be the chief master of the *Ghazal*, a form of lyric, and various attempts have been made to put some of these poems into English. But the greatness of Hāfiz, for which he is appreciated in his own land, is in the mystical consciousness that makes him one of the greatest Sūfīs. See RŪMĪ.

Hagar. Hājar in Islamic legend, who was cast out with her son Ishmael, ran to and fro between the two low hills of Safā and Marwa (a ritual repeated during the pilgrimage ever after (see HAJJ and MARWA)) and found water from which the Zamzam (q.v.) well sprang.

Haggada, Aggadah. A Hebrew term for utterance or 'narration', and applied to about a third of the *Talmud* which is non-legal. Haggada includes history and legends of the past, visions of the future and messianic salvation, metaphysical speculation and moral reflection, as well as observations on medicine, botany, astronomy, popular science and worldly maxims. These all testify to the religious and secular knowledge of the rabbis and aim at inspiring and directing men to righteous action. The name *Haggada* is also given to the text recited at the Seder (q.v.) meal at Passover.

Haiden. The hall of 'worship' in Japanese temples (see JINJA). It stands in front of the sanctuary or Honden (q.v.) and is larger and open on all sides. It is open to ordinary worshippers for their prayers, and is separate from the Heiden (q.v.) or Hall of Offerings where priests perform their rites.

Hair. See SHIKHĀ and 'AKĪKA.

Hajj. (Arabic) 'pilgrimage', the pilgrimage to Mecca which is the last of the Five Pillars of Islam (q.v.), and which every adult Muslim should perform at least once in his life. About a million people make the pilgrimage every year, but most are from Arabia and nearby countries. From farther afield, pilgrims go by air, boat, bus, lorry or on foot, the return journey sometimes taking several years. The Great Pilgrimage must be performed in the pilgrimage month, the twelfth of the Islamic year. At any other time it is a Little Pilgrimage (see 'UMRA). At ten miles from Mecca pilgrims change into a two-piece robe; women are completely veiled. All pilgrims must circumambulate the Ka'ba shrine seven times, if possible kiss or touch the Black Stone (q.v.) in its wall, and then run seven times between two little hills, Safā and Marwa (q.v.). Then all go to the plains of 'Arafāt and Mina (qq.v.) and cast stones at cairns there. These were pre-Islamic customs, but later associated with Adam and Eve, Abraham and Ishmael. A great sacrifice of animals closes the pilgrimage, and this is performed all over the Islamic world at the same time, thus making a strong ritual communal bond. See CORBAN.

Hajura 'l-Aswad. See BLACK STONE.

Hākim. Fātimid caliph of Cairo (996–1021) who was notorious for his persecution of Jews and Christians, and demolition of churches, including the Holy Sepulchre at Jerusalem. He was killed in a conspiracy headed by his sister. Darazī, one of the founders of the Druze religion (q.v.), regarded Hākim as incarnate deity, because the universal reason had passed through the prophets and 'Alī into the Fātimid caliphs. The atrocities of Hākim were explained symbolically.

Hakuin. Reputed inventor (1685–1768) or organizer of the Kōan (q.v.) system of Japanese Zen Buddhism.

Halachah, Halakah. (Hebrew) 'walking', the name given to a Jewish legal teaching and related to *Exodus* 18, 20, 'thou shalt show them the way in which they must walk'. Deriving from the oral Law as exposition of Biblical texts, Halachah was codified in the *Talmud*. The civil and ritual laws, with decrees and customs bearing on them, were distinguished from the non-legal Haggadah (q.v.). The decisions of Halakah are Halakoth.

Ha-Levi, Judah. Jewish philosopher and poet (1085–1140) of Toledo, who sought to show the superiority of Judaism over Christianity and Islam. His writings, in Arabic, distinguished between the God of philosophy and the God of revelation, and he claimed the revelation of God on Mount Sinai as the basis of all Jewish faith. Yet while Israel was the elect nation, it would lead all other peoples to God.

Hallāj. 'The wool-carder', a Persian Sūfī mystic (858–922) whose real name was Husain ibn Mansūr. Born at Tūr, he joined Sūfī teachers but left them to preach ascetic and mystical doctrines of his own. Hallāj visited Mecca but on return to Baghdad he was accused of heresy and imprisoned for some years. Finally he was charged with blasphemy for having said: 'I am the Truth' or 'the Real' (*haqq*), a title of God. Hallāj was tortured and hanged or crucified. It is said that he prayed for his enemies and in a later work attributed to him he compared his sufferings to those of Jesus, for whom, like many Sūfīs, he had a profound reverence. Hallāj, like other mystics, taught the union, if not identification, of the soul and God. He spoke of the love of God, and said, 'We are two spirits dwelling in one body.' Condemned by the orthodox, Hallāj has always been venerated by popular devotion.

Hallel. (Hebrew) 'praise', the title given to *Psalms* 113–18, which are included in the Jewish liturgy for the New Moon, and at the festivals of Passover, Pentecost, Tabernacles and Hanukkah.

Halo. See NIMBUS.

Hammurabi, Hammurapi. The most famous king of old Babylonia, who reigned for forty-three years in the eighteenth or seventeenth centuries B.C. The Laws or Code of Hammurabi were inscribed on a black basalt pillar discovered at the ruins of Susa in Persia in 1902 and taken to the Louvre. On the face there is a relief of the king standing and receiving the laws from the seated god of justice, the sun-god Shamash. The prologue of the inscription mentions

HAMMURABI

other gods: Anu, Enlil, Marduk, Ishtar. Hammurabi is said to have established law and justice and to have promoted the welfare of the people. The laws have been compared with those of Moses, with resemblances as well as differences.

Hamsa. See HANSA.

Hanafites. See HANĪFA.

Hanbal. Ahmad ibn Muhammad ibn Hanbal, or Ibn Hanbal, founder of the Hanbalite school of Islamic law, was born at Baghdad in 780. He travelled extensively in order to study the ancient traditions and was imprisoned for refusing to deny the orthodox doctrine of the eternity of the *Qur'ān*. After his release he was honoured at court and granted a state pension, gathering round him many disciples. He died in Baghdad in 855. Ibn Hanbal tried to derive every law from traditional sources and he accepted even feebly supported *Hadīth* (q.v.) traditions. He was opposed to innovation and rationalism, and today his school of Fiqh (q.v.) is the smallest, found chiefly in Arabia.

Hand Gestures. See MUDRĀ.

Hanes Taliesin. See TALIESIN.

Hanīf. Arabic name (plural *Hunufa'*), of uncertain origin, for a man who possesses the real and true religion. It occurs often in the *Qur'ān*, sometimes as identical with Muslim, and at other times of a pre-Islamic believer: 'Abraham was a Hanīf and not one of the idolaters' (2, 129). In later usage it is almost always identified with Muslim.

Hanīfa, Abū Hanīfa. Founder of one of the four orthodox schools of Islamic law, the Hanafites. Abū Hanīfa was born in Kūfa about 700 and probably died in prison in 767 for having refused to accept public office, preferring like other pious men to live quietly. He worked as a cloth merchant, but spent all the time he could spare studying the *Qur'ān* and 'Traditions'. No writings of Abū Hanīfa have survived, and his method seems to have been that of establishing rules by applying reason to tradition (see FIQH). The Hanafī school originated in Iraq, and it came to dominate in central Asia and India.

Hansa, Hamsa. (Sanskrit) 'a goose' or 'swan', or perhaps even a flamingo. The Hansa is a mythical bird, on which Brahmā in particular was said to fly (see VĀHANA). In the *Mahābhārata* the Hansa is one of the first Avatars of Vishnu. In the *Upanishads* the Hansa is a symbol of the soul, perhaps because it is both pure and migratory. It is sometimes identified with the universal Soul or Spirit, and with the gods Vishnu and Shiva.

Hanukkah, Chanukkah. 'Dedication', a Jewish special festival which lasts for eight days and commemorates the rededication of the Temple at Jerusalem in 165 B.C. The Maccabees, under Judas Maccabeus, defeated the armies of the Syrian Greeks who had defiled the Temple, and it was purified and reconsecrated. Hanukkah is celebrated by the kindling of lights, one each day, on an eight-branched candlestick.

Hanumān, Hanumat. A monkey chief and god in Hindu mythology; son of the wind, Pavana, he was able to fly through the air. Hanumān is particularly prominent in the epic poem *Rāmāyana*, the story of *Rāma*, and rendered great assistance to the hero Rāma in his war against the demon Rāvana. When Rāvana stole Rāma's wife Sītā and carried her off to his fortress in Ceylon (Lankā),

Hanumān jumped over to Ceylon and performed great exploits. Rāvana and his monsters set Hanumān's tail on fire, but with it he burnt down their city. Returning to Rāma he helped him build a bridge to Ceylon (the islands called Rāma's or Adam's Bridge, q.v.) and the army crossed over and defeated Rāvana. Hanumān continued to serve Rāma and was promised eternal youth. In pictures he is often represented in an attitude of devotion to Rāma. Hanumān is also worshipped as a god in his own right, no doubt as a relic of an old monkey cult.

Haoma. A sacred plant used in the central rites of Zoroastrian religion. It is a medicinal plant, mostly twigs, which grows in the mountains of Persia and neighbouring countries, from whence it is brought to Parsi temples in India. The plant was dried, pounded to produce a yellow liquid, and the fermented juice poured out and drunk. It was called the nectar of immortality, which gods and priests consumed. The Haoma formed part of ancient Persian religion before the time of Zoroaster's reforms; he attacked the ancient rite, but Haoma was either tolerated or introduced again to form the major part of Zoroastrian ritual, in offerings to Ahura Mazdā and the immortals. Haoma was both a sacrifice and a god, like the Hindu Soma drink (q.v.), to which it was related.

Hapi. See Apis.

Hapi, Hep. Ancient name of the river Nile, which was deified and thought to dwell in the island of Bigeh. Hapi was not only 'lord of fishes', but 'father of gods' and creator of all beings, and was exalted even above the great state god Rē' by his worshippers. He gave fertility and also was concerned with right and truth. In art Hapi was represented as of double sex, as a bearded man with female breasts. He was symbolized by water and plants. See also Apis.

Haqq. (Arabic) 'real', truth, used especially of God as the Real or Reality, and therefore regarded in Islam as blasphemous if applied to a man. Hallāj (q.v.) was crucified for using this term of himself or God within him.

Harai, Harae, Barai. 'Purification' ceremonies in Japanese Shinto. These are purifications of good and of evil, entailing the removal of evil, pollutions and disaster by prayers to the gods, the use of water and other means, to ensure a return to a pure condition for relationship with the deity.

Hara-kiri. (Japanese) 'belly-cutting', a vulgar term which has become popular in the West for the Samurai form of suicide. But the Samurai themselves used the more dignified term *Seppuku*, which was a legal and ceremonial process developing from the Middle Ages to the present century.

Harappā. Site of an ancient city in north India, whose name is often used for the whole ancient culture of the Indus Valley or plain. Harappā is on the river Ravi, a tributary of the Indus, and its great mounds were reported in 1826 and extensively excavated from 1922. The city was composed of a citadel and lower town, with straight streets, brick houses and running sanitation. There were great granaries and perhaps temples. Stone images show the worship of a mother goddess and a male deity. Here and at Mohenjodaro are small stone seals, incised with pictures of animals, some human beings and symbols such as the Swastika.

A few seals show a male figure, with several faces, sitting cross-legged in Yoga posture, perhaps a proto-Shiva (q.v.). The seals have inscriptions, not hitherto deciphered, but Finnish scholars are beginning to read signs indicating kings and gods. The Harappān culture was contemporary with Mesopotamian and more extensive, dating from about 2500 to 1500 B.C., and was largely destroyed by Aryan invaders (q.v.). See Cernunnos.

Hare. See Hari and Krishna.

Harem. From an Arabic word meaning 'forbidden' or 'sacred'. Haram is applied to the sacred areas in the holy cities of Mecca and Medina, and also in Jerusalem. Then, applied to the female apartments which are forbidden to strangers, both the apartments and their occupants are Harīm. In the early years of Islam some women, at least, were unveiled, and until the third century they could pray in mosques, with their heads covered though not their faces. Seclusion was reinforced by Persian influence, and by the time of the 'Abbāsid caliph Hārūn al-Rashīd in 786 the system of the harem was fully established, with the women separated from the rest of the house and in the care of eunuchs. By the Middle Ages the system was in force all over the Islamic world, except parts of Africa. Much of it has gone nowadays, but women are still heavily veiled in Arabia. See also PURDAH and BURQA'.

Har Govind. Sixth Guru of the Sikhs (1595–1644), he succeeded Guru Arjan and was followed by Har Rai. Har Govind was responsible for the building of the shrine Akal Takht, 'throne of the Timeless', by the Golden Temple in Amritsar.

Hari. Title and invocation of Hindu gods, like Vishnu and Krishna, as 'sin-remover'. Hari-Hara is a combination of the gods Vishnu and Shiva, representing their unity, and depicted sometimes in sculpture with each half of the figure bearing the symbols of the appropriate god.

Haribhadra. A Jain teacher of the ninth century, a converted Brahmin and opponent of both Hindu and Buddhist doctrines. He is said to have written more than a thousand books, some of which remain to this day, and was particularly important for his comparative studies of Yoga.

Harijan. See GĀNDHI.

Harish-chandra. Twenty-eighth king of the solar race in Hindu mythology and favourite example of suffering and virtue. His story is told at length in the *Mārkandeya Purāna*, where he defended the Sciences against a fierce sage Vishvamitra. The latter demanded a sacrificial gift and the king offered everything, whereupon he was stripped of his kingdom and all possessions. He went as beggar to Benares and there his wife and child were sold into slavery. Then Dharma, god of right, appeared as an outcaste and bought Harish-chandra as slave, making him steal clothing from a cemetery. His wife came there, they recognized each other and vowed to die on their son's funeral pyre. Then the gods intervened, Dharma revealed himself, and Harish-chandra and his wife went to heaven. They are said to dwell in an aerial city which is still occasionally visible.

Harivamsha. The 'genealogy of Hari' or Vishnu. A Sanskrit poem of some sixteen thousand verses appended to the great Hindu epic *Mahābhārata*. It has three parts, the first tells of creation and royal dynasties of the past, the second relates the life of Krishna, and the last indicates the future corruptions of the world in the Kali age. The chief interest of the *Harivamsha* is the second part, in which Krishna as the Avatar of Vishnu is described with his adventures in much more detail than in the epic, and it testifies to the growing cult of Krishna and the desire to have more legends of his life.

Harkishan. Eighth Guru of the Sikhs (1661–1664), who succeeded Guru Har Rai and was followed by Tegh Bahadur. He was son of Har Rai and his short term of office was comparatively uneventful.

Harmonia. (Greek) 'concord', in mythology daughter of Ares and Aphrodite, and wife of Cadmus (q.v.). He gave her a necklace, made by Hephaestus, which figured in other stories. In old age they went to Illyria and were turned into serpents or lions.

Harpies, Harpyiae. In Greek mythology the Harpies were probably originally winds, and then winged beings who snatched away persons and things, sometimes to the underworld. In Homer

they are servants of the Erinyes (q.v.); in Hesiod they are named as Aello, Ocypete and Celaeno, and are granddaughters of the Ocean. Later Virgil speaks of them as birds with the faces of women, and they are sometimes represented in this form.

Harpocrates. Greek rendering of Har-pe-khrad, Horus the Child, in the popular worship of Ptolemaic Egypt (see HORUS). The great gods of Alexandria were Osiris, Isis and Horus, and these were known as Serapis (q.v.), Isis and Harpocrates, or identified with the Greek gods Dionysos, Demeter and Apollo. Harpocrates had long been famous as a war-god, but he was also popular as a child-god and was called

HARPOCRATES

'little Apollo', 'little Heracles', or Eros. His symbol was still the falcon, as with Horus, and he was often depicted as a child in a lotus or chalice. Since he had his finger to his lips, the Greek took this to be a command to silence about the mysteries of religion.

Har Rai. Seventh Guru of the Sikhs (1645–61), who succeeded Har Govind and was followed by Harkishan. His sixteen years as Guru were devoted to strengthening the solidarity of the Sikh community against increasing external pressures.

Hārūn al-Rashīd. Most splendid of the 'Abbāsid (q.v.) caliphs, who ruled at Baghdad from 786–809. He was contemporary with Charlemagne, but more powerful and civilized, and though Frankish authors speak of exchange of embassies and gifts between the two rulers Arab writers say nothing. Under Hārūn Baghdad became the finest city in the world, and the caliph's cousin-wife, Zubaydah, set the fashion for jewelled clothing and splendid pilgrimages. The palaces of the viziers, or Barmakids (q.v.), were almost as magnificent. Artists and thinkers were attracted to the court, and the travels of merchants and sailors to spread commerce are reflected in the adventures of Sindbād the Sailor in the *Thousand and One Nights*.

Haruspex, Haruspices. Etruscan (q.v.) diviners who sought to interpret natural phenomena in mysterious ways. The size, colour and markings of sheep livers and gall-bladders were examined, as well as abnormal births and growths, and unusual heavenly phenomena. Despite criticism the work of the Haruspices became popular in Roman religion and was still seriously considered in the sixth century A.D.

Hārūt, and Mārūt. Two angels in the *Qur'ān* (2, 96/102) mentioned in connection with Suleiman (Solomon), but with the words that they and not he taught magic and false doctrine which they had received in Bābil (Babylon). Muslim legend called them fallen angels who were led astray by a beautiful woman and killed the man who discovered them. They chose to be punished in this world rather than the next and hang by their feet in a pit in Bābil, where they are still teachers of magic.

Hasan. Eldest son of 'Alī (q.v.) and Fātima, and grandson of Muhammad. After 'Alī had been assassinated in 661, his partisans proclaimed Hasan as Caliph in Iraq, but before long he renounced the title in favour of the Caliph of Syria, Mu'āwiya, and retired on a pension. Hasan died shortly afterwards at Medina and was succeeded as head of the 'Alid house by his brother Husain. The Shī'a Muslims regard Hasan as the second of their twelve Imāms or leaders, between 'Alī and Husain.

Hasan ibn Sabbāh. See SABBĀH and ASSASSINS.

Hāshim. Great-grandfather of the prophet Muhammad, and claimed as ancestor by various rulers. The Shī'a regarded the house of Hāshim as primarily the descendants of 'Alī, Muhammad's cousin who had married his daughter Fātima. But the 'Abbāsids (q.v.) were also Hāshimites through another branch. Claims to this distinguished ancestry have continued down Islamic history.

Hashish. See ASSASSINS.

Hasidism, Chassidism. The 'pious' (Hebrew) followers of Israel ben Eliezer (1700–60), known as Baal Shem Tov or the Besht, the 'Master of the Good Name'. Cossack persecutions of the Jews in the seventeenth century brought fear and depression. Besht spent years travelling among the Jews of the Ukraine and Poland, teaching faith and piety in contrast to the formalism and spiritual depression of the times. Rather than looking to the future, he stressed the presence of God in everyday life and the value of prayer. His followers used chanting and even dancing as stimuli to the ecstasy of communion with God. The leaders of the movement called themselves Zaddik, perfectly righteous (q.v.). Hasidism spread rapidly and by the middle of the nineteenth century nearly half the Jews of eastern Europe followed it, though there were fierce conflicts with the Rabbinic academies. But then the movement began to decline firmly owing to the spread of modernism. Modern mystics, like Martin Buber (q.v.), have reinterpreted Hasidism for the West.

Haskalah. (Hebrew) 'rationalism', name given to the Enlightenment movement in Judaism in the eighteenth and nineteenth centuries. Study of non-Jewish subjects led to a critical and rationalistic approach to religious as well as secular matters, and such critics were called Maskilim, 'intellectuals', and so rationalists. This led to Reform or Liberal Judaism (q.v.). See also MENDELSSOHN.

Hatha. (Sanskrit) 'force', name of a kind of Yoga (q.v.) which is chiefly concerned with physical culture, with many exercises and postures, including breath control and meditation. It has had a tendency towards occultism, with claims of levitation and ability to survive burial alive.

Hathor. The sky and cow-goddess of Egypt and, next to Isis, the one whose name occurs most often in the Pyramid texts and the *Book of the Dead*. As sky-goddess Hathor was daughter of Rē'and Nut, but also mother of Rē'. As cow-goddess her home was on the east bank of the Nile, not far from Memphis, where a white cow sacred to her was worshipped. Hathor was also a lioness-goddess, said to have come from Nubia, and wife of Horus who was a lion-god. She was also spoken of as mother and nurse of Horus. Hathor was called goddess of love and dance, lady of the underworld, and mistress of the stars. In art she was usually represented as a woman with cow horns on her head which enclosed the solar disk. See also HEKET.

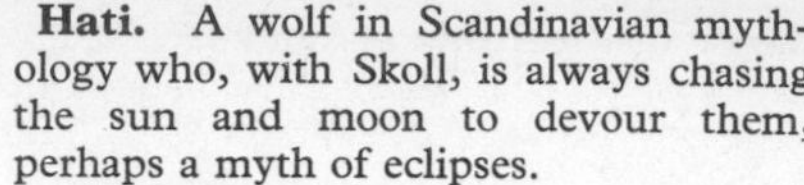

Hati. A wolf in Scandinavian mythology who, with Skoll, is always chasing the sun and moon to devour them, perhaps a myth of eclipses.

Hawd. In Islamic *Traditions* this is the Basin at which Muhammad will meet his community on the day of resurrection. The idea of the Hawd is not found in the *Qur'ān* and its origins are obscure, though it may be connected with the rivers of Paradise. Legend multiplies details, making the basin of huge size and its jars numberless; its waters are sweet as honey and it is fed by a gold and a silver spout from Paradise. The throne of Muhammad is above the Hawd and from thence he descends to intercede with God for his followers. See JANNA.

Hebat. In Hittite mythology the consort of the storm god Teshub (q.v.).

Hebe. Greek personification of 'youthful beauty', a goddess with little cult, though associated with other gods. She was daughter of Zeus and Hera, and sister

of Ares. In the *Iliad* and later, Hebe appears as cup-bearer to the gods, and in the *Odyssey* she is wife to Heracles. In some stories Hebe restores the old to youthful bloom and beauty. See AMBROSIA.

Hecate. Ancient Greek earth goddess, often confused with Artemis (q.v.). In Hesiod it is said that Zeus gave Hecate power over sea and sky as well as the earth, and that she can give victory in war, athletics, pastoral work, fishing and courts of law. This, however, is unusual and perhaps derived from a local cult. Hecate is connected with the uncanny and with haunted places, and was specially worshipped at cross-roads where her statues had three or four bodies. Thus she was related to ghosts, black magic and sorcery, though her older earth cult continued.

Hecatomb. 'Hundred oxen' sacrifice in ancient Greece, though the term is loosely used of the offering of a considerable number of animals. The official calendar at Athens began at midsummer, the Hekatombaion or month of the great sacrifice, though little is known about it except that it was in honour of Apollo and held on his day, the seventh of the month.

Hedonism. See EPICURUS.

Hegira. See HIJRA.

Heiden. The Hall of 'offering' in a Japanese Shinto temple (see JINJA). The Heiden is the building where prayers and offerings are presented by priests, as distinct from the Haiden (q.v.), or Hall of Worship, which is open to general worshippers.

Heimdall. The 'white god' of Scandinavian mythology, said to be the son of Odin and nine maidens who were sisters, though this may mean that he was to be born and to die nine times. Heimdall lived in the Rocks of Heaven (Himinbjörg), beside the quaking Rainbow-bridge (Bifrost), to guard heaven against rock-giants. Heimdall was the watchman of the gods; he could see a hundred leagues by day or night and needed less sleep than a bird. He had a Ringing Horn (Gjallarhorn) whose note could be heard throughout the worlds. When the signs of Doom (Ragnarök) appear, he will sound his horn and call the gods forth to war against the evil Loki and his monsters.

Heimskringla. History of the kings of Norway down to the twelfth century, ascribed to Snorri (q.v.).

Hekaloth. (Hebrew) 'halls', of heaven, the name of fragments of Jewish mystical literature which sought to prepare men for visionary ascensions to heaven. See MERKABAH.

Heket. A goddess of birth in ancient Egypt, usually taken to be the wife of Khnum (q.v.) with whom she joined in creating the world. She was represented as a woman with the head of a frog, and was sometimes identified with Hathor (q.v.).

Hel. The world of death in Scandinavian mythology and the goddess who ruled there. It seems that originally all the dead were thought to go to Hel (like the Greek 'Hades'), therefore Balder (q.v.) went by the Hel-way after cremation, and his brother found him in the seat of honour. When Valhalla (q.v.) is spoken of as the abode of dead warriors, the idea of Hel seems to be narrowed down. It is said that wicked men go to Hel, and even lower to the Misty Hel (Niflhel, q.v.), through dark valleys. The goddess Hel presides over this underworld and it was perhaps originally derived from the idea of burial in the earth. In myths she is said to be a monstrous being, daughter of the evil Loki. See also HELL.

Helen. In Greek mythology daughter of Zeus and Leda, and worshipped at Sparta and elsewhere. She was connected with trees and birds, as a vegetation deity, and has been called a 'faded goddess', whose cult became largely forgotten. In the *Iliad* and *Odyssey* Helen was a woman, wife of Menelaus, who was abducted by Paris and carried away to Troy, thus giving rise to the Trojan war.

Helicon. Largest mountain of Boeotia in Greece, which had a temple of the Muses (q.v.) in a valley, and other temples, theatres and statues. The spring Hippocrene (q.v.) arose just below the summit.

Helios. Greek god of the sun, though he had little cult in the early period and not much mythology. Helios was thought to drive in a chariot across the sky and float back under the earth in a huge cup along the stream of Ocean. There was a powerful non-Greek sun cult on the island of Rhodes, with a festival which had athletic contests. Helios, seeing everything, was called upon as a witness of oaths. Later he came to be identified with Apollo and other gods, and in the Roman empire the sun became the supreme God like the emperor himself.

Hell. For the Scandinavian abode of the dead, see HEL. The idea of a place of darkness, generally underground, to which the dead or the wicked go is common in many religions; see HADES, TARTARUS, ISIS, ISHTAR. For Muslim belief see JAHANNAM. In Hinduism the triple gate of hell (Naraka, q.v.) is Anger, Desire and Greed; the *Bhagavad-Gītā* says that those who reject God will never attain to him but, after revolving in successive evil births, will go on the lowest way (16, 19–21). In Buddhism, Jainism and Taoism there are many hells, whose evil beings and torments are depicted in countless paintings, though there is hope that most beings will get free eventually by rising in the round of transmigration. In Zoroastrian belief hell is presided over by Ahriman (q.v.) and demons, but it is temporary, for all souls will finally be released and the devil made powerless for ever.

Hemachandra, Hemāchārya. A leading Jain teacher and writer (1088–1173). He wrote in Sanskrit and is honoured by educated Hindus as well as Jains. During his long life it is said that Hemachandra wrote over thirty-five million verses on subjects of religion, grammar and history, and he was called 'the Omniscient' of the present era. Under the influence of Hemachandra a great king of Gujerat (Kumārapāla), was converted to Jainism, made it the state religion, prohibited the killing of animals and built magnificent Jain temples.

Henotheism. A term invented in the nineteenth century, generally ascribed to Max Müller, but by some to F. W. J. von Schelling, and derived from two Greek words meaning 'one god'. It is regarded as preliminary to, or different from, Monotheism, which means the worship of one God alone. Henotheism is used to describe religious beliefs in which one god is supreme but others exist, or each god while it is invoked is addressed as if it had all the attributes of the single and supreme God. In ancient Indian religion, for example, Indra is praised as the greatest god but there are also other deities in the pantheon. See KATHENOTHEISM.

Hepatoscopy. 'Liver observance' (Greek), a method of divination practised by the Babylonians, Etruscans and others. See HARUSPICES.

Hephaestus. The Greek god of fire and particularly of blacksmiths' fire, originally associated with volcanic fire. He was the son of Zeus and Hera but thrown out of heaven because he was misshapen. His lameness perhaps indicated the weak legs but strong arms which a blacksmith might have, which would disable him for battle but fit him for smith's work. As a divine craftsman Hephaestus was patron of human crafts, and his cult was strong in towns, particularly at Athens. His wife was Aphrodite, and he made famous works: the armour of Achilles, the sceptre of Agamemnon, and Pandora the first woman. The Romans identified him with Vulcan.

Hera. Wife of Zeus in Greek mythology, daughter of Kronos and Rhea, and mother of Ares, Hebe and Hephaestus. She was an ancient pre-Hellenic deity, the patroness of marriage and female sexual life. The stories of the amours of Zeus with other goddesses were no doubt meant to reconcile various cults with which he was connected, and the Greeks united him with Hera whose powerful cult could not be ignored. Hera was worshipped particularly at Argos and Samos, but also in many other places. Her chief rite was the sacred marriage, and she was connected with birth and childhood. The Romans identified Hera with Juno.

Heracles. The most popular Greek hero, who was sometimes worshipped as a god. His name, 'the glory of Hera' or 'glorious gift of Hera', is a human name, and the adventures and Twelve Labours of Heracles were popular stories of heroic endeavour. In private cults Heracles was naturally appealed to for victory over evil and protection. He was identified with other gods, as far away as Egypt and Spain, and this led to the theory that there were several heroes of the same name. The Romans called him Hercules. The Twelve Labours were in several groups:

killing or capturing various beasts (Nemean Lion, Hydra, Erymanthian Boar, Ceryneian Hind, Stymphalian Birds, Cretan Bull, Horses of Diomedes); then cleansing the Augean Stables and seizing the Girdle of the Amazon queen (q.v.); finally three labours conquering death: the triple-bodied monster Geryon, the infernal watch-dog Cerberus, and the Golden Apples of the Hesperides at the end of the world (see TARTARUS and separate articles on these Labours). For his death, see NESSUS.

Heraclitus. A Greek philosopher of Ephesus, who lived about 530–470 B.C. He believed that fire was the primal element from which everything else arose; there is no permanent being, since 'all is flowing'. This fitted in with belief in the transmigration of souls, as taught by Pythagoras. For Heraclitus, the strength of the soul and its perfection depended upon its nourishment by the cosmic fire, the universal reason or Logos. He was critical both of popular religion and democracy and, although his teaching had widespread influence, his followers became so extravagant that both Plato and Aristotle criticized them.

Hercules. The Roman pronunciation of Heracles (q.v.).

Hermae. Greek bronze or marble pillars of the god Hermes and other deities, found from the fifth century B.C. They were surmounted by a bust of the god, had beams at the shoulders on which to hang wreaths, and a phallus. They stood in the streets and at the gates of Athens and other cities, and were often inscribed with texts.

Hermes. One of the most ancient Greek gods, though depicted as a youth in myths. His name may derive from a stone or heap of stones by the roadside, and many images of him were stones with a head and phallus (see HERMAE). Hence he was connected with fertility, sometimes united with Aphrodite, and was Guide of Souls and a necromancer. In mythology Hermes was son of Zeus and Maia, a cunning child who on the day of his birth invented the lyre and stole Apollo's cattle. He was the messenger of the gods and in human form dressed as a herald, carrying a herald's staff. On other occasions he carried a magic wand. He was god of merchants, and even of thieves as a non-moral being. He was identified with the Roman Mercury and Egyptian Thoth. The so-called Hermes Trismegistus, 'thrice great', made Thoth the supposed author of Hermetica or Gnostic writings produced in Egypt by Greeks from the first to the third centuries A.D.

Hermod, Hermodr. In Scandinavian mythology a son of Odin and brother of Balder. After Balder's death Hermod rode on the grey horse Sleipnir, over a gold-thatched bridge spanning the river Gjöll, to the World of Death. Hermod rode for nine nights through deep valleys till he reached the bridge which was guarded by a maiden, Modgudr. She allowed him to pass after questioning, and Hermod rode on downward and jumped the gates of Hel. He found Balder and asked Hel to permit his return, which she would have allowed if all beings wept for Balder (q.v.) but the evil Loki refused to do so.

Herzl, Theodore. German Jew (1860–1904), who developed the Zionist (q.v.) ideas of Pinsker in a work entitled *Judenstaat*, 'Jewish State', published in 1895. This became the textbook of Zionism, at the first Congress held two years later, and in following years. He envisaged not only a home but a state for Jews in Palestine, and considered that this would be a blessing to all nations.

Hesiod. One of the greatest writers on Greek mythology. His dates are disputed, but are probably some time after the ninth century B.C. In *Works and Days* Hesiod told the myth of Prometheus and gave an account of the Five Ages of the World. In the *Theogony* ('genealogy of the gods') Hesiod tried to arrange ancient material according to his view of the universe in which Zeus was supreme. But, as Zeus was a late arrival, creation began with Chaos and Gaea (Earth) united by Eros and producing Ouranos (Heaven), Kronos and Zeus. Ouranos was mutilated by Kronos who in turn was overthrown by Zeus. Hesiod followed this complex genealogy by accounts of the children of Zeus and the offspring of goddesses with various mortals. Further lists were probably lost.

Hesperus. Greek for the Evening Star, Vesper in Latin. In art he appeared as a boy with a torch. Hesperus is also called father or mother of the Hesperides, the nymphs of the west. See HERACLES.

Hestia. Greek goddess of the hearth, and important because of the central place of Fire (q.v.). There was not much personalization of Hestia and so little mythology, though Hesiod made her the daughter of Kronos and Rhea. Little is known of her private cult, though animals were sometimes sacrificed, and she received the first part of public sacrifice. Hestia was called 'she of the Senate' because of the sacred hearth in the Senate House. Her name is the equivalent of the Roman Vesta (q.v.). The flame for the Olympic Games is still lit from the sacred hearth of Hestia in the ruins of Olympia.

Hevajra. Tibetan Buddhist spirit, presiding over a Tantra (q.v.) cult. To some extent Hevajra was extracted from the elements, in magic circles or Mandalas (q.v.). It is said to have been introduced from Nepal by Marpa (q.v.).

Hevioso. The So, thunder god, of the town of Hevie in Dahomey, corresponding to Shango (q.v.) of the Yoruba of Nigeria. Hevioso is one of the most popular deities of Dahomey.

Hierodouloi, Hierodules. (Greek) 'temple slaves', who belonged to the god and worked for him. In Egypt they looked after the sacred cats and collected temple taxes; in Asia Minor they worked on temple lands; in Corinth and other places the term was applied to temple prostitutes (see DEVADĀSĪS). In the Hellenistic period slaves might be sold or dedicated to a god and thus gain their freedom.

Hierophantes. (Greek) 'exponent of sacred things', chief priest. The title was particularly applied to the most venerated Greek priest, the head of the mysteries at Eleusis (q.v.). He wore a head-band and a purple embroidered robe, and held office for life, being chosen from a priestly family. The Hierophantes proclaimed a truce for the duration of the Mysteries, told all barbarians and defiled persons to keep away, and revealed the secrets to the initiates. He also had public duties in state festivals.

Hijra. (Arabic) 'migration', the removal of Muhammad from Mecca to Medina. Formerly misrepresented as Hegira and termed 'flight'. In A.D. 621 twelve men from Medina vowed to follow Muhammad and the following year seventy-five more did so. The Prophet then resolved to leave Mecca, where Muslims were persecuted, and accept an invitation to install himself at Medina, 320 kilometres north. He sent seventy followers on first in small groups (called Muhājirūn, Emigrants), and himself followed by night with Abū Bakr. They arrived in Medina on 24 September, A.D. 622. Under the Caliph 'Umar, the Hijra was fixed as the beginning of the Islamic era, but the first day of the year was selected, taking it as 16 July, A.D. 622. Islamic dating is calculated from the Hijra, but, as the year is lunar and shorter than the solar year, adjustments have to be made in comparing dates.

Hillulah. See SIMEON BEN YOCHAI.

Hillul Hashem. See KIDDUSH.

Himsā, Hinsā. (Sanskrit) 'injury', violence, killing. It is said to be of three kinds, mental, verbal and personal, and may be personified as Mischief. See AHIMSĀ

Hīnayāna. (Sanskrit) 'small vehicle', or 'low career', used, though only occasionally in Buddhist texts, to indicate the monk's way of salvation or nirvāna for himself alone. The *Mahā-yāna*, 'great vehicle' or 'career' seeks the salvation of all beings. But many *Mahāyāna* texts, such as the *Lotus Sūtra* (q.v.), say that there is only one 'vehicle'. It is said that there were eighteen Hīnayāna Buddhist sects, including the Sarvāstivādins and Mahāsanghikas (qq.v.), but only one remains. Its followers in the lands of south-east Asia prefer to call their school by the more honourable title of Theravāda (q.v.), the 'doctrine of the elders' (see BUDDHISM). Hīnayāna Buddhism is found in Ceylon, Burma, Thailand (Siam), Cambodia and Laos.

Hindarfjall. See SIGURD.

Hinduism. The name, invented by Europeans, for the religion of the majority of the inhabitants of the Indian subcontinent. Hindus call their religion Sanātana Dharma (q.v.), 'eternal truth' or 'right' (*sanātana* related to the Latin *senex*, 'ancient'). There is no church and little organization of Hinduism, and doctrines are exceedingly diverse. It has been said that a Hindu is one who accepts the *Veda* scriptures and is born into a caste, and this means that Hinduism is not a missionary religion, though it spread as far as Java and Bali in earlier times and has missionary groups today, such as the Rāmakrishna Mission. The term *Vedānta* is applied to some ancient and modern Hindu pantheistic philosophy, but there is much that is not pantheistic. There are

SARASVATĪ GANESHA GANGĀ

KUBERA UMĀ SŪRYA

countless gods and cults, but some, like Vishnu and Shiva, are virtually monotheistic. It was claimed in 1966 that there were 406 million Hindus. For the six systems of orthodox Hindu philosophy, see DARSHANA.

Hindu Mahāsabha. See MAHĀSABHA.

Hippocrene. A spring just below the summit of mount Helicon in Boeotia, Greece, which is said to have gushed out when the rock was struck by the foot of the winged horse Pegasus. Hippocrene was the inspiration of poets.

Hippolytus. (Greek) 'loosed horse', son of Theseus and the Amazon (q.v.) Hippolyte. The sea god Poseidon sent a monster which frightened the horses of Hippolytus so that he was thrown from his chariot and killed. In worship he was associated with Aphrodite, as god or hero, and laments were made for him. The Romans identified him with Virbius (q.v.) at Nemi.

Hiranya-garbha. (Sanskrit) 'golden egg' or 'womb', said in the *Rig Veda* to have evolved in the beginning and then to have established earth and heaven. In the *Laws of Manu* it is said that Hiranyagarbha was the seed of the divine Self-existent, which became a Golden Egg in which he himself was born as Brahmā, the progenitor of the world. The name became a title of Brahmā or any creating deity.

Hiranya-kashipu. (Sanskrit) 'golden dress'. An Indian demon who obtained from the god Shiva the rule over the world and prevented his son Prahlāda from worshipping Vishnu. Hence he was killed by Vishnu in his Avatar as Nara-Sinha or man-lion (q.v.).

Hiran-yāksha. (Sanskrit) 'golden eye', brother of Hiranya-kashipu, who dragged the earth down to the bottom of the sea. He was killed by Vishnu in his Avatar as a Boar, Varāha (q.v.).

Hito No Michi. See P. L. KYODAN.

Hitopadesha. 'Good advice', 'friendly instruction' (Sanskrit), the name of a collection of fables mingled with moral precepts popular with Hindus, and taken from the larger collection, the *Pañcha-tantra* (q.v.). It is said to have been compiled by Nārāyana and narrated by a Brahmin called Vishnu-sharma to some young princes.

Hittites. Until the last century only the Old Testament preserved the memory of this people of ancient Asia Minor, and those of them who were found in northern Syria. But modern excavations (particularly at the ancient Hittite capital of Hattusa, now called Boghaz Keui) have revealed many details of Hittite religion engraved on tablets in cuneiform characters. The chief deity was the Sun-goddess Arinna, followed by a storm god whose chief symbol was a bull. He was spouse of Arinna and also god of war. Particularly interesting is the mention on treaty tablets of the Indo-Aryan gods Mitra, Varuna and Indra. There was also a sun-god, called 'Sun of the sky', and an archer-god standing on a deer. Other deities survived the decline of the Hittite empire, and spread into Syria and the later Roman empire.

Hlin. One of the Scandinavian goddesses called Asynjur (q.v.), but all that is known about her is that she protected those whom the goddess Frigg wished to save.

Hoa Hao. See CAO-DAI.

Hod, Hödr, Hotherus. A blind god in Scandinavian mythology. According to Snorri when the gods were shooting at Balder (q.v.) in the certainty that nothing could hurt him, the evil Loki learnt that the mistletoe had not taken an oath not to harm Balder. So Loki gave Hod a shaft of mistletoe and with this Balder was killed. According to Saxo Grammaticus, however, Hod (Hotherus) was a human hero, son of the king of Sweden, who was threatened with death by Balder through jealousy over the maiden Nanna (q.v.). Hod and his allies fought Balder and all the gods in Denmark, defeated them and took Nanna to Sweden. Later Hod was beaten by Balder, and later still he mortally pierced Balder with his sword.

Hokekyō. Japanese name for the *Lotus Sūtra* (q.v.).

Ho Kung. See KO HUNG.

Holi. Spring festival of Krishna (q.v.).

Holy Lake of the Acts of Rāma. A Hindi poem by Tulsī Dās (q.v.), *Rāma-charita-mānasa*, made in the sixteenth century as a popular version of the Sanskrit epic *Rāmāyana* (q.v.). The holy place is the lake of the mind, into which the story of the Avatar Rāma flows to bring joy and peace. The childhood of Rāma, marriage to Sītā, exile to the forest, loss and recovery of Sītā, and return home are all recounted with charm and devotion, and this work has been one of the most popular productions of Vaishnavite religion in recent centuries.

Holy War. See JIHĀD.

Homer. The great classical Greek poet was traditionally regarded as the author of the *Iliad* and the *Odyssey*, which contain many references to the gods and goddesses, as well as heroes and common people. But the existence, date, place and life of Homer have all been questioned in modern times. Critical study might place him before 700 B.C. and, though his text may have been altered and enlarged, it seems to show a controlling mind giving unity to the epics. He may have been blind and illiterate, but many ancient epics were composed orally, such as those of India. The poems were preserved by Sons of Homer, Homeridae, who recited them at public gatherings and added their own compositions. Such were the Homeric Hymns, of varying dates, the *Hymn to Demeter* being as old or older than Homer and the *Hymn to Pan* perhaps later than 500 B.C.

Honden, Shinden. The principal shrine of a Shinto Jinja (q.v.) or temple. It is quite small, a single room, and as the dwelling of the deity it is on a higher level than the rest of the sanctuary, being reached by a staircase. In the middle of the Honden is the symbol of the deity, called a Go-shintai, 'god-entity', or Mitama-shiro, 'spirit-substitute'. This symbol is often a mirror or a cloth, but rarely an image. The shrine is relatively bare, with curtains, some green twigs, white tablets, vessels for gifts, and a mat for the priest to sit on. In front of the Honden stands the hall of worship or Haiden (q.v.).

Honen. Honen Shonin or Genku (q.v.), 1133–1212, founder of the Jodo-Shu (q.v.) or Pure Land sect in Japan. He taught that rebirth in the Pure Land of Amida (see AMITĀBHA) could only be gained by the recitation of the *Nembutsu* (q.v.), the words Namu (Amida) Butsu, 'Hail to Amida Buddha'. This indicated both the saving compassion of Amida and the faith of his follower. Before his death Honen gave a summary of his doctrine in a 'One-Sheet Document', in which he said that salvation depended neither upon meditation nor upon repetition with study, but upon simple repetition of the name of Amida without doubting his mercy. Honen and other Jodo leaders are said to have recited the *Nembutsu* sixty thousand times a day. His life was written by Shunjo.

Hongwanji. Name of some of the principal temples of Shin Buddhism in Japan. In Kyoto one is the Western Hongwanji (Nishi) and the other the Eastern Hongwanji (Higashi).

Horae. Greek goddesses of the 'seasons', who made plants and flowers grow, and were said to be present at the births of gods and heroes. They are depicted in art with suitable attributes, to be seen in the mosaic at Lullingstone in Kent. The Horae were sometimes regarded as more abstract powers, daughters of Justice and given names of Good Government, Right and Peace. See DIKÉ and IRENE.

Horse-Sacrifice. See ASHVA-MEDHA.

Horus. Sky and royal god of ancient Egypt who appears in many forms. Three principal forms were as Horus the Elder, Horus the son of Isis, and Horus the child or Harpocrates (q.v.). As the Elder, Horus was son of Atum or Geb and brother of Osiris, thus indicating an alliance between these two great gods. Then Horus became son of Osiris and Isis, and when Set slew Osiris, Horus avenged him and so became the successor of Osiris. It is generally said that Horus originated in lower Egypt, and the cow-horned Hathor (q.v.) was his wife. But he had many wives and four important sons, with heads respectively of man, dog, jackal and falcon. The falcon was always the greatest symbol of Horus, and this was combined with the sun-disk. In pictures, then, Horus is the falcon-headed god. The Eye of Horus was the moon, parallel to the Eye of Rē' as the sun.

Hoshana Rabba. 'Save, we beseech thee', from Psalm 118, 25, the name of the seventh day of the Jewish festival of Tabernacles (q.v.). In the Safed school of Kabbalistic (q.v.) mystics, and still fairly generally, this day is a time of judgement, when the divine decrees which were sealed on the Day of Atonement take effect.

Hōshin. Japanese form of Sambhoga-kāya; see TRIKĀYA.

Hosshin. Japanese term for Dharma-kāya; see TRIKĀYA.

Hotoke. Japanese term for Buddha, usually in the sense of becoming a Buddha, though occasionally used of the historic Shākyamuni (q.v.).

Hotri. A Hindu priest or sacrificer who invoked the gods or recited the *Rig Veda*. He was one of four kinds of classical priests and had three assistants.

Houris. The Arabic word *hūr* means 'white ones', and in the *Qur'ān* it indicates the clear-eyed maidens of Paradise. They are specially created perpetual virgins who, along with boys of eternal youth, attend on the faithful, among trees and streams, on jewelled couches, with choice

SONS OF HORUS

food. These physical descriptions of Paradise may be derived in part from the biblical *Book of Revelation* added to Christian or Persian pictures of angelic beings in heaven. The *Qur'ān* also speaks of the 'purified wives' of believers entering Paradise. Later legend multiplied the descriptions, but the Sūfī mystics gave the Houris a spiritual interpretation. See also JANNA.

Hozo. Japanese form of the name of Dharmakāra (q.v.), the legendary Buddhist monk who took forty-eight vows and finally became Amitābha (Amida).

Hsiao. (Chinese) 'filial piety', taught by Confucius though not invented by him. Confucius said that a youth should be filial at home, respectful to elders abroad, circumspect and sincere, and show love to all men. Parents also should help their children, and as the subjects should obey the ruler so the ruler should treat his subjects fairly. See ANCESTOR WORSHIP.

Hsien. See IMMORTALS.

Hsüan-tsang or **Chuang.** Chinese Buddhist scholar (A.D. 596–664) who made a great pilgrimage to visit the Buddhist centres in India and studied at the university of Nālanda there to learn Sanskrit and philosophy. After being away many years he returned to China in 645 with many manuscripts and relics and received a great welcome. He wrote a famous account of his pilgrimage and undertook many translations of Indian texts. Hsüan-tsang developed the teachings of the Wei Shih or Fa Hsiang, 'Mere Ideation', school in which the external world is regarded as only a fabrication of our own consciousness, and his thought had a great influence on the philosophically-minded. The Wei Shih was based on the writings of Asanga and Vasubandhu (qq.v.) who claimed that only ideation exists. The story of Hsüan-tsang, as Tripitaka, was written up in the sixteenth century in the novel *Monkey* by Wu Ch'êng-ên, with Tripitaka as the ordinary man and the supernatural Monkey as restless genius.

Hsün Tzŭ. Confucian scholar of the third century B.C. He followed on the Confucian Mencius, but was indebted to Taoist thought, and his idea of Heaven (T'ien) was more natural in the Taoist rather than the Confucian manner. Hsün Tzŭ was a naturalistic and rationalistic thinker who tried to explain the cult of ancestors and the worship of heaven and the gods in poetical and symbolical ways, though most people did not accept this. He criticized superstition, yet he was conservative towards institutions and laid emphasis on ceremonies and customary laws as means of beautifying human relationships, He regarded human nature as evil, and stressed the importance of education and law. See also LI CHI.

Huaca, Waca. 'Sacred shrine' among the Incas and neighbouring peoples of Peru, and deities connected with these shrines. It is applied to adobe pyramids, piles of stones, hills, and great temples. Each Huaca was the abode of a spirit, which needed propitiation, and high mountains were especially sacred. A stone on a hill near Cuzco was held to represent a brother of the emperor Manco Capac and to protect his dynasty. There were said to be 350 Huacas near Cuzco, on lines radiating from the Temple of the Sun (q.v., and see INTI).

Hua Yen. A Chinese Buddhist School which based its principal teachings on the *Hua Yen* or *Avatamsaka Sūtra*, the 'Garland' or Adornment of the Buddha which glorifies the Buddha and Bodhisattvas. Hence it is called the Garland School. Hua Yen is said to have been founded by Tu-shun (A.D. 557–640), who was followed by Chih-yen and Fa-tsang. It believed that all beings possess the Buddha-nature, and other Chinese schools shared this doctrine. Its teachers were dissatisfied with the negative expressions of emptiness of Mahāyāna philosophy, and taught a universal principle (*li*) derived from Confucianism. Hua Yen monks were forbidden to eat meat, and this was adopted by other Chinese sects. The school was taken to Japan in the eighth century as Kegon, where its headquarters at Todai-ji, Nara, has the largest wooden building in the world. Kegon has been one of the smallest Japanese Buddhist schools but has exercised considerable influence on Buddhist thinking.

Hubal. An idol at Mecca from pre-Islamic days. It was in the shape of a man, coloured red, and stood inside or in front of the Ka'ba shrine (q.v.). The image was consulted by divination with arrows. Some writers, but not Muslims, have thought that Hubal was a representation of Allāh. When Muhammad conquered Mecca in A.D. 630, Hubal was destroyed along with all the other idols.

Hūd. A prophet mentioned several times in the *Qur'ān*, where chapter 11 bears his name and tells his story (11, 52f). He was sent to the tribe of 'Ād as a prophet from God, but it is not clear whether the prophet and the people were

thought to be connected with the biblical revelations or whether they were purely Arabian.

Huehuecoyotl. 'Old Coyote' (a Mexican word), in Aztec mythology a backbiting and mischievous deity, associated with gaiety and sex. Sometimes he was identified with the animal deity Xolotl (q.v.) as showing the animal side of human conduct. Prisoners of war were sacrificed to him in ceremonies of great cruelty.

Huehueteotl. (Aztec) 'old god', the god of fire, often depicted as a bent old man, sitting on the ground, with a shallow bowl for burning incense on his head. He was also called Xiuhtecuhtli, 'turquoise lord' (q.v.).

Hui Hui. Chinese name for Muslims (q.v.).

Huiracocha, Viracocha. Creator god of the Incas (q.v.), who dwelt in heaven and was immortal. He created and maintained the world, but delegated some functions to other gods, such as the sun and stars. Huiracocha appears in human form and in some myths was a culture hero. At the capital city of Cuzco his image was of solid gold with arm upraised. He was particularly the concern of official religion, and in popular cults there were many other deities. In mythology Huiracocha created the sky and earth, and then huge men, but being displeased with them he turned them into the huge stone figures which are still to be seen at Tiahuanaco. Later he made normal men, gave them clothes, and taught them languages and moral codes.

Huitzilopochtli. The national god of the Aztecs, whose name meant 'humming bird on the left', since the sun came from the south, left-hand, side and was brought by the humming-bird which was his representation. One text says that Huitzilopochtli was a human being, and an early warrior was indeed deified and carried in a mummy bundle on migrations to the valley of Mexico. The identification with the sun arose because the sun is a warrior who chases the moon and stars away with a turquoise serpent as weapon. In pictographs Huitzilopochtli appears as light compared with the dark god Tezcatlipoca. Human sacrifice, principally heart sacrifice, was offered particularly to the sun god to ensure his strength. He had a great temple on the Great Pyramid in Mexico City. See COYOLXAUHQUI.

Hui-yüan. Chinese Buddhist monk (334–416), disciple of Tao-an (q.v.). He read widely in Taoist and Confucian philosophy, and helped thus to root Buddhism more firmly into Chinese thought. He established a famous monastery at Lu-shan in southern China, among the mountain scenery that accorded with Taoist love of nature. Hui-yüan is regarded as the founder and first patriarch of the Pure Land (Ching-t'u) school, and in 402 before a statue of Amitābha he made his monks vow to be born in his Western Paradise.

Huldu. 'Hidden folk', in Scandinavian mythology, especially Iceland, much the same as elves (see ELF).

Hulūl. Arabic philosophical and mystical term, meaning to 'settle in', alight, enter, and used of the soul in the body. In the further sense of an 'incarnation', as in Christian doctrine, Hulūl was rejected by almost all Islamic writers, and extreme Shī'a who seemed to accept it were regarded as heretical. They were called Hulūlīya. See TANĀSUKH.

Human Sacrifice. This practice has been found in many religions and ages, as the highest form of offering, to 'give my firstborn for my transgression' (*Micah* 6, 7). It was denounced by Hebrew prophets and Hindu practitioners of Non-violence (see AHIMSĀ), and of course never held a place in reformed religions such as Buddhism and Islam. Human beings were killed as attendants upon dead chiefs in Ancestor Worship (q.v.), and as principal offerings in First Fruits (q.v.). Some of the most notorious sacrifices were those practised in the declining Aztec empire (q.v.). See MIXCOATL. See also IPHIGENIA.

Hung Hsiu-ch'üan. See T'AI P'ING.

Hun Pic Tok. War god of the Maya, named after 'eight thousand stone knives' which were the spears of his soldiers. His pyramid temple was the most important of those in the city of Izamal (q.v.) in northern Yucatan.

Huppah. 'Bridal chamber', in Hebrew, from *Psalm* 19, 5, originally where the bride received her husband and the marriage was consummated. It developed into a square canopy of silk or other material fixed across four poles planted in the ground or held by attendants, and here in traditional Jewish practice a marriage ceremony is performed.

Hūr. See HOURIS.

Huracān. Great and ancient Maya god, called the Triple Heart of the Universe. Our word 'hurricane' comes from his name.

Husain. Second son of 'Alī and Fātima, born at Medina about A.D. 626. After the death of his elder brother al-Hasan (q.v.) he waited quietly in Mecca till a new caliph Yazīd (q.v.) was proclaimed at Damascus. Husain was then persuaded by supporters in Iraq to put himself forward as the true caliph. He set out for Iraq, but his party was surrounded by rival soldiers at Karbalā'. On 10 Muharram (10 October, A.D. 680) Husain's party was destroyed and he himself fell, wounded in many places. His head was sent to Yazīd, but was returned and buried with his body in Karbalā' (q.v.), which became a great shrine of the Shī'a Muslims, rivalling Mecca. Every year Shī'as celebrate the martyrdom of Husain with lamentations during the first ten days of Muharram, culminating in a great 'Passion Play' at the end of which the angel Gabriel delivers the key of intercession to Husain so that he may take to Paradise all who have honoured him.

Huxley, Aldous. See NEO-VEDĀNTA, VEDĀNTA and MESCALIN.

Hvergelmir. A well, perhaps meaning 'roaring kettle' in Scandinavian mythology. It was in Niflheim (q.v.), the world of death, and from the well flowed eleven rivers. According to Snorri (q.v.), Hvergelmir lay under one of the roots of the great world tree, Yggdrasil.

Hyacinthus. An ancient Cretan god, a flower-hero, perhaps also called Narcissus. When introduced to Greece various cities had months called after Hyacinthus, there were festivals, and in art the god was represented as bearded. In Greek story, however, Hyacinthus was a beautiful boy who was loved by Apollo but killed accidentally with his discus; in one version the Wind was jealous and turned the discus in mid air so that it

smashed against Hyacinthus. From the boy's blood sprang the flower of his name which is marked with letters taken as his initials or as 'aiai', 'alas'.

Hybris. In Greek thought Hybris was overweening pride of strength or passion which led to wanton violence. This brought the Nemesis of retribution of the gods to human presumption, causing some blind infatuation (see ATE) which made a man commit a rash act leading to his ruin.

Hydra. Many-headed water serpent in Greek mythology, which lived at Lerna near Argos. To destroy it was one of the Labours of Heracles (q.v.), but

when he cut off one head two or three more grew in its place. He burnt the grove to cauterize the roots of the heads, and buried its golden immortal head under a rock.

Hygieia. The Greek goddess of personified Health, generally associated in cult with her father Asclepius (q.v.), with his snake emblem; her name followed his in the Hippocratic oath taken by physicians. She is usually said to be a virgin, though she is also addressed as 'mother most high'.

Hymen. A cry, *Hymen*, *Hymenai*, made at Greek marriages and thought to be an invocation of a god named Hymen or Hymenaeus. Myths were invented to recount his adventures and connection with a happy wedding.

Hymn. The Greek *Hymnos* was a word of uncertain origin, for a song or ode in honour of gods and heroes. Hymns listed the attributes of the god, recounted his exploits, and ended with a prayer for help. There were famous hymns to Demeter (q.v.) and other gods. Similar divine songs are found in many religions, from the *Psalms* of the Bible to the Indian *Vedas* (q.v.).

Hyperion. An epithet often used of the Sun in Greek myth. But according to Hesiod he was a Titan, who married his sister Theia, and they had three children: Sun, Moon and Dawn.

Hypnos. God of sleep in ancient Greek mythology, son of Nyx (night) and brother of Thanatos (death). He lived under the earth and never saw the sun, or changed into a bird at night time. As a youth with wings he stroked the foreheads of the weary with a branch or gave them a potion. He was worshipped in Troezen.

Hystaspes. Greek form of Vishtāspa, a king of Bactria, who was converted by Zoroaster in the sixth century B.C. An Oracle of Hystaspes, mentioned by Christian writers much later, was probably not Zoroastrian but Mithraic (q.v.) and foretold the coming of Mithra at the end of the world to save the righteous and destroy the wicked by fire.

I

Iacchus. A minor Greek god, associated with the Mysteries of Eleusis (q.v.), and perhaps a personification of a ritual cry. The god and the song and the day when his image was carried all had the same name. He was said to be the son of Demeter, or Persephone, or even of Dionysos. Later the similarity of name caused him to be confused with Bacchus.

Iamblichus. Neo-Platonist philosopher (A.D. 250–325), who founded a school in Syria, and is said to have developed the Neo-Platonic (q.v.) teachings. But few works of his survive, and he seems to have introduced magical and theosophical ideas into the teaching of Plotinus.

'Ibādāt. Arabic term for religious practices, particularly the five Pillars of Islam (q.v.).

Ibādīs, Ibādīya, Abādīya.—One of the chief branches of the Khārijite Muslims (q.v.), found in Oman, East Africa, Libya and Algeria. The name is derived from one of their founders, 'Abdallāh ibn Ibād who lived in the seventh century. They hold to the election of Imāms, spiritual leaders, by secret councils. They must rule according to the *Qur'ān*, the *Traditions of Muhammad*, and the example of previous Imāms, but they are tolerant of those who hold different views, allow marriage with non-Ibādīs, and reject the violence of some other Khārijites. Their women are more emancipated than in some Muslim lands. Today they number about half a million people, mostly in

Oman where they form about seventy per cent of the population.

IBIS AND THOTH

Ibis. A sacred bird to the ancient Egyptians, especially connected with the god Thoth who was believed to be manifested in this form and worshipped as such at Hermopolis, Hermes being the Greek name for Thoth. The Ibis symbolized research and knowledge, and at death it was mummified as seen at Memphis, Thebes and Abydos.

Iblīs. The name of the Devil in Muslim belief, probably derived from the Greek Diabolos. The *Qur'ān* uses both the terms 'Iblīs' and 'Shaitan' (Satan), sometimes in the same way and meaning, but in stories of creation the Devil is always called Iblīs. Probably following Christian tradition, the *Qur'ān* says that when God had created Adam he told all the angels to bow to him, and all obeyed but Iblīs who thought it beneath his dignity to bow to a creature made of earth while he himself was made of fire. For this he was banished but begged for a postponement of his final degradation till the Day of Judgement, so he leads men astray on earth. In the end Iblīs will be thrown into hell with all his hosts, though some mystics considered he would be saved since he refused to bow down to Adam through a wish to honour God alone.

Ibn 'Arabī. Celebrated Islamic pantheistic mystic, born in Murcia in Spain in A.D. 1165 and died in Damascus 1240. Orthodox Islam said that there was only one God, but Ibn 'Arabī declared that 'there is nothing but God', God *is* everything. Creation is a perpetual state, in which something already existing in God comes into manifestation. There is no duality of the human soul and God, since it is not separate from him, and unification is simply becoming aware of a relationship of unity with God that has always existed. Ibn 'Arabī dealt more than any other Muslim thinker with the Kalima, Word or Logos, as manifested in the Perfect Man. This he saw in the Prophet Muhammad, yet not in his earthly person but in the Spirit of Muhammad of which all the other prophets were manifestations. This is not a second divine person, but God himself in perfect manifestation. Other theologians charged Ibn 'Arabī with heresy, but he had many followers.

Ibn Hanbal. See HANBAL.

Ibn Hishām. See IBN ISHĀQ.

Ibn Ishāq. Arabian scholar, born in Medina about A.D. 700 and died in Baghdad in 767 or 769. He spent his life collecting legends and traditions of Muhammad, and wrote the standard life of the Prophet, *Sīrat Rasūl Allāh*, the 'Life of the Apostle of God'. It was edited, as the English translator says, with 'impertinent meddling' by Ibn Hishām who died in Egypt about 834.

Ibn Rushd. See AVERROES.

Ibn Sīnā. See AVICENNA.

Ibn Tūmart. Muslim reformer (about A.D. 1080–1128) of Morocco, and regarded as the Mahdī of the Almohads (q.v.).

Ibrāhīm. The name of the Biblical Abraham in the *Qur'ān* and Islamic tradition. Together with Ismā'īl (Ishmael) Ibrāhīm raised the foundations of the Ka'ba (q.v.) shrine in Mecca (*Qur'ān* 2,121f). It is said that Ibrāhīm was not a Jew, nor was he a Christian, but he was a Hanīf (q.v.), a Muslim (3, 60). In later traditions Ibrāhīm was one of the six great prophets, to whom God revealed twenty portions of scripture, and was called the 'Friend of God' (Khalīl Allāh).

Icarus. Son of the craftsman Daedalus (q.v.) in Greek mythology, who was imprisoned with his father by King Minos of Crete. Daedalus made two pairs of artificial wings with which they flew away, but Icarus went too near the sun, the wax of his wings melted and he fell to his death in the Aegean sea through this 'Icarian pride'.

I Ching, Yi Ching. The Chinese *Book of Changes*, one of the most influential of the so-called Confucian Classics (q.v.). The character 'I' means change or transformation, but this is based on the constancy of the eternal principle Tao (q.v.). This Tao produces all the changes of the universe by the interaction of two complementary forces, Yang and Yin (q.v.). The *I Ching* sets out a system of diagrams, eight trigrams (q.v.) and sixty-four hexagrams derived from them, and by study men can understand the phenomena which they represent, and their relationships and changes, thus obtaining a blueprint of the universe. This work began as a treatise on divination, but it came to have great moral and philosophical significance for living in harmony with the universe. Appendices to the *I Ching* brought a synthesis of Confucian and Taoist thought, of morality and life in harmony with heaven.

'Īd. Arabic 'festival'. There are two prescribed festivals in the Muslim year: the 'Īd al-adhā, 'sacrificial festival', is on the tenth day of the twelfth month (the month of pilgrimage, Dhu al-Hijja) and is marked by sacrifices of animals performed not only by pilgrims near Mecca, but all over the Islamic world. The 'Īd al-fitr', 'festival of breaking the fast', is held on the first day of the tenth month, Shawwāl, which comes after the end of the month's fast of Ramadān. Each festival lasts several days, during which people visit their friends and the cemeteries, and have general holidays (see BAIRAM).

Idā, Ilā. Food or libation in the Indian *Rig Veda*, and then personified as goddess of speech. She instructed the first man, Manu, and gave him the rules for sacrifice. Another myth says that Idā sprang from a sacrifice performed by Manu to obtain offspring, and she married him to produce the race of Manu. In later story the sacrifice was performed wrongly, and Idā or Ilā was born, and another version says that Manu's eldest son was Ila, who through trespassing on a sacred grave was changed into the female Ilā.

Iddhi. See SIDDHI.

Ideation School. Chinese Buddhist school, known as Wei Shih or Fa Hsiang (qq.v.), a development of the Yogachāra of Asanga (qq.v.). It taught that only ideas exist and the external world is a creation of our consciousness. It was developed in China by Hsüan-tsang (q.v.), but, though it influenced the philosophically-minded its teachings were beyond most monks and laymen.

Ides. (Latin) eighth day after the Nones (before the Ides which were nine days inclusive), in the ancient Roman calendar, so the 15th of March, May, July and October, and the 13th of other months. 'Beware the Ides of March' (*Julius Caesar*), therefore the 15th. Jupiter (q.v.) was worshipped at the Ides of each month, the time of the full moon.

Idol. This word is derived from Greek, *eidolos*, meaning a form or shape, and it was comparable to the Indian *rūpa* (q.v.). In English usage it has come to be used in derogatory fashion of religious objects or aids to worship, and it is better to consider them as Images (q.v.). See also FETISH.

Idrīs. Name of a man mentioned twice in the *Qur'ān* and said to be raised to a high place (19, 57). It has been assumed by commentators that this was Enoch of the Bible, who was said not to have died, and not to be touched by Azrael (q.v.), the angel of death.

Another eminent Idrīs, and his successors, was the founder of the Sanūsī order (q.v.). The last of the dynasty, Sayyid Idrīs, ruled Libya from 1943–69.

Idunn. A minor Scandinavian deity, wife of Bragi the poet. Her chief function was to guard the magic apples of immortality which the gods ate when they wanted to renew their youth. The evil Loki enticed Idunn into a forest and the giant Thjazi stole the apples and took them off to Thrymheim, the Giant World. Then the gods became old and they forced Loki to bring back Idunn and the apples. Loki took the form of a falcon, changed Idunn into a nut, and flew off with her. The giant changed into the form of an eagle and pursued them but was destroyed by Odin.

Ifa. A West African system of geomancy (q.v.). The name is from the Yoruba of Nigeria, but derivative or similar systems are found among neighbouring and even distant peoples, among the Nupe to the north and the Bini to the east. In Dahomey it is called Fa and was borrowed from the Yoruba. The Ifa system has a protecting deity known as Orunmila, 'heaven knows salvation', but the earthly geomancy is held to have originated with a diviner named Ifa who founded the city of Ifé. There are two methods of divination, one by means of a cord which has four half nuts at each end, giving concave and convex faces. The larger system uses a board covered with sand or powder, on which the diviner marks figures of one or two marks, depending on two or one nuts that remain in his hand after a handful have been transferred from one hand to the other. Eight sets of marks are made, in two columns, corresponding to the eight half nuts on the cord. The resultant pattern is interpreted according to traditional proverbs and legends.

Ifa Oracle, sixteen combinations of single and double signs:

I	II	II	I
I	II	I	II
I	II	I	II
I	II	II	I
I	II	I	II
I	II	II	II
II	I	II	II
II	I	II	I
I	II	II	II
I	I	I	II
I	I	II	I
II	I	II	II
I	I	I	II
II	I	II	I
I	II	I	II
I	I	II	I

'Īfrīt. A powerful and evil person and in Muslim thought identified with the most hostile and malignant of the Jinns (q.v.).

Igigi. See ANUNNAKI.

Iguvine Tablets. Nine bronze tablets, found in A.D. 1444 at the ancient Iguvium, Gubbio in Italy. They date from between 400 and 90 B.C. and are engraved with the liturgy and activities of the Fratres Atiedii, a brotherhood of priests, for cleansing, sacrifices and dedications. The festivals of clans, sacrifices to Jupiter and other gods, regulations and decisions here recorded provide the most important evidence for ancient Italian religion.

Ihrām. 'Sacred state', Arabic (see HAREM). The word is used particularly of the dress assumed by pilgrims to Mecca, and this is done at one of several stations around the holy city. Men wear two white robes and women a long robe from head to foot which need not cover the face but usually has a mask over it. With such common dress all pilgrims become equal. The time of Ihrām lasts throughout the ritual of pilgrimage proper (see HAJJ), and it is forbidden to wear jewelry or perfume, cut the nails or hair, have sexual intercourse, shed blood, hunt, or uproot plants. Fasting is not prescribed.

Ijmā'. (Arabic) 'agreement', one of the four principles by which Islamic faith and practice are defined. These are the *Qur'ān*, Custom (sunna), Ijmā', and Analogy (qiyās, q.v.). Ijmā' is not the agreement of the masses, but the judgement of proper authorities on matters of faith, based upon knowledge. The Wahhābīs (q.v.) only accept the Agreement of the Companions of the Prophet, while other law schools (see FIQH) followed the Agreement of larger communities. The principle of Ijmā' allowed for development of doctrine and practice, notably regarding Muhammad and the saints, and it is claimed by many today to be a potent means for reform within Islam. See 'ULAMĀ'.

Ijtihād. (Arabic) 'opinion' or 'trying to form an opinion as to law'. This is a deduction or decision given by a Muslim teacher, Mujtahid, as distinct from the collective opinion of an authoritative group of teachers which is Ijmā' (q.v.). While some regard Ijtihād as simply individual opinion, however, the founders of the four legal schools have been reckoned as having outstanding Ijtihād and important opinions have been deduced from their principles. In modern times Sunni Muslims have sought to discover within the teachings of any of the four schools principles which can justify Ijtihād in adapting conduct to the needs of modern life.

Ikebana. (Japanese) 'flower arrangement'. *Bana* or *hana* means a 'flower' and *Ikebana* means loosely 'keeping flowers alive in vases'. The word 'flower' includes branches, twigs, reeds and grasses. It is particularly associated with Zen Buddhism (q.v.). See also TOKONOMA.

Ikelos. See MORPHEUS.

Ikhnaton. Egyptian Pharaoh of the fourteenth century B.C. sometimes called a monotheistic reformer. His name was Amenophis IV, his queen was the beautiful Nefertiti, he came to the throne at about ten years of age and died at about twenty-six. He changed his name to Ikhnaton, 'it pleases Aton', about the sixth or eighth year of his reign. He came to oppose the worship of the god Amūn (q.v.) of Thebes, destroyed his images, effaced his name from inscriptions, and left Thebes to found a new city, Akhetaton. He favoured the worship of Aton the sun, and its disk with rays shining out. While the names of some other gods were chiselled out, they were

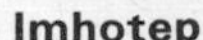

IKHNATON

not all denied, the name of Rē' was usually untouched, and it was Amūn who was particularly attacked. Ikhnaton would thus rather be a henotheist (q.v.). After his death the priests of Amūn resumed power. Ikhnaton's second successor, Tutankhaton, became Tutankhamūn (q.v.) 'living image of Amūn'. Now Aton's names were defaced, but they have remained in the rock-tombs of Tell el-Amarna (q.v.).

Ikhwān. See BRETHREN.

Ikshvāku. Legendary founder of the Indian solar race, himself grandson of the sun, who reigned at Ayodhyā at the beginning of the second or Tretā age (q.v.). He had a hundred sons.

I Li. See LI.

Illapa. Thunder and lightning, the storm and weather god of the Incas and neighbouring peoples. He was pictured as a man with war club and sling who broke the jug in which his sister kept the rain. This produced the thunderclap and thunderbolt, and the rain comes from the heavenly river, the Milky Way.

Illiteracy. See UMMI.

'Ilm. (Arabic) 'knowledge', in the broadest sense of the intellectual processes, and of arts and sciences. One who exercises 'ilm may be a canon lawyer, '*ālim* (plural '*ulamā*', q.v.), or a scholar in the widest sense.

Ilyās. The name used in the *Qur'ān* for the Biblical prophet Elias or Elijah. He called the people from Baal to the true God (37, 123f.).

Image. A word derived from Latin *imago*, perhaps from the same root as 'imitate', as an imitation or representation of a person or thing, a sculpture, statue or effigy. An image of any being is strictly prohibited in Judaism and Islam, but is common in many other religions. Images often represent deities, notably in Hinduism, or saints in Buddhism and Jainism. But the Buddha-rūpa is not necessarily worshipped and its different postures have symbolical meaning (see RŪPA). It is remarkable that African wooden sculptures frequently represent attendants rather than the deity concerned. See IDOL, FETISH and MASK.

AFRICAN IMAGE

Imām. (Arabic) 'leader' or 'pattern', an important title used in several ways. Most generally an Imām is anyone who leads congregational prayer in a mosque; he is a layman, chosen for this task by the local community. Sunni Muslims apply the term to the orthodox Caliphs, to leaders of law schools and to eminent theologians. Among Shī'a Muslims the idea of the Imām developed greatly. Basically the Imāms were twelve, or seven, beginning from 'Alī (q.v.), and at first regarded as the legitimate Caliphs. Mystical ideas were later added, the twelfth or seventh disappeared, became the Hidden Imām, and would appear later as the Messiah or Mahdī, 'the guided one'. Then there was said to be always an Imām in the world, hidden, but appearing to the faithful in time of need, and sending out his light to convert all mankind. Theories of the transmigration or incarnation of the Imām were held, but not by the majority of the Shī'a (q.v.).

Imāmī. See SHĪ'A.

Īmān. (Arabic) 'faith'. The basic idea is that of rest and security, and so trust in somebody, above all in God. Īmān is both having faith in God and his message, and the content of his message. It is sometimes used almost identically with Islām.

Imbe, Hironari. Japanese scholar who in A.D. 807 wrote an account of early Japanese myth and religion, called Kogoshui (q.v.).

Imhotep. Egyptian wise man, priest, physician and architect of the Third Dynasty, about 2780 B.C. Some two thousand years later he was regarded as a god and was popular with the Greek rulers, who identified him with Asclepius. As a god Imhotep was called the son of Ptah and Nut, he was patron of wisdom and especially of medicine and exorcism, and scribes poured libations to him before writing. His picture, common at Memphis, shows him as a seated man with a papyrus roll on his knees. To Imhotep is attributed the construction of the first Pyramid (q.v.), the famous Step Pyramid at Saqqāra.

Immortals. In Chinese Taoism various classes of immortals are named who live in the Realm of Great Purity. The best known are the Eight Immortals, Pa Hsien, though groups of other numbers were listed. The eight are: Li T'ieh-kuai (a beggar with medicine), Chung-li Ch'üan (with a beard and a peach), Lan Ts'ai-ho (as a young man or woman with a flute), Chang Kuo (on a mule), Ho Hsien-ku (a girl with a musical instrument), Lü Tung-pin (with a magic sword), Han Hsiang Tsu (with peaches) and Ts'ao Kuo-chiu (with castanets). The Eight Immortals have been popular on the stage, in art and other ways, and, although their members changed, the number eight for some unknown reason remained the most popular. The Immortals rival, and perhaps imitate, groups of Buddhist spiritual beings, and as representing figures of both sexes and different ages they give scope for representation in art and drama.

'Imrān. In the *Qur'ān* (3, 30f.) a chapter is named after 'Imrān, who was the father of Mary, the mother of Jesus ('Isā). There is perhaps a connection with 'Amrām of the Bible (Numbers 26, 59), father of Moses and Miriam. See MARYAM.

Inactivity. See WU WEI.

Inari. Shinto god of food, the name said to mean 'man of rice' or 'load of rice'. Inari is identified with various other gods: Uga-no-mitama, a son of Susano-wo (q.v.), or food-goddesses such as Ukemochi or Toyo-uke-bime; but in popular worship the god of food is most generally known as Inari. There are many temples,

which are distinguished from the other unpainted Shinto temples by being bright red. They are approached through long rows of Torii (q.v.) arches which are also painted red, and devotees place large or small Torii in front of the shrine. The most striking features are the statues of foxes which are found at all Inari shrines, of all sizes, and made of stone or other materials. Inari is thus sometimes called the fox-god, but the foxes are messengers of the deity, kindly to men, often holding keys, balls or texts in their mouths. Inari is prayed to for good harvests, for protection from evil, and any blessings.

Incarnation. Parallels to the Christian doctrine of one Incarnation have been suggested in other religions, but there are characteristic differences. The closest are the Hindu Avatars (q.v.), which are successive descents of the deity or theophanies, but although they were appearances in human bodies they were hardly historical or datable and it may be doubted whether they were limited, suffering men. The Buddhas-to-be were born on earth, after successive transmigrations, before attaining Nirvāna, but they are never incarnations of a deity. The Lamas of Tibet are incarnations of previous Buddhas and Bodhisattvas. The notion of incarnation has always been rejected by most Islamic authorities, Sunni and Shī'a. See HULŪL.

Incas. Rulers of ancient Peru whose

INCA SYMBOLS

empire had a highly developed priestly hierarchy, the chief of whom, a relative of the emperor, was known as Villac or Huillac Umu, 'speaking chief'. There were also chosen women, Virgins of the Sun (q.v.), brought up in convents, serving in temples or used as sacrificial victims. The chief Inca god was the creator Huiracocha (q.v.), who was linked with other gods and also appeared as a culture hero. The sun-god Inti (q.v.) was deity of the ruling dynasty and also connected with fertility. There were many other deities, represented in human or animal form, and household spirits guarding life and property. The Peruvians were preoccupied with life after death and had a deeply rooted ancestral cult. They held that the righteous go to an upper world in the sky, and the evil to the cold under the ground.

Incubo. In Latin notions a spirit of 'nightmare', or sometimes of buried treasure, and also identified with forest spirits such as Fauns (q.v.). This was the origin of the Incubus of medieval belief, an evil spirit that preyed on sleeping women, as the Succubus had relationships with sleeping men.

Indian Religions. India has been one of the major homes of religion and through its missionary offshoots, like Buddhism, Indian ideas have gone to the farthest extremes of Asia and in modern times all over the world. The majority religion is Hinduism (q.v.). Jainism (q.v.) flourished from about the sixth century B.C. and Buddhism shortly after. The Parsis came to India from the eighth century A.D., and the Sikhs arose in the fifteenth century. Islam flourished in India from about 1000 and became the second largest religion. The Indian census of 1963 returned 366 million Hindus, 47 million Muslims, 10 million Christians, 6 million Sikhs, 3 million Buddhists, 1½ million Jains, 125,000 Parsis.

Indigetes, Indigitamenta. Minor gods of Rome, whose title has been explained in various ways. They have been said to comprise gods of limited function, or foreign importation, or ancestral origin, but all of these derivations have been disputed.

Indra. The greatest god of the Indian Vedic scriptures, with more hymns than any other deity except Agni. He is a sky and particularly a storm god, sending out lightning and thunderbolts. He is also a great warrior and national god of the invading Aryan soldiers. Indra fights Vritra (q.v.) or Ahi, the snake or demon of drought and compels it to release the waters. He overthrows the cities of the native inhabitants of India, probably those of Harappā (q.v.) and other centres, and perhaps destroys their irrigation systems. Indra is depicted as a giant, ruddy or golden, addicted to great draughts of the sacred Soma juice, and riding in a golden chariot. Later he declines in importance, is humbled by Krishna, and today is almost forgotten except as ruler of a distant heaven, Indra-Loka, 'Indra's world'; see SWARGA.

Indrānī. Wife of Indra (q.v.), mentioned occasionally in the *Rig Veda*, and said to be blessed because her husband would never die of old age. She was chosen for her beauty among competing goddesses, but Indrānī has always played a very minor role and has had little cultus.

Indus Valley Culture. See HARAPPĀ.

Initiation. See SACRED THREAD.

Injīl. The name for the *Gospel* in the

Qur'ān and Muslim tradition, derived from the Greek word for Evangel. It is regarded as a book given by God to Jesus (5, 50) since it is also the *Injīl* in the possession of Christians (7, 156). It covers not just one *Gospel* but the four, and perhaps also the whole *New Testament*, since this is the sacred book of the Christians which in Muhammad's time had probably not been translated into Arabic. Several stories from the *Gospel* appear in the *Qur'ān*, always treated with respect, and Muslim writers used the Bible widely, though giving their own interpretations to it.

Innen. Japanese term for Karma (q.v.).

Innina, Irnina, Nin. Sumerian names for the goddess of the planet Venus, called by the Akkadians by the name of Ishtar (q.v.), the equivalent of Astarte (q.v.).

Inshallah. (Arabic) 'If it should please God' (*inshā' allāhu*), a very common expression among Muslims, indicating dependence upon the divine will.

Inti. The tribal god of the ruling dynasty of the Incas (q.v.). Although the god of the sun represented as a golden disk with a face, he was thought to be human in shape. Inti was not only the sun, but also a god of fertility. His wife was the moon mother, Mama Quilla, who was concerned with the calendar and its religious festivals. Inti ruled over lesser gods, as he was closely tied to the state religion and some of them belonged to conquered tribes. Since Inti was the sun, the king was called 'Son of the Sun' and regarded as ruling by divine right. So the king received divine honours and at death his body was mummified. He was thought to live for ever, with the wives and servants who were buried with him. The sun was represented in the temples of Inti (Sun Temples) by a golden disk, and there was an immense one in the great Temple of the Sun in Cuzco, which was removed at the Spanish invasion.

Intichiuma. An Australian ritual for increasing the families of men and animals, used by a local group of the Aranda tribe. The general Aranda term is Mbanbiuma and in western Australia it is called Talu.

Io. Priestess of the Greek goddess Hera (q.v.) at Argos. Zeus loved Io and changed her into a heifer to hide her from Hera, but the latter set the three-eyed monster Argos to watch her and when Hermes killed Argos Hera plagued Io with a gadfly. She ran away to Egypt where Zeus restored her to her natural form. In Egypt Io was identified with Hathor and Isis (qq.v.). Perhaps she was originally another form of Hera, or a moon-goddess with cow horns.

Io. Since 1850 references have been made in Maori (q.v.) religion to belief in a supreme God, Io. Since his name was not recorded earlier, it has been debated whether it was too sacred to be mentioned, or whether the notion of a supreme being was derived from Christian teaching.

Iphigenia. Daughter of Agamemnon in Greek mythology and sacrificed by her father at Aulis, perhaps because he had offended the goddess Artemis. According to Euripides she was not killed but taken away by Artemis to the land of the Tauri to become her priestess. She remained there till delivered by Athena and brought to Attica, where a cult and sacrifice at Halae were explained by this story.

Iqbāl. Poet-philosopher of undivided India, Sir Muhammad Iqbāl (1876–1938), has been called the Father of Pakistan, yet he sought a universal reform and revival of Islam. Born in Sialkot in the Punjab he became a lecturer in Lahore and a poet. Iqbāl travelled abroad, took a doctorate at Cambridge, set up as a barrister in Lahore, and became president of the Muslim League. He called Muslims to awake from their stagnation, rejecting world-denying tendencies, and insisting on progress. He wrote *The Reconstruction of Religious Thought in Islam*, and many poems.

Irene, Eirene. The personification of peace among the Greeks. She had little mythology or cult, but it is said that she was worshipped during a public festival in Athens, and a bloodless sacrifice was offered. She was called Pax by the Romans.

Iris. Greek rainbow-goddess, with no cult, regarded as messenger of the gods since the rainbow touched heaven and earth. She was daughter of a Titan Thaumas, and employed especially by Zeus and Hera.

Ironwood. A forest where Troll (q.v.) women lived, according to Snorri (q.v.), and they were called Ironwood-women. Little is known about them, but they were perhaps dangerous woodland spirits.

Irpa. Scandinavian goddess, perhaps of Finnish origin. She was worshipped particularly in Halogaland, where there were several temples with life-size images. Irpa had power over nature, especially tempests and hailstorms. See THORGERD.

'Īsā. The name of Jesus in the *Qur'ān* and used generally of him by Muslims.

This form of the name probably came from the Syriac Yeshū and ultimately from the Hebrew Yeshua. See INJĪL.

Isaac the Blind. Jewish mystic who lived at Posquières in Provence in the twelfth century and established Kabbalah (q.v.) there, gaining many disciples. He opposed the philosophy of Maimonides (q.v.), but little is known of Isaac's teaching.

Isé. The greatest religious centre of Japan, on the south-east coast, and the holy of holies of Shinto. It is dedicated to the Sun-goddess, Amaterasu-ō-mikami (q.v.), the chief deity. There are two similar precincts. The Inner Shrine of Amaterasu is said to have been founded in the third century A.D. by the emperor Suinin who appointed his daughter as high priestess. The Outer Shrine was made in the fifth century for the goddess of cereals, Toyouke-bime (see INARI). The shrines are built of wood, in antique style like log cabins, with projecting beams and ridge billets. They are renewed every twenty years, but while not old they preserve old patterns uninfluenced by the later Buddhist stone-built temples. The Isé Inner Shrine contains sacred symbols which the goddess sent to earth with her grandson: a mirror, a sword and a jewel. Isé is particularly important to the

Japanese imperial family, since the goddess has been regarded as its ancestress.

Īsh, Īsha, Īshāna. See ISHVARA.

Īsha. One of the shorter classical *Upanishads.* It opens with praise of the Lord, *Īsha,* but is fairly monistic, though with some traces of theism.

Isherwood, Christopher. See NEO-VEDĀNTA and VEDĀNTA.

Ishmael. The Biblical figure appears in Islamic tradition as Ismā'īl, also son of Abraham (Ibrāhīm q.v.). The *Qur'ān* says that together they restored the Ka'ba (2, 119/125, etc.), and tradition says that Ishmael placed the Black Stone (q.v.) in the Ka'ba and found the well of Zamzam (q.v.). Ishmael is regarded as a prophet and father of the Arabs, and it was he rather than Isaac who was prepared for sacrifice by his father. See MINĀ.

Ishmael, Rabbi. Jewish teacher of Jabneh (about 60–140), killed in the persecutions of Hadrian. He wrote a Midrash on the book of *Exodus,* called *Mekilta.* In the Middle Ages a Kabbalistic work was ascribed to him, called *Shiur Komah,* 'Measures of the Divine Stature', claiming to describe the divine body.

Ishta. See DEVATĀ.

Ishtar. The greatest goddess of Assyria and Babylonia, usually called Innina in Sumerian. She replaced the colourless Antu and became consort of the great god Anu (q.v.). Ishtar was goddess of love and fertility, with Hierodules (q.v.) attached to her temples, and also goddess of war, even represented with a beard and riding on a lion. Ishtar figured prominently in the stories of the Flood and Gilgamesh, and was closely connected with the ancient Sumerian god Tammuz as his sister-spouse. When Tammuz went to the underworld Ishtar sought for him and the two gods came triumphantly back; a typical vegetation myth, like that of Isis and Osiris. Ishtar had many temples: the chief centre was at Erech, and others at Ashur, Babylon, Nineveh and Ur.

Īshvara, Īsha. (Sanskrit) 'lord', master, husband, king, God, Supreme Being. It is applied to Krishna in the *Bhagavad-Gītā* as Lord of Beings, Lord of Yoga, and Supreme Lord, but it is most often the title of Shiva as Supreme Being.

Īshvara-Gītā. (Sanskrit) 'Song of the Lord', part of the Kūrma Purāna (see KŪRMA), in which the first eleven chapters are devoted to the praise of the god Shiva. It is inspired by the *Bhagavad-Gītā* (q.v.), but directs its praise to Shiva rather than Krishna. It dates between the seventh and eleventh centuries A.D.

Īshvara Krishna. Author of the earliest text of the Sāmkhya (q.v.) school of Indian philosophy, he lived in the fourth or fifth century A.D. His *Sāmkhya Kārikā* teaches the existence of twenty-five basic principles, of which the first is Nature or matter, Prakriti, and the last is Spirit or person, Purusha. There is an infinite number of souls in the universe, but no supreme deity, and the souls are delivered by knowledge from involvement in matter. See KAPILA.

Isis. The greatest Egyptian goddess, from predynastic times, and focus of legends, literature and mystery cults. Her name means 'throne'. She was the daughter of Geb and Nut, sister and wife of Osiris, and mother of Horus. Isis was the great wife and mother, a corn-goddess and personification of the power of the soil, married to the vegetation-god Osiris. A great magician, she restored Osiris to life. She was symbolized by a knot, a seat, cow's horns, a falcon and a star. She is represented as a woman, identified with many goddesses but especially with Hathor. When Osiris was murdered by Set, Isis mourned till she recovered his dismembered body and he was installed in the nether world. Isis became popular in the Greek and Roman worlds as sky-goddess, mistress of magic and teacher of mysteries, and her cult spread over Europe as far as Britain.

Islām. (Arabic) 'submission', 'surrender' to God, the faith and practice of religion based on the *Qur'ān.* Originally used of the religious attitude, Islām has come to mean the whole complex culture of the communities which confess the oneness of God and the primacy of his apostle Muhammad. Muslims (a word which comes from the same root as Islām) object to being called Muhammadan or Mahometan, since they do not worship Muhammad, and claim to follow Islām. The Dār al-Islām, 'House of Islām', is the Muslim world as distinct from other communities. The strength of Islām in the modern world is hard to estimate; it stretches from Senegal to Mongolia, and from Russia to East Africa, but in the absence of reliable census figures the numbers of Muslims may be estimated at about four hundred millions, though with increasing world population they may well be considerably more. See also Īmān.

Ismā'īlīs. Branches of Shī'a Muslims (q.v.), differing from the majority Twelvers (q.v.) and being known as Sab'iya, 'Seveners'. Instead of holding to twelve Imāms (q.v.) beginning with 'Ali, they hold that their seventh, Imām Muhammad ibn Ismā'il, was the final Imām who disappeared and would return at the last day. In early years Ismā'īlī doctrine differed little from that of other Shī'a, and their exoteric doctrines were conservative and close to orthodox Sunni Islam. Esoteric teachings absorbed Neo-Platonic ideas of emanations from the divine expressed in the perfect man, the Prophet Muhammad, and the Imāms who lead souls to the highest spiritual worlds. There are two principal branches of Ismā'īlīs, the Musta'lians in the Yemen but particularly strong in India, and the Nizārīs who are found in Syria, Persia, Afghanistan, India and East Africa. Some of the latter became Khojas under the rule of the Aga Khan (q.v.).

Isnād. (Arabic) a 'chain' or 'support', indicating the chain of traditional authority. A Tradition (see Hadīth) is only acceptable if the Isnād gives an unbroken series of reliable teachers, and much research has been done into the criticism of Isnāds.

Israel ben Eliezer. Jewish mystic (1700–60), also known as Baal Shem Tov or the Besht (see Hasidism).

Isrāfīl. An archangel of Islamic mythology, not mentioned in the *Qur'ān* or Traditions, but prominent in later story. The name may come from the Hebrew Seraphim. Isrāfīl is the angel who reads the divine decrees from a tablet and passes them on to the other archangels. He sounds the trumpet at the Day of Resurrection, bringing the dead back to life, and he is called Lord of the Trumpet. Isrāfīl is described as colossal in size, with his feet under the seventh earth and his head by the pillars of the throne of God; he has four wings, as the Seraphim had six. See also Uriel.

Isvara. See Ishvara.

Ithnā 'Asharīya. 'Twelvers' (Arabic, *ithna 'ashara*, twelve, or two plus ten), the name given to those of Shī'a Islam who follow twelve Imāms, as against the Sab'iya who follow 'seven'. See Shī'a.

I-Tsing. Chinese Buddhist monk who, following Hsüan-tsang (q.v.), in A.D. 671 went by sea from Canton to India to visit the centres and homeland of Buddhism. He translated Buddhist texts and wrote a Record of Buddhist Kingdoms and biographies of famous monks in the west.

Ittihād. (Arabic) 'becoming one', a technical term of Islamic Sūfī mystics for the union of the creature with the Creator. It is the 'unitive state' of other mystical doctrines, but is distinguished from 'incarnation' (see Hulūl). Some mystics spoke of the unity of two beings, but according to others human individuality disappears finally in the one divine Reality. See Fanā' and Tawhīd.

Ittōen. See Tenko-san.

Itzamna. A sky-god of the ancient Mayas (q.v.), sometimes depicted as an old man with a 'Roman' nose, hollow cheeks, one tooth and a pointed beard. Sometimes he appears between a sun and moon, or with his head appearing from the mouths of the sky snake with two heads. The main temple of Copan was sacred to Itzamna, and his head appears between two jaguars. Itzamna had a

counterpart in a sun-god with a fleshy face. He has two pyramid temples in the city of Izamal (q.v.) in northern Yucatan.

Itzcoliuhqui. 'Curved obsidian knife', an Aztec god of darkness, destruction and volcanoes, and a variant of Tezcatlipoca (q.v.).

Itzpapalotl. 'Obsidian knife butterfly', Aztec goddess, beautiful but with death symbols shown on her face. She was a demonic deity of fate, also of stars and agriculture, and in calendar pictures she presides over the fifteenth week.

Iuventas. See JUVENTAS.

Iwaïgoto. See NORITO.

Izamal. City in northern Yucatan where there were five pyramid temples to gods of the Mayas. Two were dedicated to the sky god Itzamna, on the south and west; the eastern pyramid was for Chac as god of lightning, and the northern to Kinich Kak Mo (qq.v.) as a sun god in the form of a macaw. In the centre was the temple of the war god Hun Pic Tok, which was the most important.

Izanagi and Izanami. 'The male who invites' and 'the female who invites'. The last couple of seven generations of deities in Shinto mythology, but most important as creative principles. In the Nihongi texts they stood on the floating bridge of heaven, the rainbow, and thrust a spear to the ocean from drops of which an island formed to which they descended to Japan. They built a house with a central pillar and going round it met one another and united to produce the deities. When Izanami died, her husband pursued her to the land of death, but was horrified at its pollution, was pursued by ugly females and finally by Izanami herself. Izanagi blocked up the pass with a great rock and pronounced a formula of divorce. He left his clothes there and washed himself, and from his left eye the Sun-goddess Amaterasu (q.v.) was born.

'Izrā'īl. See AZRAEL.

Izumo. Said to be the oldest sacred precinct in Japan, on the north-west coast facing Korea. The god worshipped there, Onamuchi, was son of the Storm-god Susa-no-ō (q.v.), the tempestuous brother of the Sun-goddess, Amaterasu (q.v.). It is said that Amaterasu had the shrine built for her more kindly nephew, and it has a central pillar which recalls the pillar in the house of the primal deities Izanagi and Izanami (q.v.). The Izumo shrine is made of wood, like those of Isé (q.v.), but in not such an ancient style. The barge-boards end at the tile-ridge, and do not extend in the manner of Isé.

J

Jade Emperor, Yü Huang. The supreme deity of Taoism, symbolical of jade or absolute purity. He came to predominate in the Sung dynasty, from about the tenth century A.D. The first member of the Taoist supreme Triad had been Yüan Shih T'ien Tsun, the 'heavenly honoured one of origin and beginning'; but it was said that he had abdicated in favour of Yü Huang who, from being his deputy, became the supreme Jade Emperor. Confucian scholars said that

the emperors had invented him, but for the people he was the chief object of worship, more accessible than the Confucian deity Shang-ti. The Jade Emperor was over all the gods, entrusting particular regions to the city gods, and receiving accounts from all others in the yearly festivals. Similarly the Jade Emperor kept account of human deeds, giving each his destiny and presiding over life and death.

Jagannātha. (Sanskrit) 'world-lord', a divine title applied especially to Vishnu and Krishna. The famous temple of Jagannātha is at Puri in Orissa, on the sea coast about 480 kilometres south of Calcutta. Here there are three central images, of Krishna and his brother and sister, Balarāma and Subhadrā (q.v.). They are crude wooden busts, brightly painted, and clearly representing ancient models. Every June they are taken to be bathed on a great temple cart (*rath*), and pilgrims in ecstasy used to throw themselves in front of the cart and were crushed to death, hence the term 'Juggernaut car'. Countless pilgrims arrive for the festival, which is popular because all castes are regarded as equal at the temple and all visitors have to partake of food cooked by low caste men at the shrine.

Jahannam. The Muslim name for Hell, derived from the Hebrew *Gehinnom* or *Gehenna*. The name and the idea appear frequently in the *Qur'ān* and it is spoken of in lurid terms of roasting in a scorching fire, where the damned are chained amid hot wind, boiling water and black smoke. Sometimes Jahannam is personified as a great monster brought out at the Judgement. There are held to be seven gates of hell, situated under the earth, and later descriptions of hell and heaven in the Islamic world may have inspired Dante's visions in his Inferno and Paradiso. Orthodox theologians, however, did not teach that Hell is eternal, and Sūfī mystics thought that even the most wicked would eventually be saved from it.

Jāhilīya. The name given to the state of religion in Arabia in the 'time of ignorance', before the coming of Muhammad and Islam. It was the old polytheistic and idolatrous religion, with its poets and shrines, its customs and barbarism, which needed to be changed or abolished in the new religion.

Jaidev, Jayadeva. Indian religious poet of the twelfth century, born in Bengal but wrote in Sanskrit, or perhaps in the popular Prakrit from whence his works were later translated into Sanskrit. After wandering about as an ascetic Sannyāsin, Jayadeva married and settled as the leading poet at the court of King Lakshmana. His own love for his wife, Padmāvatī, inspired his best known work, *Gīta Govinda* (q.v.), the 'song of the Cowherd'. This is a series of lyrical monologues on the loves of Krishna and Rādhā. Two hymns by Jayadeva are included in the Sikh scripture *Ādi Granth* (q.v.).

Jaimini. Reputed founder of the Mīmāmsā (q.v.) school of Indian philosophy. Very little can be said about him or the time at which he flourished, and even his century is uncertain, though critical opinion inclines to place him about the second century B.C. Jaimini's principal work is the *Mīmāmsā Sūtra* which expounds the teaching of the *Vedas* as eternal truth. This text is the ground work of the Mīmāmsā system and the basis of later commentary and theory.

Jainism. An ancient Indian religion, taught by Jinas, 'conquerors', or 'ford-makers', Tīrthankaras. The religion is eternal, but in the present eon there have been twenty-four Jinas, of whom the first, Rishabha (q.v.), lived millions of years ago and the last was the historical Mahāvīra (q.v.). Jainism has no supreme deity, though some Hindu gods are recognized, and in its temples there are images of the twenty-four Jinas. There are many living souls (jīva) which seek liberation from Karma and aim at Nirvāna. A major Jain doctrine is non-violence (ahimsā, q.v.), and not only is meat

forbidden but any occupations which might involve taking life, such as hunting and farming. There are two major sects, the Digambaras, 'space clad', and Shvetāmbara, 'white clad' (qq.v.), and these have different canons of scripture. Monastic communities are important since a layman cannot attain final Nirvāna. Jainism has had wealthy supporters and splendid temples were built, for example at Mount Abu. Its followers today in India amount to about a million and a half.

Jalāl al-Dīn. See RŪMĪ.

Jālūt. The name given in the *Qur'ān* to the Biblical Goliath (*Qur'ān* 2,250), and apparently influencing the form of the name given to Saul, Tālūt.

Jamāl al-Dīn. See AFGHĀNĪ.

Jambu-dvīpa. (Sanskrit) 'rose-apple continent', the central or southernmost of the continents which surround Mount Meru (q.v.). The south of this continent was India, the 'land of the son of Bharata', Bhāratavarsha. Jambudvīpa is also described as a circle around Mount

Meru and separated from other continents by oceans of butter and treacle.

Janaka. Mythical Indian king of the Solar race, the first Janaka. Another was king of Videha and father of Sītā, the 'furrow', wife of the hero Rāma (qq.v.). Janaka is said to have performed rites without the help of Brahmins and finally to have become a Brahmin (he was originally of the Kshatriya warrior class) and a royal sage, Rājarshi.

Janam-Sākhīs. 'Birth evidences' or 'evidences of his life' (Punjabi), a collection of stories of the life of the founder of the Sikhs, Guru Nānak (q.v.). There are several versions of these, dating from the sixteenth century onwards.

Jana Sangh. See MAHASABHA.

Janissaries. Troops of the Ottoman empire, from Turkish *yeni-cheri*, 'new troops', a name applied to infantry composed chiefly of captured Christians who became some of the best soldiers of the Ottomans. The Bektāshi sect (q.v.) was closely connected with them.

Janna. The 'garden' (Arabic), the name given most often in the *Qur'ān* to heaven, and fairly frequently called 'gardens of Eden', *jannāt 'adn*. It is twice referred to by the word *Firdaws*, 'Paradise' (q.v.). See HOURIS and HAWD.

Janus. An ancient Italian god, the spirit of the door (*janua*) and arch. Monuments at gates were called after him. Janus was a god of beginnings, named first in prayers, and the first month was called January after him. Because he looked forward and backward,

his symbol was a head with a face in front and behind, sometimes fixed on a body. See AKER.

Japanese Religions. The traditional religion of Japan is Shinto (q.v.), the 'Way of the Gods', distinguished between Sanctuary (Jinja) and Sectarian (Kyoha) Shinto. The former was the ancient polytheistic religion which was regarded as the national faith, and the latter were sects that arose in recent times. Buddhism entered Japan from Korea in A.D. 552 and rapidly dominated the country, forming an amalgam of Ryōbu (q.v.) or 'Two-aspect' Shinto which was only partially dissolved in the Shinto revival in 1868. There are some thirteen major Buddhist sects in Japan and many minor ones; the best known are Jodo, Nichiren and Zen. Confucianism also influenced Japan from China, with moral and social ideas, and with reverence for elders and ancestors. Taoist nature and magical beliefs were also potent. Christian missions were active in the sixteenth century, but banned from 1638–1872. Today they have many branches, but relatively few members. In 1962 there were estimated 78 million Shintoists, 65 million Buddhists and one million Christians.

Japji. Sikh morning prayer which every devout Sikh should repeat from memory after rising and bathing. Japji means 'remembrance', repetition (Punjabi from Sanskrit *japa*, repeated prayers). It was compiled by the founder of the Sikhs, Guru Nānak, and was said to have been revealed to him by God. It contains thirty-eight verses. The fifth Sikh Guru, Arjan, who compiled the scripture *Ādi Granth* in which the Japji stands first, prefaced it with a basic credal statement on the nature of God. This is the Mūl Mantra, 'basic mantra', opening with the declaration: 'This Being is one, he is eternal.'

Jason. Legendary Greek hero and leader of the Argonauts (q.v.). He was brought up by the Centaur Chiron and while returning home lost a sandal, in one version, through carrying the goddess Hera over a stream. He was sent to fetch the Golden Fleece and married the sorceress Medea (q.v.), whom he deserted on his return.

Jātaka. (Sanskrit) 'birth stories', which purport to be accounts of former lives on earth of Gautama the Buddha. There are 547 tales relating the adventures of the Buddha-to-be in animal and human forms, each of them ending with the phrase, 'I was that being.' The *Jātaka* contain many popular yarns from folklore and have parallels with Hindu collections such as the *Pañchatantra* (q.v.) and tales of other nations. The stories are embedded in a commentary of the fifth century A.D. said to come from Singhalese but no doubt from an older original. There is an introductory commentary, the *Nidāna-kathā*, 'Story of the Lineage', which gives the life of the Buddha and also some of his former lives.

Jāti. (Sanskrit) 'birth', family, lineage, rank, caste. The word is normally used for what we call 'Caste', distinction, rather than *varna* which is 'colour'. See CASTE.

Jayadeva. See JAIDEV and GĪTĀ GOVINDA.

Jên. 'Benevolence', goodness, love, humaneness, in Chinese thought. In Confucian philosophy Jên was both the greatest virtue and the sum of all virtues, it was a supernatural grace and the inner power of Li, ceremonial (q.v.). In the Analects (q.v.) Confucius said that Jên makes a neighbourhood beautiful, it is more important than fire or water, it is self-denial and one who seeks Jên will do no evil. The meaning of Jên was said to be to 'love men.'

Jerusalem. The city is sacred to Jews, Christians and Muslims. For its origins and history reference must be made to works on the *Bible* and history. For its place in Islam, see QUDS, AQSA, and DOME OF THE ROCK.

Jewels. See THREE JEWELS.

Jhāna. Pali term for Dhyāna meditation (q.v.).

Jibrīl, Jabrā'īl. The Arabic version of the Biblical Gabriel and the most popular figure of Islamic angelology. Although only named twice in the *Qur'ān*, tradition holds that all the *Qur'ān*, was revealed to Muhammad through Jibrīl. He appeared to the Prophet on Mount Hirā', declared his name to him, and told him to recite. Later legends said that Jibrīl showed Adam the site of Mecca, helped all the prophets, and announced the birth of John to Zachariah. He is called the Faithful Spirit and Supreme Spirit, and perhaps confused with the Holy Spirit. With three other archangels Jibrīl is active at the judgement and his name is often written with theirs on magic squares. See GABRIEL.

Jihād. (Arabic) 'striving', 'holy war', the duty of Muslims to spread Islam by force of arms, though not made into a Pillar of Faith (q.v.). In the early chapters of the *Qur'ān* composed at Mecca, the Muslims were taught to be patient under attack; later, at Medina, defensive and then offensive warfare was prescribed. Jihād against all unbelievers in the world appears, however, only after the death of Muhammad. But true Jihād is carefully defined. It must be led by an Imām or Muslim sovereign. There must be prospect of success. The enemies must first be invited to accept Islam. Monotheists, like Jews and Christians, may refuse Islam but submit to its rule on payment of a tax. Sūfīs and modern writers maintain that the true Holy War is against sin in oneself. He who died fighting the Jihād was assured of Paradise as a martyr or witness (*shahīd*).

Jihi. Japanese term for Karunā (q.v.).

Jimmu Tenno. In Japanese tradition the first emperor of Japan, from 660 B.C. Everything after that date was accepted as historically true, though writing was not introduced until over a thousand years afterwards. It was said that Jimmu unified Japan and established its government under the guidance of the gods (Kami). Critical Japanese historians now date the emergence of the dynasty about the beginning of the Christian era, and the unification only gradually proceeding till its completion about the sixth century A.D. Jimmu Tenno was said to be a great-grandson of the supreme sun goddess, Amaterasu-ōmi-kami (q.v.), and hence of divine origin, and this belief strengthened the imperial cult. Belief in the divinity of the emperor was formally repudiated in 1945.

Jina. (Sanskrit) 'conqueror' or 'victor'. Used of Buddhas, but especially of the twenty-four Jinas of Jainism (q.v.).

Jinja, Jingu, Yashiro. The Shinto sanctuary or shrine. There are many kinds and sizes of Jinja, tiny ones by the roadside or in factories, and larger ones located in beautiful surroundings, with avenues of trees and Torii (q.v.) gateways at the entrance. Since the last century a distinction has been made between Jinja Shinto, 'shrine Shinto', and Shuha or Kyoha Shinto, 'sectarian Shinto.' The regular Jinja include main shrines, halls of worship, and halls for reciting prayers, giving offerings and performing ceremonial dances; see HAIDEN, HEIDEN and

JINJA

HONDEN. The Jinja are under the care of priests who daily offer green twigs and utter formal texts, without lay assistance. But there are great seasonal festivities at every Jinja when prayers and praises are made and whole communities join in.

Jinn. Airy or fiery spirits in Muslim belief. Their relationship to the devil or Iblīs is obscure: he is said to be one of them in the *Qur'ān* but Muhammad was sent to preach to the Jinns as well as to men. They were pre-Islamic spirits whose existence was fully accepted in the new religion and few Muslim teachers doubted them, though some put forward different theories of their nature. Legend and folklore told many stories of the Jinns, their loves for mankind and their relations with saints. They could perform works of great power and Solomon was said to have built the Temple with the aid of thousands of Jinns. They appear in the *Arabian Nights* and in more religious popular novels, and the stories incorporate much material which has little to do with Islam. See 'IFRĪT.

Jinnah. See MUSLIM LEAGUE.

Jiriki. (Japanese) 'self-power', a Buddhist term used of path to enlightenment through the self-discipline of the believer. Opposed to this is Tariki, salvation by grace from Amida (see AMITĀBHA), in the Pure Land schools.

Jīva. (Sanskrit) 'life', vital breath, living soul (like our 'quick'). The Jīvātman is used of the living or personal soul, as distinct from the Paramātman or supreme and universal soul. Jīva is used especially by the Jains, where Hindus might use ātman (q.v.). Jīvanmukti, 'liberated soul', is used of one who is liberated in this present life, and for great saints.

Jizo. Japanese name of the Bodhisattva Kshitigarbha (q.v.).

Jizya. (Arabic) 'tribute', poll tax, the name given to the tax on non-Muslim peoples in an Islamic state. See DHIMMA and AHL AL-KITĀB.

Jñāna. (Sanskrit) 'knowledge', related to the Greek *Gnosis* and opposite to Ajñāna, 'ignorance'. Jñāna is knowing, knowledge about anything, but especially the higher knowledge or wisdom which is cognizance of and union with the Supreme Spirit. In the Hindu scriptures, notably the *Bhagavad-Gītā*, the discipline or method of knowledge, Jñāna-Yoga, is compared and contrasted with the discipline of works, Karma-Yoga and the discipline of devotion, Bhakti-yoga. Bhakti is exalted over Jñāna, but the way of Knowledge continues to assert itself even in the devotional schools, because the intellectual and ascetic effort involved in Jñāna gives it great prestige. Even the Gītā says that nothing purifies like Jñāna. See also VIJÑĀNA.

Jñānadeva, Jñāneshvar. Writer of western India (1275–96) who composed hymns to Vishnu as Vithoba (q.v.) and a work on the *Upanishads*. He is chiefly known for the *Jñāneshvarī*, a paraphrase of the *Bhagavad Gītā* and commentary on it, in the Maratha language, which is still very popular. According to tradition Jñānadeva died at the age of twenty-two at Alandi, and he has been regarded as an Avatar of Vishnu.

Jocasta, Epicaste. In Greek mythology wife of Laius, king of Thebes, and mother of Oedipus (q.v.). It is said that Jocasta married her son unwittingly, and when she discovered the dreadful fact she hanged herself and Oedipus blinded himself. For reference to Freud's theory, see OEDIPUS.

Jōdo. (Japanese) 'Pure Land' (q.v.), the general term for the devotional Buddhist sects which are strongest in Japanese Buddhism. Chinese Buddhist schools taught from the fifth century A.D. that Amida (q.v.) Buddha dwelt in the Pure Land of the west and called men to him by faith through grace. The Japanese Pure Land Sect, Jōdo-shu, was created or reinforced by the teaching of Hōnen (q.v., A.D. 1133–1212), who declared that recitation of the Nembutsu, 'Hail to Amida Buddha', would bring entry into his Pure Land. His disciple Shinran (1173–1263) established the Jōdo Shinshu, the True Pure Land Sect which taught a doctrine of salvation by faith alone, against traditional Buddhist monasticism, allowing priests to marry and abandon regulations since there was no salvation by works.

Jörd. Goddess of the Earth, in Scandinavian mythology, and one of the Asynjur (q.v.). She was consort of Odin and mother of Thor. Jörd was sometimes also called Fjorgyn, but it is not known how she was worshipped.

Jörmungand. See MIDGARD.

Josaphat. Medieval European version of Bodhisattva (q.v.). See BARLAAM.

Jötun, Jötnar. Giants of Scandinavian mythology, either personifications of the forces of nature or embodiments of memories of earlier inhabitants of northern Europe. The giants were said to dwell in Jötunheim, to the east, and even gods like Thor were dwarfed by them, and taking refuge in what seemed to be a great hall, found it was only the thumb of a giant's glove on the floor of Jötunheim. The giants were generally stupid, though some were very wise, and similarly while they were mild-tempered they could be roused to anger, Jötunmödi, and then perform violent actions.

Jove. A form of Jupiter (q.v.).

Ju. A 'scholar' in China, especially of the school of Confucius, and the scholar class. In the time of Confucius (q.v.) the Ju was a 'gentle' intellectual whose chief task was to conduct or supervise the correct performance of rituals, Li (q.v.). Such Ju wore wide-sleeved robes, with silk sashes, high feather hats and square shoes. Confucius recognized his debt to these teachers, and claimed only to transmit their teachings, but in time he was regarded as the founder of the Ju school, the philosophy that dominated Chinese thought from his time for twenty-five centuries. But Ju philosophy developed and took in many ideas which would have surprised Confucius, though still linked with his name.

Ju Chiao. Chinese name for Confucianism (q.v.).

Judah. Jewish Rabbi and Patriarch (135–217), called the Prince, and supreme teacher. For some fifty years Rabbi Judah was patriarch of the Sanhedrin in Galilee and is said to have been friendly with one of the Roman emperors. To give continuing authority to Jews under peace or persecution, and to clear up the confusion of rival collections of teachings on practice and ritual, Rabbi Judah made a digest of laws which came to be known as the *Mishnah* (q.v.). This was authoritative, yet left room for further development. It was accepted, after the Scriptures, as a guide of Jewish life and before Rabbi Judah's death it was the object of close study among the Jewish communities not only in Palestine but in other great centres such as Babylon.

Judah Ha-Chasid. Judah the Pious (died 1217) was the first teacher of the German school of Kabbalah (q.v.). He is said to have written the 'Book of the Pious' (*Sefer Chasidim*), which combines a profound piety with high morality.

Judaism. This term was used by Greek-speaking Jews before New Testament times, to differentiate their way of life from that of their neighbours which was called Hellenism. Paul used the term Judaism of the Jewish religion (*Galatians* 1, 13). In modern times it is common, as in this *Dictionary*, to distinguish as

Judaism the Jewish religion and life after the Exile of the sixth century B.C., and more particularly of Judaism as distinct from Christianity. This is a convenient division, but of course Judaism is continuous with the *Old Testament* or Hebrew religious life of ancient Israel. The Babylonian exile marked the end of the geographic unity of the Jews and the beginning of the Dispersion. The destruction of the Second Temple of Jerusalem by the Romans in A.D. 70 drove many Jews into exile and made the synagogue take the place of the Temple in religious life. The Hebrew term Yahadut was used from the Middle Ages. See REFORM, ZIONISM and DIASPORA.

Judo, Ju-jitsu. Judo is the correct name for the Japanese form of wrestling which was first known to the West as Ju-jitsu. Both Taoist and Zen naturalistic principles are applied: that victory comes from weakness or passivity and the strength of the attacker is manipulated to his own defeat.

Juggernaut. See JAGANNĀTHA.

Juju. A word formerly used of religious and magical objects, particularly in West Africa. The origins of the term are obscure. It has been derived from the French *joujou*, a 'toy', but the French do not use it in a religious or magical sense, preferring the term *Gris-gris* (q.v.). Another suggestion is that Juju is a duplication of the Latin *Deus*, and was applied by Portuguese traders to African objects, but this is conjecture. Juju has been used both of objects and of powers and taboos connected with them, but it is abandoned by modern serious writers on African religion. The term is vague and deprecatory, and the objects and powers described are worldwide and not confined to Africa.

Ju Lai. A Chinese name for Tathā-gata (q.v.).

Julunggul, Yulunggul. A huge python in an important myth of north Australia. Two sisters, Wawalag (q.v.), were travelling and naming plants and animals. When they arrived at a waterhole, one of them built a hut in which the other gave birth to a child. Julunggul smelt the blood and emerged in anger from the hole. Despite the songs and dances of the sisters, Julunggul entered the hut and swallowed the child and then the sisters. On bark paintings Julunggul is depicted as a curled up python with its eggs at the bottom of the sacred waterhole. Swallowing the people symbolized the onset of the monsoon, and later the python vomited them up again. See GALERU.

Jum'a. 'General assembly' (Arabic), the name for Friday and the Friday prayer which is obligatory at midday for male Muslims. This congregational prayer in a mosque consists of two prostrations of prayer (see SALĀT) and a sermon, and other prostrations and prayers may be added.

Junaid, Junayd. Sūfī mystic, native of Baghdad, who died in A.D. 910. He was one of the more sober mystics, respected by the orthodox, and giving warning of the dangers of extremism to mystics like Hallāj (q.v.). Junayd's teachings have survived in letters and short treatises in Arabic. He taught the doctrine of Fanā' (q.v.), 'passing away', but not in the pantheistic sense of the annihilation of the soul in God, but of its communion with him. After such an experience, he said, the mystic must return to daily life. His own experience was one of considerable suffering and this may have led him to beware of extremes. See also BISTĀMĪ.

Juno. An ancient Italian goddess, often identified with the Greek Hera (q.v.). Her name may be derived from a root meaning 'young woman' (*iunix*), or it may be related to Jupiter. Juno was closely concerned with the life of women and the monthly rhythms, so that she was related to the moon and sometimes called a moon-goddess. She also became a great state-goddess, both under the Etruscans and at Rome, and on the Capitol she made a triad with Jupiter and Minerva. Juno had many festivals (an important one was the Matronalia on March 1) and sacred days every month. Juno was identified with an ancient goddess of childbirth, Lucina.

Jupiter. The 'sky-father' of ancient Italy. The form *Diou-pater* is directly related to the Greek *Zeus-pater* and Sanskrit *Dyaus Pitri* (q.v.). Jupiter was the power of the sky, manifested in lightning and thunderbolts; he was a god of war but also of treaties and oaths because violation of his name might bring down a thunderbolt. He was worshipped at the Ides of each month, the full moon when the sky is brightest, and also at offerings of firstfruits. As a great sky-god Jupiter was transcendent, but not very personal; yet the Etruscans gave him special honour and on the Capitol at Rome Jupiter was associated with Juno and Minerva and presided over games and triumphal displays. His priest was the Flamen Dialis. For Jupiter Ammon, see AMŪN.

Juventas, Iuventas. Italian goddess

of the Iuvenes, young men of military age, who made gifts to her temple when first putting on the *Toga virilis*, the manly robe assumed at about fourteen years of age. Juventas had an ancient shrine on the Capitol and refused to move when other gods were installed there.

K

K. The five K's (Kakkas) are the marks of initiated Sikhs, who enter the Khālsā brotherhood (q.v.). They are: Kesh, wearing hair and beard uncut; Kungha, wearing a steel comb in the hair; Kuchha, wearing shorts; Kara, wearing a steel bangle on the right wrist; Kirpan, carrying a short sword. Wearing a turban is not prescribed, but is convenient to cover the long hair. Observance of the Five K's is part of the duty of those who are admitted into the Sikh Khālsā, and such people have the name Singh, 'lion.'

Ka. Ancient Egyptian 'spirit', 'divinity', 'genius', or 'divine power'. The word was used from ancient times but in a variety of ways. At first it seems that it was associated only with a dead Pharaoh, who awoke near his Ka, but later a Ka was said to be born with everyone. The Ka was a sign of divinity, a god was a Ka, and a king insofar as he was divine. Later anyone might become divine and so had a Ka, which existed before his body, and to which he would go in heaven when he died. The Ka was closely related to the Ba (q.v.) which can often be translated as 'soul'.

Ka. (Sanskrit) 'who?'. Used first as an interrogative pronoun, in the Hindu *Brāhmanas* the name Ka came to be regarded as the title of a god, or identified with the creating deity Prajāpati. In the epic *Mahābhārata* Ka is identified with the sage Daksha, and in the *Purānas* he appears as a god with a family of his own.

Ka'ba. (Arabic) 'cube', the sacred shrine in Mecca to which all Muslims turn in prayer daily. It is a cube-like building, about twelve metres long, eleven wide, fifteen high, with a flat roof. The whole is covered with a black cloth (Kiswa, q.v.), into which the Confession of faith (Shahāda) is woven, and a gold embroidered band goes right round, full of *Quranic* verses. Ordinary pilgrims do not enter the Ka'ba, which is only opened a few times in the year; lamps hang inside

and inscriptions cover the walls. In the eastern corner of the Ka'ba is set the Black Stone (q.v.). The building is in the centre of the great mosque and surrounded by courtyards. The Ka'ba is mentioned in the *Qur'ān* as the Sacred Mosque (al-Masjid al-Harām). No doubt it was a pre-Islamic holy place, which Muhammad incorporated into Islam when he told his followers to pray towards it instead of Jerusalem. Muslim legends attribute its foundation to Adam, restoration to Abraham and Ishmael (q.v.) and further rebuilding to Muhammad.

Kabbalah. 'Tradition', general name for Jewish mysticism. Based upon occult interpretations of the *Bible*, Kabbalah probably began in Palestine but developed in Babylonia from the sixth century A.D. Two important works were composed: the *Shiur Komah*, 'Measures of Divine Height', giving the dimensions of the deity; and *Sefer Yetzirah*, 'Book of Creation' discussing the creative powers of numbers and letters. Then Kabbalah moved to western Europe and in the thirteenth century Judah the Pious was said to have written *Sefer Hasidim*, the 'Book of the Pious', in Germany, and in Spain Moses de Leon introduced the *Zohar* (q.v.) 'Splendour', which became the textbook of Jewish mystics. In the sixteenth century other mystics, such as Isaac Luria, helped on the revival of Hasidism (q.v.). Kabbalism became very popular, and although rabbis denounced superstitions, it was a mainstay in troubles. Kabbalism speaks of God as En

Sof (q.v.), the 'Limitless', the Ten Sefiroth, 'Emanations', creation, evil, the soul, Israel, exile and the Messiah.

Kabīr. Indian mystic, followed by the sect of Kabīr-panthīs said to number about a million today. Kabīr died in A.D. 1518 but the date of his birth is not certain, perhaps about 1440. He was a weaver who lived in Benares and his caste had probably recently been converted to Islam, whence his Arabic name, 'great'. But though partly influenced by Islam, Kabīr's teaching is strongly affected by the Bhakti (q.v.) devotion of the worshippers of Vishnu, added to elements of Yoga. Kabīr believed in one God, the True Guru (q.v.), but he rejected belief in the Avatars of Vishnu. He declared that the same god was worshipped under the different Hindu and Muslim names of Rāma and Allah, and in all holy places, whether Benares or Mecca. The mystical verses of Kabīr are collected in the *Kabīr-Granthāvalī* and a later work called *Bījak*, and some are also found in the Sikh scripture, the *Ādi Granth*.

Kabod, Chabod. (Hebrew) 'glory', a divine attribute often mentioned in the *Bible*, and taken by Jewish Hasidic (q.v.) mystics as attainable in vision. By cultivating the sense of God's presence, it was hoped that the divine Kabod would reveal itself according to the needs of the time, as to the prophets in the past.

Kadariya, Kadiriya. See QADARĪYA, QADIRIYA.

Kaddish. (Aramaic) 'holy', a Jewish prayer to hallow the name of God and ask the coming of his kingdom, which marks the close of parts of the synagogue service. A Half Kaddish, used when an additional service follows, consists of the first sentences of the Kaddish. A Mourner's Kaddish declares the faith of the mourner in the greatness of God and prays for his kingdom.

Kāfir. An Arabic word meaning first 'concealing' and 'ungrateful' for the benefits of God, and so 'unbelief' and 'infidel.' The Meccans who did not believe in Muhammad were called Kāfirūn, and unbelievers in general were warned of the punishment of God. Muslim Traditions talk of the fate of unbelievers at the Judgement, and it was assumed that they would suffer eternally, though Sūfī mystics taught eventual universal salvation. Holy War (see JIHĀD) was directed against idolaters and polytheists, but not against Jews and Christians and other monotheists if they paid tax. The modern South African use of *Kaffir* for black people is particularly inappropriate since many of them are monotheistic believers.

Ka-gyü-pa. Buddhist order of Tibet founded in the eleventh century by Marpa (q.v.).

Kailāsa. The name of a mountain in the Himalayas, north of Lake Manasa. Here the god Shiva was said to have his heaven, where he sits on a tiger skin, in yogic meditation, with his wife Pārvatī and sons Ganesha and Skanda. Some myths say that the god Kuvera also has a palace on Mount Kailāsa. For Kailāsa Temple, see ELLORA.

Kairos. (Greek) 'opportunity', fitness, and so the right and opportune time. Kairos was personified, with an altar at Olympia, and represented in art as a horse. Later he had a long forelock and provided the origins of our phrase 'taking time by the forelock.' See KRONOS.

Kairouan, al-Qayrawān. City and famous Islamic centre in Tunisia, founded in A.D. 670, and named from the Persian Kārwān (related to English 'caravan'). The great mosque, founded by the Umayyad Caliphs, remodelled by the Aghlabids (qq.v.) in the ninth century and damaged several times since, has been regarded by Muslims as the fourth wonder of the world, and the fourth sanctuary in Islam, after Mecca, Medina and Jerusalem.

Kaivalya. (Sanskrit) 'isolation', perfect unity and detachment of the soul from matter and any Karma which would lead it to further transmigrations. So Kaivalya leads to eternal bliss and the emancipation of Nirvāna, in Jain and some Hindu doctrines. See KEVALA.

Kalām. (Arabic) 'speech', and by extension the theological teaching of Islam. Kalām is used of the Speech of God, or the *Qur'ān*, and there was long discussion as to whether the Speech of God was eternal or created, the orthodox view being that God has always been speaking, so the *Qur'ān* is eternal. From Kalām as speech there was a development to Kalām as theological argument, with the theologian as Mutakallim. There was considerable opposition to the use of reason in matters of faith and, though great theologians such as Ghazālī and Ash'arī (qq.v.) justified its use, they were still conservative in their application of reason and based their arguments on the *Qur'ān* as 'God said'.

Kalevala. 'Land of Heroes', national epic of Finland, in fifty songs, which was transmitted orally till 1822 when it was published by Zacharias Tepelius. It contains myths of the god of music and poetry, Wainamoinen, and his brother Ilmarinen a blacksmith.

Kālī. (Sanskrit) 'black', the black and bloody Hindu goddess, consort of Shiva. Kālī is one of the many names of the Great Goddess, Mahā-devī (see DEVĪ), and no doubt represents one of the ancient dark gods that has been absorbed into her cult. In pictures Kālī is shown as a black gaunt figure, almost naked, with fierce face and lolling tongue, a necklace of skulls and snakes, with hands holding weapons, and treading on the body of her prostrate husband Shiva. Kālī is especially popular in eastern India; Calcutta is Kālī-ghat, the 'steps of Kālī', where steps go down from her temples into the mouths of the Ganges. Animal sacrifices are still offered in these temples and there are crude images. Yet Kālī is also the Mother, to whom women pray for health and children, and trees at the temples are hung with votive gifts. See also THUGS.

Kāli-Dāsa. Greatest poet and dramatist of India, who lived in the fourth or fifth century A.D. For religious interest, his drama *Shakuntalā* gives a charming picture of simple Brahmin life in the forest, while his poem *Raghu-vamsha*, the 'dynasty of Raghu' (ancestor of Rāma), tells of divine Avatars.

Kali-Yuga. The fourth age of the world in Hindu mythology, the last and worst, in which we are now living. The Kali Yuga lasts twelve thousand divine years, but four hundred and thirty-two thousand human years. In the Kali Yuga only a quarter of righteous practices remain, sacrifices and scripture teachings cease, calamities and disease abound. At the end of the age the world is dissolved, eventually to be absorbed into the divine and then reborn in a new cycle of ages. See YUGA, KALPA and KALKĪ.

Kalkī, Kalkin. The Avatar (q.v.) of Vishnu which is yet to come, in Hindu eschatology. Kalkī will appear at the end of the present world ages (see YUGA) on a white horse and with a drawn sword, to destroy the wicked and establish right.

Kalpa. A 'day of Brahmā', a creating deity, in Hindu myth often counted as 4320 million human years. A 'night of Brahmā' is the same length, and 360 days and nights make a 'year of Brahmā'. Since the life of Brahmā is of a hundred years, only after all these have passed does the universe dissolve into the world-spirit, Vishnu or Shiva, before emerging again with another creating Brahmā in the endless round.

Kalpa Sūtra. The most complete of the six *Vedāngas* (q.v.) of Hinduism, which give short rules for performing sacrifices and ceremonial acts in the forms of Sūtras or aphoristic statements. In the Jain scriptures the *Kalpa Sūtra* is the most popular account of the life of Mahāvīra (q.v.) and other Jinas.

Kāma, Kāma-Deva. Desire or love, and the god of love, in Hindu mythology, somewhat like Eros or Cupid. Desire as creative energy is celebrated in the *Atharva Veda* as first to be born, superior to gods and men, and the origin of thought. In later writings Kāmadeva is said to be the son of various gods and husband of Rati the goddess of passion. The name of Kāmadeva is also given to the great god Vishnu, as creator, preserver and destroyer. In mythology Kāma shot the ascetic god Shiva with the arrow of Fascination, so that he resolved to marry Pārvatī to cure himself of the disease which comes from desire. The *Kāma Sūtra* is a treatise on sexual relationships, attributed to a Brahmin named Vātsyāyana of the early Christian centuries. It treats of courtship and erotic life for the benefit of both parties and says little of homosexuality compared with some other literatures. See also ĀSAVA.

Kāmadhenu, Kāmaduh. 'Cow of wishes', in Hindu mythology a cow which satisfies all desires. It was produced when the gods churned the ocean for immortal nectar (see AMRITA). Kāmadhenu, also called Surabhi, is said to have produced Nandinī, a cow of plenty which belonged to a sage named Vasishtha and had the power of giving him everything that he wanted. The 'cow of wishes' is revered as the origin of milk and curds, and helps to justify the reverence paid to the cow by Hindus.

Kamakura. See DAIBUTSU.

Kāma Sūtra. See KĀMA.

Kami. (Japanese) a word of disputed etymology, but in the Shinto religion indicating the 'gods', superior or sacred beings, objects of worship. The Kami were believed to live in heaven, air, forests, rocks, earth, waters, or in human beings who manifested the Kami by supernormal powers. It was said that there were eight million Kami. The Shinto religion is called the Way of the Gods, Kami no Michi. In Japanese houses the altar or shelf, Kami-dana, 'god-shelf', is the focus of daily worship. It is installed above the sliding screens and contains simple symbols, twigs, water, and a Shimenawa (q.v.) or rope with patterned strips of paper as symbol of sanctity. See also UJI-GAMI.

KAMI-DANA

Kamma. See KARMA.

Kamsa, Kansha. Tyrant king of Mathurā, in Hindu mythology, cousin of Krishna's mother Devakī. It was prophesied that a son of Devakī would kill him, so Kamsa tried to destroy all her children. When Krishna was born his parents fled with him and Kamsa destroyed all other male babies, thus being called the Herod of India, though the story is very different. When Krishna grew up, he destroyed the tyrant, but he figures as a demonic character in popular Indian plays.

Kanāda. (Sanskrit) 'atom-eater', name of the reputed founder of the Vaisheshika (q.v.) system of Indian philosophy, who is said to have taught that the world was formed by an aggregation of atoms. He may have lived in the third or second century B.C., but little is known about him, if in fact he existed. He is also called Kashyapa and identified with the sage of that name (q.v.).

K'ang Yu-wei. Chinese statesmen and scholar (1858–1927) who regarded Confucius as founder of a religion and strongly advocated making Confucianism the state religion of China, even after the foundation of the republic. Opposition to this move came not only from leaders of other religions, but from some of the most eminent Confucian scholars who held that Confucianism was simply an ethical and political philosophy and lacked the essentials of a religion. See CONFUCIANISM.

Kanishka. An Indo-Scythian king of the first century A.D. who helped to spread Mahāyāna Buddhism. He is said to have held a council at Purushapura (Peshawar), at which Ashvaghosha (q.v.) defeated the Theravāda Buddhists, but the latter do not recognize this council.

Kannon. See KUAN-YIN.

Kānphata. 'Ear-split', the name of an order of Indian Yogis, so called because huge earrings were inserted at initiation, and this opened a mystic channel which helped yogic powers to develop. They were traditionally founded by Gorakhnāth (q.v.).

Kanrodai. A Sacred Column, in the

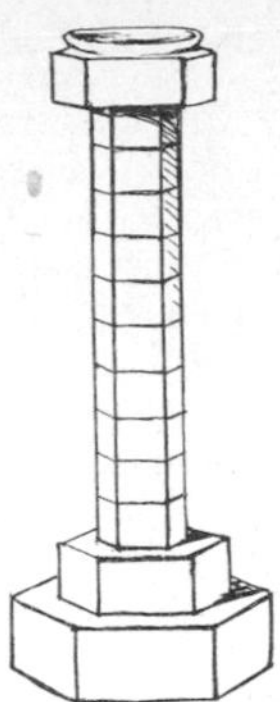

KANRODAI

Tenri-kyō (q.v.) sect of Japan. It is said to mark the place where divine revelation came to Miki, the foundress, and indicates the centre of the world. It is over two metres high, in thirteen layers, and a cup on the top is for the manna of longevity which is expected to come down; even now the spirit of Miki is said to hover there.

Kapila. The reputed founder of the Sāmkhya (q.v.) system of Hindu philosophy. In a legend in the *Mahābhārata* the sage sat in meditation in the underworld and with a flash of his eye burnt intruders into ashes. Kapila means 'the red one', is an epithet of the sun, and is sometimes identified with the fire god Agni, or the sky deity Vishnu. In the *Bhāgavata Purāna* he is called an Avatar (q.v.) of Vishnu. A *Sāmkhya Sūtra* was ascribed to Kapila, but critical opinion would place it about the fourteenth century A.D., while the earliest surviving text of the Sāmkhya school is the *Sāmkhya Kārikā* of Īshvara Krishna (q.v.) and dates from the fourth or fifth century.

Kapilavastu, Kapilavatthu. The traditional birthplace of Gautama the Buddha (q.v.), now called Piprawa in the foothills of Nepal. The birth was sited in the Lumbini Park, now said to be Rummin Dei. In 1898 a Stūpa (q.v.) was discovered near here with an inscription referring to the Buddha or an early follower.

Karaites. (Hebrew) 'readers' of scripture, a name given to a Jewish sect from the eighth century, to distinguish them from the Rabbanites (q.v.) who followed the *Talmud*. The founder of Karaism was Anan ben David who, it was said, declared himself Exilarch, supreme secular authority of Jews in Babylonia. Anan wrote *Sefer ha-Mitzvoth*, 'Book of the Precepts', in which he abandoned the Jewish way of life prescribed in the *Talmud* and claimed to base all his regulations upon the *Bible* alone. Interpreting Biblical laws literally, the Karaites forbade any fires or lights on the Sabbath, carrying any burden or food, washing or making beds. Because of troubles in Babylon, Anan set up a rigorist group in Jerusalem. A disciple in Persia, Benjamin Nahavendi, did much to consolidate Karaism, allegorizing Biblical passages. Another Persian Jew, Daniel Alkumisi, opposed allegorization. Karaism split Judaism for a time, spread to Egypt and Spain, but declined under revived Rabbanism. Small Karaite groups remain in the Crimea and Turkey and, in 1957, the remaining Egyptian Karaites migrated to Israel.

Karbalā'. A city ninety-six kilometres south-west of Baghdad, sacred to Shī'a Muslims. Here Husain (q.v.) was killed in battle, in A.D. 680, and ever since it has rivalled Mecca itself as a place of pilgrimage for the Shī'as. There are two great shrines in Karbalā': the first is the Shrine of Husain, with a golden dome and three minarets, the other with a blue dome is the shrine of Abbas, his half-brother, who died fighting at his side. Many legends are told of the sanctity of Karbalā'. Muhammad himself is said to have declared that the angels brought the dust of the place from Jerusalem, rosaries of clay tablets from Karbalā' are taken as protective charms, and visiting the shrine is held to give immunity from fire and flood. The intercession of Husain, and his role as martyr of martyrs, is central to Shī'a devotion.

Karma, Karman. (Sanskrit) 'doing', deeds, action, work (*Kamma* in Pali Buddhism). In the *Vedas* Karma was the term for a religious rite, which was bound to produce a result or 'fruit', by the law of cause and effect. But Karma was action in general and, while sacrifice was the Karma appropriate to a Brahmin priest, the Karma of a soldier was fighting, of a farmer ploughing, and of a serf service. Karma became both action and its fruit or entail, and was closely linked with the doctrine of transmigration, by which good Karma brought a good afterlife, and evil Karma a bad one. Karma is not Fate, and one's lot in future lives can be improved by effort at good Karma now, but the notion of Karma did help to explain the present inequalities of life. The idea of Karma is common to

Hinduism, Buddhism and Jainism, and release from all Karma, good and bad, was obtained by knowledge and abstinence.

Karma-yoga. The discipline of action, or spiritual exercise through work, taught in the *Bhagavad-Gītā*, along with Jñāna-yoga (q.v.), the discipline of wisdom, and Bhakti-yoga, the discipline of devotion. Karma, action, is essential to everyone, but the Yoga consists in acting without attachment to rewards or fruits; therefore it is detached work by which the bonds of Karma disappear.

Karmathians. See QARMATĪ.

Kārttikeya. Hindu god of war, also called Skanda, identified with the planet Mars. In the epics it is said that he was the son of Shiva and born of the river Ganges or of Pārvatī. He was nursed by the six Pleiades, Krittikā, and so got his name and became six-headed. In art Kārttikeya is represented with six heads, riding a peacock and holding a bow and arrow. He is also called Kumāra and in the south of India Subrahmanya.

Karunā. (Sanskrit) 'compassion'. In Mahāyāna Buddhism one of the two pillars, the other being Prajñā, wisdom. Karunā is also called the second of four sublime moods, the identifying of oneself with the suffering of other people, and it is one of four Brahma Vihāras or lordly states which come from eliminating selfish inclinations. See VIHĀRA.

Kasher. See KOSHER.

Kāshī. The old name for Benares (q.v.) or Vārānasī.

Kashyapa. An ancient Indian sage who had some part in creation. The epics say that he was son of Marīchi, the son of Brahmā, and father of Vivasvat, the father of Manu, progenitor of mankind. He married Aditi (q.v.) and twelve other women, and they gave birth to the Āditya deities and also to Vishnu in his Avatar as a dwarf. Kashyapa was a universal father and is sometimes called after the creating deity Prajāpati. He was one of the great Rishis or ancient sages. Kashyapa is also called a tortoise. For a philosopher Kashyapa, see VAISHESHIKA.

Kassapa, Kāshyapa. The name of the last Buddha of the six before the present Gotama the Buddha, according to the *Mahāpadāna Sutta* of the Pāli scriptures of Theravāda Buddhism. He is sometimes called 'of the ten powers' (*dashabala*), a title used of other Buddhas, but especially of Kassapa. Three other Kassapas were ascetics converted by Gotama with their thousand pupils. Kassapa the Great, Mahā Kassapa, with five hundred brethren, heard of the death of the Buddha, told his followers not to weep, bowed to the funeral pyre, and then arranged the recitation of the scriptures, the *Dhamma* and *Vinaya*. Another Kassapa, called Kumāra, was son of a nun and later is mentioned in the scriptures as converting heretics.

Kasuga. A Shinto deity, formerly the tutelary divinity (see UJI-GAMI) of the Nakatomi or Fujiwara family. It is enshrined at the famous centre of Nara and has become a favourite god for many people.

Katcina. See KOKO.

Katha. A Hindu sage, also the name of one of the classical *Upanishads*. In the latter comes the story of Nachiketas who obtained three boons from death, Yama, the last being knowledge of the nature of the soul and life after death. The answer was that the soul is indestructible, not only post-existent but pre-existent and eternal. This *Upanishad* had a great influence on the *Bhagavad-Gītā*, which quotes its words on the immortal soul.

Kathenotheism. A term coined by Max Müller (1823–1900), to indicate the practice by which men have regarded one god at a time as supreme, notably in the *Vedas* (see HENOTHEISM).

Kauravas. See KURU.

Kavitāvalī. Hindi devotional poem to Rāma composed in the sixteenth century by Tulsī Dās (q.v.).

Kawaté, Bunjiro. Japanese founder of a Shinto sect (1814–1883); see KONKŌ-KYŌ.

Keb. See GEB.

Kedesh, Qadesh. An Egyptian goddess of love, of west Asian origin, usually identified with Hathor (q.v.). She was represented as a naked woman, standing on a lion, with the head-dress of Hathor. Kedesh, 'the holy', was mistress of all the gods; she may have personified the temple prostitutes, and thus was identified with Astarte.

Kedushah. (Hebrew) 'sanctification', a name given to Jewish prayers which are restricted to communal worship, since it is only in community that God can be fully sanctified and witness given to his holiness.

Kegon. Japanese name of the Buddhist Garland school, known in China as Hua Yen (q.v.).

Kena. 'By whom', the title of one of the shorter classical *Upanishads*, so called after its first word. See UMĀ.

Kendo. Japanese art of fencing, influenced by Zen teachings like Judo (q.v.).

Kerbala. See KARBALĀ'.

Keridwen. See CERRIDWEN.

Keshab Chandra Sen. Modern Hindu religious reformer (A.D. 1838–84). He came from a Brahmin family of Bengal; in 1857 he joined the Brāhma Samāj (q.v.), and in 1861 gave up his post in a bank to become a minister, Āchārya, of the Samāj, giving special emphasis to philanthropy. He toured widely and adopted Christian ideals, but in 1865 separated from the leader of the Samāj, Debendranath Tagore. In 1866 Keshab founded the Brāhma Samāj of India, Bhāratvishya, using both texts from other religions and reviving the kīrtans, choruses, of the followers of Chaitanya (q.v.). Keshab opposed idolatrous ceremonies and child-marriage, but when his daughter married the prince of Kuch Bihar, at the age of thirteen and by traditional rites, there was a split in his Samāj. In 1881 his revised movement came to be known as Nava Vidhāna, the Church of the New Dispensation (q.v.). Keshab held that all religions are true, that Christ was the God-man, but that he himself was the divinely appointed leader of the New Dispensation for our times. (See MOZOOMDAR.)

Ketu. In Hindu astronomy the descending lunar orbit, represented by a dragon's tail (the head was Rāhu, q.v.). Ketu was also a comet or meteor, and ninth of the planets. At the churning of the ocean Ketu tasted the nectar Amrita (q.v.) and became immortal.

Ketubah. (Hebrew) 'writ', the Jewish marriage settlement, instituted by Simeon ben Shatah in the first century B.C. According to Jewish law the bridegroom must draw up the Ketubah before marriage to give his wife security and provide for the education of the children. This 'marriage settlement' is read out after the ring is given, and the bridegroom promises to honour and maintain his wife.

Kevala. (Sanskrit) 'single', alone, whole, absolute. In Indian philosophy the term is used of the doctrine of the absolute unity of spirit. Among the Jains it indicates the highest possible knowledge, the infinite and supreme which is possessed only by meditative ascetics called Kevalīs. See KAIVALYA.

Kevalādvaita. (Sanskrit) 'strict non-dualism'; see SHANKARA.

Khadīja. The first wife of the Prophet Muhammad, and during their twenty-four years of married life his only wife. Khadīja was a rich merchant's widow, who first of all employed Muhammad in her service. She was said to have been married twice before, with children of her own. She was about forty years of age, but bore Muhammad seven children. Their marriage was happy, and Khadīja encouraged Muhammad after his visions and during his early preachings, being virtually his first convert. Her cousin Waraqa (q.v.) was a Christian and no doubt this helped to make her sympathetic to Muhammad's teaching of one God. Her death in A.D. 619 was a grievous loss to the Prophet, and only then did he take other wives.

Khālid. A great general of early Islam. He opposed the forces of Muhammad at the battle of Uhud (q.v.), but afterwards joined the Prophet and went with him to the final capture of Mecca in A.D. 630. Khālid led the Muslim forces against the Persian empire and occupied Mesopotamia in 634. He then turned against Syria and captured Damascus in 635. Through a disagreement with the caliph 'Umar, Khālid was deprived of supreme command, but continued to help in victorious battles, was governor of Syria, and died at Hims or Medina in 642.

Khalīfa. See CALIPH.

Khālsā. 'The Pure', the Sikh order or brotherhood, instituted by Guru Gobind Singh (q.v.) in 1699. Members of the Khālsā took the name Singh, 'lion', and swore to observe the Five K's (see K's). They were also forbidden to smoke tobacco or drink alcohol, to eat the Kosher meat killed by Muslims, or to have sexual relations with Muslims. The Khālsā were called the chosen of God, and by their distinctive dress became the embodiment of the Sikh community. Not all Sikhs entered the Khālsā, and those who did not were called the 'slow adopters' (Sahaj dharis).

Khandha. See SKANDHA.

Khārijīs, Khārijites. The oldest sect of Islam and, though heretical to the orthodox Sunni, the closest to orthodoxy. The name (plural *Khawārij*) is generally taken to mean 'seceders' but may signify 'those who come out from impropriety'. The occasion of the schism was the compromise of the fourth Caliph, 'Alī, with his rival in Damascus; the Khārijī declared that God alone could judge and withdrew their support from 'Alī. They also condemned his assassinated predecessor 'Uthmān, and 'Alī himself was killed later by a Khārijī. A series of insurrections and terrorist actions followed but declined during the eighth century. The sole survivors of the Khārijī today are their moderate branch, the Ibādīs (q.v.).

Khatīb. See KHUTBA.

Khepri. The Egyptian god Rē', in the form of the rising sun, and also associated with funeral scenes. He had an ancient cult and was said to have created himself or to have emerged from Nun, the primeval watery chaos. Khepri was represented as a scarab (q.v.), or a man with a scarab on his head, and this symbolized the beetle which rolled the sun as its egg across the sky.

KHEPRI AND KHNUM

Khnum. An old Egyptian god of the upper Nile, worshipped at Elephantiné, Antinoé, and other places. He was a creator-god, the name meaning 'to create', and originator not only of gods and men but especially of the waters. Khnum appears as a man with a ram's head, and was called the ram of Rē', with four horns which perhaps symbolized four sources of the Nile. Khnum was especially revered as a creator and was associated with both Rē' and Horus.

Khoja. Name of certain Indian Muslim groups, derived from a Persian word for 'lord' or master. There are several varieties of Khojas, most of them are Nizārī Ismā'īlīs (q.v.) and follow the Aga Khan (q.v.). But some of them are Twelver Shī'a (q.v.) and a few are orthodox Sunnis; neither of the two last named are followers of the Aga Khan, and he has many non-Indian followers who are not Khojas. Khoja beliefs differ little from those of other Muslims of their particular sects, except in so far as they follow the customs of their Indian caste, particularly regarding marriage and inheritance. The Khojas are a wealthy community, concerned with the welfare of their members, and active in education and literary work.

Khonsu. A minor Egyptian god of the moon, his name perhaps deriving from a root meaning 'to pass through', as the moon passes through the sky. He was represented as a seated man, with a crescent and full moon on his head. Khonsu was said to be son of Amūn and Mut, lord of truth and oracles, and having the power to cast out evil spirits. He was one of the later gods, and sometimes identified with Thoth.

Khuddaka-Nikāya. The 'division of small books' in the Pali canon of Theravāda Buddhist scriptures, the fifth part of the second section, *Sutta Pitaka*, of the canon.

Khutba. (Arabic) 'sermon', or address, delivered by a Khatīb, spokesman or preacher. The Khutba is pronounced at the Friday midday congregational prayer, at the two great festivals (see 'ĪD), and on special occasions. The Friday prayer should be preceded by two short sermons, generally given from a pulpit (see MINBAR), by the preacher who leans on a sword or staff and afterwards prays on behalf of his audience. The festival Khutbas are much the same as regular ones, but should include instructions on the rituals of the day.

Kibla. See QIBLA.

Kiddush. (Hebrew) 'sanctification', the benediction recited in Jewish homes by the master of the house, usually over a cup of wine, before partaking of the Sabbath meal. It begins with the account of the end of creation on the seventh day, and is followed by prayers of blessing. The Kiddush is also recited at Festivals and the New Year. The *Talmud* says that the Kiddush was established by the men of the Great Synagogue before the Christian era. Kiddush Hashem is the sanctification of the divine name and is applied to every act which brings glory to God, especially martyrdom. Contrary acts are Hillul Hashem, the desecration of God's name.

Kindred Sayings. See SAMYUTTA NIKĀYA.

Kingu. Babylonian god, consort of the goddess of chaos, Tiamat (q.v.). Tiamat gave him the Tablets of Destiny, but he was defeated by Marduk (q.v.) who bound them to his own breast. At an assembly of the gods Kingu was found guilty of inciting Tiamat to revolt and he was executed; out of his blood man was created.

Kinich Kak Mo. 'Sunface fire macaw', a sun god of the Maya who was represented as a macaw coming out of the noonday sky to light the sacrificial fire. He had a pyramid temple at Izamal (q.v.) in northern Yucatan. The image of a similar winged being was found in temples at Tulum and perhaps represented the same deity.

Kīrtana. Chorus-singing in Indian worship, as expression of devotional love. From a root meaning 'repetition', the Kīrtana came to be especially popular in Bengal, associated with the followers of

Chaitanya (q.v.), but also with modern reformers such as Keshab Chandra Sen (q.v.). In a Kīrtana a soloist sings verses and assistants join in a chorus, with interludes of dancing and instrumental music. A Kīrtana may last for hours and induce states of ecstasy in the participants (see also BHAJANA.)

Kismet. A Turkish word, used in the sense of destiny or fate, and derived from the Arabic *qisma*, meaning a portion or lot. Commonly used in Islamic countries in the sense of Predestination. See QADAR.

Kiswa. (Arabic) 'robe', a black brocade curtain which covers the whole Ka'ba (q.v.) shrine at Mecca. It reaches from the flat roof to the ground, being fastened by copper rings, and has holes left for the door, water-spouts and the Black Stone.

The Kiswa is made in Egypt and taken to Mecca by pilgrims every year. The old one is taken down at the end of the preceding month and pieces are sold as relics to pilgrims by the door-keepers of the shrine. The Kiswa has the Shahāda confession of faith woven into it, in Arabic script, and a gold embroidered band running round it full of verses from the *Qur'ān*. See MAHMAL.

Kitchen God, Chinese. See SSŬ-MING-SHEN.

Klesha. (Sanskrit) 'evil', pain or defilement, sometimes translated as sin, but erroneously since there is no necessary reference to a deity. In the philosophy of Yoga five Kleshas are named, and in Buddhism ten: three of the body, four of speech and three of the mind.

Klothes. (Greek) 'spinners', goddesses who spun the thread of life. See FATE.

Kōan. A technical term of the Rinzai sect of Japanese Zen Buddhism. Derived from the Chinese *Kung-an*, a public document, a Kōan is a problem of enigmatic or nonsensical language used in meditation, it cannot be solved by the intellect and so is a means of developing intuition and attaining Enlightenment (*satori*). The Kōan system is said to come from Hakuin (1683–1768) who organized the study of the Rinzai school into six stages, beginning with five groups of Kōan. A well-known example of an enigmatic Kōan problem is, 'what is the sound of one hand clapping?'

Kōbō Daishi, Kūkai. Japanese Buddhist monk (A.D. 774–835) who introduced the Shingon (q.v.) sect from China.

Kogoshui. (Japanese) 'Gleanings of Ancient Words', an account of early Japanese myth and religion, with commentaries on words and practices. It contains some details not to be found in the more authoritative *Kojiki* and *Nihongi* (q.v.). The *Kogoshui* was written in A.D. 807 by Hironari Imbe and presented to the Emperor Heizei; since it would be discussed at court, its factual details must have been carefully stated.

Kohen. (Hebrew) 'priest', an official leader of worship in the temple of Jerusalem, before its destruction by the Romans in A.D. 70 and 135. When the temple had gone the priests (plural *kohanim*) lost their domination and were replaced as leaders by the Rabbis (q.v.), since it was forbidden to offer sacrifices anywhere other than in Jerusalem. Priestly families, however, retained some prestige and certain ritual prohibitions have remained, for example a marriage between a Cohen (kohen) and a proselyte or a divorcee.

Ko Hung. Chinese philosopher and alchemist, of the fourth century A.D., and reputed author of the Taoist classic *Pao P'u Tzu* (q.v.). It is said that Ko Hung achieved immortality, since when a friend visited him when he was over eighty he found only his empty clothes.

Kojiki. (Japanese) 'Records of Ancient Matters', the oldest Japanese book, the nearest to a sacred scripture of Shinto and sometimes called the Japanese Homer. The Emperor Temmu (A.D. 673–686) gave orders for records to be preserved, in view of the growing power of Buddhism in Japan, and in his household was Hieda no Are who could repeat many past traditions. After Temmu's death his widow Jito ordered Are's words to be written down by O-no-Yasumaro and the *Kojiki* was completed in 712. The text of the *Kojiki* is in Chinese characters, of poor quality, which could be read in Japanese, so that it was read partly in Chinese and partly in Japanese. There are several English translations. The *Kojiki* contains myths and histories, of creation, gods, men, the nation, customs and ceremonies. The *Nihongi* (q.v.) is very similar.

Kokka. See SHINTŌ.

Koko, Katcina. Mask gods of popular cults among the Zuñi of New Mexico. The Koko are the dead and ancestors from over the Whispering Water who come to bring blessings and fortune. All males belong to Koko groups and dancers number up to seventy in the public squares in summer. In winter the Koko dances take place in rectangular rooms which can only be entered through the roof. The dancers wear masks of many kinds, and represent gods as well as ancestors.

Kol Nidre. 'All vows', a Jewish prayer chanted and the name of the evening portion of the Day of Atonement (q.v.). Recalling the years of persecution it was meant to encourage those who had failed to fulfil their religious vows.

Konarak. See BLACK PAGODA.

Konkō-kyō. 'The religion of Golden Light', one of the most popular of Japanese New Religions (see SECT SHINTO). Founded in 1859 by Bunjiro Kawaté or Konkō Daijin (1814–83). The religion began in peasant surroundings, and a fearsome popular god Kon was changed into a merciful deity by interpreting the name *Kon*, 'metal', as 'Gold'. Konkō-kyō teaches that man can avoid the suffering of Karma by dependence on the 'God of the Golden Light'. It claims to be universal and monotheistic, and has more than half a million followers.

Kono-hana-sakuya-hime. Goddess of Mount Fuji in Japan who married Ninigi, son of the sun-goddess Amaterasu. See FUJI-SAN.

Koran. See QUR'ĀN.

Koré, Core. (Greek) 'Maiden', the virgin daughter of mythology, commonly called Persephone (q.v.). See also DEMETER.

Koreish. See QURAYSH.

Kosher, Kasher. 'Fit', 'clean', meat that is properly killed for Jewish usage under strict regulations. Some species are 'unclean' and prohibited altogether. That which is 'clean' must be so killed that the blood is drained off, for, according to the Bible, the 'blood is the life' (or soul, *nephesh*; *Leviticus* 17, 14).

Kozeba. See COCHBA.

Krishna. (Sanskrit) 'black' (also spelt **Kṛṣṇa**) the most popular of Hindu gods and hero of many myths. He is said to have been the eighth or ninth Avatar (q.v.) of Vishnu, but usually appears as a god in his own right. His origin is obscure and mixed, his name suggesting that he came from the older darker population, and he is often associated with cowherds. In the *Chāndogya Upanishad* a Krishna is a scholar, son of Devakī, and this name remains in later story. In the *Mahābhārata* and later *Purānas*, specially the *Bhāgavata Purāna* (q.v.), Krishna is son of Vasudeva, and hence called Vāsudeva, a wonderful and mischievous child, a youth amorous of the Gopis (q.v., milkmaids), a hero, warrior and king. Finally he dies by being shot inadvertently in the foot and returns to heaven. None of this comes in the *Bhagavad-Gītā* (q.v.) where he is the divine instructor of Arjuna and supreme Deity with little reference to Vishnu.

KRISHNA AND RĀDHĀ

Krishna Dwaipāyana. See VYĀSA.

Krishnā. See DRAUPADĪ.

Krishnamurti. The name given to one of the sons of G. N. Aiyer, a Brahmin of Madras, who was entrusted to the Theosophist Mrs Besant to be educated. C. W. Leadbeater, a colleague of Mrs Besant's, took charge of the boy and claimed that he was the vehicle of the coming World-teacher. He called him Alcyone, and in India and Ceylon proclaimed him as the expected Maitreya or Avatar, and in Europe as the coming Christ. This was in 1923, after Krishnamurti and his brother had been educated in England, and tours were made in which he was announced as the World Teacher. Krishnamurti published several books, but in 1929 he renounced the claims that had been made for him and has lived since in India and California.

Krita Yuga. The first age of the world in Hindu mythology, said to have lasted 1,728,000 years; see YUGA. It was an ideal time, of eternal righteousness, there was no malice or strife, the castes fulfilled their duties and had the same religion. It was followed by the Tretā Yuga.

Kronos. 'Time' in ancient Greek mythology, son of heaven and earth and leader of the Titans (q.v.). Kronos married his sister Rhea (q.v.) and the major gods were born of them; Kronos swallowed them all, except Zeus, through fear of usurpation, though later he vomited them up. These were probably pre-Hellenic myths, and Kronos may have been an ancient god of agriculture, to whom human sacrifices were made. The Kronia, his festival, was celebrated at harvest-time, at Athens and elsewhere. See OURANOS.

Kshatriya. The second of the four colours or classes of traditional Hindu society (see CASTE). The Kshatriya, 'endowed with sovereignty', is the ruling and warrior class. Like the other two higher classes it is 'twice-born' (*dwi-ja*), its members being invested in adolescence with the sacred thread, in their case coloured red. From the Kshatriya have come notable religious figures, partly in opposition to the Brahmin priests, such as Gautama the Buddha, Mahāvīra of the Jains, and Arjuna of the *Bhagavad-Gītā*. See RĀJA.

Kshitigarbha. A Mahāyāna Buddhist being of enlightenment, a Bodhisattva (q.v.). The name is Sanskrit, meaning 'earth-womb', perhaps because of association with the dead, but it does not appear to have developed much in India. This being, popular in China and Japan under the names Ti-Tsang and Jizo respectively, is included in late works among eight great Bodhisattvas. Kshitigarbha is especially concerned with the welfare of the dead, having vowed to deliver them all from hell, and is the special protector of dead children. He is also associated with roads and mountains. In art he appears as a monk with a staff or in six images he helps beings in the states of existence.

Kuan Ti, Kuan Kung. Popular Chinese hero and god of war, wealth and literature. The historic warrior Kuan Yü, who died in A.D. 219, fought to restore the Han dynasty for his friend the king of Shu. Kuan Yü was noted for his great strength, fierce aspect and red face, and these appear in the many statues and pictures of him. He had many adventures, which are favourite Chinese stories, but was finally executed by his enemy. His cult grew rapidly, he was called Kung (duke), and finally Ti (god or emperor), and had state worship in the Temple of Strength until 1912. Kuan Ti had many temples, as god of war and literature, and was patron of several provinces, with monthly festivals.

KUAN TI

Kuan-yin. The Chinese name for the great Mahāyāna Buddhist being of mercy, Avalokiteshvara (q.v.), whose name meant 'the Lord who looks down', or 'is seen', but it was misinterpreted in Chinese as 'seeing the sound', thus giving the form Kuan-yin. In Japan it is Kwannon or Kannon. A fuller Chinese form is Kuan-shih-yin, and under this name there were male images at an early

date. From the eleventh century Kuan-yin has been represented in China as female, though in Japan as male. She carries a child in her arms or holds a peach, a symbol of fertility; she is the popular protector of women and children, guardian of sailors, and compassionate saviour. Kuan-Yin resembles Taoist figures, such as the Empress of Heaven, or Holy Mother, but she is not correctly described as 'goddess', since she is a Bodhisattva, a being devoted to helping all others to enlightenment and peace. With Amida she is the most popular of all Buddhist objects of worship in China and Japan.

Kubera, Kuvera. In early Indian mythology a chief of evil beings or spirits of darkness, and represented with three legs and eight teeth. Later, Kubera is god of wealth and ruler of the northern regions, some authorities saying that he had a place in the heavenly Kailāsa (q.v.). Kubera once ruled in Ceylon, but was expelled by the demon Rāvana. After he had practised austerities for thousands of years the god Brahmā granted him immortality and guardianship of gold, jewels, and mystic treasures. See also YAKSHAS.

KUKULCĀN

Kuds. See QUDS.

Kuei, Kwei. (Chinese) 'spirit', in the sense of a returned or disembodied spirit. In relationship to Shên (q.v.), Kuei is the vital principle of Yin compared to Yang (q.v.). Shên is the coming into being from non-being, and Kuei is the return from being to non-being. In reference to a person Kuei is the negative aspect, and in religion it is the spirit venerated in an ancestral temple.

Kūkai. See KŌBŌ DAISHI.

Kukulcān. The Maya name for Quetzalcoatl (q.v.).

Kumāra. In Hindu mythology a name of Kārttikeya (q.v.) or Skanda, the god of war.

Kumāra Kassapa. See KASSAPA.

Kumārajīva. An Indian scholar (344–413) who went to China and founded there the Mādhyamika, Middle Doctrine, or Three Treatises (San Lun) school of Buddhism. He is said to have translated three hundred Buddhist texts into Chinese, including the treatises of his own school and other works, such as the popular *Lotus Sūtra* (q.v.). Kumārajīva expounded these texts to Chinese scholars, teaching the unreality of the self and the doctrine of the Void (*shunyatā*, q.v.). From his associates and followers came further developments, uniting Buddhist and Taoist thought. See SAN TSANG.

Kumarbi. Ancient deity of the Hurrians and Hittites, and called 'father of the gods'. In mythology Kumarbi was threatened by Teshub (q.v.), the god of storms, and made a great stone hero, Ullikummi, to fight him. Ullikummi advanced against the city of Kummiya and covered it with his shadow. The menace was seen by Hebat, wife of Teshub, who warned her husband; he sent his acolyte Tashmishu to view the situation. The acolyte was afraid and cried that all was lost and that Teshub must give up his rule over the world. But Ea, the Sumerian god of sweet waters and magic, restored order and destroyed Ullikummi's power.

Kumārila. Hindu philosopher of the eighth century A.D.; see MĪMĀMSĀ.

Kumbha Mela. 'Pitcher fair', a great Indian pilgrimage festival held every twelve years. In mythology gods and demons fought for a pitcher of Amrita nectar (q.v.) and, when the gods finally carried it off to heaven, they stopped at four places which were sanctified by its touch. The four places in turn have the Kumbha Mela; they are: Prayag (see YAMUNĀ), Hardwar, Nasik and Ujjain.

Kunapipi. See GUNABIBI.

Kundalinī. (Sanskrit) 'serpent-power', a concept in Tantric (q.v.) forms of Hinduism. The Kundalinī is believed to be a power situated in the lower parts of the body and usually quiescent, but it can be aroused by yogic practices and rises up through the great vein (Sushumna, q.v.) which runs up the spinal column and unites with a powerful psychic centre (Sahasrāra, q.v.) called a 'lotus' in the skull. So the Yogi is thought to gain spiritual power, supernatural abilities and knowledge, and finally liberation.

Kuntī. Wife of Pāndu, in the Indian epic *Mahābhārata*, and mother of the heroes Yudhi-shthira, Bhīma and Arjuna; hence they are called 'son of Kunīt' or Kaunteya. She was also known as Prithā and her sons as Pārtha.

Kuo P'o. See FÊNG SHUI.

Kurbān. See CORBAN.

Kūrma. 'Tortoise' (Sanskrit), the second or third Avatar (q.v.) of Vishnu in Hindu mythology. When the gods sought to churn the ocean to gain the nectar of Amrita, Vishnu took the form of Kūrma so that the mountain Mandara could be supported on his back. This is found in the epic *Mahābhārata* and elsewhere. There is a *Kūrma Purāna*, with seventeen thousand verses, but strangely it is not much concerned with Vishnu since the greater part inculcates the worship of Shiva and Durgā. See ĪSHVARA-GĪTĀ.

Kurozumi-kyō. The 'religion of Kurozumi', a Japanese New Religion (see SECT SHINTŌ), founded by Kurozumi Munetada (A.D. 1780–1850). He came from a priestly family, but had a special vocation in 1814 and was renowned for his piety. The Shinto background is shown in emphasis placed on the worship of Amaterasu-ōmi-kami (q.v.), who is regarded as the pervading power of the universe, with whom man should live in union. The followers of Kurozumi-kyō are reckoned at about three quarters of a million.

Kuru. Indian prince of the Lunar race, who ruled to the north of Delhi. He was ancestor of both Dhrita-rāshtra and Pāndu (qq.v.), whose sons struggled for sovereignty; usually the former's sons are called Kurus or Kauravas, though occasionally the title is applied to one of the Pāndus also. The battle between them took place at Kuru-kshetra, 'field of Kuru', site of one of India's newest universities.

Kusinārā, Kusinagara. Place of the death of Gautama the Buddha, where he passed into Parinirvāna (q.v.). It is called a 'little wattle-and-daub township in the jungle', probably because later legend thought that the Buddha should have died in a more notable place, but the fact that the name has been retained suggests its historical character. It is usually identified with the town of Kasia, in northern India.

Kūsti, Kūshti. Sacred girdle worn by Parsis, made of lamb's wool, with seventy-two threads corresponding to the number of chapters of the Yasna texts. It is first put on at the ceremony of initiation in adolescence and worn thereafter throughout life, except when bathing. See SACRED THREAD.

Kuvera. See KUBERA.

Kwang Ti. See KUAN TI.

Kwanyin, Kwannon. See KUAN-YIN.

Kyōdan. (Japanese) 'association', a term used of religious organizations, especially modern sectarian movements. See P. L. KYŌDAN.

Kyoha. See SECT SHINTO.

L

Labyrinth. A complicated building from which escape was impossible, said to have been made for King Minos of Crete by Daedalus (q.v.). The Minotaur lived there, and it is depicted on coins, vases and mosaics. It was probably at Knossos, and many later mazes were called Labyrinths.

Lachesis. In Greek mythology, one of the Moirai who spin the thread of life. It was Lachesis who assigned the lot. See FATE.

Laindjung. A spirit being of northern Australian mythology about whom there are many stories. He lived on the shores of the Gulf of Carpentaria, but his size and loud voice frightened people so that they attacked him with spears and he plunged into a waterhole to escape. While his wounds were healing, Laindjung painted his body with special designs. He emerged from the hole, changed his name to Banaidja and called the people to him. He explained the patterns of his body and told them that they should be used in the rituals of each linguistic unit. Thus the different rituals have been explained.

Lakshmana. Son of King Dasharatha, in the Hindu epic *Rāmāyana*, and half-brother of Rāma (q.v.). He accompanied Rāma in his exile, and shared his struggles. Finally to save Rāma from an angry sage, Lakshmana bore the latter's curse and walked into a river, but the gods took him bodily to heaven.

Lakshmī. Hindu goddess of fortune and wife of the great god Vishnu. She is commonly called Shrī, a title given to many gods and saints but especially to Lakshmī, and the letters of the name Shrī are written on walls, books and papers to guarantee good fortune. It is said that Lakshmī sprang from the ocean, like Aphrodite, when the gods churned it for the nectar of immortality (see AMRITA). She had a lotus in her hand and she is sometimes called Lotus (Padmā). As consort of Vishnu, when he descended to earth in an Avatar, she was incarnate also in his earthly wife, as in Sītā, the queen of Rāma. Lakshmī is a model of beauty, sometimes with four arms, but generally with two, holds a lotus in her hand, and is a gracious and kindly being. The popular festival of Dīvālī (q.v.) is largely associated with her as bringing blessing at the new year.

Lakulīsha. Reputed founder of the Pāshupata (q.v.) sect of the followers of Shiva in south India. He is said to have lived in the third century A.D., and his name is sometimes derived from the Lakula or club which he carried. His followers often regard Lakulīsha as an Avatar or Manifestation of Shiva, carrying a citron in his right hand and a staff in his left.

Lalita-vistara. The 'extended account of the sports' of the Buddha. A

Mahāyāna Buddhist scripture, first written in the popular Prākrit dialect and later put into Sanskrit and other languages. It is in mixed prose and verse, and dates from about the third century A.D. The *Lalita-vistara* is highly legendary and gives stories of the future Buddha from the time when he decided in heaven to be born on earth, down to the first sermon that he preached after he had become a Buddha at his Enlightenment. It is of little historical value, but is useful for comparison with other lives and for its picture of the role of the Buddha in Mahāyāna devotion.

Lama. Name for a superior monk (blama) or abbot of Tibetan Buddhism, but commonly now applied to any monk. The two principal Lamas of Tibet are the Dalai Lama (q.v.), until recently the temporal head of Tibet, regarded as the incarnation of the Bodhisattva Chenresi (q.v.), and the Tashi or Panchen Lama (q.v.) who claimed spiritual superiority and to be an incarnation of Amitābha. A further Bogdo Lama lived in Mongolia, to represent the Tibetan Buddhists there. Lamaism is a Western term for the religion of Tibet, not used by the Buddhists themselves, which is a form of Mahāyāna Buddhism with a mingling of the pre-Buddhist Bon religion (q.v.). The two chief sects of Tibetan Buddhism are the dominant Yellow Hat or 'Virtuous' (Gelugspa. q.v.) and the older and less literate Red Hat or 'Old Ones' (Nyingmapa). Popular devotion includes constant repetition of the formula, 'Hail to the Jewel in the Lotus' (*Om mani padme hum*). See also TSONG-KHA-PA.

Lamia. A vampire or bogey frightening children in Greek mythology. It is said that the goddess Hera destroyed Lamia's children by Zeus (Hera's husband), whereupon Lamia became wild with grief and preyed on other children.

Langar. See GURDWĀRĀ.

Lankā. Ceylon in Indian texts; see HANUMĀN, RĀMA.

Lankāvatāra Sūtra. The 'Entrance to Ceylon (Lankā) Text', one of the most important texts of Mahāyāna Buddhism. Written first in Sanskrit, its date is unknown, but it was translated into Chinese by the fifth century A.D. It is the chief canonical text for expounding subjective idealism, similar to that of the later Yogāchāra (q.v.) and is taken as basic by the Zen schools of Buddhism as well as others in Mahāyāna.

Laocoön. A prince of Troy and priest of Apollo or Poseidon in Greek legend. Snakes were sent to kill him, either because he had married against the will of

Apollo or because he opposed the Trojan wish to drag the Wooden Horse into Troy. Laocoön and his two sons were strangled in the embrace of the two huge serpents, and a famous ancient sculpture in the Vatican shows them in their death agony.

Lao-T'ien-Yeh. (Chinese) 'ancient ancestor heaven', the supreme God in popular Chinese religion (see JADE EMPEROR). He was adopted from Taoism as originally the second of a triad of deities but later effectively the chief. Lao-T'ien-Yeh was depicted as a heavenly emperor, with a court and army at his command.

Lao Tzŭ, Lao Tse. The reputed founder of Taoism, his name was Latinized as Laocius. Nowadays it is generally agreed that he was a mythical figure, to whom was ascribed the famous scripture

Tao Tê Ching (q.v.), the Classic of 'The Way and its Power'. Perhaps he was a composite figure, one member of which was Lao Tan who lived in the fourth century B.C., but this is disputed. Legend said that Lao Tzŭ was born with white hair (hence his name which means 'Old Master'), that he lived nearly two hundred years, that he worsted Confucius (q.v.) in argument, and on his departure to the west wrote down the *Tao Tê Ching* before riding on his ox into the mountains. In the early Christian era Lao Tzŭ was taken as the founder of Taoism, and later he became a member of the Taoist Triad, sometimes alongside the Jade Emperor (q.v.).

Lapiths. A people of Thessaly in Greek mythology. Their king, Peirithous, invited the Centaurs (q.v.) to his marriage, but some of them attacked the Lapith women and in a fierce battle the Centaurs were defeated. The scene is popular in sculpture.

Lares. Spirits of agriculture in ancient Italian religion, connected primarily with the land, but also with roads and houses and with guardianship of the state. Where farm lands met at crossroads (*compita*), the Lares had shrines and Compitalia festivals; they were guardians of roads, Lares Viales, and their cult was probably brought into houses by farm-workers, as Lares Familiares. Small groups of freedmen in Rome tended their shrines and celebrated their festivals, but they had no mythology. See COLLEGIUM. See also MANIA.

Lāt, al-Lāt. Ancient deity of Arabia whose name means 'the goddess'. Her principal shrine was at Tā'if, south of Mecca, where she was represented by a white stone. The sanctuary was destroyed after Muhammad conquered Mecca in A.D. 630, but veneration of the goddess remained for centuries after. The *Qur'ān* (53, 19–20) says, 'Have you considered al-Lāt, and al-'Uzzā, and the third, Manāt? Have you male offspring and he female?' This suggests that it would dishonour God to say that he only had female children in these goddesses, whereas men had male children. But Muhammad's biographer, Ibn Ishāq, said that Satan first suggested to the Prophet the addition of the words, 'these are the exalted swans [or cranes] whose intercession is approved', as if he was making a concession to the polytheism of Arabia. But Gabriel told him that God had not sent this message, which was changed to the form in which it stands now.

Latona. See LETO.

Law, Islamic. See SHARĪ'A, FIQH, FOUR SCHOOLS.

Leadbeater, C.W. Convert to the Theosophical Society (q.v.) in 1884, who settled in Madras and engaged in occult investigations. He hailed Krishnamurti (q.v.) (whom he called Alcyone in his investigations) as the coming world teacher.

Lear. See LLYR.

Lectisternium. (Latin) 'spreading couches', a feast of the gods, when couches were prepared for their images and they were entertained like human guests, in a private house or shrine. See CONSENTES DI and SUPPLICATIO.

Leda. In Greek mythology she was mother of Helen and the Dioscuroi (qq.v.), by Zeus. The famous story of Zeus turning into a swan to approach Leda has often been depicted in art.

Left-hand Worshippers. See VĀMĀCHĀRA, SHĀKTAS and TANTRA.

Legend. See MYTH.

Lemures. Roman spirits of those dead who had no relatives and were hungry, and hence were supposed to haunt houses. Black beans were thrown in the direction where they were supposed to be to get rid of them. They were fed at the Lemuria, 9, 11 and 13 May.

Leon. See MOSES DE LEON.

Ler. The Irish god of the sea; see LLYR.

Lethe. (Greek) 'forgetting', forgetfulness, oblivion. The name of the river of forgetfulness in the underworld. See STYX and OCEANUS.

Leto, Latona. One of the female Titans in Greek mythology whose name is pre-Greek. She was mother of Apollo and Artemis and so had shrines on the island of Delos (q.v.). In the hymn to Apollo of Delos, it is said that the gigantic Leto gave birth to Apollo leaning against a mountain and chose Delos because of the jealousy of Hera (q.v.) on the mainland. When Niobe (q.v.) boasted that she had more children than Leto, the latter's two, Apollo and Artemis, killed all Niobe's children.

Levitation. See HATHA.

Leza, Lesa, Resa. A name for the supreme God among some African peoples, from the northern Kalahari into Congo, and across into Zambia and Tanzania. Leza has been derived from several roots, of which the favourite is a verb meaning 'to cherish'. The Supreme Being is referred to as a Creator, Owner and Giver of rain. He lives in heaven, but comes down to earth to make mountains, rivers, trees and grass. He is regarded as living on high, tearing the sky with lightning, and ultimately incomprehensible.

Lhasa. Capital of Tibet and religious centre (see LAMA). It was traditionally founded by King Songtsen-gampo (d. A.D. 650), in whose reign Buddhism became first established in Tibet; from a temple that he built, it was called Lhasa, the 'Lord's place'. The most famous building is the Potala palace (q.v.), finished in 1694, which sits like a great mountain on top of the one on which it is constructed. It resembles a truncated pyramid, with great walls and windows, and stairways like mountain ledges. Here was the traditional residence of the Dalai Lama (q.v.).

Li. In Chinese tradition Li was ceremonial, propriety, 'rites'. It is expressed in books of rites, *Li Chi*, *I Li* and *Chou Li*, which, though put in their present form long after Confucius, yet preserve something of the state of rituals in his time. In the *Analects* (q.v.) of Confucius himself, it is said that parents should be served according to Li in their lifetime and sacrificed to according to Li after death. Rulers were told to submit themselves to Li so that Heaven would respond to their goodness. Li provided the external expression of Confucian religion, and Jên (q.v.), 'benevolence', was its inward motive force.

Liber. An Italian fertility god, especially connected with wine, and often identified with Dionysus (q.v.) whose mythology he borrowed. His festival, the Liberalia, was celebrated on 17 March and was a time of rejoicing when boys often put on the Toga. Liber had a cult in Rome with the female Libera, associated with Ceres (q.v.).

Liberal Judaism. See REFORM.

Libertas. Roman goddess who personified liberty, first of free men and later of constitutional government. She was associated with Jupiter and her cult was fairly late.

Li Chi. 'Book of Rites' or 'Records on Ceremonial', one of the five Confucian Classics (q.v.). Compiled during the first century B.C., it contains much older material, but with a mixture of Taoism and legalism it shows the syncretistic forces at work within Confucian teachings at this period. It also contains passages identical with some of the writings of the third century Confucian scholar Hsün-tzŭ (q.v.).

Lieh Tzŭ. Reputed Chinese Taoist sage, supposedly of the fourth century B.C., but, despite the book ascribed to him and references in the *Chuang Tzŭ* (q.v.), little is known of him. The *Lieh Tzŭ*, which bears his name, is reckoned as a forgery compiled centuries later, perhaps in the third century A.D., to bolster up certain Taoist ideas. In the seventh chapter, named after a historical character Yang Chu, teachings of pleasure-seeking are given which do not accord with what is known otherwise of Yang Chu; nevertheless they show developments in later Taoism. It teaches that one should live according to nature, according to oneself and not others. There is much concern about death and how to avoid it in the search for longevity and immortality. See also YANG and YIN.

Līlā. (Sanskrit) 'play', 'sport'. In Indian thought this explains the activity of the divine in the world. In the legends of Krishna his adventures with the Gopis are his Brindāban (q.v.) Lilā. In the philosophy of the Vedānta school the Lilā of the World Soul creates the cosmos as an artist makes a picture; there is no necessity, or even reality, in this play. Mahāyāna Buddhism spoke of the three worlds as the Lilā of the Bodhisattva. Mystics have spoken of the display of the divine Lilā, in relationship to the force of Shakti. Modern teachers, like Tagore, taught their pupils to emulate God, making work to be like play, Karma like Lilā.

Lilith. A demon of Assyrian and Babylonian myth, both male and female, and mentioned in the *Bible* (*Isaiah* 34, 14). In the *Talmud* Lilith was the chief female demon, a monster with long hair who seized sleeping men, like the Roman Succubus. The *Talmud* does not give many other details, but Lilith is prominent in medieval Jewish folk-lore and was regarded as particularly dangerous to children and pregnant women.

Lin-chi. Founder of the Lin-chi sect (Japanese Rinzai) of Chinese Buddhism. After great persecution in the ninth century, south Chinese Zen Buddhism developed into five traditions or Five Houses, of which the most important was that founded by Lin-chi (died A.D. 867). He studied the scriptures and engaged in dialectics. His followers developed the use of the Kung-an (Japanese Kōan, q.v.), the riddle or paradox, which leads to enlightenment. The Rinzai school of Zen in Japan has especially developed the use of Kōans.

Linga, Lingam. The phallic symbol of the Hindu god Shiva, as a straight mud, stone or marble column, often set in a Yoni (q.v.). Offerings of Ganges water or milk are poured over it. The Linga does not appear in the *Vedas*, but on seals of Mohenjodaro (q.v.) there is a Shiva-like Yogi with Linga, and it seems to have come from the fertility rites of ancient times. There were traditionally twelve Shiva-Linga centres, notably at Benares, but there are millions of these objects all over India. There is a *Linga Purāna*, a poem of eleven thousand verses, in which Shiva explains the four goals of virtue, wealth, pleasure and salvation. Although incorporating ancient fertility cults, Shiva is also the great ascetic and his Linga, rather than a human image, is the plain symbol of his presence.

Lingāyats. Members of sects of the Hindu god Shiva, founded in the twelfth century near Bombay, and first called Vira Shaivas or heroic Shiva followers. Originally they rejected the authority of Brahmins, caste-distinctions and child-marriage, but some of these have reappeared. The Lingāyats are led by teachers from any caste, called Jangamas, and have strong organization. In modern times they are active in missionary work and reclaiming those who have been converted to other religions. Every Lingāyat wears a miniature Linga (q.v.), the symbol of Shiva, in a container round his neck and holds it in the hand during worship. Their theological doctrines are little different from those of other followers of Shiva.

Lisa. A Dahomean god, male and of the sun, partner to Mawu (q.v.), the female and moon. The pair Mawu-Lisa is supreme over other twin gods. In a Capuchin catechism of 1658, made at Allada (Ardra) in Dahomey, Lisa was taken as Jesus and Mawu as God the Father.

Llyr. The Welsh form of Ler, the Irish god of the sea. He was father of Bran (q.v.) and Manawyddan (q.v.), the latter also being an Irish sea-god, Manannan, and lord of the dead. Llyr is King Lear and his other daughter Creiddylad is Cordelia.

Loa. Name of gods in the Voodoo (q.v.) of Haiti. The general explanation is that the term means 'mystery', but its origin is obscure, though perhaps derived from Dahomey. The Loas are families of gods, yet they are not arranged in the traditional divine families of Dahomean religion, but in Haiti are grouped under divinities of the same name. For example Ogou; Papa Ogou is the father, Ogou Badagri is a general whose name indicates origin from Badagry in West Africa, Ogou Ferraille is a metal divinity who protects soldiers, and Ogou Ashadé knows medicinal plants.

Lochanā. Japanese form of the Bodhisattva Vairochana (q.v.) who is also called Dainichi. It is sometimes said that Lochanā should be distinguished from

Vairochana, as the special personification of the Dharma Doctrine. But the Daibutsu (q.v.) , 'great Buddha' image of the Todaiji temple at Nara is called Lochanā (Roshana) and Vairochana (Birushana).

Lofn. A minor Scandinavian goddess, counted among the Asynjur (q.v.). She is said to have been benevolent and she obtained the permission of Odin or Frigg for those who wanted to get married; however, she has little mythology.

Logos. (Greek) 'thought', word, and in philosophy the rational principle of the universe. For the Stoics (q.v.) it was the principle in gods and men, sometimes identified with the god Hermes (q.v.) in popular religion. For Philo (q.v.) the Logos was the sum of the divine ideas, mediating between God and man, ultimately God himself in relationship with man. Thence the Logos idea entered the Fourth Gospel.

Lohans. Chinese term for the Indian Arhants, 'worthy' followers of the Buddha. Sixteen in some early texts, but generally Eighteen Lohans represent these disciples and are common figures in Chinese and Japanese temples, paintings and sculptures, as also in Tibet and Korea. The Lohans have different characteristics; they were said to rule regions assigned to them by the Buddha for the protection of the faith, and they would not leave these regions till the arrival of the next Buddha.

Loka. (Sanskrit) a 'world'. Three worlds, Tri-loka (q.v.), are commonly named: heaven, air and earth; but seven Lokas also include abodes of gods and saints. Loka-pālas were guardian spirits who supported or presided over the principal points of the compass and were identified with some of the major gods of the Hindu pantheon, generally Yama, Indra, Varuna and Kubera. Each of them had an elephant which was also called Loka-pāla, a world-protector. Lokāloka, 'a world and not a world', was said to be a range of mountains which separated this world from the outer darkness.

Lokāyata. (Sanskrit) 'world extended', materialistic, the system of materialistic or atheistic Indian philosophy taught by Chārvāka (q.v.).

Loki. A mischievous character in Scandinavian mythology. He was included among the Aesir gods (q.v.), yet he is said to have been son of a giant and father of monsters: the Fenris wolf, Hel and the Midgard snake. Perhaps he was an early spirit of the elements, a fire-god, and it is said that he could change his shape and fly through the air. Loki was the friend of the great gods Odin and Thor, yet he was mischievous and brought harm to the gods. In particular, Loki was responsible for the death of Balder (q.v.), as he gave a mistletoe shoot to the blind god Hödr (q.v.) and guided his hand so that Balder was shot and killed. Loki was captured by the gods and bound with intestines, while a snake dropped its poison on his face. His struggles cause earthquakes.

Lokottaravādin. A school of transcendental Buddhist teaching which developed early in the Mahāyāna movement. It taught that the Buddha was 'above the world' (*lokottara*), a transcendent being who only appeared to conform to human conditions, but really was above them all. Lokottaravādin doctrines are found in the *Mahāvastu* (q.v.) and many other texts.

Long House. Temple of the Iroquois of North America and centre of communal religious life. The four walls are orientated to the cardinal points and have a number of windows. Unlike the Delaware Big House (q.v.), there is no centre post. The Long House is divided into an eastern and western half, by an invisible line, and women sit on the east and men on the west. Some tribes divide the Long house according to clan groups. The winter ceremonies are thanksgivings for the harvest performed by men, and the summer ceremonies performed by women are for the crops.

Lonkā, Lunkā. Jain teacher who in 1452 separated from the parent body on the grounds that the Jain scriptures said nothing of images or temples. In 1653 began the Sthānakavāsīs (q.v.), 'dwellers in meeting houses'.

Lotus. This flower is one of the most popular symbols of oriental thought and art. In Buddhism it is the scripture of the True Law (see LOTUS SŪTRA), and Buddhas and gods are usually depicted seated

on a lotus. In the Hindu *Bhagavad-Gītā*, evil is said to slip off a wise man as water slips off lotus flowers, and the picture of the pure white or pink lotus rising from a muddy bed is very popular. The petals of the lotus appear in Mandala designs (q.v.). See also OM.

In Greek mythology the lotus or jujube was eaten by Lotus-eaters (Lotophagi), making them forget their own country and wish to stay in the lotus-land for ever.

In Egypt the lotus was the abode of the great god Rē' and a manifestation of the god Nefertem (q.v.).

Lotus Sūtra. Popular name for the *Saddharma Pundarīka*, 'True Law Lotus', the favourite Mahāyāna Buddhist scripture. Written in Sanskrit early in the Christian era, it was widely translated and used, and has been called 'the Gospel of half Asia'. The translation by Kumārajīva (q.v.) in A.D. 406 was common to China and Japan. There is a complete English translation from Sanskrit, and an abridged version from Chinese. The *Lotus Sūtra* depicts the exalted Buddha on a Himalayan peak, giving a new Vehicle of universal salvation; this offends some monks who withdraw, and the Buddha proceeds to develop his doctrines of salvation by faith. The popular twenty-fourth chapter, recited by Zen and other Buddhists, tells of the grace of the compassionate Bodhisattva Avalokiteshvara (q.v.).

Lü. Chinese name of a Disciplinary, Vinaya, School of Buddhism, founded upon the strict discipline of the Vinaya (q.v.) portion of the Buddhist canon of scripture. It was founded or elaborated in China by Tao-hsüan (595–667), who had a high reputation for learning which persisted in the Lü monasteries till modern times. It was introduced into Japan as Ritsu in the eighth century and is called Shin Ritsu or New Disciplinary School, with a small number of followers.

Lucina. Minor Italian goddess who became assimilated to Juno (q.v.). Lucina was a goddess of childbirth and so appropriately connected with a mother deity like Juno. The foundation day of the temple of Juno Lucina was 1 March, when the Matronalia festival was held.

Lug, Lugus, Lugos. Ancient Celtic deity, widely worshipped and with many characteristics. In Gaul he was patron of the 'stronghold of Lugus', Lugudunum (Lyons), and in north Britain the 'wall of Lugus' was Luguvallum. In Ireland he was father of the hero Cúchulainn (q.v.). Lug was sometimes connected with ravens since these were regarded as prophetic birds and he was a god of wisdom, like Mercury. Lug was also perhaps a sun-god and general patron of culture. He is said to have been a tall fair warrior, who carried a shield, spear and javelin. He also had medicinal art and, when his son was wounded, sang him to sleep and healed his wounds with herbs.

Lulab. 'Branch', a branch of a palm tree taken at the Jewish feast of Tabernacles (q.v.) and waved during recitation of passages from the *Psalms*, following a commandment in *Leviticus* 23, 40.

Lullingstone. Village near Orpington in Kent with the remains of a Roman villa dating from the first century A.D., with 4th century floor mosaic illustrating themes in Roman mythology. See CHIMAERA, BELLEROPHON, EUROPA and HORAE.

Lumbini. Name of the park near Kapilavastu (q.v.). in which Gautama the Buddha was born, The place was marked by a pillar erected at the orders of King Ashoka in 250 B.C.

Lumpaka See Lonkā.

Lun Yü. See ANALECTS.

Lung Wang. (Chinese) 'dragon king', a popular god, especially in north China. He controls the rain and there are many rain-making ceremonies associated with his worship. He is depicted as a huge and ugly amphibian, since he is particularly connected with floods.

Lupercalia. Roman festival at the Lupercal, a cave below the Palatine, perhaps for the god Faunus. Goats or dogs were sacrificed and youths dressed only in the skins of these round their waists ran round the Palatine city beating people, especially women, with strips of the skins called Februa (q.v.). The feast was held on 15 February, the month which took its name from this custom. The name of the youths, Luperci, suggests that the rite arose from fear of or to propitiate a wolf god (*lupus*), and that it may have come from rites of herdsmen.

Luqmān. A sage mentioned in the *Qur'ān*, which names chapter 31 after him. He was known in pre-Islamic Arabia, and later Islam saw him as a teacher of proverbs and fables. He has been identified with the Biblical Balaam, or called a nephew or cousin of Job, but the *Qur'ān* does not suggest either of these.

Luria, Isaac. Palestinian Jewish teacher (1534–72) who by uniting Kabbalah and law stimulated the development of practical Kabbalism. Luria was called the Lion, Ari, and his way of life came to be known as Lurian Kabbalah. Luria taught the contraction (*zimzum*) of the infinite En Sof (q.v.) to provide for the creation of the world, the struggle of good and evil, the transmigration and eventual salvation of souls, and ascetic practices to encourage spiritual progress. Lurian ideas and practices gained many followers at Safed in Palestine and elsewhere. See SIDDUR and SAFED.

Lycanthropy. Derived from a Greek term for becoming a 'wolf-man', this expresses a belief common in many parts of the world. Circe (q.v.) changed men into wolves and other animals, and Plato and Pliny refer to this possibility. It was said to have happened to Lycaon. Sorcerers were said to have this power and to eat human flesh while in wolf shape.

Lyceum. Gymnasium with covered walks in the eastern part of Athens, near a temple of Apollo Lukeios (perhaps 'wolf-slaying', or Lycian). It came to be called Peripatos, after the covered walks, and here the school of Aristotle (q.v.) met.

Lynceus. See ARGONAUTS.

M

M. The five M's (*makāras* in Tantra) (q.v.) Hinduism are 'five forbidden things', which are nevertheless regarded as holy and form the substance of certain Tantric rites. These are: Madya, wine; Māmsa, meat; Matsya, fish; Mudrā, hand gestures; Maithuna, sexual union. There are parallels to these rites in some forms of Mahāyāna Buddhism.

Ma. Cappadocian war-goddess, identified with the Roman Bellona (q.v.).

Maaseh Bereshith. (Hebrew) 'work of creation', a name given to mystical speculations in the *Talmud* on the first chapter of *Genesis*, and associated with Rabbi Akiba (q.v.). For Maaseh Merkabah, see MERKABAH.

Maat. Ancient Egyptian abstract goddess, personifying truth, justice and order. She was said to be daughter of Rē' and wife of Thoth, the god of wisdom. As an abstract goddess, Maat had no temples or cultus, but she was always considered as a deity and represented as a woman with the feather of truth standing upright on her head.

Mabinogion. 'Instruction for young bards', Welsh saga of kings, queens and heroes, some of whom represent earlier deities. The work consists of four prose narratives. The *Mabinogi of Pwyll* tells of a king of that name, also lord of the underworld, married to Rhiannon, 'great queen', associated with fertility. The *Mabinogi of Branwen* tells also of her brother Bran (q.v.), and their father Llyr (q.v.) or Lear, god of the sea. The *Mabinogi of Manawyddan* (q.v.) continues the story of Branwen and tells of wizards and magic. The *Mabinogi of Math* tells of the magic of Math Hen who was also a beneficent deity.

Maccabees. Jewish warriors of the second century B.C., named after their leader Judas Maccabeus (taken to mean the 'Hammerer') whose victories are celebrated in the Festival of Hanukkah (q.v.) for the Dedication of the temple to this day.

Madhva. South Indian philosopher (1197–1276). He opposed the monistic Advaita (q.v.) of Shankara and taught a frank dualism (*dvaita*, q.v.), between God on the one hand, and the world and souls on the other. The two latter were subordinate to God, who was identified with Vishnu. Madhva explained away monistic passages in the *Upanishads* as figurative, and maintained that Vishnu has full power to save or damn souls. But since God could not be approached directly, Vāyu, the wind, was the mediator for men. Some influences upon Madhva from Christians of Malabar have been suggested and also strongly repudiated. Madhva wrote commentaries on the scriptures, notably the *Vedānta Sūtra* and the *Bhagavad-Gītā*. His followers, Mādhvas, are still numerous in Bombay and Mysore, and worship Vishnu, but are regarded as more intellectual than the devotional sects.

Mādhymika. (Sanskrit) 'middlemost' or intermediate school of Mahāyāna Buddhism, midway between the realism of the Sarvāstivādins and the idealism of the Yogāchāras (q.v.). Said to have been founded in the second century A.D. by Nāgārjuna, his *Mādhyamika Kārikā* is the basic text of this school. Their ideas develop the doctrines of the early Buddhist Wisdom school. The universe was in a state of flux, which was ultimately unreal, and the only reality was the Void (q.v.) or Emptiness (Shūnyatā). But this did not lead to agnosticism, since the world had a qualified reality, and underlying all was Nirvāna.

Madrasa. A school, college or seminary for the teaching of Islamic sciences. Madrasas were closely connected with mosques from the beginning of Islam, since learning and expounding the *Qur'ān* were basic, and learning and piety have remained inseparable. Great mosques have also been schools, many of them with splendid libraries, forming the nucleus of a university like al-Azhar (q.v.) in Cairo. A teacher is a Mudarris, and often lives in or near the Madrasa, as do other holy men. In modern times education in western style has often been separated from Madrasas, though they retained the study of theology, law and Arabic language.

Madura. In the far south of India, this town is famous for its great temple, surrounded by nine Gopuram (q.v.) towers. Most of it was built by Tirumala Nayak (1623–60). It is a twin temple: to the north that of Shiva, under the name Sundareshvar, and to the south that of his consort Mīnākshī, the 'fish-eyed goddess' (q.v.). The most striking feature of the temple is the Hall of a Thousand Pillars, Sahasrasthambha Mandapam, which are nearly all different, with carvings in stone from many figures of Hindu mythology. There are statues and columns depicting Hindu saints, the five Pāndu (q.v.) brothers of the famous epic war, and many deities such as the sons of Shiva, Subrahmanya and Ganesha. Additional buildings contain the cars or Vāhanas of the presiding deities, plated in gold.

Maenads. (Greek) 'mad', women who went into ecstasy and were inspired by the god Dionysus (q.v.). They were also called Dionysiacs, Bacchae and Thyiades, 'frantic'. Their ecstatic frenzy was depicted in the plays of Aeschylus and Euripides, representing liberation from convention and union with nature.

Magga. See MĀRGA.

Maghavan, Maghavat. (Sanskrit) 'bountiful', distributing gifts, a title of Hindu gods, especially Indra. It is also used of those who pay the priests and singers at sacrifices.

Magi. Hereditary priestly class of ancient Persia, responsible for all religious ceremonies. The old Persian word *magu* was related to the Indian *magha* meaning a 'gift' or 'riches', and so the Magu was the man who received the gift or grace of God, in the religion of Zoroaster and older cults; this gift was bestowed because he belonged to the class of priests. The suggestion of Herodotus that the Magi were a special tribe is unlikely and in historical times they appear, like the Brahmins of India, to have been a class which had charge of all forms of religious ceremony. The Magu became the official exponent of Zoroastrian religion and was called by the Greeks *Magos* (plural *Magoi* and *Magi*). The Wise Men of the *New Testament* are Magoi (*Matthew* 2, 1), and in the *Qur'ān* (22, 17) the Majūs will be distinguished at the resurrection.

Magic. Word derived via Greek from the Persian Magi (q.v.), used of any enchanter and in a bad sense of quacks and jugglers. In modern usage Magic should be distinguished from Witchcraft (q.v.). Magical practices are to be found in all countries and at all levels of society, down to modern superstitions, lucky charms and astrology. Distinctions can be made between public and private magic, and helpful and hurtful magic (in intention). In most societies the good magician is a public and respected figure, giving out curative remedies, love potions, protective amulets, and the like. A practitioner of harmful or 'black magic' works in secret and is feared or hated. J. G. Frazer (q.v.) made useful distinctions of Sympathetic Magic, which works by kinship with the object used, and Contagious Magic which works by contact; both are forms of Homeopathic Magic, illustrating likeness. However, Frazer's theory that magic preceded religion is generally abandoned, since the two are mingled at many stages of culture.

Magog. See GOG.

Mahabalipuram, Mamallapuram. Ancient site on the eastern coast of India, below Madras, where the 'Seven Pagodas' are stone temples dating from about the seventh century A.D. There are fine free-standing stone sculptures of animals and a carved rock face representing the Penance of Arjuna (q.v.), with many other gods. The town is said to have been the capital of King Bali (q.v.).

Mahābhārata. 'Great (battle) of the Bhāratas', the longest of the two great Indian Epic poems, the other being the *Rāmāyana* (q.v.). It is in Sanskrit, one hundred thousand verses, the longest poem in the world. Traditionally composed by the sage Vyāsa, it was first recited at a great sacrifice, and its central importance was in recalling the heroes of the past at royal rituals. The kernel of the epic is the eighteen days' battle between the Kauravas, sons of Kuru, and their cousins the Pāndavas, sons of Pāndu. Before the battle begins, in the sixth book, comes the short but famous theological dialogue of Krishna and the warrior Arjuna the *Bhagavad-Gītā* (q.v.). The epic contains many other speeches, myths of gods, legends of heroes and sages, teachings of religion and duty (*dharma*, q.v.). Most prominent is the god Vishnu, and his Avatar (q.v.) Krishna, so that the epic is also called the 'Veda of Krishna' (*Kārshna Veda*).

Maha Bodhi. Modern Buddhist society

of 'great wisdom', founded in Calcutta in 1891 by the Ceylonese reformer Anāgarikā Dharmapāla (q.v., 1865–1933). The society now has branches in many lands and has built new temples on historic sites, notably at Sarnath, the place of the Buddha's first sermon.

Mahādeva. (Sanskrit) 'great god', a title of Shiva. He is also called Mahāyogī, the 'great ascetic'. His consort is Mahādevī, 'great goddess'; see DEVĪ.

Mahant. Ruler of an Indian monastery, Matha or Math (q.v.).

Mahāparinibbāna Sutra. 'The great scripture of the attainment of Nirvāna', by the Buddha, giving accounts of the Buddha's last days and death. It forms part of the first section of the second Basket of the Theravāda Buddhist canon (see TRIPITAKA), and contains both valuable historical references to the Buddha and also a good deal of legend.

Quite different is the *Mahāparinirvāna Sūtra* of Mahāyāna Buddhism, also called the 'Paradise Sūtra', which teaches the doctrine of the Buddha-nature innate in all beings.

Mahārishi. See RISHI.

Mahāsabha. 'Great society', the Hindu Mahāsabha is a semi-religious, semi-nationalistic organization, founded in 1920. Its ideology was expounded by V. D. Savarkar who claimed that the Hindus were both a community and a nation, and efforts have been made to exclude all that is not Hindu. In 1925 the Rashtriya Swayamsevak Sangh ('national self-rule community', RSS) was founded to build up the Hindu nation, by K. B. Hedgewar. Even non-Hindus in Hindustan must 'reverence Hindu religion and culture'. In 1951 S. P. Mookerjee founded the Bharatiya Jana Sangh, a more political society ('Indian birth community') which stands for Indian culture rather than just Hindu.

Mahāsanghika. (Sanskrit) 'belonging to the great Order', or assembly. A name given to one of the earliest groupings within Buddhism, in the fourth or third centuries B.C., which provided the starting point some time later for the much larger division of Mahāyāna (q.v.). The Mahāsanghika may have been the majority of monks, or those who represented the majority of laymen. The *Mahāvastu* (q.v.) is said to be the sole surviving part of their canon of scripture.

Mahat. (Sanskrit) the 'great', a name given in Sāmkhya (q.v.) philosophy to Buddhi (q.v.), mind or intellect.

Mahātmā. (Sanskrit) 'high-souled', magnanimous, having a noble or divine nature. This title is applied to the Supreme Spirit, to Krishna in the *Bhagavad Gītā*, to great sages and teachers. In modern times it is applied to outstanding leaders, like Mahātmā Gāndhi (q.v.). Theosophists claim that occult wisdom was revealed to Madame Blavatsky (q.v.) by Mahātmās who lived in Tibet.

Mahāvagga. 'Great section,' a name given in Theravāda Buddhist scriptures to divisions in several major works. It is the second of the three main parts of the *Dīgha Nikāya*, the third of the *Sutta Nipāta*, the first of the *Khandakas*.

Mahāvairochana. See VAIROCHANA.

Mahāvamsa. The 'Great Chronicle' of Ceylon, a document in Pali of the fifth century A.D., and based on the *Dīpavamsa* (q.v.) and Singhalese commentaries. It contains stories of the Buddha, his legendary visits to Ceylon, and a list of kings and councils.

Mahāvīra. (Sanskrit) 'Great Hero' of the Jains. His dates are uncertain, but are sometimes reckoned as 540–468 B.C. He was named Vardhamāna, son of Siddhārtha and Trishalā, of the warrior-ruler (Kshatriya) caste, like Gautama the Buddha but a little before him in time. Mahāvīra was a prince and, according to the major Jain school, was married and had a daughter. His parents followed the previous Jina, Pārshva (q.v.), and starved to death. Mahāvīra then became an ascetic and after thirteen years found enlightenment, becoming a Jina, 'conqueror', and the twenty-fourth Tīrthankara, 'ford-maker'. He taught for thirty years, gathered many followers and was patronized by kings. Many temples are dedicated to him, his statue is in all Jain temples, and meditations and devotions are addressed to him.

Mahāyāna. (Sanskrit) 'Great vehicle', or career, of universal salvation, the major part of Buddhism, contrasted with Hīnayāna (q.v.). Mahāyāna arose around the beginning of the Christian era, and one of its major scriptures is the *Lotus Sūtra* (q.v.), which teaches of 'one vehicle' of salvation for all, of grace and faith, and of the Bodhisattvas, beings of enlightenment, and notably Avalokiteshvara (q.v.). Mahāyāna does not reject the canon of scripture of Hīnayāna, but adds to it other works, such as the *Lotus Sūtra* and the *Lalita-vistara*, along with many legendary and philosophical works. The Mahāyāna countries (Tibet, China, Korea Japan and Vietnam) form Northern Buddhism.

PHOENIX HALL OF THE BYODO-IN TEMPLE, NARA, JAPAN.

A BUDDHIST NOVICE HAS HIS HEAD SHAVED.

MASK OF A BODHISATTVA,
JAPANESE, 1086–1185 A.D.,
USED IN 'GYŌDŌ' OR BUDDHIST PROCESSIONS.

MIROKU BOSATSU (BODHISATTVA),
7TH CENTURY A.D.,
KORYUJI TEMPLE, NARA, JAPAN.

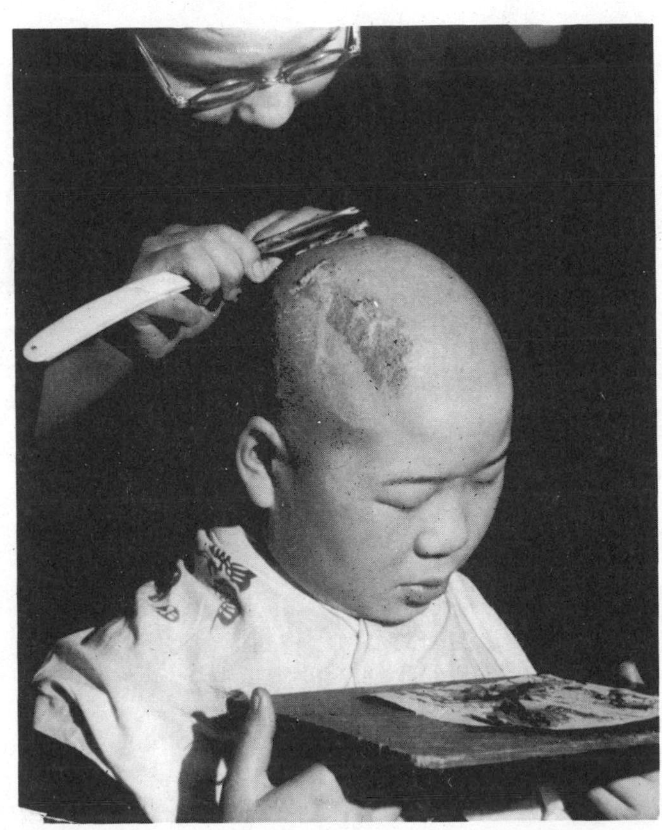

Mahdī. (Arabic) 'the guided one', the expected restorer of religion, who provides an eschatological hope for Islam. The word Mahdī does not occur in the *Qur'ān*, but fairly early there arose the hope of a restorer of the faith who would be al-Mahdī, a descendant of Muhammad, or 'Īsā (Jesus), and there has remained confusion between the coming Mahdī and the second advent of the Messiah, among orthodox Sunni Muslims. Among Shī'a Muslims the Mahdī was identified with their Hidden Imām (see IMĀM), though Jesus also might be a restorer. In the course of Islamic history various leaders have been hailed as Mahdī, one of the best known recent ones being Muhammad ibn Abdullah of the Sudan, who rebelled against Egyptian rule, set up a kingdom in Khartoum after the death of Gordon, and died of typhus in 1885. See SEVEN SLEEPERS.

Mahinda. Buddhist monk, son or near relative of the emperor Ashoka (q.v.), who traditionally took Buddhism to Ceylon. He and his followers landed on a mountain and the bare rock under which they slept is still shown at Mihintale. He preached to King Devanampiya Tissa and the monarch became the protector of the new religion, giving lands to the monastic order, and building some of the famous Buddhist monuments of Anurādhapura (q.v.). Mahinda's sister was Sanghamittā (q.v.) who brought a shoot of the Bo-Tree to Ceylon.

Mahisha. In Hindu mythology, a demon in the form of a buffalo who was killed by the fierce goddess Durgā (q.v.).

Mahmal. Arabic name for a splendid but empty litter sent at the head of the pilgrimage procession to Mecca, from various countries (especially Syria and Egypt) from about the thirteenth century. The Mahmal was borne on a camel, but had no occupant, except a *Qur'ān* or prayer book in a receptacle. In modern times the sending of a Mahmal has been interrupted by disagreements and the Wahhābī (q.v.) rulers of Arabia have demanded that there should be no accompanying music or armed guards. It did not contain the Kiswa (q.v.).

Mahomet. See MUHAMMAD.

Maia. In Greek mythology Maia was one of the Pleiades, a daughter of Atlas and mother, by Zeus, of Hermes. Her name meant 'mother' or 'nurse'.

There was a Roman goddess Maia, whose name may mean 'grow', whence she would be a fertility goddess. Rather strangely, she was associated with the fire god Vulcan (q.v.).

Maimonides. Moses ben Maimon (1134–1204), the greatest Jewish philosopher, was born in Cordova, Spain, but, owing to persecutions from the Muslim Almohads (q.v.), his family went to Fez, Morocco, and finally settled in Cairo. Hence he came to be called Moses Egyptius and he wrote his great works in Arabic. He became a physician at the court of Saladin and is said to have been invited to serve Richard Coeur de Lion. Maimonides wrote a commentary on the *Mishnah* (q.v.), a code of Jewish law, and treatises on medicine and astronomy. In his commentary he set out his creed, in thirteen articles, which are still printed in Jewish prayer books as the Thirteen Principles of the Faith (or Thirteen Creeds q.v.). Maimonides studied Arabic philosophy, which preserved Greek classics, and had a great veneration for Aristotle. In his chief work, the *Guide for the Perplexed*, he sought to reconcile rabbinic Judaism with Aristotelian philosophy. See also YIGDAL.

Maisir. Arabic name for divination by casting lots with arrows. This was a popular pre-Islamic practice and was condemned in the *Qur'ān* (2, 216/9) as pagan. Arrows were drawn out of a bag, for dividing game or before undertaking a journey or business. Later the term is used to condemn play with dice or even chess, regarded as games of chance.

Maithuna. See M.

Maitreya. (Sanskrit) 'friendly', 'benevolent'. In Pali the name is Metteya, in Chinese Mi-lo-fo, and in Japanese Miroku. This is the Buddha-to-come and important in all forms of Buddhism. In Theravāda Buddhism Gotama is said to have announced that after a decline of religion and morality there would arise an Exalted One named Metteya, a Buddha 'even as I am now', who would have thousands of disciples as Gotama had hundreds, and would restore the truth. In Mahāyāna Buddhism the future Buddha is represented as fat and laughing, holding in one hand a bag of good fortune, and in the other a rosary, each bead of which represents a thousand years which he spent doing good in previous lives. The name Maitreya is related to Mitra and Mithra, and may perpetuate these powerful Hindu and Persian deities.

Majjhima Nikāya. (Pali) 'collection of Middle Length sayings', the second section of the second main division of the Theravāda Buddhist canon of scripture. See TRIPITAKA and SŪTRA.

Majjhima Patipadā. See MIDDLE WAY.

Mājāj. See GOG and MAGOG.

Makkhali. See GOSĀLA.

Makoto. (Japanese) 'sincerity', truth, the fundamental virtue in Shinto. Makoto is called the purest manifestation of the human spirit, the source of beauty, truth and goodness. It is said to come from an awareness of the divine and to serve the gods with Makoto brings conformity to their will. With this attitude in family life there come filial piety, love to neighbours and loyalty to rulers.

Mālik. The chief guardian angel of Hell, in Islamic mythology. He is mentioned in the *Qur'ān* (43, 77), where the sinners in Jahannam (q.v.) cry, 'O Mālik, let thy Lord finish with us', and he replies, 'You are to remain.' It has been suggested that Mālik is a form of Moloch, an Ammonite deity.

Mālik. Mālik ibn Anas (died 795) was the founder of one of the four orthodox schools of Islamic law (see FIQH). His followers, called Mālikis, are found in Egypt and north and west Africa. Most of his life was spent in Medina, where he had access to many teachings and traditions of the first Muslims. His chief work, *al-Muwatta*, is the earliest Muslim law book and gives a summary of law, ritual and practice according to the customs of Medina. This provided a standard whereby matters which were not settled by formal teachings could be decided. The standard of Mālik was that of custom, rather than the reasoning which developed later. Modernists in Egypt seek to justify their adaptations of law and custom by reference to all four law schools.

Mamacocha. 'Mother Sea'. Goddess of Incas and other peoples of ancient Peru, worshipped especially on the coast and presiding over fishing. See PACHAMAMA.

Mamaquilla. 'Mother Moon'. Goddess of Incas of Peru and wife of the sun god, Inti (q.v.). She had little worship but was connected with the calendar and festivals. Eclipses of the moon were said to be due to a puma or snake trying to eat Mamaquilla, and they had to be frightened away by noise and threats.

Mamlūk, Mameluke. (Arabic) 'slave'. In Islamic history the dynasty of Mamlūk slaves was a remarkable period and lasted from 1250–1517, clearing out the remnants of the Crusaders, and checking the advance of the Mongol hordes till finally overthrown by the Ottomans. Though chiefly soldiers, the Mamlūks did much to beautify Cairo and other parts of the Islamic world.

Mana. A Polynesian word, which was said in the last century to be a vague and impersonal force, found in people and things, rather like electricity. Hence it was assumed that this was the most elementary form of religious thought and the theory of Animatism was propounded (q.v.). According to recent research it appears that Mana is rather a grace or virtue which enables people to succeed in special undertakings, a spiritual power from gods or spirits, which is transmitted through priests or chiefs. Such a notion of a special energy, or truth, given through particular officials, is common in many parts of the world. See NUMEN and MAORI.

Manabusch. 'Big Rabbit', culture hero of the Algonquin and other North American peoples. He appeared on earth and introduced all handicrafts, fought monsters, reshaped the earth after a flood and restored it to its present state. The water monsters gave Big Rabbit a medicine hut and a medicine society derives from him. Admission into the medicine hut is by enactment of the struggles of Big Rabbit with upper and lower powers.

Manannan, Manawyddan. Manannan was an Irish sea god, equivalent to the Welsh Manawyddan, and son of Ler (see LLYR). Manannan was more prominent than his father, also a sea god, and tradition speaks of several Manannans. He rode on the waves, or in a chariot which crossed them and the waves were his horses. Manannan had magical powers, gave the gods immortality, had swine which came back to life after death, invulnerable armour and an invincible sword. He was connected with the Isle of Man, named after him, where his grave was said to be situated, and where his three legs are pictured revolving in the coat of arms.

Manas. (Sanskrit) 'mind', or intellect, the rational faculty in man concerned with the relationships of subject and object. In Sāmkhya philosophy this reason is inferior to but can be illuminated by Buddhi (q.v.), the contemplative intellect or higher mind, which itself is dependent upon the ultimate Spirit or Purusha (q.v.).

Mānasa, Manasā. 'Belonging to the Mind' (manas), spiritual (Sanskrit). Name given to gods, ancestors or ascetics in Hindu mythology. There is a lake Mānasa in the Himalayas which is a place of pilgrimage and believed to be the source of the river Ganges.

Manasā was a snake-goddess of the epic and *Purānas*, whose special powers caused her to be invoked for curing snake-bite. Today she is one of the most popular deities of Bengal, even more than Kālī herself, and legends connected with her worshippers are a source of inspiration especially to women.

Manāt. Ancient Arabian goddess of 'fate' and death. Her principal sanctuary was near Mecca, on the road to Medina, where she was represented by a black stone. This was destroyed after Muhammad's capture of Mecca in 630, but Manāt was worshipped in many other places in Arabia. For reference to her in the *Qur'ān*, see LĀT.

Manawyddan. See MANANNAN.

Mandala. (Sanskrit) a 'circle' or 'round', used of heavenly bodies, groups of people and divisions of books. There are ten Mandalas or books of the *Rig Veda*. A Mandala is also a symbolical diagram, usually surrounded by a circle, in which patterns are made in sand, metal, stone or paper. Spaces in the Mandala

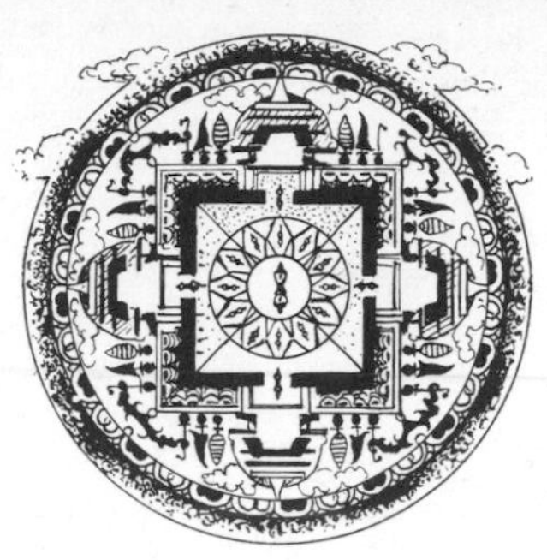

represent gods, or their symbols or abodes, and the whole is a pattern of psychic energy. Incantations are made while inscribing the Mandala and spiritual forces are believed to descend or appear. In Tantra special figures of Mandala are used called Yantra (q.v.). Mandalas are used for Hindu and Buddhist ritual and meditation, and the psychologist C. G. Jung has examined Mandala patterns as revelations of the unconscious mind.

Mandara. Great mountain in Hindu mythology which was used by the gods for churning the ocean to obtain the nectar of immortality. See AMRITA and KŪRMA AVATAR.

Mandate of Heaven. Under the Chou dynasty in the first millenium B.C., the government was justified by the concept of the Mandate (*ming*) which the rulers received from the supreme God, T'ien. A pictogram representing this shows a vassal receiving authority from an ancestral temple, and in similar fashion T'ien gave his authority to rulers, but could recall it if necessary. The concept was developed in literature (see SHIH CHING and SHU CHING) and in later literature, where man in general receives the Mandate of heaven above other creatures. The emperor received the divine Mandate in the Temple of Heaven (q.v.) in Peking.

Mandeans, Nazoreans. Members of a small but ancient religion, still to be found in Persia and south Iraq. The name Mandean comes from an Aramaic word for knowledge or gnosis, *manda*, and the language and symbolism of the religion resemble elements in Christian Gnosticism. Their own description of themselves is Nāsorāyē, a word which may mean 'observants' and refer to their special ritual of baptism. The Mandeans claim that they are descended from John the

Baptist, and that their ancestors fled to Persia when Jerusalem fell in A.D. 70. Their scriptures date from the eighth century, but contain much older traditions. They believe in God as the King of Light or Lord of Greatness and consider that the soul is imprisoned in matter. Baptism is essential, for washing body and soul, and a sacramental meal forms part of it. Mandean priests are now old and few replacements are appearing. See also NASĀRĀ.

Māndukya. The shortest of the classical *Upanishads*, consisting of only twelve verses, and the most thoroughly monistic (q.v.).

Manes. Spirits of the dead in ancient Roman religion, the name perhaps coming from a euphemistic adjective *manus*, 'good'. The word is used of the realm of the dead and for underworld gods, such as Prosperine (q.v.). Later the Di Manes were identified with family ancestors, Di Parentes, and also with individual dead people. Collectively graves were dedicated to Dis Manibus Sacrum, and individuals had their own name added to that formula.

Mani. The moon in Scandinavian mythology, son of Mundilfari and brother of the sun, Sol (q.v.). It is said that the gods were angry with Mundilfari for giving his children these names and placed them in the sky. Mani steered the moon, and arranged its waxing and waning, but there seems to be confusion between the moon and its charioteer. Mani drove round the sky by night, pursued by the wolves Skoll and Hati, which were probably eclipses.

Mānī, Manicheans. A religion founded by a Persian prince, Mānī (A.D. 216–274), who at the age of twenty began to convert members of the court to his faith. Finally he was opposed by the Magi (q.v.), Zoroastrian priests, and died in chains. Mānī claimed to fulfil the teaching of Zoroaster, Jesus and the Buddha, and identified the Saviour with the one who was revered by his followers, calling him Jesus when speaking to Christians. The distinctive belief of Mānī was Dualism (q.v.) in which he believed that the Father of Greatness is opposed by the Prince of Darkness, and the soul is imprisoned in matter. Release from evil would come by ascetic self-denial and by the Saviour of various names. This Dualism became widespread, and affected Christianity, through Augustine (who was once a Manichee) and the medieval Albigenses.

Mania. Little-known Roman goddess. Her name seems to mean 'good' (see MANES), and perhaps she was a deity of death. It was sometimes said that she was mother of the Lares (q.v.).

Mānikka Vāchakar or **Vāshagar.** A Tamil poet and mystic of Shaiva Siddhānta (q.v.). Born into a Brahmin family near Madura in the tenth century, Mānikka had a vision of the god Shiva as a Guru. He composed the *Tiruvāshagam* (q.v.), 'blest utterance', which inspired much other Tamil devotional poetry; it is sung and learnt by heart throughout Tamil country.

Manito, Mentu. American Algonquin name for spiritual or living powers. Manito applies to all kinds of spirits, the friendly and the unfriendly, and it is said that all Manitos pray because we hear the trees praying when the wind blows through them. All things are animate, including the creator God himself who sits in the twelfth heaven. See BIG HOUSE. See also WAKAN.

Manjushrī. (Sanskrit) 'beautiful lord', a great Bodhisattva of Mahāyāna Buddhism, Wen-shu in Chinese and Monju in Japanese. Not mentioned in early texts he becomes prominent in the *Lotus Sūtra* (q.v.), where he instructs other great beings, because he has eternal youth, has known many Buddhas and has

visited the depths of the sea to convert its inhabitants. Manjushrī is especially the model of knowledge and meditation, so his statues bear a sword of knowledge and a book. He is shown in yellow colour, sitting on a lion, with a blue lotus, and five curls on his forehead. Mythology gives Manjushrī a special concern with China and he is very popular there.

Man-Lion Avatar. See NARA-SIMHA.

Mantra. (Sanskrit) 'instrument of thought', sacred text or speech. In the *Vedas* the Mantras are the hymns as distinct from the priestly and wisdom portions of *Brāhmanas* and *Upanishads.* A sacred formula or mystical verse may be called a Mantra, like the favourite Gāyatrī (q.v.). In modern times, a Mantra may be a verse, a word, or an incantation used to assist in meditation or acquire supernormal powers. For Mūl Mantra, see JAPJI. See also NYĀSA.

Manu. (Sanskrit) 'thinking', man, mankind. In Hindu myth fourteen Manus were progenitors of mankind, each reigning for an 'age of Manu', Manvantara. The first Manu sprang from the Self-existent, Svayam-bhū. The seventh was saved from the Flood (q.v.) by a fish drawing his boat. The first Manu is also credited with the authorship of a famous law-book, the 'Code of Manu' or 'Institutes of Manu', *Manu-Sanhitā.* This is an ancient collection, after the *Vedas* but before the *Upanishads,* which contains myth, law and many other matters. It is said to have been originally longer than the surviving twelve books with 2685 verses. Manu is also said to have been son, or husband, of Shatarūpā (q.v.), the first woman.

Maori Religion. The mythology of the Maori was transmitted orally through chants, and resembles that of other Pacific peoples. The beginning was nothing, Te Kore, but eventually Sky and Earth emerged, Rangi and Papa (qq.v.), closely bound together with their children between their bodies. The children were gods (Atua), numbering from six to seventy in different versions. They finally separated the Sky and Earth, led by the most important god, Tane (q.v.), whose trees forced the sky upwards while other gods put in poles to keep it in place. Rain and mist show the sorrow and longing that Sky and Earth still have for each other. In Maori religion there was great respect for Tapu (see TABOO), a holiness that might be attached to any object, and offence against which could bring death. A man with Tapu had Mana (q.v.), power, which could bring success. The Maori loved carving in wood, and the meeting house was decorated with important events and beings in mythology. See also Io.

Māra. (Sanskrit) 'killing', related to death, and mortal. Although personified occasionally in Hinduism as goddess of death, Māra is rather a Buddhist figure. A Satanic tempter, he is the enemy of the Buddha and his religion, seeking to lead men astray by inflaming their passions. In Buddhist story Māra tempted the Buddha on various occasions, notably at his Enlightenment, trying to prevent him from teaching his doctrine to the world. But Māra, his army and his daughters were unsuccessful.

Marabout. A name, derived through Portuguese and French from the Arabic *Murābit,* for a saint or his descendants, especially among the Muslims of north and west Africa. In the Middle Ages a Murābit went to a *ribāt* (q.v.), a monastery where he was trained in religion and Holy War (see ALMORAVIDS). Later a Marabout was a holy man, or woman, noted for devotion or miraculous powers, and also a descendant of such a person. Marabout families have had considerable influence in settling disputes between warring groups and in protecting travellers.

Maraiin, Mareiin. Northern Australian word, meaning generally 'sacred'. Religious rituals are known by this name, mostly concerned with fertility under the direction of the Earth Mother. There are many myths connected with the Maraiin rituals.

Marcus Aurelius Antoninus. Stoic philosopher (121–180) and Roman emperor from A.D. 161. A youthful student, and Salian priest, he was adopted by the emperor Antoninus Pius and married his daughter Faustina. On becoming emperor he was engaged in warfare and died fighting German tribes. His *Meditations* express high Stoic principles and were composed as reflections during his campaigns. Several Christian writers addressed *Apologies* to Marcus, but his concern for the unity of the empire and the official state religion led to the continued persecution of Christians. See EPICTETUS.

Marduk. Tutelary god of Babylon. His temple, Esagila, 'the house that lifts up its head', was the largest of the city, with high walls and a temple-tower, Ziggurat (q.v.) or 'Tower of Babel', in the northern part of the great court. There were many side chapels of other gods. In

MARDUK

the 'Epic of Creation', *Enuma Elish* (q.v.), the primeval chaos, Tiamat (q.v.), attacks Anu and the heavenly gods. Marduk is made champion of the gods and accepts on condition that he becomes first of the gods. He takes invincible weapons and a net to catch Tiamat, and raises an army. Marduk and Tiamat meet in single combat, he slays her and places half of her body in the heavens to hold back their waters. Marduk then arranges the universe, gives the gods their places, arranges the calendar and the moon, and creates man to serve the gods. In the Assyrian version of this epic, Ashur (q.v.) takes the place of Marduk as the warrior-hero.

Marett, R. R. See ANIMATISM.

Mārga. A 'way' or path (Sanskrit; *Magga* in Pali). In Hinduism used to denote the Mārgas of Knowledge, Works or Devotion (Jñāna, Karma, Bhakti). In Buddhism it indicates the Noble Eightfold Path (q.v.). Buddhism itself is described as the Middle Way (q.v.).

Mariamman, Marai Mata. Goddess of cholera and smallpox in south India, and also regarded as bestower of many good gifts. Most of the village deities in this area have names ending in *amman* or *mata*, meaning 'mother'. The shrine of the goddess may be simply a tree under which a pot of water is placed, and prayers are made for prevention or removal of the disease. Such cults are very old and not orthodox Hinduism, but Brahmin priests regard them as manifestations of the power of Shakti, consort of Shiva, and try to remove some of the grosser elements of blood sacrifice from rituals.

Marīchi. See MARUTS and KASHYAPA.

Māriyammai. See SHĪTALĀ.

Mārkandeya. A Hindu sage, noted for his austerities and long life. He is the supposed author and part-narrator of the *Mārkandeya Purāna*, a collection of delightful narratives, such as 'the birds that knew right from wrong', and 'King Harish-chandra' (q.v.).

Markata Nyāya, Mārjāra Nyāya. See PRAPATTI.

Maror. A bitter herb used in the Jewish Seder ceremony (q.v.) to remind them that the lives of the Israelites were bitter during their captivity in Egypt.

Marpa. Tibetan Buddhist monk of the eleventh century. He sought out and translated Indian texts, and visited Nepal to be initiated into a yogic technique (Hevajra) which bestowed the ability to become a Buddha in one life. Marpa founded the Tibetan Ka-gyü-pa order of monks, and his disciple Milarepa (q.v.) was even more famous, by expressing Buddhist doctrines in Tibetan verse.

Mars. Italian god of war, and probably also of agriculture. He was chief of the pantheon (after Jupiter), had festivals in March and October, and the month of March (Martius) was named after him. In March the Salii priests (q.v.) performed a war dance in armour; in October a horse race was held in Mars' Field, the Campus Martius, soldiers were purified and the Salii danced again. The priest of Mars was the Flamen Martialis (see FLAMEN), and the wolf and woodpecker (*picus*) were sacred to him. The mythology of Mars was mostly adopted from the Greek Ares (q.v.).

Marsyas. A Phrygian god and guardian deity in local myths, associated with rivers, one of his name being a tributary of the Meander. Marsyas is said to have invented music for the flute. In Greek myth he picked up a flute which Athena had thrown away, and was then defeated in a musical contest by Apollo, who flayed him alive (perhaps a memory of ancient human sacrifice). The river was said to come from the blood of Marsyas or the tears of those who mourned him.

Mārūt. See Hārūt.

Maruts. Storm gods of the *Vedas*, friends and helpers of Indra (q.v.), and his sons or brothers. They are also called sons of Rudra, of heaven, ocean or earth. Their chief is Marīchi. The Maruts ride on the wind and guide the storm, armed with thunderbolts and lightning. In one place it is said that there are twenty-seven Maruts, and in another that they are a hundred and eighty.

Marwa. A low hill at Mecca facing another called Safā. Here Pilgrims perform the Sa'y, a ritual of going backwards and forwards seven times between these two mounds. Story connects this with Hagar (Hājar) running backwards and forwards to look for water for Ishmael. In pre-Islamic times there were stone images on each mound which pagan Arabs used to touch in their pilgrimage.

Maryam. Arabic form of the name of Mary, mother of Jesus, used in the *Qur'ān* as in the Syriac *Bible*. Maryam is the only woman mentioned by name in the *Qur'ān*, is always referred to with respect, and is called a child of 'Imrān (q.v.). See also 'Īsā.

Masada. A rocky fortress in the Judean desert where the last Jewish resistance to the Romans took place in A.D. 135. See Cochba.

Mashyē and Mashyānē. The first human couple, in Zoroastrian mythology, born of the seed of the dying Gayōmart (q.v.). They were joined together like a rhubarb plant, but separated, and then fell into sin by declaring that the evil Ahriman, and not the good god Ahura Mazdā, created the earth, water and plants. So they were condemned to hell till the last days when they will be raised by Saoshyans (q.v.), the posthumous son of Zoroaster.

Masīh. See Messiah; for **Masīhī,** see Nasārā.

Masjid. See Mosque.

Mask. Face coverings or hollow figures of the head were worn by Greek and Roman actors, and grotesque representations of faces have been worn in festivals in many countries, with humorous or terrifying effect. Gods and spiritual beings have been depicted, and in Tibetan Buddhism demonic figures fought with good beings and were eventually worsted. Masks are some of the commonest and most striking products of African art, and usually represent the dead. The masquerader or masked person normally has his whole body covered with cloth and a huge or fearful wooden or material mask over his face, and since he represents a spirit it is forbidden to speak of him as a man.

See also Image and Fetish.

ROMAN

TIBETAN

AFRICAN

Masora, Massorah. The work of the Masoretes, a name usually derived from a Hebrew root 'to hand down', and hence 'tradition.' The Masoretes, from about 500 to 1100, were Babylonian and Palestinian scholars who put the missing vowels into the text of the Hebrew *Bible*, along with accents, signs of pronunciation and divisions of sentences and paragraphs. So they tried to supply a standard text, with agreed pronunciation, based on the oral tradition of the past. They also noted all the variants of the text, counted the verses and letters, and wrote notes in the margins of their *Bibles* and also in separate books (*Small* and *Great Masora*). There were rival schools of *Masora*, and eventually that of Ben Asher of Tiberias in the ninth century prevailed and provided the standard Masoretic text.

Mastaba. Egyptian name for a tomb of a king or great person, called the Abode of Peace. A Mastaba had numerous chambers, as many as thirty, and after the Old Kingdom gave way to the more elaborate Pyramids (q.v.). Mastaba is an Arabic word for benches at doorways, and it was applied by Egyptian Arabs to the ancient tombs.

Mater. See MATUTA.

Math. Celtic deity, a master magician and lord of Gwyned, whose battles are told in the *Mabinogi* (q.v.) *of Math*.

Matha, Math. A Hindu monastery for ascetics or monks, or a college of orthodox teaching. Math is pronounced and sometimes written as Mutt. India is the home of many individual ascetics and small groups following a leader, but organized monasticism on the scale of the Buddhist Sangha (q.v.) seems to have arisen fairly late. It is perhaps significant that the philosopher Shankara of the ninth century, who combated Buddhism, founded a famous monastery at Shringeri in Mysore and others in northern India. A Math is ruled by a Mahant, who is a spiritual leader rather than a temple-priest, and even more a social and economic figure.

Mathnāwī. An epic poem, greatest work of the most celebrated Sūfī mystic of Persia, Jalālu'l-dīn Rūmī (q.v.). It is in 25,700 verses, each of twenty-two syllables, and is full of mystical teaching. There is a complete English translation, and also good selections.

Matrilineal. Descent counted through the 'mother's line', of importance in considering marriage affinity and prohibitions. See EXOGAMY.

Matronalia. See JUNO.

Matsuri. (Japanese) 'festival' or worship. Matsuri are solemn celebrations which take place at stated intervals in Shinto temples, as distinct from daily worship or Nikku. They are generally accompanied by rejoicings, rather like carnivals, but the deeper meaning of Matsuri is worship and obedience to the will of the gods. The aim of Matsuri is to bring harmony with the gods and unity of human life. The rituals include purification, prayers, offerings, songs, dances, divination and sacred meals.

Matsya. 'Fish' (Sanskrit), the Fish Avatar (q.v.) of Vishnu. In early versions this supernatural fish is tended by Manu and saves him from the Flood (q.v.); there is as yet no connection with Vishnu, but later the myth is incorporated into the ten or more Avatars, to retain the old story and strengthen the cult of Vishnu. A *Matsya Purāna*, in over fourteen thousand verses, is said to have been related to Manu by Vishnu in the form of a fish, but it is largely concerned with the worship of Shiva.

Matuta, Mater. Roman goddess of growth, and some say of dawn. At her festival, the Matralia on 11 June, women prayed for children. She had no mythology and was important for the cult which was conducted by women.

Matzah. Unleavened bread that is eaten during the Jewish feast of Passover, to commemorate the Exodus from Egypt when the Israelites baked in a hurry and could not wait to let the dough rise. All leavened bread must be removed from the house before the festival begins and Matzah is eaten during the seven or eight days that it lasts. At the Seder (q.v.) ceremony, three Matzot (the plural form) are put on a plate and used as a memorial of the Exodus. Half of one of them is put aside, hunted out by children and eaten at the end of the meal. It is called Aphikomen, a Greek word of uncertain meaning, taken to indicate a dessert.

Mawlawī. Title given especially to the Sūfī mystical teacher Rūmī (q.v.), (from *mawlānā*, 'our master), said to be the founder of the order of Dervishes (q.v.). See also MULLAH.

Mawlid. (Arabic) 'time', place, celebration of a birthday, especially that of the Prophet Muhammad. This was not observed in early days, but grew up during the Fātimid times from the tenth century and was encouraged by Sūfī mystical orders. The Prophet's birthday was said to be the twelfth day of the fourth month. Observance of the birthday spread across Islam, as a festival with processions, entertainments and recital of poems in praise of Muhammad. Birthdays of other saints have similar features. There has always been some opposition to the Mawlid, as an innovation, and it has been forbidden by the puritanical Wahhābī (q.v.) in modern Arabia, though it is celebrated in most of the rest of the Islamic world.

Mawu. A supreme being in Dahomey and Togo of West Africa, the meaning of whose name is uncertain. Mawu is the principal god, creator of other gods and men, who sends the soul into man. When linked with another deity, Lisa, the compound Mawu-Lisa is taken as moon and sun, with Mawu as female and more kindly than the fierce Lisa. There are some temples of Mawu, and a few images which, being contrary to the general African reluctance to portray the Supreme Being, may suggest that he was once one of the other gods. In a Capuchin catechism of 1658, Mawu is taken as the name of the supreme God. See LISA.

Māyā. (Sanskrit) art, 'power', unreality. The word *Māyā* has entered English dictionaries as 'illusion' and this is unfortunate, for even Hindu monists like Shankara (q.v.) only use the word as illusion in relationship to the absolute and eternal Reality. Māyā is often identified with Nature, which is the transient physical world contrasted with the unchanging Brahman. In the *Vedas* Māyā is used of power, and so of magic and even deceit, but in the *Bhagavad-Gītā* Māyā is the creative energy by which the deity comes into this world of Nature. For later philosophers like Rāmānuja, Māyā is the divine will and wisdom.

Māyā is also a name of the queen who was mother of the Buddha, perhaps in the sense of the magic power of beauty. See SUDDHODANA.

Mayas. Peoples of Yucatan, Guatemala, Honduras and southern Mexico. Only three manuscripts of their ancient religion before the Spanish conquest survive and are found in Dresden, Paris and Madrid. They have pictures of Maya gods, liturgies and calendars (q.v.). The Mayas were advanced in art and architecture, and built temples, palaces and great pyramids. Two of the principal deities were the sky-god Itzamna and the rain-god Chac (qq.v.). The Maya gods were linked with nature symbols, of which the most important was the double-headed snake, with a living head at one end and a death's head at the other end (symbolizing life and death) and its body representing the sky. Jaguar and bat gods, and many kings and priests, also figure on stelae and friezes. The Mayas believed in a succession of ages of the world, each ended by a flood, and in many heavens and hells. See IZAMAL and POPOL VUH.

BAT GOD

JAGUAR GOD

MAYA CALENDAR

MBARI

Mayauel. Mexican goddess of strong drink. According to story she saw a mouse nibbling the sap of a cactus and collected it to give to her husband, Xochipilli (q.v.). Together they introduced the gods to the drink Pulque (q.v.), the name by which it is now known. In pictures Mayauel appears naked, holding up a bowl marked with the sign 'drink it', and seated on a throne of a tortoise and a snake. On her right there is a jar of fermenting Pulque. Mayauel was also the goddess of childbirth and was venerated both by mothers and warriors.

Mayday, Maypole, May-Queen. See BELTANE.

Mazda. See AHURA MAZDĀ.

Mazdaism. See ZOROASTRIANISM.

Mazdak. Persian prophet of the fifth century A.D., one of whose principal teachings was that women and wealth should be held in common. The emperor Kavāt was infatuated with the teaching and personality of Mazdak and nearly ruined his empire. His successor in the dynasty, Khusraw I, at once put Mazdak to death by trickery and massacred his followers.

Mbari. 'Decorated' houses of the Ibo of Nigeria, specially built for the earth goddess, Ala (q.v.). They contain clay sculptures of many divine, human and animal figures, brightly painted, but the central figure is always Ala. After being built as an act of devotion, they are allowed to decay.

Mecca. The Arabian town of al-Makkah (also formerly called Bakkah) was a holy place before the time of Muhammad, but only with the mission of the Prophet, from A.D. 610, did it assume much importance outside Arabia. Mecca is situated in the middle west of Arabia, in a hot dry valley between hills, about 110 kilometres from the Red Sea. It was a trading station on the route from Yemen to Syria, and also a sanctuary which housed the Ka'ba shrine and the Zamzam well (qq.v.). The centre of the city is occupied by the 'sacred mosque' (Masjid al-Harām), with the Ka'ba in the centre, and there are religious colleges and governmental buildings. Most private houses are built to accommodate the thousands of visitors who come on the annual pilgrimage (see HAJJ). In addition to legendary attributions to Adam and Eve, Abraham and Ishmael, numerous places in the city are associated with Muhammad and his family, but other places dedicated to saints have been destroyed by the Wahhābī rulers of the city.

Medea. (Greek) 'cunning one', a sorceress in mythology, related to Circe (q.v.). She fell in love with Jason (q.v.) and helped him get the Golden Fleece by magic; she fled with him, but he later abandoned her.

Medina. (Arabic) *al-Madīnah* means 'the city', a title generally taken to have been applied to it as the City of the Prophet after his migration (Hijra, q.v.) thither in A.D. 622. However, the title may have been used earlier, though the original name of the place was Yathrib (q.v.). Medina is about 320 kilometres to the north of Mecca, more pleasantly situated and watered. Although it had no ancient shrine, it is hallowed by the mosque and tomb of the Prophet, and second only to Mecca in sanctity and as object of pilgrimage. The Mosque of the Prophet (Masjid al-Nabī) is said to have been founded by Muhammad, and the present splendid building is an improvement of several constructions. Behind the Mosque is the Hujrah, 'chamber', with the tombs of Muhammad, Abū Bakr and 'Umar, and a space reserved for the tomb of Jesus after his second coming. The fable that it is believed that Muhammad's coffin is suspended in mid air has no foundation in Muslim literature.

Medusa. A monster of Greek mythology whose gaze could turn people into stone. She lived in the far west with two immortal sisters, the Gorgo, but Perseus killed her with the help of Athena and

MEDUSA

took her head which turned his enemies to stone, including the dragon that was menacing Andromeda (q.v.). Medusa's head was said to be buried at Argos, and she was perhaps an earth-goddess of that place. See GORGON.

Mekilta. (Aramaic) 'measures', a Midrashic exposition on legal parts of the book of *Exodus* in nine tractates, from the school of Rabbi Ishmael in the second century A.D. Another *Mekilta* on *Exodus* was compiled a little later by Rabbi Simeon ben Yochai (q.v.).

Mela. (Sanskrit) 'meeting', union, and in later usage a religious fair, especially those held at the meeting of the Ganges and Jumna at Prayag. See KUMBHA MELA.

Melpomene. In Greek mythology one of the nine Muses (q.v.), that of tragedy.

Memra. (Aramaic) 'word', a term used in the Targum versions of the *Bible* to avoid speaking of God as acting in any way like a man. See SHEKHINAH and TARGUM.

Menander. See MILINDA.

Mencius. Latinized form of Meng Tzŭ, Chinese philosopher and interpreter of Confucius (q.v.). His Chinese name was Meng K'o, but he was entitled Master Meng or Meng Tzŭ. Little is known about his life or family and he is said to have lived from 372 to 289 B.C., or 390 to 305. After his death his disciples put together his teachings in the *Book of Mencius*. Like Confucius, Mencius was a teacher, who also hoped to put his ideas into practice in public office and was equally disappointed. Mencius believed that man is essentially good by nature, and that the ideal ruler would be a sage-king who had developed the nature which heaven had given him. Man should serve heaven and fulfil his destiny, and develop goodness in accordance with reason. Government should be established on benevolence, and against profit and force.

Mendelssohn, Moses. German Jewish scholar (1729–83) whose study of non-Jewish subjects had a great influence in the development of the Enlightenment movement (see HASKALAH and GHETTO). He encouraged the use of German as well as Yiddish, and paid more attention to the *Bible* than to the *Talmud*.

Mengloth. A goddess in Scandinavian mythology, apparently of healing, and perhaps a form of Frigg (q.v.). One of her maidens is the healer Eir (q.v.).

Menorah. (Hebrew) 'lamp', 'candlestick'. The golden seven-branched candlestick that stood in the Temple at Jerusalem, and stands in Jewish synagogues.

According to tradition the light of the Menorah was never extinguished till the Temple was destroyed, and a flaming Menorah has been a symbol of the unquenchable spirit of Judaism. A popular medieval work was *Menorah ha-Maor*, the 'Lamp of Life', by a Talmudic scholar of the fifteenth century, Isaac Abohab. This work consists of religious and ethical teachings illustrated by stories.

Mentu. See MANITO.

Mercury. Roman god of traders and merchandise (from *Merx* and *Mercari*). He seems not to have been an ancient Roman god and was probably introduced by Greek traders worshipping Hermes. Mercury is the Roman Hermes (q.v.), dressed like him with broad hat and herald's staff, acting as guide to the dead; nearly all his mythology is Greek.

Merkabah. (Hebrew) 'chariot', a theme of Jewish mysticism in which it was claimed that visionaries had risen above the worldly sphere to celestial regions where they learned the deepest mysteries. The father of Merkabah mysticism is said to have been Jochanan ben Zakkai of the first century A.D., but it became popular in the period of the Geonim (q.v.) when descriptions of the ascensions of mystics in their 'chariots' were given in the Hekaloth literature (q.v.). See also MAASEH BERESHITH.

Merit. See DĀNA, BODHISATTVA and DHARMAKĀRA.

Merlin, Myrddin. Bard and magician of Celtic romance. It has been suggested that he was a supreme deity of the Celts, but it is more likely that he was god of magicians or an ideal magician. There are many stories about him, but they reveal little of his origin or of worship addressed to him. See ARTHUR.

Meru. A mythical mountain in Indian cosmology, the centre or navel of the earth around which the planets revolved. Meru was compared with the cup of a lotus flower, and its four leaves were the four, or seven, continents separated from the peak by oceans, and named by the trees on their shores (see JAMBUDVĪPA). The river Ganges flowed on to Meru and thence to the continents. The gods, especially Indra and Brahmā, dwelt on its summit, as on Olympus. Meru is sometimes identified with the Himalayas or with mountains in central Asia.

Mescalin. Drug used by Indians of Mexico, derived from a root called Peyotl. Regarded as divine, it is taken to give supernormal experiences and visions, yet it is said not to be poisonous or cause addiction. Aldous Huxley, in *The Doors of Perception* (1954), claimed that he received from Mescalin experiences equal to the highest range of mystical experience, a view strongly disputed by R. C. Zaehner, in *Mysticism Sacred and Profane* (1957). See PULQUE.

Messiah. The Arabic term *al-Masīh* occurs in the *Qur'ān* and Islamic tradition as a title of Jesus (see 'ĪSĀ). It comes from Aramaic and is used without explanation or Messianic doctrine. Jesus both on earth and at his second coming is named the Messiah.

Metamorphosis. 'Change of form', from Greek. The belief in transformation or shape-shifting is found in many parts of the world. Sorcerers and witches (q.v.) are said to leave their bodies, often at night, and to change into the forms of animals or birds, returning again before dawn. In classical literature a favourite story is the *Metamorphoses* or *Golden Ass* of Apuleius, in which the curious Lucius was turned into an ass and was at last restored to human shape by the goddess Isis. See CUPID.

Metempsychosis. 'Change of soul', from Greek via Latin; see TRANSMIGRATION.

Metis. (Greek) 'counsel', wisdom. In mythology she was personified as consort of Zeus and she allowed him to swallow her so that she was always there to advise him. According to Hesiod, she was mother of Athena (q.v.) who sprang fully armed from the head of Zeus.

Mettā. (Pali) 'love', active goodwill for all beings; for Theravāda Buddhists the first of the four heavenly states or Brahma Vihāras. See VIHĀRA.

Metteya. See MAITREYA.

Mevlevi. Turkish pronunciation of Mawlawī (q.v.).

Mexican Religion. See AZTECS.

Meztli. The material Moon (see COYOLXAUHQUI) in Aztec mythology, represented as an old man with a shell on his back. He is sometimes called Tecciztecatl, 'he from the Sea Snail'.

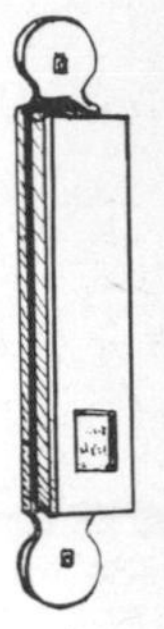

Mezuzah. (Hebrew) 'door post'. A small container with a piece of parchment, fastened on the right doorpost of the house and each room in Jewish homes. The parchment contains the words of the Shema, 'Hear, O Israel', and the instruction to 'write them upon the door posts of thy house', from *Deuteronomy* 6, 4–9. See PHYLACTERY.

Miao. (Chinese) 'temple', a generic term which may be applied to almost any kind of religious building, but is particularly used of temples of popular and Taoist gods. A Buddhist monastery is a Tzi or Ch'an Lin, though it may be called Miao if used for public worship. A nunnery is An or An-Tse. An ancestral hall is only rarely called Miao, and is known as Tsi or Tsi T'an.

Michael. (Hebrew) 'who is like God?' an angel in Jewish tradition. The name occurs only three times in *Daniel*, and once each in *Jude* and *Revelation*. Michael was the guardian angel of Israel and as such he appears in the *Talmud*. He was one of the four angels round the throne of God, standing on its right; the others were Gabriel, Raphael and Uriel. Michael and Gabriel were the most prominent, and Michael was even superior, for it was said that where he appeared the glory of the Shekhinah (q.v.) would be found. As Mīkāl his name occurs once in the *Qur'ān* (2, 98) and Islamic tradition tells of him protecting their armies.

Mi Chiao. (Chinese) 'secret teaching', a term applied to the Buddhist Tantric sect known as Chên-yen (q.v.).

Mictlan, Mictlampa. The deepest

MICTLAN

underworld in Aztec belief and the region of the dead. It was ruled by the 'lord', Mictlantecuhtli, who is depicted as a skeleton with red bones. Also associated with the stars, he was death and ruler of the dead. His consort was Mictlancihuatl who resembled him in many ways.

Middle Doctrine. See MĀDHYAMIKA.

Middle Length Sayings. See MAJJHIMA NIKĀYA.

Middle Way. The 'mean' between the extremes of sensuality and harsh asceticism (q.v.), taught by Gautama the Buddha. In his first sermon, 'setting in Motion the Wheel of Doctrine', in the Deer Park at Sarnath near Benares, the Buddha says that to avoid the two extremes he has gained knowledge of the Middle Way (*Majjhima Patipadā* in Pali), and this is identified with the Noble Eightfold Path (q.v.). See MARGA.

The Buddhist religion is sometimes called the Middle Way and since 1943 this has been the name of the journal of the English Buddhist Society.

Midgard. Our world in Scandinavian mythology, guarded by the god Thor. His greatest enemy was the Midgard snake, Midgardsorm or Jörmungand, which encircled the earth and was perhaps a personification of the sea. The Midgard serpent was said to be the offspring of Loki (q.v.), and the struggles of Thor against it as the symbol of evil are represented in art and figured in poetry.

Midrash. A method of rabbinical teaching of scripture, from a Hebrew root *dorash*, meaning 'teaching' or probing. Midrash Halakah (q.v.) referred to legal teaching, and Midrash Haggadah (q.v.) dealt with the non-legal sections of the *Bible*, that is, the moral and devotional. The Midrash method is said to have been first used by Ezra and to have continued throughout the period of the scribal teachers.

Mihrāb. The niche in the centre of the end wall of a mosque which marks the direction, Qibla (q.v.), of prayer towards the Ka'ba in Mecca. The word occurs in the *Qur'ān* of a sanctuary, but its origins are obscure. It may have derived from the usage of a Christian church for the niche where an image or a bishop's throne stood. The Mihrāb contains no image, of course, since there are none in Islam, but it may be decorated and bear the name of God or it may be quite plain.

Mīkāl. See MICHAEL.

Miki Nakayama. Japanese religious leader, born in 1798 in the village of Sammaiden in Yamato province. Her family were Jodo (q.v.) Buddhists and deeply devout. At the age of thirteen Miki was married into the Nakayama family and at nineteen was initiated into a high ritual service. She had several children and in 1838 was possessed by a deity named as Ten no Shogun, the Heavenly General. This is counted as the foundation of Tenrikyō (q.v.), the 'Religion of Heavenly Wisdom'. Miki gave away many of her possessions; after the death of her husband in 1863 she began to preach doctrines of salvation. There was persecution, but the Shinto revival of 1868 helped the new religion and a temple was founded. Miki died in 1887 and in 1908 Tenri-kyō was registered as a Shinto Sect.

Milarepa, Mila Raspa. Tibetan Buddhist monk of the eleventh century and the most famous Lama of the Kagyü-pa sect. He was a disciple of Marpa (q.v.) and is believed to have gained miraculous powers and the supreme enlightenment, or Buddhahood, in his earthly life. Milarepa had a magical trial with a priest of the old Bön religion (q.v.) and defeated him by sitting first on the holy mountain Kailāsa. His true greatness came from expressing Buddhist teaching in native Tibetan verses, which gave him great popularity.

Milinda. A Greek ruler of the Punjab named Menander, and known in Buddhism in an important Pāli work called the *Milinda-Pañha*, 'Questions of Milinda'. Composed around the beginning of the Christian era, the 'Questions' give the discussions of the king with a Buddhist monk named Nāgasena. The king is said to have become a Buddhist. Although not part of the canon of Theravāda scripture, the 'Questions' are so important that they are acknowledged as authoritative, and they form a valuable compendium of developing Buddhist teaching, considering the nature of the Buddha, the doctrine, Nirvāna, and religious and moral duties.

Millet. A name given in the Ottoman empire to religious groups which were recognized by the state. The Arabic word *milla* was used of a sect or creed, and Millet extended from this to a society. So Christians, Jews and others were Millets which paid taxes to the state on account of their position. The members of the Millet could be scattered over the empire, yet the differences between them and other Millets led to separate and isolated schools, which at best might have an uneasy peace and at worst broke out into communal quarrels and fights. The Millets were taxed more severely than the Muslims, but were exempt from fighting for the faith. The Millet system has been abolished or reduced in modern times.

Mīmāmsā. (Sanskrit) 'enquiry', one of the six schools of orthodox Hindu philosophy; sometimes called Pūrva (first) Mīmāmsā, in contrast to Vedānta (q.v.) which is Uttara, 'later' or 'higher'. Mīmāmsā is said to have been founded by Jaimini (q.v.), and his Sūtra is its earliest text. It investigates duty (*dharma*) as set forth in the *Vedas*, which are regarded as eternal and fully authoritative. A great deal was said about law, and less about salvation, but the latter was shown to consist in respect for the *Vedas* and fulfilment of their rules. Not much was said about God; some accepted while others denied or ignored him. One of the later scholars was Kumārila, by whose time the Mīmāmsā school was being absorbed into the more popular Vedānta.

Mimi. Spirit beings of northern Australian mythology, who are generally shy and harmless and do not interfere with human beings, though sometimes they may do so. They are distinguished from the malignant Namandi (q.v.), with whom they are in conflict. The Mimi are said to live in holes in the rocks, the ground or trees, as well as in termite mounds or in the sky. Paintings in the caves of Arnhem Land are said to have been done by the Mimi. In bark paintings they appear as thin beings, playing the Didjeridu, dancing, singing, sometimes cutting up the bodies of their enemies. It is said that clever doctors in the past could see the Mimi occasionally, but nobody does now.

Mimir. Wisest of men in Scandinavian mythology. He was sent as hostage in the war of the gods, Aesir and Vanir, but the Vanir were suspicious and cut off his head. It was preserved by Odin who sang charms over it and consulted it at need. Mimir had a well under the roots of the Yggdrasil tree (q.v.), where wisdom was stored; Odin came here for a drink, but had to give his eye as a pledge and this was hidden in the well. At the Doom of the gods (see RAGNARÖK) Odin again consulted Mimir's head. Mimir was therefore a forest or water spirit, and personification of wisdom.

Min. One of the oldest gods of Upper Egypt, the centre of whose cult was at Koptos where a thunderbolt was his sign. In mythology he is called son of Rē', or Osiris, or Shu. Min was god of fertility and sexual power, but also of storm, sky and moon. His great symbol was the thunderbolt, and in statues he carries this, or a whip; he has a headdress of two tall feathers, like Amūn. He was often identified with Amūn (q.v.), as Min-Amūn, and also with Horus, as Min-Horus of Koptos. The birth of Min was celebrated in an early festival and his cult developed widely.

Minā. A village in the hills east of Mecca where some of the most important rituals of Islamic pilgrimage take place (see HAJJ). Pilgrims on the road from 'Arafāt (q.v.) collect forty-nine pebbles and these are thrown at monuments in Minā. This is probably a pre-Islamic rite, but in Islam it is taken to commemorate the Stoning of the Devil by Ishmael when he was tempted to flee from being sacrificed by Abraham. Then animals are sacrificed, not only here but at the same time all over the Islamic world.

Mīnākshī. (Sanskrit) 'fish-eyed', a title of Devī (q.v.), the spouse of Shiva. In south India Mīnākshī is a goddess in her own right and, though myths try to absorb her into the cult of Shiva, there are many other stories in which she plays a separate role. It is said that she was a beautiful child, with long fish-shaped eyes, and smelt of fish, so perhaps she was a goddess of fishermen. Her temples are often next to, but separate from, those of Shiva, as at Madura (q.v.). See SUNDARESHVARA.

Minaret. Arabic *manārah* is the tower or turret of a mosque, the name perhaps being derived from that of a watch-tower. or a fire tower. The earliest mosques of Islam had no Minaret, but this graceful feature was introduced in the first century and served as a high place from which the call to prayer (*adhān*, q.v.) was made. Hence a Minaret is sometimes called Ma'dhana, the place of the Adhān call to prayer. Many mosques have several minarets and like church spires they form the distinctive skyline of Islamic towns and villages. Many small mosques, however, have no minaret and the call to prayer is made from the door of the mosque. In modern times the Muezzin (q.v.) often no longer climbs up the Minaret for all the calls to prayer, but recordings are used.

Minbar. A pulpit in a mosque, often pronounced Mimbar. It is said to have been introduced in the time of Muhammad himself, as an elevated place of three steps on which the Prophet stood to speak. Minbars may be of brick or wood, and many of them are high and elaborate, with covers, or small towers or minarets.

Minerva, Menerva. Italian goddess, often identified with Athena. When she appeared in Rome, it was in an Etruscan group with Jupiter and Juno (q.v.), the Capitoline Triad. Minerva was very popular as goddess of handicrafts, her temples were frequented by guilds of craftsmen, and her festival in March usurped the powerful cult of Mars. See DI NOVENSILES.

Ming. See MANDATE.

Minhag. (Hebrew) 'custom', Jewish local customs and usages which have been taken as formative of law, in matters of marriage, ritual or civil law. The importance of local custom among the Ashkenazim (q.v.) led to the compiling of *Minhagim*, works which detailed the customs of the east European communities and gave them authority. The differences of Ashkenazim and Sephardim (q.v.) were largely Minhagic.

Minos. Legendary king of Crete, whose Minoan civilization is reflected in some of his stories. He was said to be son of Zeus and Europa (q.v.), and his wife Pasiphae disguised herself as a cow to mate with a bull that was sent to Minos by the god of the sea, Poseidon. She bore the Mino-taur, Minos-bull, half man and half bull. This was hidden in the Labyrinth made by Daedalus (q.v.) and received a yearly tribute of young men and girls from Athens, until it was killed by Theseus.

Minyan. (Hebrew) 'count', the number of adult males, fixed at ten, which must be present for an act of Jewish public worship to take place.

Mīrā Bai. A Rājput princess of Chitor who became a poetess and mystic. Her dates are uncertain, but may have been A.D. 1547–1614. She was married young and widowed in 1565. Mīrā Bai had already become devoted to Krishna (q.v.) and was scorned because she followed a low caste saint, Raidās (q.v.). She went to live at the temples of Krishna at Brindāban and then at Dwarka where, according to legend, an image of Krishna came to life and disappeared with her into the earth. Mīrā Bai is noted for her simple devotional lyrics, which are scornful of ascetics and full of passionate feeling, mostly addressed to Krishna.

Mirāj. (Arabic) 'ladder', 'ascent', the visit of Muhammad to heaven. The only hint of it in the *Qur'ān* comes in the sura called Isrā, the 'night journey,' which says, 'glory to him who travelled by night with his servant from the Sacred Mosque to the Farthest Mosque' (17, 1). This is taken to mean a visit or vision of the Prophet from the Ka'ba in Mecca to the Temple in Jerusalem. Legend soon added details: Gabriel brought Muhammad a white mule, Burāq (q.v.), which flew through the air to Jerusalem, and then mounted to heaven. There Muhammad ascended through the seven heavens, seeing prophets at each stage, and in the highest received instructions from God on the number of times of daily prayer. Sūfī mystics took the story as a model of the rise of the soul to the divine throne. Guides in Jerusalem still point to marks in the rock floor of the Dome of the Rock as the footprints of Muhammad at his Mirāj. See AQSA and DOME OF THE ROCK.

Miroku. Japanese form of Maitreya (q.v.).

Mīrzā Ghulām Ahmad. Punjabi Muslim, who in 1880 claimed to be the expected Mahdī (q.v.), and later to be both the Messiah and an Avatar of Vishnu. He lived in Qadian and died in 1908; the Ahmadiyya movement (q.v.) was named after him. The centre of the Qadiani movement has now been moved to Rabwa in Pakistan.

Mishnah. From a Hebrew word meaning 'to repeat', the collection of Laws in systematic form made particularly by Rabbi Akiba and Rabbi Judah (qq.v.). Rabbi Judah's *Mishnah* preserved the opinions of previous important teachers, and gave an authoritative norm. The *Mishnah* is in six orders, including Ethics of the Fathers, Pirke Aboth. The subjects are: agricultural laws, Sabbath and festivals, family law, civil and criminal law, Temple laws and sacrifices, laws of cleanliness and impurity.

Mistletoe. The plant and the tree on which it grew were sacred to the Druids (q.v.), since it was white and rare. It was cut on the sixth day of the moon, by a white-robed Druid using a golden sickle. Animals were sacrificed, a feast was held, and prayers were made for divine blessing on this 'all-healing' plant. It was used for medical and magical purposes. In Scandinavian mythology it was a shoot of mistletoe which killed the god Balder (q.v.).

Mitama-Shiro. See HONDEN.

Mitegura. See GOHEÏ.

Mithra. A powerful god of ancient Persia, whose name meant 'contract' and 'friendship', and was related to the Indian Mitra (q.v.). Before Zoroaster's reform

Mithra.

Mithra shared power with the highest deity, Ahura, and is frequently spoken of as Ahura-Mithra. Zoroaster concentrated on Ahura Mazdā (q.v.), but Mithra survived as god of contracts, war-lord, and nowadays as judge of the dead. Sacrifice is still performed in the 'portico of Mithra' (Dar-i-Meher) where the sacred fire forever burns. The cult of Mithra spread to the west as Mithraism and perhaps to the east in Maitreya (q.v.), of the Buddhists. (q.v.) See FIRE TEMPLES.

Mithraism. A male cult, carried especially by soldiers, connected with the god Mithra (q.v.), but most popular in its spread to India, Mesopotamia, Asia Minor and Europe. The cult of Mithras is said to have reached Rome in 67 B.C. and it was made an imperial cult by the emperor Commodus (A.D. 180–192). Mithraic monuments were numerous on the frontiers of the empire because of the popularity of the cult among soldiers, but it declined with the growth of Christianity from the fourth century. The central act of worship was the sacrifice of a bull (Taurobolium) whose blood fell on the initiate. There was also a common meal of bread and wine with a priest representing Mithra. Under the church of San Clemente in Rome is a Mithraic altar with a scene of Mithra slaying the bull. In Queen Victoria Street, London, is the reconstructed foundation of a Mithraic temple. See also HYSTASPES.

Mitnagdim, Mithnaggedim. The opponents of Jewish Hasidism (q.v.), who saw in its intense piety and veneration of leaders a threat to the authority of the Torah and organized Jewish life. The separation of Mitnagdim and Hasidists was sharp for a time and inter-marriage between the groups was forbidden.

Mitra. A god of the Indian *Vedas*, whose name means 'friend'; he is related to the Persian Mithra. Mitra was a solar deity and a son of Aditi (q.v.). In the *Vedas* Mitra is associated with Varuna, Mitra ruling the day and Varuna the night. Together these gods uphold the earth and sky, guard mankind and punish sin.

Mitzvah. See BAR MITZVAH.

Mixcoatl. 'Cloud serpent', the god of the Pole Star in old Mexico and national god of the Chichimecs. Some of the stars were known as 'cloud serpents', Mimixcoa, as well, since all were manifestations of Mixcoatl and they served as food for the sun. Victims of sacrifice among the Aztecs were dressed as stars, since they would turn into stars; their bodies were painted white or red, with white clothes and a black half-mask which belonged to Mixcoatl. At a warrior's funeral a bundle was erected in the robes of Mixcoatl and sacrifices offered to it.

Miya. Another name for a Shinto 'temple', see JINJA.

Mjöllnir. The hammer of Thor (q.v.) in Scandinavian mythology, said to have been made for him by dwarfs. Although the meaning of the name is unknown, Mjöllnir was clearly a thunderbolt, like the Vajra (q.v.) of the Indian thunder god Indra.

Mnevis. A sacred bull worshipped in Egypt as a manifestation of the god Rē' (q.v.). Like other bulls (see APIS and

BUCHIS) he was regarded as a representation of the chief god of his city, Heliopolis. The Mnevis-bull was depicted as black and white, with the disk of the sun and a cobra between his horns. He was a symbol of fertility and also associated with Osiris.

Mobed. General name for a class of Parsi priests. Priests of higher grade are named Dastur (q.v.).

Modgudr. In Scandinavian mythology a maiden who guarded the bridge thatched with gold on the way to Hel. To her came Hermodr (q.v.) when seeking for Balder, and she said that he made as much noise riding over the bridge as five companies of dead men.

Moggallāna, Maudgalyāyana. One of the two chief disciples of the Buddha, the other being Sāriputta. They were among the first converts, and both died shortly before the Buddha. Moggallāna is said to have been famed for his supernatural powers. He was also called Kolita. Stūpas were erected for their relics, which were discovered at Sānchi (q.v.) in 1851 and re-interred there in 1953. A later Moggallāna was a Buddhist philosopher, known for his work called *Prajñapti-shāstra.*

Mogul. See MUGHAL.

Moha. (Sanskrit) 'delusion', error, ignorance. In Buddhism this is one of the three roots of evil, the others being Anger and Greed (Dosa and Rāga, in Pali).

Mohammed. See MUHAMMAD.

Moharram. See HUSAIN and MUHARRAM.

Mohenjodaro. 'City of the dead', a site in north India, which flourished about the same time as Harappā (q.v.). Stone seals found here show a horned cross-legged figure, like the later god Shiva (q.v.). See CERNUNNOS.

Mohism. See MO TZŬ.

Moira. (Greek) 'lot', portion, and so the goddess of Fate (q.v.). At first singular, and baneful doom, she becomes threefold, as the Moirai which determine birth, life and death. The three Moirai are named as Lachesis, Clotho and Atropos (qq.v.).

Moksha. (Sanskrit) 'release', 'liberation', salvation, generally from the round of transmigration. Liberation according to Hindu teachings can be obtained by knowledge (*jñāna*), works (*karma*), or devotion (*bhakti*) (qq.v.).

Mondo. Japanese word for 'questions and answers' which are found in short dialogues between Zen (q.v.) Buddhist masters and their disciples. Most of the specifically Zen literature consists of these questions and answers, together with commentaries that have been made of them; some of the Mondo are used as Kōan (q.v.) riddles to help in meditation.

Monju. See MANJUSHRĪ.

Monkey. See HSÜAN-TSANG.

Monkey-rule. See PRAPATTI.

Monks, Monasticism. See RĀHIB, SANGHA, BHIKKHU.

Monism. From a Greek word for 'one', *monos*, monism is applied to philosophical doctrines that only one being exists. It is sometimes identified with, but better differentiated from, Pantheism, the belief that God is everything or all is divine. Indian forms of Monism are described in that country as Non-duality, Advaita (q.v.). For Greek Monism, see ELEATICS.

Monotheism. From Greek *mono* and *theos*, this word is used of the doctrine that only one God exists, to the exclusion of all others. It is particularly applied to Judaism, Christianity and Islam, commonly called the three monotheistic religions. However, tendencies towards unity (as in Monism, q.v.) have appeared in many religions. Some of the great Hindu gods, such as Vishnu and Shiva, are regarded as sole deity by their worshippers, though sometimes with the admission that other gods appear as their aspects. African gods have been described as servants or aspects of the Supreme Being, in a 'diffused Monotheism.' Zoroastrian belief in Ahura Mazdā was in a single God, though perhaps with a diabolical counterpart in a kind of Dualism (q.v.). In many other religions of Asia and ancient America there was belief in a supreme or High God, but often as creator among other gods, leader of a pantheon, or president of the immortals.

Montu. Ancient Egyptian war-god of Hermonthis. He was represented as a man with a bull's head, carrying bow and arrows, a club and a knife. He was also associated with the sun, being identified with Rē' (q.v.) as 'lord of battle' or with his bull as the 'soul of Rē'.'

Moors. Name sometimes applied to Muslims, particularly those of North Africa and Spain (see MORISCOS). The Romans called the inhabitants of north-western Africa Mauri, perhaps from a Phoenician word meaning 'western', hence the country named Mauretania. The true Moors would be the Berbers who lived in northern Africa, but later the Spanish word *Moros*, and English 'Moors', came to be used of the Muslim inhabitants of North Africa and Spain. The Spanish also called the Muslims in the Philippines Moros.

Moriscos. (Spanish) 'little Moors', a term first used of Spaniards who were converted to Islam, and applied after the capture of Granada in 1492 to the Muslims who remained in Spain. From 1501 they were ordered to abandon their religion, customs and language, or leave Spain, and after 1609 those that remained were deported to North Africa under cruel conditions. European visitors to the Near East also sometimes called the Jews in those countries Moriscos.

Morpheus. The Greek god of dreams, son of Sleep. Three sons of Sleep – Morpheus, Ikelos and Phantasos – gave men visions respectively of human forms (*morphai*), animals and objects. Morpheus was properly the Former or Shaper, from the shapes that he made to appear before sleepers. The drug morphia is named after him.

Morrigan. Great queen, or night-mare queen, and war goddess of Celtic mythology. She was amorous of the hero Cúchulainn (q.v.), but when he refused her advances she became his enemy.

Moses. See MŪSĀ.

Moses de Leon. Spanish Jewish scholar of Granada (1250–1305) who is said to have compiled the great Kabbalistic work, the *Zohar* (q.v.). Moses himself said that the *Zohar* was written by a second century rabbi, Simeon ben Yochai (q.v.), and that it had been preserved in secret and came into his hands by accident. This was repudiated by other scholars, but the *Zohar* became the textbook of Jewish mysticism.

Moslem. See MUSLIM.

Mosque. Arabic *Masjid*, a 'place of prostration', the Muslim building for public worship. The word is used in the *Qur'ān* especially of the Ka'ba (q.v.), the Sacred Mosque (al-Masjid al-Harām) in Mecca (q.v.). When the Prophet migrated to Medina, one of his first actions was to buy ground for a Mosque, which became a place for prayer, a meeting-ground for

believers, a courtyard of his house, and eventually the great building which today covers the site. As Islam spread, Mosques were erected as places for worship and assembly. Mosques are usually built of stone or brick, in the form of a square, with an open courtyard in the centre. Minarets rise in front or at the corners. The wall that faces Mecca contains a niche or Mihrāb (q.v.), to the right of which is a pulpit or Minbar (q.v.). The courtyard may contain a tank or taps for ritual washings before prayer. Mosques have no images or paintings, but walls, pillars and ceilings are decorated with verses from the *Qur'ān* in Arabic script.

MOSQUE IN ISTANBUL

Mosque of Omar. See DOME OF THE ROCK.

Mother of the Book. A phrase (Umm al-Kitāb) used occasionally in the *Qur'ān* to indicate the essence or celestial archetype, the original copy with God in heaven from which the *Qur'ān* and all other scriptures, such as the *Torah* and the *Gospel*, are derived. 'We have made it an Arabic *Qur'ān*, and lo, it is in the Mother of the Book in our presence' (43, 3).

Mo-tzŭ, Mo-ti. Chinese religious and ethical teacher of the fifth or fourth century B.C. His dates and place are uncertain, but there is some agreement that he was born in the state of Lu about the time of the death of Confucius (479 B.C.). The teachings of Mo-tzŭ are contained in his 'Works', of which fifty-three chapters survive, twenty-four of them being the most important. Mo-tzŭ criticized the Confucian doctrines and ceremonies as erroneous and wasteful, and taught a universal benevolence. He believed in a righteous God (heaven) and in the Way (Tao, q.v.) of heaven. He was opposed to warfare and the luxury of princes. His followers, Mohists, were very numerous for two centuries, but declined with the growth of Confucianism, and Mohism as a movement disappeared. His more sympathetic critics said that Mo-tzŭ was well-meaning but too intellectual, and his general benevolence was considered to be detrimental to family and state.

Mozarab. 'Speakers of Arabic', *musta 'rabim*, a name particularly given to the Christians in Spain who adopted Arabic language and customs after the eighth century A.D., and their liturgical forms of Mozarabic rites. A similar name was applied to Jews in Egypt, Palestine and Syria.

Mozoomdar, Pratap Chander. Follower and biographer (1840–1905) of Keshab Chandra Sen (q.v.) and leader after him of the Brahma Samāj (q.v.).

Mu'āwiya. Founder of the Umayyad (q.v.) dynasty of Islamic Caliphs. He was son of Abū Sufyān, one of the Companions of Muhammad, and was appointed by the Caliph 'Umar as governor of Syria. Mu'āwiya opposed 'Alī (q.v.) after the death of 'Uthmān, and after the battle of Siffīn (A.D. 657) the empire was divided between them. After the death of 'Alī his eldest son Hasan gave up his rights and Mu'āwiya was hailed as Caliph.

Muditā. (Pali) 'joy', in the happiness of other beings, the third of the four heavenly states to Theravāda Buddhists. See VIHĀRA.

Mudrā. (Sanskrit) 'seal', and so a gesture, position or intertwining of the fingers. The term is used for dance positions, but particularly for symbolic positions of the hands, *hasta-mudrā*, in ritual, dancing and meditation. There are said to be twenty-four Mudrās commonly

MUDRĀS

used in Indian religious worship, though there are hundreds of combinations and meanings. The basic positions of the hands are: the open palm, the hollowed palm, the finger tips together, and the closed fist. In Buddhism statues are shown with hand Mudrās: together on the lap in meditation, uplifted in blessing, touching the earth for strength, and joined together for teaching.

Muezzin. Arabic Mu'addhin, the 'caller of the Adhān' (q.v.) or announcement of prayer. The first Muezzin of Islam was Bilāl, an Ethiopian freedman, who called the faithful to prayer in Medina from the top of the highest house near the mosque. When Muhammad conquered Mecca, Bilāl (q.v.) gave the call to prayer from the Ka'ba (q.v.). It is not certain whether minarets were introduced to give the Muezzin a higher place for the call to prayer, but they were soon used for that purpose. In small mosques the Muezzin calls from the door, and nowadays a recording often sounds from the minaret.

Muftī. A canon lawyer of Islam who gives Fatwās (q.v.), formal legal opinions on questions submitted by judges or private persons. A Muftī does not follow his own judgement, but gives it in accordance with fixed precedents, and so he must be learned in the *Qur'ān*, the *Traditions* and the writings of the schools of law. The Grand Muftī is a title given to the highest religious dignitary and for centuries the Grand Muftī of Istanbul was of great importance and called Shaikh al-Islam (q.v.).

Mughal, Mogul. The name given to the Islamic people who ruled much of India from the time of Bābur, in 1526, till the defeat of Bahādur Shah II by the British in 1857. The name Mughal is from the same root as Mongol, but the latter term is best restricted to the central Asian nomads, led by Jenghiz Khan and others. The term Great Mogul was applied to some of the outstanding Indian rulers, such as Akbar and Aurangzeb (qq.v.).

Muhājirūn. (Arabic) 'emigrants', the name applied in the *Qur'ān* to those followers of Muhammad who migrated with him in the Hijra (q.v.) in A.D. 622. See ANSĀR.

Muhammad. The founder of Islam was born in Mecca, probably in A.D. 570, the 'Year of the Elephant', when an Ethiopian army was repelled from the city. His father 'Abd Allāh was of the family of Hāshim and tribe of Quraysh, but died before his son's birth. His mother Āmina died when he was six and his grandfather 'Abd al-Muttalib when he was eight. Then he was under the care of his uncle Abū Tālib. When Muhammad was twenty-five, he married a rich widow, Khadīja (q.v.). At about the age of forty he began to have visions and hear voices, later said to come via the angel Gabriel, in which God told him to preach against idolatry and polytheism. Khadīja supported him, and his first followers included 'Alī and Abū Bakr (q.v.). Due to persecution in 622 Muhammad and his disciples migrated (see HIJRA) to Medina. There he raised successful armies, and in 630 he conquered Mecca and destroyed its idols. He died in Medina in 632 in the arms of his youngest wife Ayesha (q.v.). While Khadīja lived (till 619) Muhammad had no other wife; later he had at least nine wives, but only one was previously unmarried. In Islamic belief Muhammad is the Seal, last and greatest of prophets, and intercessor with God for Muslims on the Day of Judgement. See MEDINA.

Muhammadanism. See ISLAM.

Muharram. The first month of the Islamic year, of thirty days in length. The first day of the month is generally celebrated, and the tenth day is sacred to all Shī'a (q.v.) Muslims as the anniversary of the death of Husain (q.v.). It is a time of mourning, of performance of a Passion Play of the death of Husain, and of pilgrimage to sacred places, especially to Karbalā' (q.v.). See also *'Āshūrā'*.

Mujtahid. See IJTIHĀD.

Mukta, Mukti. (Sanskrit) 'released', saved. See MOKSHA.

Mullah. A Persian form for the Arabic term *Mawlawi*, a learned man or scholar, and so teacher and exponent of the sacred law of Islam.

Müller, Max. German philologist and religious writer (1823–1900), who became an Oxford professor and edited the translations of 'Sacred Books of the East'. Müller's theories of the origins of religion in the personification of natural phenomena have largely been abandoned, but terms that he introduced, such as Henotheism and Kathenotheism (qq.v.), have had considerable currency.

Mūl Mantra. See JAPJI.

Mulungu. A name for the supreme God found in a number of the languages of East Africa, in various forms such as Murungu, Mungu, Mlungu, Mluku, Mngu. Mulungu is used both of the Creator and of an impersonal spiritual force, particularly associated with storms, so it is said that Mulungu rains or speaks in the thunder. Sometimes associated with ancestors, in general Mulungu is not used in the plural since the divine spirit is one.

Mumbo Jumbo. In English usage, according to the *Oxford English Dictionary*, this name means a grotesque idol, and hence any object of senseless veneration. It may be further assimilated to the word 'mumble', and so indicate nonsensical speech. But according to the Scottish explorer Mungo Park who travelled about West Africa from 1795, Mumbo Jumbo was the name given by the Mandingo people to 'a sort of masquerade habit, made of the bark of trees', which was worn at nocturnal ceremonies, with songs and dances and beating of offenders against the public peace. This was clearly one of the secret societies, still common in West Africa, in which the members, chiefly male, dress in masks and robes to represent the spirits of the dead and the authority of society.

Mummu. Craftsman-god in Mesopotamian mythology, who personified technical skill. He was attendant upon the god Ea (q.v.), husband of the goddess Damkina and father of Marduk.

Mummy. The name, from an Arabic word meaning 'wax', for a body preserved after death by embalming. Practised in various parts of the world, this custom was developed in Egypt to a far greater extent than anywhere else. From an early date, the First or Second Dynasty, bodies were preserved to maintain the relationship between the soul and its double (see BA and KA). After purification a ceremony of Opening the Mouth was performed (see PTAH) and then the body was

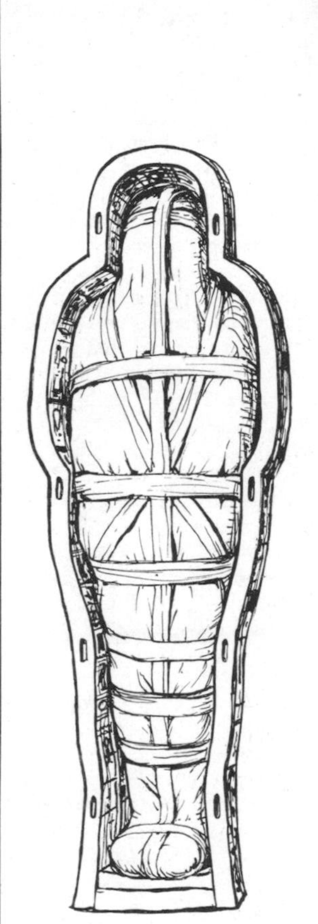

anointed, wrapped in bandages and given royal or other emblems. The ceremonies of mummification lasted many days, up to seventy, and were meant to imitate the death and restoration of Osiris (q.v.). Mummified bodies were placed in Pyramids (q.v.) with many treasures, but, while many mummies have survived and are to be seen in museums, most of their belongings were stolen in ancient times, except a few such as those of Tutankhamūn (preserved in Cairo).

Mundaka. One of the classical *Upanishads*, attached to the *Atharva Veda*. Generally monistic, it contains hints of a more personal theism, in its three short sections.

Mundilfari. Deity of Scandinavian mythology, father of Sol, the sun, and Mani, the moon. It is said that the gods were angry with him for giving them these names and placed Sol and Mani in the sky to drive the sun and moon. There is some confusion between the celestial bodies and their chariots.

Muni. Indian 'sage' (Sanskrit), ascetic or Brahmin of the highest order. The name is applied also to a Rishi (q.v.) and to people renowned for their writings, like the grammarian Pānini (q.v.). Gautama the Buddha was called Shākya-muni, the 'sage of the Shākya clan'.

Munkar and Nakīr. Names of two angels in Islamic belief who examine the dead in their graves and punish them if necessary. The names are not found in the *Qur'ān*, though there is reference to angels taking the life of unbelievers (8, 52). The origin of the names of these angels is uncertain, but later tradition taught that this interrogation in the tomb was a reality.

Murīdiya. A Murīd is 'one who is willing' (Arabic), and so applied to a disciple of a mystical Islamic order. The Murīdiya of West Africa are a powerful branch of the Qadiriya (q.v.), founded in the nineteenth century by Ahmad Bamba of Senegal and with a great centre at Touba.

The Murādiya was a Turkish order in Istanbul in the eighteenth century.

Murjites, Murji'a. One of the early sects of Islam, which has disappeared. The meaning of the name is not certain, but it has been interpreted as 'procrastinators'. The Murjites were distinguished for their quietism and forbearance, as against the fanaticism of the Khārijīs (q.v.). The chief Murjite distinctive belief was in the indelible character of faith, that a Muslim did not lose his faith through sin. A sinner did not cease to be a Muslim and there was hope for him at the Last Judgement.

Murshid. (Arabic) a 'guide', on a straight road The name given to a leader or director of a mystical order (see Sūfī).

Mūsā. The name of the Biblical Moses in the *Qur'ān* and Islamic tradition. He is the most frequently mentioned character in the *Qur'ān* (over five hundred verses) owing to the popularity of his stories and a fair amount of repetition. He is one of the prophets said to have received a book (kitāb) from God, the *Tawrat* or *Torah*, the Hebrew scriptures.

Muses. Greek gods of the arts, and later of other intellectual pursuits. According to Hesiod there were nine Muses, though their names vary and others are known. The nine Muses were: Calliope of epic poetry, Clio of history, Euterpe of flutes, Terpsichore of dance, Erato of lyric poetry, Melpomene of tragedy, Thalia of comedy, Polyhymnia of mimic art, and Urania of astronomy. The Muses were said to be daughters of Zeus and they danced at the festivals of the gods led by Apollo. They had cults throughout Greece and a Museum was a place of learning. See also Graces and Helicon.

CALLIOPE THALIA ERATO EUTERPE

Muslim. The name for the follower of Islam, and from the same Arabic root, *aslama*, 'to submit'. So a Muslim is a submitted or surrendered man, to the will of God. In the *Qur'ān* Christians are also called Muslims, when they follow the revelations of God. In English the word Muslim is often rendered Moslem, and in French it is Musulman from the Persian form of Muslim. The names Muhammadan, or Mohammedan, or Mahometan, are disliked by Muslims because they do not worship Muhammad. See Black Muslims.

Muslim ibn al-Hajjāj. One of the great collectors of the traditions of Muhammad and his companions, he was born and died at Naishapur (817–875). Muslim travelled widely and his collection, *Sahīh*, rivals that of Bukhārī (q.v.), but differs in that it is not divided into chapters, but is in fifty-two books dealing with the usual subjects of Hadīth: the Pillars of Islam, customs of Muhammad and his Companions, marriage, slavery, war, and theological matters. See also Tirmidhī.

Muslim League. Political organization founded in undivided India in 1906, meeting first at Dacca. It was English-speaking and imperially loyalist at first, led by upper and middle class Muslims seeking communalist favours. Muslim nationalists were soon attracted, such as

Muhammad 'Alī Jinnah who became leader and from 1936 gave the league a wider appeal and sought to form an Islamic state, eventually Pakistan (coming into being after the partition of India in 1947).

Muspell. A people of the south in Scandinavian mythology, who lived in a hot world called Muspellheim, which was guarded by Surt (q.v.) with a fiery sword. Muspell was taken in German texts to mean the end of the world, but to the Norse people it meant a world of fire and its rulers. At the Doom of the gods (see RAGNARÖK) the people of Muspell would come in a ship called Naglfar, guided by the wicked Loki (q.v.).

POLYHYMNIA CLIO TERPSICHORE URANIA MELPOMENE

Mustafā. Name often given by Muslims to Muhammad, from an Arabic root but used in this Turkish spelling. Several Ottoman Turkish sultans were known by this name, from Mustafā I in 1617. It was also the name of the modern Turkish reformer Kemāl Atatürk (1881–1938).

Musta'lians. A sect of Ismā'ilī (q.v.) Islam. Al-Musta'lī was younger son of the Caliph al-Mustansir, and on the death of his father in 1094 al-Musta'lī was proclaimed Caliph in place of his brother Nizār (q.v.) who was killed. This split the Ismā'ilī into two main branches, Musta'lians and Nizārīs. The Musta'lians were centred at first on Egypt, but moved in time to the Yemen and then to India. About a quarter of a million of them are now to be found in India, many in East Africa, and several thousands in the Yemen.

Musulman. See MUSLIM.

Mūt. An ancient Egyptian goddess, of Thebes and perhaps originally from Nubia. She was called Queen of Nubia, Eye of Rē', Queen of all the Gods, Ruler of Karnak. She was the wife of Amūn (q.v.) in Thebes. Mūt was the mother of the world and was said to be bi-sexual. She was often identified with Hathor. Mūt was represented as a woman with a double crown, or sometimes as a vulture.

Mut'a. (Arabic) a temporary marriage, called a 'marriage of pleasure', in traditional Islam. It was contracted for a fixed period only and entailed a reward to the woman so engaged.

Mutakallim. Theologians of Islam, exponents of Kalām (q.v.).

Mu'tazila, Mu'tazilites. A powerful rationalist theological movement in early Islam. Their name has been taken to mean 'seceders', but may mean 'intermediate'. In politics some of them separated from 'Alī (q.v.), but refused to fight against him, and in religion they sought to combine reason with faith. For some time they were the official teachers of the 'Abbāsid Caliphs (q.v.) and were largely responsible for translating Plato, Aristotle and other Greek writers into Arabic. So the Mu'tazila followed the Greek rational method, as opposed to the Traditionists who held solely to the *Qur'ān* and *Traditions* and denied the use of reason. The Mu'tazila denied that God predestines man to evil, affirmed human freewill, and asserted that the *Qur'ān* was created, in contrast to the orthodox who believed in predestination and the eternity of the *Qur'ān*. The orthodox won, particularly with the help of Al-Ash'arī (q.v.), and most Mu'tazila works were lost, but their influence remains in Shī'a Islam. See QADARĪYA and ZAMAKHSHARĪ.

Mutt. See MATHA.

Muwahhidūn. See ALMOHADS.

Mysteries. Secret cults of ancient Greece, connected with agriculture and originally leading to ceremonies for rebirth, and in later times to teachings of purity and righteousness. The principal mysteries were those of Demeter and Dionysus, celebrated at Eleusis (qq.v.). The basic theme was the capture of Koré or Persephone by Pluto, her journey to the underworld for four or six months, and return to Mother Earth, Demeter. This illustrated the disappearance or storing of corn in the winter, and its reappearance and sowing in spring. Other Mysteries were those of Orphism (q.v.). There was no fixed Mystery doctrine, and the adaptability of the Mysteries to different needs accounts for their popularity up to the end of ancient Greek religion.

Mysticism. Related to Mysteries (q.v.), this word suggests the esoteric or occult. But more importantly it is used for intuition, or the apprehension of truths beyond the reason, and supremely for union with the Deity by contemplation and self-surrender. In the latter sense Mysticism is found in many religions and is notable in the Bhakti (q.v.) cults of Hinduism, the Sūfī (q.v.) mystics of Islam, and the Kabbalah (q.v.) of Judaism.

Myth. A myth is a story of unhistorical or supernatural beings, as distinct from a Legend which refers to a historical person. Myths are found in all religions and are often taken as statements of fact; hence there are modern attempts to 'demythologize' religion. But a myth is a symbolical representation, meant to indicate a reality which is essentially beyond description, and modern psychology, as well as anthropology and theology, insists upon the importance of myth for human thought and behaviour.

N

Nabī. The Arabic word for a 'prophet' is derived from the same Hebrew form. In the *Qur'ān* twenty-eight Prophets are named, all or nearly all from the *Bible*, since a Nabī was sent to the People of the Book, Jews and Christians. These Prophets included Adam, Moses and Jesus. Muhammad himself was a Nabī for Arabs and in one verse he is the Seal (q.v.) of the Prophets. Muslims believe that Muhammad was the last and greatest of the Prophets, and nobody after him, however great, can strictly be called a Nabī. See RASŪL.

Nabu. See NEBO.

Nachiketas. A young man in Hindu story, son of Aruni, whose dialogue with death is told in the *Taittirīya Brāhmana* and the *Katha Upanishad* (see the latter).

Nafs. Arabic word for 'soul' or self, related to Hebrew *nephesh*. It is used reflexively of oneself, and also of the human soul. After the *Qur'ān* the word Nafs came to be used interchangeably with Rūh (q.v., Hebrew *ruach*), which earlier had meant breath and spirit, but both Nafs and Rūh were used of human and angelic spirits. The difference between Nafs and Rūh was like the English vague distinction of 'soul' and 'spirit', but pantheistic Sūfīs identified the human and divine Rūh.

Nāgārjuna. Buddhist teacher, reputed founder of the Middle Doctrine or Mādhyamika School (q.v.). Little is known about his life or even dates, but he probably lived in the latter half of the second century A.D. According to Chinese tradition he was the second patriarch of Mahāyāna Buddhism, after Ashvaghosha (q.v.), and other legends say that he visited the Nāgas, the sea serpents, perhaps indicating his new doctrines. Nāgārjuna's 'Aphorisms', the *Mādhyamika Kārikā*, are basic to that school, and he is sometimes called the 'Father of Mahāyāna' because he first taught its distinctive doctrine of the Void (q.v.).

Nāgas. Snakes of Indian mythology, especially indicating cobras, but in myth they are semi-divine beings with human faces, cobra necks and snake tails. They were said to live in the waters or in a city, Bhoga-vatī, under the earth. Their wives were beautiful and stories are told of them marrying men.

There were also historical people called Nāgas, who lived in the mountains and were distinct from the Hindus, and in modern times aboriginal tribes of this name live in the hills of eastern India.

Nāgasena. See MILINDA.

Nahavendi, Benjamin. Jewish rabbi of Persia who in the ninth century did much to establish the Karaites (q.v.).

Nahualli. See CHANUL.

Nakayama. See MIKI.

Nakīr. See MUNKAR.

Nakshatra. (Sanskrit) 'star', constellation, one of the twenty-seven or twenty-eight lunar mansions of Hindu astronomy. See ZODIAC.

Nakshbandi. See NAQSHBANDI. .

Nala. In Hindu mythology a king of Nishadha whose love for Damayantī (q.v.) is a favourite romance.

Nālanda. Buddhist university in north-east India, founded about the second century A.D. and continuing till the ninth century. It had a famous library and notable teachers. Long in ruins the site has been excavated in modern times. See HSÜAN-TSANG.

Nām. (Punjabi) 'name', the Sikh designation of God as the divine Name. It expresses the nature and being of God in terms which men can understand, and, in this, Nām is close to Shabad, the divine Word (see SHABDA). Guru Nānak (q.v.), founder of the Sikh religion, taught 'remembrance of the divine Name' (*Nām simran*) as an interior discipline which brings a growth towards and into God in ascending stages.

Nāman. 'Mark' or name of the Hindu god Vishnu, generally three perpendicular marks made on the forehead with sandalwood paste or ash. Sometimes it is simply a small circle or a figure like the flame of a candle, but zealots in south India may paint their whole body with the marks of Vishnu as others do for Shiva. The Nāman is marked on the skin with the right thumb and the vertical emblem of Vishnu is distinct from the horizontal lines of Shiva.

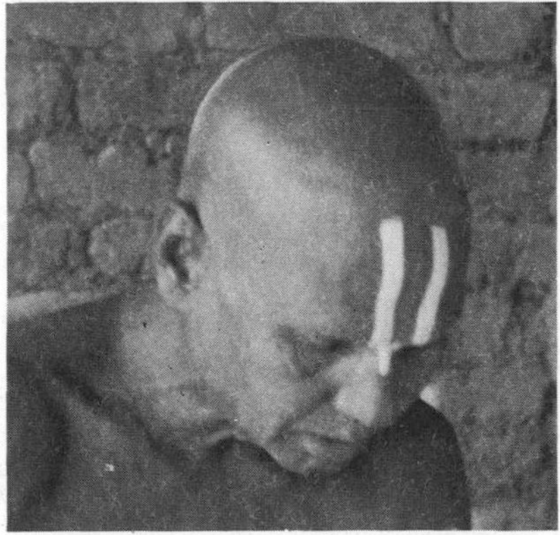

Namandi. Spirit beings of northern Australia, who are generally malignant and ill-disposed to human beings, though they prefer to attack lonely people rather than those who travel in groups. They are always in conflict with the more harmless Mimi beings (q.v.).

Nāmdev, Nāmadeva. Hindu poet and mystic who lived from about A.D. 1270 to 1344. Born in Maharashtra, he followed his father's trade of tailoring and is said to have fallen into evil ways till he was converted to the worship of Vishnu (Vitthoba) and devoted the rest of his life to him. He composed many hymns, in Hindi and Marathi, and was one of the early leaders of the Vishnu revival. Some sixty hymns of Nāmdev are included in the Sikh Scriptures, the *Ādi Granth* (q.v.).

Names. See BEAUTIFUL NAMES.

Nānak. The founder of the Sikh religion was born in Talwandi in the Punjab in 1469. In early manhood he moved to Sultanpur and from there travelled to other parts of India and perhaps beyond. Finally he settled in the village of Kartarpur and died there in 1539. Many stories are told of Nānak by his followers, who always call him Guru, 'teacher', in legendary tales called Janam-sākhīs (q.v.). Basically he was in the tradition of Bhakti (q.v.) devotion to one God, and perhaps slightly influenced by Islamic mysticism. He was a younger contemporary of Kabīr (q.v.), also a mystic and a monotheist. Nānak had a vision in which God, the Name, told him to teach the repetition of his name. His movement increased after his death, his 'followers' being called Sikhs, and Guru Nānak was said to be present in the nine Gurus who followed him. The Sikh scriptures, *Ādi Granth* (q.v.), contain nearly a thousand hymns attributed to Guru Nānak.

Nandi, Nandin. (Sanskrit) 'happy', the name of the bull of the Hindu god Shiva. Nandi is said to be the chief of

Shiva's personal attendants and guardian of animals. His white image always sits before the temples of Shiva, gazing at the shrine.

Nandinī. See KĀMADHENU.

Nanna. Nanna Nepsdottir was wife of the god Balder (q.v.) in Norse mythology. She was daughter of Gevar and was charmed by the music of the blind god Hod (q.v.). Balder saw Nanna bathing and resolved to kill Hod, but was himself killed eventually by him. Meanwhile Balder had won the hand of Nanna and they had a son, Forseti. When Balder was killed by a mistletoe shoot from the hand of Hod, Nanna died of grief, was burned with Balder in his ship in the funeral pyre, and then accompanied him to the underworld.

Nannar. An early name for the Mesopotamian moon god Sin (q.v.).

Naōjote. Ceremony for investing a Parsi child with sacred shirt and thread, from Pahlavi words meaning 'new praying' or perhaps 'new birth', indicating that after initiation the person will be qualified to offer prayers and observe religious customs as a true Zoroastrian. See SACRED THREAD.

Naqshbandī. A Muslim Sūfī (q.v.) order, founded by Muhammad Naqshband (1317–89). He was born near Bukhara and spent most of his life in the neighbourhood, in the later years of his life mending roads and caring for animals. Pilgrimages to the tomb of Naqshband used to be made from remote parts of China, and the order is popular in many middle eastern countries. The Naqshbandīs perform a silent devotion, repeating their special litany (see DHIKR).

Nara. See DAIBUTSU and NARA-NĀRĀYANA.

Naraka. The name of a Hell or place of torment for the wicked in Hindu mythology, see BRAHMĀNDA. The Code of Manu (q.v.) names twenty-one Narakas for those who accept presents from evil kings. The *Vishnu Purāna* names twenty-eight 'awful provinces' of the god of death, Yama (q.v.), to which are assigned those who revile the scriptures or neglect their duties. These Narakas are places of darkness, fear, sharp swords, scourges and a waveless sea.

Another Naraka was a son of the earth, a demonic being who stole the earrings of the goddess Aditi and was killed by Krishna. In a different version he was an evil king, an Asura (q.v.), who took the form of an elephant and seized the daughters of gods and men. He had a splendid palace and treasures and many wives, but was evil in his actions.

Nara-Nārāyana. (Sanskrit) Nara is a 'man', the primeval Man or the eternal Spirit and Nārāyana is son of the primeval Man. In Hindu myth Nara and Nārāyana are two ancient sages, sons of the god of Right, Dharma (q.v.), whose austerities were so severe that the gods became alarmed and sent nymphs to disturb their devotions. In epic poetry they are emanations of the god Vishnu, Arjuna being Nara and Krishna being Nārāyana. Nārāyana became a regular title of Vishnu. See also HITOPADESHA.

Nara-Simha. 'Man-lion' (Sanskrit), an Avatar (q.v.) of Vishnu. A demon named Hiranya-kashipu was oppressing the world and was invulnerable to gods, men and beasts. The demon's son,

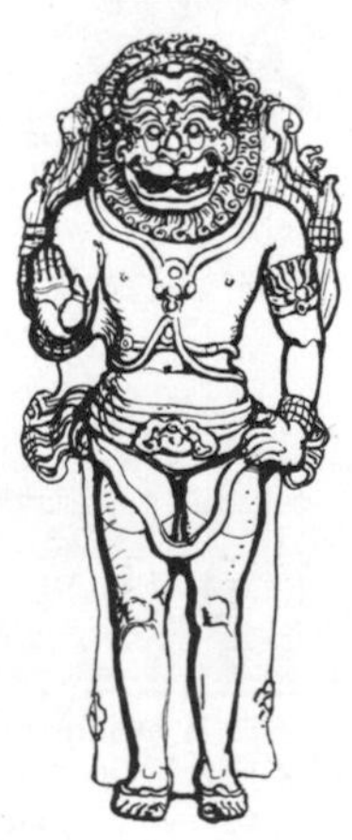

Prahlāda, worshipped Vishnu, and his father struck a stone pillar asking if Vishnu was inside it. Vishnu came out, in form neither fully man nor beast, and tore the demon to pieces. This old myth was incorporated into the series of Avatars.

Narcissus. A youth in Greek mythology who fell in love with his own reflection in water, pined away and died, being turned into the flower that bears his name. Another story says that he was punished for being cruel to Echo (q.v.). She tried to make love to Narcissus by repeating his own words, but he repulsed her and she wasted away till only her voice was left.

Nasārā. The name for Christians in the *Qur'ān* and used among Muslims still, though other titles are also used now, such as 'Īsawī and Masīhī, followers of Jesus and the Christ. The word was used in pre-Islamic times and came through Syriac from the rare Biblical title Nazarene (*Acts* 24, 5). Nasārā, or variants upon it, also appeared among the Mandeans (q.v.), probably to escape persecution since Christians were protected as People of the Book. See AHL AL-KITĀB.

Nasser, President. See BRETHREN.

Nat. A nature spirit of Burma, called Phi in Thailand. Nats are believed to inhabit trees, mountains and rivers and little wooden shrines with lamps are attached to trees, or placed under them or by rivers and hills, to honour the Nats and keep in their favour. Spirits of the dead, ghosts of good or bad, may also be propitiated in similar fashion. In Buddhist commentaries it is said that trees are inhabited by these spirits, which are not evil but may be vindictive to those who offend or neglect them.

Natarāja. (Sanskrit) 'Lord of the Dance', a title of the Hindu god Shiva who is commonly represented performing his world-shattering dance in a ring of fire. See DANCE OF SHIVA.

Nātha. (Sanskrit) 'refuge', lord, name of a Yoga sect which arose in northern India about the tenth century A.D., and whose saints are called Nātha. Its legendary founder, Ādinātha, 'first lord', is identified with the god Shiva, and the followers worship Shiva and practise forms of Tantric (q.v.) devotion. The leaders have great reputations as workers of miracles, bringing rain or drought, living without food, riding through the air, and changing shape at will. The Nāthas were severely criticized by Kabīr and Nānak, founder of the Sikhs, for their occult teachings.

Nathan. See GHAZZATI.

Nautch. An Indian female dancer, and by degeneration a courtesan. See DEVADĀSĪ.

Navarātra. (Sanskrit) 'nine nights', the period of a Hindu sacrifice, applied especially to the nine nights of reciting hymns to the goddess Durgā before the Dasharā (q.v.) festival.

Nava Vidhāna, Naba Bidhan. See KESHAB CHANDRA SEN and NEW DISPENSATION.

Nāyanārs. Sixty-three 'teachers' of Tamil Shaivism who composed hymns, from the seventh to tenth centuries, which form eleven sacred books, *Tirumurai* (q.v.). See SHAIVA SIDDHĀNTA.

Nazoreans. See MANDEANS.

Nebo, Nabu. Babylonian god of writing, son of Marduk whom he often overshadowed. He was especially favoured by Nebuchadrezzar (Nabuchodonosor II), the conqueror of Jerusalem in 586 B.C., and later Isaiah mocked at the image of Nebo being itself carried into captivity (*Isaiah* 46, 1–2). Nabu's chief temple was at Borsippa, called the 'Firm house' and its tower the 'house of seven guides of heaven and earth.' Nabu was the supreme scribe, the lord of the pen, and his symbol was the pen or stylus. In many ways he resembled the Egyptian Thoth (q.v.). He was creator of writing and so of destiny, could prolong life and revive the dead.

SYMBOL OF NEBO

Nectar. Drink of the gods in Greek mythology, though sometimes also their food (see AMBROSIA).

Nefasti. Unpropitious days in ancient Roman religion on which courts must not sit or public assemblies be held, as unhallowed, impious, and so unlucky. See FASTI.

Nefertem. A minor Egyptian god, son of Ptah and Sekhmet, who was worshipped at Memphis. He was chiefly a god of vegetation, a personification of abstract forces. In art Nefertem appears as a bearded man with two feathers on his head, and a solar disk or ram's horns.

Nefertiti. The beautiful wife of Pharaoh Ikhnaton (q.v.).

Neit, Net. One of the oldest Egyptian goddesses, worshipped in many places, but especially at Sais in the delta of the Nile. Neit is called daughter, mother of Rē', and mother of other gods as well. She was called 'mother of all the gods', 'mistress of the Mediterranean'. Perhaps she personified the primeval waters out of which the gods arose, but she was also connected with the sky since she was mother of the sun. Neit appears in art as a woman holding bow and arrows (since she was a goddess of hunting) and wearing a crown. Occasionally she appeared as a lioness or a cow. She was sometimes identified with Isis or Hathor, and in Greek and Roman times was called Athena or Minerva.

Nekhbet. One of the oldest deities of Egypt, a vulture-goddess and guardian of the South. She was said to be wife of Hapi and daughter of Rē‘, and was often identified with Hathor (q.v.). Nekhbet was represented as a woman with the white crown of Upper Egypt, or as a vulture holding a ring in her claws and flying above the king. Her chief temple was at Nekheb.

Nembutsu. Japanese form of the Buddhist invocation Namu Amida Butsu, 'Hail to Amida Buddha', repeated in the Pure Land sects (q.v.), to aid concentration on Amida and rebirth into his Pure Land. See HONEN.

Nemean Lion. A monster of Greek mythology, offspring of Selene, the moon, and with a hide proof against iron, bronze or stone. To kill it was the first Labour of Heracles (q.v.), and after several vain attempts he strangled the lion to death.

There were Nemean Games, held in the valley of Nemea in the Argolid, founded by Heracles according to some, or by Adrastus of Argos; here a fourth century temple of Zeus and a gymnasium have been excavated.

Nemesis. In some Greek mythology Nemesis appears to be a goddess like Artemis (q.v.), pursued by Zeus and changing her form to avoid him. Here she is like many other goddesses and was perhaps related to fertility cults. But in most instances Nemesis is portrayed as the personification of retribution, and she represents the anger of the gods at human presumption. Nemesis was a power, perhaps made abstract after earlier story, like Fortuna (q.v.).

Neo-Confucians. See CHU HSI, WANG YANG-MING and T'AI-CHI.

Neo-Platonism. A school of syncretistic religious philosophy which claimed to derive its origin from Plato (q.v.). The reputed founder was Ammonius Saccas (A.D. 175–242) of whom little is known; he was overshadowed by Plotinus (q.v.). From Alexandria Plotinus took Neo-Platonism to Rome; after him came Porphyry, Iamblichus and Proclus. Neo-Platonism taught the ultimate One, the Absolute Good, from whom emanations radiate throughout the universe. Matter is ultimately unreal and the soul needs to withdraw from sense objects to reach the divine source, by a 'flight of the alone to the Alone'. Neo-Platonism declined with the growth of Christian theology, yet it influenced Christian thinkers like Augustine, and mystics, and was also potent in the formulation of Islamic philosophy and mysticism.

Neo-Pythagoreans. See PYTHAGORAS.

Neo-Vedānta. 'New Vedānta', meaning a new exposition of the Hindu Vedānta philosophy, which was given in the *Upanishads* and by philosophers of the Vedānta schools, such as Shankara and Rāmānuja (qq.v.). As expounded by its western teachers, such as Aldous Huxley, Christopher Isherwood and Gerald Heard, Neo-Vedānta appears to be a thoroughgoing monism or pantheism in the tradition of Shankara. The *Upanishads* are not consistently pantheistic, Rāmānuja preferred a 'modified non-dualism', and many Hindus have repudiated pantheism in theory and action. This modern monism is also often expressed by leaders of the Rāmakrishna movement (q.v.). See ADVAITA.

Nephthys. Egyptian goddess, wife and sister of Set, and friend and sister of Isis. Although Set killed Osiris, of a rival cult, Nephthys joined Isis in bewailing him and caring for the body of Osiris. Nephthys was called the Lady of the West and Goddess of Fate, and in art was represented as a woman with the hieroglyph of her name on her head.

Neptune. Ancient Italian water-god whose festival (23 July) was celebrated by erecting branches, perhaps with the aim of inducing a supply of water during the dry season. Under Greek influence he was identified with Poseidon, the god of the sea (q.v.).

Nereus, Nereids. Nereus was an old Greek sea god, father of the Nereids, with whom he lived like a merman at the bottom of the sea. He was said to be very wise and could change into many shapes, as he did when Heracles (q.v.) wrestled with him to learn the location of the Golden Apples. See CASSIOPEIA and ANDROMEDA.

Nergal. A god of the underworld in Babylonian religion. He was believed to spend half the year in the upper world, as an aspect of the sun, and the other half below ground. The ruler of the underworld was the goddess Ereshkigal (q.v.) (or Allatum in Semitic forms), and she called Nergal before her. However, Nergal dragged her from her throne by her hair, until Ereshkigal agreed that he should share her rule over the underworld. Nergal was originally a solar deity and the myth expresses his double activity.

Nerthus. The Roman historian Tacitus, in the first century A.D., in *Germania* XL, gave one of his most vivid descriptions of a northern deity in describing Nerthus as Mother Earth. She was worshipped by seven tribes on an island which has been identified with Seeland. There was a grove, with a veiled chariot which only a priest could touch. At certain seasons the goddess was believed to be present in the chariot, and it was drawn by cows round the island. That was a time of peace when all weapons were put aside. It seems certain that Nerthus was the Scandinavian Njörd (q.v.), one of the Vanir deities, but Norse writers call him a god and either Tacitus was mistaken in his sex or he may have been regarded as female at some places or times. The other details, with the ornamental chariot, occur in Norse stories.

Nessus. One of the Centaurs (q.v.) in Greek mythology. When Heracles had married Deianeira, they came to a river and Nessus offered to carry her over as he was the divinely authorized ferryman; however, while Heracles swam across, Nessus tried to carry off his wife. Heracles shot him with an arrow and the dying Nessus told Deianeira to keep his blood and anoint Heracles' shirt with it and oil if he was unfaithful. This she did much later and, as Heracles was offering sacrifices, the oil melted and he was burnt with the poison. The shirt clung to his skin and he collapsed, but on his funeral pyre his immortal spirit mounted to the gods.

Net. See NEIT.

New Dispensation. Modern Hindu reform movement founded by Keshab Chandra Sen (q.v.), as a break from the earlier Brāhmo Samāj. It was deliberately syncretistic. In January 1881 Keshab and twelve disciples appeared with a red banner bearing the words Naba Bidhan (New Dispensation, Nava Vidhāna), with a symbol composed of the Hindu trident, Christian cross and Islamic crescent. On a table were the scriptures of Hinduism, Buddhism, Christianity and Islam, and four disciples were appointed to study each of them. The movement sub-divided before long and only survived the founder's death in attenuated forms.

New Grange. Vast tumulus in the valley of the Boyne in Ireland which, together with the neighbouring tumuli at Dowth and Knowth, provides some of the best Neolithic material in Europe. In Celtic mythology these and other *sids*, mounds, are the homes of gods and paradises. See DAGDA, OENGUS, TIR NA N-OG, TUATHA DÉ DANANN, SID.

STONES FROM NEW GRANGE

New Religions, Japanese. See SECT SHINTŌ.

New Year. The Jewish New Year festival, Rosh Hashanah, falls on the first of Tishri (September–October). It is the memorial of creation and also a time of making account to God. During the morning service in the synagogue the ram's horn (Shofar) is sounded, to proclaim God king of the universe and call men to repentance. New Year's day marks the beginning of ten days of penitence, culminating in the Day of Atonement (q.v.) on the tenth of Tishri.

Ngewo. Supreme deity of the Mende of Sierra Leone, the origin of whose name is uncertain but may mean 'high'. As in much other African mythology, Ngewo was once much nearer to the earth than he is now, but moved away due to human over-familiarity. There are no temples, but many prayers are addressed to Ngewo, either directly or through other gods.

Nibbāna. See NIRVĀNA.

Nichiren. Japanese Buddhist reformer (1222–82), and sect called after him. His name, meaning 'sun-lotus', suggests a mixture of Shinto and Buddhism, and Nichiren produced a particularly Japanese and militant form of Buddhism. Son of a fisherman, he became a monk early in life and at thirty years of age received the conviction that true Buddhism was in the Lotus of Truth, or the *Lotus Sūtra* (q.v.), as translated by Kumārajīva. He proclaimed this as the gospel for his age with the simple formula, 'Hail to the Lotus of Perfect Truth'. Nichiren held that other forms of Buddhism were in error, particularly the popular Jodo (q.v.) or Pure Land forms of faith and devotion, and he tried to persuade the government to suppress them. His fanatical zeal was continued by his followers, with his apostles Nichizo and Nichiji. In modern times Nichiren Buddhism has inspired some of the new religious sects and political movements in Japan, and the Sōka Gakkai (q.v.) today.

Nidāna. A 'fetter' or link (Sanskrit and Pali) in the chain of causation brought about by Karma. Buddhists use this term to denote the process by which one comes into existence and is bound to the wheel of life or transmigration. There are twelve Nidānas, beginning with ignorance and ending with birth. The chain is broken by overcoming desire, Tanhā (q.v.).

Nidāna-Kathā. See JĀTAKA.

Nidhogg. A cruel snake in Scandinavian mythology which gnawed the roots of the Yggdrasil tree (q.v.) and sucked the blood of corpses in the lower world, particularly those of treacherous men and murderers.

Niflheim, Niflhel. The dark Misty Hel, the world of death, in Scandinavian mythology. It was in the north, a place of mist and cold, and existed long before the formation of the earth. In Niflheim there was a well, Hvergelmir, from which eleven icy rivers flowed bringing cold to the earth.

Nihongi, Nihon-shoki. The 'Chronicles of Japan', the second most important text of Shinto, next to the *Kojiki* (q.v.). The *Nihongi* was said to have been written by Futo-no-Yasumaro no-Ason and Prince Toneri. It is about twice the length of the *Kojiki* and contains most of the myths of creation and legendary figures that appear in that work, but with different versions; often the same gods appear under different names or rendered in variant Chinese characters. The *Nihongi* was written in Chinese and, although it was the favourite text for centuries, in recent times preference has often been given to the *Kojiki* because of its more Japanese style and nomenclature.

Nikāya. (Sanskrit) 'collection', group, title used for each of the five sections of the second part, *Sutta Pitaka,* of the canon of scripture of the Theravāda Buddhists. See SŪTRA.

Nikė. (Greek) 'victory', conquest, personified as the goddess of victory. In mythology she was said to be a daughter of a Titan (q.v.), yet to have fought with the gods against the Titans, perhaps as a symbol of their victory. She was patroness

of military and athletic contests and was represented on vases and in images. There was a famous statue in Delos, and on the Athenian Acropolis (q.v.) in the small but well preserved temple of Athena Niké. The Romans called her Victoria and she was worshipped by the army along with Mars.

Nikku. (Japanese) 'daily offerings', the regular worship of a Shinto temple, as distinct from the periodical celebrations called Matsuri (q.v.).

Nīla-Kantha. (Sanskrit) 'blue-throated', an epithet of the Hindu god Shiva (q.v.), derived from the story that he drank poison, which was produced when the gods churned the ocean for nectar (see AMRITA), and thus delivered them from danger.

Nile. See HAPI.

Nimbārka, Nimbāditya, Niyamānanda. A Telegu Brahmin teacher, known under these names, but especially the first. His dates are uncertain, perhaps the twelfth century A.D., as a younger contemporary of the great philosopher Rāmānuja. Like him Nimbārka was a philosopher and mystic of the worshippers of the god Vishnu. He held to the reality and absolute existence of God, the creator of the universe, and to the individual soul of man, who was dependent upon God but not identical with him. His philosophy is known as 'dualism non-dualism' (*dvaita-advaita*). He taught 'devotion' (*Bhakti*, q.v.) to Vishnu, in the form of Krishna, and his consort Rādhā. His followers were known as Nimbārkas, flourished in western India, and still exist today.

Nimbus. (Latin) a 'storm', cloud, and so a halo or aureole, a round light behind or over the heads of gods, heroes and emperors. Light shining from a sacred person is shown in the art of many countries. The Buddha was said to have a glow of light six metres all round him, and in Assyria the gods have rays round their shoulders, no doubt from comparison to the sun. The Nimbus appeared on Etruscan mirrors and Greek vases and became common in the Roman empire on paintings and mosaics, whence it entered Christian art.

Nine Songs. See CH'U TZ'Ŭ.

Ningal. Mother of the sun-god in Mesopotamian mythology and consort of the moon-god Sin (q.v.).

Ninigi. Grandson of the Shinto supreme deity, Amaterasu-ōmi-kami, who came down from heaven and married the goddess of Mount Fuji, from them coming the Japanese royal family. He is often called the Divine Grandchild. See AMATERASU and FUJI-SAN.

Ninlil. Mesopotamian goddess, feminine counterpart of the storm god Enlil (q.v.), called Queen, Mother of the Gods, Lady of town and house. She is sometimes confused with Ishtar, or made consort of Dagon (qq.v.).

Ninmach, Nintu, Ninkhursagga. Names of the mother-goddess in Mesopotamian religion and one of the principal deities. She was especially associated with childbirth, but she was also active with Ea or Enlil (qq.v.) in the creation of the human race.

Niobe. Daughter of Tantalus (q.v.) in Greek mythology. With her husband Amphion she had twelve children but incurred the jealousy of the goddess Leto, whose two children, Apollo and Artemis, killed all Niobe's children. Niobe wept and wept, and then was turned to stone.

'Niobe all tears' (*Hamlet*) became a model of parental grief for the high infant mortality of ancient times and was often represented in art.

Niord. See NJÖRD.

Nirākāra, Nirankar. Nirākāra is Sanskrit for 'formless', incorporeal, used of the neuter Brahman, and also of the transcendent Shiva or Vishnu. It is also applied to the doctrine that perception of the outer world does not come from forms impressed on the mind. Nirankar is Punjabi, used by Sikhs to describe God as 'the formless One.' See NIRGUNA.

Nirgrantha. (Sanskrit) 'free from bonds', a name sometimes given to Jain and Buddhist mendicants. The Nirgrantha Jains are said to have been founded by Pārshva (q.v.),; the name was used later for the monks who followed Mahāvīra (q.v.) See JAINS.

Nirguna. (Sanskrit) 'without a strand' (see Guna), having no qualities or attributes. In Hindu philosophy created beings are made up of three strands or Gunas: the qualities of goodness, passion and darkness. But the absolute Brahman is often said to be without qualities or attributes, Nirguna, though theistic works such as the *Shvetāshvatara Upanishad* (q.v.) insist that God is both with and without qualities. See Saguna and Anthropomorphism.

Nirmāna-kāya. (Sanskrit) 'transformation-body', in Mahāyāna Buddhism the means by which the Buddha is manifested for the benefit of humanity. See Trikāya.

Nirvāna. (Sanskrit) 'blown out', 'extinguished' (Pali, *Nibbāna*). A technical term for an indescribable state of bliss achieved by enlightened and liberated beings after death. It was used by the Jains for the place of liberated souls at 'the ceiling of the universe'. Among Buddhists it has been said to indicate extinction, but this is not in the sense of annihilation of being. What is 'blown out' is desire, without which men would return to earth in a constant round of transmigration. Buddhist texts compare Nirvāna to the calm of a mountain peak or to a wishing-jewel. The word Nirvāna is not found in the older Hindu *Vedas* and *Upanishads*, but appears in the *Bhagavad-Gītā* and the *Mahābhārata* and has been commonly used since in the meaning of the abode of liberated souls in union with the divine.

Nitya. (Sanskrit) 'innate', eternal, constantly dwelling in or intent upon, used of a constant act or an eternal truth. Reality is defined in Hindu philosophy as Nitya, eternal, and the soul (ātman) is this, though in Buddhist thought the self is impermanent, Anitya or Anicca.

Niveditā, Sister. The name assumed by Miss Margaret Noble (1866–1911) who became the disciple of Swāmī Vivekānanda (q.v.) on his visit to England in 1896. She took the name Niveditā, 'dedicated', and settled in Calcutta, living as a Hindu and establishing a school for girls, which still exists. Her chief writing, *The Web of Indian Life*, is full of sympathy with Hindu ideals and justifications of practices, some of which Hindu reformers had rejected.

Nīya. (Arabic) 'intention', a declaration by a Muslim of sincere intention to perform an act of worship. It is particularly obligatory before formal prayer (see Salāt), but has also been held to be required before alms, fasting, pilgrimage and sacrifice. Without the act of intention the ceremony would be vain or invalid (*bātil*).

Niyati. (Sanskrit) 'fixed order', necessity, fate. In Hindu mythology Niyati was sometimes personified as a daughter of Mount Meru (q.v.). In religion it could mean obligation or self-restraint. In philosophy the determinism of Niyati was the special doctrine of the Ājīvikas (q.v.).

Nizārīs. A sect of Ismā'īlī (q.v.) Islam. Nizār was eldest son of the Caliph al-Mustansir, but on his death he was passed over in favour of his younger brother al-Musta'lī. Nizār fled to Alexandria where he gathered supporters and raised a revolt, but he was captured and killed. His infant son was taken to Persia and brought up in secrecy as the true Caliph. The schism divided the Ismā'īlīs into Musta'lians (q.v.) and Nizārīs. The Nizārīs are found today in Syria, Persia, Afghanistan, central Asia, and India, with colonies in East Africa. They are reckoned to number about a quarter of a million. Many of them are called Khojas and follow the Aga Khān (q.v.).

Njörd. One of the principal Vanir, Scandinavian deities, who dwelt in Noatun, 'ship-haven', in heaven. He ruled the wind and calmed the sea and was worshipped by sailors. He married Skadi, daughter of a giant Thyaji, who wanted her husband to live in her home at Thrymheim in the mountains. Njörd wanted to stay by the sea and, although they agreed to spend nine nights in each place, it was not satisfactory. Njörd was identical with Nerthus (q.v.) whose cult was described by Tacitus.

Noble Eightfold Path. The last of the Four Noble Truths (q.v.) taught by the Buddha in his first sermon; a scheme of moral and spiritual training which leads to deliverance from suffering and full enlightenment. The Noble Eightfold Path can be divided into three sections, and each term has the adjective Right (*sammā*). The first two, Right Views and Right Resolve, indicate an understanding of the Buddhist way and the intention to follow it. Then come Right Speech, Right Action, Right Livelihood, concerned with correct living. Finally Right Effort, Right Mindfulness, and Right Concentration or Contemplation refer to the higher levels of spiritual exertion and meditation. See also Sammā.

Noble, Margaret. See Niveditā.

Non-Duality. See Advaita.

Norito. (Japanese) 'enunciation of

sacred words', words of praise and liturgical addresses offered to the Shinto gods. They are very ancient words and lists of offerings, including formulas of blessing (Yogoto) and prayers of congratulation (Iwaïgoto), many of which date from ancient texts such as the *Engi-shiki* (q.v.). Most of the Norito are very old specimens of Japanese composition, dating from the first century of our era. The Norito-den is a Hall for reciting the ritual prayers, found in Shinto temples; see JINJA.

Norn. One or more of the Fates of Norse mythology. The Well of Fate (Urdarbrunnr) lay at the foot of the world-tree Yggdrasil (q.v.), and from here the female Fate, Urdr (q.v.), laid down the course of human lives. Though sometimes personified, Urdr is often spoken about as abstract and her name is used of death. Two other Fates were associated with her (probably later): the Present (Verdandi) and the Future (Skuld).

No-Self. See ANATTĀ.

Notarikon. In Jewish Kabbalah (q.v.), the practice of taking the letters of a word individually as initials of other words, and so producing allegorical interpretations of the *Bible*. See also GEMATRIA.

Nūh. The name given in the *Qur'ān* to the Biblical Noah. He is a very popular figure as one of the prophets, appearing in 131 verses.

Numen. (Latin) 'a nod', and hence authority and power, and especially the power of the gods. Numen was not used of personal gods till the time of Augustus, but it was the power possessed by gods. Zeus was said to nod and shake the mountains, and all things obeyed his Numen. The Senate and the Emperor could possess Numen, and men asked gods for Numen when undertaking dangerous tasks. The Melanesian Mana (q.v.) has been compared to Numen.

In 1917 the German theologian Rudolf Otto, in his book *Das Heilige* ('The Idea of the Holy') coined the term Numinous to indicate the object of religious experience, the holy and terrible power of divinity. He called this Numinous 'the tremendous and fascinating mystery' (*mysterium tremendum et fascinans*).

Numitor. King of Alba Longa in Roman mythology, who was deposed by his brother Amulius and eventually restored by his grandson Romulus (q.v.).

Nun. Egyptian nature god, sometimes identified with the river Nile, or the sea, and later with the sun. He was a counterpart to the primeval mother Nut (q.v.). Nun appears in art as a man with a beard, sometimes with the head of a frog or snake. On his head are two feathers and water flows from his mouth. See also PTAH and OGDOAD.

Nūr. (Arabic) 'light', and used in Islamic expressions that God is light. A favourite 'light' verse of the *Qur'ān* (24, 35) says that 'God is the light of the heavens and the earth, like a niche in which is a lamp'. Sūfī mystics came to speculate about the light of God descending, and the human soul ascending to the realm of light. The Light of Muhammad, Nūr Muhammadī, was a term used to denote the pre-existence of Muhammad, through whom all souls emanated, and which was transmitted from age to age in the elect.

Nusairīs. An extreme Shī'a Muslim sect in Syria. The origin of the name is disputed but it may come from Ibn Nusair of Basra, who in A.D. 867 proclaimed himself the Door (*bāb*) or manifestation of the tenth Imām of the Shī'a (q.v.). The Nusairīs adopted many Neo-Platonic (q.v.) ideas, especially those of a series of emanations of heavenly beings from the ineffable divinity, and belief in the transmigration of souls. They have secret initiations and celebrate festivals which have absorbed ancient sun and moon cults.

Nusku. Assyrian god of fire, sometimes called the child of the moon-god Sin and associated with his cult. Nusku (like the Indian Agni, q.v.) burned the offerings made to the gods, and so was their minister and messenger. He was often represented by a lamp. The chief worship of Nusku was in the temple of Enlil (q.v.) at Nippur. Nusku was intermediary between earth and heaven, but he was also called judge, counsellor, and master of destiny.

Nut. Egyptian personification of the sky, and counterpart to the god of ocean,

Nun (q.v.). Nut was Lady of Heaven, but was also associated with the underworld. Heaven was feminine and Nut was stretched out over her husband Geb, the earth-god (q.v.), and supported by Shu, 'emptiness'. Nut is represented as a woman, sometimes with outstretched wings; she also appeared as a cow with legs at the four cardinal points. She is sometimes identified with Hathor and other goddesses.

Nyambe. The name for the supreme God is found in various forms as Nyambe, Nzambi, Tsambi, Zam, and so on, in a large area of tropical Africa, from Botswana to Cameroun. The origin of the name is unknown, but it may be related to ideas of causation and greatness. The title Onyame or 'Nyame, used by the Akan peoples of Ghana and the Ivory Coast, is similar but probably unrelated. Its links are more likely with a Sudanese word *Nyam*, indicating power.

Nyāsa. (Sanskrit) 'putting down', placing, abandoning. In some forms of Hindu worship Nyāsa is the assignment of parts of the body to particular deities, pointing to the limbs and uttering the sacred texts (*Mantras*, q.v.) appropriate to the gods which thereon enter the worshipper if his adoration has been effective.

Nyāya. (Sanskrit) 'method', the Logic school, one of the six orthodox systems of Hindu philosophy. Nyāya is said to have been founded by Gotama (q.v.) whose *Nyāya Sūtras* are dated between the third century B.C. and the second century A.D. Nyāya probably originated in efforts to formulate rules of logic for use in philosophical discussion. Later there was merging with ideas of the Vaisheshika (q.v.) school and introduction of ideas of divinity

Nyingmapa. (Tibetan) 'old ones', the older of the two dominant sects of Tibetan Buddhism (see GELUGSPA), often known as 'Red Hats' from their headdress. Some of the Nyingmapa lived nearer to the people than the Yellow Hats, married and helped in village work. They were also less literate and were addicted to magic, though many of their religious and magical books have not been translated into European languages and may form the basis for teachings of 'occult Mahatmas' proposed by Madame Blavatsky (q.v.). See LAMA.

Nymphs. (Greek) young unmarried women, and by extension female spirits who were supposed to inhabit hills, trees and waters. They were daughters of Zeus, generally helpful to men, associated with healing springs, but also inhabiting wild places. There were widespread cults of Nymphs, especially in caves.

Nyōrai. Japanese form of Tathāgata (q.v.).

Nyx. 'Night' in Greek mythology, personified as a great being, daughter of Chaos. She was feared even by Zeus but advised him in making the world. Nyx had great oracular powers and was important in Orphism (q.v.). She had little worship, but was especially prominent in stories of creation and in oracles which she gave from the cave of night.

O

Obeah. Religious and magical practices of the West Indies, largely of African origin. The word may be derived from the Twi language of Ghana in which an Obayifo is a witch. See also VOODOO.

Oceanus. The great cosmic power in Greek thought, and in mythology a kindly old god. Oceanus appears in Homer as the river which encircles the world and from which all other rivers flow, especially Styx (q.v.) in the underworld. The stars were thought to rise and set in Oceanus and the sun crossed it in a golden bowl during the night on the way back to the east. Oceanus was brother and husband of Tethys, from whom came not only the rivers but three thousand Oceanids, the nymphs who were favourable to young men. See also APSU.

Odin, Odinn. The chief god of many Teutonic and Scandinavian peoples, and as patron of poetry especially praised by bards. He is called Alfather, the 'Father of all', the gods being his children, but since he fought against some of them there are mingled traditions of Odin. He was also Valfather, 'Father of the slain', who were received by Odin into Valhalla. Odin was a god of war and he promoted strife by devious means, hence he was also a source of evil. Odin had a spear, Gungnir, which never missed; a horse, Sleipnir, with eight feet which bore him through the air; two ravens sitting on his shoulders told him all the news; and Odin drank wine but ate no food. He was lord of life and human sacrifices were offered to him. Odin was specially popular in Sweden and Denmark, and in north Germany and England where the god

Wotan and Woden was largely the same. From the latter came the name of Wednesday.

Odysseus. A legendary and heroic rather than a religious figure in Greek story, though he was occasionally worshipped but not in his homeland of Ithaca. For semi-religious references, see CHARYBDIS, CYCLOPES and CIRCE; see also HOMER.

ODYSSEUS AND THE SIRENS

Oedipus. In Greek mythology the 'swollen-footed' son of Laius and Jocasta. In Homer it is said that he married his mother unknowingly and she hanged herself, but Oedipus continued as king. In the later dramatists, Oedipus was thrown out by his father and brought up by a shepherd; he went to Delphi where the oracle told him that he would kill his father and marry his mother. At Thebes he solved the riddle of the Sphinx (q.v.), killing Laius on the way. Then he married Jocasta and she hanged herself while Oedipus blinded himself and went into exile. This is the version given by Sophocles. There is little religious reference in the story, but it has become notorious in modern times through its adoption by the psychologist Sigmund Freud, in *Totem and Taboo*, (1919) as the origin of religion. There is no historical evidence for this and the theory is generally rejected except by ardent Freudians. See also ELECTRA.

Oengus. Celtic deity, son of Dagda (q.v.), though in one story he expelled his father from a tumulus at New Grange, which perhaps suggests that he had become more popular than Dagda, or was a god of a conquering tribe. Oengus Mac ind Oc, 'son of the young ones', may have been a fertility deity, but he was popular in story as patron of Diarmaid (q.v.), a hero of the Fionn saga, and helped him to defeat his enemies by changing their shapes.

Ogdoad. From Greek 'eight', a name applied in Egyptian religion to an Ogdoad of deities at Hermopolis. These were eight ancient (and some of them rather vague) gods who represented the watery abyss from which came all things. The eight were: Nun (q.v.) and Nunet, Huh and Huhet, Kuk and Kuket, Amūn (q.v.) and Amunet. These eight gods created the sun, Rēʻ (q.v.), and brought the primeval chaos to an end. See ENNEAD.

Ogma. Celtic god of poetry and eloquence, and given the title 'son of knowledge'. Eloquence and poetry were honoured by the Celtic bards and their protecting god was also called 'he of the smiling face'. He championed the Tuatha Dé Danann (q.v.) gods in their battles.

Ogŭn, Ogou. Ogŭn is the god of iron among the Yoruba peoples of Nigeria, known in Dahomey as Gu. He is a god of all metal and metal users, and thus of blacksmiths, hunters and soldiers. Cyclists and lorry drivers carry protective charms from Ogŭn and oaths are sworn in his name on metal objects. In the Voodoo of Haiti he appears as Ogou, and variants on this name appear in the Loa gods (q.v.).

Oharaë. (Japanese) 'great expulsion', a Shintō ritual for driving away sins and impurities. It is held at the end of June and December, but also at other times of trouble and before the beginning of festivals.

Ohrmazd. Name of the supreme deity among the Zoroastrians and their modern Parsi descendants. After the time of Zoroaster, Ohrmazd became the popular form of the name Ahura Mazdā (q.v.).

Oisin. See OSSIAN.

Ojin. Japanese form of Nirmāna-kāya; see TRIKĀYA.

Olcott, Henry Steel. American journalist (1830–1907), who had served as colonel in the federal army in the Civil War, and in 1875 founded the Theosophical Society in New York with Helena Blavatsky (q.v.). Later he helped in developing Buddhist education in Ceylon.

Old Man of the Mountains. Name given by Crusaders to Hasan ibn Sabbāh, founder of the Assassins (qq.v.). One of the first reports, in 1175, said that they were called Heyssessini or Segnors de Montana, and their violent methods were said to strike fear into both Saracen princes and Christian lords.

Olodumarè. A name of God among the Yoruba of Nigeria, generally translated as 'Almighty'. Split into its component parts, Ọl-ódù-marè, has been interpreted as 'the owner-of authority-that remains'. See OLORŬN.

Olorŭn. A name of God among the Yoruba of Nigeria, meaning 'the owner of heaven' (*orŭn*). See OLODUMARÈ.

Olympia, Olympus. The principal sanctuary of Zeus in Greece was at Olympia, in the heart of the Peloponnesus. It is said to have been first a shrine of the oracle of Earth, like Delphi, and was probably pre-Hellenic. The foundations and many pillars of the temple of Zeus remain, and ruins of temples to other gods. The Olympian flame is still lit at the ruined shrine of Hestia (q.v.).

The Olympic Games were in honour of Olympian Zeus, founded in 776 B.C. and held every four years, till they were abolished by the emperor Theodosius I in A.D. 393 (or in 426 by Theodosius II).

Mount Olympus is the highest peak in Greece, on the borders of Thessaly and Macedonia, and was said to be the home of the gods.

Om. The most sacred word of the Hindus, occurring first in the *Upanishads*. It is composed of the sounds A, U, M and a humming nasalization, and so it is said to represent the three oldest *Vedas*, and the triad of gods: Vishnu, Shiva and Brahmā. Om is placed at the beginning of works, like 'Hail', and at the end like 'Amen'. It is written at the head of books and papers and uttered before prayers.

Om is used also by Buddhists, and in Tibet the exclamation *Om mani padme hum* is constantly uttered, written on prayer-flags, wheels and walls, and muttered with prayer-beads. This phrase means 'Hail, the jewel in the lotus, hail', the jewel being the Buddhist doctrine and the lotus the scripture or reality.

Omar, Caliph. See 'UMAR.

Omar's Mosque. See DOME OF THE ROCK.

Omar or **'Umar Khayyām.** Astronomer, mathematician and poet of Persia (died 1123). Seventy-five verses of his *Rubā'iyāt* were translated by Edward Fitzgerald in 1859 and have remained very popular in the English-speaking world, as much for the running rhymes as for the hedonistic and even cynical sentiments expressed in them. Critics have asserted that Fitzgerald imported scepticism into Omar, paraphrasing and

even inventing lines and verses. In Persia, at least, Omar is regarded not as a sceptic but as a Sūfī mystic; the symbolism of bread, wine, love, songs and solitude can all be given mystical meaning.

Omen. Portent of good or evil, from Latin, perhaps derived from *audire*, to hear. See AUGURS.

Ometecuhtli. 'Lord of duality', in Aztec mythology, a deity above and different from all others, being both male and female. He was the maker and sustainer of all, both Fire and the Pole Star. In his male aspect he was Tonacatecuhtli, 'lord of our subsistence', creator of all and chief of gods. In his female aspect he was Tonacacihuatl, 'lady of our subsistence'.

O-mi-t'o Fo. Chinese name of the Buddhist Amitābha (q.v.).

Omoto. (Japanese) 'great foundation', a modern Japanese religious movement founded in 1892 by Mrs Deguchi. It was prohibited in 1937 but began again in 1946. It borrows elements from other religions and believes in one pervading God and in the brotherhood of men. The followers of Omoto are not many, about ninety thousand, but its influence is widespread through literature. See SEKAI-KYUSEIKYO and SEICHO NO IE.

Omphalos. (Greek) 'navel', applied to stones in the shape of a navel which were used in ancient Greek cults. The most famous of such stones was in the temple of Apollo at Delphi (q.v.) which was thought to indicate the centre of the earth. In many other mythologies the most sacred place was regarded as the navel of the earth, such as Jerusalem, Mecca or Benares.

OMPHALOS STONE

Onamochi, Onamuchi - no - kami. Shinto deity, son of Susano-wo (q.v.). His name is usually translated 'great name possessor' and he is also called O-kuni-nushi-no-kami, 'master of the great land' or 'great administrator'. In mythology he had to begin to make the land by overcoming the powers of sea, wind, animals and fire. He was taken as protector by Tendai Buddhists.

Onkelos. Aramaic pronunciation of Aquila, whose *Targum* (qq.v.) on the *Pentateuch*, perhaps dating from the second century A.D., was the oldest to be officially adopted. Aramaic is not spoken now, but pious Jews still read the *Onkelos Targum.*

Onuris. A minor god of ancient Egypt, a warrior and closely connected with Horus (q.v.). He was identified in Greek times with Ares. He is represented as a man with a beard, with a spear in his hand and four plumes on his head.

Onyame. See NYAMBE.

Opening the Mouth. Ceremony performed in ancient Egypt to enable a dead person to make the correct responses in the afterlife. See MUMMY and PTAH.

Ops. Roman goddess, probably of agriculture. Her festivals were at the end of harvest on 25 August and the autumn sowing on 19 December. The god Consus (q.v.) was celebrated on the same dates, and later he was identified with the Greek god Kronos (q.v.) and Ops with Rhea.

Oracle. From Latin *orare*, 'to speak', an Oracle denotes a message from a god, the place where such message is received, the person giving the message, and generally a holy place. There were many Oracles in ancient times, that of Apollo at Delphi (q.v.) being one of the most famous. Zeus was also an Oracle at Dodona and Olympia. Famous far beyond Egypt was the Oracle of Ammon or Amūn (q.v.) at Thebes which was visited by Alexander the Great. A modern oracle is the Ifa (q.v.) of Nigeria.

Orenda. See WAKAN.

Origins of Religion. See ANIMISM, FRAZER, FREUD, MÜLLER, TYLOR, TOTEM.

Orion. A giant and hunter in Greek mythology, since the time of Homer identified with the constellation that bears his name. Orion loved the goddess of dawn, Eos (q.v.), but the gods were jealous and Artemis killed him with her arrows. In other stories he is said to be chasing the Pleiades, since their constellation rises above the horizon just before his.

Ormuzd. See OHRMAZD.

Orpheus, Orphism. Orphism was a religious cult of ancient Greece, said to have been founded by Orpheus of Thrace. Orpheus was famous as a singer and lyre-player, who charmed even beasts and trees. His most famous myth tells of the death of his wife Eurydice (q.v.) from a snakebite and the journey of Orpheus into the underworld to persuade its lord to allow her return. This was promised on condition that Orpheus did not turn round and look at her before reaching the earth, but he could not resist so she vanished. There was an Orphic poem, 'Descent into the Underworld', and in another myth Orpheus himself was slain. The Orphics believed in punishments in the underworld and also in the transmigration of souls. According to Plato they regarded the body as evil, as a tomb of the soul, and they also would not kill animals or eat meat. Both Dionysus and Apollo were worshipped by the Orphics, and after being despised in the classical age Orphism revived to become one of the great Mysteries (q.v.) in Hellenistic times.

Orunmila. 'Heaven knows salvation', an oracular deity and protector of the Yoruba of Nigeria, often identified with the oracle of Ifa (q.v.).

Osiris. The most popular of Egyptian gods, on account of his peaceful and generous nature, and the myth of his death and rule of the underworld. Osiris was son of Geb and Nut (earth and sky, qq.v.), brother of Set and Isis, husband of Isis and father of Horus. Osiris was killed by his brother Set and his body divided into fourteen or sixteen parts. Isis sought out the pieces and buried them; in another version the assembled body was embalmed and a sycamore tree enveloped it. Horus was born later and he and Isis used words and ceremonies supplied by the magician-god Thoth. Osiris was revived and reigned in the underworld as king of the dead and lord of eternity. This story doubtless embodies vegetation myths and Osiris is depicted with corn springing from his body. Osiris is most often represented as a man with beard on a throne, wearing a pointed crown and holding the crook and flail of upper and lower Egypt.

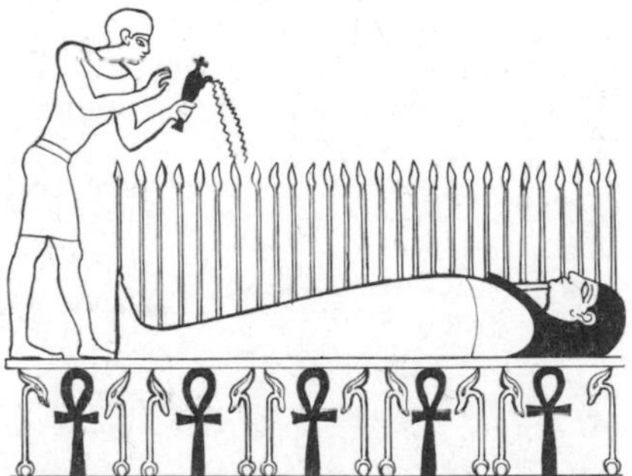

Ossian. More properly Oisin, an Irish mythical hero, son of Fionn (q.v.). Oisin was a poet and joined his father in many fights, at last being one of the few survivors. Oisin went to the 'land of youth' (Tir na n-Og, q.v.) and stayed for a long time, which seemed very short, but when he returned to earth he became an old man. He is said to have met St Patrick. In 1762-63 James Macpherson published epic poems called *Fingal* and *Temora*, supposedly translated from the poet Ossian, which were much admired by romantics. Their authenticity was challenged by Dr Johnson and others and it was shown that Macpherson had given versions of traditional Gaelic poems with liberal insertions of his own. See FINGAL.

Othman. See 'UTHMĀN.

Ouranos. The sky, in Greek mythology. The Latin form of the name was Uranus and Varuna was a related deity in Hindu mythology. Ouranos was the child and husband of Gaea (q.v.), and their offspring were the Titans and Cyclopes. Kronos (q.v.), the youngest of the Titans, castrated Ouranos so that he separated from Gaea and left room for the Titans between heaven and earth.

Outcastes. Now called Scheduled Classes or Exterior Castes, these people are outside the Indian Class system (see CASTE) and are estimated at well over sixty millions. Their definition is difficult, but generally they are said to pollute a caste Hindu by contact or proximity and are barred from wells, villages and temples. Outcastes include many subclasses, who have their own taboos. Even the lowly Doms, executioners and assistants at funerals, have artisan groups with special crafts who repudiate the scavenging of city Doms. They were probably related to our Gipsies (name derived from Egyptian) who called themselves Rom and Romany, but in Syria are called Doum. See also GĀNDHI.

Oya. Goddess of the river Niger in the mythology of the Yoruba of Nigeria, and wife of the thunder god Shango (q.v.). Shango chased her across the sky all day till she hid in the sea at night. Oya is said to be beautiful but also terrible, with a fierce beard, and sometimes she is associated with a wind that blows down trees and houses.

P

Pacceka. See PRATYEKA-BUDDHA.

Pachacamac. 'Lord of the Earth', in Inca religion who was said to create the earthquakes in the interior of the earth. His great pyramid temple rivalled that of the Sun and was a centre of pilgrimage. It overshadows the city of Pachacamac in the Lurin valley, covers about five hectares and rises to a height of about twenty-three metres. The Spanish conqueror Pizarro heard of the treasure of Pachacamac and sent his brother Fernando there. Fernando destroyed the image of the god but most of the gold had been hidden, though part was later recovered.

Pachamama. 'Earth mother' of the Incas of Peru and neighbouring peoples, who was invoked in daily rites, especially in the highlands, and presided over agriculture. See Mamacocha. Pachamama was also represented by Amaru, a mythical dragon, who lived under the earth and manifested itself in earthquakes, in fire that comes from volcanoes, and in landslides in the rainy season.

Padma. 'Lotus' (Sanskrit), the name of a *Purāna*, generally placed second in this series of Hindu stories. It deals with the period when the world was a golden Lotus, with creation, heaven and earth. The *Padma Purāna* is devoted to the god Vishnu and in it the rival god Shiva praises Vishnu.

Padmāsana. (Sanskrit) 'lotus posture', in Hindu Yoga practices; see ĀSANA.

Padma Sambhava. The 'Lotus-born', a Buddhist monk of north India who belonged to the Yogāchāra sect and was an expert in Tantric Buddhism (q.v.). In A.D. 747 he was invited to Tibet by King Khri-Srong to strengthen Buddhism which had been in that country for little over a century. Padma Sambhava built a monastery at Samye, about 48 kilometres from Lhasa, and was greatly revered by Tibetans who called him Guru or 'the second Buddha'. When his work was finished he vanished from Tibet, leaving behind him twenty-five disciples who continued his teaching. Padma Sambhava does not appear to have been celibate but had female companions, and he was an exorcist and magician. Pictures show him as rather fierce and with strongly marked features. See CHENRESI.

Paean. A hymn of praise to Apollo as Healer (Paian). Paeans were sung to other gods, such as Zeus and Dionysus, and similar chants in unison were sung by guests at meals, on military and public occasions, and in Hellenistic times to successful individuals.

Pagan. The word comes from Latin *paganus*, 'a countryman', used by Christians from the fourth century to indicate the country people who had not accepted the new faith like town-dwellers. The English word 'heathen', perhaps an inhabitant of the heaths, suggests the same notion. In modern times both 'Pagan' and 'Heathen' have been used of believers in other religions or in none, but this is unfortunate since it appears to suggest that such people are ignorant or irreligious. Most scholarly books on the comparative study of religions have abandoned both these names.

Pagoda. In Burma and other lands of south-east Asia, and China, Japan and Korea, a building constructed over Buddhist relics. The word is said to be derived from the Ceylonese Dāgoba (q.v.). In Burma there are countless Pagodas, large and small, many of them graceful white-washed conical buildings, from whose spires there hang brass leaves which tinkle in the wind. The Golden Pagoda, Shwe Dagon, in Rangoon stands about 61 metres high, is covered with gold leaf, and contains solid gold statues of the Buddha, as well as countless stone and plaster images in its shrines and courtyards. In China the Buddhist Pagodas replaced earlier towers, were erected in auspicious places (see FÊNG SHUI), and should always have an odd number of storeys. For the Seven Pagodas, see MAHABALIPURAM, see also BLACK PAGODA.

Pa Hsien. In Chinese Taoist mythology the Eight Immortals who live in the Realm of Great Purity. For their names, see IMMORTALS.

Pa Kua. (Chinese) Eight Trigrams, ascribed to the emperor Fu-shi, expressing the classical world view and used in magical practices. For these diagrams, see TRIGRAMS.

Palden Lhamo, Dpaldan Lhamo. The chief goddess of the ancient Bon (q.v.) religion of Tibet and guardian of Tibetan Buddhism, especially the Gelugspa or Yellow Hat sect. She is much like the Hindu Kālī (q.v.), being black, thin, with four hands, wielding terrifying weapons, and garlanded with snakes and skulls. See SRONG MA.

Pali. The scriptural language of Theravāda Buddhism (q.v.), in which their versions of the teachings of the Buddha and his followers are preserved (see TRIPITAKA). Hence Theravāda is sometimes called Pali Buddhism.

Pallas. A title of the Greek goddess Athena (q.v.). In Homer it is always used in the compound Pallas Athena, but later Pallas is used alone for Athena. A late legend said that Pallas was a goddess killed accidentally by Athena who made the Palladium in her memory. The Palladium was an ancient image of Pallas Athena, said to have been sent down by Zeus from heaven to Troy. Perhaps many cities had such images and in Greece Athens claimed to have the Palladium, because it was the city of Athena.

Pan. A Greek god of herdsmen, his name perhaps meaning 'the Feeder'. He was represented with legs, horns and ears like a goat, but the rest of him human. He was son of Hermes but had little mythology and was thought of as haunting mountains and caves and playing on the pan-pipe which Greek shepherds still use. When Pan was adopted by Athens, he was given a shrine in a cave on the Acropolis and annual sacrifices were held. Then his name was associated with *pan*, meaning 'all', and he came to be regarded as a universal god. For *Hymn to Pan*, see HOMER.

Pañcha-rātra. Some of the oldest forms of the worship of Vishnu in Hinduism. The name means 'five nights' and, when it first appears, the great god Nārāyana (Vishnu) saw that the five-day sacrifice would make him superior to all gods. There are also said to be five vehicles or forms of doctrine connected with different branches of the Pañcha-rātras. When they were unified, they taught belief in the one god Vishnu, advocated devotion (*bhakti*, q.v.) to him, condemned sacrifices and austerities, and taught simple forms of worship. There is a considerable Pañcha-rātra literature, and the influence of the doctrines has been great on devotional Hinduism. See EMANATION.

Pañcha-tantra. (Sanskrit) 'five books', an anonymous collection of Indian stories in five sections. The stories are said to have been told by a Brahmin priest called Vishnusharma to three princes for their education. The *Pañcha-tantra* consists of fables of animals which not only display fidelity or hypocrisy, but also study the *Vedas* and perform religious ceremonies. The tales were very popular and were translated and copied in other languages, coming to Europe in the Middle Ages as the 'Fables of Bidpai' (or 'Pilpay').

Panchen Lama. Title popularly given to one of the leading abbots in Tibetan Buddhism. The name Pan-chen Rin-po, 'Precious Teacher', was adopted in the sixteenth or seventeenth century by the Lamas of Tashi-lhunpo near Shigatse, whence they are also sometimes called Tashi Lamas. They are believed to be reincarnations of the Buddha of Infinite Light, Amitābha (q.v.), and at the death of one Lama a search is made for a successor born about the same time, as with the Dalai Lama (q.v.). Though important spiritually, (and some claimed superior to him), the Panchen Lamas were more limited to spiritual affairs than the Dalai Lama. Under modern Chinese rule, both the Dalai Lama and Panchen Ngoerhtehni were photographed in Peking in 1954, preaching, and voting for the Chinese constitution. When the Dalai Lama fled, there was some effort to put forth the Panchen as the true and loyal leader in Tibet, but from time to time rumours have circulated that he was married or dead. In 1969 it was said that the Panchen Lama had escaped from Tibet, but no countries nearby reported having received him.

Pandit. See PUNDIT.

Pandora. (Greek) 'all gifts', in mythology said to be the first woman created by Zeus to bring confusion to mankind. She was made of clay by Hephaestus and married to Epimetheus, the simple-minded brother of Prometheus. Despite the latter's warnings, she let out all evils from Pandora's Box, or store jar, except Hope which remained to console mankind. Pandora was perhaps originally an earth goddess.

Pāndu. Indian king, brother of Dhritarāshtra (q.v.), husband of Kuntī (q.v.). His five sons were the Pāndus or Pāndavas, whose adventures form a large part of the epic *Mahābhārata* in their struggle to regain the kingdom from the Kurus. The two chief sons were Yudhi-shthira and Arjuna.

Panentheism. A modification of the theory of Pantheism (q.v.), wherein it is affirmed that, while all things are in (*en*) God, he is more than a summary of the parts.

Pānini. Famous Indian grammarian of the fourth century B.C. His masterpiece was the *Ashtādhyāyī*, 'eight chapters', consisting of some four thousand sūtras or aphorisms, of two or three words only. The terseness of his system necessitated the writing of commentaries, one of the chief being the *Mahābhāshya*, 'great commentary', of Patañjali (q.v.). Pānini fixed the rules for the Sanskrit (q.v.) language, which now became known as Samskrita, 'perfected', opposed to the Prakrita, 'unrefined' or popular.

Pansil, Pancha-shīla. See SHĪLA.

Pantheism. From two Greek words, *pan*, all, and *theos*, god. Pantheism is taken to express the belief that all is God or God is all, merging all things into the divine and denying personality to God or anyone else. A modification, to allow some transcendence to God, is in Panentheism (q.v.); for Indian forms, see MONISM and ADVAITA.

Pantheon. (Greek) 'all the gods', a term used to describe all the deities, either of Greek or other peoples. The great building called the Pantheon in Rome was first built in A.D. 27 by Agrippa, and rebuilt by Hadrian in 126 and dedicated to 'all the gods'. It was re-dedicated to the Virgin Mary and all the saints in 609 and still stands.

Pao P'o Tzŭ, Pao P'u Tzŭ. A classic of Taoism, giving fundamental teachings on alchemy, magic and dietetics by which adepts sought to attain immortality. It is attributed to Ko Hung (q.v.), about A.D. 326. The work describes breathing exercises, perhaps adapted from Indian Yoga, to increase powers of body and mind. The diet should be only air and dew, natural good which was supposed to give immunity from sickness. The alchemy sought to discover liquid or eatable gold which would bestow immortality.

Papa. The 'earth' in Maori religion, female and the wife of the sky, Rangi (q.v.). From Papa was formed the first

PANTHEON

woman, who became the wife of the chief god, Tane (q.v.).

Paradise. See Janna, Houris and Tyr na n'og.

Paradise Sūtra. See Mahāparinibbāna.

Paramātman. (Sanskrit) 'supreme soul' or self, used as a title of a personal God, or of the absolute Brahman (q.v.). See Ātman and Jīva.

Parameshthin. 'Standing in the highest place' (Sanskrit), a title given to superior gods in Hindu mythology and to some distinguished mortals.

Pāramitās. 'Perfections', the six or ten stages followed by a Buddhist saint to achieve perfection (from Sanskrit, 'to cross over', transcend, become perfect). The Six Perfections are: Dāna, giving; Shīla (q.v.), moral conduct; Kshānti, resignation; Vīrya, Vigour; Dhyāna, meditation; Prajñā, wisdom. To these are sometimes added four more: skill in teaching, power over obstacles, spiritual aspiration, and wisdom. See Prajñā.

Parashu-Rāma. 'Rāma with the Axe', one of the Avatars (q.v.) of Vishnu, and sometimes reckoned sixth of ten Avatars. The story of Parashu-Rāma is told in the *Mahābhārata* and the *Purānas*. He was a Brahmin, descendant of a Vedic sage Bhrigu. He was under the protection of the god Shiva, who gave him the axe (Parashu) after which he is named. In anger he cut off the head of his mother, Renukā, for her impure thoughts, and then begged for her return to life. His conflict with the Kshatriya warrior-rulers suggests hostility between them and Brahmins. Parashu-Rāma is said to have destroyed the Kshatriya class several times. He also came into clashes with the next Avatar, Rāma-chandra, and was angered when the latter Rāma defeated him by breaking Shiva's bow. This led to his defeat and he was sometimes called 'the inferior'.

Parcae. (Latin) 'fates', Parca, Fortuna and Necessitas, often identified with the Greek Moirai (q.v., and see Fate).

Parentalia. Roman feast of departed souls, 13–21 February. On most of these days rites were celebrated for the dead of each family, Di Parentes or Parentum, and they were Dies Religiosi during which temples were closed and weddings prohibited. The last day was the Feralia, a public ritual about which little is known. See also Manes.

Pari-Nirvāna. (Sanskrit) 'complete Nirvāna', entire cessation of rebirths. This is the final state of a Buddha who has already achieved Nirvāna on earth and on passing away will not be reborn. See Nirvāna.

Parivrājaka. (Sanskrit) a 'wandering' ascetic and religious mendicant, in Hinduism and Jainism. Such men have been generally less orthodox than the forest hermits (see Vāna-prastha) who are fulfilling a stage of life's duties, and they have held very various doctrines.

Parjanya. The rain-god of the Indian *Vedas*, or the rain personified. A few hymns are addressed to Parjanya; sometimes it is combined with the wind, Vāta; later it is the guardian deity of rain and clouds and may be applied to the god Indra. Parjanya is also the name of one of the Ādityas (q.v.).

Parmenides. Greek philosopher of Elea, about 450 B.C. Like other Eleatic philosophers he taught a variety of Monism, since that which is exists without beginning or end, is single and changeless, like a sphere, and the diversity of nature is only apparent. See Zeno of Elea.

Pārshva. The twenty-second Jina or Tīrthankara of Jainism (q.v.). He was born at Benares (Kāshī) of King Ashvasena and Queen Vāmā, about 872 B.C., and is said to have lived one hundred years. Pārshva married but at the age of thirty left home, gave away his possessions, and adopted an ascetic life. He founded an order of monks, Nirgranthas, who were perhaps the first white-clad monks of Jainism. The parents of the better known Mahāvīra (q.v.) were followers of Pārshva, and like him they died of voluntary

starvation to avoid accumulating any good or bad Karma which would entail rebirth on earth. The life of Pārshva is related in the Jain scripture *Kalpa Sūtra*. See NIRGRANTHAS.

Parsis, Parsees. From the name *Pars* for Persia, these 'Persians' are the modern descendants in India of ancient Zoroastrianism (q.v.). Their religion was dominant in Persia (Iran), but the Muslim conquest in A.D. 652 made Persia a largely Muslim land. The Zoroastrians were tolerated, and occasionally persecuted, and in the eighth century a minority emigrated to Gujerat in India; since the seventeenth century they have been mostly concentrated in Bombay. Small groups are found elsewhere, some in East Africa. In India they number about 125,000. The Parsis hold to Zoroastrian teachings, mingled with some Indian beliefs and customs. They are noted for their 'Fire Temples' (q.v.), where the sacred flame forever burns, and for the Dakhmās or 'Towers of Silence' (q.v.) where the dead are exposed. The Parsis are a small but active and educated minority and they have played a considerable role in Indian life. See GABARS.

Pārtha. A common name in Hindu epic mythology, applied to the three elder Pāndus or Pāndavas, as sons of their mother Prithā or Kuntī (q.v.). See ARJUNA.

Parthenon. The most famous Greek temple, built under Pericles in Athens (447–432 B.C.) on the Acropolis hill and still preserved, though without a roof or many of the original sculptures, some of which are in the British Museum. It was dedicated to the 'virgin' (*parthenos*) goddess Athena and originally contained a great statue of Athena by Phidias. Friezes represented the Panathenaic Procession, the birth of Athena, and her struggle with Poseidon for the land of Attica. See ACROPOLIS and ATHENA.

Pārvatī. 'The mountaineer', a goddess daughter of the Himalayas, and one of the names of the consort of the god Shiva. Shiva at first scorned Pārvatī for her dark colour, since she was an ancient Indian goddess, and she took to rigorous asceticism which made her body glow and disturbed Shiva. In order to test her, he appeared as a dwarf and vilified Shiva, whereupon Pārvatī defended him. They were married and had two children, the

PĀRVATĪ, SHIVA AND FAMILY

six-headed Kārttikeya, and the elephant-headed Ganesha (qq.v.). Pictures show the family amid the Himalayan snows.

Paschal. See PASSOVER.

Pāshupatas. A sect of followers of Shiva, named after his title as Pāshupati, 'lord of animals.' On Mohenjodaro (q.v.) seals there sometimes appears a figure like Shiva, surrounded by animals, and this is regarded as his first representation in art. The Pāshupatas taught a doctrine of 'difference non-difference', a modification of monism (q.v.), in which Shiva is the supreme Lord and cause of all things. They taught a Yoga discipline, simple ascetic rules, and union with Shiva through meditation. Some branches degenerated into magical and immoral practices and gained a bad reputation, but more enlightened ones were active in education from the twelfth century.

Pasiphae. In Greek mythology a daughter of Helios, the sun god, and wife of Minos (q.v.), king of Crete, Her name meant 'all-shining'. She fell in love with a bull sent by the sea god Poseidon, disguised herself as a cow with the help of Daedalus, and bore the half-human half-bull, Minotaur (q.v.).

Passion Play. For Shī'a Muslims the re-enactment of the death of Husain. See HUSAIN and MUHARRAM.

Passover, Pesach. Chief festival of the Jewish year, named from the occasion when God 'passed over' the Israelites in Egypt (*Exodus* 12, 27). From Hebrew *Pesach* came the name of Paschal Lamb for the animals that formerly were sacrificed at this time. It was a spring festival, both of newborn lambs and of the barley harvest, and celebrated the Exodus of the Hebrews from Egypt. Passover begins on 19 Nisan (March–April), and lasts eight days, during which time all leavened food must be kept out of Jewish houses. It is introduced by a service at home, Seder (q.v.), which recalls past history and looks to the future.

Pātāla. In Indian mythology the seven subterranean regions, abode of demons and Nāga snakes (q.v.). It was the lowest part of the 'world egg', the universe. See BRĀHMANDA.

Patañjali. Indian philosopher and reputed author of the *Yoga Sūtras* (q.v.). Patañjali was not the founder of Yoga, which on the evidence of remains at Harappā (q.v.) and elsewhere seems to have been in existence for many centuries; but he collected ideas associated with Yoga, joined them to the Sāmkhya (q.v.) philosophy, and produced the short work, in four chapters or books, attributed to him. The date of Patañjali is much disputed, and two or even three Patañjalis have been suggested – a grammarian, a Yoga writer and a commentator. The first two are probably the same, and the commentator came later. Part of the argument for a late date depends upon possible criticisms of Buddhism in the fourth book, but this itself may be later than the earlier books. Suggestions for the date of Patañjali range from the second century B.C. to the fifth century A.D., with probability nearer the first period. See also PĀNINI.

Pātimokkha. (Pali; Sanskrit, **Prātimoksha.**) A term perhaps originally meaning 'binding', and used in the sense of freeing from punishment, but the explanations are obscure and debatable. The Pātimokkha forms part of the first section of the *Vinaya Pitaka* (q.v.), the first of the three divisions of the Buddhist canon of scripture. It is composed of 227 rules, which are recited at the fortnightly or weekly fast days (Uposatha, q.v.) at the new and full moon, by Buddhist monks and nuns. The basic rules of the Pātimokkha may go back to the Buddha himself, or his immediate disciples, since they agree in several Pali and Sanskrit versions.

Patrilineal. Descent counted through the father's side, important in rules and taboos of affinity for marriage. See EXOGAMY and MATRILINEAL.

Patta. (Sanskrit) a 'tablet', a copper plate for inscribing orders. Also used by followers of Vishnu of metal and stone plaques which have pictures of the god and his Avatars. See YANTRA.

Pavana. (Sanskrit) the 'wind', or god of the wind. In Hindu epic mythology he was father of Hanumān (q.v.), the monkey god.

Pax. (Latin) 'peace', personified as a goddess at a late date, and identified with the Greek Eirene (q.v.). Temples to Pax were built around the beginning of the Christian era.

Peepul. See PIPAL and BO-TREE.

Pegasus. A winged horse in Greek mythology who carried the thunderbolt of Zeus. His mother was the dying Gorgon (q.v.). Pegasus was tamed by the hero Bellerophon and helped him to fight the Chimaera (q.v.) and the Amazons, but he threw Bellerophon off when the hero tried to fly to heaven. See HIPPOCRENE.

Peking. See TEMPLE OF HEAVEN.

Pekwin. 'Place of speech', the chief

religious figure of the Zuñi of New Mexico, responsible for the material and spiritual welfare of the people. His power comes from the 'sun father', and his task is the observation of the solstices. In December he watches the movements of the sun and in due course announces that everyone must plant 'prayer sticks'. These are of different forms and sizes and varied colours, according to the gods and the status of the worshipper. Each has a tuft of feathers at the end. The prayer sticks are placed at shrines and in maize fields and their feathers waft up prayers to the gods for fertility.

Penates. The guardian spirits of the store cupboard (*penus*) in ancient Rome, worshipped along with the Lares and Vesta (qq.v.). The Di Penates were the most important spirits of the household and also had a public worship as Penates Publici. Penates and Lares were regarded as beneficent; food was set aside for them and thrown on the fire in offering.

Pentateuch. (Greek) 'five books', the first five books of the *Bible*: *Genesis, Exodus, Leviticus, Numbers* and *Deuteronomy*. See TORAH.

Pentecost. From the Greek 'fiftieth' day, this Jewish festival comes seven weeks after Passover. Called Shavuoth, the Feast of Weeks, it was the wheat harvest festival of the ancient Hebrews. In later synagogue times Pentecost came to be associated with spiritual harvest and was the season of celebrating the Giving of the Law on Mount Sinai; in recent years synagogues have been decorated with plants and flowers. A consecration or confirmation service may be held for boys and girls at Pentecost.

People of the Book. See AHL AL-KITĀB.

Perfections. See PĀRAMITĀS.

Peripatetics. The school of Aristotle (q.v.) was Peripatos, a 'covered walking place', or Lyceum (q.v.), but it does not mean, as often supposed, that Aristotle walked about while teaching. The members were named Peripatetics; in their first period they did important scientific research, but did not pursue so ardently the philosophical speculations of Aristotle. This was taken up in the second period (from Andronicus onwards in the first century B.C.) and the philosophy was systematized to prepare the ground for the scholastics of the Middle Ages.

Perkunas, Pērkons. Ancient Lithuanian and Latvian god of thunder, who was also supreme god. His relationship with the sky-god, Dievaitis and Dievs, is not clear; sometimes the two deities seem to have been identified and at others the sky-god was superior. In one myth the thunder-god used his hammer (like Thor) to deliver the sun from captivity, and in another he forged the sun and threw it into the sky.

Persephone. Ancient Greek goddess, identified with Koré (Core), another 'maiden' daughter of the corn. In Latin Persephone was mispronounced as Prosperina. The most famous story tells of the love of Hades (Pluto) for Persephone, her abduction while gathering flowers, the search made by her mother Demeter (q.v.), Persephone eating pomegranate seeds in the underworld, and her return to her mother. However, through eating the seeds, she was forced to spend three months every year with Hades as his queen. This was a myth of the agricultural cycle and priests identified the place of Persephone's disappearance with Eleusis (q.v.), where Mysteries re-enacted the story. In another tale Persephone bore a child Zagreus (q.v.) to Zeus, but the jealous Titans tore him to pieces. There was little worship of Persephone, usually called Koré, apart from that of Demeter.

Perseus. Greek mythological hero, son of Zeus and Danaë (q.v.). He was cast out with his mother and brought up by

King Polydectes. Perseus fetched the head of the Gorgon Medusa (q.v.), released Andromeda (q.v.) from a sea-monster and married her. He returned the Gorgon's head to Athena and his flying shoes and cap of darkness to Hermes. He accidentally killed his grandfather Acrisius and became king of Tiryns.

Pesach. See PASSOVER.

Peyotl. See MESCALIN.

Phantasos. (Greek) 'dream', appearance. One of the sons of sleep, in mythology, and brother of Morpheus (q.v.), which sent visions of inanimate objects. Thus it is a mere image, a Phantasma, phantom or fantasy.

Pharmakos. (Greek) 'remedy', and so a scapegoat which took away bad luck. In some places a human scapegoat was chosen and killed, in reality or pretence. At the Thargelia (q.v.) in Athens every year, a male and a female Pharmakos were sent out of the city to carry away evil.

Phi. See NAT.

Philo Judaeus. The most famous Jewish philosopher of Hellenistic Egypt, who lived chiefly in Alexandria from about 25 B.C. to A.D. 40. Philo sought to reconcile the Jewish scriptures with Greek philosophy, and he wrote extensive commentaries on the *Bible*, interpreting its teachings and characters with Greek ideas, especially those borrowed from Plato. Taking further the Jewish notion of the Wisdom of God, Philo spoke of the Logos (Word) as a 'second God', or 'son of God', which was the means of divine creation and activity in the world. God himself was regarded as pure being, of whom nothing could be said. The concept of Logos had little effect on Jewish thought, but it probably influenced the *Gospel of John*, and Philo's writings were closely studied by Christian writers, in Alexandria and elsewhere, seeking to unite Hebrew and Greek thought.

Phoebe. (Greek) 'bright one', a female Titan, daughter of Earth and Heaven, mother of Leto (q.v.) and grandmother of Artemis. Her name was sometimes used in later writers for the Moon and also for Artemis and Diana when they were identified with the moon.

Phoebus. (Greek) the 'bright one', an epithet of Apollo as sun god (q.v.).

Phoenicians. Phoenician cults in ancient times were chiefly agricultural, concerned with spirits of the earth, climate and vegetation. Excavations at Ras Shamra-Ugarit since 1930 have revealed fragments of tablets with poetic mythology in which the principal role is played by Baal, a rain and fertility god, and next by Anath (q.v.), a warrior-goddess. This confirms the Biblical picture of Jezebel, wife of Ahab, who came from Sidon bringing cults of Baal and Asherah. Other gods were El or Elyon, Anat, Ashtart, and after the Ugaritic period appear the names of Adonis and Melkart. The Phoenicians, as a seafaring people, had a group of maritime gods, notably the sea-god Yam, pictured with a man's body and a fish tail, and under Greek influence identified with Poseidon bearing a trident. Asherah was also known as Elat, consort of El, and among the Phoenicians in Carthage she was called Tanit. (See also EL and CARTHAGE.)

Phoenix. Greek name for Phoenician, and for 'purple' or deep crimson since the discovery of this colour was attributed to the Phoenicians. Herodotus described a fabulous Egyptian bird of this name which rose out of the fire to new life, and this was taken by pagans and Christians as a symbol of resurrection. An elegiac poem *Phoenix*, often ascribed to Lactantius (A.D. 250–317), is a curious mixture of pagan and Christian thought on the fabulous bird which pre-figured the resurrection of Christ.

Phylactery. The Greek word for an amulet (from a root 'to guard') is used for the Hebrew Tefillin (singular: Tefillah, 'prayer'). Two leather boxes contain slips of parchment with four scriptural texts, which say that 'thou shalt bind them for a sign upon thine hand and they shall be for frontlets between thine eyes' (*Deuteronomy* 6, 8; see MEZUZAH). They are bound on the forehead and left arm by straps and worn during morning prayer, though not on Sabbaths and festivals. The texts exhort man to love God with heart and soul and might, and they are a reminder of the need for his constant service. See photograph opposite.

Picus. For the Romans this was the woodpecker, sacred to the god Mars, but also said to be an early king who was changed into the form of a bird.

Pietas. The Roman attitude of respect to parents, relatives, country and gods. She was personified and had a temple in Rome; sometimes she was accompanied by a stork as a symbol of filial piety.

Pilgrimage. Pilgrimage to sacred places, for devotional needs and gaining merit, is a feature of most religions. For Islamic pilgrimage to Mecca, see HAJJ.

For Hindus the most sacred place is Benares, but there are other sacred sites which pilgrims visit, from the Himalayas to the extreme south at Rameshvaram (q.v.). Seven especially sacred places are at Benares (Kāshī), Mathura, Ayodhyā, Hardwar, Dwaraka, Ujjain and Kanchipuram (Conjeeveram). Buddhists, Jains and Sikhs all visit towns and shrines connected with the lives of the founders and holy men. Often the holy place is a very ancient sanctuary, perhaps associated later with some historical character.

Pillars of Islam. There are five pillars (arkān) of Islam. The first is Faith (īmān), summarized in the Confession (shahāda) of the unity of God and the apostleship of Muhammad. The second is Prayer (salāt). The third is Almsgiving (zakāt). The fourth is Fasting (saum), from all food and drink during the daylight hours of the month of Ramadān. The fifth is Pilgrimage (hajj) to Mecca at least once in a life An attempt was made to add Holy War (jihād), but that was not generally agreed. See separate articles.

Pilpay. Corruption of Bidpai and his fables. See PAÑCHATANTRA.

Pinda. (Sanskrit) a 'ball' of rice which is offered to the departed fathers (see PITRIS) in ceremonies held some ten days after cremation. Libations of water and vessels of milk are also provided to help the departed soul on its journey to the afterlife, and to cleanse the mourners from impurity. See SHRADDHĀ.

Pinsker, Leo. Jewish nationalist (1821–91) who, reacting against anti-Semitism, saw the cure in founding a national state for the Jews. He headed a movement called Choveve Zion, 'Lovers of Zion'. It spread widely and after his death the name Zionism (q.v.) was coined for the expression of his ideas.

Pīpal. Hindi form of Sanskrit *pippala*, the sacred Bo-Tree (q.v.), a species of fig (*ficus religiosa*).

PĪPAL LEAVES

PHYLACTERIES

Pīr. A Persian word for an elder, and used for a Murshid (q.v.) or spiritual director. In India a Pīr indicates a Muslim saint or teacher, in contrast to the Hindu Guru.

Pirke Aboth. See MISHNAH.

Pishāchas. Fiends, the most malignant spirits in Hindu mythology. They are said to have been created from stray drops of water which fell from the production of gods and men.

Pitaka. (Sanskrit and Pali) 'basket', and applied to the three baskets which form the canon of Pali Buddhist scriptures, the *Tripitaka* (q.v.). This is used in the sense of 'handing on' tradition, as baskets of earth are passed by builders from hand to hand. The word Pitaka is not found in these scriptures, but inscriptions of the third century B.C. tell of the Petaki as 'reciter of the Pitaka'.

Pitris. The 'fathers', ancestors (Sanskrit, like Latin *Patres*), in Hindu belief. The name is applied to departed forefathers, and also to the first progenitors of mankind and to certain offspring of gods. Yama (q.v.), the god of the dead, is king of the Pitris, and their world is Pitri-Loka. See SHRADDHĀ and PINDA.

Plato. Greek philosopher, born about 429 and died in 347 B.C. in Athens, of a distinguished family. He was a disciple of Socrates (q.v.), most of whose teachings are found in Plato's writings, so that it is difficult to know how much is from Socrates and how much from Plato. After the death of Socrates in 399 Plato travelled abroad, to Italy, Sicily and Egypt, but about 385 he founded the Academy (q.v.), a college in a gymnasium on the outskirts of Athens dedicated to a hero Academus. Plato wrote many books and letters, including twenty-five dialogues which are preserved. The *Republic* teaches both philosophical search into the nature of the Good and sketches the ideal state with its rulers. The *Phaedrus* and *Timaeus* speak of God, nature and the soul, and the *Phaedo* is chiefly concerned with immortality. For Plato the highest realities are 'universals', which exist as 'forms' or 'ideas': such are beauty, justice, truth and, above all, the Good. The influence of Platonism has been immense – on Neo-Platonism (q.v.) and on European philosophy down the ages.

Pleiades. See ORION, ENLIL and KĀRTTIKEYA.

P. L. Kyodan. 'Perfect Liberty Association', a Japanese religious movement founded as a Shinto sect in 1926 by Tokuharu Miki and then called Hito no Michi. It was prohibited in 1937, but began again under its new name in 1946. Like many modern sects it claims to believe in one supreme spirit, but also accepts Karma (q.v.) and the influence of the ancestors upon believers. With the motto 'life is Art', this movement gives great importance to material and social activities, with schools, hospitals, games' centres and golf courses, as well as temples and ancestral shrines.

Plotinus. Philosopher of Neo-Platonism (q.v.), born in Egypt about A.D. 205, went to Rome at the age of 40, and died in Italy about 270. His life is known from a memoir written by Porphyry (q.v.). Plotinus was 50 years of age when he wrote a series of essays to expound his doctrines to his pupils, and these were arranged by Porphyry into six groups of nine, or *Enneads* (q.v.). The *Enneads* expound physics and cosmology, psychology, metaphysics, logic and epistemology. Plotinus taught that all modes of being come from a single impersonal force, which he called the One or the Good. By expansion or overflow from the One come descending grades of reality, down to nature and man who is potentially immortal. Sometimes criticized for mysticism, to others Plotinus is the greatest philosopher between Aristotle and Aquinas.

Pluto, Plutus. Pluto is a name of Hades (q.v.), the god of the underworld, in Greek mythology. Plutus is personified 'wealth', associated with the earth-mother Demeter, as is Pluto. Both of them have associations of abundance and fertility.

Pollux. See DIOSCUROI.

Polydaemonism. A term used by some writers on comparative religion in the late nineteenth century and early twentieth century, but now generally abandoned. Polydaemonism was used generally, to describe spirits of any kind, as the Greek word *daimon* (q.v.) meant a spirit or genius. However, it came to denote the respect paid to evil spirits as contrasted with good (demons or devils against gods) and for the latter Polytheism was preferred. But the notion of complete wickedness of a Devil, as in Jewish, Christian, Islamic and Zoroastrian thought, is foreign to many peoples of the world. The 'demons', *asuras*, of Hindu mythology have a disconcerting habit of turning out to be ascetics after all or at any rate they can rise in the scale of existence. African spirits were often called 'devils' by earlier writers, but now both this diabolism and fetishism (q.v.) are discarded as misleading descriptions.

Polydeuces. See DIOSCUROI.

Polyhymnia. In Greek mythology one of the nine Muses (q.v.), that of mimic art.

Polytheism. From the Greek for 'many gods', Polytheism is the term used to describe belief in and worship of many gods, or more than one. It does not necessarily imply that all the gods are of equal status, and there is generally some hierarchy of power or myth, sometimes with a Supreme Being who is not, however, the only god. A variety of Polytheism is in Henotheism (q.v.). The religions of ancient Egypt, Greece and Rome are often called polytheistic, as are those of modern Africa or India. In the latter case, at least, worshippers of Vishnu or Shiva may claim that their deity is not simply chief of many, but the sole God, of whom other divinities are but names or aspects. African religion has also been said to be polytheistic and monotheistic by turns, or even to be 'diffused monotheism', though this is disputed. See MONOTHEISM.

Pomona. Roman goddess of fruit (*poma*), especially apples, represented as a buxom girl with fruit. Her cult was a minor one and had no known festival, but her sacred place, Pomonal, was just outside Rome. A late story said that she was married to Vertumnus (q.v.).

Pontifex, Pontifices. (Latin) 'skilled in the magic of bridge-making', and so a priest who knew the ritual of public worship. Originally the Pontifices were advisers to magistrates, but they became pontiffs of the state cult (see COLLEGIUM). Their college included the Flamens and Vestals (q.v.), and at the head was the Pontifex Maximus, a title taken over by the Pope of Rome.

'Pope', Taoist. See TAO SHIH.

Popol Vuh. 'Book of the community', the sacred book of the Quiché Maya of central America. It was written shortly after the Spanish conquest, by a Maya of the ancient kingdom of Quiché in Guatemala, and contains mythology and traditions, and chronologies of kings down to A.D. 1550. This original manuscript was lost and its author unknown, but 150 years later a transcription was made by a Dominican, Francisco Ximénez, and other versions have appeared since. See CHILAM BALAM.

Porphyry. Philosopher (about A.D. 232 to 305), born in Tyre, studied at Athens and became disciple of Plotinus (q.v.) in Rome. He edited the *Enneads* (q.v.) of Plotinus and was important in the development of Neo-Platonism. Not an original thinker, Porphyry did valuable work in quoting and preserving many fragments of older writers.

Poseidon. A great Greek god, first of earthquakes, since he was often called 'earthshaker', but later and principally god of the sea. In mythology Poseidon was one of the three sons of the Titan Kronos (q.v.), and was swallowed by his father but later spewed up. The three brothers drew lots for rule of the world and the sea fell to Poseidon. His consort was Amphitrite, and he fathered Pegasus on Medusa the Gorgon (q.v.). Poseidon built the walls of Troy, alone or with Apollo, and quarrelled with Odysseus, upsetting the hero's journey home to Ithaca. The Romans identified Poseidon with Neptune.

Posture. See MUDRĀ.

Potala. Monastery-palace in Tibet, completed 1694 on a hill near Lhasa (q.v.)

by the Dalai Lama, Nag-wan lo-zang. It was named after the mythical residence of the celestial Avalokita (q.v.) which is believed to be the Bodhisattva incarnate in all Dalai Lamas. In normal times the Potala palace was a religious and political centre, and residence of the Dalai Lama (q.v.).

Potlatch. Ceremonial exchange of feasts between communities of Indians in British Columbia, entailing competitive display and exchange of valuables, even destruction of valuable property to achieve social effect. The host clan might give away all its possessions, but custom ruled that all its gifts should be returned in duplicate within a year, so that clan property was 'killed' in order to be 'reborn' bigger than before.

Prahlāda. The virtuous son of the demon Hiranya-kashipu in Hindu mythology. Prahlāda was an ardent devotee of the god Vishnu, but was persecuted by his father, whereupon Vishnu came in his Avatar as Man-lion (see Nara-simha) and slew the father. Prahlāda succeeded as king in his father's place and later was united with the gods.

Prajāpati. (Sanskrit) 'lord of creatures'. The name is used in the *Vedas* as an epithet of various gods, but later for an abstract deity, a primal creator or creative activity. Later still, Prajāpati is used for the creating God and for Vishnu and Shiva in that character.

Prajñā. (Sanskrit) 'wisdom', used in the abstract sense or sometimes personified as a goddess, especially Sarasvatī (q.v.). In Buddhism Prajñā (Pali: *Praññā*) is one of the six perfections or Pāramitās (q.v.).

The *Prajñā-Pāramitās* are a group of Mahāyāna Buddhist scriptures concerning the 'Perfection of Wisdom'. The earliest of these may date from the first century B.C. and they lie behind the teachings of Nāgārjuna (q.v.) and the doctrine of the Void. One of the best known is the Diamond-cutter (q.v.), *Vajracchedikā*, which in brief verses states the unreality of all things. Despite their idealistic and void teachings, the 'Perfection of Wisdom' sūtras speak of wisdom personified as a gracious being, similar to the Hindu belief.

Prakrit, Prakrita. See Pānini and Sanskrit.

Prakriti. (Sanskrit) 'making before', the original or natural form of anything. In the Sāmkhya (q.v.) philosophy, Prakriti is Nature, as distinct from Purusha, soul or spirit. Prakriti is eternal and self-existing, as matter in its primal form, and it is the first of twenty-five categories, of which soul is the last and different from all the rest. From Prakriti all the categories emanate, except soul. See also Buddhi.

Prāna. 'Breath', life, the breath of life (Sanskrit). In Indian thought breath has great significance, so that it is personified in the *Atharva Veda* and has a hymn addressed to it; later Prāna is identified with the universal Brahman. In Yoga it is the first of the five vital airs, or a generic name for all five; it is the divine life in the body.

Prapatti. (Sanskrit) 'falling down', resignation or surrender, to God. Prapatti is particularly the teaching of worshippers of Vishnu who claim that there is no way of receiving the grace of God but by complete surrender to him. Vadagalia and Tengalai sects differ in opinion whether salvation is obtained by the 'monkey-rule' (*markata nyāya*), as a young monkey co-operates with its mother by clinging to her, or by the 'cat-rule' (*mārjāra nyāya*), as a kitten is carried by the scruff of its neck and is completely dependent on its mother.

Prashna. 'Question' (Sanskrit), one of the short early *Upanishads*, consisting of dialogues between a teacher and his disciples.

Pratyeka-Buddha. Sanskrit (Pali: *Pacceka*), a 'single' or 'separate' Buddha. In the third section of the Theravāda Buddhist canon of scripture, the *Abhidhamma*, comes a description of this independent or separate Buddha. The Pratyeka-Buddha has attained enlightenment by himself and is concerned with gaining the truth for himself alone. He cannot preach the doctrine to others, as a complete Buddha does. He is sometimes called a 'lonely rhinoceros', and this description is apt for those hermits who were only intent on their own liberation from the world. There are many legends of such beings in later literature, but they did not have great importance in the development of Buddhism.

Pravara. (Sanskrit) 'best', term used for the names of legendary sages mentioned in daily prayers of Brahmins, the founder of their Gotra (q.v.), and also other remote ancestors. The Pravaras form a further restriction to marriage, banning it with a member of another Gotra if he and the proposed partner had one Pravara name in common.

Prayer Beads. The use of beads on a thread to assist in repetition of a divine name or prayer is worldwide, and probably originated in India. Prayer beads appear in Buddhist, Jain and Hindu art from the early centuries. Hindus chant the hundreds or thousands of names of Vishnu, Shiva and the like, while Jains

similarly praise their Jinas. 108 is a favourite number of beads as a sacred multiple (12 x 9), and Buddhists take the two halves to represent fifty-four stages of becoming a Bodhisattva. In Japan the Pure Land sects use thousands of beads to praise Amida Buddha. Sikhs and Parsis use beads also, and in Islam the chain of ninety-nine beads represents the ninety-nine Beautiful Names of God (q.v.). It was probably through Islam and contacts at the crusades that the rosary came into medieval Christendom, said to have been introduced by St Dominic (1170–1221), but developing under both Cistercian and Dominican influence. See SUBHA.

Prayer Flags. Pieces of cloth used in Tibet and northern India by Buddhists, on which are inscribed or printed texts and sacred or magical pictures, and the sacred phrase *Om mani padme hum*, 'hail, the jewel in the lotus, hail' (see OM). Such flags flutter from poles in the fields, from houses and from temples.

Prayer Sticks. See PEKWIN.

Prayer Walls. Walls in Tibet and northern India inscribed with sacred texts and pictures of gods and spirits, and revered by Buddhists (see PRAYER FLAGS and WHEELS). Some of them belong to the pre-Buddhist Bon (q.v.) religion and are circumambulated anti-clockwise, whereas the Buddhist prayer walls must be walked round keeping the holy wall or shrine to the right.

Prayer Wheels. Prayer or praising wheels are used everywhere in Tibet and

among Buddhists in northern India. They are inscribed with prayers and the sacred phrase *Om mani padme hum* (see PRAYER FLAGS), and this is multiplied as the wheels turn. The prayer wheels are in many styles, small hand wheels which are turned as people walk, paper lanterns in temples and houses, large wooden cylinders turned by hand, wheels on chimney cowls, and wheels in rivers.

Predestination. See FATE, KARMA, KISMET, QADAR.

Pretas. (Sanskrit) 'departed', the dead. Used especially of the spirit of a dead person before funeral rites were performed, the word came to mean a ghost thought to haunt cemeteries and other places.

Priapus. A god of fertility from the Hellespont region, whose cult spread to the rest of Greece after Alexander's wars brought new ideas. He was symbolized by a phallus, like the Indian Linga (q.v.). Priapus was said to be the son of Dionysus, and the great oriental deity Aphrodite was often regarded as his mother. The ass was sacrificed to him, as a symbol of lust. In later times Priapus was a god of gardens, a scarecrow and a guardian.

Prithā. In Hindu epic poetry another name for Kuntī (q.v.), mother of three of the Pāndus who are often called Pārtha after her.

Prithivī. (Sanskrit) 'the broad', a name for the wide earth in the *Vedas*, and personified as the earth mother of all beings. With Dyaus (q.v.), the sky, the earth is joined to indicate the parents of all, called Dyāvā-Prithivī. However, these primal beings are sometimes said themselves to have been created, or Prithivī is called the first of created beings. There are also three earths, as there are three heavens, and our world is called Bhūmi. Prithivī is said to have received her name from a sage or king called Prithī, or Prithu, who milked the earth as a cow and fed all mankind.

Proclus. See NEO-PLATONISM.

Prometheus. (Greek) the 'fore-thinker', one of the Titans and a popular demi-god. Originally he was a trickster, sometimes opposed to Zeus, connected with the creation of man and the invention of fire. Hesiod says that Zeus hid fire from man; Prometheus stole it and brought it back to earth. Zeus then chained Prometheus to a rock where an eagle ate his liver all day, but since he was immortal it grew again every night. But Prometheus stayed chained to the rock till he was delivered by Heracles. See EPIMETHEUS and AESCHYLUS.

Prosperina. Roman mispronunciation of Persephone (q.v.).

Proteus. A minor sea god of the Greeks who tended fishes and seals. He was servant of Poseidon (q.v.), the great sea god, and could change into all manner of 'Protean' shapes but, if he was held fast till he returned to his true form, Proteus would answer any questions. According to Euripides, Proteus was a king of Egypt who took charge of Helen until her husband Menelaus arrived.

Psyche. (Greek) 'the soul', conceived in Homer as a kind of double of the body, of similar size and clothes. The philosophers regarded the Psyche as a divine being different from the body, and in Orphism (q.v.) the body was its tomb. All Psyches could now be regarded as female, and from the fifth century B.C. Psyche appears in art as a beautiful maiden pursued, and sometimes tormented by, Eros (q.v.). Later still Psyche is a goddess, perhaps imported from the east.

Psychopomp. (Greek) 'guide of souls', one who led the dead to the underworld, used as an epithet of Charon, Hermes and Mercury (qq.v.). See also SHAMAN.

Ptah. Egyptian god, apparently not one of the oldest but achieving greatness after his association with the great centre at Memphis. His name may mean 'the opener', and as a god of the dead Ptah played an important part in the ceremony of 'Opening the Mouth', a ritual performed for a dead person to enable him to make the right responses and live again in the afterworld. Hence also Ptah had a close connection with the death and resurrection of Osiris (q.v.). Ptah came to be regarded as creator of all beings, associated with the water deity Nun, and called Ptah-Nun. The Greeks called him the craftsman Hephaestus (q.v.), and the Romans Vulcan. Ptah was always represented as a man, often with a beard and holding a sceptre.

Pūjā. (Sanskrit) 'worship', honour or reverence paid to gods and superior beings. Pūjā today in India is used generally for ceremonial worship, whether daily offerings of flowers, water, and incense to images, or symbols of a god, or more complex rites in a temple or on an anniversary. In early times there was animal sacrifice, but now this is very largely confined to the worship of Kālī (q.v.). Recitation of sacred texts is always recommended, and the names of deities and the sacred syllable *Om* (q.v.) are repeated. Priests who perform special ceremonies are called Pūjāris.

Pulque. Agave beer, fermented juice of the maguey cactus in Mexico. The goddess of Pulque was Mayauel (q.v.), who bore a bowl of the frothing intoxicant. Other gods were the 'four hundred rabbits', Centzon Totochtin, who were supposed to be seen in the mountains of the moon and whose worship was strongest in the state of Morelos, with drinking bouts and orgies. See MESCALIN.

Pundit. The Sanskrit *pandita* means a learned or wise man, a scholar or philosopher. He may be, though not necessarily, a Brahmin.

Pundra. See CASTE MARKS.

Purāna. (Sanskrit) 'ancient', traditional, general name for collections of Hindu myths and legends. The *Purānas* are part of the 'remembered' (*smriti*) religious texts, of less authority than the *Vedas* and following the epics. They are said to have been compiled or arranged by Vyāsa, reputed composer of the epic *Mahābhārata* (q.v.), but they probably all date from the Christian era. There are said to be eighteen *Great Purānas*, six each for the gods Vishnu, Shiva and Brahmā, though there is much overlapping. There are also numerous lesser *Purānas* and some modern works under this name. The *Purānas* develop much of the mythology of earlier works, especially Vishnu and Krishna in the *Vishnu Purāna* (q.v.) and the *Bhāgavata Purāna* (q.v.) respectively, part of the latter being still very popular.

Purdah. From Persian and Urdu *pardah*, a veil or curtain, and so used for the seclusion of women behind a veil or in private apartments. In India the system of Purdah was adopted from the Muslims and in ancient times the *Rig Veda* shows that at least unmarried girls went about freely. Arab travellers remarked that Indian queens were often to be seen unveiled, though no doubt they were carefully guarded. Purdah has been restricted or abolished now, but seclusion of women often remains. See HAREM and BURQA'.

Pure Land. In the great Mahāyāna Buddhist text, the *Lotus Sūtra* (q.v.), Sukhāvatī or Sukhākara is named as the 'world of bliss' or 'pure land' where Amitābha (q.v.) dwells in the west. Into this Western Paradise the devout were reborn. Later Sanskrit Mahāyāna texts, especially two called *Sukhāvatī-vyūha*, give great praises of the Buddhas, the bliss of their heavens and their superiority to those of other sects. The Pure Land school was introduced into China by Hui-yuan (q.v.), about A.D. 400, and into Japan by Honen in the twelfth century. The Pure Land doctrine teaches salvation by faith alone in Amitābha, rebirth in his Paradise, and then easy attainment of Nirvāna. Simple repetition of his name achieved this. The Pure Land sects are strongest in Japan, as Jodo (q.v.). See NEMBUTSU. In China they are known as Ching T'u.

Purim. Jewish festival celebrated on the fourteenth of Adar (February–March) in memory of the deliverance of the Jews from the plots of Haman in Persia, as described in the *Book of Esther*. The name is said, in *Esther* 9, 24, to come from the word 'lot' (*pur*), which Haman had cast against the Jews. Purim is the most joyous Jewish festival, marked by reading the *Book of Esther* in the synagogues, by feasting, distribution of gifts to friends and the poor, and by masquerades in the streets.

Purohita. A priest 'placed in front' (Sanskrit), commissioned in ancient India as a family chaplain or domestic priest of a nobleman. As well as leading royal sacrifices, the Purohita advised on temporal matters.

Purusha. (Sanskrit) 'person', man. One of the most famous hymns towards the end of the *Rig Veda* (10, 90), the *Purusha Sūkta* or 'Hymn of Purusha', describes him as a cosmic giant. This macrocosmic Person surpassed the earth and filled the heavens, was sacrificed by the gods, and from his body came the three early *Vedas*, the four classes of men, and the gods of nature. Later Purusha is used as a divine title, in the sense of Spirit, and Krishna is called the Purushottama, the supreme spirit or soul. In Sāmkhya (q.v.) philosophy Purusha is the ultimate soul or spiritual reality, in relationship with Nature or Prakriti (q.v.).

Pūrva Mīmāmsā. See MĪMĀMSĀ.

Pūshan. A god of the *Vedas*, probably named from a root meaning 'nourisher', a guardian of men and multiplier of cattle. He is connected with the sun, surveying everything, and also with the moon and with the storm god Indra. Pūshan is listed among the twelve Ādityas (q.v.).

Pushkar. 'Blue lotus-flower', the name of a sacred lake and temple in Rajasthan, said to be the only remaining temple of the once important god Brahmā in India. In front of the image of the four-faced god many silver coins are set in the concrete floor.

Pwyll. See MABINOGION.

Pyramids. The pyramids of Egypt were royal tombs, of which about eighty have survived intact or in ruins, many of them built between the third and sixth Dynasties, from 2815 to 2294 B.C. The earliest was the Step Pyramid at Saqqāra, attributed to Imhotep (q.v.), about 2780, for King Zoser. The famous group at Giza is dominated by the Great Pyramid of Cheops, the Greek form of the name of Khufu; it was 146 metres high and its base covered an area of thirteen acres. Nearby is the famous Sphinx (q.v.), a knoll of rock 20 metres high and 72 metres long, fashioned into the form of a recumbent lion with a human head, probably King Chephren. See EGYPTIANS, CHEOPS and MASTABA.

Comparable but different from the Egyptian pyramids were the Ziggurats (q.v.) of Mesopotamia, the sun temples of the Aztecs (q.v.) and the great Buddhist pyramid monument at Borobudur (q.v.). See also MAYAS and IZAMAL.

Pythagoras. Greek philosopher of Samos, of the sixth century B.C. He founded a religious society at Croton in southern Italy, but had to leave that place. The Pythagorean order was destroyed in the fifth century, though there were followers till the fourth. A Neo-Pythagorean school existed in Italy and Alexandria in the first century B.C., and was finally merged in Neo-Platonism (q.v.). Pythagoras wrote no books, though later some were attributed to him. He believed that the soul was a divine being imprisoned in the body (see PSYCHE), and that it transmigrated into further human, animal or plant lives, but could be delivered by the discipline of purity. He taught a way of life disciplined by study. Pythagoras interpreted the world through numbers, of which he made a systematic study, and discovered the intervals of the musical scale. His supposed visits to many places, as far apart as India and Druidic Britain, are probably apocryphal.

Pythia, Python. See APOLLO and DELPHI.

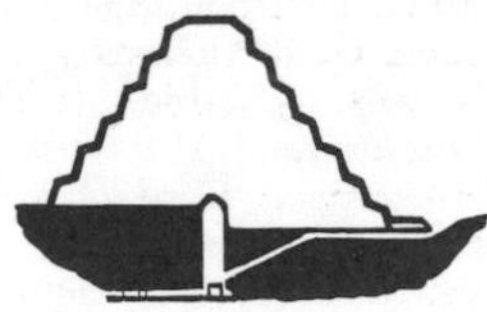

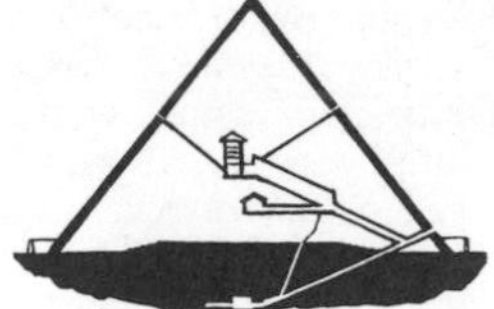

SECTIONS OF PYRAMIDS OF ZOSER AND CHEOPS

Q

Qadar. (Arabic) 'determination', 'decree', expressing the Muslim belief in predestination. The *Qur'ān* speaks of God writing down what will happen to men: 'we decreed for the children of Israel in the Book' (17, 4). There were great debates on predestination and freewill in early Islam and, strangely, opponents of extreme predestination were called Qadarīya (q.v.). A mediating orthodox position was given by Ash'arī (q.v.), who believed in the divine decrees, and that God alone had the power of creation and action, but that man could acquire or appropriate this action, so having some moral responsibility for his deeds.

Qadarīya. The name given to opponents of the Islamic doctrine of extreme predestination (see QADAR). There was said to be a statement of Muhammad which declared that 'they are the opponents of God in Qadar'. Ash'arī (q.v.) gives the question, 'why have you named us Qadarīya?' and answers, 'because you claim that you yourselves determine your actions, and not your Lord.' The name Qadarīya came to be applied to the rationalists in general known as Mu'tazila (q.v.), but they objected to the nickname and said it should be applied rather to those who maintained the decree (Qadar) of God over all things. Another version of the origin of the name is that it came not from 'decree' (qadā'), but from 'power' (qadr), and referred to human power in freewill.

Qadesh. See KEDESH.

Qādī. A judge who traditionally should decide all cases of civil and criminal law. However, from early days the Qādī was particularly concerned with religious questions, and today, in the majority of Muslim countries, most other legal matters are decided by secular authorities.

Qadiani. See AHMADIYYA.

Qādiriya. One of the most popular religious orders of Islam in the Near East and Africa. Founded by 'Abd al-Qādir (1077–1166) whose school in Baghdad became very popular and whose teachings spread to Syria, Egypt and the Yemen, and later throughout the Islamic world where he is one of the most revered saints, being called Emir of God and Sultan of Saints. Al-Qādir's doctrine was fairly orthodox, but with mystical interpretations of the *Qur'ān* and repetition of words and texts hundreds of times (see PRAYER BEADS). His school soon spread to North Africa, and from the nineteenth century has been powerful in West Africa. One branch of it, the Murīdiya, led by Ahmad Bamba, founded one of the greatest Islamic centres in tropical Africa at Touba in Senegal. In modern times the African Qādiriya seems to have lost some ground to the Tijānīya (q.v.).

Qarmatī, Qarmatians. A name of obscure origin given to rebellious factions and secret societies in Mesopotamia in the ninth century. Later the title was applied to movements for social reform and justice in the eastern Islamic world from the ninth to the twelfth centuries, and to mystical doctrines connected with them. They had supreme leaders (Imāms, q.v.) whose names were never pronounced. They adopted Gnostic speculations, in which there are successive cycles of world events, with succeeding Imāms, looking therefore to the dawn of a new age. Members of the Qarmatī were admitted by initiations, in which they were sworn to secrecy. Their power was great, supported by the Fātimid (q.v.) dynasty, but declined before the Crusades.

Qayrawān. See KAIROUAN.

Qetesh. See KEDESH.

Qibla. (Arabic) 'opposite', the direction in which all Muslims must pray. This is not simply towards Mecca but towards the Ka'ba (q.v.) shrine there. At first Muhammad and his followers accepted the Jewish practice of praying in the direction of Jerusalem, but at Medina a change was made and the *Qur'ān* says, 'we shall put you in possession of a Qibla that will satisfy you, turn your face in the direction of the Sacred Mosque' (2, 139). At all times of prayer Muslims must make their Qibla to the Ka'ba. In mosques this direction is indicated by the Mihrāb (q.v.) prayer niche. It is customary to slaughter animals ritually facing Mecca and the dead are buried with this Qibla.

Qisma, Qismet. See KISMET.

Qitfīr. The Biblical Potiphar in Islamic tradition, not named in the *Qur'ān*, but in the sūra of Joseph simply mentioned as 'he who bought him, being from Egypt' (12, 21). Later story gave special attention to Potiphar's wife, under the name of Zulaika (q.v.).

Qiyās. (Arabic) 'comparison', analogical reasoning. The fourth principle for determining Islamic faith and practice; the others being *Qur'ān*, *Tradition*, and *Agreement* (Ijmā', q.v.). Qiyās is the reasoning of the learned from the analogy of other doctrines or practices. It must not be contrary to anything in the *Qur'ān* or *Traditions*, but if these authorities do not give guidance for action then analogy may be used. For example, gambling is forbidden, but not playing chess, which some severe teachers (but not all) regard as a game of chance.

Qubbat al-Sakhra. See DOME OF THE ROCK.

al-Quds. The usual Arabic name for Jerusalem (q.v.), meaning 'the holy', like Hebrew *qodesh*.

Questions of Milinda. See MILINDA.

Quetzalcoatl. Mexican god, whose name among the Aztecs meant 'most precious twin', since he was the planet Venus which is a morning and evening star, and the morning star was the Quetzal or precious one. The Maya called him Kukulcān, a translation of his name. Quetzalcoatl is shown adorned with jewels, with cape and headdress of feathers, and above him a feathered snake (his symbol). He was ruler of the

wind and also teacher of human beings in useful arts. Great temple-pyramids were built to him, but only priests and nobles could enter there. After living on earth, Quetzalcoatl wandered away, sailed over the sea, or disappeared into the sky like Venus. When Cortes arrived from Europe, the Mexicans thought he was Quetzalcoatl returned and this made his conquest and destruction of the rival religion easy. See TEZCATLIPOCA and FEATHERED SERPENT.

Quinquatrus. (Latin) 'fifth day after' the Ides (q.v.) of March, and so denoting a festival of Mars celebrated on 19 March which later by a misunderstanding was extended to five days (until 23 March). The festival also came to be associated with Minerva even more than Mars, since 19 March was supposed to be the birthday of her temple. See SALII.

Quirinus. A god of the Sabine tribes which lived on the Quirinal hill before Rome was built. Later he forms a third with Jupiter and Mars and resembles the latter as a warrior. His festival on 17 February was the Quirinalia, but the origin of the name of the god is obscure. His priest was the Flamen Quirinalis.

Qur'ān. (Arabic) 'reading' or 'recitation', the sacred book of Islam, and regarded as the very Word of God. It was revealed to the prophet Muhammad, beginning on the Night of Power (*Qur'ān* 97), and generally taken to be the 27th of Ramadān, and celebrated on that day in the month of fasting. It came as an 'Arabic Qur'ān' for the Arabs who had as yet no scripture like Jews and Christians. Translations are made nowadays, but only the Arabic is regarded as the true *Qur'ān*. It is in a rhyming prose, in lines

of uneven length, which are learnt by heart and chanted throughout the Muslim world. There are 114 chapters or sūras, the shortest generally being earliest, but arranged at the end of the book. The chapters all have a name in Arabic, but numbers are common now. It is said that Muhammad was illiterate, but the *Qur'ān* was written by his followers on scraps of material and gathered together shortly after his death. The third caliph, 'Uthmān, had an authoritative version made which replaced all other copies.

Quraysh. The Arabian tribe to which Muhammad belonged and which played a prominent part in early Islamic history. Hence the ruler or Sharīf of Mecca should always be of the Quraysh tribe, though this authority was usurped under Turkish rule. See BADR.

Qurayzah. A Jewish tribe at Medina in the time of Muhammad. At first they supported him, but after a Meccan attack on the town they were suspected of treachery. They were seized and condemned, and Muhammad allowed another chief Sa'd to decide their fate. All the Qurayzah men, some six hundred, were executed and their wives and children sold into slavery. Two other Jewish tribes of Medina had earlier been expelled from the town.

Qutb. (Arabic) a 'pole' or 'pivot'. The name given to an important spiritual being or especially holy man. Saintly hierarchies are headed by a Qutb, who is the pole-saint or pivot of the world. In Delhi the Qutb Minar is an ancient Islamic tower of victory. See also WALĪ.

R

Ra. See RĒ'.

Raba. Jewish rabbi (299–352) who was one of the Babylonian Amoraim (q.v.), and opponent of Abbaye.

Rab Ashi. Jewish rabbi (died A.D. 427) who directed the Babylonian Academy for over fifty years, editing the *Mishnah* and preparing much of the *Talmud*. His work was continued by Rabina II (q.v.).

Rabb. (Arabic) 'lord', master. Applied to gods before Islam, it is a regular name for Allāh in the *Qur'ān* and after. Tradition says that because of this a slave should not call his master Rabbi but Sayyidī, 'prince', owner.

Rabbanites. The name given to general teachers of the *Talmud* (from *Rabbi*) from the eighth century, to distinguish them from the narrow literalism and rigorous legalism of the Karaites (q.v.). The Rabbanites not only met the danger of Karaism by more intensive Talmudic and Biblical study, but they also faced challenges from rationalism and began the study of philosophy and the natural sciences. One of their great teachers was Saadya ben Joseph (q.v., 892–942), of Fayyum in Egypt who became head (Gaon) of the Babylonian Academy at Sura. His great work *Emunoth Wedeoth* ('Faith and Knowledge') was the earliest attempt at providing a rational basis for Jewish faith and practice. He wrote a great deal against Karaism and this led to its eventual decline.

Rabbi. (Hebrew) 'master', a title given to Jewish teachers and after the destruction of the Temple in A.D. 70 used to indicate ordained or authoritative exponents of the Law. Rabbi Judah (q.v.) was the 'Rabbi' or teacher *par excellence*. The Rabbi today is not a priest, but he conducts services, preaches sermons and instructs the young. Rabbinism, or Rabbinic Judaism, is the name generally given to the teachings of the Rabbis after the fall of Jerusalem and in the Middle Ages, to adapt the teachings of the *Bible* and the *Talmud* to their times. For Islam, see RABB. See also KOHEN.

Rābi'a al-'Adawīya. An early Muslim woman mystic or Sūfī. She was a freedwoman but poor, and lived most of her life in Basra in Mesopotamia. Born about A.D. 717, she died in 801. She was an ascetic and celibate, and was called 'a second spotless Mary'. Rābi'a taught the love of God, her Beloved, for his own sake rather than for any reward. She was fond of symbolic actions and walked through the streets with water and fire in her hands, saying that she was going to quench the flames of hell with water and warm up paradise with fire. Miracles and visions are attributed to her and there are several biographies, the fullest being that of the Persian poet 'Attār (q.v.).

Rabina, Rab Abina. Jewish rabbi (died A.D. 500) who continued the work of previous Amoraim (q.v.), especially that of his predecessor Rab Ashi (q.v.). He was the last to teach the *Torah* on an oral basis and the *Talmud* is regarded as closing with him.

Rabindranath. See TAGORE.

Rādhā. The favourite Gopī (q.v.) and mistress of Krishna while he was living among the cowherds. She left her husband, Ayana-ghosha, to dance with Krishna and disappeared with him. The loves of Krishna and Rādhā, their separations and longings, are vividly described by Jayadeva in his poem *Gīta Govinda* (q.v.). The words of love are taken as symbolical of the love of God for the soul, the latter being Rādhā. Rādhā came to be worshipped as a goddess, or an Avatar of Lakshmī (q.v.) as Krishna was of Vishnu. Some mystics, such as Chaitanya (q.v.), dressed as Rādhā at times to represent the soul's love for God.

Radhakrishnan, Sarvepalli. Born in 1888, Radhakrishnan is one of the most versatile of modern Indians and has been a cultural ambassador for his country. The first holder of the Spalding Chair of Eastern Religions and Ethics in the university of Oxford, he went from there to become President of India, and finally retired. Radhakrishnan is a prolific and charming writer, and his books are full of quotations, ranging easily from Shankara to Teresa, from Confucius to Luther. Among his many writings *Eastern Religions and Western Thought* or *An Idealist View of Life* are perhaps the most representative, but he has written long commentaries on Indian Philosophy, the *Upanishads*, the *Brahma Sūtra* and the *Bhagavad-Gītā*. Radhakrishnan's philosophy is largely the monism of Shankara (q.v.), though in deference to the modern scientific viewpoint he claims to give more room to the reality of nature. His translations sometimes paraphrase the text in favour of monistic philosophy.

Rādhā Swāmī. Indian sect, which calls itself a Satsang, 'company of pious people', as do the Sikhs (see SATSANG). Its first Guru was a baker from Agra named Tulsī Rām or Shiva Dayāl Sahib (1818–78). The Supreme Being is said to have revealed himself to the first Guru, under the name Rādhā Swāmī. Literally this title means 'Lord of Rādhā', that is, Krishna (see RĀDHĀ), yet this sect rejects all the Hindu gods and holds to its teachers, or Sant Satgurus, who receive revelations by the Word or Shabda (q.v.) of Rādhā Swāmī.

Rāga. (Sanskrit) 'love', beauty, a musical note or harmony. Six Rāgas or musical modes were enumerated, each arousing some affection and having its female consort called Rāginī. Seven or twenty-six Rāgas have also been mentioned.

In Pali Buddhism Rāga is 'greed', one of the three cardinal vices; see MOHA.

Raghu. Indian legendary king of the solar race, and ancestor of the hero and Avatar Rāma. The *Raghu-vamsa*, 'the race of Raghu', is a famous poem in nineteen cantos by Kāli-dāsa (q.v.).

Ragnarök. The 'fate of the gods' in Nordic mythology, sometimes called 'twilight of the gods' and also the 'fate of mankind.' The idea of doom pervades the mythology and with the passage of time evil increases, heroes are killed, morality declines and demons break loose. The gods are killed by their foes, the sky is rent, the sun turns black, and the earth slips into the sea. Yet some gods survive and the earth will rise again, while the ancient wisdom is restored. Such notions are common to many cultures, and there are Christian influences in some accounts of the Ragnarök, as when it is said that the world will be destroyed by fire, and the demons who are bound till the last days resemble fallen angels.

Rāhib, Rahbānīya. A Rāhib is a 'monk' in Islam, mentioned in the *Qur'ān* as consuming the wealth of the people, yet not counting himself great (9, 34; 5, 85). The followers of Jesus were said to have 'kindness and mercy and monasticism' (*rahbānīya*; 57, 27). Early Islam rejected monasticism and a late tradition said 'no monkery in Islam', yet the Sūfī mystics often left the world and lived in communities which, however, were rarely as enclosed as some of the Christian fortresses or enclosed monasteries.

Rahīm. (Arabic) 'merciful', or the Compassionate Rahmān (q.v.). With the latter name it appears at the head of every chapter of the *Qur'ān* but one (9) and is therefore one of the most frequently repeated attributes or praise-names of God on Muslim lips. See ALLĀH.

Rahmān. (Arabic) 'merciful' or 'compassionator', a title of Allāh (q.v.). Used also as a proper name, like Allāh, Rahmān may have been an old pre-Islamic divine title. With Rahīm it occurs in the invocation to Allāh at the head of every chapter but one of the *Qur'ān*.

Rāhu. A Daitya or demon in Indian mythology, who swallows the sun and moon to cause eclipses. When the gods churned the ocean for the nectar of Amrita (q.v.), Rāhu drank some of it; this was revealed by the sun and moon to Vishnu who thereupon cut off Rāhu's head. However, he had become immortal through the drink and was fixed in the sky as a dragon, taking revenge on sun and moon and giving birth to comets and meteors. In astronomy Rāhu is the dragon's head, with Ketu (q.v.) the tail and descending lunar orbit.

Rāhula. Son of Gautama the Buddha (q.v.) and Yasodharā. His father left him shortly after birth to seek enlightenment. When Rāhula was fifteen years old, he entered the Sangha to become a monk and is said to have been an eminent Arahat.

Raidās. Indian mystic of the fifteenth century, also called Ravidās or Rohidās. He was a low caste leather-worker, and was opposed by Brahmins, but was accepted by many followers and taught Princess Mirā-bāi (q.v.). Raidās composed devotional verses to Vishnu and his Avatars, which were so popular that forty-one of his hymns are included in the Sikh scripture, *Ādi Granth.*

Rainbow Serpent. See GALERU.

Rāja. 'King', chief (Sanskrit). The Rāja, 'royal', class was the Kshatriya (q.v.). A royal sage was a Rājarshi. A favourite form of Yoga is Rāja Yoga; see YOGA.

Rajas. (Sanskrit) 'passion', force, the second of the three Strands or Gunas (q.v.) in Hindu philosophy, especially Sāmkhya (q.v.).

Rājasūya. (Sanskrit) 'royal sacrifice', the consecration and series of sacrifices traditionally performed by Indian kings to imbue them with divine power. Such a sacrifice is described in the *Mahābhārata* epic for the coronation of Yudhishthira (q.v.). During the ceremonies the king was identified with various gods, especially Indra, Prajāpati and Vishnu, and he was regarded as one of the gods himself. See ASHVA-MEDHA and VĀJAPEYA.

Rak'a. (Arabic) 'prostration', a section of the formal prayer of Muslims. See SALĀT.

Rākshas, Rākshasas. Evil spirits or goblins of Hindu mythology. Some were relatively innocuous, called guardians of the waters (from a root *raksh,* to guard). Others were enemies of the gods, and the worst haunted cemeteries and afflicted mankind. The chief of the last was Rāvana (q.v.), who opposed the divine hero Rāma. Even these evil beings were sometimes said to have been born from the foot of the god Brahmā, and it may be that the Rākshas in the epic poems represent indigenous tribes in south India and Ceylon against whom the Aryan warriors were fighting. They were said to be of many shapes, some grotesque and some beautiful, and they received many epithets: thieves, blood-drinkers, black-faced (names also given to other enemies).

Rāma. There are three Rāmas in Hindu stories: Bala-rāma, Parashu-Rāma (qq.v.), and Rāma-chandra. The last is the most important and noble. Son of Dasharatha and Kaushalyā, who reigned at Ayodhyā, Rāma was the seventh Avatar of Vishnu and appeared at the end of the second or Tretā age. His story is partly told in the *Mahābhārata,* but more fully in the *Rāmāyana* (q.v.). Rāma had four brothers, in youth performed heroic feats, and married Sītā (q.v.). Defrauded of succession to the throne he retired to the forest with Sītā and his brother Lakshmana. Sītā was stolen by the demon Rāvana and carried off to Ceylon. Rāma gained the help of the monkey god, Hanuman, and crossed to Ceylon (Lankā) by 'Rāma's bridge', a chain of islands.

Sītā was recovered but underwent an ordeal to prove her chastity. Then Rāma and Sītā returned to reign at Ayodhyā. Finally Rāma went into a river and returned to Vishnu in heaven. The worship of Rāma is popular and has not the erotic associations of the Krishna cult. The name Rām is used in salutations and prayers.

Rāma-charita-mānasa. See TULSĪ DĀS. and RĀMĀYANA

Ramadān. The ninth month of the Muslim calendar and a time of fasting. It is named in the *Qur'ān* (2, 181/185) as the month 'in which the *Qur'ān* was sent down', in which those who are healthy should fast, from dawn when a white thread may be distinguished from a black, till they can no longer be distinguished at night. All adult healthy Muslims fast from food and drink all day in Ramadān, but they may eat at night. A few modern lands, like Tunisia, relax the restrictions for workers. The month's fast ends with a festival, 'Īd al-fitr (q.v.). In India the month is called Ramazan. Since the Islamic year is lunar, and shorter than the solar year, the time of Ramadān gets earlier every year. When it falls in the summer, it makes a very long fasting day for those who live in northern or southern climates. See SAUM.

Rāmakrishna. Modern Hindu saint (1834–86), born in a poor Brahmin family at Kamarpukur in Bengal, with the name Gadādhar Chatterji. He was uneducated but went to Calcutta to serve in temples there. While at the new Dakshineshvara temple of Kālī, he began to have visions and states of ecstasy (*samādhi*). His parents took him home to be married to a young girl and she followed him back to Calcutta later but the marriage was never consummated. As Sārada Devī, or the Mother, she is honoured as an Avatar. He became an ascetic (*sannyāsi*) and took the name Rāmakrishna, by which he is known with the title Shrī or Paramahamsa. He had visions of Kālī, but also of other religious figures, including the Buddha and Christ. Rāmakrishna was concerned with the multiplicity of religions and taught that they were all paths to the same goal. He attracted disciples, including Keshab Chandra Sen and Vivekānanda (qq.v.), the latter founding the Rāmakrishna Mission.

Rāmakrishna Mission. A modern eclectic Hindu movement founded by Vivekānanda in 1897, to propagate the teachings of Rāmakrishna (q.v.). It began with two Maths or monasteries, at Belur near Calcutta and Mayavati in the Himalayas, where young men were trained for the mission. Centres are now found throughout India and in many western countries, particularly America. The teaching is generally monistic, a Neo-Vedānta (q.v.), but two distinctive marks of the organization are the Mission and the emphasis on social work. Schools, publishing houses, dispensaries and relief centres have been opened. The headquarters is at Belur, where a temple in styles of several religions houses an image of Rāmakrishna, called the 'presiding Deity', and relics of his life, while smaller shrines are dedicated to his wife Sārada Devī and to Vivekānanda.

Rāmānanda. Hindu saint of the late fourteenth and early fifteenth century. He was a follower of the philosophy of Rāmānuja (q.v.), but devoted to mystical practices. Rāmānanda taught in Benares, but is said to have travelled all over India. He used the vernacular Hindi and appealed to the masses. Kabīr (q.v.) is said to have been his disciple and one hymn by Rāmānanda is in the Sikh scripture, *Ādi Granth*.

Rāmānuja. South Indian philosopher of the eleventh century A.D. A Tamil, born near Madras, he travelled widely and finally settled down to teach in the great temple at Shrirangam. Rāmānuja wrote great commentaries on the *Upanishads*, the *Bhagavad-Gītā* and the *Brahma* or *Vedānta Sūtra*. He opposed the strict non-dualism or monism of Shankara (q.v.), and taught a 'qualified non-dualism' (*vishisht-ādvaita*) or 'difference non-difference' (*bhedābheda*). God, the world and selves are real, but the two latter depend on God and are his body. God is the eternal and perfect Brahman, but personalized as Vishnu. Salvation is not dissolution into Brahman, but devotion to Vishnu. Hence there is a place for the Avatars, which reveal the grace of God. Rāmānuja gave philosophical respectability to the devotional cults of Vishnu and was more significant to religious life than rival philosophers. See ADVAITA.

Rāmāyana. The 'story of Rāma', the second great epic of India after the *Mahābhārata* (q.v.). It is in Sanskrit, attributed to a sage named Vālmīki and composed somewhere about the beginning of the Christian era. It is in seven books or sections and fifty thousand lines, but the first and last books are probably of later date. The *Rāmāyana* tells of the adventures of Prince Rāma (q.v.), his birth, youth, marriage, exile, pursuit of Rāvana, rescue of Sītā, reign, final years, and death. It is much more of a unity than the longer epic and gives a lofty example of heroic behaviour. It has remained popular for devotion to Rāma as an Avatar of Vishnu.

Another version of the *Rāmāyana*, the 'Holy Lake of the Acts of Rāma', was composed in Hindi by Tulsī Dās (q.v.) in the sixteenth century. This depends upon Vālmīki's poem but alters and adapts it to even greater devotional purposes; it is also popular.

Rām Dās. Fourth Guru of the Sikhs (1534–81), he succeeded Guru Amar Dās and was followed by Arjan (qq.v.). Rām Dās founded the city of Amritsar (q.v.) and dug the tank in which the Golden Temple was later situated. Over six hundred of his hymns are in the Sikh scriptures, *Ādi Granth*.

Rāmeshvara. 'Lord of Rāma', one of the twelve great Lingas (q.v.) set up to Shiva, rather strangely by Rāma who was an Avatar of Vishnu. The place is at Rāmeshvaram at the southern tip of India. by the straits leading to Ceylon where Rāma's Bridge (Adam's Bridge on English maps) is a chain of islands said to have been made by Rāma and Hanuman. The temple at Rāmeshvaram is magnificent and a great place of pilgrimage for visitors, many of whom visit shrines from the extreme north in the Himalayas to here in the far south.

Ramman, Rimmon. The 'thunderer', Syrian form of the storm god known in Mesopotamia as Adad (q.v.). His temple in Damascus is mentioned in the *Bible* (2 *Kings*, 5, 18).

Ram Mohan Ray or **Mohun Roy.** Modern Hindu reformer, born into a Brahmin family in Bengal in 1772, of deeply religious parents who were followers of the Vaishnavite teacher Chaitanya. Ram Mohan later studied the religions and languages of Islam and Christianity: Arabic, Persian, Hebrew and Greek. After service with the East India Company, he retired and settled in Calcutta to devote himself to religion. He denounced widow-burning (*sati*) and polygamy, and sought to reform Hinduism. In 1828 with some friends he founded the Brāhma Samāj or one-God society (q.v.), which combined elements of different religions in public services. In 1830 he sailed for England and died and was buried in Bristol in 1833. Ram Mohan Ray was more an innovator than an original thinker, and was important for his influence on his followers, such as Keshub Chandra Sen and Debendra Nath Tagore.

Ran. Scandinavian goddess, wife of the sea-god Aegir. The sea was called the 'land of Ran' and the waves were said to flow out of her mouth. She was dangerous and drew sailors into her net, so that 'faring to Ran' meant death by drowning. Ran had nine daughters, personified waves, the 'horses of the sea'. They tossed ships up to the sky and wept at the death of Balder (q.v.).

Rangi. The 'sky' in Maori religion. He was male and closely joined to the earth, Papa, their children being bound between the bodies of their parents. There were up to seventy of these children and they forced the sky and earth apart. They were led by Tane (q.v.), creator of vegetation whose trees forced Rangi upwards and the other sons fastened him up with poles. Rain and mist continue to express the longing of Rangi and Papa for each other. See ATUA.

Raphael. (Hebrew) 'healing of God', one of the four archangels of Jewish tradition. Raphael does not appear in the *Bible*, but in the apocryphal *Book of Tobit* he is sent to heal Tobit's eyes. In the *Talmud* he is one of the four angels who surround the throne of God, standing behind it, corresponding to the tribe of Ephraim. As a prince of healing he was said to have visited Abraham to heal him after circumcision. See GABRIEL.

Rashi. Title of Rabbi Sholomon ben Isaac, abbreviated from those names (Ra-Sh-I). A French Jew, born at Troyes about A.D. 1040, he exercised a great influence on Jewish thought, and especially during the Crusades which began towards the end of his life and brought some of the first persecutions of Jews in central Europe. He died in 1105. Rashi commented on nearly all the *Talmud* and his explanations of terms and concepts have been guides to students ever since. See TOSAFOTH.

Rashīd. See HĀRŪN AL-RASHĪD.

Rashīd. See RIDĀ.

Rashnu. The 'judge' or Requiter of the dead in Zoroastrian religion. In the *Gāthās* (q.v.) of Zoroaster it is the supreme God, Ahura Mazdā himself, who judges men; it may be that Rashnu was the judge before the Zoroastrian reform, or that he was only an epithet of Ahura Mazdā and later became the judge. In later Zoroastrian tradition the souls of the departed come to the Bridge of the Requiter. There Rashnu weighs their deeds in a balance, judging impartially both rich and poor, not respecting persons since he is the just judge and himself the Requiter. The souls of the saved pass over the bridge, which for them is very wide, but the souls of the damned fall off the razor-sharp bridge into various hells, where they remain till the final resurrection. See CHINVAT.

Rashtriya Swayamsevak Sangh. 'National self-rule community,' a Hindu national society founded in 1925 and demanding even from non-Hindus a reverence for 'Hindu religion'. See *Mahāsabha*.

Ras Shamra Ugarit. Site in Syria of excavations which since 1930 have contributed fragments of tablets bearing mythological texts which throw much light on the religion of the ancient Phoenicians (q.v.).

Rasūl. (Arabic) 'messenger', apostle. In the *Qur'ān* it is said that each community (*umma*, q.v.) has a Rasūl (10, 48, etc.) and God sends one messenger to each. Muhammad came as Rasūl to the Arabs who had not yet had a messenger, and others given this name in the *Qur'ān* included Noah, Lot, Ishmael, Moses and Jesus. Others are called Prophet (*Nabī*) but not Rasūl, and it seems that Rasūl is a narrower term, rather like 'Apostle' in Christianity. Muhammad is called both Nabī and Rasūl, but in the confession of faith Allāh is hailed as the sole God and Muhammad as the Rasūl of God. See NABĪ.

Ratha, Rath. (Sanskrit) 'chariot', applied to the light chariots of warriors, and also to the vehicles of gods. In later Hindu usage a Rath is the chariot or car of a temple in which the image of a deity is placed for ceremonial and occasional processions and lustrations. See JAGANNĀTHA.

Rati. (Sanskrit) 'love' or 'desire', the Venus of Hinduism and wife of the god of love, Kāma (q.v.), whence she is also called Kāmi. Other names are Revā and Prīti, and she is called 'vine of love' and 'fair-limbed.'

Ratna-sambhava. (Sanskrit) 'jewel existence', a name given to one of the seven Dhyāni-Buddhas (q.v.).

Rāvana. The demon-king of Ceylon or Lankā, in Hindu mythology. He was ruler of the Rākshas (q.v.) and is said to have had ten heads and twenty arms. Rāvana appears particularly in the *Rāmāyana*, where he abducts Sītā, wife of Rāma, and carries her off to Ceylon. After long battles Rāma slew Rāvana and rescued Sītā, who had preserved her chastity against the demon. On the death of Rāvana the gods praised Rāma as Vishnu, for he had saved heaven and earth from destruction. In the Dasharā festival (q.v.) in September-October, huge effigies are made of Rāvana and his allies, filled with crackers which explode when fiery darts are sent against them.

Rāzī. Islamic theologian and philosopher (1149–1209). He travelled widely in Persia and India and settled at Herat in Afghanistan where he founded a Madrasa school and was called Shaikh al-Islam. He wrote a commentary on the philosophy of Ibn Sīnā (see AVICENNA) and opposed the Mu'tazila heresy (q.v.) in his commentary on the *Qur'ān*. Rāzī was a famous preacher but also a rational exponent of orthodox philosophy.

Rē'. The great state god of ancient Egypt, called Ra by the Greeks. He was in nearly every sanctuary and had more myths than any other god, but was centred at Heliopolis and from there became the state divinity The name Rē' indicated the sun, of which he was the personification. Rē' created himself, or arose out of the primaeval water, as a child from a lotus, or was born from an egg. He had many titles, such as 'begetter of gods' and 'light of the world'. He is represented in many forms, as a beetle like the sun, a falcon, or a man. Most often he is shown as a man with a falcon's head and the sun's disk on the head. He is associated with many gods, and the Eye of Rē', which later was the goddess Hathor, was the sun itself, parallel to the Eye of Horus as the moon.

Red Hat. See NYINGMAPA and LAMA.

Reform. Name for modern movements within Judaism, also called Liberal Judaism. They began with the Enlightenment (see HASKALAH), the study of non-Jewish subjects and a critical attitude to the past. The first Reform Temple was built by Israel Jacobsohn at Seesen in Germany in 1810. Emphasis was made on modernizing synagogue services, using the vernacular in place of much Hebrew, introducing instrumental music, reading the Prophets as well as the Law, uniting men and women in family pews, and confirming girls as well as boys (see BAR MITZVAH). The universal aspect of Judaism was stressed, with less reference to the election of Israel and the restoration of the Temple or the coming of a physical Messiah. Great dissension was aroused, but most countries now have Reform or Liberal communities as well as Orthodox, the latter being in the majority. In the United States there is a strong Conservative movement, which is moderately reforming, and a radical Reconstructionist movement.

Refuge. See THREE JEWELS.

Regin. See FAFNIR.

Reincarnation. See TRANSMIGRATION.

Reiyukai. (Japanese) 'soul friend association', one of the modern Japanese movements and an offshoot from Nichiren (q.v.) Buddhism. It was founded in 1925 by Kakutaro Kubo and has split up into numerous sub-sects. Its teaching is Mahāyāna Buddhist, following the *Lotus Sūtra* (q.v.), with a strong social emphasis. More than three million members are claimed, but many of them remain attached to their parent Buddhist or Shinto temples. See RISSHOKO-SEIKAI.

Relic. Relics are found in most religions, associated with holy men, saints and martyrs. They are often part of the body or clothing of the saint, or any object connected with him. In general they indicate the historical life of the saint, though they may also illustrate some legendary event. But there are also foot-

RELIC OF SHRINE

steps of celestial gods, such as Vishnu, in India, and huge footsteps of more historical characters like the Buddha. The relic is normally enclosed in a small or large shrine (see STŪPA) and pilgrims visit it to pay their devotions and offer prayers for help.

Remus. In Roman mythology one of the grandsons of Numitor, who founded Rome with his brother Romulus (q.v.). It is said that he was killed for jumping over the newly built walls of the city. Greek authors generally called him Rhomos, but the name Remus may be derived from Rome.

Reshef, Resheph. Phoenician god of 'lightning', fire and war. He was called great God and Lord of the heavens. He was represented with the head of a

gazelle, or in Egypt, where his cult was adopted, as a bearded man with a crown from which sprang gazelle's horns. Syrian workers in Egypt dedicated tablets to Reshef, and associated him with the goddess Kedesh (q.v.). His name survives in the ruins of Arsouf, north of Jaffa.

Responsa. Jewish Latin term for 'Questions and Replies' (*Sheeloth u-Teshuboth*), mostly correspondence of individuals and communities with teachers (see GEONIM) on religious, legal and social matters. These teachings came to be accepted as authoritative and were passed down to succeeding generations.

Revenant. A French term for one who has 'returned' from the dead, and so a ghost or apparition. It may be loosely applied to a Zombie (q.v.), but there is a difference since a Revenant has no necessary connection with witchcraft.

Rhea. One of the ancient Greek Titans, who with her brother Kronos (q.v.) ruled over the planet Saturn. They had six children, five of whom Kronos swallowed but later vomited up; these were: Hestia, Demeter, Hera, Hades and Poseidon. The last was Zeus, but Rhea hid him in Crete and wrapped a stone in swaddling-clothes for Kronos to swallow. The oak was sacred to Rhea, and some have equated her with Dione or Diana, goddess of an oak cult. The Romans identified her with Ops (q.v.).

Rhea Silvia was a Vestal Virgin, violated by Mars to whom she bore the twins Romulus and Remus (q.v.); she was imprisoned while they were thrown into the Tiber.

Rhiannon, Rigantona. Celtic deity, consort of the sea god Manawyddan (see MANANNAN), whose tale is told in the *Mabinogion* (q.v.). A magician caused her to disappear, along with a castle, but Manawyddan overcame the magician and restored his wife.

Ribāt. Fortified Islamic monastery, originally a place for keeping horses, a caravanserai, but quite early applied to a religious and military establishment. The origins of the name are uncertain. The Ribāt prepared men for the Holy War (see JIHĀD), the defence and extension of Islam. The trained man was a Murābit, now popularly called a Marabout (q.v.), and in modern times a peaceful individual. See ALMORAVIDS.

Ribhu. Skilful and semi-divine beings in Indian mythology, perhaps rays of the sun or seasons of the year. They were said to be three: Ribhu, Vibhu and Vāja; they were artisans who made Indra's chariot and a fine sacrificial cup. They may have been deified workmen, or divine artificers like Tvashtri (q.v.).

Ridā, Muhammad Rashīd. Islamic reformer from Tripoli in Lebanon who went to Egypt in 1897 and became the disciple and friend of Muhammad 'Abduh (q.v.). He edited a reformist monthly journal *al-Manār*, in which 'Abduh's commentary on the *Qur'ān* appeared, completed by Ridā. He also wrote a long biography of 'Abduh, and continued his social and reforming teaching. He died in 1935.

Right-hand Worshippers. See SHĀKTAS and TANTRA.

Rig Veda. (Sanskrit) 'Veda of praise' (from a basic form *Rich*; and see also VEDA), the most sacred and ancient scriptures of Hinduism. Sometimes claimed as the world's oldest 'scriptures', excavations at Harappā (q.v.) show that they must have been composed later, perhaps between 1500 and 1000 B.C., thus later than the religious texts of ancient Egypt and Mesopotamia. Also they were not written down for many centuries, being passed on orally, and the earliest manuscripts are from about the fourteenth century A.D. The *Rig Veda* consists of 1017 hymns (or 1028 with some additions) arranged in ten books or Mandalas ('circles'), the hymns consisting of various numbers of verses (mantras). The *Vedas* are psalms of praise to the many gods of the Aryan Indians, the most popular being Agni and Indra. In the tenth book come the beginnings of speculation, about the origins of the universe and man, with a famous 'Hymn of Creation' and a 'Hymn of Man'. The *Vedas* are revealed or 'heard' (*shruti*) scriptures, received from the gods by ancient seers. Their use is confined to the top three castes or classes.

Rimmon. See RAMMAN.

Rinzai. One of the two main schools of Japanese Zen (q.v.), the name being derived from the school of the Chinese teacher Lin-chi (q.v.). The Rinzai monks are especially given to the use of the Kōan (q.v.) paradoxes, while members of the opposite school, Sōtō, prefer sitting in silence (*zazen*) and performing the works of everyday life. Rinzai has had considerable publicity, through the many writings of the late D. T. Suzuki, but has less followers than Sōtō. Rinzai was introduced to Japan by Eisai in the twelfth century.

Rishabha. The first of the present cycle of twenty-four Jinas of Jainism (q.v.), whence he is sometimes called Ādi-Nātha, 'primal helper'. The story of Rishabha is highly legendary and he is said to have lived eight million years. A version of his life is in the *Kalpa Sūtra*, where he is credited with teaching men the seventy-two sciences, of which writing was the first and arithmetic the most important. Otherwise the life is modelled, with appropriate exaggerations, on that of the more historical Mahāvīra. Rishabha appears in many statues of the twenty-four Jinas in Jain temples, and receives offerings like the others. In Hindu devotional legend, in the *Bhāgavata Purāna*, Rishabha was a righteous king who had a hundred sons, but he handed over the kingdom to his eldest son Bharata and took up a life of extreme asceticism.

Rishi. (Sanskrit) a singer of hymns, a poet or 'sage' (sometimes spelt ṛsi). The Rishis were the seers who received the *Vedas* from the gods. There were said to be seven Rishis, beginning with Gotama, sometimes identified with the seven stars of the Great Bear, or with seven senses, or seven vital airs. Ten Rishis are also mentioned as subordinate creators of gods and men. In later use any wise or holy man may be called a Rishi or Mahārishi, great sage.

Risshoko-seikai. (Japanese) 'society for establishing righteous and friendly association', one of the modern Japanese movements which broke away from Reiyukai (q.v.) in 1938. It is Mahāyāna Buddhist, following the *Lotus Sūtra* (q.v.). In recent years it has made many converts, through its thousands of trained teachers, and claims over a million members.

Rita. (Sanskrit) 'law', 'order', especially religious rule and custom. In the *Rig Veda* divine and human order is indicated by Rita and the moral god Varuna is especially concerned with its observance. In later times Rita is largely replaced by the concept of Dharma (q.v.), right and duty.

Ritsu. Japanese name for the Disciplinary or Lu (q.v.) school of Buddhism.

Rohita. 'Red' (Sanskrit), a red horse, horse of fire or the sun in Hindu mythology. In the *Atharva Veda* Rohita is celebrated as the sun or fire.

Romulus and Remus. Legendary founders of Rome, the name Romulus meaning 'Roman'. They were twin brothers, children of Mars and the Vestal Virgin Rhea Silvia (q.v.). They were thrown into the Tiber by Amulius, who had deposed his brother Numitor, Rhea's

father. The twins were suckled by a she-wolf (some say also by a woodpecker; both sacred to Mars) and brought up by herdsman Faustulus and Acca Larentia, also a goddess. When Romulus and Remus grew up, they killed Amulius, reinstated Numitor and founded a city of their own on the Palatine hill in what was later Rome. Romulus built the walls, invited fugitives there and stole wives for his men from the Sabines. After reigning forty years Romulus disappeared in a storm and was said to have become the Sabine god Quirinus. Remus had been killed earlier jumping over the wall. Romulus and Remus are often represented in art as twins suckled by a wolf, as in Roman pictures and statues.

Rongo. God of agriculture and peace in Maori religion. When sweet potatoes were planted, Rongo, as their fertilizing deity, was brought near a fire to make sure of a good harvest. See ATUA.

Rosary. See PRAYER BEADS.

Roshana. See LOCHANĀ.

Rosh Hashanah. (Hebrew) 'beginning of the year', the Jewish festival of New Year (q.v.).

Roshi. Japanese term for an 'old teacher', the title of the master of a Zen (q.v.) monastery who instructs pupils in Za-zen. He may be the abbot or head of the monastery or give himself completely to instructing his pupils.

Rubā'īyāt. (Persian) 'quatrains', a form of verse in stanzas of four lines in which the first, second and third lines rhyme. The most popular example of this verse in English is in Edward Fitzgerald's version of the *Rubā'īyāt of Omar Khayyām* (q.v.).

Rudra. A storm god of ancient Hinduism, whose name probably meant the Howler or Terrible. He is closely associated with the warrior and storm god Indra, and with the fire Agni. Rudra is father of lesser storm spirits, Rudras and Maruts (q.v.). Later he is said to have had eleven sons, which were symbolical of the ten vital breaths and the heart or mind. Rudra was both destructive, bringing disease to men and cattle, and kindly, bringing healing. He is called 'auspicious' (*shiva*), and the great god Shiva took over both the kindly and terrible aspects of Rudra's nature, while Rudra as a god virtually disappeared.

Rūh. (Arabic) 'breath', spirit, like the Hebrew *ruach* used of the breath of life and Spirit of God. In the *Qur'ān* Jesus ('Īsā) is called 'a *rūh* from God' (4, 169/171), perhaps in reference to the manner of his birth, but the title Spirit is applied to Jesus again in later Islamic usage. The *Qur'ān* also speaks of the Holy Spirit, or perhaps rather the Spirit of Holiness. It is not always easy to distinguish spirit from soul, as in other religions also. See NAFS.

Rukminī. Daughter of Bhīshmaka, king of Vidarbha, she fell in love with Krishna (q.v.), but her brother was an enemy of Krishna and got her engaged to King Shishupāla. Krishna seized her from the temple on her wedding day and married her. She bore him nine sons and a daughter, but he had many other wives, though Rukminī was chief. On Krishna's death Rukminī with other wives burnt herself on his funeral pyre.

Rūmī, Jalāl al-Dīn. Greatest of Persian Sūfī mystics, born at Balkh in 1207 and died at Konya in 1273. After travelling to famous centres, including Mecca, Rūmī met a Sūfī named Tibrīzī and decided to devote himself to mystical studies, settling at Konya, where his tomb is in the monastery that he founded. He is credited with the foundation of the Dancing or Twirling Dervishes, though there existed Dervish orders (q.v.) before him, dancing round a leader as planets round the sun. Music held an important part in their ceremonies, which is unusual in Islam. Rūmī's principal work was the composition of the *Mathnawī*, a long poem in six books, full of legends, maxims and Sūfī teachings, including a number of stories of the poverty of Jesus. Rūmī sought to rcconcilc religions, and said that 'the lamps are different but the Light is the same'. All men, even Satan, would be saved because all served God secretly. The Mathnawī has been called 'the *Qur'ān* of Persia', and much of it is learnt by heart in Persia, while there are numerous translations. See HĀFIZ.

Rūpa. 'Form' (Sanskrit) of any being, as the outward appearance or shape. The Hindu gods may assume a form or appearance or colour on occasion, and may be depicted with a multitude of forms. In Buddhism the Rūpa is one of the five constituents or Skandhas (q.v.). A Buddha Rūpa is an image, in which the Buddha is represented in various attitudes, usually seated and cross-legged, sometimes sitting with legs down, and sometimes standing or lying down to pass into Nirvāna. See MUDRĀ. For Rūpa-kāya, see TRIKĀYA.

Ryōbu Shinto. Japanese 'two-fold' or 'dual' Shinto, the fusion of Shinto and Buddhism made in the ninth century by Dengyo Daishi and Kōbō Daishi. The Shinto gods (Kami) were identified with Buddhist Bodhisattvas, and many Shinto shrines were taken over and embellished in the interests of Buddhism. This mixture was also called Shinbutsu. Ryōbu Shinto lasted till 1868, when Shinto was restored as the state religion and Buddhism was declared foreign and persecuted. However in 1872 liberty was established in Japan for all religions. Until 1945 there was strong pressure from Shinto for dominance, but Buddhism and Shinto have been so long intertwined that many mutual influences remain.

S

Saadya ben Joseph. Jewish philosopher (A.D. 892–942), who has been called the 'father of Jewish philosophy'. Born in Upper Egypt, his great knowledge caused his appointment at an early age to the Gaonate ('Eminence', see GEONIM) of the Babylonian Academy at Sura. Saadya was influenced by Islamic Kalām (q.v.), justifying the use of reason in theology, and he taught the unity of reason and faith. He also compiled one of the earliest Jewish Prayer Books for use in Egypt. His philosophical work, 'Faith and Knowledge' (*Emunoth Wedeoth*), was the first systematic effort at giving reasonable grounds for religious life. See RABBANISM.

Sabazius. A god of Phrygia and Lydia, sometimes identified by Greeks with Dionysus. The cult spread to Athens by the fifth century B.C., though derided by some writers. Later Sabazius was identified with the Lord Sabaoth of the *Bible*. He was often called Zeus Sabazius, bore the thunderbolt of Zeus and was accompanied by his eagle or by a snake.

Sabbāh, Hasan ibn. Persian Muslim, said to have been of Arab origin, born about the middle of the eleventh century and died 1124. He went to Egypt, and became a strong supporter of the Nizārī (q.v.) Shī'a sect. Returning home he took possession in 1090 of the mountain fortress of Alamūt and other strong places, and founded the order of the Assassins (q.v.). He did not invent assassination, which had been recommended by some Islamic sects as a religious duty before his time, but he gave them a focus at Alamūt, and was called by the Crusaders 'the Old Man of the Mountains' and by his followers 'our lord' (*saiyidnā*). He wrote several works, but they were destroyed when Alamūt was sacked by the Mongols in 1256.

Sabbatai Zevi. See SHABBETHAI ZVI.

Sābians, Sabeans, al-Sābi'a. The name given to groups of people who three times in the *Qur'ān* are named along with Jews and Christians as believers in God. They have been identified with the Mandeans (q.v.), the Elkasites, the Zoroastrians, or with star-worshippers of Harran. The latter, in Mesopotamia, would not qualify for the Quranic title of 'People of the Book', since they worshipped many gods and had idols, but under Muslim rule they claimed protection as the Quranic Sābians and they flourished until the thirteenth century. The true Sābians were most likely the Mandeans, as followers of John the Baptist and owners of scriptures.

Sabines, Sabini. Ancient inhabitants of Italy, to the north of Rome, who were renowned among the Romans for their religion and superstitions, so that numerous Roman gods and customs were said to have been derived from them. The legend of the Rape of the Sabines tells how Romulus invited them to a festival and stole their women for his own men. After centuries of wars the Sabines were finally merged with the Romans. See ROMULUS and QUIRINUS.

Sab'īya. 'Seveners'; see ISMĀ'ĪLĪS.

Saboraim. Hebrew root, 'to reflect', a name given to Jewish teachers who from the sixth century reflected on the teachings of the Amoraim (q.v.) which were in the *Talmud* and expounded them with additions.

Sacred Thread The ceremony of initiation (Sanskrit, *upanayana,* 'drawing near'), in which a Hindu boy became a full member of one of the three main castes, and 'twice born' (q.v.). The heart of the ceremony was to invest the body with the sacred thread (*yajñopavīta*) which hung from his left shoulder to his right hip and was always worn from then onwards. The thread is made of three cords of nine twisted strands each; of cotton, hemp or wool, and white, red or yellow, for Brahmins, Kshatriyas and Vaishyas respectively. Originally designed for the threee upper classes, it came to be restricted chiefly to the Brahmins and to males only.

There is a similar Parsi investiture, Naōjote (q.v.), in which a boy is clothed with a sacred shirt, Sudreh or Sadreh, and a sacred thread, Kūsti (q.v.). The Kūsti is made of wool, in fine strands, and tied round the boy's waist during the utterance of scriptural texts by the officiating priest.

Sadaqa, Sadaqāt. (Arabic) 'alms', the practice of special charity in Islam. Sadaqa is sometimes identified with the religious Pillar or duty of Zakāt (q.v.), which is a fixed and obligatory rate of almsgiving intended for the poor; but the proper use of Sadaqa is spontaneous or voluntary giving of alms as an act of charity.

Saddharma Pundarīka. See LOTUS SŪTRA.

Sādhana. (Sanskrit) 'fulfilment', 'worship', 'demonstration'. A name given to a course of discipline or spiritual

teaching, leading to fulfilment or realization of life. In Buddhism it is a method of Tantric (q.v.) training of the faculties to realize their potentiality. Tantric texts called Sādhanas, dating from about A.D. 500, describe this tradition and the spiritual beings connected with it.

Sādhāran. 'General', the name of that portion of the Brāhma Samāj (q.v.) which separated from Keshab Chandra Sen (q.v.) in 1878 and sought to organize this reform society in a more representative manner than under their old leader. Of the early missionaries, one of the most eminent was Shiva Nath Shastri, and many tours of India brought large numbers to the movement. The theistic, philanthropic and educational work of the Brāhma Samāj was continued.

Sādhu. (Sanskrit) 'good', 'holy', a general term for a holy man in India. The name is applied to many kinds, from extreme ascetics to common wonder-workers. There are many schools of Sādhus, and the philosopher Shankara (q.v.) tried to organize them into 'ten names'. Most Sādhus are initiated in youth, though some may enter the life later. Many carry a staff (*danda*, see DANDINS) or trident, wear a saffron robe or simple loincloth, or go naked. Some shave their heads, while others have long matted hair and beards, and smear their bodies with ashes. Some Sādhus live in solitude, and others in monastic communities, the majority are celibates, but some have female companions. Among the Jains a Sādhu is one of the fifth class of the five supreme categories of beings, a saint or ascetic. See also SANT.

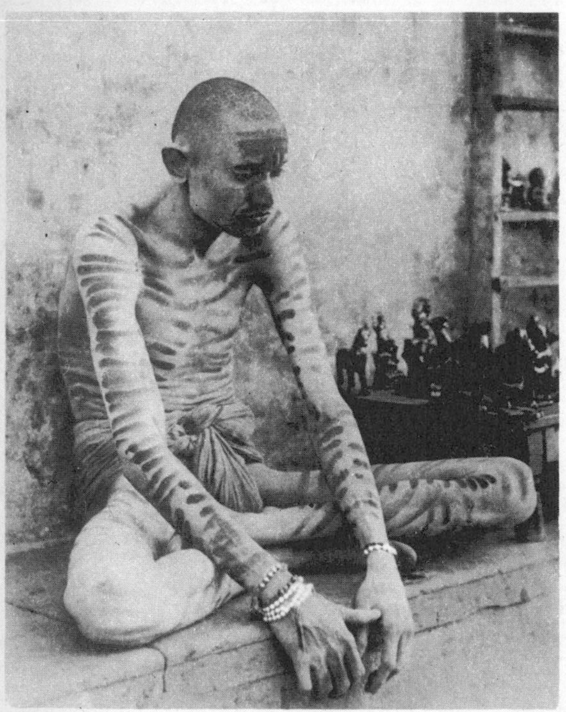

Sa'di. Persian Sūfī mystic (1193–1291), born and died in Shiraz. In his travels he was captured by Christians, ransomed by a chief of Aleppo and married his daughter. His poems are famous throughout Persia and neighbouring countries, especially the *Gulistan* or 'Rose Garden', *Pand Nameh* or 'Book of Counsel', and *Bostan* or 'Garden of Perfume'. Here human images are used for the relationships of the soul and God.

Sadreh. See SACRED THREAD.

Safā. A low mound at Mecca, probably meaning the 'stones'. In pagan times there was an image of a god Isāf here, which pilgrims used to touch, and then go to the neighbouring hill and image of Marwa. In the ritual of Islamic pilgrimage it is part of the ceremony to run backwards and forwards seven times between these hills, as Hagar ran looking for water for Ishmael. See MARWA.

Safed. Palestinian centre which saw a great development of the teaching of the Zohar (q.v.). One of the leading mystics of Safed was Moses Cordovero (1522–76), whose book the 'Orchard' (*Pardes*) is a rational exposition of Kabbalistic doctrines. He was overshadowed by Isaac Luria (q.v.) who elaborated Zoharic ideas. From Safed the teachings of Kabbalism spread throughout Palestine and across much of Europe.

Saga. Scandinavian goddess, one of the Asynjur (q.v.). She was said to dwell in a great abode called Sokkvabekkr, where with Odin she drank the water in golden cups. Saga has been identified with Frigg (q.v.).

Saga. (Old Norse) 'story', narratives of the Middle Ages, from Iceland and Norway, which tell of legendary and mythical characters in human and divine story. The more historical are those of Snorri (q.v.) and the *Sturlunga Saga* of Sturla. More imaginary are those of Njala, a foresighted lawyer, and the *Grettis Saga* (q.v.). The *Eddas* (q.v.) are more mythologies than Sagas and of more significance to religious knowledge.

Saguna. (Sanskrit) 'having Strands', with attributes or qualities. In Hindu philosophy all created beings are said to have three strands or Gunas (q.v.), but the absolute Brahman or deity has no attributes. Yet it is difficult for religion to believe in a God who has no attributes, of whom nothing can be said, and so the theistic *Shvetāshvatara Upanishad* (q.v.) says that the power of the divine was hidden 'in its own qualities' (*sva-guna*, 1, 3). See NIRGUNA.

Sahaja, Sahaj. Sanskrit and Punjabi terms for 'born together' and thence a state of mystical union with God or of supreme beatitude. It is used in Sikh and other Indian mystical writings.

Sahaj Dharis. (Punjabi) 'slow adopters' a term used by Sikhs of those who do not enter the brotherhood of the Khālsā (q.v.).

Sahasrāra. (Sanskrit) 'thousand-spoked', the name of a cavity supposed to be in the top of the head and to resemble a reversed lotus. In the anatomy of Hindu Tantra (q.v.), the coiled or serpent power, Kundalinī (q.v.), can only very occasionally rise up above the heart to the Sahasrāra, but the latter is a centre of psychic energy, and union of the Kundalinī with the Sahasrāra brings liberation.

Sahīh. See MUSLIM IBN AL-HAJJĀJ.

Saichi, Saichō. Name of Dengyō Daishi (q.v.), founder of Japanese Tendai Buddhism.

Saints, Muslim. See WALĪ and SHIRK.

Saiva, Saivite. See SHAIVA and SHAIVISM.

Saiyid. See SAYYID.

Saktas, Sakti. See SHAKTI.

Sakha. See SHĀKHĀ.

Sākyamuni. See SHĀKYAMUNI.

Sālagrāma. See SHĀLAGRĀMA.

Saladin, Salāh al-Dīn. Famous Muslim ruler, a Kurd born in Mesopotamia in 1138. He came to prominence in campaigns in Egypt where he became sultan in 1174. He defeated the Franks at the crucial battle of Hattin in 1187 and took Jerusalem in the same year, allowing the Frankish defenders to leave peaceably. He died in Damascus in 1193, admired by foes and friends, and patron of arts and religion. See AYYŪBIDS.

Salām, Salaam. (Arabic) 'peace', related to Hebrew and Aramaic *Shālōm* and *Shelām*. *Salām 'alaikum*, 'peace be upon you', is found in the *Qur'ān* (6, 54) and has remained the common form of greeting in Muslim lands down to this day. The reply is: *Alaikum es-salām*. *Salām* has a religious value, and in addition is used to describe a litany uttered from minarets on Fridays. In India seven *Salāms* from the *Qur'ān* are recited or written down for protective purposes.

Salāt. (Arabic) 'prayer', in the sense of ritual or regular acts of prayer. Salāt is one of the Pillars of Islam (q.v.), which every adult Muslim is required to perform five times a day: at dawn, midday, afternoon, sunset and night. The prayer need not be performed in a mosque, but at home or wherever the person may be, but he must face towards the Ka'ba in Mecca and pray on a prayer mat. It must be preceded by ritual ablutions, or washing face and head, hands and arms, and feet, and also by a declaration of pious intention (*nīya*). The first chapter of the *Qur'ān*, Fātiha (q.v.), is recited in Arabic, followed by kneeling, prostration and ascriptions, to form a section (*rak'a*) of prayer. Two or more *Rak'as* may be performed in each act of prayer. See JUM'A and DUĀ'.

Salii, Salians. Ancient minor priesthoods of Italy, so-called from the dances (from Latin *salire*, 'to dance') which they performed beating shields and singing hymns. Their hymn, *Carmen Saliare*, has only survived in fragments. The Salii were in two companies of twelve each, and were associated with the war god Mars. They wore ancient war dress and were prominent in the festivals of Quinquatrus (q.v.) and Armilustrium, on 19 March and 19 October, which opened and closed the campaigning season.

Salmān. A companion of Muhammad and popular figure of Islamic legend. He was a Persian, said to have been a Christian as well as a Zoroastrian before going to Medina and becoming a Muslim. He advised Muhammad to dig a Trench for the battle of that name, by which the Muslims were protected from Meccan attack in 627. Shī'a Muslims claim Salmān as a champion of the claims of 'Alī to be Caliph, and he is also said to be a founder of Sūfī mysticism.

Samādhi. (Sanskrit) 'putting together', concentration of thought or intense contemplation. In Yoga this concentration is the eighth and last stage of meditation, and in Buddhism it is the fourth stage of meditation or the last stage of the Noble Eightfold Path (q.v.), Sammā Samādhi. See GORAKHNĀTH.

Samana, Sāmanera. Pali term for an ascetic, and especially a Buddhist monk of the lowest order. The Sanskrit Shramana was also applied to a Jain ascetic, who was later more usually called a Yati. (q.v.)

Sāma-Veda. The *Veda* of 'chants', one of the three principal *Vedas* (q.v.). It is composed of two major parts, with six and nine books respectively. There are 1549 verses, all of which, except some 78, are to be found in the *Rig Veda* (q.v.). The *Sāma-Veda* is therefore highly repetitive. Like the *Rig Veda* it praises many gods, but in particular the ritual juice, Soma. Its verses were chanted by priests at Soma rituals, but to others their interest is small apart from the *Rig Veda*.

Sambandar. Tamil religious poet (died A.D. 660). He was a devotee of the god Shiva, is said to have sung his praises at the age of three and to have died at seventeen. His poems are contained in the *Tevāram* hymns of Shaiva Siddhānta (q.v.).

Sambhoga-Kāya. (Sanskrit) 'enjoyment-body', that manifestation of the ultimate Buddha by which the doctrine was communicated to the exalted Bodhisattvas (q.v.), as distinct from the Nirmāna-kāya (q.v.) which revealed it to the world. See TRIKĀYA.

Sambodhi. Buddhist term (Sanskrit and Pali) for the wisdom bringing the highest stages of an Arahat. It is the 'perfect enlightenment' of a Buddha, also called Sammā Sambodhi.

Samhain, Samuin. Ancient Celtic feast, held at the end of October and beginning of November. In Ireland it was celebrated on the shores of lakes. Samhain marked the beginning of winter, as Beltane (q.v.) marked the onset of summer. Samhain meant 'summer end', and bonfires were lit to strengthen the powers of the waning sun. These are perpetuated in the bonfires of November 5, still popular in Britain. In the Christian calendar Samhain was merged into All Saints' Day on November 1.

Samhitā, Sanhitā. (Sanskrit) 'collection', union by grammatical rules. The term is used especially of the text of the *Vedas* since the separate words were joined (*sandhi*) by euphonic rules and underwent changes to form a continuous text. There are *Samhitās*, verse recensions, of the *Rig*, *Sāma* and *Atharva Vedas*, and two types, 'Black' and 'White' in the *Yajur Veda*. Other arrangements of verses could be called *Samhitās*, such as texts in the *Purāna* tales (q.v.).

Samkhāras. See SAMSKĀRAS.

Sāmkhya, Sānkhya. (Sanskrit) 'enumeration' or 'count'. Perhaps the oldest of the six systems of orthodox Hindu philosophy. It is said to have been founded by Kapila (q.v.), a legendary sage perhaps of the seventh century B.C., but the earliest text is the *Sāmkhya-kārikā* of Īshvara-Krishna (q.v.) of the third or fourth century A.D. Sāmkhya is mentioned in the later classical *Upanishads* and the *Bhagavad-Gītā*, though at that date it was probably a method rather than a clearly defined system and school of philosophy. Sāmkhya enumerates twenty-five basic principles (*tattva*), of which the first is Prakriti, matter or nature, from which the next twenty-three principles develop. The twenty-fifth, and independent, is the Person or Spirit, Purusha. The dualism of Prakriti and Purusha dominates Sāmkhya thought, with little room for God, though in later ages some theism emerges. Sāmkhya also taught the doctrine of three Gunas (q.v.), elemental qualities within matter, a notion which influenced much other Indian thought. See also YOGA.

Sammā. (Pali) 'supreme' or 'right'. In the Buddhist teaching of the Noble Eightfold Path (q.v.), each step is described as Sammā, 'right' or perfect. In the absolute sense it means 'supreme'.

Samnyāsi. See SANNYĀSI.

Samrāj, Samrāt. (Sanskrit) 'full rule', universal reign, the state of a Hindu king when he was free from allegiance to any other ruler. This was sealed by the Vājapeya sacrifice (q.v.).

Samsāra. (Sanskrit) 'going through', transmigration, the passage of the soul through a series of earthly lives. See TRANSMIGRATION.

Samskāras. Hindu personal religious ceremonies, from a root word meaning 'putting together' or 'making perfect'. There are twelve Samskāras which traditionally were enjoined on the orthodox Hindus of the three upper classes, from the conception of a child to marriage, and one of the most important was investiture with the Sacred Thread (q.v.). By extension the Samskāras may be other purificatory ceremonies and faculties of mind or qualities. In Buddhist thought the Samskāras (Pali: Samkhāras) are the aggregates, the grouping of mental properties which compose awareness, and the fourth of the five Skandhas (q.v.), the elements which form a being.

Samuin. See SAMHAIN.

Samurai. Japanese 'guardians' or 'warriors'. They were attached to a Daimyō, 'great name', a feudal lord to whom they must be loyal to death. In the feudal period only the Samurai could carry swords. For the code of the Samurai, see BUSHIDŌ.

Samyutta Nikāya. (Pali) 'collection of kindred sayings', the third section of the second main division of the Theravāda Buddhist canon of scripture. See TRIPITAKA and SŪTRA.

Sanātana Dharma. (Sanskrit) 'eternal right', truth, religion. A term used in the *Bhagavad-Gītā* for the eternal laws of family (1, 40). Sanātana is related to Latin *senex*, for age and elders, and has a similar meaning of tradition. Sanātana Dharma is the term often used by Indians nowadays for their religion which the West has called Hinduism (q.v.).

Sānchi. A centre of famous Buddhist buildings in western India near Bhopal and Bhilsa, sometimes called the 'Bhilsa Topes', the word *Tope* being derived from *Stūpa* (q.v.). On a hilltop there stand the stūpas, the largest being over twelve metres high, encased in stone, and said to contain Buddhist relics. The original building was erected during the reign of the emperor Ashoka (q.v.) in the third century B.C. The whole Stūpa is surrounded by a stone railing, with four ornamental stone gateways, lavishly carved with scenes from Indian mythology; these gates were added during the first century B.C. Another smaller stūpa contained the relics of two disciples of the Buddha, Moggallāna and Sāriputta (qq.v.). These were discovered in 1851 and taken to the Victoria and Albert Museum in London, but in 1953 they were returned to Sānchi and re-interred in a new shrine.

Sandhyā. 'Twilight' (Sanskrit), a daughter of the creator god Brahmā in Hindu mythology and one of the wives of Shiva. In a *Purāna* story Sandhyā was pursued by her father and changed into a deer, whereupon he changed into a stag. Shiva shot an arrow which cut off the stag's head, and this head remains in the fifth mansion of the sky, while the arrow is in the sixth mansion. Sandhyā as the 'joining together', twilight of morning and evening and noon period, is the name given to religious acts performed by Brahmins at these Sandhyā services, especially repeating the Gāyatrī mantra (q.v.). Between each Yuga (q.v.), world age, there is a Sandhyā twilight.

Sangha, Samgha. (Sanskrit) an 'assembly'; a Hindu gathering of sages, a Jain monastic fraternity or sect, and the Buddhist society and order of monks (see BHIKKHU). Founded by the Buddha himself, the Buddhist Sangha may well claim to be the world's oldest monastic order. It is the last of the Three Jewels (q.v.), recited daily by Buddhists: 'I go to the Sangha for refuge.' The Sangha is entered by initiation, but members may leave if they wish and monasteries are often open to laymen. The Sangha is strong in Theravāda (q.v.) Buddhism in south-east Asia, now much weakened in China and Tibet, and different in Japan where many monasteries are more like colleges than secluded retreats.

Sanghamittā. In Buddhist legend a nun said to be sister of the monk Mahinda who himself was supposed to be a son of the emperor Ashoka (q.v.). A Ceylonese princess, Anulā, wanted to become a nun but at that time nobody in the island was qualified to consecrate her and so Sanghamittā was fetched. Perhaps more importantly, Sanghamittā brought a branch of the sacred Bo-tree (q.v.), from Gayā where the Buddha had been enlightened underneath its shade. It was planted at Meghavana and still survives, being claimed as the oldest tree in the world, since the parent tree was destroyed.

Sanjaya. The charioteer of King Dhrita-rāshtra in the *Bhagavad-Gītā* (q.v.). He was also an ambassador to the Pāndu warriors before the outbreak of the war in which he drove his master. Although Dhrita-rāshtra was blind, he was offered supernatural vision to see how the battle went, but he knew there would be great carnage and could not bear the sight. So Sanjaya told him all that went on and, in theory, recited the *Bhagavad-Gītā* in which, however, he himself speaks only most of the first chapter, part of the eleventh, and the conclusion of the eighteenth.

Sankara. See SHANKARA.

Sānkhya. See SĀMKHYA.

San Lun. See KUMĀRAJĪVA.

Sannyāsi, Samnyāsi. (Sanskrit) 'laying aside', one who has given up worldly

affairs. A Sannyāsi traditionally is a Brahmin who has entered the fourth stage or Āshram (q.v.) of life and has abandoned the world to become a mendicant. The term is more widely applied to any religious ascetic or beggar. A female mendicant or nun is a Sannyāsinī.

Sanskrit. Classical language of the Hindu scriptures, from Samskrita, 'perfected', as opposed to Prakrita, 'unrefined' or popular. The oldest forms are in Vedic, which is rather like the relationship of Homeric to classical Greek, some forms having gone out of usage. The grammarian Pānini (q.v.) laid down rules for the language in the fourth century B.C. The first Sanskrit grammar in a European language was compiled by a Jesuit, Hanxleden, from 1699–1732. The first direct translation of a Sanskrit text into English was in 1785, the *Bhagavad-Gītā* by Charles Wilkins. Sanskrit has long since been replaced by popular vernaculars, such as Hindi, but it has been revived for study as a classical language and there have been moves to introduce it as a common Indian language. It is related to Greek and Latin.

Sant. In Indian religion one who controls his senses, but later used to designate any religious beggar, and often synonymous with Sādhu (q.v.). Sant, however, also indicates a sect of central India, and more generally those who believe in a supreme God, but not in his Avatars (q.v.), such as Kabīr and Nānak (qq.v.).

Sāntideva. See SHĀNTIDEVA.

San Tsang. The *Tripitaka* (q.v.) or Chinese version of the canon of Buddhist scripture; however, it differs from the Theravāda *Tripitaka* in having four rather than three main divisions, and in including many more Mahāyāna than Theravāda texts. The *San Tsang* includes the *Vinaya* (*Lü*), the *Sūtras* (*Ching*) and the *Abhidharma* (*Lun*), and also many Miscellaneous Works (*Tsa*) by Chinese Buddhists. It includes many important Mahāyāna texts, translated from Sanskrit by Kumārajīva (q.v.) and others. The oldest Buddhist work in Chinese still extant is the *Diamond Sūtra* (q.v.), printed in A.D. 868.

Sanūsī, Senussi. A conservative African Islamic order, founded by Muhammad ibn 'Alī-al-Sanūsī (1791–1859). He was born in Mustaghanim, Algeria, and studied at Fez, Cairo and Mecca. Finally Sanūsī settled at Jaghbub in Libya and built a monastery which became a renowned Islamic centre. He was a great scholar, with a library of eight thousand books, and he sought to bring his followers back to the original purity of Islam. He founded a missionary order, Sanūsiya, which became involved in struggles against the colonial invasions of Italy and France. There were several wars and the present head of the order, Sayyid Idrīs, had to flee from Italian rule into Egypt and did not return to Libya till its liberation in 1943. He ruled the new state till the nationalist revolution in 1969. The Sanūsiya are orthodox Muslims, of the Māliki school, and have a conventional form of Sūfī mysticism.

Saoshyans, Sōshyans. (Pahlavi) 'he who brings benefit', the 'Saviour' of Zoroastrian eschatology. In the *Gāthās* (q.v.) it seems that the future saviour is Zoroaster himself, but in later Zoroastrian belief the Saoshyans is the last of the posthumous sons of Zoroaster, born miraculously from his preserved seed. He is therefore still a hero and not a god, and represents the human race. The supreme God, Ahura Mazdā, entrusts the resurrection of men to Saoshyans, and he first raises Gayōmart, the ancestor of all men. Saoshyans then sacrificed a bull, Hadhayans, and from its fat a white Haoma (q.v.) liquid was prepared as a drink of immortality which gave a 'second life' to men who would die no more. In Zoroastrian and Mithraic liturgy, both drinking Haoma and sacrificing the bull procured immortality.

Sārada Devī. Bengali woman (1855–1920), who at the age of six was married to the nineteenth century Hindu saint Rāmakrishna (q.v.). At that age the marriage is binding but the couple do not live together and, although the young bride joined her husband at his temple in Calcutta when she was eighteen, the marriage was never consummated. Her name was first Sāradamani, changed to Devī, 'goddess', when she was regarded as a saint in her own right, referred to as Holy Mother and an Avatar of the Great Mother (see DEVĪ). At the Rāmakrishna centre at Belur, north of Calcutta, there is a temple with an image of Sārada Devī, and she is adored by worshippers.

Sarapis. See SERAPIS.

Sarasvatī. An Indian river identified with a goddess of the waters. In the *Rig Veda* she is associated with various deities, and later is identified with speech, Vāch, and so is goddess of eloquence. Later still she is regularly regarded as the wife of the creator divinity Brahmā, and so also named Brahmī. Sarasvatī is said to have invented the Sanskrit language and letters, and to be patron of letters, arts and sciences. In art Sarasvatī is represented as a gracious lady, with two arms or more, and holding a lute. She is goddess of intellectuals, and books and pens are placed in front of her images.

Sarasvatī, modern Hindu reformer, see DAYĀNANDA.

Sarcophagus. (Greek) 'eating flesh'; a limestone which consumed animal substances was often used in classical times for making coffins, and so a Sarcophagus was a coffin. Greek coffins were of stone, wood, lead or clay, and decorated in similar fashion to temples. Roman coffins were sometimes in the shape of altars or basins. Wooden sarcophagi have rarely survived, but there are many still visible in stone or lead. See MUMMY and CREMATION.

Sāriputta, Sāriputra. One of the two principal disciples of Gautama the Buddha (the other was Moggallāna), and also known as Upatissa. He was called 'Captain of the Dhamma', and said to be next to the Buddha himself in 'Turning the Wheel of Doctrine'. Several dialogues in the Buddhist scriptures are attributed to Sāriputta. His relics were found in a stūpa at Sānchi (q.v.) and re-interred there in 1953.

Śārīraka Sūtra. (Sanskrit), 'text of the embodied self', another name for the *Vedānta Sūtra* (q.v.), so called because it considers the embodiment or manifestation of the eternal Self.

Sarvāstivāda. (Sanskrit) 'all things are real', the name of a Buddhist school or groups of schools. In some lists the name is a general one which covers seven sub-sects, but clearly in early Buddhism the Sarvāstivādins were among the most important schools, and partly from them arose new tendencies which developed into Mahāyāna (q.v.). The Sarvāstivādins, sometimes called Realists, came nearer than most Buddhists to rejecting the common belief in universal impermanence. They were especially insistent on the real existence of past events, otherwise these would have had no causal efficacy to produce future events. In course of time the Sarvāstivādins merged with the Mahāyāna and much of their scripture survives in Chinese translations.

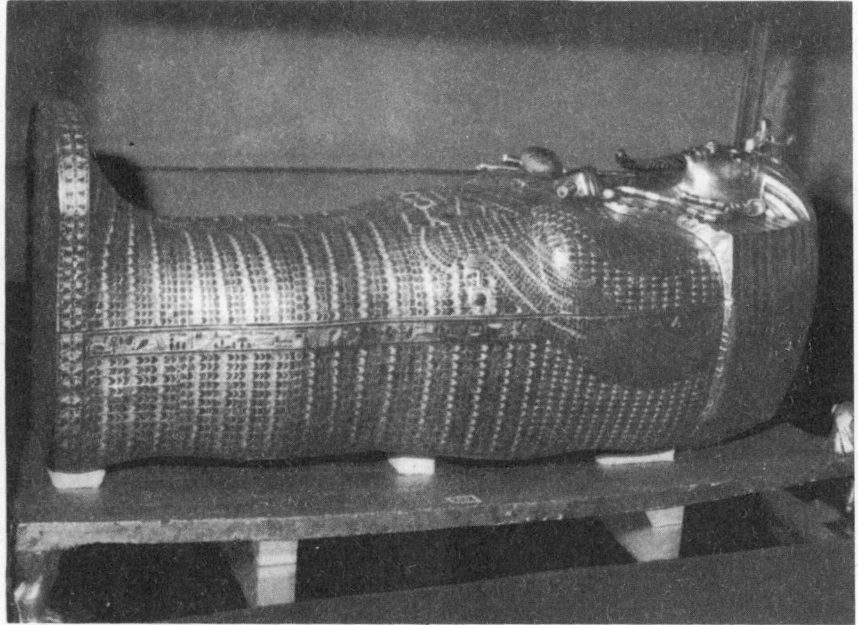

Sāsana. Pali Buddhist term for 'doctrine', the Dhamma which was taught by Gautama the Buddha.

Sasportas, Jacob. Learned rabbi of Amsterdam (1610–1698), who in 1664 was for a year spiritual head of the English Sephardi Jews. He wrote an important work on legal problems, but was even more significant for exposing the claims of the pseudo-Messiah Shabbethai Zvi (q.v.).

Sastra. See SHĀSTRA.

Sat. (Sanskrit) 'being', existence, and

hence the good or true. It is used of a good or wise man. In Indian philosophy Sat is true being, reality, essence, and is used of the self-existent or universal spirit, Brahman. The opposite is Asat (q.v.).

Satan. See SHAITĀN.

Satapatha. See SHATAPATHA.

Satarūpā. See SHATARŪPĀ.

Satī, Suttee. Originally the Sanskrit name for a 'virtuous woman', it came to be applied to a widow who burnt herself with her deceased husband on his funeral pyre. The custom has been practised in many parts of the ancient world, from China to Mesopotamia, and is hinted at in the *Rig Veda*. Greek accounts mention it in India and memorials are found at later periods. Mediaeval Indian writers said that Satī would bring deliverance from the sins of the couple. It was supposed to be voluntary, but contemporary accounts show that it was not always so. Satī was abolished in the British provinces of India in 1829 and in other states later.

Satis. Water goddess of ancient upper Egypt, her name meaning to 'scatter' or 'sow seed' perhaps referred to the fertilizing floods of the Nile. She was called Queen of the Gods and daughter of Rē' (q.v.), and in art was depicted as a woman with a crown and cow's horns. In later times she was identified with Isis. The centre of the worship of Satis was on the island of Elephantiné in the Nile and she was also worshipped at Aswan, though no temple devoted to her alone has survived.

Satnāmīs. A Hindu Vaishnava sect whose name (*nām*) for God is the one Reality (*Sat*). It is said to have been founded or organized about 1750, by Jag-jīvan-dās, whose tomb is at Katwa near Lucknow. Sub-sects include outcastes, like Chamars, and are strict vegetarians.

Satori. The 'enlightenment experience' (Japanese) of Zen Buddhism (q.v.). This is the goal of the Zen adept, who uses Kōan and Mondo (qq.v.) to attain it. The coming of Satori may be in a flash, and may be brief or the fullness of Nirvāna. It is regarded as a state of consciousness in which man passes beyond the present world of differences and discrimination to absolute peace.

Satsanga, Satsang. Sanskrit and Punjabi term for 'association with the good', a congregation or fellowship of true believers. It is used by Sikhs and also by some other groups, such as Rādhā Swāmīs (q.v.).

Sattva. (Sanskrit) 'goodness', brightness, the most refined of the three elementary substances or Strands (see GUNAS) of Hindu and especially Sāmkhya (q.v.) philosophy.

Saturn, Saturnalia. Saturn was a Roman god, perhaps of autumn sowing, and identified with the Greek Kronos (q.v.). His festival, the Saturnalia, was on 17 December, when there was considerable licence. Slaves could do as they liked, for a time, there was a Lord of Misrule, and presents were exchanged. Some of this was transferred into Christmas and New Year festivities. Saturn was also a planet from which Saturday is named.

Satya. (Sanskrit) 'true', real, truthfulness, virtue. A name of various Hindu saints and deities. It is used in compounds, such as Satyaloka, Satyagraha (qq.v.). See SAT.

Satyagraha. 'Truth-force', soul-force, a name introduced by Mahātma Gāndhi (q.v.) to express the positive side of his non-co-operation or non-violence movements. It was suggested in South Africa by Maganlal Gāndhi, in the form Sadagraha, and changed by the Mahātma to make a clearer reference to Satya, 'truth'.

Satyaloka. (Sanskrit) 'world of truth', the highest of the seven heavens in Hindu mythology, said to be the abode of the creator deity Brahmā, and so also called Brahmā-loka.

Satyrs. In Greek mythology Satyrs were spirits of woods and hills, and partly horse or goat in nature. They were often confused with Sileni (q.v.), but the latter were older and had horse-ears, while Satyrs were more goatlike, like Pan.

Saum, Sawm. (Arabic) 'fasting', rest. Fasting is prescribed in the *Qur'ān* (2, 179f.) and is one of the Pillars of Islam (q.v.). It is obligatory on all healthy adults for the whole of the daylight hours of the month of Ramadān (q.v.).

Savitri. A sun god in the *Vedas*, who has many hymns addressed to him. He is the god of the most holy verse of the *Vedas*, sometimes called by his name but more commonly known as Gāyatrī (q.v.).

Saxo Grammaticus. Danish historian and mythologist, who wrote *Gesta Danorum* about 1200. While including many of the same gods and heroes as the older Snorri (q.v.), Saxo gives more earthly locations to people and places of the supernatural world.

Sa'y. An Islamic ritual, undertaken during the course of the pilgrimage (see HAJJ), during which the pilgrims go seven times between the two low hills of Safā and Marwa (qq.v.), as Hagar is said to have done when searching for water for Ishmael.

Sayadaw. A Burmese title of respect, especially applied to heads of Buddhist monasteries, but also used at times for other distinguished persons.

Sayo Kitamura. See TENSHŌ-KŌTAI-JINGU-KYŌ.

Sayyid. (Arabic) 'prince', chief or owner. It is used in the *Qur'ān* of John the Baptist (3, 34/39). But the chief sense of Sayyid is of one distinguished by his birth, and particularly of a descendant of Muhammad. In Shī'a Muslim lands Sayyid is only used of descendants of Muhammad through Hasan and Husain. See SHARĪF.

Scandinavian Religion. The Scandinavians were related to the Germanic or Teutonic peoples of central Europe, who invaded England as Angles and Saxons. Their religion was similar but our knowledge is more extensive of Scandinavia. Stories of gods and heroes are found in the *Poetic* and *Prose Eddas* (q.v.), and particularly in the divine poem *Voluspa* (q.v.) which describes the gods and the final doom (see RAGNARÖK). Other sagas contain many traditional stories, but also throw light on religion. The *Prose Edda* distinguished two groups of gods, Aesir and Vanir (qq.v.), though later they are merged. Odin is both a hero and a god, fighting the Vanir but admitting Njörd and Frey into temples. Thor and Tyr, Balder and Loki, and many other divine beings played important roles (see separate articles). There were sacred groves for the gods, but also many temples mostly of wood but some of stone. Images of gods stood round the altars, where blood was shed and perpetual fire burned. Prayers were offered, rituals to preserve the seasons, and oaths were sworn in these sacred places.

Scapegoat. See PHARMAKOS and THARGELIA.

Scarab. A beetle (Latin, *scarabaeus*) reverenced by the ancient Egyptians. Models of Scarabs were cut out of many gems and semi-precious stones, often blue, sometimes set in gold. Inscribed with the thirtieth chapter of the *Book of the Dead* (q.v.), they could take the place of the heart in mummies. The Scarab was the special symbol of the sun-god Khepri (q.v.), who was 'he who rolls', causing the sun to roll across the sky as a beetle rolls its egg.

Scylla. In Greek mythology a monster who dwelt in a cave opposite the whirlpool of Charybdis (q.v.). She had six heads and twelve feet, and ate fish but could devour men off passing ships. The hero Odysseus got past her with difficulty. Later ages said that Scylla was a natural rock in the Straits of Messina.

Seal. A title of Muhammad, applied once in the *Qur'ān* (33, 40) where it is said that Muhammad is 'the messenger of God and the seal (*khātam*) of the prophets'. The term is not explained here and it may mean that he confirms what other prophets have said before. But in Islamic belief Muhammad is the last of the prophets, sealing up the succession, and no prophet appears after him. Even the Shī'a, who greatly revere Muhammad's cousin 'Alī, call 'Alī the friend of God and Imām (leader) but not prophet. Legend also said that Muhammad had a 'seal of prophecy', a large mole on his back, which was recognized when he was a boy by a Christian monk named Bahīra.

Sebek. A water-god of ancient Egypt, symbolized by the crocodile with which he was often identified. Since crocodiles are fearsome and destructive, Sebek was feared and regarded as the personification of evil powers and death itself, and he was associated with Set (q.v.). In art Sebek appears as a crocodile, or a man with a crocodile's head.

Sebha. See SUBHA.

Sect Shinto. A name particularly applied before 1945 to varieties of new religious associations in Japan. Religious independence was not always allowed, and new movements had to assimilate themselves to Shinto patterns and were called Sectarian Shinto (Kyōha or Shuha) to distinguish them from Sanctuary or Shrine (Jinja) Shinto. Now such movements are commonly called 'New Religions', and in 1960 it was said that there were more than 126 of them. They generally have a recognized founder, organizations that in some ways resemble churches, and particular doctrines and practices. See separate articles, such as: ANANAI-KYŌ, ITTŌEN, KUROZUMI-KYŌ, KONKŌ-KYŌ, SŌKKA GAKKAI, TENRI-KYŌ.

Seder. (Hebrew) 'order', the name of the Jewish service held at home on the first and second nights of Passover (q.v.). It is the most important domestic ceremony and the ritual is known as Seder Haggadah. At the Seder unleavened bread, bitter herbs and wine recall the travails and deliverance of the Exodus. Strangers are welcomed and a cup is reserved for Elijah. Children ask questions to elicit the teaching of the distinctiveness of the occasion.

The *Seder* or *Siddur* of Rav Amram was the first complete Jewish Prayer Book, compiled by Amram Gaon (died 874), for Spanish Jews. Another was produced by Saadya Gaon (892–942) for Egyptian Jews.

Sefer ha-Mitzvoth. (Hebrew) 'Book of the Precepts', published in 770 by Anan ben David in Aramaic, setting out his Karaite (q.v.) teachings, very different from those of most rabbis as prescribed in the *Mishnah* and *Talmud*.

Sefer Hasidism. (Hebrew) 'Book of the Pious', a medieval work of Jewish Kabbalah, attributed to Judah ha-Hasid (died 1217, q.v.).

Sefer Yetzirah. (Hebrew) 'Book of Creation', Jewish magical and mystical work, attributed to Abraham, but probably compiled in the eighth century AD or later in Babylon. It is concerned with speculations into cosmology, and introduces the notion of ten Sefiroth (q.v.), the rays which emanated from God at creation, adding to this mystical notions of the letters of the alphabet as means of divine utterance.

Sefiroth. A term of Jewish Kabbalistic mysticism, of uncertain origin. It may be derived from 'sapphire' (Hebrew, *sappir*), the colour of rays which shone from God at the creation, or from a word meaning 'to number', since there are numbered principles, ten rays and twenty-two letters of the alphabet. There were ten Sefiroth, rays or ideas or forms, in which all beings were originally made. In the Zohar (q.v.), the Sefiroth are channels of light which are projected into time by En Sof (q.v.), the Infinite. The last Sefirah is also the Shekhinah (q.v.), the indwelling of God in the world.

Seicho No Ie. (Japanese) 'house of growth', one of the modern religious movements in Japan. It was founded by Masaharu Taniguchi in 1934, from the Omoto (q.v.) movement. Its teachings are similar in some ways to those of Christian Science and there is emphasis on healing by faith. All men are said to be sons of God and, when they realize that, they enter great developments. Much propaganda is done through literature and over a million members are claimed.

Sekai-kyuseikyō. (Japanese) 'world Messianic church', one of the modern Japanese religious movements, a break away from Omoto (q.v.), founded by Mokichi Okada, who claimed to have been sent to establish paradise on earth and to abolish poverty, disease and strife. There is an emphasis, as in Taoism and Zen (qq.v.), on natural beauty and the importance of living according to nature. The movement claims about half a million members.

Sekhmet. (Egyptian) 'the powerful', a fiery goddess, representing the destructive heat of the sun. She was contrasted with the beneficent sun's powers of Bast (q.v.), though often identified with her. Sekhmet was the wife of Ptah and mother of Nefertem and Imhotep. She was depicted as a woman with the head of a lioness, bearing a solar disk and cobra. The chief centre of her cult was at Memphis.

Selene. The Greek moon-goddess. She was not worshipped, but in mythology she was the daughter of the Titan Theia, or daughter and wife of the sun. In poetry and magic Selene was almost identified with Artemis or Hecate (q.v.). The rising moon was a prosperous time, the full moon suitable for love potions, and the waning moon for evil magic. In Hellenistic times the moon was regarded as the abode of souls.

Selli, Selloi. Inhabitants and priests of the Greek oracle at Dodona (q.v.), called in Homer those of 'unwashed feet' who lie on the ground.

Semele. Greek heroine or goddess, perhaps from Zemelo a goddess of the earth in Thrace and Phrygia. She was pursued by Zeus and conceived Dionysus but Hera was jealous and advised Semele to ask Zeus to reveal his own true shape; when he did this, she was killed by the fire of his thunderbolts.

In one story Zeus descended into Hades and brought Semele up to Olympus. Dionysus had already been made immortal by the thunderbolts but was yet unborn and Zeus hid him in his thigh till he was mature. See ZAGREUS.

Semiramis. Daughter of a Syrian goddess Atargatis or Derceto (q.v.), according to Greek mythology. She was cast out at birth and tended by doves till shepherds found her. She married Ninus, king of Assyria, and built Babylon. After her death Semiramis changed into a dove which was sacred to her. It is thought that the historical basis for the legend was in Sammuramat, wife of an Assyrian king Shamshi-Adad V, who herself was regent from 810–805 B.C.

Seneca, Lucius Annaeus. Stoic philosopher, born at Cordoba in Spain in 4 B.C., he studied in Rome and was a tutor to Nero, accumulating a large fortune in imperial service. In A.D. 65 Seneca was accused of complicity in a conspiracy against Nero and was forced to take his own life. The text of his famed orations has not survived, but there are extant *Dialogues* which are chiefly ethical and philosophical. Seneca said that the sufferings of the good are only apparent, that anger was futile and a Stoic should be impassive. His thought is not original or consistent and his life differed from some of the principles which he expounded, but Seneca was respected by some Christian writers and his style and thought have long commanded attention.

Senussi. See SANŪSĪ.

Sephardim. The name traditionally given to the Jews of Spain and Portugal, derived from the name Sepharad in the prophecy of *Obadiah*, verse 20, and interpreted as Spain. Until the fourteenth century the Jews in Spain were generally well treated and prosperous, but under the Inquisition many were killed or converted and in 1492 the remainder, some three hundred thousand, were expelled from the peninsula. Most of them went into the Turkish empire, in North Africa and Palestine, and some to western Europe and later to America. There the Sephardi communities followed local customs which differentiated them from the Ashkenazim (q.v.) of eastern Europe and they still have Spanish words in their dialects.

Seppuku. (Japanese) 'ritual suicide', vulgarly known as Hara-kiri (q.v.).

Septuagint. (Greek) 'seventy', the name of the most important Greek version of the Hebrew *Old Testament*. It is said to have been made by seventy-two translators, at the order of Ptolemy Philadelphus (285–246 B.C.) and, it is added, done by them on the island of Pharos in seventy-two days, but these traditions are not now literally believed by most scholars. Septuagint is often written LXX, and is called by Jews the *Targum of the Seventy* (see TARGUM). The *Septuagint* arranges its books differently from the order of the Hebrew *Bible* and includes other books (*Apocrypha*), which circulated among Greek-speaking Jews. The *New Testament* frequently quotes the *Septuagint* and it was used by many later Christian writers.

Serapis. The state god of Egypt during the period of the Greek Ptolemies whose worship then spread throughout the Mediterranean and to Britain. He was depicted as a man with curly hair and beard, with a sort of basket (*modius*) on his head. Sometimes he was in the form of Osiris, to Greeks and Romans he was the equivalent of this deity, and sometimes he appeared as the Apis-bull (qq.v.). The bull was sacred to Ptah at Memphis, but was also regarded as the soul of Osiris, and the joint god was called Osyrapis and later Serapis. He was a god of fertility and also of the underworld, and in the latter function seemed akin to the Greek Mysteries. It is said that Ptolemy Soter sought to found a religion which would combine both Greek and Egyptian elements, and so united Osiris and Eleusis, but Serapis was thoroughly Egyptian. The greatest Serapeum was in Alexandria and there were many others, the next being at Memphis.

Sesha. See SHESHA.

Seshat. A goddess of writing in ancient Egypt whose name means 'writer'; she was wife or sister of the secretary-god Thoth (q.v.). Seshat was also patroness of arithmetic and architecture. She was depicted as a woman with a staff and star on her head, a pen in one hand and a palette in the other. She measured the king's life on a palm branch and helped him mark out the plans of buildings. The Greeks identified Seshat with Clio, the muse of history and epic poetry.

Set. One of the most ancient and popular gods of Egypt, called Lord of Upper Egypt in pyramid texts, where his capital was Ombos. Set was son of Geb and Nut, and husband of Nephthys. He was the god of storm and, unlike Horus the sky-god, was dangerous, Like the storm he was violent, had red eyes, and was a warrior who taught the use of bows and arrows. Set was notorious for his conflict with Osiris (q.v.), whom he killed, dividing his body into fourteen or sixteen parts, which were later reassembled by Isis and Horus. The pig, which Egyptians hated, was sacred to Set, and his cult-animal has been interpreted as a pig or a dog. Set was depicted as a man with the head of his cult-animal, or wholly as that animal, and more rarely as a hippopotamus or a snake. From being originally a storm-god, the conflict with

Osiris made Set unpopular and he only played a minor role in worship. See THUERIS.

Seveners. Sab'iya (Arabic), the name given to those Shī'a Muslims who reject the majority belief in Twelve Imāms (see TWELVERS and SHĪ'A) and hold that the number of visible Imāms ceased at the seventh, Muhammad ibn Ismā'il, about 762. See ISMĀ'ĪLĪS.

Seven Sleepers. The Christian legend, of seven young men of Ephesus who were walled up alive during the Decian persecution in A.D. 250 and awoke a hundred years later, has remained in Islam. The *Qur'ān* (18, 12–25) says that they were young men who believed in God and withdrew to a cave, with their dog at the threshold, remaining there 309 years. In Islamic tradition the Seven Sleepers will arise with the Messiah at his return with the Mahdī (q.v.) and will die as martyrs in Jerusalem. This chapter of the *Qur'ān* is recited all over the Islamic world at the Friday communal prayer and is the chief one repeated at that time on the Egyptian state radio.

Shabbethai Zvi. Jewish mystic and pseudo-Messiah (1626 to about 1676). Born in Smyrna, he studied the Zohar (q.v.), and in 1648 declared himself privately to be the Messiah. He was banished to Egypt and gained wealthy supporters in Raphael Chelebi and Nathan Ghazzati. Shabbethai declared himself openly Messiah at Gaza and Salonica and had a large Jewish following from the masses who had suffered under violent persecutions in eastern Europe. His chief critic was Jacob Sasportas of Amsterdam, a learned Talmudist, who in 1664 was for a year head of the English Jews. Shabbethai's followers, feeling the end of the world to be near, engaged in excesses which offended the pious. The Turkish authorities imprisoned Shabbethai, he became a Muslim and died in exile in Albania. The collapse of his movement drove many Jews to embrace Hasidism (q.v.). A sect of followers of Shabbethai survives, known as Dönmeh, 'apostates', to the Turks, but to themselves as 'believers', as they hope for the reappearance of their Messiah.

Shabda. (Sanskrit) 'sound', 'word', applied by Hindus to the sacred syllable Om (q.v.). Among the Sikhs, in the form Shabad, it is used to indicate a hymn of the *Ādi Granth*, and generally of the divine Word as revelation. See also SUBUD.

al-Shāfi'ī, Muhammad ibn Idrīs. Founder of the Shāfi'ī school of Islamic law (see FIQH), which is followed in Syria, lower Egypt, southern Arabia, East Africa and Indonesia. Shāfi'ī was born in Gaza in 767 and brought up in Mecca. He was of the Quraysh tribe and distantly related to the prophet Muhammad. About 810 he set up as a teacher in Baghdad, but died in Egypt in 820. Shāfi'ī took an intermediate position between rigid traditionalism and the invention of new laws, but he laid down strict rules for the use of 'analogy' (see QIYĀS). He made a systematic collection of traditions, distinguishing between those that were in force and those that had been abrogated. Shāfi'ī was a voluminous writer and his first work, *Usūl*, 'fundamentals', contained the principles of civil and canon law.

Shahāda. (Arabic) 'testimony', witness. The title of the Islamic confession of faith: 'there is no god but God; Muhammad is the Apostle of God.' This is the first of the five Pillars of Islam (q.v.). The Shahāda is expressed in fighting for Islam, especially in dying for it, and a Muslim who dies in Holy War is a Shahīd, a 'witness' or martyr. For the Shī'a, Husain (qq.v.) is the supreme Shahīd.

Shaikh. (Arabic) an 'old man', over fifty years of age, a head of a family or tribe. Nowadays it is a title of respect for one in authority, especially religious leaders or teachers, and heads of religious communities. From the tenth century the title Shaikh al-Islam, 'leader of Islam', was a greatly honoured title reserved for teachers and mystics. It was applied especially to the Grand Muftī (q.v.) of Constantinople, who for centuries had outstanding religious importance. In modern times the political influence of the Shaikh al-Islam had declined, though appeal was made to him in religious and legal matters, but in 1924 the Turkish nationalists abolished this title along with all the offices of the old Caliphate (q.v.). See also WALĪ.

Shaitān. (Arabic) from the Hebrew word for Satan. In the *Qur'ān* the word Shaitān is used both in the singular and the plural. The Shaitāns in some ways are like the Jinns (q.v.), but they are of the tribe of Shaitān, prompting men to evil, and unbelievers have them as companions. Shaitān is a fallen angel, who tempts men but has no real power or authority over them. His name is often used alternatively to that of the Devil, Iblīs (q.v.).

Shaiva Siddhānta. 'The doctrine of Shaiva', the name of an important school of worshippers of Shiva (q.v.) in southern India. Earlier Shaivite texts were written in Sanskrit, but in the Tamil country of the south these were supplemented and superseded by texts in Tamil, by the fourteenth century. The chief scriptures of Shaiva Siddhānta are known as *Tirumurai* or canon and consist of collections of hymns. Among them are: the *Tirumandiram*, composed by Tirumular about the seventh century; *Teveram*, including songs by Appar, Sambandar and Sundarar; and *Tiruvashagam* by Mānikka Vāchakar (q.v.). Shaiva Siddhānta teaches the reality of God and souls, without identifying them as do the monists. The harsh and immoral character of Shiva is changed to one of justice and love. As the only God he punishes sinners, but reveals himself in grace as the teacher of his beloved. See NĀYANĀRS.

Shaivism. The religion of the worshippers of the Hindu god Shiva (q.v.). Shaivism is particularly strong in southern India and most of the extreme ascetics are Shaivite. The Shaivites generally worship under the symbol of the Linga (q.v.). Some of the most clearly monotheistic expressions of Hinduism are in the Tamil works of Shaiva Siddhānta (q.v.). Shaivism also flourished in Kashmir, known as Trika from its possession of three scriptures, but its teachings were monistic, like those of Shankara (q.v.). See also LINGĀYATS.

Shākhā. (Sanskrit) 'branch', limb, division or school of the Hindu *Vedas*. There were said to be five Shākhās of the *Rig Veda*, each with its own text and interpretation. In more modern times the Brahmin class was divided, among other ways, according to the versions of the Vedic texts which were accepted as authoritative by different families.

Shāktas. Worshippers of the divine female energy of the Shaktis (q.v.) in Hinduism. The Shāktas are among the most important of Hindu religious associations, and their doctrines are contained in the *Tantras* (q.v.). They are divided into two main groups, the right-handed and the left-handed, Dakshināchārīs and Vāmāchārīs. The right-hand Shāktas have comparatively open and regular rituals, but those of the left-hand deliberately break normal rules and follow the Five M's (see M).

Shakti. (Sanskrit) 'energy', the power of a Hindu god personified as his wife, and worshipped by the Shāktas (q.v.). Various numbers of Shaktis are listed: three, eight or fifty, in addition to the principal goddesses. Thus as well as his regular consort Lakshmī, Vishnu may be reckoned as having fifty other forms of Shakti, and so has Shiva in addition to his regular Durgā. The male and female deities represent universal powers, and the female is often more potent than the male. No doubt Shakti worship assimilated ancient Indian cults of Mother Goddesses to the more male Aryan pantheon, and in Shākta rituals the cult of the Yoni (q.v.) perpetuated ancient fertility symbols and ceremonies.

Shākyamuni. (Sanskrit) 'the sage of the Shākyas', a title of Gautama (q.v.) the Buddha frequently found in Sanskrit texts, and particularly common in northern or Mahāyāna Buddhism. The Shākyas or Shākiyas probably lived on the Indian side of the borders of Nepal in the Himalayan foothills.

Shālagrāma. A black stone used as symbol of the Hindu god Vishnu, in worship and in funeral ceremonies. It contains a fossil ammonite whose spiral markings indicate the presence of the god. In some parts marriage ceremonies are performed between the Shālagrāma and the Tulasī plant (q.v.) which represents Lakshmī, consort of Vishnu. See AMMONITE.

Shalush, Shalash. A Hurrian goddess, of ancient Asia Minor, who was introduced into the Babylonian pantheon as consort of Adad, and also was associated with Dagon (qq.v.).

Shaman. An ecstatic religious leader, primarily of Siberia, whence the name Shaman comes, from the Tungusic language. In modern times the name Shaman has been applied to many kinds of priest, medicine man, magician and sorcerer, but it is best to confine it to the dominating religious ecstatic, in Siberia or elsewhere. He may or may not be a priest of a religious cult, but he is above all a master of ecstasy and Shamanism is the 'technique of ecstasy'. The Shaman obtains his powers both through his own abnormal experiences and through initiation by another Shaman. He goes into a trance, in which it is believed that he visits upper or nether worlds, flies through the air and guides souls or searches for those that are lost through sorcery or witchcraft. In so doing he re-enacts traditional journeys and encounters with gods and demons. So he is a Psychopomp (q.v.), a guide of souls. See also CH'U TZ'Ŭ.

Shamash. 'The sun', solar deity of ancient Babylonia. He was said to be son of the moon-god Sin, as day succeeds

SHAMASH

night. Shamash is often depicted on Babylonian seals with ray s coming from his shoulders, and in Assyria he was symbolized by a winged disk, symbol of royalty. Shamash was worshipped by all classes of people, but was especially concerned with communal justice; on the pillar which bears the Code of Hammurabi (q.v.) it is Shamash who gives laws to the king. He had temples in many places, and chief centres were at Sippar and Larsa.

Shango. The storm deity of the Yoruba people of Nigeria. He is identified with the fourth king of the ancient capital town of Oyo and is said to have been fierce in character and a powerful magician. After his own lightning had destroyed his family Shango is said to have hanged himself; in another version he went up to heaven on a chain. His consort was Oya (q.v.), the river Niger. The symbol of Shango is the axe and neolithic axes are said to have been cast down by him as thunderbolts. The ram is also sacred to him. Shango is akin to the Dahomean thunder deity, So or Hevioso. In the Caribbean and South America, Chango features in Voodoo (q.v.) cults as the thunder, a great general riding a horse, a protector from sickness whose sacred day is Wednesday. In Haiti, Shango is Saint Barbara, de pite a differ-

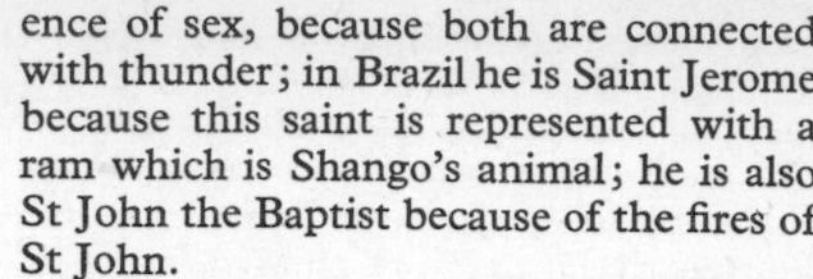

ence of sex, because both are connected with thunder; in Brazil he is Saint Jerome because this saint is represented with a ram which is Shango's animal; he is also St John the Baptist because of the fires of St John.

Shangri-la. See WESTERN PARADISE and PURE LAND.

Shang Ti. (Chinese) 'lord on high', 'supreme God'. In early times Ti was worshipped as a god and founder-ancestor but, when the Chou dynasty was established in the twelfth century B.C., its claim to power was strengthened by uniting the ancestral Ti with a heavenly deity T'ien (q.v.) and insisting on the righteous life demanded by Shang Ti, the 'supreme Ti'. In time the name Shang Ti declined in popularity, except in royal rituals, and by the period of Confucius the supreme being is named as T'ien. Down to modern times, the emperor, the son of heaven, performed a great annual sacrifice to Shang Ti at the altar of heaven at the winter solstice. (See TEMPLE OF HEAVEN.)

Shankara, Shamkara, Shankarāchārya. The most famous Hindu philosopher of the Vedānta schools, who lived from about 788 to 820. Born into an orthodox Brahmin family in Malabar, he travelled widely over India and died in the Himalayas. Shankara sought to reform and purify religion, and founded four Maths (q.v.) or monasteries. But his chief work was the exposition of the Vedic scriptures, their reduction to a consistent system and the propagation of an uncompromising monism, Advaita or Kevalādvaita, 'strict non-dualism'. Shankara wrote commentaries on the *Upanishads*, the *Brahma Sūtra* and the *Bhagavad-Gītā*, emphasizing their non-dualistic elements. Also, unusually for a philosopher, he composed hymns to gods such as Vishnu and Shiva, but these were concessions to popular need and Shankara thought that the truly enlightened man would pass beyond them to identity with Brahman. He has been called the Aquinas of Hinduism; or Rāmānuja (q.v.) may be compared to Plato and Shankara to Aristotle. Modern leaders of his school may also bear the title Shankarāchārya, 'Shankara teacher.' Shankara is also a title of the god Shiva.

Shāntideva. Buddhist poet and mystic of the seventh century A.D. Said to have been born a prince at Surat in western India, he renounced his throne to become a monk and many miracles are related of his life. He composed a poem of twenty seven verses, followed by a long commentary, called *Shikshā-samuchaya*, 'collection of rules of instruction', in which the training and ideals of Bodhisattvas (q.v.) are set out. His further poem *Bodhicharyāvatāra*, 'path of training for enlightenment', is a beautiful dedication to the service of others and has been called the finest poem in Buddhism, comparable to the *Imitation of Christ*.

Sharī'a. (Arabic) 'path', and technically the canon law of Islam, as a clear way to be followed. In a non-technical sense the word occurs in the *Qur'ān*; 'we gave you a Sharī'a (open way) in religion' (45, 17). Later Sharī'a came to mean all the commandments of God concerning human activities; Fiqh (q.v.) was the science of Sharī'a, sometimes used synonymously with it. Sharī'a applied chiefly to Muslims and only to a limited extent to non-Muslims in Islamic territory. Even at the height of its application to civil and commercial law, there were distinctions between religious and secular authorities. Since the nineteenth century the scope of Sharī'a has been severely limited, abolished altogether in Turkey in favour of European codes of law and limited in many other Islamic countries to marriage and religious matters.

Sharīf. (Arabic) 'noble', exalted, of a freeman who could claim illustrious ancestry, especially descent from the family of Muhammad and his grandsons Hasan and Husain. The Sharīfs (*ashrāf*) often wore green turbans as marks of distinction. See SAYYID and BARAKA.

Shāstra. (Sanskrit) 'command', 'book', the name given to any manual of teaching or sacred book. It is particularly applied to the *Dharma-shāstras*, or law books, but also to works on Vedānta philosophy, *Vedānta-shāstras*, or poetry, *Kāvya-shāstras*, (see DHARMA and MANU).

Shatapatha. (Sanskrit) 'having a hundred paths', the name of a Brāhmana (q.v.) said to have a hundred paths or sections. It is attached to the *White Yajur Veda* and ascribed to the sage Yājña-valkya (q.v.). The *Shatapatha Brāhmana* is one of the most interesting of these Hindu writings, with curious myths and important speculations which are continued in the *Upanishads*.

Shatarūpa. (Sanskrit) 'the hundred-formed', the first woman in Hindu mythology. In one account she was daughter of the creator-god Brahmā and mother of the first man, Manu; in another version she was the wife of Manu (q.v.).

Shavuoth. See PENTECOST.

Shawabti. See USHEBTI.

Shawl, Prayer. See TALLITH.

Sheba, Queen of. See BILQĪS.

Sheik. See SHAIKH.

Shekhinah, Shechinah. (Hebrew) 'indwelling', 'presence', of God, a term coined by the *Talmud* to emphasize the omnipresence of the deity. In mediaeval Kabbalism (q.v.) human sin separated the Shekhinah from the absolute God, En Sof (q.v.).

Shema. (Hebrew) 'hear', the primal confession of faith of Judaism. The name is taken from the first word of *Deuteronomy* 6, 4: 'Hear, O Israel, the Lord our God, the Lord is one.' The Shema occurs in all public and private devotions, on waking in the morning and retiring at night, at the time of death and at all festivals. See MEZUZAH and PHYLACTERY.

Shemoneh Esreh. (Hebrew) 'eighteen', the name of the eighteen blessings, now nineteen, which form the main section of Jewish morning, afternoon and evening prayers. See AMIDAH.

Shên. (Chinese) 'spirit', 'power'. Shên can mean heavenly spirits or unfathomable spiritual power, the vital force in heaven and earth. It is often linked with Kuei (q.v.); in relation to the vital principles of Yang and Yin (q.v.), Shên is the efficacy of Yang and Kuei that of Yin. Shên is also used of mental power, style and rhythmic vitality.

Sheriff. See SHARĪF and BARAKA.

Shesha. King of the snakes or Nāgas (q.v.) in Hindu mythology, a snake with a thousand heads on which the god Vishnu rests and sleeps under their covering hoods in the intervals between the creations of the world. At the end of every age Shesha breathes out fire to destroy everything, till a new creation emerges through Brahmā from Vishnu's

body. Shesha is also named An-anta (q.v.), the 'endless'. In other myths he was used as a rope with which the gods turned a mountain to churn the sea, to obtain the nectar of immortality, A-mrita (q.v.).

Shī'a, Shī'ites. (Arabic) the 'party' or 'followers' of 'Alī, (q.v.), whom they regard as the first true Caliph or Imām (q.v.). This great schism within Islam had political and social as well as religious sources, varied fortunes over the centuries, and is today the state religion of Persia (Iran), strong in Iraq, Pakistan, India and the Yemen, and in minorities elsewhere such as East Africa. To the confession of faith (Shahāda, q.v.) the Shi'a add, 'Alī is the friend of God.' They believe in a series of Imāms, leaders who now hidden will reappear. The two major Shi'a divisions are between the Twelvers (Ithnā 'Asharīya) and the Seveners (Sab'īya). The Twelvers believe in Twelve Imāms: 'Alī, Hasan, Husain, 'Alī Zain, Muhammad al-Bāqir, Ja'far, Mūsā al-Kāzim, 'Ali al Ridā, Muhammad al-Taqī, 'Alī al-Naqī, Hasan al-'Askarī, Muhammad al-Mahdī. The last-named went into hiding and will re-appear as the Mahdī (q.v.). The Seveners or Ismā'iliya (q.v.) follow seven Imāms of whom the last was Ismā'īl. The Shi'a form less than one fifth of the total Muslim population of the world.

Shide. Folded strips of white paper, originally cloth, which hang from the Shimenawa (q.v.) sacred rope in a Shinto temple. Sometimes thin sheets of brass are used. They were offered to the gods and serve a decorative and propitiatory purpose.

clearly dated, but they existed before Confucius (q.v.). He was traditionally credited with collecting them, but while this is now disputed it is likely that Confucius and his followers used the *Shih Ching* for moral teaching. The *Shih Ching* speaks of the Mandate (q.v.) of Heaven (T'ien) given to the Chou rulers who were regarded as its sons; it teaches filial piety and also reveals the prevalence of magical belief and practice. In some of the later poems the troubles of the time give rise to the thought that T'ien does not pity man, who must strive to free himself from suffering. See also SHU CHING.

Shikhā. The name, of doubtful derivation, of a tuft of hair on top of the head of a devout Hindu, sometimes said to indicate the spot from which the soul leaves the body, through the sagittal suture or junction of the skull bones. Every morning an orthodox Hindu binds up the Shikhā while reciting the *Gāyatrī mantra* (q.v.).

Shikhara. (Sanskrit) 'pointed', the spire or tower of a Hindu temple. The Shikhara generally stands over the central shrine of the temple complex and may be pointed or dome-like; it is often much smaller than the soaring towers of the gates or Gopurams (q.v.).

Shīla. 'Custom', 'conduct' (Sanskrit and Pali). Among Buddhists 'moral conduct' is one of the six or ten perfections (see PĀRAMITĀS). There are also Five Precepts or rules of moral conduct, Pancha-shila or Pansil, which are basic to the life of every Buddhist, lay or monk. These are: non-injury, not stealing, chastity, not lying, temperance. In modern times politicians have sometimes enunciated five principles as Pansil or Pancha-shila.

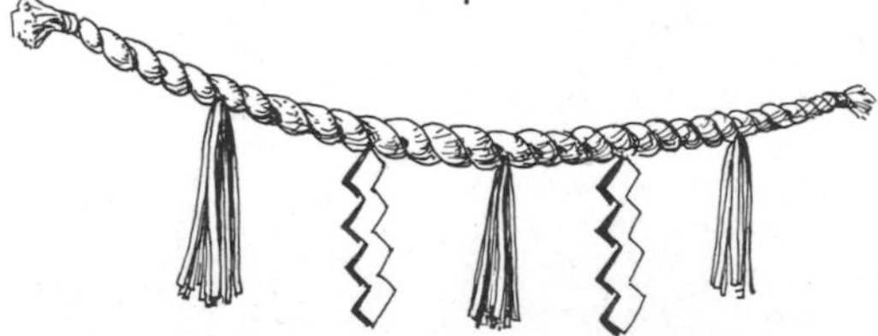

SHIDE ON SHIMENAWA

Shih Chi. See SSŬ-MA CH'IEN.

Shih-chia-mo-ni-fo. Chinese name for the Buddha Shākyamuni (q.v.).

Shih Ching. (Chinese) 'Book of Odes' or classic of songs. These are ancient poems which shed much light on Chinese religion and practice in the early part of the first millenium B.C. None can be

Shimenawa. A rope of rice-straw which hangs over the doors of Shintō temples and occasionally private houses. The origin of the name is obscure, some deriving it from 'straw rope' and others from 'forbidden', as taboo. The Shimenawa may be as small as a string or very large, it may encircle holy places or be placed over the door of a house while its occupant is away on pilgrimage. Normally it hangs at the entrance to temples and shrines. From the Shimenawa hang strips of folded paper, Shide similar to the Goheï (qq.v.). See also KAMI.

Shin. A shortened form of Jōdo Shinshu See JŌDO

Shinbutsu. See RYŌBU SHINTŌ.

Shingon. (Japanese) 'true word', from Chinese Chên-yen derived from a Sanskrit word for a magic formula. Although originating in India, this form of Buddhism became most popular in Japan thanks to the work of a great scholar Kōbō Daishi or Kūkai (774–835). He studied in China, concentrated on the 'secret teaching' (*mikkyō*) and took it back to Japan as Shingon. Shingon is highly syncretistic, and Kōbō Daichi is also often said to have founded the mixture of Buddhism and Shinto which appeared in Ryōbu Shintō (q.v.). The various gods and demons were identified with the great Buddha of Light, Vairochana (q.v.). This led to a mystical pantheism in which the whole universe is an expression of Vairochana as the ultimate reality. Shingon has remained one of the most powerful forms of Japanese Buddhism. See CHÊN YEN.

Shinnyō. Japanese form of Tathatā; see TATHĀGATA.

Shinran. Japanese Buddhist monk (1173–1263), disciple of Hōnen (q.v.), who established the 'True Pure Land School', Jōdo Shinshu (see JŌDO). His doctrine was of salvation by faith alone and he was opposed to the asceticism and celibacy of traditional Buddhist monasticism.

Shintai, Go-shintai. See HONDEN.

Shintō. Japanese form of a Chinese term, Shen-Tao, 'the way of the gods', to distinguish the original religion of Japan from Butsu-Tao, 'the way of Buddha'. In pure Japanese the term is Kami-no-Michi, the 'way of the Kami' or gods. Shintō indicates the belief in and worship of the Japanese gods and the culture associated with them. The oldest records of their mythology are in the *Kojiki* and *Nihongi* (qq.v.), which begin with the 'age of the Kami', wherein the sun-goddess, Amaterasu-ōmi-kami (q.v.) emerges as supreme and as ancestress of the emperor. Shintō is generally divided into two main branches, Jinja (q.v., shrine) or Kokka (state), and Sect (q.v.) or Kyōha Shintō. In the long period of Buddhist domination Twofold or Ryōbu (q.v.) Shintō prevailed. The association of Shintō with nationalism led to its dominance in the early part of this century and then to disestablishment after 1945, but it remains powerful in Japanese tradition and culture (see ISÉ). For Emperor-worship, see JIMMU TENNO.

Shirk. (Arabic) 'associating', joining another god with God, or worshipping another in polytheism. This is the gravest sin in Islam and the *Qur'ān* says that God will not forgive the association of anything with himself (4, 51). The Wahhābī (q.v.) denounce the veneration given to saints and prophets by fellow Muslims as Shirk and say that Muhammad himself can only be an intercessor on the Day of Judgement by special permission of God.

Shītalā. Indian village goddess (Sanskrit, 'cool'), concerned with smallpox, and worshipped for its cure or prevention. She is one of the greatest village goddesses (see GRĀMADEVATĀ) and in Tamil country is called 'Mother Death' (Māriyammai). Women are among her special worshippers, interceding for their sick children. In Bengal, Shītalā is represented by a block of stone, a pot of water, or an image with the face covered with pustules. During epidemics gifts of rice, fruit and sometimes animals are offered to the deity.

Shiur Komah. Jewish Kabbalistic work, 'the Measures of the Divine Stature', which attempted to give the bodily dimensions of God. It was attributed to Rabbi Ishmael (q.v.) of the second century, but was clearly much later, and the philosopher Maimonides condemned it as a forgery and unworthy of study.

Shiva, Siva. (Sanskrit) 'kindly', 'auspicious', one of the greatest Hindu deities, and often regarded as one of the triad in which the others are Brahmā and Vishnu. Shiva does not appear in the *Vedas*, but in the *Shvetāshvatara Upanishad* (q.v.) he is an attribute and identified with the storm-god Rudra. In Mohenjodaro (q.v.) culture, however, several seals depict a cross-legged figure, with three faces and horns, among animals; all of these are paralleled in later art about Shiva. The god is called Mahādeva ('great god'), Mahā-yogī ('great ascetic'), Nata-rāja ('Lord of the Dance') (q.v.). He is Nīla-kantha, 'Blue-throated' from the poison that he drank that would have destroyed the world. He is daubed with ashes, wears animal skins, has snakes over his head, stands on a demon, and is accompanied by the bull Nandi. Shiva's wife is Pārvatī or Durgā (qq.v.), and their

THE BURNING GHAT, SHOWING A BODY READY FOR BURNING BESIDE THE RIVER GANGES AT PATNA, INDIA.

GARUDA, WINGED CARRIER OF VISHNU. NEPAL. (LEFT)

BRAHMIN PRIEST GIVING LESSONS IN THE HOLY SCRIPTURES ON THE BANKS OF THE RIVER GANGES AT BENARES, INDIA.

children are Ganesha and Kārttikeya; their heaven is on Mount Kailāsa. In the *Mahābhārata*, *Purānas* and later there is great rivalry between Shiva and Vishnu, though sometimes they are united. For his followers, see SHAIVISM and SHAIVA SIDDHĀNTA.

SHIVA AND PĀRVATĪ

Shivājī. Indian patriot, champion of the Marathas (in the seventeenth century) against the oppressions of the Mughal emperor Aurangzeb (q.v.). He was persuaded to visit the Mughal court at Agra and was angered at the enforcement of court etiquette on him, escaped, and compelled his recognition as Rajah. He died in 1680, having created a nation and defended Hinduism against its detractors.

Shofar. (Hebrew) 'ram's horn', used in Bible times in processions and at festivals. The Shofar is blown in modern synagogues in the liturgy of the New Year (q.v.) as a proclamation of the divine kingship and a call to repentance on the Day of Atonement and it also ends the fast of that day. The Shofar is sounded on some other occasions as a special memorial and anticipation of the trumpet of the Messiah.

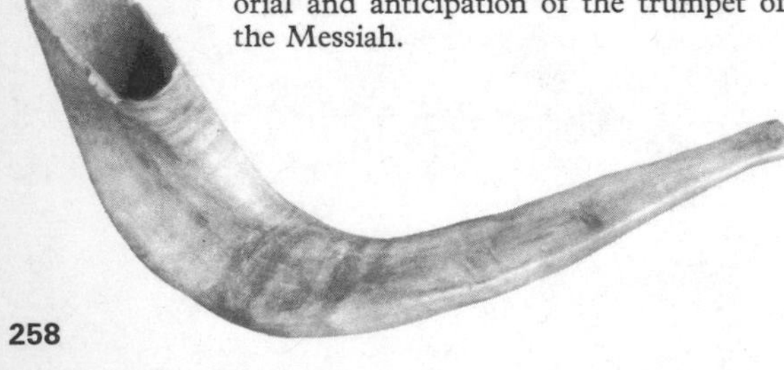

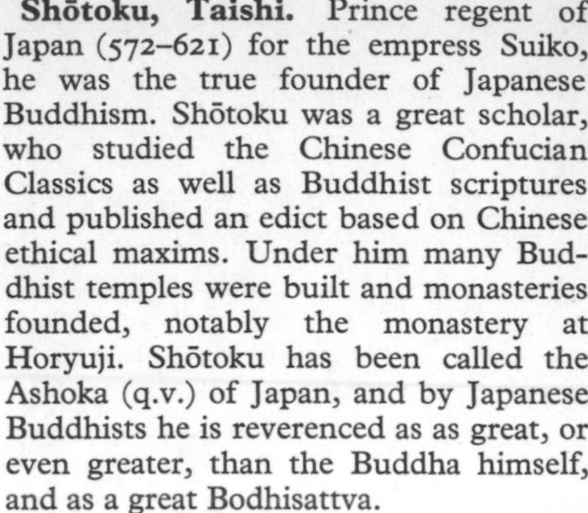

Shōtoku, Taishi. Prince regent of Japan (572–621) for the empress Suiko, he was the true founder of Japanese Buddhism. Shōtoku was a great scholar, who studied the Chinese Confucian Classics as well as Buddhist scriptures and published an edict based on Chinese ethical maxims. Under him many Buddhist temples were built and monasteries founded, notably the monastery at Horyuji. Shōtoku has been called the Ashoka (q.v.) of Japan, and by Japanese Buddhists he is reverenced as as great, or even greater, than the Buddha himself, and as a great Bodhisattva.

Shrāddha. (Sanskrit) 'faithful', a Hindu memorial ceremony for the dead. It is not the funeral but follows it between the tenth and thirty-first days and at other intervals. The sons, grandsons and great-grandsons of the dead person pour libations of water, offer vessels of milk and balls of rice (*pinda*). The aim is to give peace to the departed and to link the dead and living community by this ritual. Music and feasting follow and successive Shrāddhas are performed according to the financial ability of the family. See also CREMATION.

Shramana. See SAMANA.

Shrauta Sūtras. (Sanskrit) 'heard texts', short verses containing rules of ceremonial and sacrifice, also known as *Kalpa Sūtras* (q.v.).

Shrī. (Sanskrit) 'fortune', 'prosperity.' The name of Lakshmī (q.v.), wife of Vishnu, who is often invoked in books, prayers and at her Dīvālī (q.v.) festival as Shrī. The name is also used as a title of other gods and goddesses, of holy books and of saintly men. From thence it becomes a title of respect, like 'reverend'.

It is often written at the beginning of books, documents, letters and examination papers, in the Sanskrit form.

Shrī-vaishnavism is a name given to worshippers of Vishnu, especially in southern India. Shrī co-operates with Vishnu in removing sins and is often identified with him, though sometimes also with the human soul in a loving relationship with Vishnu.

For Shrī-yantra, see YANTRA.

Shruti. (Sanskrit) 'heard', a term applied to the most sacred and 'inspired' scriptures of Hinduism, the *Vedas* and *Upanishads*, which were 'heard' from the gods by the ancient seers. Shruti works are distinguished from later 'remembered', Smriti (q.v.), works which though authoritative have come from human authors. But some of the latter, such as the *Bhagavad-Gītā*, spoken of as Smriti, have in fact long been regarded as being on the same high plane as Shruti.

Shu. (Egyptian) 'emptiness', the atmosphere personified as Shu. He stood on the earth, Geb, and with his arms upheld the heavenly goddess, Nut. Shu is called father of Nut, and in another story he reigned with Geb as a king on earth.

Shu Ching. (Chinese) 'Book of Documents', or Classic of History. Its text has been much disputed, but seven sections in a 'modern script' are generally accepted as authentic. Confucius is credited with editing the *Shu Ching*, along with other Classics, but this is doubtful. The *Shu Ching*, like the *Shih Ching* (q.v.), reveals something of the religious beliefs and practices of the Chou dynasty in the early part of the first millenium B.C.. Heaven, T'ien, bestows its Mandate (q.v.) on kings, to put down crime and establish good government. So the new dynasty justified its assumption of power, but showed that the rule of the people was the concern of God.

Shūdra. The fourth of the four traditional classes of Hindu society (see CASTE). The name Shūdra is of uncertain origin; it was applied to a man of the lowest of the four original classes, but such a person is regarded as of higher rank than many of the modern low castes in India. According to the 'Hymn of Man' in the *Rig Veda*, the Shūdras came from the feet of the cosmic giant, Purusha (q.v.). In the *Laws of Manu* it is said that there was only one occupation prescribed to the Shūdra, namely, to serve the other three classes meekly.

Shuha. See SECT SHINTO.

Shūnya. (Sanskrit) 'void', emptiness. A Buddhist technical term for the doctrine which holds that the visible world has no self-substance, and the ideal world has no limitations of individuality. It is a monistic theory, no doubt influenced by Hindu monism (q.v.), which abolishes the notion of duality and proclaims the essential oneness of everything. While especially the teaching of philosophical schools of Mahāyāna Buddhism, Shūnya is also mentioned in the Theravāda canon in the explanation of meditation on a state empty of phenomenal relationships.

Shvetāshvatara. Name of a Hindu sage and an important *Upanishad* attributed to him. It is one of the later of the classical *Upanishads* (q.v.) and shows the revival of theism after early Upanishadic monism (q.v.). Creation cannot be the result of chance, fate or nature; it depends upon a personal God. This God is named as Rudra, with the attribute of Shiva, 'kindly'. So the *Shvetāshvatara* has been called a Shaivite tract. It is, however, of great importance as mediating between the monism of the earliest *Upanishads* and the theism of the *Bhagavad-Gītā*, which quotes it at times. At the end of its six short chapters, this *Upanishad* closes with a brief description of Yoga and a mention of Bhakti devotion.

Sibyl, Sibylline. The Greek Sibylla was said to have been a wandering prophetess, whose presence was attested at different places, and later there were numerous Sibyls with various names. They were located from Persia to Italy, and the Cumaean Sibyl, whose oracular cavern may still be seen, was famous. The

prophetic utterances were preserved in verse, often written on palm-leaves, and collections of these formed Sibylline Oracles. In Rome the Decemviri (q.v.) were in charge of them. After the Capitol was burnt in 83 B.C., involving the destruction of the Sibylline Books, a new collection was made from several sources. Later there were forgeries and Jewish and Christian interpolations. The influence of these latter, together with a prophecy of the Cumaean Sibyl in the *Fourth Eclogue* of Virgil, increased the respect for the Sibyls in medieval and later Europe. Michelangelo depicted them in the Sistine Chapel. See also VOLUSPA.

Sid, Sidh. Mound or tumulus which in Celtic mythology was regarded as a home of the gods. When the ancient deities were defeated, Dagda (q.v.) divided the Sids among them and they retired into them. Dagda was lord of a Sid, which was a sort of wonderland, full of things that never failed. See NEW GRANGE.

Siddha, Siddhi. (Sanskrit) 'fulfilment', 'perfection', the acquisition of supernatural powers by performance of ascetic or magical paths. There are said to be eight or ten of these powers (in Pali Buddhism called Iddhis), and both Yoga and Tantra (qq.v.) claim to provide the way.

In Hindu mythology there are thousands of Siddhas, beings of great purity who dwell in ethereal regions. In Jainism they are the purified and disembodied souls who dwell in Nirvāna at the summit of the universe in endless bliss.

Siddur. (Hebrew) 'arrangement', the name of the Jewish prayer book, arranged for worship throughout the year. The *Siddur Ari* was prefixed to the Sephardi prayer book, containing customs from Luria and the Safed mystics (qq.v.).

Siegfried. See SIGURD.

Sif. The wife of the god Thor (q.v.) in Nordic mythology. The evil Loki cut off her hair, so Thor forced him to go to the dwarfs or black elves and make them forge a golden head of hair which grew like ordinary hair.

Sifra. (Aramaic) 'book', applied to Rabbinic commentaries on *Leviticus* and other Pentateuchal books. They aimed at applying the general teaching of the Law to new cases.

Sigrdrifa. See BRYNHILD.

Sigurd, Siegfried. A hero of Scandinavian, German and Burgundian mythology. He was son of Sigmund and distantly descended from the god Odin. In one version he was a foundling, who

was fed by a hind. In the *Edda* (q.v.) it is said that Sigurd rode to the mountain Hindarfjall, Hind-mountain, which was surrounded by flames and woke a Valkyrie (q.v.) whom Odin had put to sleep with a sleep-thorn, learnt occult wisdom from her and was betrothed to her. The Valkyrie was, or was confused with, the swan-maiden Swanhild or Brynhild (q.v.). Sigurd's subsequent marriage to the Burgundian Gudrun was discussed by medieval poets. Sigurd was famed for killing the dragon Fafnir (q.v.), with the help of Odin, both to gain the dragon's gold and to learn its wisdom. In *Beowulf* it was Sigmund who killed the dragon. The dragon's blood covered Sigurd and made him invincible, except for one spot that the blood did not reach. The Niflungar, black demons or Burgundians, struck Sigurd on this spot. He was burnt on a pyre along with Brynhild who rode down to Hel to follow him.

Sikh. (Punjabi) 'disciple', a follower of Gurū Nānak (q.v.), the founder of Sikhism. The Sikh religion arose in the devotional atmosphere of central India and the Punjab, which believed in a supreme God but rejected the idea of his Avatars (see SANT and KABĪR). Nānak was followed by nine other Gurūs, of whom the fifth, Arjan, compiled the basic scripture, *Ādi Granth* (q.v.), and the tenth, Gobind Singh, founded the inner group of initiates, the Khālsā (q.v.). The Sikhs have built many temples and their religious centre is at Amritsar, with its famous Golden Temple. The Sikhs dominated the Punjab, suffered under Mughal oppression, tried to found a separate state in 1947, were expelled from

Pakistan, and form one of the most active and advanced communities in India numbering over six millions. Many Sikhs have migrated to East Africa and Europe, and in 1968 there were thirty-five Sikh temples in Britain.

Sikha. See SHIKHĀ.

Sikhara. See SHIKHARA.

Sīla. See SHĪLA.

Sileni. Spirits of the wild in Greek mythology, often confused with Satyrs (q.v.). The Sileni were older and were depicted with horse-ears, sometimes with horse-legs and tails, pursuing nymphs.

Silenus was said to have been caught by King Midas and made drunk, and often the behaviour of the Sileni was rowdy.

Silvanus. A Roman land god, of vague functions, often identified with the Sileni.

Simchat Torah. See TABERNACLES.

Simeon ben Yochai. A Jewish rabbi of the second century A.D. (100–160?), who compiled *Midrashim* (q.v.) on Pentateuchal books. After the revolt of Bar Kozeba had been crushed by the Romans in A.D. 135, Simeon fled with his son and it is said that they hid for thirteen years in a cave. In the thirteenth century Moses de Leon (q.v.) claimed that Simeon had written the mystical *Zohar*, instructed by the prophet Elijah. Simeon is the chief teacher of this work, and the supposed anniversary of his death is still celebrated as Hillulah, 'marriage', indicating the union of his soul with the Shekhinah. His tomb at Meron in Galilee is the scene of great rejoicing at this time. See also MEKILTA.

Sin. Babylonian moon-god and guardian of the city of Ur. In early Sumerian lists his name is Nannar, son of Enlil, but he seems to hold a relatively independent place. Since the name Sin is Semitic, it has been thought that the cult was brought by nomads into Babylon, or perhaps united with an earlier cult. Sin is male, and father of the sun, Shamash, since night comes before day. He was lord of the calendar and so his sacred number was thirty; he was also a god of vegetation. His wife was Ningal. In art Sin appears riding on a winged bull.

Sindbad. See HĀRŪN AL-RASHĪD.

Sindī, Abū 'Alī. Islamic mystic of the ninth century, about whom little is known except that he was taught the duties of Islam by Bistāmī (q.v.) in exchange for instruction in divine truths. From this, and his name which suggests that he came from Sind in India, it is deduced that al-Sindī was a convert to Islam from Hinduism and brought with him some of those pantheistic doctrines which, contrary to the original spirit of Islam, deeply affected the Sūfī mystics.

Singh. 'Lion', from Sanskrit *sinha*, a title taken by Sikhs when they become members of the brotherhood of the Khālsā (q.v.).

Sīra. See IBN ISHĀQ.

Sirens, Sirenes. In Greek mythology these were half women and half birds; according to the *Odyssey* they lived on an island near Scylla and Charybdis (qq.v.). Their enchanting songs attracted sailors, who then were wrecked and died. Odysseus only got past them on the advice of the enchantress Circe (q.v.). The Sirens were sometimes called daughters of the Earth or lived in Hades and they accompanied the dead to the underworld, so that it has been thought that they were birds originally imagined to be inhabited by the souls of the dead. In early art they were represented as monsters, but later as beautiful mourning beings.

Sisyphus. In Greek mythology a son of Aeolus (q.v.) who was tormented in Hades by having to roll a rock to the top of a hill from whence it always rolled down again. No reason for this is given in Homer, but later it was said that he had offended Zeus and received eternal punishment. He is also said to have been a trickster who bound up death (Thanatos) so that nobody died till the latter was rescued by Ares.

Sītā. (Sanskrit) 'furrow', the daughter of earth, Bhūmi, and deity of agriculture. In the *Rāmāyana* (q.v.), she is the wife of Rāma, and daughter of Janaka, king of Videha, but she is still said to have sprung from a furrow and at the end she descends again into the earth. Sītā is also regarded as an Avatar of the goddess Lakshmī, consort of Vishnu of whom Rāma is an Avatar. Rāma won her hand by bending a great bow of Shiva and she was his only wife, their life still being taken as a model of marital affection. Sītā accompanied Rāma into exile, was abducted by the demon Rāvana and carried off to Ceylon. Eventually she was rescued by Rāma and Hanumān, underwent an ordeal to prove her chastity, and reigned with Rāma in Ayodhyā.

Sitala. See SHĪTALĀ.

Siva. See SHIVA.

Sjofn. One of the goddesses known as Asynjur (q.v.) in Scandinavian mythology She was said to turn the thoughts of men and women to love, but little else is known about her.

Skadi, Skathi. Scandinavian giantess, daughter of Thyazi, and also goddess of snow-shoes. Her father was killed by the gods and Skadi arrived in armour seeking vengeance. She was allowed to choose a husband among the gods; looking at their legs only, she chose the most beautiful which she thought belonged to Balder, but they were Njörd's (q.v.), the sea-god. The couple were married but could not agree whether to live in the mountains or by the sea and they separated. Skadi is rather a masculine goddess, of winter and darkness, and may have been a deity of destruction.

Skanda. Hindu god of war and the planet Mars, son of Shiva and Pārvatī, and also named Kārttikeya (q.v.).

Skandha, Khandha. A constituent element of being (Sanskrit and Pali). In Buddhist thought the Five Skandhas are the elements which make up a personality in a life, during the process of transmigration, and they are inherent in all forms of life. The Five Skandhas are: Rūpa, form or bodily shape; Vedanā, sensation or feeling; Samjñā or Saññā, perception; Samskāra or Sankhāra, the elements and aggregates of consciousness; Vijñāna or Viññāna, consciousness or the thought-faculty. At death the Skandhas dissolve and are not carried over into the next life, the link between the two lives being Karma (q.v.). See also ANATTĀ.

Skidbladnir. The magic ship of the god Frey (q.v.) in Scandinavian mythology. It was made by the dwarfs, of so many pieces that it could be folded up and put in a purse, yet it was so big that all the gods could get in it. It always had a following wind, by similar magic.

Skirnir. In Scandinavian mythology the servant of the god Frey (q.v.), who was sent by his master to woo the beautiful giantess Gerd (q.v.).

Skoll. A wolf, in Scandinavian mythology, who with his fellow Hati was always chasing the sun and moon to devour them, perhaps a reference to myths of eclipses. See SOL and MANI.

Skuld. One of the Norns, Fates, (q.v.) in Scandinavian mythology. They lived in a hall under the Yggdrasil world tree, and perhaps Skuld represented the Future. Elsewhere she is named as one of the Valkyries, the battle-maidens. The original Fate was perhaps Urd (q.v.), Skuld and Verdandi being added later.

Sleipnir. Supernatural horse of Odin (q.v.) the great Nordic deity. He is said to have been born of the trickster Loki (q.v.) and Svadilfari, and perhaps was originally a fertility deity in his own right. Sleipnir was a grey horse with eight legs, who galloped through the air and over the sea. After the death of Balder his brother Hermod (q.v.) rode Sleipnir to the world of death to seek the return of Balder.

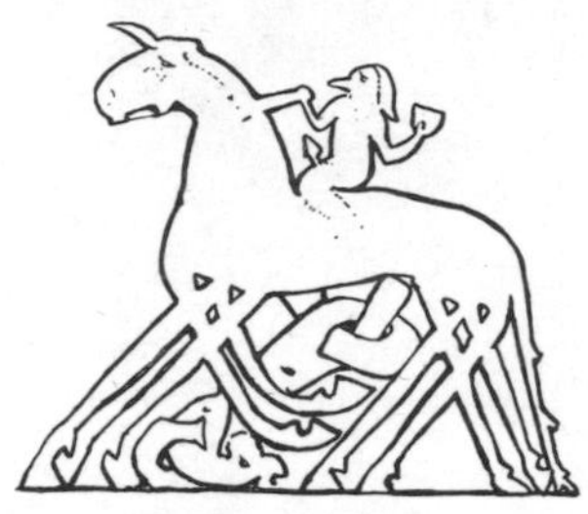

Smārta. Belonging to the Smriti (see SHRUTI). The name is given to an orthodox Brahmin who follows the Smriti usages, and there are *Smārta Sūtras* which embody these. The term Smārta is also applied to those who follow the Advaita (q.v.) teaching of Shankara (q.v.), recognize all the gods but as manifestations of the one Brahman, and follow strictly the rules laid down in the Smriti.

Smriti. (Sanskrit) 'remembered', a name given to the whole body of religious and legal teaching which comes after the Shruti (q.v.), the 'heard' *Vedas* and *Vedānta*. Smriti includes the epic poems, laws of Manu, *Purāna* tales and many other works. Strictly the *Bhagavad-Gītā* is Smriti, as part of the great epic *Mahābhārata*, but this has been called the 'fifth *Veda*', and the prestige of the Gītā is so great that it is treasured equally with or above much of the Shruti.

Snorri Sturluson. An Icelandic chief (about 1179–1241) whose *Edda* (q.v.) is the most valuable source of knowledge about Scandinavian mythology. Snorri was a Christian layman, educated by clergy, but, although his view of the old gods is coloured by Christian teaching, he preserves much valuable material from oral and poetic traditions. The first section of his *Prose Edda*, the 'Deceiving of Gylfi' (*Gylfaginning*), tells how a Swedish king Gylfi went to the gods in their city, Asgard, and asked them questions about the beginning and end of the earth, men, giants and gods. Snorri travelled widely and in his later life turned to history, the *Saga of Olaf* and a history of Norwegian kings, *Heimskringla*, being ascribed to him.

Snotra. One of the Scandinavian goddesses called Asynjur (q.v.), but little is known about her except that she was gentle and prudent.

Socrates. Athenian philosopher (469–399 B.C.). Son of Sophroniscus and Phaenarete, he married Xanthippe late in life, a lady notorious for her bad temper. Socrates served in the army and was noted for his courage, which also showed itself in political life later when he defied the Thirty Tyrants. He was accused of introducing strange gods and corrupting youth. Probably he did criticize the immoral myths of some Greek gods, but his religious views seem to have been fairly orthodox and he constantly believed himself to be inspired by a divine spirit (*daimon*, q.v.). His questioning nature, insistence on the definition of terms, and posing of profound religious and philosophical questions may well have unsettled young and old. He was tried and condemned to death, refused to escape, and took poisoned hemlock. His life is described by both Plato and Xenophon. It is difficult to know how much in the Platonic dialogues, put in the mouth of Socrates, came from the master, but he had a great influence on the development of philosophy, ethics and logic. See PLATO.

Sodales. Minor priesthoods in Rome (Latin, 'companions' or 'associates'), ranking below the Collegia (q.v.). The chief were the Fetiales (q.v.) who made treaties and declared war. Then came the Salians (q.v.), priests of Mars, the Luperci (q.v.), who conducted a February ritual, and the Fratres Arvales who had charge of agricultural rites. There were other Sodales, but little is known of them except their name.

Sōka Gakkai. 'Creative-value Study Society', a Japanese religious and political society of recent foundation but considerable power. Arising out of the forceful Nichiren (q.v.) school of Buddhism, Sōka Gakkai was founded in 1930 by Jōzaburo Makiguchi. During the Second World War it was suppressed, but has revived and spread since 1947. It has been said to use coercion to gain converts, and was intolerant towards other religions, notably Christianity; recently it is claimed that this attitude has been modified. Sōka Gakkai is popular among both the poor and ruling classes, having members in the Japanese Senate, and claims over a million adherents.

Soker. Ancient Egyptian god of the dead, especially at Memphis, and often associated with Ptah and Osiris (qq.v.), as Ptah-Soker-Osiris. Soker was worshipped in many other parts of Egypt but came to be absorbed in Ptah and Osiris. He was depicted in art as a falcon or a man with a falcon's head.

Sokkvabekkr. The abode of the goddess Saga (q.v.) in Scandinavian mythology, a great place where she and Odin drank from golden cups.

Sol. The Latin name for the sun, given to an old Roman deity about whom little is known apart from a festival on 11 December. Later he was identified with the Greek Helios (q.v.). Sun-worship came across from the east and became popular in Rome under the name of 'invincible sun', Sol Invictus. In the third century A.D. efforts were directed to make his cult supreme, though the worship of Jupiter and older gods continued. The worship of Sol Invictus was the chief rival of Christianity and, when the latter finally triumphed, the birth or dedication (*natalis*) day of the sun was taken over for the celebration of the birth of Christ, the eternal Sun, whose Christmas festival was first celebrated in Rome about A.D. 360. See YULE.

In Scandinavian mythology Sol was one of the goddesses known as Asynjur (q.v.). She was the sun, or charioteer of the sun, and sister of the moon, Mani. They drove round the sky by day and night, pursued by the wolves Skoll and Hati, perhaps representing eclipses.

Soma. The juice of a plant (perhaps *Asclepias acida*) whose stalks were crushed and fermented and then offered to the gods in ancient India. Soma is personified as a deity, and, along with the fire Agni (q.v.), formed one of the principal elements in ritual. Hence many Vedic hymns, the whole of the ninth book of the *Rig Veda* and much of the *Sāma Veda* are in praise of divine Soma. Soma is closely similar to Haoma (q.v.) of Persia and the use of the latter in Parsi ritual has survived while Soma ritual has disappeared. In later mythology the name Soma was applied to the moon, credited with parents and wives, who were the stars. There was a Lunar race of men, and a Moon-world, Soma-loka.

Sopdu. Minor Egyptian god of warlike character, whose home on the east of the Delta of the Nile protected the land from Asian invaders. His name perhaps meant 'sharp-toothed'. He was identified with Horus (q.v.) as a solar deity. In art Sopdu was depicted as a man with a beard and two tall feathers on his head, or as a falcon with similar feathers.

Sophists. First of all 'wise men' in Greek, and then applied to wandering teachers who gave instruction for money. Some of them, like Protagoras (born about 485 B.C.) claimed to teach virtue and the relativity of knowledge and were respected. Others were less honoured because of their rapacity in amassing fortunes in teaching and their general sceptical attitude. They were criticized by Plato and later writers and their name, not indicating a particular school but applied to mercenary teachers, came to have bad associations, though some of them were men of noble character.

Sophocles. Greek dramatist (496–406 B.C.), whose plays on Oedipus and Electra (qq.v.) have been interesting to modern theorists of the origins of religion in hatred for parents. See FREUD.

Sorcery. A practitioner of harmful Magic (q.v.), not a witch. The word comes from Latin *sors*, a 'lot', used of casting lots, consulting oracles, prophecy. See also LYCANTHROPY.

Sōshyans. See SAOSHYANS.

Sōtō. The largest sect of Japanese Zen (q.v.) Buddhism. The Japanese word is derived from the Chinese *Ts'ao-t'ung*, itself a contraction of the names of the two founders of the sect in the ninth century A.D. Sōtō is distinguished from Rinzai (q.v.) by the greater number of followers, more popular forms of worship, avoidance of Kōan (q.v.) problems, and working out Zen in daily life and art.

Spenta Mainyu. The 'bountiful' or 'holy spirit' in Zoroastrianism opposed to the evil or 'destructive spirit', Angra Mainyu (see AHRIMAN). One of these brings life and the other death, and they stand eternally opposed to each other, in complete contradiction or Dualism (q.v.). In the *Gāthā* (q.v.) scriptures the Bounteous Spirit appears as distinct from the Supreme Being, Ahura Mazdā, but later they are identified. Spenta Mainyu is one of the Bounteous Immortals, Amesha Spentas (q.v.).

Sphinx. The Sphinx of Gizeh in Egypt is a figure carved out of rock, a recumbent lion with a human head, probably representing the Pharaoh Chephren, about 2600 B.C. (see PYRAMIDS.) The Greek word *Sphinx* came from a root meaning 'the Throttler' and was used of a she-monster who asked the Thebans a riddle about the three ages of man and devoured all who failed to solve it, till Oedipus solved the riddle and the Sphinx committed suicide or was killed. Sphinxes appear in Greek art, often as beautiful women, guarding tombs or as enigmatic messengers of the gods.

Spinoza, Baruch. Jewish philosopher (1632–1672) of Holland, but excommunicated for supposed atheism. He taught that God was the absolute, eternal and necessary being, but held a logical monism (q.v.) in which all things are of a single substance.

Sraddha. See SHRĀDDHA.

Sramana. See SAMANA.

Sraosha. In early Zoroastrianism Sraosha was a genius of hearing and obeying, from a word meaning to 'hearken', implying 'obedience'. It expressed the relationship of Zoroaster to Ahura Mazdā. Later Sraosha becomes a personal deity, who is both God's hearing the words of men and his instrument for judging and punishing evil men and spirits. With Mitra he assists at the judgement when men's deeds are weighed in the balance of Rashnu (q.v.). So Sraosha is a mediator between Ahura Mazdā and men, standing before him in the heavenly court, and conducting the righteous over the Bridge of the Requiter to heaven. Sraosha survived into the Islamic period in Persia and was sometimes identified as Surūsh with the archangel Gabriel. The Manichees (see MĀNĪ) identified him with their Column of Glory which unites heaven and earth.

Sri. See SHRĪ.

Srong Ma, Srung Ma. (Tibetan) 'guardians' of the Buddhist doctrine, title of some of the chief gods of the ancient Bon (q.v.) religion of Tibet. They are also known as Chos Skyong, 'protectors of the religious law'. The Srong Ma include gods and goddesses, and also some other (sometimes harmful) non-Buddhist spirits. See PALDEN LHAMO.

Sruti. See SHRUTI.

Ssŭ-ma Ch'ien. Chinese historian (died about 80 B.C.) and called 'the Herodotus of China'. His 'Historical Records' (*Shih Chi*) came to hold a place in education second only to the Classics (q.v.). Particularly important is his biography of Confucius, the first attempt (and almost the only major one) to arrange the events of the life of Confucius in a chronological order, although it was written some four hundred years after the death of his subject. In other biographies Ssŭ-ma Ch'ien has a gift for enlivening incident and character, and writing with great style.

Ssŭ-ming-shen. (Chinese) 'kitchen god', whose altar is near the hearth or cooking place. In popular belief he makes a report to Heaven at the end of the year on the conduct of all members of the house, and so his face is smeared with sweet things at that time to persuade him to make a good report.

Steropes. One of the three Cyclopes (q.v.) in Greek mythology. Also one of the Pleiades and, further, a daughter of King Cepheus.

Sthānakavāsī. A reformed sect of the Jains (q.v.). In 1452 Lunkā or Lonkā Sā, a Jain of Ahmedabad, found that image-worship was not mentioned in the scriptures of the Shvetāmbaras, and with his followers he separated from the parent body on this issue. In 1653 a stricter reform from this sect was initiated by the Sthānakavāsīs, 'dwellers in meeting-houses' or monasteries. They are also called Dhundiās or 'searchers'. The Sthānakavāsī claim to be closest to primitive Jain practice, use the Magadhi rather than the Sanskrit language for their scriptures, and reject the use of all images. There are a number of sub-sects, all reject images, but in many ways they resemble the original Shvetāmbaras.

Sthenno. (Greek) the 'strong', one of the Gorgons (q.v.) in mythology, an immortal living in the far west.

Stoics. A philosophical school founded about 300 B.C. by Zeno (q.v.) of Citium, and named after a public hall in Athens called the Stoa Poikilé or 'painted porch' where Zeno and his successors taught. Zeno taught the basic principles of early Stoicism and his system was elaborated by Cleanthes and Chrysippus. The main doctrines were: virtue comes from knowledge; the only good is to live in harmony, with reason (and some said with nature); not to be virtuous is the only evil. These principles demanded courage, since pain and death are not evils; chastity since pleasure is not a good; and justice since the virtuous man is impartial. Some of the most famous later Stoics were Epictetus, Seneca and Marcus Aurelius (qq.v.).

Stonehenge. (Saxon) 'hanging stones', one of the finest groups of prehistoric monuments in Europe, near Amesbury in Wiltshire. Romantic theories that connected Stonehenge with the Druids (q.v.) have long been abandoned by serious scholars. The first banks and stones of Stonehenge were erected between 1900 and 1700 B.C., blue stones were brought from Wales about 1600, and sarsen stones from Marlborough about 1500. The Druids are not mentioned till over a thousand years later, and not in connection with Stonehenge. The open part of the Stonehenge horse-shoe is in a line with the sunrise on Midsummer's Day, June 24, and this supports the theory that it was a primitive sanctuary of sun-worship. See top photograph p. 266.

Stools. In parts of Africa, especially

STONEHENGE

 BUDDHIST STŪPA AT SĀNCHI

West Africa, stools have a personal and religious meaning, often as the shrine of one's soul which becomes an ancestral shrine at death (see ADAE). The Golden Stool of Ashanti was said to have been brought down from heaven in the eighteenth century by the priest Anotchi and to embody the soul of the nation. It was covered with gold and had bells, chains and masks fastened to it. The Golden Stool was hidden in wartime, came to light in 1921 and was restored to the royal palace in Kumasi where it remains.

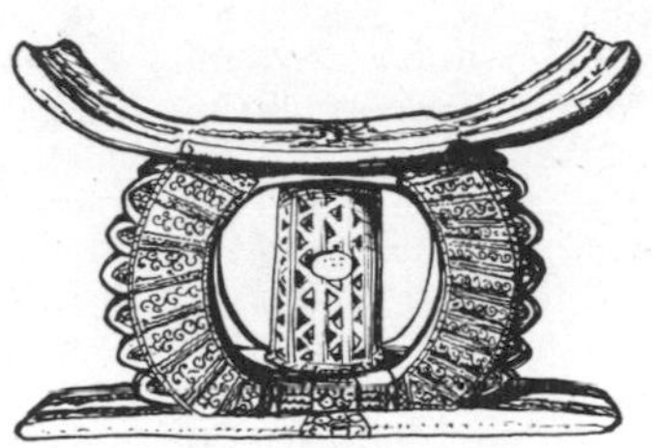

Stūpa. A mound of bricks or earth, originally erected for burials, and used by Buddhism for containers of relics of the Buddha and some of his leading followers. The name is of uncertain derivation, but it comes to indicate a relic-chamber, usually covered by a large hemispherical dome. The emperor Ashoka built Stūpas at some of the principal places associated with the birth, life and death of the Buddha. These were later enlarged and beautified, and a splendid one remains at Sānchi (q.v.). and see bottom photograph opposite In Ceylon the Stūpa became the Dāgaba (q.v.), and in Burma and beyond the Pagoda (q.v.). Stūpas contain bones, hair or clothing attributed to the person celebrated, and these show that he is regarded as a historical person. They are still visited by pilgrims, who place flowers and small gifts in front of them. A Stūpa is also sometimes called a Tope; it was formerly also called a Chaitya, a funeral mound, monument or temple.

Stymphalian Birds. In Greek mythology brazen man-eating birds in the Stymphalian marsh; to kill them was one of the Labours of Heracles (q.v.). Athena gave him some brass castanets. Frightened by these, many of the birds were shot by Heracles as they flew away. In some versions the birds were women, daughters of Stymphalus, who refused hospitality to Heracles so that he killed them.

Styx. (Greek) the 'hateful' or horrible, a river of Arcadia which was believed to go underground and form one of the nine rivers of the underworld. Gods and mortals swore their most sacred oaths by it. See LETHE and OCEANUS.

Subha, Sebha. Prayer beads (q.v.) used in Islam, probably used first by Sūfī mystics and derived from India. Subha are made of wood, bone or mother of pearl and are in three groups of thirty-three beads, for reciting the Ninety-Nine Names of God (see BEAUTIFUL NAMES). They are also used for remembrances (see DHIKR), and a thousand beads have been recorded for recitations of the Bismillah (q.v.).

Subhadrā. In Hindu mythology the daughter of Vasudeva (q.v.), sister of Krishna and wife of Arjuna who carried her off at Krishna's suggestion. She is also associated with Krishna as Jagannātha (q.v.), and her image and car accompany his at ceremonies at the temple at Puri.

Subrahmanya. A name of Kārttikeya (q.v.), Hindu god of war, especially popular in this form in southern India.

Subud. From the Indian forms Shabda (q.v.) and Shabad, for the divine Word revealed to man, Subud has been taken as the title of a religious movement from 1933, founded by Muhammad Subuh, which has spread from Java. In the scripture *Susila Budhi Dharma*, this is expounded as the Way of Submission to the Will of God, teaching the conditions for communion with the great life that proceeds from the one God.

Succubus. See INCUBO and LILITH.

Suchness. See TATHĀGATA.

Suddhodana. Father of Gautama the Buddha, of the Shākya (q.v.) tribe, and said to have ruled the kingdom. His wife was named Māyā, and in the oldest traditions their child was born naturally, rather than as miraculous birth, though Māyā had visions of the coming greatness of her child.

Sudra. See SHŪDRA.

Sudreh, Sadreh. See SACRED THREAD.

Sūfī. A mystic of Islam, the name being derived from the *sūf* or 'cloak of white wool' which mystics wore after the model of Christian monks. Mystical movements began in Islam at least from its second century (eighth century A.D.), partly in reaction against the formalism of orthodox teaching and social and political oppression. Despite some claims to the contrary, the Sūfī movement was as much Arab as Persian, though it greatly developed in the latter country. Some of the most famous Sūfīs were Rābi'a, Hallāj, Ghazālī, Rūmī, Ibn 'Arabī, Hāfiz and Omar Khayyām (qq.v.). Sūfī doctrines taught the immanence of God and sometimes a pantheism that perhaps came from Hinduism; there were also teachings from Neo-Platonism. Hallāj was executed for blasphemy, but Ghazālī helped to make the Sūfī movement orthodox. Sūfī communities have flourished in many parts of the Islamic world and, although banned in Turkey (for superstition and as rival organizations to the state), similar devotional movements continue to appear. See also DERVISH.

Sukha. (Sanskrit) 'happiness', ease, bliss. In Hindu mythology it is personified as a child of Dharma, or one of the nine Shaktis of the god Shiva. In Buddhism it is the opposite of pain, Dukkha.

Sukhāvatī. See PURE LAND.

Sukkoth. See TABERNACLES.

Sulaiman. The name of the Biblical Solomon in the *Qur'ān* and a popular figure in Islamic legend. The *Qur'ān* calls him an apostle, who knew the language of birds and ants (27, 16f.), and to him came the Queen of Sheba, later called Bilqīs (q.v.). It is said that Solomon built the temple with the help of thousands of jinns and his supernatural powers are exaggerated in medieval story.

Another Sulaiman was an Umayyad caliph (715–17) who besieged Constantinople but failed to take it.

Sulaiman the Magnificent was the most splendid Ottoman emperor (1520–66), who called himself Sultan of Sultans and Shadow of God on earth. He beautified Constantinople (Istanbul) and had built the famous Sulaimaniyah or Blue Mosque higher than the adjoining cathedral of Santa Sophia which was built by Justinian.

Sumanakuta. See Ādam.

Sumedha. The name of the Buddha-to-be in a previous life, when as a Brahmin he met the Buddha Dīpankara (q.v.) and took a vow to become a Buddha himself.

Sundarar. A Tamil devotee of Shiva in the ninth century, whose hymns are in the *Tevāram* (q.v.). He was married twice and many miracles are told of his life. See SHAIVA SIDDHĀNTA.

Sundareshvara. (Sanskrit) 'beautiful lord', a name of the Hindu god Shiva, under which he is worshipped in the famous temple at Madura with his consort Mīnākshī (qq.v.). It is said that Mīnākshī's fishy smell disappeared when Sundareshvara appeared to her, showing that he was her lord.

Sunna, Sunni. (Arabic) 'custom', used of Islamic traditional ways and particularly of that of Muhammad. The Sunna came to mean the theory and practice of orthodox Muslims, Sunni, especially in opposition to the Shī'a schism (q.v.). It is a standard of faith and conduct, expounded by orthodox teachers. The Sunni recognize the first three Caliphs; Abū Bakr, 'Umar and 'Uthmān, as 'rightly guided', while the Shī'a reject them in favour of 'Alī as first Caliph or Imām. All Sunni follow one of the four orthodox schools of law: Hanafī, Shāfi'ī, Mālikī and Hanbalī (see FIQH). Over eighty per cent of modern Muslims are Sunni.

Sun Worship. A practice in many lands; see AMATERASU, ATON, RĒ', STONEHENGE, SŪRYA.

Sūnya. See SHŪNYA.

Superman, Marks of. Thirty-two marks of a Great Person (Mahā-Purusha) are listed in the Buddhist scriptures. If a child has them, he will either become a Lord of the Wheel, a universal king, or he will become a Buddha who removes the veil from the eyes of the world. These marks were seen on the body of the infant Buddha by a sage called Asita (q.v.). See also CHAKRAVARTIN.

Supplicatio. (Latin) 'public prayer', day of humiliation or thanksgiving on occasions of special adoration of the Roman gods, so named from the kneeling prostration of the worshippers. Sometimes it was associated with a Lectisternium (q.v.), a feast of the gods, but was generally distinguished from it.

Sūra, Sūrah. The name of the chapters of the *Qur'ān*, sometimes derived from a root meaning 'line' or 'order'. The *Qur'ān* has 114 sūras, all of which have names in Arabic, generally from a word or major theme in their contents; European editions of the *Qur'ān* use numbers of chapters and verses instead.

Surabhi. (Sanskrit) 'sweet-smelling', name of a mythical cow in Hindu mythology, mother of cattle and the Rudras, storm spirits, and sometimes identified with Kāmadhenu, the cow of plenty (q.v.).

Surt, Surtr. 'The Black', in Scandinavian mythology, a wicked giant who guarded the southern hot world called Muspell. The Sons of Muspell were demons of destruction who at the Ragnarök (q.v.), 'end of the world', boarded the ship of death and followed Surt against the gods. Surt with a fiery sword fought with Frey, who had given away his magical sword, and finally Surt burnt up the earth with fire.

Sūrya. The sun, in Hindu mythology, sometimes identical with Savitri (q.v.). He is an important god in the *Vedas*, sometimes called son of Dyaus, a heavenly god, and Ushas the dawn is his wife. His twin sons are the Ashvins (q.v.). The solar race, Sūrya-vansa, was said to come from his grandson Ikshvāku. There is a famous work on astronomy, *Sūyra Siddhānta*, said to have been revealed by Sūrya. See BLACK PAGODA.

Susanowo, Susano-ō. The storm god of Shinto mythology, the 'Valiant-swift-impetuous'. He ruled the ocean, while his sister the sun-goddess, Amaterasu-ōmi-kami (q.v.), ruled heaven and earth. Susanowo ravaged Amaterasu's rice-fields and polluted her sacred observances, so that she hid in a cave and all the world was in darkness – a myth of eclipse, or night, or winter. Finally the gods rallied to Amaterasu and Susanowo was banished to Izumo on the north coast of Japan, where he ruled over the domain of the invisible. The sanctuary at Izumo (q.v.) is one of the most ancient in Japan, in traditional wooden style.

Sushumna. Sanskrit name for a vein or artery, perhaps the carotid, which according to Tantric anatomy was a passage for the breath or spirit. At the top of it was the Sahasrāra psychic centre; the Kundalinī serpent power passed up through the Sushumna to unite with the Sahasrāra and bring liberation. See KUNDALINĪ and SAHASRĀRA.

Sūtra, Sutta. (Sanskrit) 'thread', 'row', and so a short verse or aphorism, and a collection of such rules and sayings. There are many Hindu *Sūtras* on varying subjects, but the '*Sūtras*' generally indicates those which are connected with the *Vedas*: *Kalpa Sūtras* about ritual, and *Grihya Sūtras* relating to domestic rites. See also KĀMA.

The Pali word *Sutta* indicates the second Basket or section of the Buddhist canon of scripture, the *Sutta Pitaka*. It contains five parts, Nikāyas: Digha, Majjhima, Samyutta, Anguttara and Khuddaka. These are largely discourses attributed to the Buddha, though clearly expanded and of uncertain dates.

Sutta Nipāta. (Pali) 'collection of verses', one of the oldest and most popular works of Theravāda Buddhism, and part of the second section of the canon of scripture. The *Sutta Nipāta* is in five parts, with varied numbers of verses. The third part, Mahāvagga, tells of the Buddha's renunciation of the world, his temptation by Māra (q.v.), and the visit of the sage Asita (q.v.) to the infant future Buddha.

Suttee. See SATĪ.

Sva, Swa. (Sanskrit) 'self', one's own, used in compounds. So Sva-dharma is one's own duty and particular property, one's class duty. Sva-bhāva is one's own condition, natural state, inherent disposition. In Hindu philosophy the latter term is used not only of individuals but of the notion that the universe was created and sustained by the natural action of substances through their own inherent properties.

Svayambhū. 'Self-existent' (Sanskrit), a name of the creating deity in Hindu thought, sometimes identified with Brahmā. See MANU.

Svetāmbaras. (Sanskrit) 'clothed in white', one of the two major divisions of the Jains, from the white robes worn by monks, in opposition to the Digambaras (q.v.) who were 'sky-clothed'. See JAINS.

Svetāsvatara. See SHVETĀSHVATARA.

Swāmi, Svāmī. A member of a Hindu religious order, and a general title for a holy man.

Swanhild. See BRYNHILD.

Swarga, Svarga. The heaven of Indra in Hindu mythology, said to be situated on Mount Meru (q.v.). It is used as a general name for heaven or paradise. In Jainism Swarga is divided into twenty-six regions; there are twelve Devalokas (q.v.), worlds of the gods where Indra is the chief; above these are nine worlds where gods are equal, and then five highest abodes for gods on the verge of attaining liberation. In these heavens joy predominates, though pain may also be felt, and there is rebirth from them to the world again. Above Swarga is the highest region which is called Moksha, liberation, attained by ascetics who are completely freed from Karma.

Swastika, Svastika. A mark of good fortune, whose name may be derived from Sanskrit, 'well-being'. It is ancient, and appears on the seals of the Harappā (q.v.) civilization, about 2000 B.C. It is found in many parts of the ancient world, and is to be seen on the Roman mosaic at Lullingstone, Kent. Among the Jains it is an especially auspicious symbol, connected with the seventh Jina and marked on objects and utensils of worship. Sometimes it is called the Jaina Cross or Buddhist Cross.

The origins of the Swastika are disputed, a favourite theory being that it represents the sun, or the wheel of Vishnu, with spokes or rays bent. The correct form is with the limbs bent to the right. The reverse form was used in Bön (q.v.) Tantric rites and in black magic; this form was the one adopted by the Nazis.

Sweat Baths. See TOZI.

Syn. One of the Scandinavian goddesses called Asynjur (q.v.). She was concerned chiefly with justice, and at the Thing, the people's gathering, she acted as defence and kept the door of the hall to bar intruders.

Synagogue. Jewish place of worship, from Greek 'bringing together', assembly. The origins of the Synagogue are uncertain, but since they appear after the Exile of the leaders of Judah to Babylon in 586 B.C., it seems that they arose from the necessity of worshipping in a strange land. In the Holy Land itself the attempts that were made (from the time of King Josiah about 620 B.C.) to centralize sacrificial worship in the Temple at Jerusalem meant that other temples or 'high places' were suppressed. Eventually they would be replaced by Synagogues and for centuries Jews worshipped there regularly, with occasional visits to the Temple. During the Dispersion, and after the destruction of Jerusalem by the Romans, the Synagogues were the centre of Jewish religious life and have remained so down the ages. They are simple buildings, with the scrolls of the Law in an Ark (*Aron ha-kodesh*) cupboard at the wall facing Jerusalem. In Orthodox Jewry women sit separately from men, but in reformed congregations they are mixed. See ARK and BIMAH.

T

Tabarī. Arab historian (A.D. 839–923), who died in Baghdad. He is said to have learnt the whole *Qur'ān* by heart by the time he was seven, and then travelled to neighbouring countries gathering traditions. He wrote a standard commentary on the *Qur'ān* which is still used, but his greatest work was a history of the world, beginning with patriarchs and prophets and ending in A.D. 915.

Tabernacles, Booths. Third and autumn harvest festival of Judaism (see PASSOVER and PENTECOST), celebrated from the fifteenth to the twenty-second of Tishri (September-October). During this time Booths (*Sukkoth*) are erected of palm and other branches. Meals are taken there in memory of the booths in which the Hebrews lived during their journey through the wilderness after the Exodus, and in which they celebrated this at later deliverances, 'all the congregation of those that came again out of the captivity made booths, and dwelt in the booths.' (*Nehemiah* 8, 17). Tabernacles is a joyful festival, thanking God for his providence and inviting the poor to the feast. It ends on the eighth or ninth day with the Rejoicing of the Law (*Simchat Torah*), with processions of the scrolls and the calling of boys under thirteen to the reading of the Law under a canopy.

Tablets of Destiny. In Mesopotamian mythology possession of these tablets gave the owner power over the destiny of all things, and the sovereignty of heaven depended upon them. In the myth of Zu (q.v.) the bird-god stole these emblems of royal power, and several gods refused to recover them until one, whose name is not clear, did so and restored the tablets to Enlil. In the myth of Tiamat (q.v.) she gives the Tablets to her husband Kingu and he is defeated by the god Marduk who binds them on his own breast.

Taboo, Tabu. English forms of a Polynesian word, generally pronounced *Tapu* and accented on the first syllable. It was first noticed by Captain Cook, who in 1784 wrote of the Atui people of the Sandwich Islands that they spoke of '*taboo*, or, as they pronounced the word, *tafoo*'. Later investigation found *Tapu* from New Zealand to Tahiti, *Kapu* in Hawaii, *Tabu* in Fiji, and *Tabaka* in Malagasy. The meaning of Taboo is generally that of prohibition, because of a sacred or dangerous character of the

Taboo object. It may be derived from a compound word meaning to 'mark thoroughly', or at least that indicates its nature as marked off, prohibited, shown as sacred. Taboo has been used very widely in modern writings to denote persons or things set apart, banned, cursed, prohibited or consecrated. See MAORI.

Tabulae Iguvinae. See IGUVINE TABLETS.

Tafsīr. (Arabic) 'explanation', commentary, the general term for commentaries on the *Qur'ān* such as those of Baidāwi, Rāzi, Tabari and Zamakhshari (qq.v.). These are huge but uncritical explanations of texts and words, aimed at settling points of law and theological doctrines.

Tagore, Thakur. A famous Bengali family, foremost among the reformers and revivers of Hinduism. Debendra Nath (1818–1905) joined the Brāhma Samāj (q.v.) in 1842 and became its leader, compiling extracts from Hindu scriptures called *Brāhma Dharma* or 'Brāhma Religion'. After the schism of Keshab Chandra Sen in 1865 (q.v.), Debendra continued the older movement as Ādi (or original) Brāhma Samāj. His 'Autobiography' shows the spiritual progress of an educated nineteenth century Hindu. His fourth son was Rabindra Nath Tagore (1861–1941), a leading national, poetical and religious thinker. He took part in the independence struggle and resigned a knighthood after a massacre at Amritsar in 1919. His songs and hymns in Bengali have revived that literature and he himself translated a considerable part into English. His short book of religious poetry, *Gitanjali*, 'Song Offerings', breathes a mystical spirit which is at once Indian and universal, and it may be remembered as his finest work.

Tahrīf. (Arabic) 'corruption', alteration of the sense of a document. It is used in religious debate, and particularly occurred in discussions with Jews in Medina over differences between their traditions and scriptures and those put forward by Muhammad. While not denying that the Torah came from God, the *Qur'ān* declared that 'those who have Judaized alter words from their position' (4, 48).

T'ai Chi. The 'supreme ultimate' or 'transcendent absolute' in Chinese philosophy. Borrowed from Taoism, the concept was developed by Neo-Confucian scholars from the tenth century A.D. Particularly interesting was the use of an ancient diagram, T'ai-chi T'u, to express the production of Yang and Yin (q.v.) and their interaction. The Supreme Ultimate produced the Yang through movement, and having reached its limit came to quiescence which produced the Yin. By the complementary actions of Yang and Yin all things were produced and maintained. The T'ai-chi diagram is found everywhere in China, decorating gates and houses, household utensils and furnishings, and is used in exorcist symbols. These two inter-locking or separated symbols have spread throughout the world, in Indian and Persian carpets and curtains, and on clothing, scarves and ties in the west, with the constant pear-shaped pattern.

T'ai Hsu. Buddhist monk (1889–1947) who sought to reform and revive Chinese Buddhism. He tried to educate and purify the monasteries and priesthood, to use Buddhist property for the benefit of the people and to reconstruct Buddhist doctrine. T'ai Hsu was active in the formation of lay associations for the study of Buddhist texts, and he sought to reconcile Buddhism with modern science.

T'ai I. (Chinese) 'Grand Unity', a Taoist divinity mentioned in the 'Songs of Ch'u' (see CH'U TZ'Ŭ) and declared in the second century B.C. to be the greatest God. Later Taoist teachers worshipped a Triad of supreme gods: the Grand Unity (T'ai I), Heavenly Unity (T'ien I), and Earthly Unity (Ti I). See JADE EMPEROR.

T'ai P'ing. (Chinese) 'great peace', a revolt of Chinese peasants in 1850–65 which almost broke the Manchu dynasty and was suppressed with the loss of about twenty million lives. Although basically a rebellion of oppressed peasants, it had religious aspects and its leader, Hung Hsiu-ch'üan, was influenced by Christian ideals. See BOXERS.

T'ai P'ing Tao. See CHANG CHÜEH.

Taittirīya. (Sanskrit) for the 'pupils of Tittiri', a school of the *Yajur Veda*. The *Taittirīya Upanishad* is one of the shorter classical *Upanishads* (q.v.) and forms part of the *Krishna* or *Black Yajur Veda*. It is an important source of monistic philosophy, is still recited in many parts of

Taj Mahal

India and has often been commented upon. For the *Taittirīya Samhitā*, see YAJUR VEDA.

Taj Mahal. A monument, not a temple, at Agra in India. It was built by the Mughal emperor Shah Jehan, from 1630, as a tomb for his favourite wife Mumtaz-i-Mahal, the 'Elect of the Palace'. The Taj Mahal is classic perfection, one of the wonders of the world, built of white marble with inlaid black lettering and coloured stones. The central dome with its metal pinnacle is 74 metres high and four marble minarets are 40 metres high. On either side of the Taj are two fine buildings of red sandstone and marble. Inside the Taj is a marble trellis screen enclosing the tombs of Shah Jehan and Mumtaz-i-Mahal, the latter bearing the ninety-nine Beautiful Names of God (q.v.) in Arabic black marble lettering.

TALLITH

Takbīr. (Arabic) the formula Allāhu Akbar (q.v.), 'God is most great', which is part of every act of formal prayer for Muslims.

Taliesin. Legendary Welsh bard, who perhaps lived in the sixth century A.D. Poems attributed to him and a story, *Hanes Taliesin*, of the fourteenth century give tales of the gods, including Cerridwen and Tegid Voel (qq.v.). Taliesin may have been a god of poetry, with a beautiful chair in Caer Sidi to which he went with Arthur. He is said to have had the power to change his form and was reborn several times.

Talisman. A charm or amulet (q.v.), or magical figure of astrology. The word comes from Arabic *tilsam* derived from a late Greek word *telesma*, meaning a rite.

Tallith, Talis. 'Prayer shawl' used by male Jews at morning prayer in synagogues. It is made of woven wool or silk and has fringes at the four corners, according to *Numbers* 15, 38: 'make fringes in the borders of their garments.' See TZITZITH. For Small Tallith, see ARBA KANFOTH.

Talmud. The encyclopedic collection of Jewish traditions supplementing the *Bible*, from a Hebrew root 'to study'. It grew out of the *Mishnah* and *Gemara* (qq.v.) and was completed in two forms about the fifth century A.D. The Palestinian *Talmud* was in Western Aramaic and, in addition to its interpretations of the Law, it gives much information on the state of the Jews when Christianity was becoming the religion of the Roman empire. Nearly three times as long is the Babylonian *Talmud*, in Eastern Aramaic, produced by the more free academies in Babylon; it is not only fuller but much better arranged than the Palestinian *Talmud*. From the *Talmud* derive the social and religious laws of modern Jews, even after reform, and their principles of law and morality. After the *Bible* it is the unifying force of Jewry, allowing it to adapt itself to many varying conditions.

Talu. Western Australian name for the fertility ritual known elsewhere as Intichiuma (q.v.).

Tālūt. The name given to the Biblical King Saul in the *Qur'ān* (2, 247f.). It may have originated from similarity to the name given to Goliath, Jālūt (q.v.). Tālūt had charge of the ark and routed the army of Jālūt, who was killed by David. Muslim legend added many details and included stories of the relationships of Saul and David.

Tamas. (Sanskrit) 'darkness', mass, the third and lowest of the three constituent qualities of beings (see GUNAS) in Hindu Sāmkhya philosophy (q.v.).

Tammuz. Ancient Mesopotamian god, whose Sumerian name meant 'true son', Dumu-zi. He was the vegetation deity of a famous myth and ritual in which he died and descended to the underworld. His sister-spouse Ishtar went to search for him and the two divinities returned triumphantly to earth. This represented the dying and rising corn, like the Greek Mysteries of Persephone and Demeter (qq.v., and see also OSIRIS and ISIS). When the cult declined officially in Babylonia and Assyria, it remained among ordinary people and was found in Syria and Canaan. In Syria Tammuz was identified with Adonis, the Rās Shamra texts (q.v.) refer to his cult. *Ezekiel* 8, 14 speaks of 'women weeping for Tammuz', no doubt part of the ritual imitating Ishtar's weeping search for the god.

Tamo, Putitamo. Chinese form of the name of the Buddhist monk Bodhidharma (q.v.).

Tanāsukh. (Arabic) 'transmigration' (q.v.), reincarnation. Although the notion was foreign to early Islam, as to Judaism and Christianity, it became popular among some Shī'a Muslims, especially in India, the classical home of transmigration. The Ismā'īlīs believed that souls could not be reborn till they were released through their Imām (q.v.) and ascended to the world of light. Only a few extremists believed in Tanāsukh in the sense of Incarnation (q.v., and also HULŪL).

Tāndava. (Sanskrit) 'frantic dance', the world-shattering Dance of Shiva (q.v.).

Tane. The most important god (see ATUA) in Maori religion, creator of vegetation and vanquisher of darkness. When the gods were struggling to get free from the embrace of earth and sky, Rangi and Papa (qq.v.), it was the trees of Tane which forced upward the primeval father while the other gods fastened the sky up with poles. Tane made a female out of earth and breathed life into her. She, or her daughter the Dawn Maiden, became the wife of Tane.

Tangaroa. God of the sea in Maori religion: see ATUA.

T'ang Huan-chang. See WU SHAN SHÊ.

Tangi. A Maori ritual for speeding a departed soul to the land of the spirits (Te Reinga), making sure that it left the body and was equipped for its journey. It was a great and long ceremony in which people from different villages might join. The corpse was placed in front of the meeting house and the bones were not finally buried until decomposition had taken place.

Tanhā. (Pali) 'desire', craving (Sanskrit, *trishnā* q.v.). It is the thirst for attachment to the sensual world and continued existence in it, which is the cause of suffering as analysed by the Buddha in the Four Noble Truths (q.v.).

Tanit. Goddess of Carthage, wife of Baal Hammon, corresponding to the Phoenician Elat as her husband did to El (q.v.). Tanit was called mother and had colleges of priests. Later she was named Juno and Caelestis. See CARTHAGE and PHOENICIANS.

Tanna, Tannaim. Jewish scholar, and scholars, of the first two centuries of the present era, who specialized in teaching *Mishnah* (q.v.). The name means 'teach' or 'repeat', from the Aramaic root similar to the one from which *Mishnah* comes, and the Tannaim were the Palestinian and Babylonian scholars whose teachings are in the *Mishnah* and later in the *Talmud*.

Tano. River god of the Ashanti and neighbouring peoples of Ghana, whose worship used to extend far away from the river. He is one of the most popular deities, said in mythology to have fought with death, and he possesses his priests in order to bring messages to men. There are temples of Tano and wayside shrines at which offerings are made.

Tantalus. A mythical Greek king, son of Zeus and an earth nymph, Pluto. He was father of Niobe (q.v.) and ancestor of the royal line of Pelops. Tantalus offended the gods, perhaps by stealing their food and giving it to men. He was condemned to everlasting punishment but, as he was immortal, he could not be killed, so he was 'tantalized' by being placed in water up to his chin with fruit hanging over his head; when he tried to drink or eat, the water and fruit disappeared. Another version says that a great stone was hung over his head, always ready to fall, so that he lived in perpetual fear.

Tantra. (Sanskrit) 'system', 'rule', the name of a class of Hindu religious and magical works and practices derived from them. The texts are chiefly dialogues between the god Shiva and his spouse or Shakti called Devī or Durgā (see SHĀKTAS), which deal with five subjects: creation, destruction, worship, superhuman powers, union. Great prominence is given to the energy of the female Shakti. Each Shakti has a kindly and fierce, white and black, nature and similarly the Tantrists or Shāktas are divided into the Right-hand and Left-hand worshippers. The latter in particular seek for magical and sexual powers through the five M's (see M). Tantra worship has been particularly prominent in Bengal and eastern India. From there Tantra entered Buddhism and became important in Tibet, where the Left-hand Path follows Indian Tantric practices, and the Right-hand Path has elaborate exercises to develop Siddhis or Perfections. See also KUNDALINĪ and BLACK PAGODA.

Tao. A fundamental concept of Chinese thought, indicating broadly the 'way, path, eternal principle.' For Confucius (q.v.) the original meaning of a road or path, the Way of Man, is extended into the Way of Heaven, which it has ordained for man to walk in. This is the Way for good men to follow, bringing conformity to the will of Heaven, and producing wisdom, propriety and righteousness. With the Taoists (q.v.) Tao becomes the unity under the plurality of the universe, the unnamed and indefinable principle behind all things. It becomes a mystical concept which leads to a search for harmony with Tao, through ascetic practices and also magic. (See also MO TZŬ and CHUANG TZŬ.)

TAOIST SHRINE

Tao-an. Chinese Buddhist monk (A.D. 312–385), propagator of the faith and student of the scriptures. He collected many texts and commentaries, founding a famous centre in northern Hupei and developing Mahāyāna Buddhist wisdom literature. In addition to attracting monks and scholars, Tao-an stressed the devotional side of Buddhism with particular emphasis on the coming Buddha, Maitreya (q.v.). He set many translators to work on Chinese versions of monastic rules and Mahāyāna texts. His most famous disciple was Hui-yüan (q.v.).

Taoism. The name given to one of the most basic and characteristic ways of

Chinese religion. Tao Chia, the 'Taoist School', is only mentioned as such from the first century B.C., but the movement existed centuries before, though its attribution to the legendary Lao Tzŭ (q.v.) is now thought unlikely. The Taoist canon, *Tao Tsang*, comprises about 1,120 volumes, some two hundred of which were in existence by the seventh century A.D. Taoism basically was a following of Tao (q.v.), in a nature mysticism, which degenerated into magic only too often, with search for the elixir of immortality and islands of the blest. There were many temples and gods, which incorporated ancient cults, but have now been mostly suppressed. After decline in imperial favour Taoism went into secret societies, such as the later Boxers (q.v.). In 1957 a Chinese Taoist Association was formed, under strict governmental control. (See also TAO, TAO TÊ CHING, CHUANG TZŬ, LIEH TZŬ.) For priests and Taoist 'Pope', see TAO SHIH.

Taoist Triad. See T'AI I.

Tao-shêng. Chinese Buddhist monk (A.D. 360–434). He was a follower of Kumārajīva and gave great attention to the texts about Nirvāna, claiming that it is a present reality. All beings possess the Buddha-nature, which can be realized by knowing one's true self. So there is no future Pure Land, but Buddhahood is within us. Though disliked as heretical at first, much of this doctrine came to be accepted by Ch'an and other schools of Chinese Buddhist thought.

Tao Shih. (Chinese) 'Taoist master', a priest of Taoism, in early times itinerant but later presiding over a district. The priest was often married, though under the influence of Buddhism those who lived in monasteries were usually celibate. The title T'ien Shih, 'celestial Master', was taken by reformers and leaders, especially after Taoism became the official religion of China in the fifth century A.D. Some of them were regarded as 'Popes' of the Taoist 'church' by Taoist sects down to this century.

Tao Tê Ching. The 'Classic of the Way and its Power', one of the most important of Chinese religious and philosophical writings. Formerly attributed to Lao-tzŭ (q.v.), which would have placed it in the sixth century B.C. and so before Confucius, it is now generally thought to be the work of an anonymous quietist of the fourth or third century B.C., though it may contain some older material. The *Tao Tê Ching* has eighty-one (a magical number) short chapters, and is concerned with the Tao. Tao is indefinable and ungraspable, though it is the mother of the ten thousand visible things. The wise man both engages in 'actionless activity' (*wu wei*, q.v.) and yet works on all creatures. He seeks the void and quietness, needs no morality, and avoids war and weapons. This gentle classic has been influential through wars and revolutions, until recently, and perhaps even now, being treasured by many people.

Tao Tsang. See TAOISM.

Tapas. (Sanskrit) 'heat', and then 'austerity'. The power of religious asceticism (q.v.) was a form of heat; Hindu myths often tell of the Tapas of ascetics which was so great that the gods were afraid of their position and sent envoys to distract the holy men from too severe asceticism.

Tapu. See TABOO.

Tāra. A supernatural female figure, especially of Tibetan mythology. Probably from an Indian goddess, Tāra nevertheless developed in Buddhist contexts as a Bodhisattva (q.v.) and her images combine Hindu and Buddhist features. Tāra is the female counterpart of Avalokiteshvara (q.v.) and is especially important in Tantra (q.v.) forms of Buddhism. Tāra has sometimes been identified with Kuan-yin, the Chinese female form of Avalokiteshvara, but in origin they were different.

Targum. A 'translation' (Hebrew) of the scripture among late Biblical and post-Biblical Jews. The *Targum of the Seventy*, or *Septuagint* (*LXX*), was so-called because it was said to have been made by seventy scholars into Greek in Egypt in the third century B.C. The *Targum of Onkelos* (Aquila) was an Aramaic translation of the second century A.D. still used by some Jews, and there is debate whether he was the same Aquila who produced a famous Greek version of the *Old Testament* used by Origen and other Christian scholars. The *Targumim* try to avoid anthropomorphic expressions in the *Bible* and speak of Memra, 'Word', instead of God when that occurs in a manner suggesting an action like a man.

Tariki. (Japanese) 'external strength', used of salvation by the grace of Amida, when 'one's own strength' (Jiriki, q.v.) had failed.

Tarīqa. (Arabic) a 'path', used of the spiritual path or system of rites for the communal life of the Muslim Sūfī (q.v.) mystical orders (plural *turuq*). The rules of monastic life were distinctive by their Dhikr (q.v.) litanies, initiation into the order by senior teachers, and connection with the tomb of the founder or saint who was venerated.

Tarpeian Rock. A cliff in Rome from which traitors and murderers were thrown. Some located it above the Forum and others near the temple of Jupiter Capitolinus (see CAPITOLINE TRIAD) so that it was perhaps at the southern side of the Capitol.

Tartarus. Underworld or Hell in Greek mythology, perhaps from a Cretan root meaning 'far west'. It was said to be a foul and dark abyss below Hades, though later writers identify it with Hades. Tartarus was a primal being, produced by Earth or united with her to bring forth monsters. The final Labour of Heracles (q.v.) took him down there, guided by Athena and Hermes. Near the gates of Tartarus Heracles found his friend Theseus fixed to a cruel chair, and released him; he slaughtered cattle to feed the ghosts and nearly choked the guardian dog Cerberus. On his return Heracles made a wreath from a tree planted by Hades – the silver aspen, the leaves of which are dark on the outside like the colour of Hell itself.

Tasawwuf. Islamic mysticism, from the word Sūfī (q.v.).

Tashi Lama. Name of the chief Lamas of Tashi-lhunpo, near Shigatse in Tibet, and borne by them since the seventeenth century. See PANCHEN LAMA for more detail.

Tathāgata. A title of the Buddha, used by his early followers and also put into his own mouth about himself. A Sanskrit word, its origin and meaning are doubtful. It may mean one who has 'thus gone' (*tathā-gata*), or 'thus come' (*tathā-āgata*), meaning 'one who has come and gone like former Buddhas'. Among Mahāyāna Buddhists preference is given to the meaning, 'one who has fully realized Thusness or Suchness' (*tathatā*), a term indicating the ultimate and unconditioned.

Tathatā. See TATHĀGATA.

Tattva. (Sanskrit) 'truth', reality, in Sāmkhya philosophy (q.v.) the twenty-five principles, twenty-four with Nature (Prakriti) and Spirit (Purusha) the twenty-fifth.

Tat Tvam Asi. 'That thou art', a famous Sanskrit phrase repeated nine times in the *Chāndogya Upanishad* (chapter 6). The pupil is told of his identity with the reality behind all things, the universal Soul or Self (*ātman*, q.v.). This is sometimes claimed nowadays as the central and determinative declaration of philosophical Hinduism, absolute pantheism or monism (q.v.). It was taken as such and expanded by Shankara, but Rāmānuja said that the words 'that' and 'thou' showed some difference between God and the soul or 'qualified non-dualism', and Madhva declared that it meant 'not that', plain dualism (see articles on these writers).

Taurobolium. See MITHRAISM and CYBELE.

Taurt. See THUERIS.

Tawhīd, Tauhīd. An Arabic term meaning 'making one' or 'asserting one-ness'. In Islamic thought Tawhīd means primarily the unity of God, expressed in the witness: 'there is no god but God.' This means that God has no partners and is oneness in himself, in unicity: unique-ness and unity. Yet this absolute trans-cendentalism led among the Sūfīs to pantheism or monism (q.v.). The infinite distance between God and man can be annihilated by God, for he is one in the sense that there is no other; God is all. So to the Sūfīs Tawhīd meant the absolute divine nature, which is realized in the passing away of human nature. By Fanā' (q.v.), 'passing away', the mystic is lost in God and almost is God, saying, 'when you see me you see him.' This was repu-diated by the orthodox, and for such sayings Hallāj (q.v.) was put to death; however, Sūfī pantheism persisted. See ITTIHĀD.

Tawhīd-i Ilāhī. (Arabic) 'divine monotheism', or Dīn ilāhī, 'divine faith', the synthesis of religions made by the Mughal emperor Akbar (q.v.) and pro-claimed in 1582.

Tê. A Chinese term meaning 'power' or 'virtue'. In early usage Tê can mean bad as well as good, rather like the Indian Karma in the sense of the effects of one's deeds here in this life. Tê has the idea of potentiality, used of planting seeds, and so indicating a latent power. In the *Tao Tê Ching* (q.v.) it is the power of Tao. Among the Confucians Tê came to mean virtue in the sense of good conduct.

Tea Ceremony. The Japanese 'tea and hot water', Cha-no-yu, is the cere-monial preparation and taking of tea, which has not only a social but a spiritual purpose, seeking to induce a mood which leads to peace or enlightenment.

Tecciztecatl. See MEZTLI.

Teetotalism. See ABSTINENCE and KHĀLSĀ.

Tefillin. 'Prayers', term for the signs or remembrances, generally rendered by the Greek word Phylacteries (q.v.), which are worn by Jewish men at weekday morning prayers. See also AMIDAH.

Tefnut. Ancient Egyptian goddess personifying moisture, who with her husband Shu (q.v.) separated heaven and earth. Originally she had no temples or rites, though revered in many places and later acquiring priests and shrines. Tefnut was said to be the daughter of Rēʿ, and mother of Geb and Nut. She was called Eye of Rēʿ and Left Eye of Horus. She was also goddess of the dead. Tefnut was principally identified with the lioness-goddess Hathor, and in art she sometimes appears as a woman with the head of a lioness, with the solar disk and cobra on her head.

Tegh Bahadur. Ninth Guru of the Sikhs (q.v.), who ruled the community from 1664–75. He died a martyr, at the hands of the Mughal emperor Aurangzeb (q.v.), and was succeeded by his son Gobind Singh who founded the Khālsā brotherhood.

Tegid Voel. Ancient Welsh deity, whose story is told by Taliesin (q.v.). He dwelt in Lake Tegid, with his wife Cerridwen (q.v.) and their children Creirwy, Morvran and Avagddu (q.v.). The lake was perhaps an underwater wonderland full of magical objects.

Teiresias. See TIRESIAS.

Tell el-Amarna. Ancient capital of Pharaoh Ikhnaton (q.v.), long in ruins and deserted when the priests of Amūn regained power. In 1887 clay tablets were found there with cuneiform writing, giving correspondence in the Babylonian language. These and other tablets and papyri have been invaluable in rediscovering part of the history and religion of ancient Egypt and its neighbours, with references to the Habiru (perhaps the Hebrews). See ATON.

Tellus. Ancient Roman goddess of the earth and the dead, though her temples were built at a late date, from the third century B.C. She had no Flamen priest (q.v.), but a festival on 15 April, the Fordicia, and sacrifices were made for neglect of rites to the dead.

Temenos. (Greek) the 'domain' of a god or king, and particularly used for the sanctuary or consecrated precinct round the altar of a temple, It could include the temple also, with its images and gifts.

Temple of Heaven. The Hall of Annual Prayers in Peking where once the emperors of China, the Sons of Heaven,

received the Mandate (q.v.) of Heaven to rule. The complex of buildings enclosed within a double red wall, with five thousand cypress trees in the approaches and enclosure, are relatively modern, from the fifteenth century when the Ming emperors made Peking the national capital. The Temple of Heaven has blue-tiled roofs, symbolizing the three circular heavens. There is also a Hall of Prayer for Good Harvests, and a Circular Mound Altar. Also in the city are an ancient Altar of Land and Grain, a Hall of Worship and a Gate of Heavenly Peace. Once used in great state rituals, these buildings now feature in Communist rallies, with not dissimilar purpose.

Temple of the Sun. The most sacred shrine of the Incas of Peru, known as the Coricancha, parts of which are still preserved though much altered. It was a great building or group of buildings around a courtyard, with gabled thatch roof and only one outer door. It was lavishly furnished, with golden objects on the walls, images of the chief gods, and bodies of past emperors. There were smaller shrines round about and rooms for priests. Adjacent to the temple was a great square where national ceremonies were performed and to which sacred objects were brought from the temple. The monastery of Santo Domingo was built upon the lower walls of the temple.

Temurah. In Jewish Kabbalah (q.v.), the practice of substituting one letter of the *Bible* for another, and producing a mystical meaning. See TZIRUF and GEMATRIA.

Tendai. See T'IEN-T'AI.

Tengalai. See PRAPATTI.

Tenko-san. Japanese religious reformer (1872–1968), who abandoned a business career to found a community of Ittōen, the Garden of the One Light. From a Buddhist (particularly Zen) background, Tenko-San developed a group of about three hundred people at Ittōen, near Yamashina, Kyoto, devoted to both meditation and service.

Tenri-kyō. 'The Religion of Divine Wisdom', the most powerful of the modern Japanese sects or New Religions (see SECT SHINTO). Founded by Miki Nakayama (q.v.) after her 'possession' in 1838, it was registered in 1908 as a Shinto Sect. The great new centre of the religion is at Tenri, named after the religion, which is believed to be the centre of the world (Jiba). The central pillar (Kanro-dai, q.v.) of the main shrine is prepared for the coming of 'heavenly dew' to bring in the promised age of peace and goodwill, and even now the spirit of Miki Nakayama is said to be there. Tenri-kyō claims over ten thousand churches and two million members; it has a university, library and museum, and thousands of

INCA SUN TEMPLE

missionaries. There is a close community spirit, and the magnificent buildings have been erected by voluntary labour in a spirit of service.

Tenshō-kōtai-jingu-kyō. 'The Religion of the Heaven-shining Great Deity-Dwelling', one of the latest developments of Sect Shinto (q.v.). Founded in 1942 by Sayo Kitamura, it is popularly called the 'dancing religion', because ecstatic dancing takes place during worship. Kitamura goes into a trance state and chants her messages. To her followers she is a successor to the Buddha and the Christ, and is called 'Great God' (Ōgamisama). The teaching is of repentance and unselfish service, and claims over a hundred thousand followers.

Teotl. Aztec word meaning 'stony', and so permanent and powerful, used of the gods and goddesses generally. See HUEHUETEOTL.

Te Reinga. See TANGI.

Terminus. (Latin) 'boundary mark', and especially the spirit (see NUMEN) of such marks, which were erected with sacrifices and strengthened by an annual festival on 23 February, the Terminalia. There was a god Terminus who embodied the power of all boundary-marks. It was said that a Terminus on the Capitol in Rome was there before the building of the temple to Jupiter and had to be incorporated in it, with an opening in the roof since the Terminus must be under the open sky.

Terpsichore. In Greek mythology one of the nine Muses (q.v.), that of dance.

Teshub. Storm god of the Hurrians and Hittites, also called Tessub. In Egyptian texts Teshub is identified with their thunder god Set. He is the same as Adad (q.v.) with his bull. The Hittites gave him a leading place in their pantheon. He is called Lord of the land of Hatti and Lord of Aleppo. His consort was Hebat. In mythology Teshub appears in conflict with Kumarbi (q.v.), the father of the gods, who sends his son, the stone giant Ullikummi, against Teshub. Hebat warns her husband, but both are threatened till Ea, the Sumerian god of magic, restores order.

Teteoinnan. See TOZI.

Tethys. The wife of Oceanus (q.v.) in Greek mythology, daughter of Heaven and Earth. She bore the rivers, including the hateful river of the under-world, Styx (q.v.) and the more gracious thousand Oceanids.

Tetragrammaton. The 'four letters' (Greek) of the Hebrew most holy name of God, YHWH. From the time of the Exile, at least, this name was never uttered and other names were substituted, such as Adonai and Elohim. In time its pronunciation was forgotten, and when Christians came to use it they introduced vowels from the other names, to produce *Jehovah* (with Continental value to the

consonants), though the true pronunciation may have been more like *Yahweh*, a name that is used in modern Christian scholarly books. The Tetragrammaton appears in Kabbalistic writings where it is given mystical explanations.

Tevāram. A collection of Tamil hymns in honour of the Hindu god Shiva, dating from the seventh to ninth centuries, and containing compositions by Appar, Sambandar and Sundarar (qq.v.).

Tezcatlipoca. 'Smoking Mirror', or more correctly, 'It causes the Black Mirror (night) to shine,' one of the two most prominent deities in the Mexican pantheon, the other being Quetzalcoatl (q.v.). He was a local deity of the Toltecs, adopted by the Aztecs. The earth was brought down from heaven by these two gods, and when the sky fell Tezcatlipoca and Quetzalcoatl changed into two trees and erected it again with the help of four other gods. So they are called rulers of the sky, but they also came into conflict when Tezcatlipoca as a warrior expelled his priest-king rival. The two gods represent different aspects of divinity, Tezcatlipoca personifying its negative and dark aspect, being lord of the night, cold and north, and a great magician. His symbol was the jaguar, whose spotted coat may have been taken to represent the starry sky. See ITZCOLIUHQUI.

Thag. See THUG.

Thales. Greek philosopher of Miletus in the sixth century B.C. He was considered one of Seven Sages and laid the foundations for scientific philosophy. He saw all things as modifications of water, from which the world comes and in which it floats; yet, impressed by the magnetic powers in matter, he said that 'everything is full of gods'.

Thalia. (Greek) 'abundance', as one of the three Graces (q.v.), and also one of the nine Muses (q.v.), that of comedy.

Thanatos. (Greek) 'death', generally abstract and with little personification or mythology. He is sometimes called the brother of Sleep (Hypnos, q.v.) and together they carry men away. Later Heracles wrestled with him; also Sisyphus (q.v.) bound Thanatos till he was rescued by Ares.

Thargelia. Ancient Greek festival, known from the Ionian islands to Asia Minor, held on the 7 Thargelion (May–June). It was preceded by a procession of a scapegoat (q.v.), the Pharmakos, 'remedy', who was then expelled or killed. The festival which followed was in honour of Apollo and Artemis, and the principal rite was offering Thargela, the firstfruits of the crops and the first bread baked from the harvest. See also FIRSTFRUITS.

Theia. A Titaness in Greek mythology, wife of her brother Hyperion (q.v.), bearing him the Sun, Moon and Dawn.

Themis. Greek goddess, whose name, probably meaning 'steadfast', led to her identification with Earth, Gaea (q.v.). Hesiod calls her a daughter of Earth and elsewhere she is a consort of Zeus. Once she was connected with the oracle at Delphi and as prophetess she warned her son Prometheus of his coming fate. Later Themis was taken to mean established custom and law; she became more abstract, as Right or Justice, and she was invoked as guardian of oaths.

Theogony. (Greek) 'genealogy of the gods', and used especially of the religious writing of that name by Hesiod (q.v.).

Theos. (Greek) a 'god', and especially one of the great gods of mythology; in a more abstract sense he might be called a Daimon (q.v.). With the definite article it indicates the god of a particular place, as Athena at Athens. The origins of the word are unknown; in usage but not in etymology it may be compared with the Indian Deva (q.v.).

Theosophy. A term applied to some speculative systems which claim possession of a hidden wisdom, from two Greek words meaning 'divine wisdom'. It was once used of the mystical philosophy of the German enthusiast Jakob Boehme or Behmen (1575–1624). Nowadays it is generally applied to the Theosophical Society founded in 1875 in New York by Colonel Henry Olcott and Madame Blavatsky (qq.v.). This was said by the latter to be spiritualism under another name, composed of occultists and cabbalists. It is certainly eclectic and claims to combine the wisdom of all ages and religions, with special revelations from 'Occult Mahatmas' in Tibet. The headquarters of the society moved to Adyar in India, but there are branches in many countries. After Madame Blavatsky, one of the most important Theosophical writers was Annie Besant (q.v.).

Thera. Pali Buddhist term for an 'elder', a senior member of the Sangha monastic order, who is honoured for age or ability. See THERAVĀDA.

Thera-gāthā, Therī-gāthā. 'Verses of the Elders', male and female, two popular collections of poems in Theravāda Buddhism. They form part of the fifth section, *Khuddaka-Nikāya*, of the *Sutta Pitaka* or Teaching Basket of the canon of scripture. The Theras are monks or Bhikkhus (q.v.) and the Therīs are nuns, Bhikkunīs. The poems sing of the glory of attaining peace and many are of considerable literary merit.

Theravāda. (Pali) 'the Doctrine of the Elders', the name of the form of Buddhism which prevails in south-east Asia: Ceylon, Burma, Thailand, Cambodia and Laos. Sometimes called Hīnayāna, 'small vehicle' or career, by the Mahāyāna (q.v.) school, this opprobrious name is disliked by the Theravāda, who claim to preserve the teachings of original Buddhism. These are in the Pali language and are the canon of scripture called *Tripitaka* (q.v.). By the third century B.C. Buddhism had divided into a number of sects, said to number eighteen outside Mahāyāna, but of these Theravāda is the sole survivor. It is also sometimes called the Southern School of Buddhism, from its geographical location. See also HĪNAYĀNA.

Theseus. Greek hero, especially of Athens. Despite the claim that Theseus was a son of the sea-god Poseidon, or of Aegeus (q.v.), his life and exploits belong rather to national legend than religion. For his fight with the Minotaur, see MINOS, ARIADNE and DAEDALUS. He married Hippolyta, queen of the Amazons (q.v.).

Thesmophoria. A women's festival of ancient Greece, in honour of the earth-mother Demeter (q.v.), the Thesmophoros, 'law-giving'. It was held in October–November and aimed at promoting the fertility of the corn which was about to be sown. Women made bowers and beds of plants, sacrificed pigs and mixed the remains with seed-corn.

Third Eye. The Hindu god Shiva (q.v.) is often represented with a Third Eye (Tri-lochana) in the middle of his forehead, contained in or surmounted by a crescent moon. With this Third Eye he destroyed the gods at one of the dissolutions of the universe, and burnt to ashes Kāma, the god of love, for inspiring amorous thoughts in Pārvatī, Shiva's consort, when the god was engaged in austerities. Other Indian statues have a Third Eye or protuberance between their eyes (see URNĀ), It has been claimed that Tibetan adepts received such an eye, or hole to give them supernatural vision. In 1956 a book entitled *The Third Eye* purported to describe this and to be written by a Dr Lobsang Rampa who, according to his publisher, was a Devonshire man named Hoskins.

Thirteen Principles, Creeds. These articles of Jewish faith were formulated by Maimonides (q.v.) in the twelfth century and are used in Jewish daily prayer still. The Principles are as follows: Faith in God as Creator, God is a Unity, he has no Form, he is the First and Last, it is right to pray to him alone, all the words of the Prophets are true, Moses was the chief of the prophets, the whole Law is the same that was given to Moses, this Law will not be changed and there will never be any other, the Creator knows every deed and thought of men, he rewards those that keep his commandments and punishes others, the Messiah will come, there will be a resurrection of the dead.

Thirty-two Marks. See SUPERMAN.

Thor. The 'Thunderer', the great Scandinavian storm-god, called Donar in Germany and Thunor by Saxons. Thor was a great giant with red beard, carrying a hammer, Mjöllnir (q.v.), which was the

lightning-bolt, forged for him by dwarfs. He was the strongest of the gods, with a mighty girdle, iron gloves, walking or driving a chariot drawn by goats, and the rolling of the chariot was the sound of thunder. Thor is much like the Vedic Indra (q.v.), and by Christian writers was identified with Jupiter and Heracles. His parents were said to be Odin and Earth, Jörd. Thor was also a god of fertility, since storms produced rain which fertilized the land. In mythology he fights giants, trolls and dwarfs. He had many temples and images in Scandinavia. Our Thursday is named after him, since offerings were made on this day. Sacrifices were chiefly animal and vegetable, but Vikings made human sacrifices to Thor to ensure success in their raids.

Thorgerd. Scandinavian goddess, perhaps of Finnish origin and worshipped in Halogaland. The life-sized image of Thorgerd stood beside that of Thor, wearing amulets. She had power over storms and caused hail to come down. See IRPA.

Thot, Thoth. Probably one of the oldest Egyptian gods, arbiter and secretary of the gods. He was said to be self-produced, though some legends said that he was born of Rē' or Horus. Thot was the god of wisdom, inventor of writing, codifier of laws, author of the *Book of the Dead* (q.v.), recorder of deeds, friend and guide of the dead. The Greeks identified him with Hermes (q.v.). Thot was symbolized by the ibis and the ape, and most usually was represented by a human figure with the head of an ibis, crowned with a crescent moon. He also appeared with a bull's head or in the form of an ape. Thot was also identified with the moon-god, guarding the moon and measuring time by its changes. A dead Pharaoh was said to be united with Rē' by day and with Thot at night. See SESHAT.

Thou art That. See TAT TVAM ASI.

Thread. See SACRED THREAD.

Three Bodies. See TRIKĀYA.

Three Jewels, Threefold Refuge. The first lay convert to Buddhism, a householder, who listened to the Buddha just after his enlightenment, is credited with uttering first the Threefold Refuge which is recited by Theravāda Buddhists every day:

I go to the Buddha for refuge,
I go to the Dhamma (doctrine) for refuge,
I go to the Sangha (assembly and monks) for refuge.

These three, Buddha, Dhamma and Sangha, are the Three Jewels or Gems, *Triratna* in Sanskrit, or Threefold refuge, *Trisharana*.

Thrymheim. Mountain home of the giant Thyazi (q.v.) in Scandinavian mythology.

Thueris, Taurt. Ancient Egyptian goddess of childbirth, and so a benevolent deity, her name meaning 'great one'. She was a goddess of heaven and protected women, being called daughter of Rē'. But as she was often depicted as a hippopotamus or a mixture of hippopotamus, crocodile and lion, Thueris was called wife of the evil Set and also partook of his dangerous character. She had her own temple at Thebes and important festivals.

Thug, Thag. A member of a secret fraternity with the Hindi name Thag, perhaps from a root meaning 'to conceal'. The members worshipped the goddess Kālī (q.v.) under her title of Bhavāni or Bhowani, and offered to her blood sacrifices, often male human beings. In Thug tradition Kālī ordered her followers to strangle their victims with yellow scarves, giving them the hem of her robe for the purpose. The Thugs are mentioned from the twelfth century and became notorious as assassins in the nineteenth, till put down by British campaigns, from 1831, led by William Henry 'Thuggee' Sleeman. The human sacrifices have long ceased, but the chief place of pilgrimage at the Kālī temple of Mirzapur, near Benares, is still popular and goats are offered to the goddess.

Thyaji, Thjazi. A giant in Scandinavian mythology who dwelt in the mountains at Thrymheim. He stole the apples of Idunn (q.v.) on which the gods depended for their existence and renewal. His daughter Skadi married the god Njörd.

Ti. See T'IEN and SHANG TI.

Tiamat. Dragon and monster of the

ocean and chaos in Mesopotamian mythology. In the creation epic *Enuma Elish* (q.v.), Tiamat prepared to attack Anu and the heavenly gods by giving magical powers to her second husband, Kingu, and entrusting him with Tablets of Destiny. Marduk (q.v.) was appointed champion of the gods, and he made a net to catch Tiamat and got the winds to help him. The two powers met in single combat, Tiamat was slain and split in two, half of her being fixed up as the sky to hold back the heavenly waters. Kingu was seized and killed, and the Tablets of Destiny taken by Marduk for himself. See also APSU.

Tiber. The Roman river was deified, like many other rivers throughout the world (see GANGES), and often depicted in art as an old man reclining on a couch with two female attendants.

Tibet. See LAMA.

T'ien. Chinese name for Heaven and the supreme God. In ancient China T'ien and Earth were supreme objects of worship, and the Chou dynasty in the twelfth century B.C. strengthened the concept of T'ien by equating it with Shang Ti (q.v.), the supreme Ti. In the *Shu Ching* (q.v.), T'ien is spoken of as both destructive and compassionate, overthrowing evildoers or unfaithful rulers, and bestowing the Mandate of Heaven (q.v.) on the righteous Chou princes. Elsewhere T'ien was said to see and hear everything; from brightness above he looked down with care on the earth, his power was far-reaching, he protected and blessed the virtuous and punished the wicked, he created all people and ordained their natures. Although questions were later asked about the value of sacrifices, yet T'ien remained either as God who received worship or as an immanental power within all things.

T'ien Shih. (Chinese) 'celestial master', a title taken by Taoist leaders, sometimes regarded as 'popes' of Taoism. See TAO SHIH.

T'ien-t'ai. A school of Chinese and Japanese Buddhism, named after a monastery in Che-kiang province in China. In

Japan it is called Tendai. The school was founded by Chih-I in the sixth century and taken to Japan by Saichō (Dengyō Daishi) at the beginning of the ninth century. Chih-I sought to reconcile the different schools, including both devotion and discipline and trying to find a place for every point of view. This comprehensiveness remains characteristic of T'ien-t'ai, which seeks to view the three thousand aspects of being as parts of a single unity. It teaches the Middle Way between extremes and includes both almost pantheistic and almost theistic expressions of faith.

Tijānī. One of the most active religious orders in African Islam, founded by Ahmad al-Tijānī (1737–1815), named after a Berber tribe in Algeria called Tijāna. Born in southern Algeria, Tijānī travelled abroad as far as Mecca but finally settled in Fez in Algeria and was buried in his monastery there. The Tijānīya have been important in modern times, since they taught a liberal outlook, use of worldly comforts and submission to authority. There are centres throughout North Africa and the Sudan and considerable expansion has taken place in West Africa.

Tilaka, Tīkā. See CASTE MARKS.

Tiloka. See TRILOKA.

Tipitaka. See TRIPITAKA.

Ti-ratana. Pali form of Sanskrit *Triratna*, 'Three Jewels' (q.v.).

Tiresias. A blind seer of Thebes according to Greek mythology. In one story he saw Athena bathing and was struck blind, but in another version Tiresias changed sex. Hera, wife of Zeus, was angry and blinded him; Zeus recompensed Tiresias by giving him the power of prophecy and long life. Even in Hades his ghost was still wise.

Tirmidhī. Islamic writer (died A.D. 883 or 893), author of one of the collections of *Traditions*. Little is known of his life, but he is said to have travelled widely in Arabia, Mesopotamia and Persia collecting stories of Muhammad and his companions. His work is shorter, but less repetitious, than the collections of Bukhārī and Muslim (qq.v.).

Tir na n-Og. 'Land of youth' in Celtic mythology, also called 'Land of the living' (Tir na m-Beo), 'land under the waves' (Tir fa Tonn), or the 'pleasant plain' (Mag Mell). It might be an island, or under the sea, or one of the tumuli (see NEW GRANGE). Visitors to this happy land would find it under the rule of a benevolent deity, such as the sea god Manannan, and enjoy perpetual youth during the stay there. But on return to earth one would find his friends long since dead and himself become old (see OSSIAN).

Tīrtha. A 'ford', or bathing place (Sanskrit), and so an Indian place of pilgrimage on the bank of a sacred stream. Also a sacred object, or worthy person. See TĪRTHANKARA.

Tīrthankara. 'Ford-maker' or guide, one of the twenty-four Tīrthankaras or

Jinas of the present age in the belief and worship of Jainism (q.v.).

Tirukkural. (Tamil) 'sacred couplets', the name of a collection of moral sayings in verse, dating from the fourth or fifth century and attributed to Tiruvalluvar. See SHAIVA SIDDHĀNTA.

Tirumandiram. Part of the Tamil Shaivite canon of scripture, the *Tirumurai* (q.v.), comprising three thousand verses by a mystic named Tirumūlar of the seventh or eighth century. It contains much Tantric (q.v.) material.

Tirumurai. (Tamil) 'canon' of scriptures of the Tamil followers of the god Shiva, an anthology in eleven books of hymns by sixty-three Nāyanārs or Teachers. The texts include the *Tevāram*, *Tirumandiram* and *Tiruvāshagam* (qq.v.). See SHAIVA SIDDHĀNTA.

Tiruvāshagam. (Tamil) 'blest utterance', devotional poetry by the Shaivite mystic Mānikka Vāchakar (q.v.). It forms part of the Tamil Shaivite canon of scripture, *Tirumurai* (q.v.). Mānikka's work has inspired many other mystics and the book itself is adored by worshippers. It praises the god Shiva and his appearance in human form to bring salvation to men of all classes.

Ti-sarana. Pali form of Sanskrit *Trisharana*, 'threefold refuge' (see THREE JEWELS).

Tishah b'Ab. See AB.

Titans. Ancient gods of Greece,

children of Heaven and Earth, who were said to have existed before the Olympian pantheon. Thus their leader Kronos (q.v.) was the father of Zeus, the supreme God of classical times. The meaning of the name Titan is disputed and the lists of these gods contain both Greek and non-Greek names. Hesiod mentions Kronos, Rhea, Oceanus, Coeus, Crius, Hyperion, Iapetos, Theia, Themis, Mnemosyne, Phoebe and Tethys.

Ti-tsang. Chinese name of the Bodhisattva Kshitigarbha (q.v.).

Tiu, Tiw. See TYW.

Tjurunga, Churinga. Among the Aranda of Australia a word indicating sacredness and applied to symbolic objects. Tjurunga are objects of stone or wood which are venerated as symbols of past heroes, mediating their power. They are rubbed on sick people, taken by hunters for good luck and lent to strengthen friendship. At initiation men touch the Tjurunga for the first time, and so come into contact with the heroes who dwell in the eternal Dreaming (q.v.). Many Tjurunga had patterns on both sides, not always identical. The Tjurunga were associated with spiritual beings, since the ancestors changed into rocks or stone

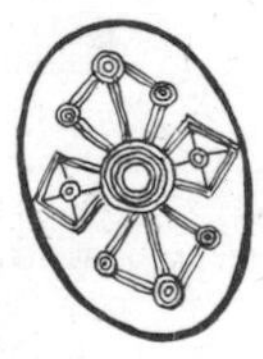

Tjurunga and their weapons into wooden Tjurunga. In central Australia everybody was represented by a Tjurunga which was regarded as his immortal body.

Tlachtli. Mexican Ball Game, played widely over central America, representing the movements of the planets and hence the changes of fate. It was played with a solid rubber ball, about 15 centimetres in diameter, in a temple court shaped like a capital letter I. Along the stone walls were rings through which the ball could just pass. Players were in two teams, wearing gloves and helmets, and bouncing the ball with their hips only. Sacrifices, even human ones, were offered to the gods before the game and the winning team could take the clothes from opponents and spectators.

Tlaloc. 'Lord of Sources of Water', the rain god in Mexican mythology and, an ancient fertility god. Once the most important deity, Tlaloc became in classical Aztec times simply a nature god, controller of clouds and rain. He has four pitchers from which he pours out rain and when he breaks them there is thunder and lightning. He lives in an earthly paradise in the south, amid rainbows, flowers and butterflies. The consort of Tlaloc was Chalchihuitlicue, 'precious jade skirt', who presided over springs and streams.

Tlauixcalpantecuhtli. 'Lord of the house of dawn', in Aztec mythology, the morning star, Venus. A variant of Quetzalcoatl (q.v.).

Tlazolteotl. 'Goddess of filth' among the Aztecs, who was believed to eat up filth, that is sin, especially sexual sin. Her priests heard the confessions of those who were taken in adultery. She had four aspects, the phases of the moon, and her third aspect was the Power of Purification which swept away sin.

Tnatantja. 'Totem pole' (q.v.) of the Aranda and other peoples of central Australia. It was a short or long stick or spear, decorated with bands of colour and stripes of down, often with a horizontal cross-piece from which Bullroarers and Tjurunga (qq.v.) were suspended. The

TLACHTLI

TLALOC

TLAZOLTEOTL

tops of the Tnatantja were decorated with feathers. They were essentially male symbols.

Toga Virilis. (Latin) 'robe of manhood', the citizen's cloak, often taken by boys at the Liberalia, feast of the god

Liber (q.v.), when a contribution was made to the temple of Juventas (q.v.), the goddess of young men of military age.

Tohunga. A Maori priest, who was also of chiefly rank (Rangatira). There were different kinds of Tohunga, according to their functions in knowledge, healing or magic, and a powerful Tohunga might be more influential than a village chief. The priests were mediums of the gods, bringing messages from them by whistling, and they guided the important rituals of agriculture, hunting, war, building and sickness. See ATUA.

Tokonoma. Japanese term for an alcove in the chief room of a house, formerly used for the image of a god or Buddha, and still used as a shrine for a beautiful object, such as a single picture or vase with one or two flowers. See IKEBANA.

Tonacatecuhtli, Tonacacihuatl. See OMETECUHTLI.

Tonatiuh. 'Ruler of Fate', the sun god in Aztec mythology. He cast himself into the fire and with him went all the heroes who had died in his service. The present sun gave power to his warriors, but he was a thirsty god because of his great heat and so he received the blood and human hearts which were offered in daily sacrifices.

Tope. See STŪPA and SĀNCHI.

Torah. (Hebrew) 'teaching', and hence instruction, doctrine, law, and law book (*Deuteronomy* 28, 61, 'the book of this law'). *Torah* is used of the whole Jewish law, the continuing revelation of God. Basically the *Torah* was the law revealed to Moses and contained in the five books attributed to him (see PENTATEUCH). The word is also used of the scroll on which these laws are written and which is to be found in the ark in every synagogue.

Torii. Gateway framework, of two posts supporting two horizontal lintels

which mark the entrance to Shinto temples and sometimes stand before sacred rocks, bridges or holy objects. The meaning of Torii is said to be that they represent perches for birds (*tori*), recalling help that the birds gave to the gods in mythology. Formerly Torii were made of unpainted wood, but later they were made of stone, bronze and now of concrete. The Torii at the temples of Inari (q.v.) are painted bright red. All main temples have at least three Torii and some have many more. As worshippers pass under them, they bow and salute the gods. The shapes of Torii differ considerably and there are more than twenty types.

Tortoise Avatar. See KŪRMA.

Tosafoth. (Hebrew) 'additions', supplements to the commentary of Rashi (q.v.) on the *Talmud*, made by Jewish scholars known as Tosafists in the twelfth and thirteenth centuries. They analysed statements in the *Talmud* in order to work out new principles for their own times. Most of the Tosafists belonged to French schools, but their method spread to Germany, Spain and England.

Tosefta were additional or 'external' (baraitha) teachings to the *Mishnah* (q.v.) which were made and preserved in the third century, and which shed much light on the development of the law.

Totem. A word from the Ojibwa Indian languages of northern America. A kindred expression, *ototeman*, meaning 'he is a relative of mine', expressed membership in a clan and restrictions on marriage (Exogamy, q.v.). Ojibwa clans mostly had animal names, but they did not believe members of the clan to be descended from this animal nor was it worshipped. There has been much confusion between the collective animal naming system and a further belief in guardian spirits. Writers such as Frazer (q.v.) assumed that Totemism was the earliest form of religion, and the psychologist Sigmund Freud (q.v.) declared that religion, art and morals arose from primitive savages killing and eating their father, symbolized later as a totemic animal. All such theories are now abandoned, for there is no historical or anthropological evidence for such totemic feasts, and the origins of religion are probably diverse and certainly lost in the mists of prehistory. See TNATANTJA. For Australian Totemism, see AUSTRALIA and TOTEM POLES.

Totem Poles. Tall heraldic posts especially of the Haida people on Queen Charlotte Islands in British Columbia, are well known as showing the crests of kinship groups and privileges of chiefs. Standing up to 24 metres high, they distinguish groups by their crests and emphasize distinctive features of the animals with which the group is associated. These 'totem' poles are relatively modern, evolving with the use of metal tools during the nineteenth century. Some tribes on the Alaska coast had Eagle or Thunderbird crests in carving in the late eighteenth century.

The Australian 'totem pole', called Tnatantja (q.v.) in Aranda, was in many shapes and sizes. It could be a short or long stick, or several spears tied together, ornamented with colour and down. Many Tnatantja poles had cross-pieces and often with Bullroarers (q.v.) and Tjurunga (q.v.) attached to them. The 'totem pole' was a male symbol and featured in dramatic acts at great ritual centres connected with the supernatural beings of mythology (see AUSTRALIA and BUGAMANI).

Tower of Babel. See ZIGGURAT.

Tower of Silence. See DAKHMĀ.

Tozi. 'Our Grandmother' in Aztec mythology, also called Teteoinnan. She was mother of the gods and had a popular festival in August in which midwives and women healers participated. She was a goddess of healing who personified the powers of nature. In Mexico the cure for all ills was the sweat bath, to which people went to cleanse their souls as well as their skin. Tozi was patroness of the sweat baths and each bath had her image above the doorway.

Traditions, Muslim. See HADĪTH.

Transmigration, Reincarnation, Rebirth, Metempsychosis. The belief that the soul or some power passes after death into another body. It was taught among the Greeks by the Pythagoreans and Orphics; Plato used it as the theme of the myth of Er at the end of *The Republic*; it is in Virgil's *Aeneid* and Caesar said that the Druids held it. The belief was unknown to the *Bible*, attacked by Augustine, though perhaps favoured by Origen, and condemned by implication at the Council of Lyons in 1274. It appeared in Kabbalism and a few modern poets and philosophers. Transmigration (Sanskrit, *samsāra*) is characteristically Indian and may have come from the Indus Valley culture. It was unknown to the *Vedas*, but appears in the *Chāndogya Upanishad* (5, 10), where the next life depends upon one's present Karma. It is a potent belief also in Jainism and Buddhism and spread through the latter to China and Japan. Though classical Buddhism taught no continuing soul, the link between one embodied existence and another depended on Karma. For Islam, see TANĀSUKH.

Tretā Yuga. The second age of the world in Indian mythical chronology (see YUGA). It was a time when sacrifice began but righteousness started to decline, men sought for rewards and were no longer given to austerities, The Tretā Yuga lasted 1,296,000 years and was followed by the Dwāpara Yuga. The Avatar Rāma appeared in the Tretā Yugā.

Triad, Taoist. See T'AI I, LAO TZŬ and JADE EMPEROR.

Trident, Tridandin. The trident (*trishūla*) was a weapon of the Hindu god Shiva and is carried by his followers or planted in the ground when a Shaivite Sannyāsi sits in meditation. A sect of

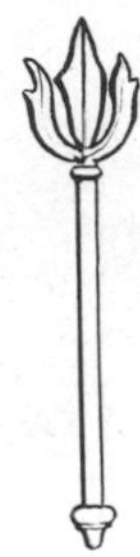

Shaivites are the Tridandins, bearers of triple batons, who carry a stick with three knots. They are subdivided into ten and are known also as Dashanāmi (those with ten names).

Trigrams, Eight. Pa Kua, Chinese diagrams, representing elements and fate. They were attributed to the emperor Fu-shi (2852 B.C.) and are worked out and multiplied in the *I Ching* (q.v.) from the eight categories into many sub-categories. These have been very popular in cosmology and divination. The Eight Trigrams are:

Chen, heaven	Kwen, earth
Kan, thunder	Kan, mountain
Li, fire	Khan, water
Teu, steam	Sun, wind

Trikāya. Mahāyāna Buddhist doctrine of 'three bodies' (Sanskrit). In this theory the transcendental Buddha was the ultimate being as Dharmakāya, 'body of law' or doctrine, the basic truth. But in manifestation the Buddha appeared in his Sambhoga-kāya, 'body of bliss' or 'community', to the celestial Bodhisattvas; and he appeared in this world in Nirmāna-kāya, 'body of transformation' to help mankind. The latter is also called Rūpa-kāya, 'form body' and, although in theory there is a triad or trinity, in practice most importance is given to the dualism of Rūpa-kāya and Dharma-Kāya. See also ASANGA and HUA YEN.

Trilochana. See THIRD EYE.

Triloka. (Sanskrit) 'three worlds', earth, air and sky, with their inhabitants. The god Vishnu, as a solar deity, took three giant strides across the three worlds. In Buddhism the three worlds (Pali: Tiloka) are the field of the senses, the field of invisible yet existent form, and the formless world.

Trimūrti. 'Three formed', Sanskrit term for a triad of gods in Hindu mythology. In the *Vedas* various gods are associated, but in the epic *Mahābhārata* the three are chiefly Brahmā, Vishnu and Shiva. In course of time Brahmā practically disappeared and the Trimūrti was regarded as a threefold representation of either Shiva or Vishnu, according to their followers. In the *Bhagavad-Gītā* the other gods are all manifestations of the one Krishna-Vishnu. In a famous stone image, in the Elephanta caves near Bombay, Brahmā the creator, Vishnu the preserver and Rudra the destroyer are all manifestations of the supreme Shiva.

Trinity. See TRIKĀYA, TRIMŪRTI, T'AI I.

Tripitaka, Tipitaka. 'Three baskets' (Sanskrit and Pali), the canonical scriptures of the Theravāda or Hīnayāna Buddhists, in the Pali language. The title is used in the sense of 'handing on', as baskets of earth in building are passed from hand to hand, so the traditions are passed down the ages. The *Tripitaka* is therefore composed of three sections: the *Vinaya Pitaka* (q.v.), or Discipline Basket which gives the rules for the Sangha assembly and Order; the *Sutta Pitaka* (see SŪTRA) or Teaching Basket; and the *Abhidhamma Pitaka* (q.v.), the higher doctrine or metaphysics.

For the Chinese Tripitaka, see SAN

TSANG, and for the man Tripitaka in the novel *Monkey* see HSÜAN-TSANG.

Triratna. See THREE JEWELS.

Trishnā. (Sanskrit) 'desire', said in mythology to be a daughter of death. In Buddhist thought it is the thirst for attachment to the world which causes craving and so suffering. See TANHĀ.

Trishūla. See TRIDENT.

Tritons. Greek sea beings or mermen. The name is not Greek and is obscure (see AMPHITRITE), and the Tritons play only a small part in legends and artistic decorations. Tritons were said to play

conches or a 'wreathed horn' (Wordsworth), and occasionally took human form.

Trolls. A name given to dwarfs in Scandinavia, called Trows in Orkney. In earlier times they were evil beings, like witches, and Thor (q.v.) is said to have fought giants and troll-women. The latter are often mentioned, dwelling in the Ironwood forest. In the *Grettis Saga* there was a terrible fight between Grettir and a giant troll-woman and only at the last minute did he manage to cut off her arm and throw her into a river.

Troy. The famous city and its siege by the Greeks belong to legend rather than mythology or religion, but see articles on AGAMEMNON, HELEN, ODYSSEUS and HOMER.

Ts'ao-t'ung. See SŌTŌ.

Tsong-kha-pa. A reformer of Tibetan Buddhism (1355–1417). He built the Gahldan monastery near Lhasa and founded the reformed sect, Gelugspa, 'Virtuous', or Yellow Hat. He tried to purify Tibetan Buddhism from earlier superstitious elements and the Gelugspa doctrine seeks to establish the teachings of Mahāyāna Buddhism. See LAMA and ATISA.

Tu. God of war in Maori religion; see ATUA.

Tuatha Dé Danann. (Celtic) 'the People of the Goddess Danu', the ancient gods of the Irish. They conquered the Fomorians (q.v.), but later were overcome by the Milesians and retreated into the tumuli near the river Boyne. The Tuatha Dé Danann were a group of deities under the goddess Danu (q.v.) and Dagda (q.v.) was a great father to them.

Tukā Rām. Hindu mystical poet in the Marathi language, who lived most of his life in western India (1607–49). He was a devotee of the god Vishnu, under the form of Vithobā (q.v.), and gave away all his goods to become a wandering ascetic. His hymns are simple pleas to God for salvation from evil within and without, speaking of the divine love with a gentle piety.

Tulasī, Tulsī. Sanskrit name of the sacred Basil, a shrub venerated by the followers of Vishnu and Lakshmi in India. Pious worshippers water the plant every day and circumambulate it for purification. The Tulasī is a representation of the goddess Lakshmī and there is an annual ceremony of its marriage with the Shālagrāma stone (q.v.) which represents Vishnu.

Tulsī Dās. Medieval Indian poet and mystic (about 1543–1623). Born at Ayodhya or Rajapur, Tulsī came from a Brahmin family about which little is known. He was married and went to Benares to continue studies in ancient Sanskrit texts. Tulsī already had a devotion to Vishnu under his Avatar of Rāma, and in his thirties he translated the Sanskrit epic poem *Rāmāyana* (q.v.) into his own Hindi language, under the title of *Rāma-charita-mānasa*, 'Holy Lake of the Acts of Rāma'. Later he wrote *Kavitāvalī*, poems (named after the metre) to Rāma and *Vinaya-patrikā*, 'letter of petition' to Rāma. These three works have been translated into English. They had a great influence in spreading devotion to Rāma in northern India. Tulsī's verse is attractive for its deep piety and its monotheistic teaching.

Tūlūn, Ibn. Founder of the short-lived Tūlūnid dynasty (868–905) in Islamic Egypt and Syria. His father was a Turk and the son was sent to Egypt as governor for the 'Abbāsid caliphs, but he made that country independent for the first time since the Greek era. Ibn Tūlūn made Egypt the seat of a splendid court and a centre of art. The mosque that still bears his name is one of the greatest monuments of Islam, with a striking circular minaret with an outside staircase.

Many verses of the *Qur'ān* are inscribed on the wooden frieze below the timbered roof of the mosque cloisters.

Tung Chung-shu. Chinese philosopher (about 179–104 B.C.) who was largely responsible for making Confucianism the state doctrine. He asked the Han emperor that all which was not within the field of the disciplines or arts of Confucius should not be allowed to progress further. However, Tung Chung-shu borrowed ideas from other than Confucian sources, particularly in adopting the teaching of Yang and Yin (q.v.) whose interaction produced everything. In his book *Ch'un Ch'iu Fan Lu*, 'Luxuriant Dew of the Spring and Autumn Annals', he spoke of man as the highest creature, receiving the Mandate of Heaven (q.v.) and the ethers of the universe constituting the Yang and Yin.

Tung Shan Shê. Modern Chinese 'society for Common Good', founded by Chiang Ch'ao-tsung and others in 1922 to unite the three Chinese religious schools and worship Confucius, Lao Tzŭ and Shākyamuni. See Wu Shan Shê.

Turīya. (Sanskrit) the 'fourth' state, in Hindu philosophy the condition of pure impersonal spirit or Brahman.

Tushita. Sanskrit name of a class of Hindu celestial beings, said to number twelve or thirty-six, and identified with the Ādityas (q.v.). In Buddhist cosmology the Tushita heaven is the fourth of six heavens of the world of desire. From the Tushita heaven the latest Buddha descended for his last birth on earth.

Tu-shun. Chinese Buddhist monk (A.D. 557–640), reputed founder of the Hua Yen or Garland school (q.v.).

Tutankhamūn. 'Living image of Amūn', Egyptian Pharaoh, second successor to the reformer Ikhnaton, who abandoned the god Aton and left the new city Akhetaton for Thebes where he was buried. His name was first Tutankhaton, 'living image of Aton'. He was buried in the Valley of the Kings, in a secret valley, and his tomb, alone of more than sixty, escaped discovery till modern times. An excavation in 1922, led by Lord Carnavon and Howard Carter, revealed magnificent equipment, with golden dress, chambers and chariots, now in the national museum in Cairo. See Amūn and Ikhnaton.

T'u Ti. (Chinese) 'earth god' or tutelary deity. Each of the local gods had a small part of the earth over which it ruled, and so each parcel of land had its little open altar (T'u Ti Miao) where incense and offerings were brought every day. Above the altar might be the whole family of deities, with T'u Ti Kung in the middle. Homes and families too had their shrines and protective deities and, although many of these have now disappeared, some remain, and ancestral shrines are particularly important.

Tvashtri, Twashtri. The most skilful workman and heavenly artisan in Hindu mythology, comparable to the Greek Hephaestus and Roman Vulcan (q.v.). In the *Rig Veda* Tvashtri bears a great iron axe and forges the thunderbolts of the storm god Indra, though he also occasionally opposes Indra. As a creator Tvashtri was said to form husband and wife and give them children. He knew all the worlds and gave their forms to all creatures. So he was invoked for blessings and prosperity. Tvashtri was sometimes identified with Vishva-karman, the all-maker, and with Prajā-patī, the lord of creatures.

Twelvers. Those Shī'a Muslims who follow twelve Imāms. See ITHNĀ 'ASHARĪYA and SHĪ'A.

Twice-born. The name of the initiated members of the three upper classes in Hindu society: Brahmins, Kshatriyas and Vaishyas (see CASTE). Nowadays it is especially applied to Brahmins. The title is derived from Sanskrit *dvi-jā*, 'twice-born', as applied to members of the three classes after an initiation ceremony in adolescence. See SACRED THREAD.

Twilight of the Gods. See RAGNARÖK.

Twins. See DIOSCUROI and ASHVINS.

Tyche. (Greek) 'fortune', generally in a good sense. In the Homeric *Hymn to Demeter* she is a companion of Persephone, and Hesiod included her among the Oceanids. Tyche was often an abstraction, but came to be personified, especially in Hellenistic and Roman times, when she was identified with Fortuna (q.v.). But she had no mythology and little worship.

Tylor, Edward B. British anthropologist (1832–1917), who was renowned for his theory of the origins of religion in Animism (q.v.), set out in his book *Primitive Culture* (1871).

Tyw, Tyr. Tyw was the Anglo-Saxon name for a popular Teutonic god, called Tyr in Scandinavia and Zio in Old High German. Tyw was a great god of war and Latin writers identified him with Mars. He was called 'god of battles', and heroes bore titles compounded with his name. Tuesday is called after him. Once as elevated as Odin (q.v.), Tyr came in time to be regarded as his son. Tyr was said to be one-handed, since his hand was bitten off in a fight with the Fenris-wolf (q.v.). At the Doom of the gods Tyr fought Garm, the watchdog of Hel, and each slew the other.

Tzaddik. See ZADDIK.

Tziruf, Chiluf. In Jewish Kabbalah (q.v.), the practice of transposing the letters of Biblical words and making anagrams from them. See TEMURAH and GEMATRION.

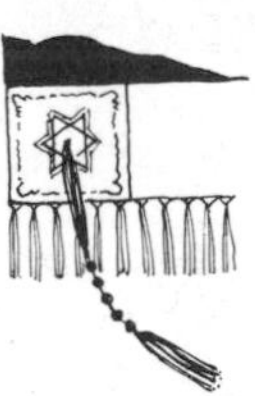

Tzitzith, Zizit. (Hebrew) 'remembrances', fringed garments worn by Jews, from *Numbers* 15, 39: 'it shall be unto you for a fringe, that you may look upon it and remember all the commandments of the Lord.' The Tzitzith are threads with a cord of blue entwined and fastened to the four corners of the Arba Kanfoth and the Tallith (qq.v.).

Tzŭ Ssŭ. A grandson of Confucius, of the fifth century B.C., who is said to have been a minister of two states and to have taught Mencius (q.v.). To him is attributed, the doctrine of the 'mean' or middle way, Chung Yung (q.v.).

U

Ubar. 'Gong' or drum used in rituals of Australian aboriginals. In one myth the Ubar is said to have belonged originally to women and it represented the womb of the Fertility Mother, so that the sound of the Ubar was the Mother's voice. In another story the first Ubar was made by a poisonous snake, Jurawadbad, and he hid inside it to take revenge on his wife and her mother. They put their hands inside it and he bit them so that they died.

Previously women had performed all sacred rituals, but from that time they were forbidden to take part in men's ritual. Bark paintings (q.v.) show men with feather headdresses taking part in Ubar rituals, and between them is the gong which is beaten with the stump of a root. It holds a central part in some of the most important rituals in the northern territory.

Udāna. (Sanskrit) 'breathing upwards'. In Yoga terminology one of the five vital airs which work upwards from the throat. In Buddhism the title of one of the works in the *Khuddaka-Nikāya*, in the second section of the canon of scripture, *Sutta Pitaka*. This is a collection of eighty Udānas, solemn utterances of the Buddha, regarded as some of the oldest teachings. They are chiefly in verse, and each one has a prose account of the circumstances in which it was uttered.

Udāsīs. A sect of Sikhs (q.v.) who practise celibacy and asceticism. They were originally followers of Sirī Chand, one of the two sons of the founder of the Sikh religion, Gurū Nānak (q.v.). The name is said to be derived from their emphasis on *udās*, a 'sorrowful' condition of isolation from the world, or isolation from a 'sorrowful' world. Udāsīs gave up their families, wore their hair long or shaved it off, wore the sacred thread (q.v.) like Hindus, and observed Hindu rites at birth, marriage and cremation. The Udāsīs claim many followers and have an important temple near the great Golden Temple of the Sikhs in Amritsar.

Ueuecoyotl. See. HUEHUECOYOTL.

Ugarit. See PHOENICIANS.

Uhud. A hill outside Medina, site of the second great battle between Muhammad and a large army from Mecca, on 23 March 625. The Meccans came to avenge their defeat of the year before at Badr (q.v.) and to destroy the power of Muhammad. After some fierce fighting, in which over seventy followers of Muhammad were killed and the Prophet himself wounded, the Meccans withdrew having failed to defeat Muhammad decisively. Their own losses were a problem to the Muslims, and the *Qur'ān* says, 'what befell you on the day when the two hosts met was by the permission of God, in order that he might know the believers' (3, 160). But the survival of the greater part of their forces led to their eventual victory and the triumph of Islam.

Uitzilopochtli. See HUITZILOPOCHTLI.

Uji-gami. 'Ancestor god' of Japanese Shinto families, sometimes called 'surname-deity'. The Uji-gami was originally a common ancestor, but came to be regarded as the Kami (q.v.) who protected all those connected with or living near his family (see also KASUGA). In modern times the Uji-gami has been considered as the deity of one's birthplace, and census returns have been made of those enrolled at the shrine of the Kami of their residence. The worship of the Uji-gami has strengthened the love of home and the soil, and at New Year celebrations those who cannot return home have a lump of earth from their home Uji-gami sent to them. An Ujiko is a child of the Uji-gami, or a 'clan member', and the word is sometimes used of the worshippers at a Shinto shrine.

Uke-mochi. Japanese Shinto goddess of food. In mythology when she turned her face towards the land, rice came out; when she turned to the sea, fishes emerged; and when she faced the mountain, animals and birds came out. She has temples of her own, but is often identified with the rice god Inari (q.v.).

'Ulamā', Ulema. Collective name for teachers of Islamic law and theology. The word is the plural of the Arabic '*alīm*, one who possesses '*ilm*, knowledge and learning (q.v.). The 'Ulamā' generally expressed the Agreement of the Muslim people which was the foundation of their religion (see IJMĀ'). So they gave final decisions on matters of law, doctrine and constitution. Governments tried to control the 'Ulamā', but private scholars could be independent. So the role of the 'Ulamā' often has been to express the will of governments but also to keep checks upon them.

Ullikummi. A great stone hero of Hittite mythology, whose stone body grew secretly in the ocean, but the sun warned Kumarbi, father of the gods. Ullikummi came out of the sea and covered Kumarbi's city with his shadow, but his power was destroyed by the magic of the god Ea. See KUMARBI.

Ulysses. See ODYSSEUS.

Umā. Hindu goddess, wife of Shiva, and daughter of the Himalayas. She first appears, without other introduction, in the *Kena Upanishad*. The other gods had tried to discover the nature and power of the divine Brahman but failed until Umā appeared and revealed that it was indeed Brahman who gave the gods their glory. Thereafter Umā is the wife of Shiva in her gentle aspect, and identified with Pārvatī (q.v.).

'Umar, Omar. The second Caliph of Islam, according to the orthodox Sunni Muslims, and founder of the Arab empire. He became a Muslim in A.D. 618, at about thirty years of age, and after the Hijra (migration) of the Islamic community to Medina in 622 he was one of the chief advisers of Muhammad. His daughter Hafsa became a wife of the Prophet. Abū Bakr, who succeeded Muhammad as first Caliph, died after only two years, in 634, and was followed by 'Umar. Arab conquests had already begun and under 'Umar Mesopotamia, Syria, Palestine and Egypt were invaded. After the submission of Jerusalem 'Umar gave orders for clearing the old Temple site and building the shrine which has sometimes been called the Mosque of 'Umar (see DOME OF THE ROCK). 'Umar was assassinated by a Christian slave in 644. Shī'a Muslims dislike him for having taken precedence over 'Alī (q.v.) as Caliph.

'Umar Khayyām. See OMAR KHAYYĀM.

Umayyads. The first dynasty of Islamic Sunni Caliphs, after the first four Rightly Guided Caliphs (see CALIPH). They were descended from the powerful Meccan family of Banū Umayya, to which 'Uthmān (q.v.) belonged. His cousin Mu'āwiya is reckoned as the first Umayyad Caliph, ruling from Damascus, the ancient capital to which the centre of Islamic power moved. The Umayyads were competent administrators generally, and saw their empire extend into the heart of France in the west and central Asia in the east. Yet discontent among Arab tribesmen and non-Arabs of conquered territories led to a revolution and the downfall of the Umayyads, bringing the Caliphate of the 'Abbāsids (q.v.). The Umayyad Caliphate lasted from 661 to 750.

Umma. (Arabic) 'people', community, from a Hebrew word *umma*. In the *Qur'ān* this word is used in many senses, but the chief reference is to racial or religious bodies of people with whom God is concerned. Every Umma has its messenger (see RASŪL) and these appear on the day of judgement, as Jesus will to the People of the Book (4, 157). The variety of Ummas and divisions of religious communities were problems: 'had God so willed he would have made you one community, but he has not done so in order that he might try you, so strive to be foremost in doing good' (5, 53). After Muhammad the spread of Islam across much of the ancient world led to the Umma being enlarged from Arab peoples to all Muslims and this created the strong sense of community which has characterized Islam.

Umm al-Kitāb. See MOTHER OF THE BOOK.

Ummī. A word used in the *Qur'ān* about Muhammad and his people and related to Umma (q.v.). The direct sense would be 'belonging to the community' and so 'the messenger, the native (ummī) prophet' (7, 156/157). But this has been taken to imply 'common', in the sense of illiterate or lacking a Scripture. This verse is often quoted to support the Islamic belief that Muhammad could not read or write, and thus the *Qur'ān* was not his own work but the direct revelation and Word of God. So strong has been this opinion that Ummī in Arabic has come to mean 'illiterate'.

Umm Kulthūm. A daughter of Muhammad; her sister Ruqaiya had married 'Uthmān (q.v.), the future third Caliph; after her sister's death Umm Kulthūm married 'Uthmān so that he was twice connected with the Prophet.

'Umra. The lesser pilgrimage to Mecca for Muslims, different from the Great Pilgrimage (see HAJJ). It seems originally to have been performed in the seventh month of the year as an additional ceremony, perhaps of spring. Now it may be performed at any time, on first visiting Mecca or returning after a long absence, as a special act of piety. Pilgrimage robes are worn (see IHRĀM), but may be put aside after visiting the Ka'ba. 'Umra is not one of the five Pillars of Islam and does not dispense the worshipper from the obligation of Hajj.

Unicity. See TAWHĪD.

Untouchables. See OUTCASTES.

Upādāna. (Sanskrit) 'acquiring', learning, in Buddhism 'clinging to existence'. For Buddhism this is the ninth link of twelve in the chain of existence. See NIDĀNA.

Upanayana. See SACRED THREAD.

Upānga. See ANGA.

Upanishads. In Sanskrit *upa-ni-shad* is literally 'near-down-sit' and means a 'session' at the feet of a teacher. The secret or mysterious nature of much teaching led to *Upanishad* being regarded as esoteric or mysterious doctrine. The *Upanishads* are sacred Hindu scriptures, formally the third part of the *Vedas*, following the *Brāhmanas* (q.v.). Like them they are Shruti (q.v.), 'heard' or revealed and authoritative scripture. The *Upanishads* are the Vedānta, 'end of the *Vedas*', a term also applied to the later school of orthodox Hindu philosophy which was partly based on the *Upanishads*. There are said to be 108 *Upanishads*, but many of them are late and of narrow importance. The oldest 'classical' *Upanishads* date from about 800 to 300 B.C. The earliest ones, *Brihad-āranyaka* and *Chāndogya*, are mostly in prose, but later classical *Upanishads* such as the *Katha* and *Shvetāshvatara*, are in verse (qq.v.). The major themes of the *Upanishads* are the divine Brahman, the Ātman, soul or self, transmigration and Karma.

Upaveda. (Sanskrit) 'secondary knowledge', the names of writings which are subordinate to the *Vedas* (q.v.) of Hinduism. There are four of these: *Ayur-Veda*, the science of medicine; *Gāndharva-Veda*, the science of music and dancing; *Dhanur-Veda*, the science of archery; *Shastra-shāstra*, the science of arms. According to some writers the fourth should be *Sthāpatya-Veda*, the science of architecture.

Upekkhā. (Pali) 'equanimity', serenity, the fourth of the Buddhist heavenly states of mind or Brahma Vihāras. See VIHĀRA.

Uposatha. The fast and rest day (or 'sabbath') of Theravāda Buddhists. The Pali name corresponds to Sanskrit Upavasatha, a 'waiting' or 'fasting' day preparatory to offering sacrifice. The Buddhist Uposatha was held at the new and full moon, and later the eighth and twenty-third days were added to make a weekly rest day. On this occasion the Pātimokkha (q.v.) rules of the monastic life are recited and the Dhamma or teachings are expounded to lay people who may be present.

Uraeus. Latin word from the Greek representation of the ancient Egyptian word for a cobra. This snake appears in Egyptian art from ancient times and was a symbol of royalty. It was often used in

images of the gods and the solar disk of Rē' had a Uraeus twined round it. Some of the goddesses appeared in the shape of a Uraeus. See BUTO.

Urania. In Greek mythology one of the nine Muses (q.v.), that of astronomy.

Uranus. See OURANOS.

Urd, Urdr. In Scandinavian mythology one of the three Fates or Norns (q.v.), who dwelt under the Yggdrasil tree with the well of fate (Urdarbrunnr). Her name may mean 'turn', as if spinning the threads of fate. Sometimes Urd is personified, but is often abstract, her name also being used for death. Urd was perhaps the original fate, Verdandi and Skuld being added later. Her name is the same as 'weird', hence the English expressions 'fulfil my weird' and the 'weird sisters'.

Uriel. (Hebrew) 'light of God', the name of one of the four angels (q.v.) that, according to the *Talmud*, surround the throne of God. Uriel was on the left of the throne, corresponding to the tribe of Dan in the north. As the divine light, Uriel was the means whereby the knowledge of God came to men. Uriel is sometimes used as the name of the Islamic archangel Isrāfīl (q.v.).

Ūrnā. (Sanskrit) 'wool', a circle of hair between the eyebrows. In Hindu, Buddhist and Jain imagery the Ūrnā was represented as a protuberance or jewel between the eyes of the image and it was held that this gave a 'Third Eye' of spiritual vision. Some modern writers have pretended that a hole was made in the forehead of adepts, particularly in Tibet, for bestowing a 'third eye' (q.v.) of supernatural power. But it is doubtful whether

either the practice was genuine or the result successful. In Hindu mythology a third eye burst out of Shiva's forehead when his wife put her hands over his eyes. Shiva was called 'three-eyed' (Trilochana) and with this destructive third eye Kāma, the god of love, was turned to ashes.

Urvashī. A celestial nymph in Hindu mythology, mentioned first in the *Rig Veda*. In later epic and story Urvashī is so beautiful that she is sent by the gods to distract men whose ascetic practices have become so great as to be dangerous. Similarly she was sent to tempt the warrior Arjuna (q.v.), but he disregarded her charms.

Ushas. The Dawn in Hindu mythology, whose Sanskrit name was related to the Greek Eos (q.v.). Ushas was the daughter of Dyaus, the heaven, and sister of the Ādityas. She is addressed in beautiful verses in the *Rig Veda*, as the friend of men, the daughter of the sky, the visitor of all homes, bringing wealth and despising neither small nor great. Ushas was the young goddess, never aging though she made men grow old.

Ushebti. Small model of a mummy used in ancient Egypt to summon the dead to work in the fields. Originally Shawabti, in the *Book of the Dead* (q.v.), the word as Ushebti came to mean 'answerer' who responded to the morning call instead of the dead person. In later times there were many Ushebtis for one dead person.

Usūl. (Arabic) 'roots', principles, especially applied to branches of Islamic learning. Thus the Principles of Religion, Usūl al-dīn, is the study of theology considered under Kalām (q.v.). The Usūl al-Hadīth is the science of Tradition (see HADĪTH) and Usūl al-Fiqh is the method of jurisprudence (see FIQH).

Utgard. The 'outer world' in Scandinavian mythology, beyond Midgard (q.v.). Apparently it was thought to contain the Land of the Giants (Jötunheim), the Land of the Elves (Alfheim), the Land of the Dark Elves (Svartalfheim) and perhaps the Land of the Vanir (q.v.), Vanaheim or Vanaland. A great extent of water separated Utgard from Asgard, the world of the gods, and Midgard, the world of man. In this water swam the Midgard-Serpent who encircled Midgard by clasping his tail in his mouth. Below Utgard was Niflheim where dwelt the goddess Hel. One root of the world-ash tree Yggdrasil was in Utgard, another in Asgard and the third in Niflheim. Utgard was thought to be a very cold region and mountainous, the dwelling of mountain elves and frost giants.

'Uthmān, Othman. The third Caliph of Sunni Islam, succeeding to 'Umar (q.v.) in 644. 'Uthmān belonged to a powerful Meccan family called Umayyad and was an important convert in early Islam since he was a rich merchant. He married Muhammad's daughter Ruqaiya, and after her death another daughter, Umm Kulthūm. 'Uthmān played a minor part till he became Caliph in rivalry to 'Alī (q.v.). He gave orders for the preparation of an official version of the *Qur'ān*; this was imposed on all Islamic communities, giving rise to discontent when other copies were destroyed. Revolts broke out and 'Uthmān was killed by Egyptians in 656. His death was followed by the division of Islam, with his cousin Mu'āwiya as first Umayyad (q.v.) Caliph sending armies against 'Alī and his Shi'a followers. 'Uthmān was the last Caliph to rule from Medina, and the Umayyad empire ruled from Damascus.

Utnapishtim. Perhaps meaning 'I have found life', or the 'Faraway', the Mesopotamian hero of the Flood (q.v.). In ancient tradition he was the only mortal who had received the gift of immortality from the gods. In the Babylonian tablets Gilgamesh determined to find Utnapishtim to gain the secret of immortality. When he found him, the latter told the story of the Flood, how he built a ship at the directions of the god Ea, took in his family and all kinds of animals, and landed on Mount Nisir. He told Gilgamesh that his plea was hopeless, but there was a magic herb at the bottom of the sea which could make the old young again. Utnapishtim is the Sumerian Ziusudra (q.v.).

Uttara Mīmāmsā. (Sanskrit) 'later Mīmāmsā' (q.v.) or enquiry. The philosophical school generally called Vedānta (q.v.).

'Uzair. Arabic form of the Biblical Ezra who is mentioned once in the *Qur'ān*: 'the Jews say that 'Uzair is the son of God' (9, 30). Muslim tradition quotes legends in support of this.

'Uzzā. A goddess of ancient Arabia, 'strong' or powerful, generally identified with Venus or the morning star. Her chief shrine was south of Mecca where there were three acacia trees and a sacred stone. Al-'Uzzā is referred to in the *Qur'ān*, along with Manāt and al-Lāt (qq.v.). The principal shrine was destroyed after Muhammad conquered Mecca in 630, but belief in al-'Uzzā long survived.

V

Vāch, Vāc. (Sanskrit) 'speech', the personification of speech and an abstract goddess of ancient Hinduism. In the *Rig Veda* she inspired the sages, Rishis (q.v.), and later Vāch was called 'mother of the *Vedas*'. She is an abstract power, like the impersonal Brahman, the creative word which took over some of her work. In the *Brāhmanas* the creative power of Vāch becomes personified in her union with Prajāpati, the 'lord of creatures', bringing forth the universe and its creatures. In later mythology Vāch is daughter of Daksha and mother of the Gandharvas, or identified with the goddess Sarasvatī, the deity of wisdom and eloquence, and wife of the creating god Brahmā.

Vāchaspati Mishra. Hindu philosopher (about A.D. 840), who wrote a commentary called *Bhāmatī* on the Vedāntic writings of Shankara. He also wrote on the Sāmkhya, Yoga and Nyāya doctrines (qq.v.).

Vadagalai. See PRAPATTI.

Vāhana. (Sanskrit) 'vehicle', a symbol of a Hindu deity. Most of the Indian gods have animal Vāhanas, on which they ride or which accompany them. Thus Brahmā has the Hansa, goose or swan; Vishnu has the Garuda eagle; Shiva has the bull Nandi; Indra has an elephant; Ganesha has a rat and Durgā has a tiger. See MADURA and JAGANNĀTHA.

Vaikuntha, Vikuntha. The heaven of Vishnu in Hindu mythology, said to be in the northern ocean or on top of Mount Meru (q.v.). It is also called Vaibhra.

Vainateya. (Sanskrit) 'child of Vinatā' (q.v.), in Hindu mythology another name of the celestial bird Garuda, vehicle of the god Vishnu. See GARUDA.

Vairochana. In Hindu mythology Virochana was a title of the sun, from a Sanskrit root meaning 'shining', and Vairochana was applied to his descendants and various gods. But in Mahāyāna Buddhism five great Buddhas, or Jinas, were produced by contemplation from an original or Ādi-Buddha (q.v.). The two most important were Amitābha (q.v.) (or Amida) and Vairochana. This solar deity perhaps entered Buddhism through the connection between the Buddha and light, and in Chinese the name is Ta-jih, great sun. In Java Vairochana was regarded as the supreme Buddha, and so he is to the Shingon sect in Japan, where he is represented by a huge statue at Nāra. He is also called Mahā-Vairochana, 'great'. As Dainichi or Lochana (q.v.) he was said to be identical with the Shinto sun-goddess, Amaterasu (q.v.) and so helped the formation of Ryōbu Shinto (q.v.).

Vaisākha, Vesak. See WESAK.

Vaisheshika. One of the six orthodox schools of Indian philosophy. The name comes from Sanskrit *vishesha*, 'particularity', whence it is sometimes called the

Atomistic school. Vaisheshika emphasizes individuals and particulars and a plurality of souls which must be assumed since consciousness cannot be identified with the body. The founder of the system is said to have been Kanāda (q.v.), or Kāshyapa, whose *Vaisheshika Sūtra* was composed after 300 B.C. Kanāda does not mention God, but later writers felt that atoms by themselves could not produce an ordered universe and that the *Vedas* had been divinely revealed. An idea of God was introduced similar to that of the Nyāya school (q.v.).

Vaishnava, Vaishnavism. See VISHNU.

Vaishya. The third of the three upper classes of Hinduism (see CASTE), a farmer and merchant, from a Sanskrit root *vish* for a house and one who settles on the land. The Vaishyas, like the other two classes, were twice-born, being invested with a yellow Sacred Thread (q.v.). Their work was said to be to till the fields, protect the cattle and engage in trade. Though not so dominant as the Brahmin priests and Kshatriya rulers, many famous men have come from the Vaishyas: in modern times Mahātma Gāndhi.

Vājapeya. (Sanskrit) 'drink of strength' or battle, a form of Soma drink (q.v.), sacrifice offered by Hindu kings and Brahmins. It helped to raise an ordinary ruler to the position of Samrāt, a monarch free from allegiance to others, and also rejuvenated the forces of an ageing king. See RĀJASŪYA.

Vajra. (Sanskrit) 'thunderbolt', especially the discus-shaped thunderbolt of the Hindu god Indra. In Tibetan Buddhism it is bell-shaped and called Dorje, whence the town of Darjeeling is the 'place of the thunderbolt'. In art Vajrapāni, 'thunderbolt-handed', or holding a thunderbolt, is applied to Indra, and in Mahāyāna Buddhism to a graceful attendant on the Buddha, painted, for example, in the caves at Ajanta (q.v.). See MJÖLLNIR, the thunderbolt of the Scandinavian god Thor.

Vajra-cchedikā. See DIAMOND SŪTRA and PRAJÑĀ.

Valhalla, Valhöll. The 'Hall of the Slain' in Norse mythology, the dwelling of all dead warriors. It stood in Gladsheim, the 'world of joy', its tiles were golden shields and its rafters spears, swords gave it light and there were breastplates on its benches. Valhalla had over five hundred doors and eight hundred warriors went through each. It was the favourite abode of Odin, who was called Valfather, 'father of the slain'. Odin dwelt there with his wolves and ravens, living only on wine, but the warriors feasted on boar's flesh and goat's milk every day. They fought each other daily in the courtyard, but at night their wounds were healed and they ate in peace. Odin had ordained that men should be cremated and, as their horses and chariots were burnt on the pyre, the warriors rode in triumph to Valhalla.

Valkyries. 'Choosers of the slain' in Norse mythology, who selected those who had fallen in battle to be received into the 'Hall of the Slain', Valhalla (q.v.), by Odin, the Valfather. The Valkyries were Odin's war-maidens, also called 'battle-maids' and 'wish-maidens', fulfilling the will of Odin. They carried swords and spears and rode over air and sea, sometimes in groups of nine. Ravens and kites were their birds because they fed on corpses. Belief in the Valkyries may have

come from Germanic women who rode to battle, like Amazons, and sometimes heroines were also called Valkyries, like Brynhild the swan-maiden. Sometimes the Valkyries were described as weaving, like Fates, with human entrails for wool.

Vallabha. Hindu philosopher (1481–1533), son of a Telugu Brahmin of southern India, but born near Benares. He studied the *Vedas* under teachers of the Madhva (q.v.) school, was devoted to the god Vishnu and visited many shrines connected with him. He married and had a son, but in later life renounced the world to become a Sannyāsi (q.v.). He is said to have had eighty-four chief disciples and to have written eighty-four books. Vallabha taught the monistic (q.v.) identity of the soul and Brahman, but with the intention of increasing Bhakti (q.v.) devotion to Krishna. He regarded Krishna as the personification of the Supreme Being, and he himself is held to be an Avatar of Krishna in western India where his followers are now most numerous. He is called Āchārya, 'leader', or Vallabhāchārya. See VISHNUSWĀMĪ.

Vālmīki. Traditional author of the Indian epic poem *Rāmāyana* (q.v.), himself taking part in some of the scenes which he describes.

Vāmāchāra. (Sanskrit) 'left hand practice' or doctrine, Tantric worship of Shakti or female energy, performed in secret, as opposed to the 'right-hand practice', Dakshināchāra. See SHĀKTA.

Vāmana. (Sanskrit) 'dwarf', the Dwarf Avatar of Vishnu. See DWARF and BALI.

Vānaprastha. (Sanskrit) 'forest dweller', the third stage of life for a Brahmin, after those of student and householder, now abandoning house and family for an ascetic life in the forest. See ĀSHRAM and PARIVRĀJAKA.

Vanir. A class of ancient Scandinavian gods, whose name is of uncertain meaning. In the *Prose Edda* they are distinguished from the principal gods, the Aesir (q.v.). The Vanir lived in Vanaland or Vanaheimr and were chiefly gods of fertility. Formerly there was war between them and the Aesir, and Odin led his hosts against them, but eventually they tired of fighting, lived in peace with their neighbours and later were included with Aesir. Njörd, Frey and Freyja were Vanir.

Var. One of the Scandinavian goddesses known as Asynjur, but little is known about her except that she heard oaths made by men and women and punished the perjurers.

Varāha. 'Boar' (Sanskrit), the third or fourth Avatar (q.v.) of Vishnu in Hindu mythology. In the *Brāhmanas* there is a story of a boar who lifted the earth out of the primeval waters. Later this story is attached to Vishnu. The demon Hiranyaksha dragged the earth into the sea (perhaps a Flood story), Vishnu took the form of a boar and after a thousand years killed the demon and raised the earth up again. The Varāha Avatar is a favourite subject in painting and sculpture. There is a *Varāha Purāna*, of ten thousand verses, narrated by Varāha to the Earth.

Vāranasī. See BENARES.

Vardhamāna. First name of the Jain saint later called Mahāvīra (q.v.). Vardhamāna means 'increasing' and is said to have been given as his name since the family's wealth had increased after his conception.

Varna. (Sanskrit) 'colour', the name applied in the *Rig Veda* and later texts to the four classes (see CASTE) of society, which were partly distinguished no doubt by the lighter-skinned Aryans taking precedence over the darker Dravidians (qq.v.).

Varuna. God of the sky (Sanskrit) in ancient Indian mythology, related to the Greek Ouranos (q.v.) and Latin Uranus. In the *Rig Veda* he is a lofty deity, though not mentioned in many hymns. Varuna is called king of the universe and his particular concern is the upholding of order (*Rita*, q.v.), so that he knows the paths of birds and ships and also the behaviour of men whose sin he punishes and virtue he rewards. Later Varuna strangely declines from this high estate and already in the *Bhagavad-Gītā* (10, 29) he is chief of water-creatures; finally he has little importance in practised Hindu religion.

Vasishtha. A sage of the Indian *Vedas*, reputed to be the author of many of their hymns. He owned a Cow of Plenty (see KĀMADHENU), and in several stories was in conflict with another seer, Vishva-mitra. (q.v.).

Vasubandhu. Buddhist philosopher, of about the fourth century A.D., who with his brother Asanga (q.v.) is said to have founded the Yogāchāra school (q.v.). He lived in Peshawar and was favoured by the king, perhaps Chandragupta I. A 'Life of Vasubandhu' says that he was first a Hindu, but became a devout Mahāyāna Buddhist and wrote treatises and commentaries on the scriptures.

Vāsudeva. A title of Krishna (q.v.) in the *Mahābhārata* and occurring frequently in the *Bhagavad-Gītā*. It seems to be derived from the name of Krishna's earthly father, Vasudeva, though it has been maintained that there was an ancient cult of Vāsudeva which later came to be attached to the worship of Krishna who was then given this patronymic. The grammarian Pānini, in the fourth century B.C., writes of Vāsudeva as an object of worship.

Vāta, Vāyu. Names of the 'wind' (Sanskrit) in ancient Hindu mythology. In the *Rig Veda* not many hymns are addressed to Vāyu, but he is often associated with the storm god Indra and they ride in the same chariot. In the *Hymn of Purusha* (q.v.) Vāyu is said to have come from the breath of Purusha. In the *Vishnu Purāna* he is king of the Gandharvas (q.v.). There is a *Vāyu Purāna* which deals with the ages past and future and is devoted to the god Shiva.

Vātsyāyana. Indian Brahmin sage, author of the *Kāma-sūtra* (see KĀMA).

Veda. The most ancient and sacred scriptures of the Hindus. The name comes from a root *vid*, meaning 'to know', related to Latin *videre* and English 'wit', and has the meaning of 'divine knowledge'. Though sometimes claimed to be as much as ten thousand years old, critical opinion tends to date the *Vedas* between 1500 and 800 B.C., since thev refer to the geography of the Indus Valley where the Aryans (q.v.) arrived between the eighteenth and fifteenth centuries. The *Vedas* are mainly hymns in praise of the gods, chanted by Brahmin priests, but they were not written down for many centuries. Preserved by amazing feats of memory for over two thousand years, there is no manuscript of the writing of the *Vedas* till the fourteenth century A.D. For the four *Vedas*, see separate articles on the ATHARVA, RIG, SĀMA and YAJUR VEDAS.

Vedanā. Pali Buddhist term for 'sense reaction', the seventh link of the chain of causation. See NIDĀNA. Vedanā, as sensation, is also one of the Five Skandhas (q.v.).

Vedāngas. (Sanskrit) 'members of the the *Veda*', a term applied to subjects and works subsidiary to the *Vedas* and necessary for their understanding, mentioned by Manu (3, 184) as the province of learned men. There are six Vedāngas: Shikshā, pronunciation or phonetics; Chandas, metre; Vyākarana, grammar, represented by Pānini (q.v.) especially; Nirukta, glossary or etymology; Jyotisha, astronomy, for fixing the calendar of ceremonies; Kalpa, ceremonial, rules written in *Kalpa Sūtras* or *Shrauta Sūtras*.

Vedānta. (Sanskrit) the '*Veda's* end'. Title first of all to be applied to the *Upanishads* (q.v.). Secondly, the name is given to the sixth and most important of the orthodox schools of Hindu philosophy, called Vedānta or Uttara Mīmāmsā, 'later Mīmāmsā'. The Vedānta philosophers based their teachings on the *Upanishads* and the *Vedānta Sūtra* (q.v.) of Bādarāyana. They included the fully non-dualist (*advaita*, q.v.) Shankara, the modified non-dualist Rāmānuja, and the dualist Madhva (see separate articles). Vedānta has continued to be of great importance, and is seen in modern teachers such as Swāmī Vivekānanda and Dr Radhakrishnan (qq.v.). In modern times also it has been common to use the term Vedānta for a kind of Shankarite monism, sometimes called Neo-Vedānta, and Aldous Huxley and Christopher Isherwood have expounded such a pantheism as a 'perennial philosophy' (see NEO-VEDĀNTA).

Vedānta-Sāra. (Sanskrit) 'essence of the Vedānta'. Name of some works on Vedānta philosophy, especially a treatise by Sadānanda Yogīndra and a short commentary by Rāmānuja (q.v.).

Vedānta Sūtra. Indian philosophical work, attributed to Bādarāyana, which with the *Upanishads* forms the basis of Vedānta (q.v.) philosophy. Also called *Brahma Sūtra* (since it discusses Brahman) and *Shārīraka Sūtra* (because it considers the 'embodiment' or manifestation of the unconditioned divine). The *Vedānta Sūtra* consists of 555 short pithy verses in Sanskrit, some of only two or three words; therefore, commentaries are needed to bring out the implications and the great Vedāntic philosophers commented on it, notably Shankara and Rāmānuja (qq.v.).

Vegetarianism. See AHIMSĀ.

Vehicle. See MAHĀYĀNA and HĪNAYĀNA, also VĀHANA.

Veiling. See BURQA', HAREM and PURDAH.

Vendidad. See VIDĒVDĀT.

Venus. Italian goddess but not originally Roman and obscure in early centuries. Perhaps an abstract power, from a noun meaning 'charm', Venus would be the power that made gardens charming and fertile. In classical Rome Venus came to be identified with the Greek and oriental Aphrodite (q.v.), goddess of love, fertility and luck. In the imperial cult she was Venus Genetrix, the mother.

Verdandi. In Scandinavian mythology one of the three Fates or Norns (q.v.) who lived in a hall under the Yggdrasil tree. Verdandi was perhaps the Fate of the Present, and her name may have been added to that of the original Urd (q.v.).

Vergil. See VIRGIL.

Vertumnus. A god of the Etruscans to whom merchants made offerings, but little is known of his person or functions. A late story said that he was married to Pomona (q.v.).

Vesper, Vesperugo. Latin forms of the Greek Hesperos (q.v.), the evening star.

Vesta, Vestal Virgins. Vesta was the Roman goddess of the hearth, akin to the Greek Hestia (q.v.). Her temple was a round building, like an ancient hut, which contained a fire which never went out, an eternal flame (see PARSI, FIRE TEMPLES). Vesta was served by Vestal Virgins, in historical times usually six but earlier two or four. They were chosen by the Pontifex Maximus (q.v.) and represented daughters of the royal house. The Vestal Virgins served from five to thirty years and had to remain virgins, though some did marry at the expiry of their term. They wore bridal dress and received many honours, but if they let out the sacred fire they were scourged;

for unchastity they were entombed alive, but could be saved if successful in an ordeal. Little is known of Vestal ritual, but if the fire went out it was rekindled by rubbing sticks together in the ancient fashion.

Vibhu. See RIBHU.

Victoria. (Latin) 'victory', the equivalent of the Greek Niké (q.v.). There was no early worship of Victoria; later she was associated with Jupiter and was worshipped by the army. She had a temple on the Palatine hill from the third century B.C. and an altar in the senate house from about the first century, which disappeared with other pagan cults in the fourth or fifth centuries A.D.

Vidar, Vidarr. The 'silent god' of Scandinavian mythology, son of Odin. He was perhaps a god of the woods, since he dwelt in Vithi, a place of trees and grass. Vidar was very strong and at the Doom of the gods, when most of them were killed and Odin himself was swallowed by the Fenris wolf, Vidar placed his foot on the wolf's lower jaw and tore out its gullet. Then he survived into the new age.

Vidēvdāt. (Pahlavi) 'law against the daevas' or demons, the last of the books of the Zoroastrian *Avesta* as it now exists. Sometimes incorrectly called *Vendidad*, it was compiled by Magi priests and deals with ritual purification, giving lists of fantastic punishments for infringements of laws. The *Vidēvdāt* is a thoroughly dualistic work, attributing all evil to the wicked Ahriman who is in eternal opposition to the good Ohrmazd (qq.v.).

Vidhi. (Sanskrit) a 'rule', formula, or direction for performing a Hindu rite, especially in the *Brāhmana* (q.v.) texts. Later used for any prescribed act or for grammatical rules.

Vidyā. (Sanskrit) 'knowledge', in the general sense of learning, but especially of spiritual wisdom and philosophy. There are said to be four Vidyās or sciences: the three *Vedas*, logic and metaphysics, government, and practical arts which include agriculture and medicine. A fifth was sometimes added, *ātma-vidyā*, knowledge of the soul or spiritual truth. Knowledge has been personified and identified with a goddess, especially Durgā. See AVIDYĀ.

Vihāra. Buddhist and Jain term for a hall where monks met and walked about, from a Sanskrit root for 'walk about'. Nowadays it is used for any retreat house, monastery, or even for a temple. Vihāra is also a state of life or mind, and there are four Buddhist Brahma Vihāras, heavenly states of mind and methods of meditation: Love (*mettā*), Compassion (*karunā*), Joy (*muditā*) and Serenity (*upekkhā*).

Vijñāna. (Sanskrit) 'wisdom', in the fuller sense of experience, what we learn from life, above simple knowledge (see JÑĀNA). In Buddhism Vijñāna (Pali: Viññāna) is consciousness, the empirical mind, the highest of the five Skandhas (q.v.). It is also a link in the chain of causation (see NIDĀNA).

Vijñānavāda. (Sanskrit) 'doctrine of understanding', a name for the Buddhist Yogāchāra (q.v.) teaching that only mind has reality.

Vinatā. A daughter of the sage Daksha in Indian mythology and a wife of Kashyapa, to whom she bore Garuda, the celestial bird of Vishnu, named after her Vainateya.

Vinaya. The *Vinaya Pitaka*, 'discipline basket' (Sanskrit); it is the first of the three *Pitakas* or sections of the canon of scripture of the Theravāda Buddhists (see TRIPITAKA). It is in three parts: *Suttavibhanga* which includes the *Pātimokkha* rules (q.v.); *Khandakas*, subdivided into *Mahāvagga* and *Chullavagga*; and *Parivāra* which are summaries and arrangements of rules for teaching and learning.

Vinaya Patrikā. (Hindi) 'letter of petition', a devotional poem to the god Rāma, by the sixteenth century mystic Tulsī Dās (q.v.).

Vinoba Bhave. Hindu leader (born 1895), disciple of Gāndhi and one of the closest to his spirit, in poverty and concern for the landless. He goes on foot through India, expounding the doctrine of Bhudan, ('land gift') or Gramdan, trying to persuade landlords to give away land to needy peasants. So far nearly four million acres have been dedicated in this way. Vinoba seeks to replace the class struggle by love and persuasion and yet to facilitate a sort of village communism as an alternative to the industrialization and development economies of the political rulers.

Viracocha. See HUIRACOCHA.

Vīra-shaivas. (Sanskrit) 'heroic Shiva followers', name of a Shaivite sect also called Lingāyats (q.v.).

Virbius. A minor Italian deity, identified sometimes with Hippolytus; since Hippolytus was associated with Aphrodite so Virbius was with her Italian counterpart Diana. In the shrine of Diana at Nemi Virbius was also worshipped and Sir James Frazer (q.v.) made this the starting-point of his famous but much disputed *Golden Bough*. Frazer said that Virbius was 'clearly' the archetype of the priests of Diana, that it was 'natural to conjecture' that they were married to the goddess also, and so the priests guarded the 'sacred bough' or tree at the shrine and were ritually killed by their successors.

Virgil. Latin poet (70–19 B.C.) who was not only outstanding in literature but influential in Christian thought as one of the noblest pagans. In his *Eclogues*, 'select poems', there is a prophecy of the birth of a boy under whom the world would be at peace. This may have been the expected child of Antony or Octavian, but was later taken to refer to Christ. His religious feelings, and this apparent Messianic reference in *Eclogue* iv, made Dante choose Virgil as his guide in the *Divine Comedy*. Virgil's *Georgics*, 'husbandry', and *Aeneid*, the story of the wanderings of Aeneas from Troy to the foundation of Rome, express his piety and humanity.

Virgin Birth. See GYMNOSOPHISTS and SUDDHODANA.

Virgins of the Sun. The 'Chosen Women', Aclla Cuna, of the Incas of South America. These were girls selected at ten years of age from all over the empire and trained in convents, Aclla Huasi, in Cuzco and other cities. From their numbers superior officials (*mama cuna*) were chosen, and all were vowed to chastity (see VESTAL VIRGINS). The Virgins of the Sun had various functions: some served in the temples, others became victims of sacrifice, and others became wives of the Inca or senior state officials. They all came under the rule of a chief priestess, Coya Pacsa, who was regarded as the earthly wife of the sun god, Inti (q.v.). See CAPAC COCHA.

Visākhā. Famous Buddhist laywoman, who received the title 'chief of almsgivers'. She was converted by the Buddha in her youth and was married to the son of Migāra who at first did not believe, but on the arrival of the Buddha he was converted and saluted his daughter-in-law as mother. Visākhā was very rich and sold her costly headdress to build a monastery at Sāvatthī, where the Buddha often stayed. The story is told in commentaries on Buddhist scripture.

Vishnu. One of the greatest gods of Hinduism and to his devotees the sole deity, of whom other gods are but aspects. Vishnu appears in only a few hymns of the *Rig Veda*, taking three strides across the universe, as a solar deity. But he develops in the *Brāhmanas*, and in the *Mahābhārata* (q.v.) he is a supreme deity alongside Shiva. These two, with Brahmā, form the triad or Trimūrti (q.v.). The name Vishnu in Sanskrit may derive from a root meaning 'to pervade'; this may have helped to link him with the theory of Avatars (q.v.) by which Vishnu was held to appear in many forms, notably Krishna and Rāma, under which he is widely worshipped today. Vishnu is a kindly deity, represented riding on the bird Garuda or reclining on the snake Ṣhesha. His consort is Lakshmī or Shrī and their abode the Vaikuntha heaven. The followers of Vishnu are Vaishnavites or Shrī Vaishnavas.

Vishnu Purāna. One of the most important of the *Purānas* (q.v.), traditional Hindu mythologies, perhaps compiled about the sixth century A.D. It is in six books and seven thousand verses, dealing with creation, myths of gods and Avatars (q.v.) of Vishnu, and legends of early men and rulers.

Vishnu-sharma. Brahmin priest who is said to have related the popular stories contained in the *Pañcha-tantra* and *Hitopadesha* (qq.v.).

Vishnu-swāmī. A Hindu teacher, perhaps of the twelfth or thirteenth century. He was a devotee of Vishnu and, having renounced the world at an advanced age, he went to teach at Kanchipuram or Conjeeveram, where he had seven hundred principal followers. Vishnu-swāmī is said to have founded the system of monistic (q.v.) identity between the soul and Vishnu, later revived by Vallabha (q.v.). However, this has been disputed and Vallabha himself did not refer to Vishnu-swāmī as originating his system. The sect of Vishnu-swāmīs is particularly strong in southern India, where they have special devotion to Krishna and Rādhā.

Vishtāspa. See HYSTASPES.

Vishva-devas. (Sanskrit) 'all gods', a class of Hindu deities in the *Vedas*. They are of inferior order, called 'bestowers of rewards', and arranged in lists of nine or ten in which the names vary.

Vishva-karma. (Sanskrit) 'all-maker', a title of powerful Hindu gods, personified in the *Rig Veda* as the creator of the universe with eyes, faces, arms and feet on every side. In later texts Vishva-karma is a general artificer and provider, sometimes identified with the craftsman Tvashtri (q.v.).

Vishva-mitra. Legendary Indian sage, who was born into the warrior or Kshatriya class but by his austerities raised himself to the priestly Brahmin class and was regarded as one of the seven Rishis or seers. His aggressive nature appeared in his quarrels with Vasishtha and Harishchandra (qq.v.).

Vishva-rūpa. 'All forms' (Sanskrit), a title of Vishnu in Hindu texts, as omnipresent, universal.

Vishveshvara. (Sanskrit) 'lord of all', a title of powerful Hindu gods, especially Shiva and applied also to his emblem of the Linga (q.v.).

Visperad, Visparat. A short Zoroastrian liturgy to 'all chiefs' or lords, which is a series of invocations to many beings. It is mostly contained already in the *Yasna* (q.v.).

Visuddhi. (Pali) 'the path of Purity', title of a famous work on Buddhist doctrine by the celebrated teacher Buddhaghosa (q.v.).

Vithi. A land full of trees and tall grass in Scandinavian mythology, home of the silent god Vidarr (q.v.).

Vithobā, Vitthala. A Hindu god worshipped in the Deccan and generally believed to be an Avatar (q.v.) of Vishnu or a form of Krishna. Images of him stand on a brick with arms crossed. No offerings are made to the image, but worshippers embrace it and believe that the deity favours them with love. The popularity of Vithobā was increased by the hymns composed by the Maratha poet Tukārām (q.v.). See JÑĀNADEVA.

Vivasvat. A name of the sun, 'shining forth' (Sanskrit) in Hindu mythology. Also one of the eight Ādityas, son of Kashyapa and father of Manu (qq.v.). Thus he is one of the parents of the human race.

Vivekānanda. Modern Hindu leader (1862–1902). Named Narenda Nath Datta, he was a Bengali of Calcutta, educated at a Christian college and eminent in philosophy. In 1882 he met Rāmakrishna (q.v.) and was his chief disciple. After the master's death he became an ascetic and took the name Vivekānanda 'discernment-bliss'; disciples added the title of Swāmī. Then he travelled abroad and made a great impression at the Parliament of Religions in Chicago in 1893. His message of the truth of all religions, but on a basis of pantheism, provided both attraction and criticism. One of his English converts was Sister Niveditā (q.v.). A further important move by Vivekānanda was the foundation of the Rāmakrishna Mission (q.v.) in 1897, named after his master, from the Christian model of social service, but thoroughly Hindu in intention. His lectures and writings were extensive.

Vohu Manah. (Old Persian) 'Good Mind', one of the Bounteous Immortals (Amesha Spentas, q.v.), of Zoroastrian belief. Vohu Manah stood close to God, Ahura Mazdā, and was regarded as his hypostasis or emanation, being simply the mind of God. Vohu Manah worked intimately with Asha, truth, and these two were more closely united with Ahura Mazdā than any other Immortals.

Void. See SHŪNYA.

Volcanus. See VULCAN.

Völund. A semi-divine being in Scandinavian mythology and an archetypal smith, like the Greek Hephaestus (q.v.). Many heroes, such as Beowulf, had swords that were forged by Völund. In the *Eddas* (q.v.) Völund is called Lord of the Elves, though he does not seem to be like them. He made marvellous things for King Nidud, but when the monarch tried to keep him on his island Völund made wings and flew away, like Daedalus (q.v.).

Voluspa. 'Sibyl's Prophecy', the most famous poem of the *Eddas* (q.v.), in Old Norse. It is uttered by a sibyl (*volva*) who tells Odin and other gods and men about the beginning of the world, the gods and the coming Doom of Ragnarök (q.v.). Though a valuable source of information about ancient Scandinavian religion, the *Voluspa* is influenced by Christian ideas, especially in its description of the Doom.

Voodoo. Religious and magical practices in the southern states of America and the West Indies, especially Haiti. The word almost certainly derives from West Africa where in the Ewe and Fon languages of Togo and Dahomey *vudu* or *vodŭn* is the regular word for a god. Slaves from these regions were taken to Haiti and neighbouring lands. In Voodoo mythology many West African gods reappear: Shango (q.v.), Legba, Ogou, and the like. However, there is a veneer of Roman Catholicism, many old gods bearing Christian names or titles, such as Virgin Charity and St Elizabeth. Similarly the ritual songs are in a mixture of Ewe and other African languages and French and English. The symbolism is also mingled. In Haiti, where Europeans have disappeared, Voodoo is no longer an African or European religion, but is the national religion with its own development. There is Voodoo Rada, still similar to the African religion, and Voodoo Petro which is entirely Creole. See also OBEAH, LOA and ZOMBIE.

Vör. One of the goddesses called Asynjur (q.v.) in Scandinavian mythology, but all that is known about her is that she was wise and saw all secrets.

Vortumnus. See VERTUMNUS.

Votum. (Latin) a 'promise' to a god, a vow or religious engagement. In many religions, prayers to gods are accompanied by promises of gifts or services if the prayer is granted. So the *Bhagavad-Gītā* says, ' with this you prosper the gods and they will prosper you' (3, 11). The practical nature of Roman religion was seen in the public use of vows, which obliged men to keep their promises if the gods favoured them. Magistrates did this in the name of the State, offering to dedicate an altar or temple, perform sacrifices or organize games if the god gave success, victory or health. There were frequent vows for the health of the emperor or his safe return from war. Votive gifts are the tokens of such promises now fulfilled by a temple offering.

Vrindāvan. See BRINDĀBAN.

Vritra. A demon of darkness or drought in ancient Indian mythology, 'covering' or possessing the clouds and keeping back the waters. The Vedic god Indra (q.v.) is pictured battling with Vritra's clouds, which are like castles, and shattering them by his thunderbolt. Vritra is often identified with Ahi, the serpent of the sky, and associated with other demonic spirits which bring flood or drought.

Vulcan, Volcanus. Fire god of ancient Italy, perhaps derived from volcanic fire; his temple should always be outside a town. He was worshipped on 23 August, the Volcanalia, when fish were thrown into a fire. The chief purpose of

the worship of Vulcan was to avert fires, and for mythology in classical times he was identified with the Greek god Hephaestus (q.v.).

Vyāsa. A 'compiler', arranger (Sanskrit), the name given to many Indian authors, but applied especially to Veda-Vyāsa, the traditional and semi-divine arranger of the *Vedas*. He is also said to have compiled the *Mahābhārata*, including the *Bhagavad-Gītā*, and the *Purānas*, and to have founded Vedānta philosophy. Vyāsa was said to have been dark in colour and called Krishna, 'black', and Dwaipayana from his birthplace. The *Purānas* mention twenty-eight Vyāsas as Avatars (q.v.) of Vishnu who descended to earth in different ages to promulgate the Vedic teaching.

Vyūha. (Sanskrit) 'manifestation', emanation, applied in Indian theology to the Vyūhas of deities, especially Vishnu. See EMANATION.

W

Waca. See HUACA.

Wahhābī. Member of an Islamic community founded by 'Abd al-Wahhāb (1703–87). The term is not used by its members, who call themselves 'unitarians' (*muwahhidūn*), and they claim to be orthodox Sunni Muslims following the legal system of Hanbal (q.v.). 'Abd al-Wahhāb was a conservative reformer, opposed to any innovations in Islam, especially the cult of saints (see *Walī*), and insisting on the letter of the *Qur'ān*. He forbade smoking of tobacco, shaving the beard, and games of chance, even chess. He was religious guide to the family of Ibn Sa'ūd which gradually conquered Arabia. Medina was captured by the Wahhābīs in 1804 and Mecca in 1806, but lost again to the Turks. The Wahhābīs strengthened their hold on the desert of Arabia but not till 1924 did they finally occupy Mecca. The puritanical Wahhābī ideas have dominated Arabia in modern times and their preachers have travelled as far as India. See SHIRK.

Wahy. (Arabic) 'revelation', a term used in the *Qur'ān* for general divine revelation, in earlier prophets, and especially in Muhammad who was sent to tell people of the revelation he had received from God. This revelation was incorporated in a divine book, the *Qur'ān*, and aimed at warning men to turn from sin and believe in God.

Wainamoinen. See KALEVALA.

Wakan. American Sioux Indian name for a sacred power, comparable to Manito (q.v.) of the Algonquin and Orenda of the Iroquois Indians. Wakan was used for any unusual quality, in men or animals, and it was also applied to natural objects, such as trees, moon and stars.

Walī. A Muslim saint, from an Arabic word 'to protect', which is often used of a friend. 'Alī (q.v.) is called by the Shī'a the 'friend of God' (*walī Allāh*). In the devotional sense the Walīs are the intermediaries between God and man, often classed in a hierarchy of which the highest saint is the Unique Pole (*qutb*) (q.v.). Theologians insist that the saints are inferior to Muhammad and the prophets, and the *Qur'ān* knows nothing of their cult, but popular sentiment brought a great range of saints and holy men into the devotions of Islam. Some of the Walīs are historical figures, but others are hardly distinguishable from ancient spirits of trees and wells and their worship has been condemned and suppressed in Arabia by the Wahhābīya (q.v.). However, it flourishes in many other lands, from North Africa to India.

Wandjina, Wondjina. Ancestral spirit beings of Australian aboriginal mythology, especially the Kimberley region. They were heroes of the Dreaming era (q.v.), who are believed to have left

their shades on rock walls in paintings and engravings. Some of the paintings are up to five metres long, with eyes and nose but no mouth, with a band round the head and a red or black outline round the body. They are named creator-heroes, kindly beings, who were the first people, each one making part of the land. The Wandjina are prayed to by clan leaders for increase of the family, animals and plants, and especially for rain after the dry season. To repaint a Wandjina engraving is thought to bring rain and to retouch figures of animals or plants increases that species, so that the painting is a ritual through which life is strengthened. See also GALERU.

Wang Yang-ming. Neo-Confucianist (1472–1529). He identified reason with mind, from which moral teachings followed. The doctrine of Mencius (q.v.), that man is essentially good by nature, was revived, and this became the basis for teaching that knowledge and conduct are identical. It was the duty of man both to exercise his mind and manifest virtue. In the nineteenth century Wang Yang-ming was honoured for providing a spiritual interpretation of life over against materialism.

Waningga. Sacred objects of Australian aboriginals, sometimes called a 'thread cross', made by tying two or three sticks into a cross and stringing bands of hair or fur across the frame so made. A spear could be used as an upright pole, and feather-down patterns decorated the base. Small Waningga were stuck into the hair of performers and others carried on their backs. They were used over most of the desert areas of central and western Australia. The Waningga could symbolize a ceremonial centre, or represent a storm-cloud or honey-ant nest from which spiritual beings were believed to have emerged.

Waqf. (Arabic) 'to prevent', to protect something and keep it from false ownership. In Islamic law (see FIQH), it is applied to state land on which previous owners pay a tax and to religious donations which yield income. So Waqf is an endowment which brings in a reward for good purposes.

Waraqa. An Arab of Mecca, cousin of Khadīja (q.v.) wife of Muhammad. In Muslim tradition he is called a Hanif (q.v.), but also said to have been a Christian who had copied the *Gospels* in Hebrew, perhaps in Syriac, since it seems that there was no Arabic *Bible* translation at that date. After Muhammad's early visions Khadīja told her cousin about them and he declared that Muhammad must be the prophet of his people. Waraqa was not converted to Islam, since he died in the second or third year of Muhammad's mission.

Wat. In Thailand (Siam) the term for a

Buddhist Vihāra (q.v.), a monastery and temple. See ANGKOR WAT.

Wawalag. Two sisters in an important myth of northern Australia. They came from the south and in their travels gave names to edible plants, animals and reptiles. The elder sister, Mirirmina, asked the younger to make a bark hut because she was about to give birth to a baby. This was done near a waterhole where there dwelt an immense python called Julunggul (q.v.). He smelt the blood of the afterbirth and came to punish the women. The younger sister danced and sang powerful songs to drive him away, but Julunggul forced his way into the hut and swallowed the child and then the sisters. On bark paintings the sisters appear, as an old and young woman, with patterns on their bodies and the blood of the birth. They also wear girdles as decorations.

Wazit. A snake goddess of the Delta in ancient Egypt, later called by Greek writers Uto and Buto. See BUTO.

Weeks. See PENTECOST.

Weird. See URD.

Wei Shih. The 'mere ideation' school of Chinese Buddhism, also known as Fa Hsiang (q.v.).

Wen-ch'ang. Ancient Chinese god of 'literary glory'. He was perhaps at first a northern tribal god of thunder, who became mingled with the Wen-ch'ang constellation which was linked with the patronage of literature. Another version is that he was a historical hero, Chang Ya-tzŭ (265–420?), who after his death was honoured to assist the Lord of Heaven in affairs of literature and official documents. The followers of Wen-ch'ang until recent times were represented in his temples as young students or writers, carrying a scroll or a box of books. The image itself was sometimes terrifying, or was a young man with a scroll in his hands, bestowing success in examinations or bringing failure to those who were badly prepared.

Wen-shu. Chinese name of the Bodhisattva Manjushrī (q.v.).

Wepwawet. A minor god of ancient Egypt whose name meant 'opener of roads'. He was a war god and associated with the king, for whose troops he opened the way. He was also associated with the gods Osiris and Rē', as opener of the way to the west and protector of the dead. He was worshipped at Abydos and represented in art as a wolf or a man with the head of a wolf or jackal.

Wesak, Vesak. Ceylonese term, from Sanskrit Vaisākha, for the month of April-May, in which a festival celebrates the birth, renunciation, enlightenment and death of the Buddha. These are all supposed to have taken place on the same day of the month, the full moon of Wesak.

Western Paradise. A concept of Mahāyāna Buddhism which named a 'world of bliss' (Sukhāvatī) or Pure Land (q.v.) of Amitābha Buddha, who dwelt in the Buddha-fields or the western sky. It is a popular belief in the Pure Land schools of Buddhism and is the idea behind the Shangri-la in *The Lost Horizon* by James Hilton.

Wheel. A sacred symbol in many ages, notably in Persia, India and the Buddhist world, as a symbol of the sun, of life, of eternity, and of transmigration. Shiva dances in a wheel of fire, and the temple at Konarak (see BLACK PAGODA) has stone wheels. The Indian national flag contains a wheel. The Buddha's first

sermon 'Set in motion the Wheel of the Law' (*dharma-chakra*). Tibetan banners and paintings depict the Wheel of Life (*bhava-chakra*), with six spheres indicating heavens, earths and hells. In the centre are cock, snake and pig, representing the three cardinal sins of lust, malevolence and greed. Tibetans use prayer-wheels, prayer-flags and prayer-walls (qq.v.) as devices to help in the repetition of invocations.

White Horse. In Chinese Buddhist legend the emperor Ming-ti after a dream sent to India for Buddhist scriptures, relics and priests, and these were brought back on a white horse. They were installed at Loyang, in Honan, the first Buddhist centre in China, where a White Horse Temple (Peh-ma-tien) was built.

Witch, Witchcraft. Many meanings have been attached to these words (from Old English *wicca*), but generally nowadays they are distinguished into harmful charms and spells (which are more properly sorcery or bad Magic (q.v.)), and supposed practices of flying by night and devouring human souls. The theory that the latter might have had some real foundation in the survival of old pagan practices into medieval Europe is now generally abandoned for lack of evidence that such rituals were nocturnal or cannibalistic. Although the belief in forms of witchcraft, such as night-flying and spiritual cannibalism, is found in many parts of the world, produced by dreams and sexual fantasies, yet it seems to be simply a creation of the imagination. There are witch-doctors or witch-hunters, concerned with curing people thought to be bewitched, but, despite confessions, and modern so-called revivals, there were no witches. See METAMORPHOSIS.

Wizard. A name for a male Witch (q.v.).

Woden, Wotan. See ODIN.

Wongar. Australian word for the aboriginal concept of Dreaming (q.v.).

Woodpecker. See PICUS.

Word of God. See KALĀM and QUR'ĀN.

Wu Hsing. (Chinese) 'five agents', the basic elements of the universe: wood, fire, earth, metal, water. Four of them occupied the four cardinal directions and controlled the four seasons, while earth was at the centre and the benefactor of all. The interaction of the Five Agents gave rise to the myriad things of the universe, engendered by Yang and Yin (q.v.). In popular Taoism the Five Agents were spirits which operated in divination.

Wu Jên. Chinese name for a Shaman (q.v.).

Wu Shan Shê. Modern Chinese 'society for the Intuition of the Good', founded in 1915 by T'ang Huan-chang. The aim was to make a synthesis of all religions, the three traditional ones of China, along with Islam and Christianity. See TUNG SHAN SHÊ.

Wu Wei. (Chinese) 'not acting', inactivity. A Taoist concept which means not simply inaction or passivity, but even more non-assertion, non-artificiality, and following nature. So the *Tao Tê Ching* (q.v.) says that 'the Sage relies on actionless activity (*wu wei*) and teaches without words, but he works upon the myriad creatures'. This quietism could lead back to nature, either to search for magical medicines, or to a gentle yet influential living.

X

Xenophanes. Greek philosopher of the sixth century B.C., claimed as the first philosophical theologian, though some of the Indian Upanishadic thinkers might have a better claim. Xenophanes was a poet and an original writer; like Plato after him he criticized the immoral and anthropomorphic stories of the gods found in Homer and Hesiod. He believed in one God, who controls the universe by thought without himself stirring. More a critical than a systematic thinker, Xenophanes has been called the founder of the Eleatic monistic school of philosophy, but this is disputed.

Xenophon. Greek historical and political writer (about 430 to 354 B.C.). He was a disciple of Socrates, but not so close as Plato, and Xenophon's interest for religion and philosophy lies in his writings about Socrates, which supplement Plato's accounts. These are the *Apology*, *Memorabilia* and *Symposium*.

Xipe Totec. The 'flayed one' of Mexican mythology, god of the west and of agriculture. He was said to have had himself skinned alive, in the way that the maize sheds its skin when shoots are breaking out. Xipe Totec was represented by the mask of a skinned human face, often with an eye hanging out to show extreme pain suffered by the god. His feast was on 22 February and captives were skinned alive at his temples to help on the process of growing corn.

Xiuhtecuhtli. 'Turquoise lord' of Mexico, an ancient fire god and patron of warriors and kings. He was also known as 'old god', Huehueteotl (q.v.), and had female emanations worshipped in many places. One of these was a butterfly, Itzpapalotl, as a symbol of the flame of the fire god. His festival was on 1 August, when slaves were roasted alive, but also when young people climbed a greasy pole

to win prizes. Xiuhtecuhtli was a form of the supreme deity, the pivot of the universe and lord of the pole star. His fire burnt in the middle of every hut and at every temple.

Xochipilli. 'Flower prince', a vegetation god of Mexico, and originally a Mixtec sun god whose helmet-mask represented a jungle fowl whose voice is the first at dawn. The Aztecs honoured

Xochipilli as a god of music, dance and ball players.

Xochiquetzal. 'Flower plume', Mexican goddess of flowers and fruit and mother of the maize god. She was goddess of sexual love, of children and twins. She was also goddess of the underworld, symbolized by flowers, and marigold flowers are still laid at graves on All Souls Eve as they were in ancient times.

Xolotl. Mexican god of the evening star, as a 'monster' animal with backward turning feet. As the evil form of the planet Venus he was said to have pushed the sun down into night, but he also brought both man and fire from the underworld. See HUEHUECOYOTL.

Y

Yad. (Hebrew) 'hand', a name used for a hand-like pointer used in Jewish worship in reading the Law.

Yahadut. A Hebrew term used for Judaism (q.v.) since the Middle Ages.

Yāhūd, Yāhūdī. Arabic term for the Jews, used from the time of the *Qur'ān* where they are recognized as a People of the Book, Ahl al-Kitāb (q.v.).

Yahweh. See TETRAGRAMMATON.

Yahyā. The name for John the Baptist in the *Qur'ān*. The origins of the form of this name are uncertain; the Mandeans (q.v.) also use the name but perhaps derived it from Arabic. The *Qur'ān* has two accounts of the annunciation of the birth of Yahyā to Zachariah (Zakarīyā') and chapter 19 gives fifteen verses to this, comparable to the account in *Luke's Gospel*, and ending with Yahyā receiving a Book from God.

Yajñā. 'Sacrifice', worship, prayer (Sanskrit), in Indian scriptures. In the *Purānas* it was personified, killed at a sacrifice and raised to the heavens to become the constellation 'deer-head'.

Yājña-valkya. A Hindu sage to whom is attributed the *Yajur Veda*, the *Shatapatha Brāhmana* and the *Brihad-āranyaka Upanishad.* In the *Upanishad* he teaches at the court of King Janaka (q.v.), argues with other Brahmins and instructs his first wife Maitreyī in the nature of the soul. He is sometimes said to have originated Yoga doctrine.

Yājūj. See Gog and Magog.

Yajur-Veda. The 'sacrificial *Veda*', the second of the most ancient Hindu texts called *Vedas* (q.v.). The *Yajus* (*Yajur* in compounds) consists of texts, often identical with verses of the *Rig Veda*, with additional prose instructions for priests arranged for purposes of sacrifice. The Yajur-Veda is divided into two collections of texts: the *Taittirīya Samhitā*, or 'Black (Krishna) Yajus', so called because texts and comments are confused; and the *Vājasaneyi Samhitā*, or 'White Yajus', because the texts are clear and orderly; in both collections, however, the order of sacrifices is similar.

Yakshas. Semi-divine beings in Hindu mythology, attendant on Kubera, god of wealth (q.v.). Generally benevolent, they sometimes appear as evil imps. Female Yakshīs or Yakshinis attend on Durgā (q.v.).

Ya'qūb. The name for the Biblical Jacob in the *Qur'ān* and Islamic tradition. He is mentioned among the prophets and appears of course in the chapter devoted to his son Joseph (Yūsuf).

Yam. God of the sea among the Phoenicians (q.v.), represented with the body of a man and a fish's tail. The Greeks identified him with Poseidon. He was married to Astarte, but coming into conflict with the god Baal lost both his wife and his gold.

Yama. God of the dead in Hindu mythology, whose name probably came from a Sanskrit word meaning 'restrainer'. In one story with his twin sister, Yamī, he was originator of the human race, and as the first man to die he found out the path to heaven. Soon he became lord and god of the dead, with two dogs each with four eyes guarding the path to his abode. In the *Rig Veda* he does not punish the dead, and in the *Upanishads* Yama is death itself engaging in dialogues with mortals (see Katha). In the epics Yama is judge of the dead, and according to their acts the departed either rise to their dead fathers or descend to one of twenty-one hells. He is dressed in blood-red clothes and holds a noose to bind souls after drawing them from the body. See also Yima.

Yamato. Former name for the region of Nara and later used of Japan as a whole, and in compound words such as Yamato-Damashii, the 'soul of Japan'.

Yamunā. The river Jumna in India. In mythology Yamunā is personified as a daughter of the sun. The junction of the Yamunā and the Ganges at Prayag, or Allahabad, is a great place of pilgrimage where visitors bathe in the sacred waters. See Kumbha Mela.

Yāna. (Sanskrit) 'vehicle', path, career. For Buddhists this is the means of attaining knowledge, the vehicle that bears across the stream of transmigration. The *Lotus Sūtra* (q.v.) speaks of one way, Eka-yāna, to beatitude. Elsewhere we read of the Great Vehicle and the Lesser Vehicle; see Mahāyāna and Hīnayāna.

Yang and Yin. Symbols and categories of Chinese thought, which appeared in philosophy from about the fourth century B.C. Yang means literally the 'sunny side' of a hill and Yin the 'dark side'. So Yang is the male, bright, positive principle, and Yin is the female, dark and negative principle. However, although a form of Dualism (q.v.), Yang and Yin do not correspond to the Zoroastrian antithesis of good and evil, for they are both interdependent forces, Yang being the power of Heaven and Yin that of Earth; also all life comes from the harmony of these two forces, Yang dominating in the summer and Yin in the winter. The Yin-Yang philosophy appears in Taoist treatises such as *Chuang Tzŭ* and *Lieh Tzŭ*, with the aim of attaining a balance between the two principles. The interaction of Yang and Yin is expressed in the diagram of T'ai-chi (q.v.), the Supreme Ultimate, which is a very popular symbol.

Yang Chu. Legendary Taoist figure, of about the fourth century B.C. He is said to have taught pleasure-seeking, though his views may have been distorted by Lieh Tzŭ (q.v.).

Yantra. Sanskrit name for a diagram of mystical significance, used in Hindu, and particularly Tantra, ceremonies. Yantras are generally metal patterns, of various sizes and shapes, bearing intricate symbols and Mantras (q.v.) or 'seed-letters' of one syllable which are held to have occult power. The Yantras are used chiefly by followers of the goddess Shakti; worshippers of Vishnu use Pattas, which are metal or stone plaques bearing pictures of Vishnu and his Avatars (q.v.).

The most potent Yantra is the Shrī-yantra, with four entrances with guardians, male and female symbols, sanctuaries for gods, and the whole enclosed within lotus petals or wavy lines.

Yashiro. Japanese term for Shinto temple buildings, see JINJA.

Yashts. Zoroastrian texts also known as the 'Little Avesta' (*Khurda Avesta*). They are hymns addressed to many gods, some of which had existed before the reforms of Zoroaster and others had been ignored by him. But there are even statements that the supreme Ahura Mazdā (q.v.) asked the help of these lesser gods and this shocked the later Zoroastrians so that there is no Pahlavi translation of the Yashts now surviving.

Yasna. The principal liturgy of ancient Zoroastrianism, which forms one of the three chief divisions of the Avesta (q.v.). The *Gāthās* (q.v.), generally attributed to Zoroaster himself, form part of the *Yasna*, but this book goes beyond them in teaching the presence of the divine in everything. Ahura Mazdā (q.v.) remains the sole object of worship, but many other gods are revived to share his glory, and all that does not participate in the divine is the evil spirit, Angra Mainyu, and his attendants. In the *Yasna* there are long and monotonous invocations of all the divine beings, and they begin with the confession of faith, 'I confess myself a worshipper of Mazdā, a Zoroastrian', which has remained in Parsi use down to today.

Yasodā. Foster-mother of Krishna in Hindu mythology, and wife of the cowherd Nanda.

Yasodharā. The name generally given to the wife of Gautama the Buddha, though in the *Lalita-vistara* (q.v.) she is called Gopā. Other stories revel in the courtship and marriage of the young couple, Gautama's abandonment of her after the birth of their son Rāhula, and how, when he had founded the Sangha, Yasodharā became one of the first nuns or Bhikkhunīs.

Yasukuni. A Shinto shrine in Tokyo for the souls of dead patriots, whose adoption by the state has been opposed. A granite Torii (q.v.) at the south entrance is thirteen metres high and the largest in Japan.

Yathrib, Yathrippa. Former name of the town of Medina (q.v.) in Arabia. It occurs once in the *Qur'ān* (33, 13), but the name al-Medina appears there several times as 'the city'. Tradition says that Yathrib was changed to Medina, as 'the city' of the Prophet, but it may already have borne this name at an earlier date.

Yati. A 'striver' or ascetic (Sanskrit). In Hindu mythology the name is given to Yatis who were associated with sages called Bhrigus in the work of creation. In Jainism a Yati is a class of ascetics of low order; see SAMANA.

Yazatās. 'Beings worthy of praise' in Zoroastrian religion. Not mentioned in the hymns of Zoroaster himself, they occur from the *Yashts* (q.v.) onwards. The Yazatās were spiritual beings, most of them gods revived from ancient religion, and Zoroaster himself was the only man to be included in their number. There were two classes of Yazatā, those of the spiritual world and those of the physical world, but all were spiritual beings. There were thirty of the latter, presiding over material nature and giving their names to the thirty days of the month.

Yazīd. The second Caliph of the Umayyad Islamic dynasty (q.v.), who reigned from A.D. 680 to 683. He tried to seize Husain (q.v.) to prevent a revolt from spreading, but his troops killed Husain so Yazīd has remained notorious for Shī'a Muslims, who re-enact his role annually in the festival of Muharram.

Yazīdī, Yezidi. A tribal group and religion, related to the Kurds of Iraq and neighbouring lands. Their name is sometimes said to have derived from a founder, Yazīd, but is thought more likely to come from Persian *īzed* (for Yazata, q.v.), an angel or god. So they call themselves 'worshippers of God' and also use the names Dāsin and Dawāsin, perhaps from Nestorian Christians. Opponents have called them 'devil-worshippers', quite unjustly, though they might be called 'angel-worshippers'. Their doctrines include minor spiritual beings, but the two chief ones are God and a fallen angel who will be restored to divine favour. Even if influenced by Zoroastrian, Manichean and Christian ideas, the Yazīdīs do not believe in a devil, evil or hell. In their art peacocks are prominent, representing angels. They have priests and a ruling prince, the Mīrzā Beg. Their chief national and religious sanctuary is the tomb of their principal saint, Shaikh 'Adī (q.v.).

Yellow Hat. Popular name for the Gelugspa, 'virtuous ones', order of Tibetan Buddhism. See GELUGSPA and LAMA.

Yellow Scarf. See THUG.

Yellow Turbans. See CHANG CHÜEH.

YGGDRASIL

Yggdrasil. The World Tree, or tree of fate, in Scandinavian mythology. In the *Voluspa* (q.v.) poem the world-tree has nine divisions corresponding to the nine worlds. It is an ash tree, glowing with light and watered from Urd's well where the three Norns dwell. Later Yggdrasil is called Mimir's tree, from the name of the wisest of the gods; under its roots which went down to the world of frost-giants was Mimir's well. There was also a well of fate, where the female fates decided men's lives. An eagle sat on top of the tree and a dragon, Nidhogg, gnawed at its roots, while a squirrel, Ratatosk, ran up and down telling the dragon what the eagle said. Yggdrasil was already decaying and at the Ragnarök Doom it will shake and creak. Other versions say that its branches spread over heaven as well as earth and, though there are many sacred trees in other mythologies, Yggdrasil is one of the most impressive.

Yi Ching. See I CHING.

Yiddish. The vernacular language of most of the Ashkenazi (q.v.) Jews, a mixture of Hebrew, Aramaic, German and other languages. Used from the Middle Ages for prayers, translations of the *Bible*, rituals, poems and tales, it has both been criticized in modern times as jargon and also used for popular education and literature. See MENDELSSOHN.

Yigdal. (Hebrew) 'magnified' by God, the most popular Jewish hymn, sung at the opening and closing of synagogue services, like Adon 'Olam (q.v.). It was written in 1404 by Daniel ben Judah Dayyan, and is based on the thirteen Articles of Faith (or Thirteen Creeds) formulated by Maimonides (q.v.). There are various settings to the *Yigdal* and one has passed into Christian use as the tune Leoni.

Yima. The first man in Zoroastrian tradition, akin to the Indian Yama (q.v.). Yima was the first king and reigned for a thousand years, but he sinned and was sent by Ahura Mazdā with wicked humanity underground. He dug a hole and dwelt in a subterranean paradise, but eventually he would re-emerge to re-people the earth in the last days. The stories are very confused; Yima is said to have forfeited immortality, yet as a deathless being he could not die. He is said to have sacrificed a bull, yet some books make no reference to this. In some ways he is a god on earth, corresponding to the Wise Lord, Ahura Mazdā, in heaven.

Yin. See YANG.

Yo Ching. Chinese 'Classic of Music', said to have been one of Six Classics but to have been lost early in the Han dynasty (206 B.C. to A.D. 220), leaving Five Classics. See CONFUCIANISM.

Yoga. A Sanskrit word related to English 'yoke' and having its two meanings of 'joining' and 'controlling', as well as many other refinements of meaning. Yoga is very ancient and may be seen in a cross-legged figure on MOHENJODARO

seals (q.v.). Later the *Bhagavad-Gītā* (q.v.) is the scripture of Yoga, teaching 'knowledge-yoga' (*jñāna-yoga*), 'work-yoga' (*karma-yoga*), and 'devotion-yoga' (*bhakti-yoga*), as well as 'mind-yoga' (*buddhi-yoga*) and 'meditation-yoga'(*dhyāna-yoga*). Yoga developed in the Yoga philosophy of Patañjali (q.v.) and his *Yoga Sūtra* (q.v.). Later forms of Yoga exercise, physical and mental, are in *Rāja* or 'royal' Yoga, teaching a mastery of mind, and *Hatha* (q.v.) or 'force' Yoga, giving especial attention to physical postures. Yoga exercise has paid attention to control of breath, in varied rhythms, of which a basic one is two-four-one, for breathing in, holding breath, and breathing out. See also Āsana.

Yogāchāra. (Sanskrit) 'observance of Yoga', the name of a Mahāyāna Buddhist school. It taught a form of idealism, in which the visible universe is an expression of eternally evolving mind. It is also known as the Vijñānavāda (q.v.), 'understanding', school. See also Lankāvatāra Sūtra, Asanga and Vasubandhu.

Yoga Sūtra. A short Hindu book, attributed to Patañjali (q.v.) of the second century B.C., and the basic text of the Yoga system of Hindu philosophy. The *Yoga Sūtras* are in four divisions, each of about fifty verses, though the last is shorter and probably later. The Sāmkhya (q.v.) system is accepted, with its discrimination of Purusha, spirit, from Prakriti, nature. But whereas Sāmkhya had no God, the *Yoga Sūtras* offer a Lord, Īshvara, as an object of meditation. This Īshvara is a particular soul, unconditioned, omniscient, and teacher of the ancients, but he is only one among many souls and is not essential. The same notion appears in the early chapters of the *Bhagavad-Gītā*, but that scripture then proceeds to praise Krishna increasingly as the Supreme Being, both immanent and transcendent.

Yogī, Yogin. A practitioner of Yoga (q.v.).

Yoginī. In Hindu mythology a female demon, one of eight attendant on the goddess Durgā (q.v.).

Yogoto. (Japanese) 'formulas of blessing', prayers to ensure that the reign of the emperor will flourish. See Norito.

Yom Kippur. See Atonement.

Yoni. (Sanskrit) 'female sexual organ', corresponding to the Linga (q.v.) and symbolized in Tantric cults of Hinduism and Buddhism.

Yüan Shih T'ien Tsun. See Jade Emperor.

Yudhi-shthira. Eldest of the five sons of Pāndu in the Indian epic *Mahābhārata*, and also son of the god Dharma. His mother was Kuntī and so he is sometimes called Kaunteya. Yudhi-shthira quarrelled with his cousin Duryodhana over succession to the throne and lost everything in a gambling match. With his brothers and their common wife Draupadī (q.v.) he retired to the forest for twelve years, finally returning to fight for the throne in the great battle at Kurukshetra which is the main subject of the epic. His side was successful, though nearly all were killed. Finally he was enthroned, performed a horse-sacrifice, and set off to heaven followed by a dog. He refused to enter heaven without the dog, who then turned into his father Dharma. Yudhi-shthira was the most conscientious of the heroes, the very 'king of righteousness' (dharma), and his scruples over fighting and injustice challenge even the god Krishna.

Yuga. An 'age' of the world (Sanskrit) in Hindu mythical chronology. There are four of these: Krita, Tretā, Dvāpara and Kali (see separate articles). Between each Yuga is its Sandhyā, 'twilight', and the four together make a Mahā-yuga, 'great age'. It is sometimes said that the Avatars (q.v.) of Vishnu appear one in each Yuga, but this is not worked out consistently. In the *Bhagavad-Gītā* Krishna says that he appears 'age after age' (*yuge-yuge*, 4, 8).

Yü Huang. See Jade Emperor.

Yule. Term of uncertain origin, Old Norse Jol, for a midwinter Teutonic and Scandinavian festival. It lasted three nights, when the dead were commemorated and even believed to be participants in the feast. In Sweden a great boar was sacrificed and when its head was brought before the king vows were made upon it. Odin was said to be the god of Yule and was called Jolnir. In the Middle Ages Yule was roughly identified with Christmas, as had been done with the Roman feast of the sun. See Sol.

Yulunggul. See Julunggul.

Yūnus. Name of the Biblical Jonah in

the *Qur'ān* and Islamic tradition. He is named four times in the *Qur'ān* and also called 'he of the fish'; one chapter (10) is called after him.

Yūsuf. The name of the Biblical Joseph (of the *Old Testament*) in the *Qur'ān* and Islamic tradition. Chapter 12 of the *Qur'ān* is entirely his story, called 'the best account' and 'one of the stories of the unseen', and including Joseph's dreams, sale by his brothers, temptation by Potiphar's wife (see ZULAIKA), imprisonment, interpretation of dreams, honour by Pharaoh, and reconciliation with his brothers and father. In Islamic legend the trials and temptations of Yūsuf are favourite tales and he is called 'the truthful', al-Siddīq. Yūsuf has been called the Adonis of the East, in his resistance to temptation by Zulaika, and their story is related in a favourite Persian poem of *Yūsef wa Zulaikhā*'.

Z

Zabūr. A word used in the *Qur'ān* of the Psalms, where David is singled out among others, with Moses and Jesus, as receiving a holy book from God: 'To David we gave the Zabūr' (17, 55/57). The origin of the term is uncertain, but it was used in pre-Islamic times in the sense of 'writ'.

Zaddik. (Hebrew) 'righteous', a concept of Hasidism (q.v.) introduced by Ber or Baer of Meseritz (1710–72) who claimed that only the perfectly righteous Zaddik could offer effective prayer and that ordinary people should attach themselves to him to gain spiritual favours. The Zaddikim came to be regarded as especially pure or possessing supernatural powers, and until today their homes are meeting places for the Hasidim, where meals are taken together and hymns and prayers are fervent

Zagreus. In Greek mythology Zeus as a serpent begat Zagreus, also called Dionysus, on Persephone, but his wife Hera was jealous and got the Titans to tear the child to pieces. Athena managed to rescue his heart and Zeus swallowed it and in due time another Dionysus was born, from Zeus and Semele.

Zaid. The name of several important men in early Islamic history. Zaid ibn Hāritha was a slave taken from a partly Christianized Arab tribe, bought by Khadīja and presented to her husband Muhammad. After the boy had refused to accept ransom, Muhammad freed him and adopted him, whence he was known as Zaid ibn Muhammad. He was one of the first converts to Islam, and died in battle in 630.

Zaid ibn Thābit was one of Muhammad's secretaries and was commissioned by Abū Bakr (q.v.), the first Caliph, to collect the fragments of the *Qur'ān* together, according to traditional story. Disputes arose over other collections and the third Caliph, 'Uthmān (q.v.) commissioned Zaid again to revise the *Qur'ān* and prepare an authoritative version, which was then imposed throughout the Islamic community.

For Zaid ibn 'Alī, see ZAIDĪS.

Zaidīs. A sect of Shī'a Muslims (q.v.), distinguished from the larger Twelvers and Seveners by their conservative and practical aims. After the death of Husain (q.v.), his grandson, Zaid ibn 'Alī, revolted against the Umayyad (q.v.) Caliphs in an effort to regain leadership for the followers of 'Alī, but he was killed in street fighting in Kufa. The Zaidīs took part in several more uprisings, but finally settled down as the group of Shī'a closest to the orthodox Sunnis. Today they remain only in the upper Yemen, where they sometimes describe themselves as the 'fifth school' of the four orthodox schools of religion. They are puritanical, rejecting mysticism, forbidding Sūfī orders, and their chief difference from the Sunni is the Zaidī claim that Zaid was a true Caliph or Imām.

Zainab. One of Muhammad's wives, who was formerly wife of his adopted son Zaid ibn Hāritha (q.v.). The latter divorced her so that the Prophet could marry her and this was justified in the *Qur'ān* (33, 36–7).

Zakarīyā'. The name of the Biblical Zachariah in the *Qur'ān*, who appears in the stories of Mary (Maryam), and John the Baptist. See YAHYĀ.

Zakāt. The duty of almsgiving in Islam, which is one of the five obligatory Pillars of Islam (q.v.). The Arabic root means 'purity' or 'virtue'. Almsgiving is insisted upon in the *Qur'ān*: 'observe the Prayer and pay the Zakāt' (2, 40, etc.). Zakāt came to be regarded as a religious tax, destined for the poor, orphans, travellers, beggars and slaves. It was collected by Muslim authorities, from Muslims only, for regulated distribution, though sometimes diverted by state rulers for their own purposes. Nevertheless, Zakāt has remained as an Islamic duty and is especially observed in the provision of food for the poor and strangers at the end of the fast of Ramadān.

Voluntary and not obligatory gifts of alms (*sadaqāt* q.v.) have always been highly esteemed in Islamic communities.

Zamakhsharī. Islamic theologian and philologist (1075–1144). He was a Persian but championed the superiority of the Arabic language. His principal work was a commentary on the *Qur'ān*, which was widely read by the orthodox although at the beginning he stated the Mu'tazila (q.v.) belief that the *Qur'ān* was created. Zamakhsharī was one of the greatest commentators of Islam, paying special attention to grammatical exposition. Baidāwī (q.v.) tried to surpass him in orthodoxy and, less successfully, in grammatical matters and variant readings. See also TAFSĪR.

Zamzam. Sacred well in Mecca, in the south-east corner of the courtyards of the Ka'ba (q.v.), where it is surmounted by a dome. It is said to be the well opened by the angel Gabriel for Hagar and Ishmael when they were dying of thirst in the desert, and it is also called Ishmael's well. Pilgrims to Mecca drink its brackish water and take it home as holy water for the sick. The name Zamzam may have been derived from the sound of the water seeping through the rock: *zam-zam*. No doubt it was a pre-Islamic holy well, and with the sacred Black Stone of the Ka'ba combined to make Mecca an ancient place of pilgrimage.

Zand. See ZEND.

Zandīks, Zindīqs. The Persian name Zandīk (Arabized as Zindīq) was used by Muslim writers of those who followed the teaching of the Zand, the 'commentary' on the Zoroastrian *Avesta* scriptures, rather than the *Avesta* itself (see also ZEND AVESTA). It was applied particularly to Manichees (q.v.) who were dualists, and other heretics who were materialists in teaching the eternity of the world and denying the creator.

Zarathushtra. See ZOROASTER.

Za-zen. 'Sitting at meditation', Japanese term for the form of meditation practised in the monasteries of the Zen school (q.v.). The posture is similar to the seated meditation position of Yoga, but there are various methods of breathing and the mind is fixed on some problem or Kōan (q.v.). Za-zen is generally practised in a hall of meditation called Zendo.

Zemelo. See SEMELE.

Zemzem. See ZAMZAM.

Zen. Schools of Japanese Buddhism, sometimes called 'meditation sects'. The name is derived from Chinese Ch'an, which was a mixture of Buddhism and Taoist nature philosophy. It was said to have been introduced from India by Bodhidharma (q.v.) though this has been disputed, and to come from the Sanskrit word for 'meditation' (*dhyāna*). But meditation is a practice of all Buddhists and the special emphasis of Zen has been an independence of texts, waiting for the 'enlightenment experience' (*satori*) and application to daily work and art. So Zen has influenced calligraphy, painting, flower arrangement, tea drinking (q.v.), and swordsmanship. It is divided into two major sub-sects, Rinzai and Sōtō (qq.v.).

Zend Avesta. Name formerly wrongly taken to denote the Zoroastrian scriptures. These are *Avesta* (q.v.), but Zend or Zand means 'commentary', and the commentaries on the scriptures were different from and inferior to them. See ZANDĪK.

Zendo, Sodo. (Japanese) 'meditation hall', of Zen monks. Generally it is a long room, with platforms on both sides on which monks sit in Za-zen (q.v.) and also sleep. The platforms are covered with straw mats and the monks face each other across the room.

Zeno. Zeno of Elea was born about 490 B.C., and as pupil and friend of Parmenides (q.v.) supported his theory of monism.

Zeno of Citium (335–263 B.C.) came from Cyprus to Athens and after studying at the Academy founded the Stoic school (q.v.). He taught in the Stoa Poikilé, a public hall, attendance at which Zeno tried to restrict to philosophers. According to Zeno, virtue is the only real good and moral weakness the only evil. Poverty, pain and death are indifferent, so that the wise man is always happy.

Zervan. See ZURVĀN.

Zethus. In Greek mythology a son of Zeus and Antiope (q.v.), and twin brother of Amphion (q.v.). With his brother Zethus was reared by a shepherd and became a herdsman.

Zeus. Father of gods and men in Greek mythology, not a creator god, but rather a deity of the sky and weather. The name is related to Sanskrit Dyaus (q.v.) and Saxon Tyw (whence our Tuesday), and means 'sky' and 'brightness'. In Greek myths Kronos, 'time', was youngest son of Heaven and Earth and leader of the Titans. Kronos married his sister Rhea and they had six children of whom Zeus was the youngest, saved by his mother by being hidden in Crete. In the classical period Zeus was regarded as the highest god, married to Hera (q.v.), and philosophers tried to rid the myths of immoral and grotesque ideas; the loves of Zeus for goddesses and mortals having been notorious (see DANAË, IO, LEDA, EUROPA, SEMELE, PERSEPHONE). Although the poet Aeschylus and the Stoic philosophers regarded Zeus as the highest power and principle, in popular religion he was less important except as a god of the weather or the chief civic deity who was given respect but little worship. His chief temple was at Olympia (q.v.).

Ziggurat, Ziqqurat. Sacred building found in most ancient cities of Mesopotamia, generally as a rectangular tower which rose like a pyramid in steps by diminishing stages to the top where there was a chapel, in which sacred marriage and new year ceremonies were held. The Ziqqurat was not a royal tomb, like Egyptian pyramids (q.v.), but it might be said that the dead body of a god lay there till emerging at the New Year festival. The Ziqqurat was not strictly a temple either, the dwelling of a god permanently, but it was a sacred place and was central to some of the great Babylonian rituals. It was thought to link heaven and earth, and this idea probably lies behind the Biblical stories of the Tower of Babel and Jacob's dream of a ladder between heaven and earth.

Zikr. See DHIKR.

Zimbabwe. Ruined stone buildings, of African construction, in land now occupied by the Shona people of east central Africa. Some of the largest have been called 'temple' or 'acropolis' and they have been given romantic interpretations in Rider Haggard's *King Solomon's Mines*, but their original connections are unknown. Carvings in the ruins, especially stone birds, resemble birds carved by Bantu peoples today to represent the thunder, and stone bowls are like wooden bowls now used in divination.

Zimzum. (Hebrew) 'contraction', a Kabbalistic doctrine which considers that creation came after a contraction or limitation of the infinite, En Sof. It was the particular doctrine of Isaac Luria (q.v.).

Zindīq. See ZANDĪK.

Zio. See TYW.

Zionism. Nationalistic Jewish movement, called for by Leo Pinsker (q.v.,) (1821–91) of Odessa, and made into a world movement by Theodore Herzl

ZIMBABWE CARVING

(1860–1904). The first Zionist Congress was held in 1897, the name Zionism having been coined by Nathan Birnbaum in 1892. The idea was to have a national home for the Jews, or a Jewish state, and there was much opposition at first from those Jews who were being well integrated as citizens of their own lands, or who thought the idea of a state was too narrow (see ASHER GINZBERG). There were small settlements in Palestine, where there had always been some Jews, but the Balfour Declaration of 1917 pledged British support for a 'national home' in the ancestral land. It was the Nazi persecution of Jews, from 1933, that forced many out of Germany and neighbouring lands and led to widespread immigration into Palestine and the establishment in 1948 of the state of Israel.

Ziqqurat. See ZIGGURAT.

Ziusudra, Ziudsuddu, Sisouthros. Sumerian name of the king who was hero of the Flood (q.v.), also known under the name of Utnapishtim (q.v.).

Zizit. See TZITZITH.

Zodiac. Late Greek word for 'signs' and figures, in a circle, applied to the sky where the apparent movements of sun, moon and planets take place. The Signs of the Zodiac are the twelve equal parts of the heavens through which the sun passes, and named after the constellations: Aries, Taurus, Gemini, Cancer, Leo, Virgo, Libra, Scorpio, Sagittarius, Capricorn, Aquarius, Pisces. Ancient India charted the heavens by means of 27, later 28, Nakshatras, stars or lunar mansions. The system of constellations and their names differed widely from those of the West, which in time took to Asia the Signs of the Zodiac.

Zohar. The greatest work of Jewish Kabbalism (q.v.), whose title means 'the Splendour'. It was written about the fourteenth century and ascribed to Moses de Leon (q.v.), who himself claimed that it had been written by the second century Talmudic scholar Simeon ben Yochai (q.v.) and who appears in the *Zohar* as the principal teacher. The *Zohar* is written partly in Hebrew, partly in Aramaic, and is in the form of a commentary on the *Pentateuch*, seeking to reveal its hidden and mystical meanings, by literal and allegorical interpretations. The *Zohar* teaches of God as the infinite En Sof (q.v.) and the ten channels of light emanating from him, Sefiroth (q.v.) . The separation of the Shechinah (q.v.) from En Sof and the final restoration of unity are described. The divine names, destiny of the human soul, nature of evil, redemption, Torah and Messiah are all discussed.

Zombie, Zambi. A term used in Haiti and other parts of America for the 'living-dead', those whose soul has been eaten by a witch (q.v.). The corpse is said to have been revived by a sorcerer. The name is derived from *zumbi*, a word from the Congo, taken across to America by slaves. Originally used for the spirits of the dead, ghosts and 'revenants', it has a rather different sense in connection with witchcraft. In slang use a Zombie is a half-awakened or stupid person.

Zoroaster. Greek form of the name of Zarathushtra the Persian prophet and reformer of the seventh and sixth centuries B.C., often dated as 628–551 B.C. His work was done mostly in eastern Persia, but he was perhaps a native of Rhages in Media, near modern Teheran. The prophetical teachings of Zoroaster himself are held to be preserved in the *Gāthās* (q.v.), the oldest part of the *Avesta* scriptures. His message began with a vocation in which the supreme God, Ahura Mazdā (q.v.), called him, and Zoroaster went on to deny the existence of other gods and insist on free will, the importance of the good life, and the certainty of heaven and hell. After preaching unsuccessfully he fled to the east, where King Vishtaspa was converted to the reformed religion. The prophet was then about forty years old and continued his mission with varying success till his death in conflict with priests at seventy-seven. See ZOROASTRIANISM.

Zoroastrianism. The religion founded by Zoroaster (q.v.), as a reform of ancient Persian polytheism into a monotheistic or dualistic system. The old Persian religion was rather like that of the Aryan Indians, as seen in the *Rig Veda* (q.v.), and much of this reappeared after Zoroaster, when the old gods became different classes of spiritual beings (see YAZATĀS and MITHRA). The Magi priests (q.v.) spread Zoroastrianism of their own kind into the central and western parts of the Persian empire. In the Sassanian period, A.D. 229–652 Zoroastrianism became the state religion and attempts were made to return to Zoroastrian purity. The conquest of Persia by Islam led to the decline and almost total disappearance of the religion in the land of its origin, where today only a few thousand Zoroastrians or Gabars (q.v.) remain. The majority, numbered at about 125,000, who follow this ancient faith are the Parsis of India (q.v.). See also ZURVĀN.

Zoser. Egyptian monarch, first king of the Third Dynasty (about 2,780 B.C.), who made his capital at Memphis and was buried in the famous Step Pyramid or Mastaba at Saqqāra. See PYRAMID.

Zu. A storm bird in Mesopotamian mythology, who stole the Tablets of Destiny from the god Enlil (qq.v.). Zu is

half man half bird. One of the gods, whose name is not clear, recovered the tablets and brought Zu captive to Enlil for judgement.

Zulaika, Zalīkhā. The name of Potiphar's wife in Islamic tradition. Neither she nor her husband (later called Qitfīr) are named in the *Qur'ān*, but the story of her temptation of Joseph is briefly told in the chapter of Yūsuf (12, 21–34). See YŪSUF.

Zurvān. Pahlavi name for 'infinite time' and treated as the heresy of Zurvānism, or Zurvāniya, by Persian writers. Zoroastrianism explained the problem of evil by positing the existence of an evil spirit, Ahriman, in opposition to the good Ohrmazd or Ahura Mazdā, who thus had no responsibility for evil. This Dualism (q.v.) had its own problems, and these were solved by positing Zurvān, Time, as the father of both Ohrmazd and Ahriman. Orthodox Zoroastrians opposed this as heretical innovation and the very name Zurvān was expunged from Persian writings, though some camouflaged Zurvānite views have remained and have been pieced together in modern times. See also ZANDĪKS.

Egyptian Dynasties

B.C.	
3100–2600	Dynasties I–III
	Unification of north and south Egypt
	Zoser (Djoser), and Imhotep. Step Pyramid at Saqqāra
2600–2180	Dynasties IV–VI Old Kingdom
	Cheops (Khufu). Great Pyramid at Giza
	Chephren (Khafre). Pyramid and Sphinx at Giza
2180–2000	Dynasties VII–XI First Intermediate Period
2000–1780	Dynasties XII–XIII Middle Kingdom
1780–1580	Dynasties XIV–XVII Second Intermediate Period
1580–332	Dynasties XVIII–XXXI New Kingdom
	Ikhnaton (Akhenaten, Amenophis IV), and Queen Nefertiti, Aton reform, capital Akhetaton (Tell el-Amarna).
	Tutankhamūn
	Ramses II (Hebrew captivity?)
332	Alexander the Great's conquest
	Greek Ptolemy rulers
30	Roman period
A.D. 639	Islamic conquest

Ancient Egyptian historical reckoning is based upon the system of Manetho, an Egyptian priest who wrote in Greek during the reign of Ptolemy II. He divided the list of Egyptian Pharaohs into thirty-one dynasties. This scheme has been generally followed by modern scholars and dates are calculated from archaeological investigation.

Islamic Dates and Dynasties

A.D.	
570–632	Prophet Muhammad
632–661	'Rightly Guided' Caliphs of Sunni Islam: Abū Bakr, 'Umar, 'Uthmān, 'Alī
661–750	Umayyad Caliphs (Damascus: Syria, Arabia, Iraq, Persia, India, North Africa, Spain, France)
	756–1031 Spanish Umayyads
750–1258	'Abbāsids (Baghdad: Iraq and beyond)
	Hārūn al-Rashīd
	868–905 Tūlūnids (Egypt and Syria)
	909–1171 Fātimids (North Africa, Egypt, Syria)
	1169–1462 Ayyūbids (Egypt, Syria, Yemen)
	Saladin

	800–909	Aghlabids (Africa and Sicily)
	1058–1147	Almoravids (Africa and Spain)
	1130–1269	Almohads (Africa and Spain)
	1250–1517	Mamlūks (Egypt and Syria)
	1038–1307	Seljuq Turks (Persia and Iraq)
1281–1924	Ottoman Turks (Turkey, Balkans, Arab lands)	
	1206–1634	Mongol Khans (Mongolia and North China)
	1526–1858	Mughals (India)
		Bābur
		Akbar
		Aurangzeb
		Bahādur Shāh
1924	Istanbul Caliphate ended by Mustafā Kemāl	

Chinese Dynasties

B.C.	
2696–2206	Legendary emperors
2205–1122	Hsia and Shang Dynasties
1122–221	Chou Dynasty, feudal and classical age
	Confucius
	Lao Tzŭ?
	Mencius
	Chuang Tzŭ
206–A.D. 220	Han Dynasty
265–419	Chin (Tsin) Dynasty
420–588	Divided North and South
618–907	T'ang Dynasty
907–960	Five Dynasties
960–1279	Sung Dynasty
1280–1368	Yüan (Mongol) Dynasty
1368–1644	Ming Dynasty
1644–1911	Ch'ing (Manchu) Dynasty
1912	Republic
1949	Communism

Further reading list

General
Parrinder, G., (ed.): *Encyclopedia of the World's Religions* (Hamlyn)
Finegan, J.: *The Archaeology of World Religions* (Princeton)
Eliade, M.: *From Primitives to Zen* (Collins)

The Ancient World

James, E. O.: *Prehistoric Religion* (Thames & Hudson)
Pritchard, J. B.: *Ancient Near Eastern Texts* (Princeton)
Cerny, J.: *Ancient Egyptian Religion* (Hutchinson)
Ions, V.: *Egyptian Mythology* (Hamlyn)
Hooke, S. H.: *Babylonian and Assyrian Religion* (Hutchinson)
Gray, J.: *Near Eastern Mythology* (Hamlyn)
Zaehner, R. C.: *The Dawn and Twilight of Zoroastrianism* (Weidenfeld & Nicolson)
——: *The Teachings of the Magi* (Allen & Unwin)
Hinnells, J.: *Persian Mythology* (Hamlyn)
Rose, H. J.: *Ancient Greek Religion* (Hutchinson)
——: *Ancient Roman Religion* (Hutchinson)
Pinsent, J.: *Greek Mythology* (Hamlyn)
Perowne, S.: *Roman Mythology* (Hamlyn)
Graves, R.: *The Greek Myths* (Penguin)
Russell, B.: *A History of Western Philosophy* (Allen & Unwin)
MacCulloch, J. A.: *The Celtic and Scandinavian Religions* (Hutchinson)
MacCana, P.: *Celtic Mythology* (Hamlyn)
Davidson, H. R. E.: *Scandinavian Mythology* (Hamlyn)
Ross, A.: *Pagan Celtic Britain* (Routledge)

Islam

Watt, W. M.: *Muhammad, Prophet and Statesman* (Oxford)
——: *Islamic Philosophy and Theology* (Edinburgh)
Rahman, F.: *Islam* (Weidenfeld & Nicolson)
Arberry, A. J. (trs.): *The Koran Interpreted* (Oxford)
Nicholson, R. A.: *The Mystics of Islam* (Routledge)
Lewis, B.: *The Arabs in History* (Hutchinson)
Smith, W. C.: *Islam in Modern History* (Oxford)

India

Zaehner, R. C.: *Hinduism* (Oxford)
—— (trs.): *Hindu Scriptures* (Everyman)
Ions, V.: *Indian Mythology* (Hamlyn)
Basham, A. L.: *The Wonder that was India* (Sidgwick & Jackson)
Zimmer, H.: *Philosophies of India* (Bollingen)
Jaini, J.: *Outlines of Jainism* (Cambridge)
Thomas, E. J.: *The Life of Buddha* (Routledge)
Conze, E. (trs.): *Buddhist Scriptures* (Penguin)
Zürcher, E.: *Buddhism, its Origins and Spread* (Routledge)
McLeod, W. H.: *Gurū Nānak and the Sikh Religion* (Oxford)
Singh, K., ed.: *Selections from the Sacred Writings of the Sikhs* (Allen & Unwin)

Far East

Smith, D. H.: *Chinese Religions* (Weidenfeld & Nicolson)
Hughes, E. R. (trs.): *Chinese Philosophy in Classical Times* (Everyman)
Christie, A.: *Chinese Mythology* (Hamlyn)
Chan, Wing-tsit: *Religious Trends in Modern China* (Columbia)
Hoffmann, H.: *The Religions of Tibet* (Allen & Unwin)
Hammer, R.: *Japan's Religious Ferment* (Student Christian Movement)
Piggott, J.: *Japanese Mythology* (Hamlyn)
Watts, A.: *The Way of Zen* (Pelican)

Africa, America, Australasia

Parrinder, G.: *Religion in Africa* (Penguin)
——: *African Mythology* (Hamlyn)
Mbiti, J.: *African Religions and Philosophy* (Heinemann)
Krickeberg, W., etc.: *Pre-Columbian American Religions* (Weidenfeld & Nicolson)
Burland, C. A.: *The Gods of Mexico* (Eyre & Spottiswoode)
——: *North American Indian Mythology* (Hamlyn)
Nicholson, Irene: *Mexican and Central American Mythology* (Hamlyn)
Osborne, H.: *South American Mythology* (Hamlyn)
Elkin, A. P.: *The Australian Aborigines* (Angus & Robertson)
Berndt, R. M.(ed.): *Australian Aboriginal Art* (Collier-Macmillan)
Poignant, R.: *Oceanic Mythology* (Hamlyn)

Acknowledgements

Acknowledgements are due to the following for supplying photographs:

Aerofilms and Aero Pictorial Ltd.; Associated Newspapers Ltd.; Australian News and Information Bureau; Barnaby's Picture Library; Black Star; Bord Failte Photos; British Museum; Canadian Information Services; J. Allan Cash; Mark Edwards; Egyptian State Tourist Office; Guildhall Museum; Israel Government Tourist Office; Japan Information Centre; Japanese Embassy; Keystone Press Agency Ltd ; National Museum, Melbourne; Janet March Penney; Douglas Pike; Paul Popper Ltd.; Radio Times Hulton Picture Library; Royal Embassy of Cambodia and Tunisian Embassy.